"Governments across the w
public financial manageme
questions that get asked in t.
lenges of managing public money and will inspire and inform reform ideas across the globe for years to come. Academics and practitioners alike should keep a copy close at hand. I certainly will."

Matt Andrews, Associate Professor of Public Policy, Kennedy School of Government, Harvard University; author of *The Limits of Institutional Reforms in Development: Changing Rules for Realistic Solutions*

"Faced with growing debt and an uncertain macroeconomic outlook, many governments are experimenting with institutional innovations such as new budgetary rules and fiscal councils. Yet the naïve import of reforms has uncertain benefits. This much-needed book seeks to avoid simplistic prescription, and fosters awareness of the coherence and context of budget institutions. It is an indispensable guide for postcrisis fiscal designers."

Joachim Wehner, Associate Professor of Public Policy, London School of Economics and Political Science; author of *Legislatures and the Budget Process: The Myth of Fiscal Control*

"This timely volume helps us all better understand the bow wave of public financial and fiscal policy reforms that have been initiated by thoughtful practitioners in nations around the world. Thanks to the chapters by leading public finance analysts, we now have a comprehensive conceptual framework to assess the practices adopted by individual nations, often in the heat of a financial crisis. This couldn't come at a better time, as leaders and analysts alike will need better guideposts to help nations achieve more sustainable and rationalized public finances in the tumultuous years to come."

Paul L. Posner, Director, Public Administration Program, George Mason University

"This helpful volume analyzes the key public financial management innovations that took place over the past two decades. Grouping these innovations loosely into three categories—information, processes, and rules—the authors argue that public financial management is an integrated framework with its own architecture, logic, and connections. There may not therefore be a direct link between individual innovations and outcomes, and general advice is not likely to fit any specific country. The book also poses some intriguing questions, such as what is the likelihood that innovations developed in more advanced economies will work in developing countries."

Irene S. Rubin, Professor Emeritus of Public Administration, Northern Illinois University; former editor-in-chief, *Public Administration Review*; author of *The Politics of Public Budgeting and Balancing the Federal Budget: Eating the Seed Corn or Trimming the Herds*

"In the wake of the financial crisis public resources are particularly scarce. Thus, effective and efficient use of taxpayers' money requires sound financial management and full transparency: citizens, parliaments, and financial markets deserve a clear picture of where public finances stand. This book provides an impressive overview of country practices, reforms and innovations in the area of public financial management. This timely publication is a rich source for practitioners in public administrations as well as for the academic community and the interested public."

Gerhard Steger, Director General of the Budget, Austrian Ministry of Finance; Chair, OECD Working Party of Senior Budget Officials

"The most comprehensive and informative guide on public financial management! It is well-timed as well. I certainly believe that it will be well received in the Asian region, including Korea, where the importance of PFM is being recognized more than ever."

Won-Dong Cho, President, Korean Institute of Public Finance

"In this comprehensive survey of current trends in public financial management, the authors present and analyze PFM instruments and practices from around the world. Their analysis is firmly empirical, based on a broad spectrum of sources, and the presentation is balanced; no reader is left with the impression that sophisticated techniques can replace political commitments and hard work. This anthology will for a long time remain a rich source of information for both practitioners in ministries of finance and academic researchers."

Per Molander, former Director-General; architect of Swedish budget reform of the 1990s

Public Financial Management and Its Emerging Architecture

EDITORS
Marco Cangiano, Teresa Curristine,
and Michel Lazare

INTERNATIONAL MONETARY FUND

Cover design: IMF Multimedia Services Division

Cataloging-in-Publication Data
Joint World Bank–International Monetary Fund Library

Public financial management and its emerging architecture / editors, Marco Cangiano, Teresa Curristine, and Michel Lazare – Washington, D.C. : International Monetary Fund, ©2013.
p. ; cm.

Includes bibliographical references.

1. Finance, Public—Management. I. Cangiano, M. (Marco). II. Curristine, Teresa, 1970– III. Lazare, Michel. IV. International Monetary Fund.

HJ9733.P83 2013

ISBN: 978-1-47553-109-1 (paper)
ISBN: 978-1-47551-219-9 (ePub)
ISBN: 978-1-47551-220-5 (Mobipocket)
ISBN: 978-1-47551-221-2 (PDF)

Publication orders may be placed online, by fax, or through the mail:
International Monetary Fund, Publication Services
P.O. Box 92780, Washington, DC 20090, U.S.A.
Tel.: (202) 623-7430 Fax: (202) 623-7201
E-mail: publications@imf.org
Internet: www.imfbookstore.org

Contents

Foreword

Public financial management (PFM)—the fine art of budgeting, spending, and managing public monies—has undergone a "revolution" since the late 1980s. This uniquely interdisciplinary combination of economics, political science, public administration, and accounting has seen an influx of innovative ideas and reforms that have sought to address some of the perennial challenges of managing public finances.

To constrain the likely temptation to increase expenditure and spend, rather than save, in times of plenty, countries have introduced fiscal rules and fiscal responsibility laws. To understand and plan for the impact of today's policy choices on finances in the years ahead, governments have adopted medium-term budget frameworks. To help guard against over-optimistic economic and budgetary estimates, some countries have established independent fiscal councils. To shift the focus of decision making from how much money programs receive to the results they can achieve, many governments have introduced performance budgeting and management initiatives. To better understand the true state of public finances and underlying risks, some governments have sought to increase the comprehensiveness and coverage of fiscal reporting and accounting and have introduced risk management techniques. This profound wave of change in the ways public spending is managed largely started in Australia, New Zealand, and the United Kingdom and has since then passed through virtually all advanced economies, and to some extent, has also reached emerging market economies and low-income countries.

While the field of PFM has changed dramatically over the last two decades, very little has been written about this revolution, with the exception of a few specialized articles. In filling this gap in the literature, this book takes advantage of the unique perspectives provided by IMF public financial management experts, who, over the last two decades, have gained practical experience with many if not all of these reforms and are well placed to draw lessons, make sense of the PFM revolution, and share their cross-country experiences of what has worked in practice and what has not.

The book poses critical questions about these reforms and evaluates what they have accomplished and the issues and challenges they have encountered, including with the global financial and economic crisis. The crisis highlighted the critical importance of a sound public financial management framework in ensuring that well-designed fiscal policies are effectively implemented. But it also demonstrated the underlying limitations of some countries' PFM frameworks and the flawed design and weak implementation of some PFM innovations, as well as their failure to entrench themselves. Based on these experiences, this book draws general lessons to help guide reformers in their pursuit of the next generation of PFM reforms.

The IMF remains committed to working with all its member countries to provide advice and assistance on public financial management, drawing on its deep experience of working on these issues all over the world. I hope that this publication will help countries meet the challenges of managing public finances in an increasingly complex and uncertain global environment.

Christine Lagarde
Managing Director
International Monetary Fund

Acknowledgments

The idea for this book came from a conversation with Professor Allen Schick in which we discussed how public financial management has developed over the past two decades. Subsequent conversations led to the conclusion that Professor Schick and the staff of the IMF's Fiscal Affairs Department had rich and unique academic and practical experiences to share on how public financial management reforms have evolved and the emerging state of the discipline at the beginning of the twenty-first century. Special recognition goes to Professor Schick for his role in propelling the project and acting as a sounding board for all of us.

This book was a joint effort involving the staff of the two Public Financial Management Divisions of the Fiscal Affairs Department. A large number of friends and former colleagues contributed by reviewing and commenting on various versions of the chapters as well as by participating in a number of lively internal seminars. The work of the entire Fiscal Affairs Department, under the leadership of its Director, Carlo Cottarelli, has provided a stimulating environment in which parallel projects have kept our eyes open, particularly to the views of the nonspecialists. There was, however, no substitute for the many interactions with member countries and colleagues from sister institutions. These interactions provided a much-needed reality check as the elements of the public financial management architecture started to emerge. Participating compatriots included past and present generations of public financial management specialists of the Fiscal Affairs Department, who have generously given us their time, wisdom, and experience, in an attempt to make this book accessible to the uninitiated. In addition to the chapter authors and the staff of the two Public Financial Management divisions, we wish to thank the reviewers, Xavier Debrun, Manal Fouad, Greg Horman, Bacari Kone, Florence Kuteesa, Lewis Murara, Peter Murphy, Sailendra Pattanayak, Mario Pessoa, Dimitar Radev, and Xavier Rame, for their insightful comments and suggestions. We also wish to express our gratitude to our administrative assistants Molly Abraham, Tracy Bowe, Veronique Catany, and Sasha Pitrof for their support, and especially Melinda Weir, who was instrumental in bringing the project to completion. We are very grateful to Michael Harrup of the IMF's External Relations Department for coordinating the production of the book. We thank all of you and especially our families and friends for their patience and support throughout this project.

Marco Cangiano, Teresa Curristine, and Michel Lazare

Abbreviations

CBA	central budget authority
CBO	Congressional Budget Office (United States)
CEMAC	Central African Economic and Monetary Community
CFI	central fiscal institution
CMU	cash management unit
CPIA	Country Policy and Institutional Assessment
DMO	debt management office
ECCU	Eastern Caribbean Currency Union
EITI	Extractive Industries Transparency Initiative
EU	European Union
FMIS	financial management information system
FRL	fiscal responsibility law
G-8	Group of Eight advanced economies
G-20	Group of Twenty advanced economies
GAAP	generally accepted accounting principles
GDP	gross domestic product
GFSM	*Government Finance Statistics Manual*
HIPC	Heavily Indebted Poor Countries
IFI	international financial institution
IPSAS	International Public Sector Accounting Standards
IT	information technology
MTBF	medium-term budget framework
MTDS	medium-term debt management strategy
MTFF	medium-term fiscal framework
NCoA	National Commission of Audit (Australia)
NDP	national development plan
NPM	new public management
OECD	Organisation for Economic Co-operation and Development
PB	performance budgeting
PEFA	Public Expenditure and Financial Accountability
PFM	public financial management
PI	performance information
PIP	public investment program
PPP	public-private partnership

ROSC	Report on the Observance of Standards and Codes
RRA	resource revenue account
SGP	Stability and Growth Pact
SOE	state-owned enterprise
T-bill	treasury bill
TSA	treasury single account
UN	United Nations
VAR	value at risk
WAEMU	West African Economic and Monetary Union

INTRODUCTION

The Emerging Architecture of Public Financial Management

MARCO CANGIANO, TERESA CURRISTINE, AND MICHEL LAZARE

If a single word could encapsulate public financial management (PFM) in the first decades of the twenty-first century, it would be *innovation*. This book takes stock of key, groundbreaking practices that have emerged over the past two decades in this uniquely interdisciplinary field, including, among others, fiscal responsibility laws, fiscal rules, medium-term budget frameworks, fiscal councils, new fiscal risk management techniques, and performance budgeting. It evaluates what these innovations have accomplished and how they have changed the way we think of PFM—from how governments administer their budgets to how they manage their fiscal policy and public finances. The aim of the book is to sketch the elements of PFM and highlight their interdependence, while being accessible to as broad an audience as possible, but in particular to policymakers who must deal with the increasing complexity of managing public resources.

Although the book was conceived and written in the midst of a grave financial crisis, it is not about the crisis. Nor is it a PFM handbook or manual, which would merely describe PFM practices. Rather, this book poses critical questions about innovations, what has been achieved, the issues and challenges that have appeared along the way, and how the ground can be prepared for the next generation of PFM reforms. The focus is mainly, but not exclusively, on advanced economies—where most of the innovations discussed in this book originated. Innovation has always been an aspect of PFM. The current wave of reforms is different, however, because of the sheer volume and pace of innovations, their widespread adoption, and the sense that they add up to a fundamental change in the way governments manage public money.

WHAT IS PUBLIC FINANCIAL MANAGEMENT? AN EVOLUTIONARY DEFINITION

PFM in the narrowest, and perhaps most traditional, sense is concerned with how governments manage the budget in its established phases—formulation, approval, and execution. It deals with the set of processes and procedures that cover all aspects of expenditure management in government. It is also interdisciplinary, drawing from economics, political science, and public administration, as well as accounting and auditing. But as its relevance in fiscal policymaking has evolved over time, so has its definition. The simple passage from *expenditure* to *financial* management has broadened its focus from the narrowly defined budget to all aspects of managing public resources, including resource mobilization and debt management, with a progressive extension to the medium- to long-term implications and risks to public finances from today's policy decisions. The coverage of PFM has thus expanded from the narrowly defined central government budget to all levels of government and the broader public sector, including state enterprises and public-private partnerships.

Furthermore, PFM is now seen as an "umbrella" definition, covering a set of systems aimed at producing information, processes, and rules that can help support fiscal policymaking as well as provide instruments for its implementation. Having in place inappropriate budgetary processes and rules can cause unsustainable increases in expenditure and unbudgeted liabilities. Poor or nonexistent financial information, as can result from unrealistic projections of economic growth or nondisclosure of fiscal risks, can undermine government finances. It is this linkage of policies and processes that highlights the importance of PFM and has stimulated recent innovations in PFM practices. That said, PFM is not a substitute for fiscal policymaking; it cannot provide answers to questions about the optimal level of public indebtedness, the proper size of government, and the fair distribution of resources.

The key objectives of public financial management—maintaining a sustainable fiscal position, the effective allocation of resources, and the efficient delivery of public goods and services—have long been established in the literature.[1] The emphasis of this book is on the set of systems, processes, and rules that can counter the well-documented deficit bias inherent in the political process.[2] As the book argues, information on past, current, and future fiscal developments is of paramount importance in this regard—without sustainable public finances, effectiveness and efficiency run the risk of becoming secondary objectives. In this respect, PFM has certainly evolved from its traditional focus on financial compliance and control to become a key foundation for macrofiscal analysis and policymaking.

It is important to dispel a potential misunderstanding of the meaning of the first PFM key objective, maintaining a sustainable fiscal position. This objective should not be seen as, and certainly does not imply, a bias toward fiscal tightening. It is a way to achieve legitimate macroeconomic objectives, most notably inclusive and balanced growth, in an orderly fashion without prejudging the state of public finances, which may, in turn, have negative repercussions on macroeconomic stability and growth.

---

[1] Since the early 1990s, these objectives have been the standard PFM objectives used in academia and by the IMF and the World Bank and other international financial institutions.

[2] The deficit (and debt) bias has been analyzed and explained by various authors as a common pool resource problem (Weingast, Shepsle, and Johnsen, 1981), a prisoners' dilemma (Hallerberg and von Hagen, 1997), time inconsistency and principal-agent relationships (Kydland and Prescott, 1977).

PURPOSE OF THIS BOOK

The objective of this book is to assess selected PFM innovations and reforms introduced during the past 20 years. It aims to explain how reforms have worked; to examine the issues that have emerged in their design and implementation; to compare experiences with expectations; and to provide an understanding of how differences in government capacity affect PFM initiatives. The hope is that readers will take away an enhanced understanding of the prospects and problems associated with contemporary PFM reform.

The PFM literature has grown rapidly in this period, but it is fairly specialized and addresses a specific audience.[3] Very few attempts have been made to take stock of how PFM has evolved over the last two decades.[4] This period has also seen the introduction of a number of PFM diagnostics, most notably the 1998 IMF Code of Good Practices on Fiscal Transparency, with the associated diagnostic, Reports on the Observance of Standards and Codes (ROSCs), and the 2002 Public Expenditure and Financial Accountability (PEFA) assessment.[5] It is also somewhat surprising—and disappointing—that despite the hundreds of thousands of civil servants and practitioners involved in this area around the globe, PFM is virtually absent from any economics or even public finance curricula; a multitude of specialized courses can be found in political science or public administration, and in accounting, auditing, and project evaluation, but very few attempt to bring together the interdisciplinary approach modern PFM requires. This book attempts to fill this gap in the literature.

What are the key PFM innovations discussed in this book? They include, among others, new legal frameworks to promote fiscal responsibility, fiscal rules, medium-term budget frameworks (MTBFs), fiscal councils, new fiscal risk management techniques, performance budgeting, and accrual reporting and accounting. How have these reforms emerged over the past two decades? Some general facts and trends about their development are highlighted in the following:

- The number of countries with fiscal rules rose from 5 in 1990 to 76 in 2012.
- The number of countries with MTBFs increased from fewer than 20 in 1990 to more than 130 in 2008.

[3] Pretorious and Pretorious (2008) provide a comprehensive review of PFM literature, but are mainly focused on the *vexata quaestio* of how best to sequence PFM reforms in developing countries. See also Diamond (2012a) for a contribution to this topic.

[4] Many handbooks and manuals were published in the late 1990s and early 2000s, largely driven by the need to deal with transition economies. See Premchand (1993); Schick (1998); Allen and Tomassi (2001); World Bank (1998); Potter and Diamond (1999); and Schiavo-Campo and Tomassi (1999).

[5] The IMF's Code and associated *Manual on Fiscal Transparency* were issued in 1998, modified in 2007 (see IMF, 2007), and substantially revised in 2013. The PEFA program was founded in 2002 as a multidonor partnership between the European Commission, the IMF, the World Bank, the French Ministry of Foreign and European Affairs, the Norwegian Ministry of Foreign Affairs, the Swiss State Secretariat for Economic Affairs, and the U.K. Department for International Development. Its aim is to assess the performance of public expenditure, procurement, and financial accountability systems.

- The number of countries with fiscal councils grew from about 6 in 1990 to about 25 in 2013. A sharp increase has occurred recently, with ten or more such councils having been created since 2008.[6]
- With the emergence of new fiscal reporting standards, the number of countries reporting at least a financial balance sheet to the IMF increased from 21 in 2004 to 41 in 2011.
- By 2007, 80 percent of Organisation for Economic Co-operation and Development (OECD) countries produced performance information, and in 2011 nearly 70 percent had a standard performance budgeting framework.
- Since 1999, 111 "Fiscal Transparency ROSCs" have been conducted, covering 94 countries, and by the end of 2012, 285 PEFA assessments had been undertaken, covering 135 countries.[7]

The word *architecture* is used in the title of this book to convey how PFM elements are interconnected and mutually dependent and how they can be melded into a comprehensive structure. Borrowing from Premchand's analogy, PFM is "like weaving a Persian carpet, where every tiny knot is as important as the grand design itself" (Premchand, 1993, p. 6). *Emerging* points to the fact that the past 15–20 years have seen the adoption of a number of innovations, some of which have now become part of the PFM lexicon, whereas others have been abandoned and others are still being tested. It also emphasizes the time dimension, given that innovations require lengthy gestation and implementation phases; it stresses how PFM is an open system in which waves of innovation are bound to take place at irregular intervals as the demand for better management of public resources increases. Finally, *emerging architecture* implies that the focus of this book is on the selected elements that have emerged in the last two decades and can now be seen as building blocks of modern PFM—along with others that are not specifically covered in this book but are also important.[8]

Looking at PFM as an integrated framework or system can illuminate important issues. For instance, when reforms are launched in isolation from one another, interested governments may not be aware of their interdependence.[9] Viewed in isolation, each innovation has its own constituency, terminology,

[6]This is the number of fiscal councils as of February 2013. For more details see the IMF Fiscal Council Database (forthcoming), as well as IMF (2013).

[7]For more details on the ROSCs, see IMF (2012). In 2013, the IMF substantially revised the Code of Good Practices on Fiscal Transparency and the corresponding diagnostic tool, the ROSC. A revised ROSC is due to be launched at the end of 2013.

[8]Essential aspects of PFM that are more focused on budget execution, such as treasury single account, commitment control and reporting, and government financial management information systems, have been developed and implemented for some time. Nonetheless, they remain critical because quite a number of countries still lack these essential features of the PFM armory. Besides the manual referenced in note 5, short and accessible material on these aspects can be found in the Technical Notes and Manuals series the IMF Fiscal Affairs Department has been producing for the last few years. They are all available via the IMF PFM blog at http://blog-pfm.imf.org/.

[9]For instance, information contained in financial statements helps in compliance with fiscal rules; changing the basis of budgetary controls from input to output can promote efficiency in the delivery of public goods and services.

information requirements, and procedures that may get in the way of others. This is when government expectations for improvement are frustrated, leading to administrative overload and reform fatigue. Properly designed, an integrated PFM agenda can highlight interdependencies among elements and enable government to select the course that fits its needs and capacity. The system frame of reference also highlights the persisting tendency among public finance specialists and policymakers to split policy design from implementation. In modern and increasingly complex economies, one cannot be conceived without the other.

Finally, advanced economies have been fertile breeding grounds for PFM innovations, but low-income countries have been the main venues for comprehensive reform efforts. The profound differences among countries do not mean that PFM improvements are beyond the reach of countries beset by significant shortcomings. The differences do suggest, however, that innovators should be mindful of sequencing issues and capacity constraints. Architecture is always important; in low-capacity countries, it is critical.[10]

PUBLIC FINANCIAL MANAGEMENT IN THE WAKE OF THE FINANCIAL CRISIS

The ongoing financial and economic crisis has proved to be quite a test for PFM. It has revealed how many reforms were far from being well entrenched. For instance, expenditure control mechanisms turned out to be weaker in practice than expected, and some countries in financial distress saw expenditure arrears increase very rapidly. Numerical fiscal rules and targets have proliferated in the past 15 years, and have often been seen as a means for addressing all fiscal problems—chiefly rising deficits and debt levels but also accountability and responsibility gaps—while relegating other vital PFM elements to a supporting role (Wyplosz, 2012). But the record to date is far from compelling, with the overall lackluster performance of numerical rules that were introduced in isolation rather than as part of a more coherent expenditure framework. It is most welcome and timely that the European Commission has focused on other essential PFM elements as part of its Fiscal Compact.[11]

The crisis has focused attention on two aspects of PFM that have been somewhat neglected in the last two decades but are at its very core: budgetary institutions and fiscal transparency. A well-established body of theoretical and

[10] It is important to stress that there is no automatic relationship between low capacity and low income. Certain advanced economies have revealed, particularly in the wake of the financial crisis, lower-than-expected PFM capacity, whereas capacity in a number of emerging market economies and even low-income countries has been growing quite rapidly.

[11] On December 13, 2011, the reinforced Stability and Growth Pact entered into force with a new set of rules for economic and fiscal surveillance. These new measures, the so-called Six Pack, comprise five regulations and one directive proposed by the European Commission and approved by all 27 member states and the European Parliament in October 2011. The Six Pack was followed in March 2012 by the intergovernmental agreement—not an EU law—the Treaty on Stability, Coordination and Governance, the fiscal part of which is commonly referred to as the Fiscal Compact. The treaty is binding for all euro area member states.

empirical analysis shows how budgetary institutions can influence fiscal outcomes.[12] From the perspective of this book, institutions are defined as the laws, procedures, rules, and conventions—including the bodies created by those norms—that influence fiscal policy decision making and management. Strong institutions can improve fiscal performance by highlighting the need for sustainable policies, exposing the full cost of public interventions, and raising the cost of deviating from stated fiscal objectives. By increasing the credibility of announced policies, strong institutions can also foster more favorable macroeconomic conditions and improve market confidence, which further support the restoration of fiscal sustainability.[13]

Key among the institutional arrangements are those that allow governments to have a full understanding of the current state and future evolution of the public finances, including exposure to contingent risks. But some governments are simply unaware of their true fiscal state and the exposure of their public finances for sheer lack of available information, despite concerted efforts to develop a set of internationally accepted standards for fiscal reporting and to monitor and promote the implementation of those standards at the national level. Thus, the understanding of many governments' underlying fiscal positions and the risks to the fiscal positions remains inadequate.

As discussed in a recent IMF paper (IMF, 2012), the financial crisis revealed that, even among advanced economies, governments' understanding of their current fiscal position was inadequate, as shown by the emergence of previously unrecorded deficits and debts and the crystallization of large, mainly implicit, government liabilities to the financial sector.[14] To paraphrase Rajan (2010), public finances were also sitting on *fault lines* largely because governments had substantially underestimated the risks to their fiscal prospects. Finally, the sharp deterioration of the fiscal stance that accompanied the crisis and the related need for fiscal adjustment have increased the incentives for governments to engage in activities that cloud the true state of their finances. As argued in quite a few chapters of this book, much remains to be done in this area because fiscal reports can be manipulated, thus circumventing fiscal rules and objectives.[15]

---

[12] Positive causality between the quality of budget institutions and fiscal outcomes has been demonstrated in numerous studies covering countries with different income levels, constitutional systems, and geographical locations. See, for example, von Hagen (1992); von Hagen and Harden (1996); Alesina and others (1999); de Haan, Moessen, and Volkerink (1999); and Debrun and others (2008).

[13] Although well beyond the purposes of this book, it may not be sheer coincidence that the debate on the role of institutions in generating growth and alleviating poverty has been reinvigorated in the last few years. See, for instance, Acemoglu and Robinson (2012) and the comments it has generated by, for instance, Sachs (2012) and Diamond (2012c).

[14] Although not explicitly discussed in this book, fiscal transparency—defined as the clarity, reliability, frequency, timeliness, and relevance of public fiscal reporting and the openness to the public of the government's fiscal policymaking process—is a critical element of and permeates effective modern fiscal management.

[15] Irwin (2012) discusses accounting devices and fiscal illusions in the wake of the crisis.

STRUCTURE OF THE BOOK

This book is divided into four parts. Its organizing principle is described by Schick in Part I, An Overview of Contemporary Public Financial Management Reforms. He draws a distinction between the different categories of innovations. The first category is major innovations that have introduced new or reinvigorated ideas and initiatives into PFM and that focus on specific issues such as the management of fiscal risks. The second category comprises reforms to the basic supporting PFM infrastructure, for example, accounting and budgeting frameworks. Modernizing this supporting infrastructure is important for providing the information and capacity to successfully implement the major innovations. This is echoing to some extent a back-to-basics theme often heard in many debates on PFM reforms in advanced as well as in developing contexts.

Accordingly, and following the architectural theme of this book, Part II discusses Designing and Building: PFM Innovations and Reforms. Part III focuses on Strengthening the Foundations: Modernizing the PFM Infrastructure. Part IV, Adapting to the Environment: PFM Reform in Developing Countries, brings to the fore selected aspects relevant particularly, but not exclusively, to designing PFM reforms in developing countries.

Part I. An Overview of Contemporary Public Financial Management Reforms

In the overview chapter, "Reflections on Two Decades of Public Financial Management Reforms," Schick promotes a better understanding of how PFM innovations operate, how they interact with each other, and how they can be integrated into a comprehensive PFM structure. This chapter provides an original framework relating innovations to the three key PFM objectives and to three common levers or instruments—new information, process adjustments, and restrictive rules—used by reformers to achieve their objectives. The first two levers operate through changing the incentives and the behavior of politicians and public servants and the third by imposing restrictions on actions and decisions.

The chapter uses this framework as a lens through which to assess the major innovations and supporting reforms that are discussed in detail in Parts II and III. New information is essential for nearly all major innovations. Information on fiscal risks, evaluations of programs, and projections of debt and deficits can provide politicians and managers with new perspectives and motivate them to change existing policies. Schick argues, however, that in most cases information alone is not sufficient to influence behavior.

Politicians and managers are less likely to disregard new procedures than new information. The main issue is whether the new procedures will change behavior or become just another task that managers must complete. For example, a procedural requirement to include performance information in budgeting and management processes can be used by managers to improve results or it can be seen as another technical requirement with little impact on decision making.

When the first two levers do not work, preferred procedures may be codified into rules, such as fiscal limits on debt or deficit, that constrain government actions. Rules have several advantages, the most obvious being that they cannot be disregarded as easily as new information and permissive procedures. Nevertheless, to work, rules have to build on innovations in information and process and not be a substitute for them.

Schick stresses that a government should apply constrictive rules only when it has a good understanding of why enhanced information and processes do not work. He cautions that not every procedure should become a constraining rule because it may end up limiting the discretion of democratically elected leaders, introducing rigidity into the PFM system, and becoming an end in itself rather than a means to an end.

The chapter concludes the discussion on levers by acknowledging that there is no "automatic transmission belt" that converts levers into modified behavior and changed behavior into substantive outcomes. PFM is an open system exposed to many economic and political factors that affect incentives and behavior of politicians and public servants. Therefore, this chapter and this book stress the importance of a country's underlying political and administrative culture and institutions and the role of political and managerial leadership in successfully implementing reforms.

As the 2008–09 crisis emanated from the financial sector, PFM has largely been a bystander since the onset of the crisis and during its initial stages. The real test for PFM was in the precrisis years in which, Schick argues, some innovations did not yield the expected results. Under unfavorable economic conditions, spending was increased to stimulate the economy, but when conditions were more favorable, spending was not lowered. In sum, in good times governments did not save. The average gross public debt-to-GDP ratio for the Group of Seven nations rose from 35 percent in 1974 to more than 80 percent in 2007, just before the crisis (Cottarelli and Schaechter, 2010). Schick concludes that PFM can make a difference to fiscal and budgetary outcomes, and the still-emerging lessons from the crisis about PFM innovations can improve them and contribute in the future to averting or at least better managing the next crisis. Key among the lessons is the need to redesign fiscal rules and improve fiscal risk management to look beyond the government sector.

Part II. Designing and Building: PFM Innovations and Reforms

Chapters 2 through 6 examine different innovations—fiscal responsibility legislation, numerical rules, MTBFs, fiscal risk management, and independent fiscal agencies—that concentrate on promoting fiscal responsibility. Although the objective is the same, different levers and approaches are used. Chapters 2 and 3 focus on codifying procedures and rules. MTBFs, discussed in Chapter 4, seek to contribute not only to fiscal sustainability, but also to the two other PFM objectives of effective allocation of resources and efficient delivery of services, and can use all three levers—new information, changing procedures, and rules—to influence behavior. Chapters 5 and 6 emphasize fiscal sustainability and the role and importance of information and analysis. Performance budgeting and information, covered in Chapter 7, are expected to contribute to the goals of effective allocation of resources and efficient service delivery. Performance budgeting relies on new information and changes in procedures to improve performance.

Van Eden, Khemani, and Emery explore in **Chapter 2** how fiscal responsibility laws (FRLs) can support more sustainable and transparent fiscal policies. Since the 1990s, there has been a significant growth in the number of countries that have developed fiscal responsibility provisions, which embed in law an agreed-on set of arrangements intended to promote fiscal discipline, transparency, and accountability. This chapter argues that design choices are critical to the success of FRLs and explores different design options. In designing FRLs it is important to start with modest and flexible frameworks then gradually move to more prescriptive legal requirements for fiscal policy. Building up PFM capacity is an additional reason to take a gradual approach. The more complex the law, the greater the capacity needed. This chapter concludes that FRLs, in conjunction with the other innovations discussed in this section (MTBFs, a new generation of numerical fiscal rules, and independent fiscal councils), can play an important role in strengthening fiscal outcomes. When adopting these laws, however, reformers should not stride too far ahead of societal acceptance and recognition of the importance of fiscal sustainability.

In **Chapter 3**, Budina, Kinda, Schaechter, and Weber take stock of the development and use of numerical fiscal rules—long-lasting constraints on fiscal policy through the application of numerical limits on budgetary aggregates. This chapter provides a systematic compilation and comparison of numerical fiscal rules and their design elements. In particular, it reviews trends—from the mid-1980s through early 2012—in the types and number of rules, as well as their combinations and main characteristics. This review includes discussions of the legal bases, enforcement, coverage, escape clauses, and provisions for cyclical adjustments. The chapter also examines the next generation of fiscal rules emerging in the aftermath of the 2008–09 global economic and financial crisis. To be effective, it is important that rules be an integral part of the budget formulation and execution cycle and have the necessary supporting institutions. Despite widespread application, fiscal rules are not without challenges, including relative rigidity in adjusting to shocks and the potential to generate incentives for creative accounting. The next-generation fiscal rules, which are attempting to address some of these issues, tend to be more complex, thus creating new challenges in design, implementation, and monitoring. Given their relatively high degree of complexity, their effectiveness will also depend on country-specific institutional capacity.

A key issue in PFM is the inability of government to look beyond a one-year time horizon when making decisions on current or proposed policies and expenditures that have fiscal implications for many years ahead. To help address this concern, over the last two decades more and more countries have developed MTBFs. Harris, Hughes, Ljungman, and Sateriale in **Chapter 4** define MTBFs as "a set of institutional arrangements for prioritizing, presenting, and managing revenue and expenditure in a multiyear perspective." There is no single MTBF model. Countries have taken a range of approaches. Preconditions for a successful MTBF include a credible and predictable annual budget, accurate medium-term macroeconomic and demographic projections, established fiscal objectives and rules, and a comprehensive top-down budget process. This chapter stresses the importance of design for success. Using original empirical research, it tests the impact of the different types of MTBF on fiscal outcomes and allocative efficiency. It also examines how selected MTBFs have been adjusted to help governments respond to, and deliver, both fiscal stimulus packages and fiscal consolidation.

The global financial crisis dramatically illustrated the importance of managing the fiscal risks to which public finances can be exposed. Budina and Petrie in **Chapter 5** assess the trends since the early 1990s toward more active disclosure and management of fiscal risks. They explore in detail how a fiscal risk management cycle tool can help governments identify, analyze, and incorporate risks into the budget, and disclose, mitigate, and monitor those risks. Since 2000 some progress has been made on disclosure of information on fiscal risks, and a few countries have developed fiscal risk statements. The IMF guidelines for fiscal risk management provide countries with risk disclosure and management principles. Although some countries have made advances, risk management for many others remains at a basic level. As the crisis illustrates, many challenges in improving risk management remain. Key among them is the lack of a systematic and centralized approach to identifying risk; simply put, many governments have no basic information on the range and magnitude of risks to which they could be exposed. The chapter concludes that in the wake of the crisis, the ability to identify and analyze risks has become more critical than ever. The priorities and capacities for strengthening risk management, however, will depend on individual country circumstances and conditions.

Another trend emerging since the crisis is an increased emphasis on independent scrutiny and analysis of governments' fiscal policies, plans, and performance and the corresponding growth in independent fiscal agencies. Among these, fiscal councils are hailed as a mechanism for promoting fiscal responsibility. Hemming and Joyce, in **Chapter 6,** review the justification for establishing independent institutions and councils, the different roles and functions they perform, and the requirements for their success. Councils do not exercise influence through formal procedures or rules but by providing independent information and analysis that can influence policymakers and the public. The theory is that independent review improves fiscal transparency, which can, in turn, enhance fiscal discipline. Fiscal councils can be advisory bodies reviewing and commenting on government fiscal policies, and/or auditing bodies that verify the reliability of government information, including the quality of their forecasts. This chapter presents a number of factors influencing the success of a fiscal council, including guaranteed independence, formal influence, political support, clear legal backing, and technically qualified staff. It concludes that although, in principle, fiscal councils can play a role in promoting fiscal discipline, it is too early to disentangle their impact on fiscal outcomes.

Curristine and Flynn in **Chapter 7** examine governments' continuous quest for improved public service efficiency and performance. Performance tools—performance management, measurement, and budgeting—have become an integral part of how governments do business. These tools all depend on performance information (PI) to measure, monitor, and improve performance. Nearly all OECD countries have developed PI and many have introduced procedures to integrate it into accountability, budgeting, and management processes. The issue is getting this information used in decision making. Information is not an end in itself but a means to better performance. In many countries it has proven more challenging to ensure the use of PI in budgeting than in management. This challenge arises from problems in aligning incentive structures, political economy issues, and informational and institutional constraints. This chapter also discusses how PI can be used in fiscal stimulus and consolidation, arguing that the approach to its use will depend on many factors, including speed and depth of consolidation, existing performance budgeting systems, the quality of PI, and the political willingness to use it. The chapter concludes by highlighting selected countries' experiences with spending reviews.

Part III. Strengthening the Foundations: Modernizing the PFM Infrastructure

Part III builds on one of Schick's themes—the critical role of information—by focusing on developments that have taken place in public accounting and reporting, cash and debt management, and public investment. It also sheds some light on accrual-based budgeting, a reform that only a limited number of countries have attempted. All the reforms discussed in this part contribute to all three PFM objectives. They are important for supporting the innovations discussed in Part II; for example, improving fiscal reporting supports better management of fiscal risks and enhanced transparency.

Blondy, Cooper, Irwin, Kauffmann, and Khan in **Chapter 8** examine the trends in fiscal reporting over the past decade. Government reporting on its fiscal position, whether in financial statements, fiscal statistics, or other documents, is vital to PFM and contributes to its three objectives. This information is essential for governmental decision making and for accountability. Significant changes have occurred in this area in the past decade. The comprehensiveness of reports has improved because many governments that in the past reported only cash flows and debt now report assets and liabilities. The adoption of accrual-based reporting has been motivated by the realization that cash reporting does not reveal costs in a timely manner, which in turn spurred the development of new accrual-based international statistical and accounting standards. Another important development is the extension of coverage of reports beyond just the central government, to include local governments and more public entities in an effort to limit off-budget spending. Despite these developments, reporting before the crisis gave few warnings of the looming problems; the risk posed by the financial sector was largely ignored in fiscal reporting and statements. The crisis emphasized both the importance of fiscal reporting and the need for further improvements, including increased focus on government balance sheets.

Gardner and Olden in **Chapter 9** discuss how governments' management of their financial assets and liabilities has evolved since 1990. The chapter focuses on changes in how governments have managed their cash and debts during this period. Significant changes have been driven by the increased volume and complexity of financial markets, by innovations in information and communication technologies, and by new institutional designs and capacity building. There is also a greater awareness of the need to integrate the management of all government financial assets and liabilities. Increasingly, debt management offices have been given responsibility for cash management. This chapter argues for an integrated as opposed to fragmented approach to cash and debt management for a variety of reasons. Integrated management creates incentives to manage all government financial resources in a portfolio, avoids sending confused signals to the markets, and consolidates scarce resources by allowing streamlining of information technology systems and back-office facilities. In addition to discussing recent trends, this chapter examines current challenges and specific issues facing emerging and developing economies. It also addresses how countries that had already developed effective systems before the crisis have benefited from them during the course of the crisis.

Fainboim, Last, and Tandberg in **Chapter 10** examine the changes in public investment management during the past 20 years. Even before this period, the management of public investment had undergone noteworthy changes. Against a global decline in public investment, the authors observe the abandonment of national plans and planning ministries in advanced economies in favor of decentralizing this function to sector ministries and the elimination of dual budgeting. The chapter considers how some of the PFM innovations discussed in Part II of this book, including MTBFs and performance budgeting systems, have affected the way that governments manage their public investments. Despite the mainstreaming of public investment into government management and budgeting, its unique nature still requires some specialized tools. This chapter discusses selected new and revamped public investment management tools. It also addresses changing approaches to financing public investment, concentrating on public-private partnerships and highlighting the importance of understanding and managing the risks created by these contracts. Public investment management and planning has significantly benefited from PFM innovations. However, despite these benefits, procyclicality and the stop-and-go nature of public investment persist, as made evident during the crisis.

Khan in **Chapter 11** discusses accrual budgeting. Although many governments have introduced accrual accounting, only a few have adopted accrual budgeting. These are countries that already produce ex post financial reports for central government on an accrual basis. No single model of accrual budgeting exists. Countries have adopted different frameworks suitable to their country contexts. This chapter examines why accrual budgeting can be a useful reform and how it works in practice, and notes the different country approaches. This chapter considers the potential benefits and challenges of accrual budgeting, along with the prerequisites for successful implementation. Among these prerequisites are a phased approach to implementation, political support, a sound cash budgeting system, and technical capacity.

Part IV. Adapting to the Environment: PFM Reform in Developing Countries

Although much of the focus of this book is on advanced economies, this part explores issues and challenges in implementing PFM reforms in developing countries. It stresses the importance of adapting PFM innovations to the environment and individual countries' contexts and capacities. Each of these chapters discusses the sequencing of reforms, the impact of context and differing institutional and technical capacities, and the influence of political economy factors on PFM reform prospects in developing countries. These considerations also apply to advanced and emerging economies.

Fedelino and Smoke in **Chapter 12** examine an underresearched topic: the links between PFM and decentralization reforms. Conceptually, the link between these reforms is strong and mutually beneficial. In practice, however, this link is rarely established. Decentralization reforms and PFM reforms are often formulated as independent initiatives managed by different agencies with different goals—thus, uncoordinated and not sequenced. This lack of synchrony creates inconsistencies in government systems and operations and sends mixed signals to key actors. This chapter argues for more integrated analysis and better coordination in the development and execution of PFM and decentralization reforms. It emphasizes the importance of more systematic and formal analysis to help reformers understand the implications of country context for the links between PFM and decentralization.

In **Chapter 13,** Dabán and Hélis explore how well-designed and sequenced PFM reforms can help natural resource–rich countries manage their public finances and avoid the resource curse. This chapter asserts that weak institutions in the preresource period, combined with poorly designed, opaque, and rigid resource-specific operational mechanisms, have contributed to the curse in some countries. The few countries that have successfully avoided the curse already had strong institutional and PFM systems in the preresource era. Resource-specific mechanisms, when poorly designed, can reduce the efficiency of government spending and result in fragmentation and delay in the budget process. By explaining the unique challenges of managing finances in natural resource-rich countries, this chapter develops a PFM framework and sequenced reform path for these countries, seeking to enhance rather than replace or bypass existing budgetary institutions so as to preserve the integrity of the budget process.

Finally, Allen in **Chapter 14** presents an analytical perspective on the current debate about the challenges of reforming budgetary institutions in developing countries. The chapter explores the factors that determine the development of budgetary reforms and what can be learned from advanced economies about prioritizing and sequencing reforms. Advanced-economy experience shows that reforming budget institutions is a very slow and challenging process, closely related to wider societal, political, and economic institutional developments. Further complications are that reforms require a willingness on the part of politicians to make hard choices; incentives for reform among politicians and public servants are weak; ministries of finance tend to be weak; and fragmented budgets are a common problem. This chapter asserts that transplanting advanced-economy approaches to reforming budget institutions into the alien environment of developing countries is likely to be unsuccessful. Although there are some exceptions, they are rare. The chapter argues that the more successful improvement strategies have a relatively short time horizon, focus on narrow and specific objectives, and involve a large element of trial and error.

WHERE DO WE GO FROM HERE?

In line with the leading theme of this book—the emerging architecture of PFM reform—this section refrains from providing any firm conclusions. The hope of this book is instead to distill a number of considerations for decision makers, international public finance specialists and practitioners, and the public at large.

- Modern PFM comprises a set of increasingly complex processes, rules, systems, and norms that are intrinsically linked to one another. Heated discussions on individual innovations often ignore this simple tenet and confuse the trees with the forest. Every reform needs a champion but very few champions have the vision to see how each innovation is interconnected with others and how only a harmonious assembly of all the bits and pieces has the chance to ultimately provide the answers and solutions sought.
- The relative emphasis on PFM's three key objectives—maintaining a sustainable fiscal position, effective allocation of resources, and efficient delivery of public goods and services—has shifted from the effectiveness and efficiency arguments to fiscal sustainability. Once again, these three objectives should not be addressed in isolation. For a long time, however, the sustainability aspect was neglected, with the obvious result that a string of "good years" was wasted with no strengthening of fiscal positions while precious time and resources were invested in other—and with the annoying benefit of hindsight, arguably less important—aspects of PFM.

- The importance of the particular context—historical, political, and geographical, but also human capital—in which a country decides to manage its public finances better cannot be stressed strongly enough. There are no magic bullets or cookie-cutter approaches to strengthening PFM, and any attempt to import innovations that may have worked elsewhere should be carefully assessed and subjected to an "on-the-ground" reality check. The same applies to political economy considerations and reforms aimed at addressing more systemic public administration or governance aspects.
- The importance of information also cannot be overly stressed. In still too many instances, countries have been caught by surprise because the coverage—either of institutions or of transactions—of fiscal activities was not fully captured. The focus is not only on past and current fiscal developments, but even more forcefully on future developments. The progress made on reporting standards is part of the effort to define better ways to convey an accurate picture of public finances for various purposes, from aggregate demand management to accountability.
- Related to the point above is the current emphasis on extending the horizon of fiscal policy by adopting medium- to long-term frameworks aimed at making clear the impact of today's policy decisions on tomorrow's outcomes. A better appreciation of fiscal risks—in a nutshell, all factors that can explain outcomes different from planned—has now been widely accepted, although the practice is still lagging.
- Information can also be a double-edged sword. Although it has to fulfill many purposes, including international comparability, actors are always tempted to make information an end in itself instead of a means to help policymakers design and implement the best responses to society's needs. Numerous examples of information overload have proved frustrating to those involved in its production and those incapable of making good use of it. Information alone may in many cases not be sufficient to change key actors' behavior.
- A plethora of discussions, theories, and approaches to the sequencing of PFM reforms have arisen since the mid-1990s. We may have come full circle with the obvious conclusion that "it depends on a number of country-specific factors."[16] "Basic first" seems to be the prevailing view at this stage, but it should not lead to oversimplification and a too-rigid approach; individual countries may occasionally leapfrog and make the most of available technologies and lessons from early reformers. External factors, most notably political economy aspects but also human capital, can help explain why reforms tend to take longer than initially planned and in many instances turn out not to be sustained over time, causing undesirable backsliding.

---

[16] See Diamond (2012a, 2012b) and Tomassi (2012) for recent work on development of a guidance note for sequencing PFM reforms in the context of the OECD Development Assistance Committee, and Schick (2012).

Viewing PFM as an integrated framework and taking account of the considerations discussed above are essential in the wake of financial and economic crisis and, possibly, in trying to prevent the next one. As is often the case, however, it may be necessary but not sufficient. Bringing about a paradigm shift whereby responsible and accountable policymakers make decisions taking account of long-term considerations and the implications for the entire public sector on the basis of the best available ex ante and ex post information may require more than full implementation of the innovations discussed in this book. We should not forget, however, that many of them remain to be adopted or fully absorbed by most countries. This is therefore the agenda for the immediate future. Nevertheless, if the past provides any lessons, other innovations will come along to strengthen PFM's emerging architecture.

Finally, does this book provide an architectural design for modern PFM? We hope so. As noted at the outset, the objective is to identify PFM's constituent elements, along with a number of considerations that should be taken into account in designing the PFM framework most suited to addressing the needs of a particular society. Going beyond that would be pretending to have discovered a magic formula that does not and cannot exist. In assembling some of the innovations discussed in this book, the ultimate design will have to take into account individual countries' specific contexts and the need for flexibility to adapt to sudden changes in circumstances. Architects and engineers have learned over the years to design buildings that can withstand earthquakes, so future PFM frameworks will be well equipped to manage public resources when facing increasingly strong tremors. We are getting there; we are just not there yet.

REFERENCES

Acemoglu, Daron, and James Robinson, 2012, *Why Nations Fail: The Origins of Power, Prosperity, and Poverty* (New York: Crown Business).

Alesina, Alberto, Ricardo Hausmann, Rudolf Hommes, and Ernesto Stein, 1999, "Budget Institutions and Fiscal Performance in Latin America," *Journal of Development Economics*, Vol. 59, pp. 253–73.

Allen, Richard, and Daniel Tomassi, eds., 2001, *Managing Public Expenditure: A Reference Book for Transition Countries* (Paris: Organisation for Economic Co-operation and Development).

Cottarelli, Carlo, and Andrea Schaechter, 2010, "Long-Term Trends in Public Finances in the G-7 Economies," IMF Staff Position Note 10/13 (Washington: International Monetary Fund).

Debrun, Xavier, Laurent Moulin, Alessandro Turrini, Joaquim Ayuso-i-Casals, and Manmohan S. Kumar, 2008, "Tied to the Mast? National Fiscal Rules in the European Union," *Economic Policy*, Vol. 23 (April), pp. 297–362.

de Haan, Jakob, Wim Moessen, and Bjorn Volkerink, 1999, "Budgetary Procedures—Aspects and Changes: New Evidence for Some European Countries," in *Fiscal Institutions and Fiscal Performance*, ed. by James Poterba and Jürgen von Hagen (Chicago: University of Chicago Press).

Diamond, J., 2012a, "Guidance Note on Sequencing PFM Reforms." Available via the Internet: https//www.pefa.org/.

———, 2012b, "Guidelines for Sequencing PFM Reforms, Background Paper 1." Available via the Internet: https//www.pefa.org/.

———, 2012c, "What Makes Countries Rich or Poor?" *New York Times Review of Books*, June 7.

Hallerberg, Mark, and Jurgen von Hagen, 1997, "Electoral Institutions, Cabinet Negotiations, and Budget Deficits in the European Union," NBER Working Paper No. 6341 (Cambridge, Massachusetts: National Bureau of Economic Research).

International Monetary Fund (IMF), 2007, *Manual on Fiscal Transparency* (Washington). Available via the Internet: http://www.imf.org/external/np/fad/trans/manual/index.htm.

———, 2012, *Fiscal Transparency, Accountability, and Risk* (Washington).

———, 2013, "The Functions and Impact of Fiscal Councils" (forthcoming; Washington).

Irwin, Timothy, 2012, "Accounting Devices and Fiscal Illusions," IMF Staff Discussion Note 12/02 (Washington: International Monetary Fund).

Kydland, Finn E., and Edward C. Prescott, 1977, "Rules Rather than Discretion: The Inconsistency of Optimal Plans," *Journal of Political Economy*, Vol. 85, No. 3 (June), pp. 473–92.

Potter, Barry, and Jack Diamond, 1999, *Guidelines for Public Expenditure Management* (Washington: International Monetary Fund). Available via the Internet: http://www.imf.org/external/pubs/ft/expend/index.htm.

Premchand, A., 1993, *Public Expenditure Management* (Washington: International Monetary Fund).

Pretorius, Carol, and Nico Pretorius, 2008, *Review of Public Financial Management Reform Literature* (London: Department for International Development).

Rajan, Raghuram G., 2010, *Fault Lines: How Hidden Fractures Still Threaten the World Economy* (Princeton, New Jersey: Princeton University Press).

Sachs, Jeffrey, 2012, "Government, Geography, and Growth: The True Drivers of Economic Development," *Foreign Affairs*, September/October.

Schiavo-Campo, Salvatore, and Daniel Tommasi, 1999, *Managing Government Expenditure* (Manila: Asian Development Bank).

Schick, A., 1998, *A Contemporary Approach to Public Expenditure Management* (Washington: World Bank).

———, 2012, "Basics First Is Best Practice," IMF Public Financial Management Blog. http://blog-pfm.imf.org/.

Tommasi, Daniel, 2012, "The Core PFM Functions and PEFA Performance Indicators, Background Paper 2." Available via the Internet: https//www.pefa.org/.

von Hagen, Jürgen, 1992, "Budgeting Procedures and Fiscal Performance in the European Communities," European Commission Economic Papers No. 96 (Brussels: European Commission).

———, and I.J. Harden, 1996, "Budget Processes and Commitment to Fiscal Discipline," IMF Working Paper 96/78 (Washington: International Monetary Fund).

Weingast, B.R., K.A. Shepsle, and C. Johnsen, 1981, "The Political Economy of Benefits and Costs: A Neoclassical Approach to Distributive Politics," *Journal of Political Economy*, Vol. 89, No. 4, pp. 642–64.

World Bank, 1998, *Public Expenditure Management Handbook* (Washington). Available via the Internet: http://www1.worldbank.org/publicsector/pe/handbook/pem98.pdf.

Wyplosz, Charles, 2012, "Fiscal Rules: Theoretical Issues and Historical Experiences," in *Fiscal Policy after the Financial Crisis*, ed. by Alberto Alesina and Francesco Giavazzi (Chicago: University of Chicago Press).

PART I

An Overview of Contemporary Public Financial Management Reforms

CHAPTER 1

Reflections on Two Decades of Public Financial Management Reforms

ALLEN SCHICK

This chapter provides an overview of contemporary public financial management (PFM). In doing so, it prepares the ground for the succeeding chapters, which discuss in detail specific PFM reforms and challenges. It frames PFM within a logical structure that links (1) the major innovations and reforms (fiscal rules, medium-term budget frameworks, risk management, and performance budgeting) to (2) the core objectives of PFM (to maintain a sustainable fiscal position, effective allocation of resources, and efficient operation of public services), and to (3) PFM levers or instruments for changing behavior and outcomes (information, processes, and rules). The major innovations discussed in this chapter seek to address one or more of the core PFM objectives and to apply one or more levers to change the incentives and behavior of politicians and public servants.

PFM reforms employ new information, process adjustments, and constrictive rules as levers for changing behavior and outcomes. Reform arguably adheres to a logical sequence, beginning with enriching the information available to policymakers (expecting that better information will produce better outcomes), then using processes to induce policymakers to make prudent and effective decisions, and culminating in rules proscribing or prescribing appropriate actions. This chapter applies similar questions to each innovation: Do adjustments to information suffice to achieve desired outcomes? Is it appropriate and necessary to establish formal rules? The chapter also examines how the basic PFM infrastructure—accounting, budgeting, and organizational frameworks supporting the management of public money—has been modernized.

This chapter draws on insights discussed in the other chapters. In line with the overall theme of this book, its aim is not to propose new reforms, but to identify good practices and to assess issues in implementing and melding them into a comprehensive PFM framework. The success of reforms depends in large measure on whether they become institutionalized as the means of managing public finance. Some PFM reforms have taken root—others have not, because implementation has been ineffective, they fit poorly within existing PFM structures, or they were not embraced by those responsible for making them work.

PFM reforms have been stress-tested by the global financial and economic crisis. The test lies not so much in crisis-induced responses but in the actions and policies in place before the crisis, when countries made program and budget decisions that ignored future costs and risks. In some advanced economies, the crisis highlighted institutional weakness and the need to reform existing institutions or introduce new ones. This story is still unfolding.

This chapter is divided into six sections. The first maps a PFM framework and examines PFM core objectives; the second looks at the three key PFM levers and instruments; the third assesses major PFM reforms and evaluates them according to changes to information, processes, and rules; the fourth addresses approaches to modernizing the basic PFM infrastructure; and the fifth discusses critical issues in reforming PFM, including differences in the capacities of advanced economies and low-income countries and whether contemporary PFM reforms can change incentives, behavior, and substantive outcomes. The final section discusses PFM and the global financial and economic crisis and what lessons can be learned for the next generation of PFM reforms.

1.1. MAPPING THE PFM FRAMEWORK

PFM is often regarded as an umbrella term for a variety of loosely related processes for managing government finances, including one set of processes for estimating economic conditions and prospects, another for allocating public money, and a third for reporting financial results. PFM sprawls across many fields and practices. It draws from economics and public finance, accounting and auditing, policy analysis and program evaluation, public administration, political economy, and political science. These fields (and others) contribute to managing public finance, but they are rooted in different professional orientations and skills.

A unifying PFM framework must cover major policy questions, such as the fiscal position of government, as well as operational issues, such as the provision of specific services. The framework must be useful to practitioners but must also provide a basis for scholarship and research.

Possible frameworks include the categories on which IMF and Public Expenditure and Financial Accountability (PEFA)[1] diagnostic tools and surveys are based. Although they differ in approach, these diagnostics share a critical assumption—that there is a right way to manage public finance, not necessarily best practice, but better than that achieved by many countries. The IMF Code of Good Practices on Fiscal Transparency[2] identifies four sets of criteria for one aspect of PFM: clarity of roles and responsibilities, an open budget process, public availability of information, and assurances of integrity. PEFA has six somewhat different categories: credibility of the budget; comprehensiveness and transparency; policy-based budgeting; predictability and control in budget execution;

[1] PEFA was launched in 2002 by a consortium of financial and development institutions that included the IMF; the World Bank; the European Commission; and French, U.K., Norwegian, and Swiss government agencies.

[2] The IMF Code was issued in 1998 and revised in 2007 and 2013. It has been extensively applied by the IMF to assess country practices and identify areas in need of improvement.

accounting, recording, and reporting; and external scrutiny and audit. Both instruments have been widely and effectively applied in assessing PFM capacity and in prodding governments to upgrade their practices. However, their focus on process calls into question their utility as the organizing framework for PFM.

Good process is essential in PFM to avoid defective results. Budgets that exclude or misreport expenditure will generate deficits above planned levels; governments that lack the means to evaluate programs will have portfolios of ineffective programs; and service-providing agencies that have inaccurate accounts or poorly trained staff will deliver inferior services. Yet, quite a few governments have comprehensive budgets and accurate accounts but excessive deficits, evaluative capacity but rigid budgets that impede a shift of resources to more productive uses, and a rich array of performance measures but inefficient services. In other words, a good process can also produce bad outcomes. Although processes matter a great deal in PFM because they generate and transmit information that shapes the behavior of key actors, they are inherently insufficient because PFM is an open, permeable system, the outcomes of which are swayed by numerous external events and pressures. Precisely because the process is not determinative, assessing the degree to which outcomes fulfill the purposes served by good financial management practice is essential.

1.1.1. PFM Objectives

These purposes have been distilled since the mid-1990s into PFM's three basic objectives, which are arrayed from highly aggregate policies to discrete actions.[3]

Government Should Maintain a Sustainable Fiscal Position

The balance between revenues and expenditures, the debt level, and other fiscal aggregates should promote economic stability and be sustainable during the medium term and beyond.

This objective may denote that the aggregates should not simply be the sum of revenue and spending actions, but that firm limits, set in advance, should drive budget decisions through top-down procedures that constrain spending bids. This objective is not well served by annual budgets that measure policy implications only for the year immediately ahead, or by the cash basis of accounting that recognizes only liabilities for which current payments are made.

Various PFM innovations detailed in this and later chapters contribute to this objective, including fiscal rules and frameworks, the accrual basis, medium-term expenditure frameworks, long-term sustainability projections, baseline estimates, fiscal risk analysis, statements of contingent liabilities, and independent fiscal projections and assessments. One of the critical questions facing PFM architects is whether this crop of innovations sufficiently counters economic and political pressures.

---

[3] Although it has antecedents in work by Musgrave (1959) and others, the typology used here was devised by Campos and Pradhan (1996).

Effective Allocation of Resources to Sectors, Ministries, and Programs

Public money should be allocated on the basis of evidence of program effectiveness and in furtherance of the priorities of government.

Achieving this objective has been hampered for decades by the entrenched incrementalism of public budgets.[4] Efforts to explicitly reallocate funds from less to more effective uses have not been notably successful, nor has a parade of reforms been able to weaken incrementalism's hold on budget policy. In many countries, the spread of entitlement programs has made the national budget more rigid and less amenable to reallocation than was the case several years ago.[5] Governments invest more in policy analysis and program evaluation than in the past, with usually only a marginal impact on allocations.

Medium-term budget frameworks are the main innovation for countering this predicament. These frameworks seek to protect future fiscal space against incremental pressures and give politicians and program managers incentives to reallocate resources within constrained budget targets.[6] Contrary to past reforms that tried and failed to uproot incrementalism, medium-term budget frameworks concede that budgets are based principally on past expenditure, but aim to significantly expand the margin for reallocation. Strategic planning, program budgeting, outcome indicators, bidding funds, forced cutbacks, and fundamental expenditure reviews have been introduced or retooled to promote effective allocation. Despite these innovations, reallocation may be the most difficult PFM task.

Efficient Provision of Public Services

Government should achieve value for money in delivering public services and should be attentive to the quality and accessibility of services.

Services are critical points of contact between citizens and government. Citizens know government by way of the services it provides or fails to provide. The depressed level of trust and confidence in governments and leaders has spurred efforts to improve service delivery, and has exerted pressure on governments to do more without increasing tax burdens. Improving public services extends beyond PFM to the overall competence and orientation of public management, especially to the motivation and performance of public employees.[7] In fact, fundamentally reorienting public management, including financial management, has been new public management's (NPM's) principal objective (see Box 1.1). It may be feasible to improve public management without embracing NPM doctrine, but it almost surely is not feasible to transform the way government manages its finances without also changing the way government manages its staff.

---

[4] The classic statement on incrementalism was formulated by Wildavsky (1964).

[5] In some countries, such as Brazil and Colombia, major entitlements are embedded in the constitution. For upward of 85 percent of total central government expenditure, the amount spent is determined by statute or constitution.

[6] The concept of fiscal space was initially formulated by Heller (2005). See also Schick (2009a).

[7] Issues in improving public services are discussed in Shah (2005).

BOX 1.1 Age of Innovation: New Concepts and Approaches in Public Financial Management

The end of the postwar boom occurred when governments in advanced economies were becoming sensitive to the financial stresses of aging populations and to the future costs of the pension rights and health benefits they had conferred on citizens during the good times (Tanzi and Schuknecht, 2000). Another, almost concurrent, development was a significant decline in citizen trust in national leaders and institutions (Pharr and Putnam, 2000; Dalton, 2004). These trends impelled some governments to explore new means of managing the public sector, chiefly through innovations that came to be labeled new public management (NPM), and some to import market methods and practices into public management. Significantly, though they were anchored in different principles and orientations, managerialists and marketers found common cause in PFM innovations.

During the past 30 years, many advanced economies have adopted PFM innovations, but few have implemented a full suite of reforms. Moreover, few have embraced the tenets of NPM or market instruments;[a] instead, they have favored innovations (e.g., performance measurement, accrual accounting) that can be grafted onto existing PFM arrangements and require no fundamental realignment of financial management. Market and managerial doctrines make demands that most governments find impractical or unacceptable. Market-oriented reforms strive to introduce prices, competition, and choice in the provision of public services. These include governments having the option of purchasing services from public or private providers, a shift from career to term public employment, fees for various services, and the right of citizens to opt out of certain public services. This is not an appealing menu of reforms for governments that have grown on the conviction that public services should be publicly provided. When market-type reforms have been suggested, strong opposition has come from many quarters, especially from public employees and civil service unions. Piecemeal market-oriented reforms have been adopted in some countries, but the overall record has been disappointing to those who believe that without genuine competition and choice, government performance will inevitably be suboptimal.

Managerialist innovations have fared somewhat better, if only because they reinforce the idea that public services should be publicly provided. Unlocking managerial potential by deregulating administrative and financial controls is a cornerstone of NPM, as is stronger accountability for actions and results. NPM purports to "let managers manage" by liberating them from inefficient constraints and procedures and to "make managers manage" by reviewing their performance against expectations. Managerial innovations include global operating budgets that permit managers to decide the inputs they purchase, strategic plans that set objectives, and performance targets that notify managers of what is expected of them. Managerialism has advanced furthest in well-run governments with a high-performing public service, low levels of corruption, and little political involvement in administrative matters. Countries that lack these enabling conditions cannot safely devolve managerial responsibilities from the center of government to operating units, but they can adopt selective performance-improving innovations.

Although they have provided ideas and momentum for innovation, neither market doctrine nor managerialism provides a fully satisfactory architecture for PFM practices. Few governments have fully devolved financial control to spending units, and fewer have marketized public services. A structure that excludes most countries might provide useful ideas for reform, but cannot fuse all relevant elements of financial management into a comprehensive template. The market and managerial designs share a more fundamental shortcoming: neither deals with the aggregate fiscal position of government—total revenues and expenditures, the financial balance, and the debt level. In short, they do not deal directly with deficit bias. Governments have had to seek other means for regulating fiscal policy, such as fiscal rules and medium-term budget frameworks.

---

[a] The concepts and applications of NPM are critiqued in Pollitt (2000) and Talbot (2010).

Efforts to improve services have been centered on performance-oriented initiatives, including output targets and indicators, performance budgets and performance contracts, performance-related pay, efficiency savings that assume ongoing productivity gains, and performance reports and audits. Accrual accounting along with strengthened internal control and audit capacity and integrated financial information systems have also been on the PFM reform agenda. Whether this impressive list of innovations has changed the culture of public management is an open question.

Although they have political aspects, the foregoing objectives are drawn from economic concepts and research. PFM also has an explicitly political dimension—managing public finance not only pursues sustainable public finances and efficiency but also encompasses responsiveness to citizen preferences and enhanced accountability and democratic institutions. Box 1.2 provides a brief discussion of approaches to strengthening financial accountability.

1.2. PFM LEVERS AND INSTRUMENTS

This section examines the three key levers of PFM: information, processes, and rules. Achievement of PFM objectives depends on those who manage public finance—primarily political leaders for fiscal matters, political and managerial policymakers for effective allocation, managers and staff at all organizational levels for efficient services. All this adds up to a massive effort to transform the behavior of just about everybody who leads or works in government. Spenders have to be recast into rationers, program defenders into program evaluators, and service providers into performance experts.

This is an immense undertaking that the political economy literature boils down to a matter of changing incentives—the signals and impulses that shape what people do and how they behave. In truth, it is exceedingly difficult to change incentives or behavior, partly because as an open system PFM does not have dominion over the myriad influences that determine actions and outcomes. There is no sure pathway from incentives to behavior. If there were, more countries would have disciplined fiscal positions, governments would routinely allocate funds only to effective programs, and efficient services would be the norm.

This section is predicated on the notion that understanding how PFM innovations work may deter governments and reformers from taking avoidable missteps and thereby boost the success rate. Almost all PFM reforms can be distilled into the following contention:

> To change behavior and results, governments must change the information available to participants, the manner in which the information is processed, and the constraints under which the participants act.

Beyond these changes, PFM branches out in different directions. One direction regards information and process as sufficient to change behavior. The other regards formal rules constraining the actions of public finance managers to be essential to producing desired behavioral modifications. The first approach would counter budgetary myopia by presenting information on the medium- to

BOX 1.2 Strengthening Financial Accountability

Information is the main tool for ensuring financial accountability, but incentives and rules, particularly accounting standards and principles and the audit process, are vital elements. National governments now commonly publish audited financial reports; the accuracy and timeliness of these statements often are regarded in well-managed countries as indicators of public financial management (PFM) quality. However, when the media and civil society pay little attention to audits and adverse findings are routinely ignored or explained away, politicians and managers have no incentive to take corrective action. Some countries have sought to strengthen PFM by arming auditors with greater independence and more resources, but what happens to audits after they are published may be more important than the process by which they are prepared.

Maintaining financial accountability usually requires some degree of legislative capacity to scrutinize public accounts, probe irregularities, and feed findings and information into budget and appropriations work. Public Accounts Committees have played these roles in Westminster-type parliaments for decades, but a more recent trend has been to relocate the national audit office (once situated within the executive branch in many countries) to the legislature. This approach strengthens checks and balances, transparency, and the legislature's capacity to hold public officials to account. Depending on the political system, this orientation may open the door to fundamental changes in executive-legislative relations or merely supply compliant legislators with more information.

Managing public finance has traditionally been a closed, insular process in which agencies of government communicate with one another to determine the budget, monitor transactions, prepare reports, and regulate the behavior of participants. The closed character of PFM systems has been reinforced in many countries by government's near monopoly on relevant information, the legislature's limited role, and the technical, sometimes dense nature of financial data and documents. Citizens and groups have usually been passive bystanders, except on those occasions when a financial issue gains public attention.

Efforts to make public finance more transparent have clustered around three sets of initiatives. One has been to make PFM processes and actions more accessible through the Internet and other means; the second has been to enlarge the legislature's role in discussing financial policies; and the third has been to open key issues to public participation before decisions have been made. The first has made most headway, undoubtedly because it does not directly challenge established institutions; progress on the second has depended on the form of government; and the third has found limited application through participatory budgeting in a few countries. In addition, many of the innovations discussed in this chapter, including explicit fiscal constraints, ex ante specification of performance targets, and accrual-based accounts, have the capacity to make government finance more transparent and political leaders more responsible.

long-term impacts of current decisions; the second would bar actions projected to breach medium-term fiscal targets. When particular PFM innovations are discussed later in this chapter, two related questions will be repeatedly asked: Do adjustments in information suffice? Is it appropriate to establish formal rules?

1.2.1. Information

Managing public finance equates to managing information. At every stage of the process, information is generated, classified, compiled into documents, and transformed into policies, actions, and financial results. Those who work in PFM are both producers and consumers of information.

The basic assumption is that changing the mix of information changes the behavior of public finance managers. Each objective identified earlier requires its own pool of information, as does each contemporary PFM innovation. As the footprint of government has expanded, PFM information requirements have escalated to the extent that the expanding portfolio of information can impair PFM's capacity to alter behavior. The more information thrust upon public finance managers, the more they can ignore. Often implicitly, but sometimes explicitly, managers differentiate useful information from essential information. Essential information tends to be more carefully prepared, more timely, and more easily applied than desirable information. This pattern explains why the quality of information on the fiscal year immediately ahead is usually much better than that on future years, and why data on inputs tend to be more reliable than data on outputs.

One of the challenges in PFM reform is to transform information from "useful" to "essential." Can government rules make desirable information essential? The case for doing so seems compelling because good-to-have information is easily disregarded, whereas information prescribed by rule is harder to ignore. Yet, there are substantial grounds for proceeding cautiously in applying the rule sanction.

The Cost of Information Affects Its Availability

At issue here are the expense and the effort to produce new data. Data internal to an entity generally entail little difficulty or cost; data that are external can be costly. This distinction can be illustrated by reference to managing a hospital, though the issue fits just about all public services.

A well-run hospital commands data on the number and remuneration of staff, the number of patients admitted and discharged, the number of beds and the occupancy rate, and so on. No special effort has to be undertaken to acquire these input, workload, and output statistics, and compiling them into useful formats requires only modest cost. However, data on outcomes and impacts lie outside the walls of the hospital. A hospital can know everything about its internal operations, but not know whether patients take prescribed medications after discharge, whether low-income residents have access to its facilities, or whether the hospital's services are suited to the community's age structure. This example suggests why many governments may have experienced analogous difficulty obtaining reliable outcome and impact data, and it behooves them to take account of cost and difficulty in establishing information requirements. The issue is not whether the information is desirable but whether the cost of acquiring the data is justified.

PFM Information Demands Risk Overloading Central and Line Agencies

The cumulative effect of PFM innovations has been to increase information demands on both central agencies and sectoral departments. Innovations generally add rather than subtract information and are promoted independently of one another. Adopting the accrual basis does not eliminate cash accounting, a multiyear framework still requires detailed annual budgeting, and adding outputs to the list does not obviate the need to keep track of inputs. Modern information technology and integrated financial systems can ease the load, though they occasionally have the opposite effect.

Critical PFM systems, such as the budget, have limited capacity to process information. Deadlines abound; when one task is completed another approaches. In contrast to what is the case in most other policy arenas, doing nothing or slipping a deadline is not an option. Governments cannot wait for better information on program results before allocating resources, nor can they sift through all the new types of information to make rational decisions. More governments than would care to admit it claim to have program or performance budgets but still tally up the cost of salaries, travel, equipment, and other line items to set expenditure levels.

Overload can be averted by purging PFM systems of older types of information. Elimination of some old forms and reports when prescribing new ones is useful. Although determined efforts may slow the increase in the volume and variety of data, they rarely eliminate overload completely.

Information Stirs Conflict

Overload is a function not only of the amount of information, but also of the intensity of conflict generated in allocating resources, evaluating programs, and exploring policy options. Although conflict is endemic in budgeting and other PFM activities, so, too, are mechanisms that dampen conflict and facilitate closure. Incremental behavior is a ubiquitous strategy for containing conflict, reducing it by narrowing the scope of decisions and by protecting existing claims on resources. Conflict can also be mitigated by reducing the types of data generated and reviewed in compiling the budget. The resulting allocations might be suboptimal, but they are made in a timely, less stressful manner.

Many PFM innovations have the opposite effect. They bring more issues, interests, and perspectives into play and challenge the expedient routines that smooth things over and pave the way to agreement. Modern financial management doctrine counsels governments that it is not enough to take account of this year's finances, but that they must consider the future as well, review existing programs and not settle for comfortable incrementalism, and take account not only of the financing needs of agencies but of how well programs are doing. These and other contemporary PFM reforms can greatly intensify conflict.

Governments handle conflict overload in much the same way they handle information overload. They ignore information or fail to produce it. Getting the job done is uppermost, even if it means cutting informational corners. Sometimes they do more. They disarm the information and make it suit different purposes than those for which it was designed. They transform strategic plans into platforms for demanding more resources and align programs to fit the organization chart rather than to achieve the objectives. Spending units stuff performance budgets with information showing they are doing more and need more resources, and use unduly optimistic assumptions in projecting the future cost of current decisions. They soften medium-term budget frameworks'

(MTBFs') hard constraints by treating them as floors rather than as ceilings on future expenditure. These ploys transform ambitious PFM reforms into little more than attractive display cases. The displays enable government to boast that it has a state-of-the art performance budget, or to proudly exhibit its medium-term budget frameworks. But the inside is empty.

Expanded conflict is not an incidental by-product of PFM innovation—it is essential for public finance discipline and for more effective allocations and more efficient public services. Although rarely articulated, the PFM agenda that rests on the avoidance of conflict often leads to excessive deficits, rigid allocations, inefficient services, and closed systems. In this circumstance, stirring the pot is beneficial, even if it complicates completion of PFM's essential tasks.

Yet, because governments do need to get things done, the challenge is to manage both conflict and public finances, to maintain a stable fiscal course while accommodating some political demands, to favor existing programs while expanding the space for new allocations, to upgrade public services without demoralizing public employees, to make financial decisions more transparent while enabling government to function. These balancing acts have led PFM architects to settle for half a building because they lack the wherewithal for a full-fledged structure.

Asymmetric Interests Spawn Asymmetric Information

Adversarial relationships are common between those who possess information and those who control resources. Principals (ministers individually or in cabinet, and senior officials in central agencies or departmental headquarters) depend on agents who run programs and deliver services for much of the information that goes into allocative decisions. Principals seek better information to enable them to reach intelligent decisions; agents seek to portray their programs in a favorable light to obtain bigger budgets. Principals often try to reduce their dependence on agents by establishing their own or independent sources of information. Their best efforts, however, cannot rid financial management of embedded information asymmetries.

Despite the superior authority of those who allocate resources, agents generally have the advantage because they know more about how programs work and control information provided to others. Interdependence (one side has the money, the other the information), the ongoing character of the relationship (the various parties interact in each budget cycle), and the perceived need for agreement (the government must present a budget) motivate the parties to cooperate and to settle for less than they want—less information for allocators, less money for spenders.

PFM innovations purport to lessen the problem of asymmetric information by augmenting the supply of data that is processed, including data on effectiveness and efficiency, and by vesting control of some critical information in central agencies. For example, although spending agencies generally estimate resource needs for the year ahead, central agencies run the econometric and program models that generate baseline projections for that same year. Similarly, central agencies may evaluate programs, devise outcome measures, survey citizen attitudes on the quality of public services, target outputs and other performance indicators, and compare operational efficiency across agencies.

However, few central agencies strive to do all these things. If they did, relationships with spending agencies would likely become more adversarial, and the spending agencies might become more cunning in providing information to superiors. Moreover, centralizing information runs counter to the new public management argument that gamesmanship diminishes and performance improves when those who operate government services have fuller managerial responsibility for the resources they consume and the results they produce. More fundamentally, the use of new information by spending units is likely to increase if they have ownership of it. For these reasons, some countries with advanced PFM systems have opted to decentralize information control, despite the asymmetries that limit the capacity of principals to allocate resources intelligently.

The four issues raised here call into question blind faith that information itself will transform the behavior of public finance managers. Knowing that one program is more effective than another does not suffice to reallocate money, nor does heightened awareness of a program's unsustainable fiscal future inevitably embolden government to behave more prudently. To make a difference, information must be processed in ways that change the behavior of those who handle public money.

1.2.2. Processes

In PFM, process is the conversion of information into decisions, actions, or documents. Every significant PFM innovation alters one or more procedures, usually in tandem with changes in information. Drawing a distinction between process that is permissive, that is, made available to government, and process that is mandatory, that is, government must apply the prescribed methods, is important. Specific procedural innovations will be examined later in this chapter (and the chapters that follow). This section sets out general characteristics of processes and the elements subject to modification through PFM reforms. These elements include the structure of decisions, the roles and relationships of participants, the time frame for action or decision, the authority of participants' actions, and the scope of decisions. One or more of these elements is always in play in PFM adjustments; they are the moving parts of PFM systems. Before each of these is commented upon, consideration is given to why routine is important in PFM processes.

Process as Routine

One of PFM's distinctive characteristics is that most procedures are repeated year after year, with little change. For example, auditors have their routines for reviewing accounts and reporting on financial condition, and budget makers for allocating resources and monitoring expenditures. Repetition of the routines year after year reduces conflict, simplifies tasks, stabilizes roles and relationships, and coordinates the numerous chores that must be completed. Players do not have to fight over procedures or improvise new ones each year. This part of their work is done before a single decision has been made, except in those cycles when some procedures are modified. Routine pacifies PFM processes and facilitates timely action.

A PFM innovation may be said to have arrived when it is embedded in procedure. Examining the extent to which new procedures have been incorporated into ongoing routines is a useful means of assessing whether innovations have been truly incorporated into PFM. A government that must decide every year whether to evaluate programs is one for which program evaluation is not yet fully part of its resource allocation repertoire. For a time, Australia was one of the few countries that made effective use of program evaluations because it had an "evaluation strategy" that routinely fed evaluative findings into the stream of budget decisions. Routine is expressed not only in the headline processes, but perhaps even more importantly in the manner in which the new procedures are linked to the old. An MTBF cannot accomplish much as a freestanding procedure; it constrains current decisions only when it is integrated into the annual budget.

Process as routine, however, has another side. It can deaden not only conflict but also political and managerial support and attention, and thereby risks becoming just another item on each year's checklist. Reformers frequently tinker with their new machinery to keep the procedures fresh and vital and to avoid making them so routine that they lose the capacity to influence behavior. One of the challenges in PFM is to embed innovation into ongoing routines while retaining the interest and engagement of political and managerial leaders. Spicing routine with improvisation may be a sensible formula for attracting top-level attention while keeping the process on track.

Structure of Decisions

The first step in processing financial data is to classify the information into the form that will be used for decisions or other actions. PFM reform conventionally assumes that changing classifications will inevitably transform the way decisions are made. A line item budget will produce decisions on inputs—the amounts spent on salaries, travel, accommodations, and other items. Shifting to a program budget will generate decisions on objectives—the amounts government spends to reduce poverty, improve environmental quality, and achieve other public objectives.

However, the link between processes and decisions is not as straightforward as reformers believe, because all complex PFM systems work with multiple classifications. National governments typically organize expenditures by line items (even if they have a program or performance budget), administrative units, economic categories, and sector or function. Other classifications may be by region, gender, age, or income of recipients, and may be mandatory or discretionary. However, although a government may maintain multiple classifications, it can have only one basis for authoritative decisions.

One common error in PFM reform is to mistake display for decision, to assume, for example, that the presentation of the budget in a program or performance format provides evidence that the government has such a budget. In most countries administrative units are the authoritative classification for accounting, budgeting, and other financial management processes. Organizations—not programs—spend money and deliver services and are the principal units of accountability. A genuine program budget would disregard organization boundaries and group all activities and expenditures serving the same objective into a single category. In practice, however, most governments that claim to have program budgets actually align programs according to definable organizational units. For example, they might relabel the bureau of water quality as the water quality program, but not include within it water quality activities conducted by other administrative entities.

Several implications flow from these characteristics of classification. First, governments that have sound administrative classifications may wish to consider whether introducing a program classification is dictated by a genuine desire to change the decision process and accountability relations. Otherwise, this reform can stretch into years and may end up being a mere presentational change, particularly if there is disagreement within government about objectives or about the optimal program structure. Second, PFM reforms should focus on improving management within government departments and agencies, because these entities determine how public money is spent. Third, good financial management would be promoted by supplementing the main classifications with schedules and statements that highlight important issues or provide insight into the way public money is managed, including schedules that focus on objectives and results.

Roles and Relationships

PFM innovations enlarge the circle of participants, redistribute power and responsibilities, and alter relationships between spenders and controllers. Some tasks become more centralized, others less so. Central organs generally become more active and authoritative with respect to financial aggregates, but less so with respect to the operations of line agencies and provision of services. Participants on the periphery of the national government, including subnational officials, may gain greater influence and possibly a formal role in the process. In some countries, independent fiscal agencies or legislative entities have carved out significant roles in producing and reviewing economic, financial, or program data, and in generating alternatives to government recommendations (see Chapter 6 for more details on independent fiscal agencies).

Certain basic tasks can be performed only at the center, such as issuing the authoritative economic projections used in setting key fiscal aggregates, establishing formal fiscal targets and constraints, and allocating resources to sectors or departments. Data and advice may flow in from many sources, but must be processed by central authorities into rules and policies that effectively guide or constrain spending units. A real problem arises, however, in the many countries with fractured centers and with different entities responsible for macroeconomic analysis, budget work, and treasury functions. Matters may be further complicated by establishment of a policy unit at the center of government, or by a more active role by the cabinet in fiscal policy. In these situations, effective coordination or a clear division of responsibilities is essential for the center to play an authoritative role.

The tasks yielded by the center have to be picked up by departments and agencies. These tasks may include control of inputs, ongoing program and expenditure review, and establishment of departmental priorities. The objective is to make department managers into rationers rather than claimants. Of course, this is much easier said than done, notwithstanding the facile notion that each department head should behave as a budget director. In this idealized process, devolution would extend from department headquarters to field operations and service delivery, with each unit controlling its own budget and the total of all the budgets accommodated within the government's fiscal envelope. In reality, the situation is likely to be messier, with a fuzzy division of labor between allocators and spenders and more friction than PFM architects foresee.

Time Frames

The fiscal year is the standard time frame for managing public finances. With few exceptions, financial reports and audits, as well as budget allocations and appropriations, are provided annually, and the period during which authorized funds are available for expenditure is a single fiscal year. PFM reformers regard the single fiscal year as an artificial time boundary that can destabilize public finance and degrade both the quality of allocations and the efficiency of operations. One year is too short for informed decisions, affecting the future, but too long for fluid operation of government agencies. The preferred solution is to adjust fiscal processes within a year, between years, and for the longer term. Thus, three different timing adjustments may be made by PFM-inspired reforms.

Within-year adjustments respond to the widespread practice (mostly in low- and middle-income countries) that limits the amount that each spending unit can obligate or disburse each quarter, bimonthly, or during some other short period. These limits, often less than the amounts appropriated, are ostensibly intended to align outlays and revenues, but they also enable the government to reserve money for further spending initiatives during the year. Whatever the motive, the short time frame leaves spending units uncertain about what funds will be available during the year and forces managers to cope by hoarding or concealing funds, accumulating arrears, and making hidden cuts in activities. These survival tactics drive up costs and degrade performance, but they enable spending units to muddle through until the next allotment arrives.

The PFM solution is to give spending units funds for the entire year, possibly reserving a small fraction for contingencies. This approach is taken in most developed countries, but it might not suit less-affluent countries whose finances can be destabilized by unexpected declines in revenue or increases in expenditures.

The second type of adjustment permits spending units to carry over unspent operating money to the next fiscal year and even to spend in advance a small portion of the next year's funds during the current year. The fiscal year survives, and the amount that may be carried forward or prespent is quite small, and normally limited to operating and investment funds. Although not yet widespread, between-year adjustments may be harbingers of innovations that undermine the centrality of the fiscal year in public finance.

The third type of adjustment extends the fiscal horizon to the medium term, usually the next three to five years, within a framework that compels government to account for the future fiscal implications of current program and budget decisions. A three- to five-year time frame is inadequate for gauging the long-term sustainability of a government's fiscal position. For this purpose, some innovative governments now project revenues, expenditures, and other fiscal variables 30 or more years ahead. These innovations are discussed in greater detail in the next section.

Scope of Decisions

PFM innovations have expanded the financial matters covered in government accounts, budgets, and other statements. Not long ago public finance encompassed the cash inflows and outflows of government. Financial performance was measured by actual receipts and expenditures during a specified period. Noncash transactions were not recognized, nor were liabilities due in later periods.

Over time, the reporting of financial transactions and condition has undergone significant expansion (see Chapter 8). An important development has been adoption of the accrual basis (usually in modified form) as the standard for government accounts. The accrual basis, which does not eliminate cash accounting, recognizes revenue not yet received and liabilities not yet paid out. Only a few governments budget on the accrual basis (see Chapter 11).[8]

The treatment of fiscal risk has received a great deal of attention in recent years and expands application of the accrual basis to contingent liabilities (Brixi and Schick, 2002; IMF, 2009). Contemporary governments are holders of an enormous range of risks for society, some explicitly recognized in guarantees and insurance schemes, some based only on the expectation that government will provide assistance if certain contingencies occur. Expensing fiscal risks poses a number of difficult questions considered later in this chapter and in more detail in Chapter 5. Failing to expense risks may impel governments to take on more risks because they are deemed to be costless.

---

[8]The U.S. General Accounting Office reported in 2000 that six countries (Australia, Canada, Iceland, the Netherlands, New Zealand, and the United Kingdom) had adopted some form of accrual budgeting (US GAO, 2000; Blondal, 2004).

1.2.3. Rules

Reliable information and sound procedures can, and often do, produce subpar or unwanted outcomes. For example, a government that produces reliable medium-term economic and financial projections may have budget deficits and public debt that exceed preset targets and risk destabilizing the country's fiscal position. Similarly, a budget system that classifies expenditures according to outputs and requires administrative units to justify spending bids according to actual or expected performance may nevertheless allocate money by the cost of inputs. These examples are part of a pervasive problem identified in *A Contemporary Approach to Public Expenditure Management*: due process does not ensure satisfactory PFM results (Schick, 1998).

The inherent shortcomings of information- and process-based innovations has spurred PFM reformers to devise rules that constrain political and managerial decision makers and dictate substantive outcomes. PFM rules may be proscriptive or prescriptive, barring certain actions and outcomes, or dictating the decisions to be made and actions to be taken. Rules are pervasive in PFM work. Some of the most important pertain to the recognition of financial stocks and flows on government accounts, aggregate spending and revenue policies, the treatment of contingent liabilities in the budget and other financial statements, and actions to be taken when financial results deviate from authorized levels.

The transformation of information and process into constrictive rules is well illustrated by the evolution of medium-term budget frameworks. The initial step in many MTBF countries was informational, preparation of multiyear economic forecasts, usually as an internal exercise in government. The next step was procedural, inclusion of out-year spending and revenue estimates in the annual budget. The final step is establishment of medium-term fiscal constraints that limit current budget decisions.

The metamorphosis of MTBF gives rise to a difficult issue—how to differentiate rules-centered reforms from those that focus on information or process. After all, legislation and regulations typically drive government agencies to change the information content and procedures of PFM systems. Lengthening the time frame of budgeting from one to three or more years and injecting performance information into the PFM stream often occurs in response to rule changes adopted by parliament or central government agencies.

Evidently, a thin, sometimes fuzzy line separates the three levers discussed in this section. Nevertheless, it is feasible to distinguish PFM instruments by defining information and process as procedural innovations, and rules as substantive changes in actions or outcomes. Economic and baseline projections and medium-term budgets alter PFM procedures; fiscal constraints seek to alter revenue, spending, or deficit policies.

Inasmuch as a key aim of PFM reform is to improve outcomes, codifying preferred outcomes in substantive rules seems sensible. Yet, there is good reason for proceeding cautiously in this area. Premature establishment of rules may have unforeseen or unintended side effects and may unduly reduce flexibility and judgment in PFM policies, and rules established prematurely may suffer from insufficient information or enforcement.

Substantive Rules Tie the Hands of Political Leaders and Managers

By predetermining certain outcomes, rules purge affected PFM actions of political or managerial judgment. A rules-based performance budgeting system would require governments to allocate more funds to activities or projects that have produced or that promise results, and less to those that have serious shortfalls in actual or projected performance. Strictly applied to education programs, government would be bound to take money away from low-performing schools and to spend more on high performers. In practice, sensible budget allocators often do the opposite, increasing funds to weaker schools in an effort to narrow the performance gap. Understandably, few governments have rules-based performance budgets, but many have performance-informed budgets.

Skill in managing public money rests in good part on the experience of decision makers, their ability to probe beyond the data to glean opportunities to create public value, and their capacity to translate public sentiment into budget allocations. To be sure, relying on political and managerial judgment often opens the door to willful disregard of results, but locking politicians and managers into a PFM straitjacket is not an effective antidote.

Substantive Rules Invite Evasion and Financial Legerdemain

When there are no rules, there is no impulse to evade them, but when government constrains financial actions or outcomes, wily spenders may have ample incentive to hide uncomfortable facts from central agencies. In view of the asymmetric information relationship (discussed earlier) between claimants and guardians, evading substantive rules is not difficult.

Evasion of fiscal limits takes several forms: setting up off-budget and special accounts that are excluded from budget totals, building up unreported arrears, delaying payment of bills, basing fiscal totals on unduly buoyant economic forecasts, increasing the pension rights of public employees in exchange for lower salaries, and issuing guarantees in lieu of direct expenditure. An MTBF's hard constraint on future spending can be undermined by raising allowable totals when it is rolled forward each year. Technically, doing so conforms to MTBF rules, but the effect is to vitiate the fiscal constraint at the heart of medium-term budget policy.

Rules can have salutary effects even when some are routinely evaded. What matters is the extent of evasion. A small off-budget fund that gives managers a little cash for routine expenses not covered in the budget may improve performance, whereas a large one may call into question the reliability of budget accounts.

Rigid Rules Have Unintended Side Effects

Substantive rules prescribe or proscribe future actions. They may be promulgated under one set of conditions, and implemented under very different conditions. The main types of fiscal rules adopted by the European Union and many countries before the financial upheavals of recent years illustrate this point. The rules were based on the assumption that economic conditions would be stable and that cyclical downturns could be accommodated within their allowable fiscal parameters.

Sometimes, unintended effects occur because of loosely drawn rules or willful disregard of their intent. Few countries have adopted accrual-based budgets, but at least one found that spending agencies were using depreciation allowances to finance program operations. An MTBF can unintentionally damage a country's fiscal position if medium-term expenditure levels are treated as floors rather than as ceilings for future expenditures.

*****

Are PFM's levers effective? The preceding discussion pointed to deficiencies in PFM's arsenal of information, processes, and rules. None alone suffices to ensure that public finances will be managed efficiently, with due regard for the future or for program results. It would be a mistake, however, to leap to the conclusion that these instruments do not have salutary effects on the behavior of public financial managers or on substantive outcomes. Arguing that the levers may not be sufficient does not justify the conclusion that they do not make a difference. Because the levers are imperfect, PFM modernization is perennially a work in progress. This is a restless field, continually in search of better information, sturdier processes, and more-workable rules. The next section addresses how PFM innovations have applied new information, processes, and rules to achieve their objectives.

1.3. MAJOR PFM INNOVATIONS AND REFORMS

Each of the three PFM objectives identified early in this chapter is associated with one or more contemporary innovations. Fiscal rules seek to stabilize a government's fiscal position and, in combination with medium-term budget frameworks, to promote effective allocation. Program evaluation and performance budgeting, along with outcome measurement, also may contribute to improved allocation; performance budgeting has also been promoted to upgrade public management and operational efficiency. Most of these innovations are discussed in the chapters that follow. This section assesses PFM reforms as they relate to the three levers of change (information, processes, and rules) and their impact on incentives and behavior.

1.3.1. Fiscal Rules

Fiscal rules are numerical targets or limits that seek to transform budgeting from an open-ended process in which aggregates are set at the end, after spending bids have been submitted and reviewed, into a disciplined process that sets the totals at the start and enforces them throughout preparation and implementation of the budget. Although this is a highly popular reform—in 2012, 76 countries had fiscal rules—many countries have found it exceedingly difficult to enforce these rules (see Chapter 3). Doing so depends not only on timely information and effective procedures, but also on political commitment to operate according to the rules.

The basic problem of fiscal rules is that they run counter to the incentive of politicians to curry favor with voters by spending more and not taxing enough to cover the increase, even at the expense of chronic deficits and escalating public debt. Fiscal rules would be redundant if politicians lacked a propensity to accumulate deficits, or if they were inhibited by other features of the PFM system. The key question, then, is whether rules that are effective only to the extent that they are enforced by vote-seeking politicians can prevail against political incentives. First-generation rules introduced before the global financial crisis generally have been ineffective. If they had been effective, many countries would have been able to ride out the crisis on a sounder fiscal basis (Schick, 2010). Of course, the crisis itself was not a fair test of fiscal rules, but the calmer, seemingly stable period before the crisis was. During the precrisis years, many advanced economies had sizable deficits despite favorable economic conditions. In fact, most of the fiscal rules then extant (such as the European Union's Stability and Growth Pact) allowed deficits or were breached. Those rules were not sufficiently constrictive because the allowable maximum deficit came to be regarded as the acceptable or normal deficit. The rules gave policymakers misguided incentives to borrow more during good times and to disregard the risks that government would face when the economy weakened.

In accord with the theme of this chapter, the potential impact of informational requirements and procedural changes on incentives and behavior is briefly discussed. The chapter then turns to the rules themselves and examines various options for disciplining public finance.

Lack of Information Is Not the Main Problem

Fiscal rules are a major exception to the generalization that injecting new information into the stream of PFM work drives behavioral changes. Policymakers already have most of the information needed to make prudent fiscal decisions. In all advanced economies, political and managerial leaders have timely data on current and projected revenues, expenditures, financial balances, and debt—in current and real terms and as shares of GDP. However, as discussed later, issues remain with coverage of reporting entities, treatment of contingent liabilities, and disclosure and management of fiscal risk. The main problem, then, is not a lack of information, but reluctance to let unpleasant fiscal facts get in the way of popular budget policies. In the political contest between rosy assumptions and hard facts, the former usually prevail, at least until capital markets render their verdicts.

Fiscal policymakers obtain certain information from external sources that bears on fiscal policy and on government propensity to take on debt. Interest rates on public debt and the ease with which government floats its bonds signal to policymakers whether they are on the right course and probably exert stronger influence than do budget data. During the easy money years before the crisis, financial markets spurred governments to borrow more. Unfortunately, sudden reversals in market signals as the crisis unfolded gave some fiscally stressed countries little time to adjust, and within a remarkably brief period some went from capital glut to capital shortage.

Although lack of information is not the main spur for irresponsible fiscal behavior, schemes are afloat to improve the reliability and relevance of fiscal signals. One such scheme is for government to establish an independent body that produces its own fiscal and economic projections and analyses to counter government's temptation to use unduly buoyant assumptions. The United Kingdom recently moved in this direction (see Chapter 6). It is not evident, however, that independent forecasts make much difference. The U.S. Congressional Budget Office has issued independent fiscal advice for more than 35 years, but despite the recognized quality of its work, the United States has had chronic and sometimes very large deficits, except in those years when political leaders have determined to steer a disciplined fiscal course.[9]

Framing Fiscal Decisions

Every government that establishes fiscal targets has procedures for setting them. Some countries have freestanding targets that are determined independently of the budget or of other policy processes. The limits are fixed in law or in a government pronouncement, or imposed by a supranational authority. In other countries, fiscal rules are integrated into a framework that includes the process for setting them, their linkage to the budget, and the manner in which they are to be enforced or adjusted. Typically, the framework is incorporated into a medium-term expenditure process covering the next three to five years (see Chapter 4).

Fiscal rules tend to be more effective when embedded in a framework than if they derive from freestanding pronouncements.[10] Framework-based rules are generated by a process that takes account of economic conditions, the budget situation, and political preferences; they therefore are likely to be vested with greater feasibility and stronger commitment than rules that are fixed in advance without regard to a particular year's circumstances. Because they may be adjusted annually or biennially, framed rules are more sensitive to shifts in political sentiment and other relevant conditions. Moreover, in contrast to freestanding rules, frameworks typically include means of enforcement connected to budget actions.

These considerations bolster the argument that supranational rules, such as those promulgated by the European Community, are inherently weaker than country-specific arrangements. The former lack frameworks; the latter often have them. However, supranational rules can feasibly be tied to an enforcement process that includes accounting standards and close oversight of country policies by regional or international bodies along with authority to take corrective action in case of an actual or prospective breach. The new set of European Commission

[9] Joyce (2011) reviews the history and performance of the Congressional Budget Office.

[10] Recent literature suggests rules cannot work without supporting institutions (Wyplosz, 2012).

Directives and the recently launched Fiscal Compact attempt to address these shortcomings (see Chapter 3).[11]

The ease of adjusting frameworks to changing conditions suggests that the type of process and intensity of political commitment matter a great deal. The ease of adjusting the targets may tempt politicians to mold them to their preferences, in which case pliable rules become accommodating rather than constraining. Arguably, governments comply with framed rules because they can bend the rules to their interests, not because frameworks tie their hands.

Transparency and political accountability are the principal weapons against opportunistic behavior in framework-centered countries that lack fixed rules. Politicians, the argument runs, pay a price at the polls if they raise deficit or debt targets. It may be that frameworks are effective only in countries that have attentive media and leaders who willingly tether their policy ambitions to fiscal discipline. Fiscal responsibility frameworks have been effective in Australia, Brazil, New Zealand, and Sweden, all of which have these supporting conditions. However, when these conditions are absent, frameworks may lack the potency to whip fiscal policy into line. These frameworks are discussed in greater detail in Chapter 2.

Proscriptive Rules That Override Political Incentives

When available information and new procedures do not curb opportunistic behavior, government may seek recourse in binding rules that legally restrict deficits or other fiscal aggregates and provide for corrective action in case of violation. To be effective, these rules would have to deter types of behavior that enable leaders to profess fidelity to fiscal limits while evading them. Some evasions, such as shifting funds between fiscal years or from one level of government to another, are easy to detect and deter. Others, such as manipulating economic assumptions, are less transparent and more difficult to guard against. The most difficult challenge occurs when the economy is booming, resources are plentiful, and deficit and debt levels appear prudent, but revenue and expenditure policies are setting the stage for future fiscal stress. The following paragraphs begin with the easy cases and end with difficult situations.

One convenient evasion route is for the national government to shift certain responsibilities and expenditures to subnational governments. In federal systems, and in unitary countries with decentralized revenue and expenditure authority, subnational governments can have a large impact on the country's overall fiscal posture. Moreover, some countries permit subnational governments to issue debt that is explicitly or implicitly guaranteed by the national government.

The interdependence of national and subnational finances and the incentive to evade limits by shifting expenditures or debt to other levels of government lead to the conclusion that fiscal rules should cover all levels of government. Implementing a comprehensive rule would require uniform accounting and

---

[11] See http://ec.europa.eu/economy_finance/articles/governance/2012-03-14_six_pack_en.htm.

reporting systems at all levels, as well as central capacity to monitor local revenue and spending trends and to intervene when necessary to keep consolidated finances on course. One possible impediment is that comprehensive fiscal rules may be perceived as an effort to recentralize government finance. To some extent this has occurred in Brazil; it is a federal country with powerful states, but it now has a comprehensive fiscal responsibility process anchored in law and operating through detailed bimonthly reports from state and municipal governments. These reports are consolidated into government-wide statements and disclose whether the country is meeting its fiscal targets (Alson and others, 2007).

A second form of evasion involves shifting recognition of revenues, expenditures, or debt from one fiscal period to another. The obvious remedy is to devise fiscal targets that span the medium term, but there are at least two ploys for circumventing a three- to five-year frame: schemes that entitle employees (or citizens) to pensions or other benefits that will be paid 20 to 50 years in the future and contingent liabilities that may become due beyond the medium term.

The manipulation of assumptions is a serious issue that pervades fiscal rules and other aspects of macroeconomic management. Every fiscal target pertains to an uncertain future open to multiple assumptions. Because fiscal targets, as well as most other PFM policies and actions, depend on point estimates rather than statistical ranges, a degree of judgment, sometimes arbitrariness, is used in selecting underlying assumptions. Often, small changes in these assumptions radiate to very large changes in fiscal or budget projections. When basic assumptions are tainted by political influence, fiscal discipline is undermined and rules become ineffective.

No airtight bulwark prevents politically motivated prevarication, but several types of arrangements may discourage baseless assumptions. Transparency helps, especially when it includes publication of the range of plausible estimates and data on the sensitivity of fiscal outcomes to changes in economic conditions. A strong professional ethic that shields fiscal experts from political influence or an independent staff that is walled off from government may promote honesty in economic forecasts and assumptions. Ultimately, however, commitment by government leaders to maintain a prudent, stable fiscal course is an essential element of rules-based regimes.

The final issue is the incentive of political leaders to exploit favorable economic conditions in ways that put the country's fiscal future at risk. When the economy is booming, nominal fiscal rules that are not cyclically adjusted give politicians license to boost spending and cut revenues. The obvious solution would be for government to adopt cyclically adjusted rules that effectively constrain tax and spending policy during the good times when resources are plentiful and political demands are hard to resist. Chile is a classic example of introducing a cyclically adjusted rule linked to the price of copper, its main natural resource (Blondal and Curristine, 2004). A more recent example is the 2012 European Commission Fiscal Compact. When conditions are favorable, it behooves government to aim for a declining debt-to-GDP ratio and to set aside significant reserve funds. If it does not, a cyclical downturn will generate deficits in excess of the level permitted by fiscal rule, and a steep or prolonged recession (such as the one experienced since 2007) may threaten to destabilize the country's finances.

However, because of the inherent complexity of cyclically adjusted rules, their dependence on external variables (economic performance), and the incentive to spend up to the allowed limit, some observers have urged adoption of expenditure-based rules or ceilings that limit the year-to-year increase in spending (including tax expenditures) (Anderson and Minarik, 2006). This limit would not be affected by cyclical movements. Most versions of an expenditure-based rule would exempt automatic stabilizers, and some would also exempt spending increases based on population changes. This type of rule would be of limited value to any country that has a fundamental imbalance between revenues and expenditures and that can rebalance public finance only by making substantial cuts in existing programs.

1.3.2. Medium-Term Budget Frameworks

The advent of fiscal rules and other developments have called attention to the inherent inadequacy of short time frames for stabilizing fiscal conditions, planning and implementing policy initiatives, and assessing the sustainability of current revenue and spending policies. Many countries have devised medium-term budget frameworks that establish tentative spending (or fiscal) levels for each of the next three to five years. Medium-term budget frameworks are discussed in detail in Chapter 4.

The frameworks do not displace annual financial decisions and reports. The fiscal year persists as the principal time frame for allocating resources, except in the few countries that have biennial or multiyear budgets. The connection between annual budget decisions and three- to five-year allocations has vexed many, perhaps most, of the countries that have introduced MTBFs. In blueprint, the annual budget is supposed to (1) be for the first year of the MTBF and (2) establish firm spending constraints for each of the subsequent years. In practice, the budget and the MTBF often are separate policy instruments and not a single, integrated process. Instead of setting expenditure ceilings, the MTBF establishes floors that generate upward pressure on future spending levels. Some national governments have separate offices for managing the budget and managing the MTBF. The large budget staff operates ongoing routines and makes authoritative allocations; the small MTBF staff projects spending levels for each of the next several years. In this arrangement, the budget staff is, by a wide margin, likely to be much more powerful, even in countries where the MTBF unit is on display.

Using Existing Information in New Ways

To operate an MTBF and to project long-term fiscal sustainability, government must stretch conventional types of information from a single year to a multiyear frame. In annual budgeting, a key question is "what will it cost next year to continue the activities that have been funded this year?" Finance and sectoral ministries address this question by subtracting temporary or expiring activities from base expenditures, adding estimated price increases, and adjusting for variables such as changes in the number of persons receiving pensions and other income supports. Most advanced economies have socioeconomic models that estimate these changes, along with baseline projections that show the impacts on the next year's budget. In constructing baselines, some governments distinguish between mandatory and discretionary expenditures; others do not regard this information as useful in making allocative decisions. Almost all countries have parallel techniques for projecting revenues and for estimating the fiscal gap that the government faces or the incremental resources available for policy initiatives.

Although baselines are now a routine part of budget work in most advanced economies, they bespeak the formal incorporation of incremental logic into allocative policymaking. With the baseline as its starting point, the principal budget task for government is to allocate fiscal space—resources unencumbered by past decisions. Of course, government has the option of allocating less than the baseline indicates, but doing so is often politically difficult.

Baselines are a vital part of MTBFs. The technique remains essentially the same, but government makes these projections for each of the next three to five years instead of just the next one. Greater uncertainty seeps into the projections and the assumptions that underlie them, and there is greater likelihood of variance between estimated and actual economic and budget conditions. The big difference, however, between one year and three to five years is that incrementalism is even more strongly embedded in resource decisions. Assumed price and workload changes are added to the base for each of the next several years before a single expenditure decision is made. The margin for spending initiatives is also enlarged, as government estimates unencumbered resources for each of the three to five years in the MTBF horizon. This larger margin enables government to make advance spending commitments—policy initiatives above the baseline—in excess of what an annual budget would permit.

Thus, using information about an uncertain future, an MTBF both strengthens incrementalism's grip on resources and spurs government to "prespend" future increments. This can be a risky combination if the assumptions on which the MTBF is based turn out to be unduly optimistic.

The MTBF Process Is Effective Only If It Actually Constrains Spending

In many countries, an MTBF is the centerpiece of PFM reform, around which other innovations such as program and performance budgeting are organized. Obviously, MTBFs would not warrant the acclaim they have garnered if they only built increments into the baseline and future policy initiatives and spending increases into the budget. In fact, an MTBF is a complex process that aims to constrain spending initiatives and to embolden spending units to trade away existing expenditures to enlarge the space available for policy initiatives. The true test of an MTBF—arguably the only one that matters—is whether it effectively accomplishes these twin objectives.

In the MTBF process, government uses baseline projections of revenues and expenditures to (1) estimate the fiscal space available in future budgets, (2) determine changes in revenues and expenditure policies, and (3) allocate available space among departments or other claimants for financial resources. The estimated space is supposed to be a "hard constraint" on spending initiatives, both for government as a whole and such designated spending categories as sectors or ministries. The term "hard constraint" denotes that neither the government nor spending units may take any action that would breach preset ceilings. In contrast to annual budgeting that permits government to adopt spending initiatives without regard to effects on future budgets, an MTBF limits policy changes to amounts that can be accommodated within medium-term constraints. The government and spending units can opt to enlarge future fiscal space by curtailing existing expenditures, thereby freeing up an equivalent amount for program enhancements.

An MTBF envisions a transformed central fiscal office as the enforcer of its hard spending constraint. Freed from line item monitoring and control, this office would maintain the baseline, advise government on fiscal space and spending constraints, allocate space among departments and other units, make and review policy recommendations, "score" trade-offs and spending changes recommended by sectoral departments, compile the annual budget and ensure compliance with medium-term fiscal constraints, and roll the MTBF forward each year by updating the baseline. This full menu of responsibilities can be managed only if the central fiscal office divests some traditional tasks and focuses on the MTBF process.

If hard constraints and trade-offs are properly managed, MTBF has the potential to live up to its billing. However, if the budget is disconnected from the MTBF, constraints become soft targets rather than firm limits and are regarded as floors when the MTBF is rolled forward. These shortcomings pervade many MTBF systems and open the door wide to the risk, mentioned earlier, that defective medium-term budget frameworks may damage the government's fiscal position.

Can Fiscal Rules Harden MTBF Constraints?

The weakness of MTBF constraints arises out of the political incentive to be myopic, that is, to initiate spending programs or changes in revenues with no regard for future fiscal implications. Political myopia cannot be cured simply by adding information and years to the budget framework; policymakers must also be deterred from putting short-term interests ahead of future fiscal stability. The central fiscal office cannot be the only guardian at the gate, warning against popular initiatives that would breach MTBF constraints, or against proposed trade-offs that would add to future deficits. Without strong allies and adequate instruments, the central fiscal office could be bypassed or neutralized when the MTBF gets in the way of political ambitions.

Linking a country's fiscal rule to its MTBF has the potential to harden budget constraints. As explained earlier, rather than being a freestanding target, an MTBF-based fiscal rule would be framed with reference to political economy conditions. And rather than relying on budget procedures alone to enforce the constraint, government would have a legal or constitutional basis for limiting expenditure or other fiscal variables. As envisioned here, the fiscal rule would drive the MTBF, and the MTBF would drive the budget. This tight coupling of rules, frameworks, and budgets does not ensure absolute fidelity to fiscal constraints, but it does increase the probability. Compliance might also be strengthened by entrusting key MTBF tasks, such as constructing the baseline and measuring the budget impact of proposed or adopted policy changes, to an independent body. Procedural adjustments work only when country leaders are committed to budgeting on a multiyear basis within predetermined constraints. When they are not, they can easily to convert an MTBF into a platform for spending increases.

Fiscal Instability and Shocks

Medium-term fiscal decisions are most effective during stable times when modest economic growth yields revenue increases that finance incremental expenditures. In these benign circumstances, government can prudently make and implement advance spending commitments for each of the next several years, adjusting amounts and priorities when it rolls the MTBF forward. During stable times, the adjustments are likely to be relatively small spending increases above the levels set in the previous year's MTBF.

Instability disrupts the MTBF process, both when the economy produces large, unpredicted revenue surges that enable the government to increase spending well above the levels projected in its medium-term budget framework and when economic contraction compels it to roll back projected expenditures. In the former case, bountiful financial resources spur political leaders to disregard previously established constraints; in the latter, inadequate resources force government to renege on promised program expansions. Alternatively, government may decide to muddle through with short-term fixes that tide it over until fiscal conditions restabilize.

Fiscal shocks of the magnitude experienced during the recent financial crisis can pull governments in opposite directions. On the one hand, shocks may prod government to adopt stimulative policies; on the other, shocks may induce government to establish new medium-term plans for consolidating public finance through fundamental changes in revenue and expenditure policies. Small fixes are not useful, and short-term policies that compress fiscal consolidation within a single year are likely to be economically infeasible and politically untenable. A medium-term budget framework can enable government to establish credible commitments for staged revenue and expenditure adjustments during the next several years.

Low-income countries that are highly sensitive to swings in commodity prices, interest rates, and donor aid may find it difficult to implement medium-term budget frameworks effectively. Some of these countries have difficulty maintaining a fixed fiscal posture for a single year. Although it makes a great deal of sense for them to plan future development, staying the course may be near impossible when they are buffeted by adverse economic conditions.

Devising Long-Term Sustainability Policies

Extending decision frames three to five years ahead has been a significant PFM accomplishment, but the medium term is much too short for assessing the sustainability of the government's fiscal position. To do so, the time horizon must stretch across generations, especially in countries that face an aging population and long-term pension and health care commitments. However, in contrast to the medium term, for which government can set firm spending limits, for periods that extend 30 or more years into the future innovative governments generally can only make projections.[12] They cannot establish aggregate spending limits this far ahead.

Essentially, therefore, contemporary sustainability work rests on the expectation that governments will be motivated to change current policies—for example, raising the minimum age for full pension benefits—once they are armed with estimates of future debt, tax, or deficit levels. The prospect of bad news in the distant future will, it is hoped, spawn good policies. Although it may be expedient to procrastinate and pretend that things will turn out better, the very bleakness of long-term forecasts will jolt recalcitrant governments to change course.

Is this mere wishful thinking? Is it realistic to expect politicians driven by short-term interests to behave as stewards of their country's fiscal future? The answer is clearly "yes" for some countries, but probably "no" for others. Countries that have boldly revamped pension and other policies to shore up their future finances can be readily identified.[13] However, most countries that have trimmed social insurance or health care expenditures have acted to secure short- to medium-term savings, not to ensure long-term sustainability. Of course, permanent policy changes made to alleviate the risk of sovereign debt default can produce significant improvements in a country's fiscal outlook.

When projections alone do not suffice to alter the country's long-term fiscal course, government can deploy several procedures and rules to encourage action or to forestall policies that would make matters worse. Fiscal gap analysis shifts the focus from the distant future to the near term by estimating the present value of the long-term gap between revenues and expenditures. Alternatively, government can adopt a fiscal rule that proscribes any policy change estimated to cause the gap to widen. This type of rule would not correct existing unsustainable policies, but would, if strictly enforced, block new policies that might adversely affect the country's fiscal future.

---

[12] Australia produces an intergenerational report; the United Kingdom and New Zealand have long-term budget models; the European Commission publishes long-term projections of the budget outlook for member countries; the U.S. Congressional Budget Office produces long-term budget projections. For a discussion of these and other practices, see, for instance, Schick (2009c); US CBO (2011); and Commonwealth of Australia (2010).

[13] One of the most innovative reforms, partly copied by a few countries, is Sweden's "automatic balance mechanism," which adjusts the value of pensions to changes in life expectancy rates and in economic conditions (Settergren, 2001; Valdes-Prieto, 2000).

1.3.3. Fiscal Risks

A country's fiscal condition depends not only on policies that prescribe future payments, but also on fiscal risk, particularly contingent liabilities,[14] that may expose it to additional expenditures. Fiscal risk is the probability that fiscal outcomes may differ from planned results and it clearly has many dimensions (Cebotari and others, 2009). The discussion that follows focuses on contingent liabilities that pervade modern economies and come in many guises. Governments in all advanced economies indemnify households against unemployment, disability, illness, and other income losses or expenses; many indemnify firms against assorted risks such as changes in prices, interest rates, and exchange rates, and natural or environmental disasters. Governments also accumulate contingent liabilities by guaranteeing personal and business loans and various other transactions. Chapter 5 discusses in more detail approaches to managing and controlling fiscal risks.

Few governments adequately disclose these liabilities and similar risks in their budgets or other financial statements. The time horizons of annual budgets and medium-term budget frameworks are too short to account for the downstream risks that governments take when they establish pension rights and other entitlements, issue or guarantee loans, or contract to make good on shortfalls in financial performance. Moreover, conventional budgets record only cash flows; they do not account for the buildup of liabilities, contingent obligations, or the future cost of past commitments.

Shifting risk to government is often an efficient way of promoting economic activity and protecting citizens against devastating losses. But it also can be a means of evading fiscal constraints by shifting expenditures off the budget. In many cases, contingent liabilities can substitute for direct expenditures, but with the critical difference that the latter are recognized on financial statements and the former usually are not. For example, government can promote home ownership through grants that are on budget, or by guaranteeing mortgages that usually are off budget. Similarly, it can directly finance road construction through budgeted expenditures or through off-budget guarantees embedded in public-private partnerships (PPPs).

The choice of policy instrument is not driven solely by efficiency considerations, but is strongly influenced by how various arrangements are treated in the budget. Conventional arrangements give politicians both incentive and opportunity to provide benefits to voters and groups in forms that hide the true cost. It is highly probable that the popularity of PPPs derives in part from substitution of guarantees for direct expenditures. When they opt for contingent liabilities in lieu of expenditures, governments create fiscal illusions, beneficiaries have inducements to behave in morally hazardous ways, and fiscal risks escalate (Irwin, 2012).

[14] A contingent liability may be explicit or implicit. An explicit liability is recognized in law or contract; an implicit liability is a "moral obligation" based on expectations that government will indemnify even when it is not legally required to do so. See Brixi and Schick (2002), Table 1.1, for examples of the various types of liabilities.

Controlling fiscal risks brings all three instruments discussed in this chapter into play. Governments need better information as well as new procedures and rules to forestall actions that make current fiscal conditions appear to be more favorable at the expense of future budgets.

A Fiscal Risk Database

As recently as the mid-2000s, most national governments were ignorant of the contingent liabilities and other financial risks they had accumulated. They had no system for compiling this information and few tools for assessing the risks to which they were exposed. They usually were informed when risks came due and payment was required, but by then it was too late to regulate their liability effectively. Now, however, many advanced economies have systems in place for identifying and tabulating fiscal risks. The fiscal risk matrix, which distinguishes between direct and contingent liabilities and between explicit and implicit liabilities, is a clear, easy-to-use tool for classifying the different types of risks facing governments.[15]

Most governments have difficulty compiling a reasonably complete list because the process for taking on risk is fragmented. One set of guarantees may be embedded in education policy, another in a housing program, a third in crisis-driven efforts to aid small firms or exporters, and so on. Often the guarantees are managed by sectoral departments rather than by a central agency. Therefore, the government lacks a mechanism for trading off among proposed risks and for tracking the status of existing risks. Establishing a database would be facilitated by centralizing management of contingent liabilities and certain other risks in the finance ministry or another central agency.

To manage fiscal risks governments need two types of information: (1) an assessment of risk before liability is assumed and (2) an inventory of outstanding contingent liabilities, along with estimates of payments that may come due. The two types are interconnected because a government can prudently take on new risks only if it knows the risks to which it is already exposed. The best, and often the only, time to limit exposure effectively is before government issues guarantees or enters into other contingent obligations.

Assessing risk is inherently difficult because the future is uncertain and multiple variables can affect the outcome. Sometimes historical guideposts, such as past default rates or the performance of contractors on PPPs, can ease the task, but this information often is either unavailable or unreliable. When it comes to risk, the past can be a misleading guide. Ideally, government would take on new risks with its eyes wide open to estimates of the full range of losses it might suffer, along with an assessment of the sensitivity of these estimates to different scenarios. Typically, however, governments rely on point estimates, which frequently turn out to be wrong, sometimes to a degree that destabilizes government finance.

[15] In addition to the fiscal risk matrix, IMF staff have proposed that governments add a "statement of fiscal risks" to the budget or other financial documents (Cebotari and others, 2009).

To assess the probability of future losses, distinguishing between pooled and concentrated risk is useful. Risk is pooled when government has a relatively small exposure to each of a large number of contingencies, as, for example, when it insures home mortgages or student loans against default. In these circumstances, probability models can enable construction of reasonably accurate estimates, except in those circumstances in which vast numbers of loans are imperiled by systemic risk. However, when risk is concentrated, as is usually the case in PPPs, probability models offer little guidance because a single event can expose government to very large losses. The inherent difficulty of estimating potential losses should induce governments to proceed cautiously, with full acknowledgment of "bad case" scenarios, before it contracts for PPPs or other concentrated risks.

The estimation difficulties that vex government when it is deciding whether to take on risks persist after it has accepted liability, but with the further complication that rather than assessing particular risks, it must consider the entire portfolio of risks it is holding. Few governments currently have sufficient information to compile a reasonably comprehensive statement of contingent liabilities, or to estimate potential losses, though many have fuller knowledge than they had a decade ago. It may be useful for governments to apply simple value-at-risk methods rather than complex models to estimate possible future losses. For example, a government can classify all known contingent liabilities into four categories, such as low (10 percent probability of loss), moderate (30 percent), high (50 percent), and very high (90 percent), and then multiply the volume of contingent liabilities in each category by its percentage to estimate total losses. Although this is a fairly crude method, it is easy to apply and sensitizes government to potential future payouts (Irwin, 2007).

Estimating contingent liabilities and losses poses knotty problems for government. One set of problems pertains to the treatment of implicit liabilities, for which the government has no legal obligation to indemnify losers but a strong expectation exists, sometimes based on past actions, that it will. Recognizing these risks on a statement of contingent liabilities will likely increase moral hazard and the probability of future payments. However, disregarding them would understate the risk to government.

A related question is whether estimating the probability of losses would generate behavioral changes that increase the risk to government. For example, would publishing data on the probability that government will have to indemnify bank depositors spur a run on risky banks? Arguably, the same analysis would also identify low-risk, soundly capitalized banks and thereby bolster confidence in financial institutions. On balance, government should favor transparency when it has a preexisting legal obligation to make good on losses and when failure to disclose would likely increase its exposure.

Procedural Innovations to Limit Risk

Information rarely suffices to protect government against pressure to assume fiscal risks, especially when no visible, upfront costs are apparent. In fact, proponents of guarantees often claim that government is profiting from taking on more risk when it books origination fees as current revenue. To counter these pressures, it is prudent for government to establish procedures that limit risk taking and recognize probable payments before they come due. It should be noted, however, that despite recent innovations, the treatment of contingent liabilities is among the least standardized areas of public financial management, and despite various existing and evolving reporting standards a satisfactory treatment has yet to be agreed upon.

Some governments have established a parallel budget-type process that limits the total volume of guarantees outstanding, as well as the volume issued during the fiscal year. These limits can be set for all guarantees or can be allocated among sectors or departments, as is done in budgeting for direct expenditures. Others have integrated contingent liabilities into their regular budgets, so that issuance of guarantees reduces funds available for expenditure by an equal amount (in cash-based budgeting) or by the present value of estimated future payments (in accrual-based budgeting). A variant of this approach would limit issuance of contingent liabilities to the amount provisioned for future losses. Some countries have set limits on payments for losses in their budgets, but preset limits are ineffective when actual losses compel higher payouts.

Rules to Constrain Risky Behavior

Regardless of the approach, a strong case can be made for limiting contingent liabilities by establishing an aggregate constraint within an overall fiscal rule and enforcing that constraint through an MTBF. Admittedly, the difficulty of estimating future payouts impairs extension of standard fiscal rules and frameworks to contingent liabilities. Yet it is feasible to compel proposed guarantees to compete against one another within a preset constraint that limits both the volume of contingent liabilities and estimated losses.

1.3.4. Government Performance

Fiscal rules, medium-term budget frameworks, and risk management procedures facilitate achievement of the first two objectives—maintaining a sustainable fiscal position and effective allocation—identified early in this chapter. Performance budgeting (PB) also aims to contribute to effective allocations and to the third objective, efficient provision of public services. A different set of innovations centers on improving administrative management and the provision of public services.

Several reforms contribute to this third objective. To be effective, these innovations must be connected to a broad agenda of administrative improvement that seeks to transform the culture and operational mores of government organizations. Recruiting and motivating staff, modernizing information systems, continuing efforts to improve, being willing to remedy perceived shortcomings, and maintaining capacity to shift money from less to more efficient uses—these and much more are the essence of vibrant, efficient organizations and of quality services. No government can budget for results if it does not also manage for results.

Without exception, governments that have made most progress in the difficult task of orienting their budgets to results are those that have transformed public management.

More than half a century of effort in many countries validates the conclusion that allocating resources on the basis of actual or expected results is a truly difficult task. Good performance is not the only consideration in allocative decisions and often not the most compelling one. Political and distributional influences weigh heavily on these decisions, as do bureaucratic inertia and past budget policies. The space for improved performance is limited by impediments to reallocation, but in normal times almost all government budgets have some space. The aim of performance-oriented systems is both to expand this space and to ensure that it is put to productive use (see Chapter 7).

These systems come in many forms, but for the present discussion they can be arrayed along a spectrum from the least to the most demanding definition. The least demanding version merely requires that the budget and related documents contain information about results. This requirement can be satisfied by inserting performance-relevant data into the budget, without explicitly linking them to resource decisions. The data may pertain to outputs, impacts, outcomes, or other information on the results obtained through public expenditure. Typically, but not always, the addition of performance data is accompanied by purging some line item detail from the budget. The expectation is that publication of performance information will spur budget makers to allocate funds on the basis of results. The other end of the spectrum is occupied by budgets that explicitly link each increment in expenditure to an increment in results, and quantify how changing the amounts spent will be reciprocated by changes in the volume of outputs or other performance measures. Numerous variations that differ in how they link resources and results can be found along this spectrum.[16]

Many governments can legitimately claim to have performance budgets if the criterion applied is publication of performance data; few, however, tightly connect the amounts spent to substantive results. Depending on the test used, one might conclude that performance budgeting has become standard practice in well-managed countries or that it has made little headway.

The questionable impact of performance budgets has led some reformers to shift discussion from systems to results and from a government-wide perspective to particular programs and objectives. They argue that the true test of performance-oriented reforms should not be whether government has a formal performance budget, but whether focusing on opportunities to remedy shortfalls in performance actually generates better results. For example, if data on school dropouts, student performance on standard tests, or literacy rates impel political

[16] Performance-informed budgeting is used by the Organisation for Economic Co-operation and Development and the World Bank to define reforms in which performance information is used to inform budget decisions. It does not automatically link results to funding. See OECD (2007) and Arizti and others (2010),

leaders and educators to reallocate education funds to more productive uses, the government can be said to budget on the basis of performance, even though it lacks some key performance-budgeting elements. This orientation may be especially useful for low-income countries that generally have insufficient capacity to mount a full performance-budgeting effort, but want to remedy serious deficiencies in performance.

Information Requirements Depend on the Approach Taken

Government cannot budget on the basis of performance if it lacks information on the results expected to ensue from public expenditure. These results are typically expressed in quantities, either as outputs (such as the number of persons or percentage of the eligible population served) or as outcomes (such as changes in health). There is enormous variation among governments both in the labels applied to these types of data and in the types of results measured. Differentiating between outputs and outcomes has been a contentious issue, leading analysts to wonder whether the labels have become more important than the results. Some governments have constructed frameworks that purport to link objectives, outcomes, outputs, activities, and inputs in a logical sequence. The neatness of these frameworks is impressive, even though the connection between outputs and outcomes is rarely as straightforward as the designers of these systems claim.

Much more attention has been paid by governments to generating performance indicators than to using them. The facile assumption that once performance information is available governments will budget on this basis is not warranted. As discussed earlier, performance data compete with other, often more powerful influences on budget decisions. Performance information does not itself dictate whether government should spend more or less. Suppose the evidence shows that many students have failed to acquire basic education tools. A strong case can be made either to cut or to augment the money allocated to failing schools. Deciding which is the better course requires qualitative contextual and quantitative data.

The claim that allocations will be based on performance information is low in the loose definition of PB but rises as the spectrum progresses toward the strict definition. A budget that shows how changes in resources will change results is purposely designed to promote due consideration of performance in allocating public funds. However, this demanding version gives rise to a different set of problems: government often lacks the capacity to estimate the effects of marginal changes in expenditures on results. Few governments have cost accounting systems that (1) distinguish between fixed and variable costs and between marginal and average costs, (2) divide outputs into standard units, and (3) fully allocate costs to these units. In many cases, relying on rough estimates of incremental impacts may be adequate, but governments that strive to apply PB systematically to improve substantive results should consider upgrading their cost accounting and allocation processes.

Building Performance into Budget Processes

Asymmetries in information beset all PB systems because budget allocators are dependent on spenders for essential information. Dependence escalates when budgeting shifts from financing inputs to producing substantive results. In well-run countries, central agencies usually generate much of the data required to compile input-based budgets; however, they must rely on spending units for essential data on the volume of outputs and the cost of producing desired outcomes. For PB to work, service providers must supply central officials with information that may put their budgets at risk. In fact, line managers typically have incentives and means to hide or hoard information, to spin data in ways that suit their interests, and to prevaricate. The more demanding PB is in linking resources and results the greater vulnerability it has to agency problems. Agents have relatively little incentive to distort performance data that are displayed in the budget but do not drive allocative decisions, but much more incentive when resources are distributed on the basis of reported or expected results.

Process adjustments can ease dependence on agent-controlled information, but not eliminate it altogether. One obvious solution is for central authorities to establish their own performance-monitoring and evaluation channels. Doing so can be costly, is not likely to cover all relevant elements of performance, and may expose central staff to capture by sectoral interests. The opposite tactic would be to decentralize various types of decisions by giving line agencies a pool of money they can spend without having to receive central approval in advance. This approach is favored by new public management doctrine, which argues that once freed from central control, managers have much less reason to dissemble and much more opportunity to apply their professional skills and judgment to the tasks at hand. However, absent fundamental changes in human resource management, confidence in the performance of line managers, whose interests and perspectives inevitably differ from those at the center of government, may be unwarranted.

Two other process adjustments have been associated with PB systems: performance auditing and performance targeting, with the former currently applied in only a small number of governments, whereas the latter is more widely applied. Some innovative governments have extended the methods of financial auditing to the audit of results.[17] The basic idea is that spending units must support statements of results with documented evidence in the same manner they do for financial statements. Independent auditors review performance statements to determine whether they meet accepted standards. This approach has encountered substantial difficulty because there are no generally accepted standards for performance evidence.

---

[17] Performance auditing has been promoted by the International Organization of Supreme Audit Institutions. In 2004, it issued *Implementation Guidelines for Performance Auditing*. The guidelines and country reports are available at INTSAI.org.

Whereas performance auditing adds to the complexity of PB, performance targeting seeks to simplify the process by selecting a small number of indicators for close scrutiny, specifying expectations in advance when resources are allocated, and comparing results to targets. The agency problem is greatly diminished because principals have a lead role in defining the targets and they need pay attention to only a small number of indicators. But performance targeting pays a price for simplicity. For one, major elements of performance are likely to be outside central purview; for another, the targets can distort results by inducing managers to concentrate on measured aspects of performance and to ignore others.

It Is Premature, and May Be Infeasible, to Prescribe Performance-Centered Rules

Major PFM innovations have been accompanied by changes in rules governing the allocation of resources or the compilation of financial data. PB is the principal exception. It is not encoded in either allocative or informational rules. Governments do not have to favor high-performing programs in their budgets and few measure performance according to prescribed criteria. The absence of rules is reflected in the shift in labels from performance budgeting, which was the term in vogue a generation ago, to performance-informed budgeting, which is now the more popular label.

Although technical impediments may hamper allocating in accord with evidence on results, the main difficulty is the need to consider multiple factors in distributing public funds to programs and agencies. Even if it had the capacity to rank programs from the most to the least productive, government would still have legitimate reasons for spending more on some low-ranked programs. The most government can do is to add performance information to the mix, thereby enabling it to claim that it has performance budgets even when it fails to budget on the basis of performance.

1.4. MODERNIZING PFM INFRASTRUCTURE

As discussed in the previous section, major PFM innovations focus on specific issues, such as the fiscal position of government, its management of financial risk, and the substantive results of public expenditures. These innovations cannot be successfully implemented without a supporting infrastructure of information and processes, specifically the accounting and budget frameworks and administrative capacity to handle broadened demands on government. This infrastructure has to be modernized apace with other reforms. This section focuses on accounting rules and procedures, features of the budget system, and the role of central fiscal agencies.

1.4.1. Accounting Framework

Accounts are the basic building blocks of PFM systems. They determine much of the content and classification of the information processed in managing public finance and they affect PFM's core objectives as well as many of the specific issues discussed in this book. They also provide a clear illustration of how authoritative rules can transform data from information that is useful into information that is essential, and how the absence of such rules can impair use of potentially valuable information.

Government accounts recognize two types of financial stocks and flows: the money received or disbursed during a fiscal period, and the money earned or liabilities accrued during the period. Each basis provides useful information, and one cannot substitute for the other. The cash basis reports the nominal surplus or deficit and borrowing requirements and the short-term impact of government finances on the economy. The accrual basis reports government's assets and liabilities and its fiscal position without regard to when the funds are actually received or paid. The cash basis shows the money spent by agencies in producing public services; the accrual basis shows the resources they have consumed. (See Chapter 8 for more details).

The accrual basis serves all major PFM objectives. It provides a fuller account of government's fiscal position because it includes unliquidated liabilities that will be paid in future periods and disregards accounting tricks that shift the recognition of receipts or disbursements from one period to another. It improves allocation because programs or departments are charged with the cost of resources they consume, regardless of the account from which payment is made. Similarly, it sensitizes managers to cost and may give them greater incentive and opportunity to operate efficiently. Finally, it bolsters financial accountability because citizens have a clearer picture of the cost of public programs and activities.

The accounting and statistical reporting standards promulgated by international bodies have established accruals as the authoritative basis for financial reports of national governments. In the past, accrual information was "good to have," now it is "must have." Accounting rules and procedures provide terms for converting accrual data into actionable reports and statements.

But are these sufficient to change incentives and behavior? For example, would deterioration in its balance sheet constructed on the accrual basis impel government to change revenue or expenditure policies? For a small number of countries, the answer may be a qualified "yes." These are countries that have extended the accrual basis beyond accounting statements to the budget and manage finances in terms of the cost of resources consumed and liabilities accrued. Even in "cutting edge" countries, the answer must be qualified because (1) almost all these governments also report finances on a cash basis, which has greater weight in fiscal and political policy; and (2) significant social insurance and health care liabilities of government are excluded by widely accepted accounting rules from accrual-based financial statements. Only contractual obligations, such as civil service pensions, are recognized on these statements, not liabilities arising out of mandated transfer payments. One important consequence of this exclusion is that the accrual basis provides little insight into long-term fiscal sustainability and only weak incentives for government to adopt policies that strengthen its fiscal future.

This is why long-term fiscal projections that accompany budget documents and financial statements are important, as argued elsewhere in this chapter. One of the key arguments in support of the accrual basis is that cash flows can be manipulated to portray a more favorable fiscal position than is warranted by accelerating revenue collections or deferring payments. But accruals also can be manipulated by changing underlying assumptions, especially for the valuation of assets and for demographic and economic trends. In fact, deception may be more difficult to uncover in accruals when it is buried under layers of assumptions.

The accrual basis may inadvertently damage financial control in countries that appropriate funds for noncash charges such as depreciation. The concept is that agencies should finance major repairs and replacement of assets out of funds accumulated in depreciation accounts. Instead, however, sometimes agencies shift these funds to other operational uses, and then seek new appropriations to replace depreciated assets.[18] The simple solution is to not appropriate cash for noncash items, and to maintain strong controls that bar agencies from financing cash expenditures out of noncash appropriations. Either way, the accrual basis adds considerable complexity, and may impair the capacity of politicians and voters to comprehend government finances.

These issues do not arise for the vast majority of countries that use the accrual basis for reporting to international bodies or for satisfying audit requirements, but actively manage public finances via cash flows. They budget and appropriate on the cash basis, and even in those cases in which spending units are charged for pensions or other indirect or overhead items, there is little discernible impact on managerial behavior. These charges are offset by an equivalent amount added to each account, but managers have no control over the amount—they cannot do anything to increase or decrease it, nor can they trade off between these charges and other expenses.

To sum up by using the distinction drawn earlier, accruals are essential for financial reporting but only good to have for agency and program management. Cash is essential for fiscal management because government must pay its bills and be mindful of the interactions between its finances and the economy.

1.4.2. Budget Framework

In most countries, the accounting system frames key features of the budget process and the reverse also holds true. But the two systems do not completely mirror one another. Many national governments report financial results on the accrual basis, but few budget on this basis, as is discussed in Chapter 11. Moreover, budgeting frames a number of issues arising out of its essential character as an instrument of allocation that do not pertain to the form of accounts.

The key question is whether governments can have both annual budgets that allocate benefits and medium-term and longer perspectives that constrain current decisions. Can governments be induced or required to forgo expedient budget

[18] Australia faced this problem when it introduced accrual budgeting (Kelly and Wanna, 2004).

policies in order to safeguard the country's fiscal future? This is much more a political than a technical question.

Budgeting Still Is a Means of Incremental Allocation

In concept, and usually legally as well, the budget allocates all resources that become available for expenditure. In reality, national budgets routinely continue almost all existing programs, with incremental (usually positive but sometimes negative) adjustments. This clash between budget doctrine and practice has triggered a decades-long quest for more comprehensively rational budget systems. It also has confirmed the durability of incremental norms and behavior and the difficulty of rooting them out.

Of course, occasional deviations from incremental patterns occur, most likely when the government has windfall revenues or a financing crisis, or when it launches new programs. Spending units also make ongoing adjustments that do not show up in aggregate data and may be made outside the budget process. For example, an agency may shift posts made redundant by the introduction of new information technology systems to other tasks without formally notifying budget authorities of the change. In other words, budgets are incremental, but not always to the extent the incremental label connotes.

The task of modern PFM systems is not to mount a frontal attack on incrementalism but to expand the boundaries of effective allocation by ensuring that the increments are optimally allocated and by spurring reallocation from less to more productive uses. The tools of PFM have often been deployed to ease incremental tendencies, but not always with success. Evaluation of existing programs, analysis of policy options, outcome indicators, and other measures of results provide the informational basis for intelligent allocation, and MTBF procedures and rules encourage trade-offs between existing and proposed programs. To succeed, they must reckon with the incentives that account for incrementalism's grip on national budgets.

Two considerations lead budget participants to favor incremental allocations, even when they decry the failure of budgeting to take a hard look at existing programs. They want to contain both political and bureaucratic conflict, and they want to complete essential tasks on or close to schedule. Spending agencies have an additional incentive—to protect existing resources and interests. Major PFM innovations during the past half century that have disregarded these incentives have failed; medium-term budget frameworks that recognize the incentives that underpin incrementalism have a better chance to succeed.

Composition of Expenditure

Yet another way can be detected in which the budget's comprehensive scope masks the reality that it does not frame all expenditure. In advanced economies, standing legislation that establishes a right to payment from the government drives half (or more) of total national expenditure. Some mandatory payments go to households in the form of income support and other entitlements, some to subnational governments in the form of revenue or expenditure assignments. In all advanced economies, these payments account for a much higher share of national expenditure than they did as recently as a decade ago.

Although the budget does not ordinarily determine these expenditures, it does account for them and occasionally influences the amounts spent. Through program reviews connected to the budget cycle, governments do frequently tinker with entitlement rules, sometimes to adjust amounts or to retarget payments. Adjustments have become routine elements of budget allocation in quite a few countries, even during stable periods. Nevertheless, transfer payments are more sensitive to demographic and economic trends than to budget decisions.

The information required for entitlement budgets differs from that conventionally produced for administrative budgets. The latter rely principally on data internal to the spending unit's mostly operational details. The former depend on external, mostly socioeconomic data, such as the country's age structure, employment levels, and trends in medical costs. Inevitably, as the relative weight of entitlements has increased, operational details (line items) have receded in importance, and econometric modeling has become a critical feature of national budgeting.

Procedures and rules can be adjusted to fortify politicians willing to discipline entitlements. Because they cover all expenditure, fiscal rules may give politicians incentives to take a hard look at existing entitlements. Of course, fiscal rules have this effect only if they are enforced, which has not always been the case. Incentives can also be changed by enabling politicians to enact cutbacks in entitlements as part of the process of formulating the budget.

1.4.3. Role of Central Fiscal Institutions

PFM operates in all echelons of public management and sprawls across multiple administrative entities, including the audit office and units responsible for maintaining government accounts and managing cash flow and debt obligations. The concern here is with entities situated at the center of government that manage the budget and related fiscal processes and the responsibilities entrusted to them.

Macroeconomic Management

It has long been accepted that national governments cannot responsibly manage revenues and expenditures unless they have capacity to project key economic indicators for the budget period or beyond and to estimate the impact of these forecasts on revenues and expenditures. Economic projections are rarely accurate, but the error may be of little consequence if the variance is small or if the government can easily adjust to it. Neither of these favorable conditions is common in low-income countries, which tend to have highly volatile economies and budgets. Some fiscally stressed countries practice repetitive budgeting; they remake the budget several times a year in response to the latest economic or financial news.[19] Some advanced economies have had similar experiences during the Great Recession, redoing their budgets during the year as deficits and risk premiums on their debt soared.

The risk of error occurs not only in projecting the economic future, but also in estimating the sensitivity of revenues, expenditures, the deficit, and other budget variables to changes in economic conditions. Although government economists and outside experts often issue similar economic forecasts, they sometimes project significantly different fiscal aggregates. At times, opportunistic politicians may issue unduly optimistic forecasts, leading some to argue that independent experts should be assigned responsibility for economic and budget projections, either as the basis for the government's forecasts or as alternatives to them. This issue is gaining prominence because of efforts under way to strengthen enforcement of fiscal rules.

Challenges to Central Fiscal Agencies

Relying on independent experts is only one of the contemporary challenges to the authoritative status of central budget agencies. Not long ago the finance ministry (or a similar entity) stood virtually unchallenged on budget and economic policy. It had a near monopoly on fiscal data and analyses, the media rarely assigned specialists to monitor economic and budget developments, and organized groups lacked expertise to question the government's assumptions. This was certainly the case in most parliamentary regimes in which the legislature made minor or no changes to the budget submitted by government. However, in many countries, the situation is quite different today—an increasing number of legislatures have established their own budget economic analysis staffs and adopt substantive amendments to the budget (Wehner, 2006, 2010). In addition, interest groups, the media, and independent experts vigilantly monitor the budget in many advanced economies.

The finance ministry also faces challenges within government—from presidential policy staffs that may be closer to the center of power, from the cabinet and sectoral ministers who have their own experts, and in planning-centered countries, from national planners who bring a different perspective on budget and other policy issues. Finally, the assumptions and policy advice of central fiscal experts are now routinely questioned in many countries by interest groups and nongovernmental organizations, which have their own experts to spin fiscal policy their way.

Fiscal debate is less orderly and much noisier than it once was, but surely with significant gain in democratic accountability. Matters have become more transparent, fiscal numbers buried under layers of complex assumptions can be questioned, and misleading or erroneous pronouncements can be exposed. Finance ministries have been taken down a notch or two and now have well-placed rivals, but they still are the dominant players in fiscal policy, especially when crisis strikes and the government must mobilize for rapid action.

---

[19]The concept of repetitive budgeting was introduced by Caiden and Wildavsky (1974).

Top-Down Budget and Policy Guidance

Central fiscal agencies relate to sectoral departments and agencies in two seemingly different ways. One is through "bottom-up" review of spending bids, the other via "top-down" policy guidance. Although they are characterized as opposite approaches, elements of both coexist in all resource allocation systems because each side has something the other wants or needs. Those at the top control allocations, those below control much of the information required for intelligent allocation. This interdependence fosters both cooperation and conflict, with the balance of power shifting from one year to the next depending on fiscal and political characteristics.

Top-down versus bottom-up also connotes whether fiscal aggregates are set before spending bids are submitted or after. In a pure top-down arrangement, central fiscal authorities set firm limits on total expenditure at the start of the process and disaggregate these amounts to departments or spending units, each of which is required to bid for resources within its preset limit. This form of budgeting replaces the bottom-up approach that enables spending units to submit unconstrained bids. To enforce preset constraints, some countries formally divide budget work into two separate stages.[20] Top-down limits are set during the framework stage, and bids, within these limits, are reviewed during the estimates or appropriations stage.

Switching to a top-down system consists of more than issuing fiscal guidance in advance; it requires divestiture by central agencies of some previously performed tasks to focus on fiscal and other policy matters. One should be mindful, however, that withdrawal from detailed expenditure oversight can leave the budget office without sufficient information to make informed decisions and without sufficient leverage to manage the country's finances. As they reposition from expenditure control to promoters of good fiscal and allocative performance, central agencies risk a loss of power and status if they fail to establish new roles and relationships.

Central Agency Roles and Capacities

In striving to improve allocation, the natural role for the central agency is to invest in program evaluation and policy analysis, review the effectiveness of existing programs, and explore options for new ones. A critical issue is whether to centralize responsibility for evaluation or to rely on sectoral departments to conduct their own assessments. Neither course is especially promising. No matter how well staffed it is, the central agency cannot be as informed of, or as sensitive to, policy and political nuances as is the spending department. Decentralizing evaluation has its own shortcomings, rooted in the understandable instinct of departments to protect their programs. One possible way out of

---

[20] Sweden adopted a two-stage process in 1996. In the first stage, the government aggregates spending ceilings as well as 27 subceilings on sectors and funds. In the second stage, the government submits the budget and the Riksdag (parliament) votes appropriations.

this dilemma is for the central agency to oversee the evaluation process, but for departments to conduct the evaluations. An approach, effectively used by Chile, is for the central agency to draw on completed evaluations in allocating budget resources, while also commissioning in-depth studies that may influence future budgets.

Central agencies must also define their role in devising and using outcome or other results-based indicators and targets. If departments have full discretion, the risk is significant that they would opt for measures oriented to their activities rather than the objectives of government and for easy-to-reach targets that do not challenge them to improve performance. Nevertheless, central agencies cannot unilaterally enforce measures and targets; ideally, they should consult with departments, advise them on recommended measures, and prod them to produce accurate and relevant data.

However, at least two circumstances might arise for which strong leadership from the center may be welcome, perhaps even necessary. One occurs when high-priority programs or policies cut across departmental lines and central leadership is required to coordinate action and monitor progress toward achieving government objectives. This is often the case with respect to government's social agenda. The other occurs when, either because of economic crisis or a major shift in political orientation, the government mounts a fundamental review that aims to make significant changes in departments and programs. These reviews must be led from the center, at least for setting expenditure targets and national priorities and overseeing results, though actual conduct of the reviews may be hived off to departments.

Central agencies can also carve out a management role that promotes the efficient operation of agencies and delivery of public services. One facet of this role entails advising line departments on good management practice; another involves establishing output and efficiency targets that prod operating units to improve performance. Here, too, the division of labor and power between central authority and operating entities may be unclear or contested, especially if the government professes to have devolved managerial discretion to subordinate entities.

1.5. CRITICAL ISSUES IN REFORMING PFM

Most PFM innovations were initiated in advanced economies and radiated over time to countries with less-developed economic and public management systems. The initiating countries have generally had greater success than those that followed, but their gains from modernizing public financial management have inevitably been less because they already had well-developed PFM systems. PFM is perennially a work in progress, driven by dissatisfaction with existing methods or the promise that new rules, processes, and information—the three levers for influencing the behavior of participants and substantive policies—will produce better outcomes.

As a work in progress, PFM must reckon with a number of issues that will shape future reform efforts. One set of issues goes to the heart of PFM reforms and questions whether adjustments to information, processes, and rules suffice to alter the behavior of policymakers and the outcomes that flow from their actions. This question emerged in discussing particular PFM innovations; full resolution of the issues requires a comprehensive assessment of whether analytical tools should be transformed into decision rules. Another set of issues pertains to the application of PFM practices devised in advanced economies to less-developed countries that are not yet endowed with full managerial capacity. A final set of issues arises from the still-unsettled fiscal crisis that has roiled many countries. This is discussed in Section 1.6.

1.5.1. Do the Levers Change Behavior and PFM Outcomes?

Adjustments to information, processes, and rules are the three levers identified earlier for transforming PFM. The first two operate through changes in incentives and behavior, the third through restrictions on PFM actions and decisions. Confining innovation to these categories suggests that despite the large number of reforms it has spurred, PFM has a limited toolkit that may be inadequate to produce the far-reaching changes it envisions. Examining each lever on its own, as well as in reference to core PFM objectives, is useful.

Information

New information is not inherently transformative. It can be a resource that exposes political and managerial leaders to fresh ideas and perspectives and emboldens them to deviate from existing policies, even when it is expedient for them to stay on the same course. Alternatively, these leaders can ignore, withhold, or spin information that challenges the status quo. They can use deficit or debt projections to promote fiscal consolidation, or ignore these warnings and make decisions that increase future deficits and debt. Policymakers can justify either action, but tough decisions typically generate more conflict, even when they are based on information of the type generated by PFM reforms. Political and administrative costs are incurred when new information is allowed to steer budget policies.

PFM reforms have an easier road when politicians and managers are not the only producers and users of critical information. At least three other sets of influencers have the potential to stimulate use of PFM information. First, autonomous entities, such as the audit office or an independent fiscal agency, can invest critical information with authority and objectivity, thereby making it difficult for government to ignore fiscal realities. This approach is likely to be effective when influence shapers, such as the media and interest groups, pay attention. Second, international and regional organizations can pressure conflicted governments to act. Third, market players can induce policy change by demanding higher risk premiums or by refusing to purchase public debt when governments fail to respond to relevant information. Some of the countries most severely affected by the financial crisis ignored the first set of signals, did not receive or parried the second set, and were driven to act by the third. The clear lesson is that markets often have the strongest voice, but ignoring the first two can adversely affect the government's fiscal position and force it to make more difficult fiscal adjustments.

Processes

Process reforms compel the use of certain types of information in carrying out prescribed PFM tasks and also impose various procedural requirements. The key issue in all process reforms is whether the new procedures will change behavior or come to be treated as just one of the chores government must complete to fulfill formal requirements. Politicians and managers are less likely to disregard new procedures than new information, but they can drain any innovative process of utility by treating it as a technical exercise that has little bearing on decisions. No less than in the case of new information, the fate of PFM reforms rests in the hands of users.

It often is difficult for reformers to discern how PFM innovations adopted by governments are actually used. How does one distinguish between an MTBF that is window dressing and one that effectively reshapes fiscal and program decisions? Appearances can be deceiving in PFM innovations. A government that wants to maintain the status quo while professing to embrace change can accomplish these seemingly conflicting aims by establishing a special unit isolated from ongoing PFM work to manage its reforms. Other tricks are to run new processes through protracted pilot tests or to insist that implementation begin with efforts to devise the perfect information or measurement system. These stratagems often are regarded by outside sponsors as evidence of commitment and progress, even though their actual effect is to thwart reform.

Procedural innovations rarely succeed when they lack well-placed champions to mobilize interest and support and clear away political and bureaucratic obstacles. Arguably, the ideal champions are those at the top of government, but political leaders rarely engage in PFM reforms after launch. Although they may endorse reform at the outset, they generally have little or no involvement during implementation. During this stage, those whose interests are threatened can subvert innovations by capturing them and elbowing out reformers.

Introducing new procedures confronts governments with a difficult question: What requirements should be eliminated or altered in existing procedures to accommodate the new ones? One appealing option is to operate parallel processes—the new alongside the old—until such time as the innovations are sufficiently accepted and embedded to form the single process by which the government manages its finances. The main difficulty with this tactic is that the existing and innovative approaches are not likely to be on equal footing. If, as often happens, line managers come to realize that the preexisting system is still the way things get done, they will disengage from innovation. A seemingly riskier approach is to sweep out the old (when it is incompatible with the new) and install innovative PFM procedures, even though they have not been fully tested or accepted by those who have to make them work. Most innovative governments combine elements of old and new, which increases work and information burdens and may provoke opposition to reform or doubt about the government's commitment. One way to mitigate these risks is to shed some older features when installing the new ones, thereby signaling that innovations are here to stay. Even in favorable circumstances and with skillful implementation, procedural innovations might not be adequate. The process might be novel, but not the behavior of those who manage it, or the results that flow from it.

Rules

Reformers, therefore, may seek to activate the final PFM lever by codifying preferred procedures into rules with which public managers must comply. The accrual basis is one such rule, fiscal limits are a second, and sometimes medium-term budget frameworks are a third. Currently, quite a few potential rules—permissive procedural innovations—can be formulated into constraints on government action. The following possibilities are mentioned to illustrate the potential reach of rules, not to advocate their adoption: (1) an intertemporal fiscal constraint that would bar changes in expenditure (or revenue) policy that would cause deterioration in the long-term financial balance; and (2) a fiscal risk rule that would limit the volume or cost of explicit contingent liabilities. Both of these potential rules would address a perceived deficiency in contemporary PFM practice: an intertemporal rule would counter myopic budget policies, and a fiscal risk rule would counter the temptation of governments to treat risk as costless or as less costly than direct expenditures.

All proposed rules, including those illustrated here, have potential advantages, the most persuasive of which is that they cannot be brushed aside as easily as enhanced information or new procedures. Nevertheless, governments should proceed cautiously in converting procedural innovations into decisional rules. Caution is in order because rules constrain the discretion of democratically elected leaders, rigidify the management of public finance, often add to information and work burdens, and can open the door to inefficient or unwanted policies. Not every analytic tool should be recast into a decision rule (Schick, 2009b). Would-be rule makers should consider how a rule might misfire before squeezing the trigger. The two illustrative rules make sense on their own terms, but they can have adverse consequences.

An intertemporal rule relies on highly uncertain, and often volatile, long-term assumptions concerning interest rates, life expectancy, trends in health care use and inflation, and other variables. It is highly sensitive to the discount rate. Using projections to inform policymakers of potential intergenerational implications of current fiscal commitments differs enormously from using them to restrict current policy options. In view of the fallibility of critical assumptions and the lack of generally accepted methods for constructing long-term projections, it is premature to impose intergenerational rules.

A fiscal risk rule requires comprehensive information on the volume of outstanding and proposed contingent liabilities; well-grounded assumptions about prospective defaults, recoveries, and other relevant variables; and estimates of future costs. Some governments have the capacity to compile relevant data and construct reliable cost estimates. Many do not.

For rules to be effective, they have to build on innovations in information and process, not substitute for them. In PFM, as in other arenas, rules work when governments compile and apply relevant data through ongoing procedures that ensure the reliability, completeness, and relevance of information and embedded procedures enable it to take informed actions. Government should apply constrictive rules only when it has a firm grip on why better information and processes are not doing the job.

1.5.2. Sequencing Matters

Sequencing matters even though there is no right sequence for all times and places. Is there an appropriate sequence for introducing PFM innovations? What criteria should be used in assessing the readiness of governments for advanced PFM practices? In simple terms, the choice is between best and basic practices, between leapfrogging innovations on the one hand and using a building-blocks approach on the other. Multiple options exist between best and basic, both in the content of reforms and in the manner in which they are implemented.

This chapter has focused on the elements of a sound PFM system. The number and variety of these elements give rise to difficult challenges in many countries. What is the appropriate strategy for modernizing PFM in countries with serious deficiencies in existing practices? The question radiates in many directions, including methods of assessing each country's PFM shortcomings and its readiness for reform, dependence of reform programs on allies and champions, the capacity of administrative units to absorb change, difficult decisions on what information and procedural requirements should be subtracted when new ones are added, the resources needed to mount a successful reform campaign, the extent to which political leaders should engage in the effort, and the motivation and skills of public managers and employees. These and other issues are critical because a faulty implementation strategy can doom well-intentioned innovations, even those boosted at the outset by strong political and managerial support. In this writer's observation, more promising reforms have been undermined by missteps in implementation than by problems in design, more by insensitivity to constraints than by failure to exploit opportunities.

Many—perhaps most—implementation issues are country specific; resolving them depends on knowledge of a country's political and administrative culture, current PFM practices, and the interests and views of key players. Generalized advice does not offer much useful guidance for a country that must find its own way through a tangle of constraints and opportunities. But two issues that have broad application across many countries have occasioned lively debate within the PFM community.

The first is whether a government that has multiple PFM deficiencies should proceed on many fronts at once or should opportunistically target particular reforms. The second is whether there is a logical or necessary progression from one set of innovations to another. The first issue pertains to workload, the capacity of a country to manage multiple innovations concurrently, the second to sequence, the capacity of a country to master advanced PFM techniques if it cannot perform simpler tasks. Many reforms have been doomed by overloading fragile administrative units with more new challenges than they can handle or by bewildering those who must perform the new tasks. The obvious solution is to match reform to capacity, even if doing so slows the pace of innovation and risks loss of interest or support before the full slate of new practices has been embedded. Matching reform to capacity is more easily said than done because reformers often disagree in their assessments of the scope of innovation that a country can absorb. Moreover, reformers—both senior country officials and outside experts—have strong incentives to take on more innovation than is prudent, sometimes because it burnishes their reputations or advances their careers, sometimes because they sense a need to remedy critical deficiencies quickly.

Getting the sequence right is an even tougher challenge, for it opens the door to unresolved disputes about whether deficient governments would be better served by striving for state-of-the-art innovations or by adopting an incremental, capacity-building strategy. Over the years, this writer has urged that highly deficient countries begin by emphasizing basic capacities, and use these as building blocks for more ambitious innovations. This argument has gained traction in the platform approach to PFM. Platforms bundle various reforms in a series of sequenced stages that range from basic to advanced. When a country masters the skills in a lower platform, it can graduate to the next higher platform, thereby enabling it to prepare for ambitious innovations while overcoming capacity limits.

In practice, platforms may be more metaphor than reality, for they sometimes resemble conventional timelines used to schedule actions (or milestones), typically over a two- to five-year period. A basics-first strategy is not a counsel for failure; in countries with deeply embedded PFM deficiencies, it is the only path to success.

1.6. EMERGING LESSONS FROM THE GLOBAL FINANCIAL AND ECONOMIC CRISIS

PFM has been stress-tested in many countries by the 2008–09 financial meltdown and its aftermath, which has disrupted entrenched routines and transformed fiscal surpluses into deficits, or relatively small deficits into much larger ones. Fiscal rules have been brushed aside and have provided neither constraints nor guidance for political leaders faced with economic stagnation or decline. Time horizons have narrowed in response to short-term pressures, even in countries with operational MTBFs. Fiscal risks that were disregarded or underestimated before the crisis have materialized, and national governments have struggled to stabilize both public finances and economic conditions.

Although the final accounting is not in, and the full cost of output losses and public debt increases is not yet known, it is timely to begin assessing the procedural and policy implications of the crisis. Some countries and supranational institutions, most notably the European Union, have already made adjustments to PFM rules and systems and many others are likely to follow.

Despite ongoing controversy about steps to resolve the crisis, it is not too early to explore reforms to avert the next one. This section aims to provoke fresh insights, not to settle issues that are not yet ripe for definitive conclusions. Looking at the crisis experience to date, what lessons can guide next-generation PFM reforms? This section presents three related hypotheses that may clarify requirements for these reforms. The first two are within the ambit of PFM; the third spills over to broader economic and financial issues. First, PFM routines are primed to deal with ordinary fiscal and budget conditions, not with shocks emanating from the mismanagement or collapse of financial institutions, nor with the consequent loss of confidence in the capacity of national governments to correct profound imbalances. Second, the modernized lineup of PFM instruments failed during the normal times that preceded the crisis. Third, breakdown occurred principally in other areas of financial governance, such as the buildup of private debt and imprudent accumulation of risk, not in the management of public money. The subsequent subsections will present the case for these arguments. If valid, they suggest two main conclusions. First, PFM was largely a bystander at the onset of and during much of the crisis, but its failures during the precrisis years were important contributors to subsequent breakdowns. Second, remedying PFM's inadequacies will facilitate economic consolidation and fiscal recovery, especially in the most severely affected countries. However, future reforms will have to cast a wider net and take account of economic conditions and financial markets.

The most economically advanced countries have not been equally afflicted by the crisis. Differences in experiences bolster the argument that countries with sturdy PFM systems are more likely to escape severe fiscal distress than those with weaker capacity. It is important to note, however, that some heavily impacted countries, such as Iceland and Ireland, appeared to have had strong fiscal positions and robust PFM systems before the crisis struck. This anomaly suggests the need to venture beyond PFM frameworks to assess and safeguard the financial condition of government.

This section embraces the two seemingly contradictory points of view, that PFM is not a shockproof system and that it makes a difference in fiscal and budgetary outcomes. The following subsections examine PFM from three time perspectives—during, before, and after the crisis.

1.6.1. The Crisis: Fiscal Shocks and Breakdown of Routine

The first hypothesis is that PFM was largely irrelevant during the crisis because it was never meant to deal with shocks. As discussed throughout this chapter, in normal times PFM routines are repeated year after year with little change.

Routine broke down during the crisis. Dismal fiscal conditions drove heavily affected countries to abandon stable routines and to patch together improvised procedures to confront the crisis. Some have been compelled to rebudget several times during the fiscal year in response to the latest projections or to turmoil in capital markets. Some have replaced the regular budget with emergency packages assembled by the ministry of finance (or other central authorities) without the usual participation of spending agencies or civil society. Under pressure from supranational authorities, governments have proposed or enacted opportunistic cuts in existing programs and promised benefits, usually without informed assessment of fiscal or socioeconomic effects.

PFM's main innovations do not fit easily into crisis-spawned makeshift processes. Little reward comes from proclaiming the integrity of fiscal rules when deficits and debt are spiraling out of control and the government has no effective means of keeping them within preset limits. In the short to medium term, closing the gap between actual and rules-based deficits and debt depends as much (or more) on the performance of the economy as on the performance of government. Pressure to right the country's fiscal problems comes more from capital markets and the international community than from data showing the extent to which projected deficits exceed rules-permitted levels. Credible commitments on future fiscal outcomes can restore confidence to capital markets, but it is exceedingly difficult to invest rules with sufficient credence when the economy is shrinking, unemployment is soaring, and each economic news bulletin compels upward adjustments of debt and deficit projections.

Medium-term budget frameworks and precrisis projections were ignored or torn up when economic and fiscal conditions deteriorated. Governments unable to keep to budget plans for the current year or the one immediately ahead certainly were unable to stay on course for the next three to five years. Countries that produced medium-term budget frameworks before the crisis continued to do so, some out of habit, some to show that fiscal conditions would improve in the out years. It is fair to say, however, that each country's fiscal future depends more on political and economic developments than on medium-term budget frameworks. Uncertainty is the perennial nemesis of multiyear budget plans, but the problem is much greater when economic prospects are clouded by crisis.

The crisis has driven political leaders and senior managers to produce savings wherever they can be found. Performance metrics and program budgets are not high on the "to do" list for deadline-sensitive budget cutters. Investing in these systems (as has occurred in a few countries) diverts attention from critical tasks and gets in the way of dealing with the crisis. In some situations, basic PFM reforms have been necessary to account for the country's true fiscal condition, but improving the reliability and timeliness of financial statements has been much more urgent than crafting a performance budget.

For good reason, dealing with the crisis has mattered more than showing fidelity to fiscal rules, using an extended time frame for budgeting, or bringing performance budgets into the picture. The time has not been ripe for modern PFM to demonstrate its potential. As conditions improve, however, the contemporary

PFM agenda may be able to play a constructive role in improving the management of public funds. For it to do so, however, PFM reformers have to take a hard look at how their prized innovations work and adjust those features that have not lived up to expectations.

1.6.2. Precrisis: The (Not So) Golden Age of PFM Reforms

The second hypothesis posed earlier deals with the precrisis years and argues that the great harvest of PFM innovations did not yield expected results. From the perspective of the crisis, it is difficult to recall the good times that preceded it. Almost all high-income countries experienced sustained growth during the first years of the new millennium. These also were years during which a benign contagion swept the PFM reforms of the previous decades from their countries of origin across continents.

Buoyant economic conditions and strong PFM systems should have produced favorable fiscal outcomes during the precrisis years. Looking back at that period, a striking number of countries incurred financial deficits and failed to reduce public debt burdens. More than two-thirds of the member countries of Europe's Economic and Monetary Union breached agreed-on fiscal limits once or more during 2000–07. In fact, both the euro area and the Organisation for Economic Co-operation and Development community as a whole had aggregate fiscal deficits every one of those years. In the absence of political, economic, or market constraints, governments distributed both their growth dividends and borrowed funds to maintain or expand their budget footprint. The seeds of future fiscal trouble were sown during those good precrisis years.

As discussed in the previous sections, PFM reforms rely on three instruments—information, processes, and rules. Before the crisis, information clearly was not enough. Most advanced economies knew more about their fiscal condition, program results, and agency performance than they did one or two decades earlier. But whether enriched information made significant differences to policies and outcomes is questionable. The coexistence of well-informed budget makers and subpar budget outcomes should have spurred reformers to reexamine their assumptions and expectations. New information has to compete with old for attention in the congested fiscal calendar. Information that enlarges conflict, which is characteristic of much new PFM information, is often ignored or deflected. An information-based strategy is undermined by principal-agent symmetries.

Changing processes to alter incentives and behavior is the next line of attack, but the incentives proffered by PFM reforms are inherently weak compared with those embedded in conventional practices. Before the crisis, incentives to change were weak, money was easy, interest rates were low, and capital was plentiful. Governments spent the dividends of economic growth and more.

Politicians and managers have multiple, often contradictory incentives. Political leaders adopt disciplined fiscal positions when they expect to be rewarded by voters if they comply with fiscal limits and penalized if they do not.

Suppose, however, that voters who favor fiscally disciplined government also want bigger programs and more benefits. Because the effects of cutting programs are much more visible, immediate, and direct than cutting the deficit, politicians have an incentive to disregard or disable the fiscal controls and do what it takes to satisfy voters. The case for MTBF rests in part on the expectation that ministers and managers are motivated to reallocate funds from less to more effective uses. However, blame-avoiding politicians and managers have stronger reasons to keep to the status quo, even if the end result is subpar allocations. The problem is not that incentives do not matter—they do—but politicians and managers are swarmed by conflicting motives, some beyond PFM's reach.

Ignored information and inadequate processes and incentives bring us to PFM's ultimate weapon for changing behavior and getting results—formal rules that constrain politicians or managers. Within the PFM framework, rules are most pervasive with respect to fiscal policy but are rarely applied to performance budgets. MTBF has rule-like features that are rigorously enforced in only a few countries. As discussed earlier, MTBFs can have a built-in rule, a "hard constraint," which is relatively easy to enforce for the current budget. However, problems are greater for future budgets because some governments have tended to raise expenditure ceilings routinely when they roll the MTBF to the next year, treat out-year spending ceilings as floors, and make overly optimistic projections.

Rules have been most prevalent in fiscal policy, but have fared the worst. With few exceptions, country-specific fiscal rules did not distinguish between the growth and contraction phases of economic cycles. Discipline was not forthcoming when conditions were weak because the economy needed stimulus, nor when conditions were favorable because incremental resources and borrowed funds were plentiful and interest rates were low.

The clear lesson from the crisis is that rules have to be flexible to accommodate changing economic circumstances. To work, they must constrain revenue and spending policies when the economy is buoyant and constraint seems counterintuitive. Stronger monitoring of country budgets sufficiently early in the process is needed to deter fiscally imprudent policies and to enable affected governments to take corrective action. Each country has to find its own way in monitoring and enforcing limits on aggregates. A few have established independent agencies, and others will likely follow this growing trend in the years ahead. Some have embedded new rules and procedures in their constitutions; others rely on ordinary laws or on supranational regulations.

One of the most difficult issues is how to respond to breaches without being either too soft and accommodating or too rigid and unyielding. Automatic adjustments dictated by arithmetic rules may appear to be a responsible antidote to political pressure, but they may force government to act in ways that damage the country's economic prospects or social policies. The key to sound fiscal policy is rules that fortify prudent political decisions, not rules that crowd out political judgment. Balancing enforcement and judgment is always difficult. Recent experience teaches that greater weight should be given to enforcement, but not to the extent of purging judgment.

Yet, a small number of economically advanced countries did exercise discipline when the economy was buoyant by running surpluses or reducing public debt. Within this cohort, some were barely bruised by the Great Recession, but others were devastated by it. Sorting out the differences among countries is necessary to the design of next-generation rules.

1.6.3. After the Crisis: Can the Next One Be Averted?

The final hypothesis is that the crisis resulted in large part from developments outside the pale of public financial management. It follows, therefore, that averting future crises will require measures that extend beyond PFM.

Improvements in information will not suffice. Gaps in data or in analysis of financial matters should be filled, but it is naive to assume that governments will make the right decisions simply because they have better data. Data are enablers, but must be accompanied by the will to use them. Processes are important, but they have to combat powerful incentives that arise out of political habits and circumstances and cannot be easily manipulated by PFM's procedural adjustments. Political commitment undergirds all effective applications of fiscal rules, medium-term budget frameworks, and performance-shaped allocations. This commitment explains why some countries have only been nicked by the Great Recession whereas others have been devastated by it. Rules can fortify politicians and managers who want to do the right thing. But they cannot invent commitment where there is none.

Most countries lie between these poles; leaders have the commitment to be good stewards of the country's finances, but political or budget pressures seem to get in the way. Rules are potentially efficacious in these countries, but only if they are well drawn, internalized (accepted as fair and workable), and enforced. Correction of today's design flaws in the next generation of fiscal rules should include a shift from nominal to cyclically adjusted measures, extension of time frames beyond a single year, expenditure limits, and strengthened monitoring and enforcement. MTBF reforms might include hardened fiscal constraints to safeguard against treating this year's limit as next year's floor, greater caution in out-year economic forecasts, ring-fenced contingency reserves, and new means to defy incrementalism in budget allocations. Performance budgets require considerable preparation before resources and results can be coupled together by a rule.

Owing to damage done by recession and crisis, better fiscal rules warrant first place on the PFM agenda. But the final hypothesis leads to the conclusion that, though highly desirable, sound fiscal rules are insufficient. Several countries that were well within allowed limits before the crisis were devastated by the financial turmoil. A country's reported fiscal position is not an adequate account of the fiscal risk it harbors. Under current budget and accounting rules, the reported position also can be viewed as the tip of the fiscal iceberg, the portion that is visible, concealing the portion below the budget line. The fiscal tip is sometimes not its most critical part. The fiscal crisis had devastating effects because of risks below the budget line. Some risks were held by government in the form of direct or contingent liabilities that came due when financial institutions collapsed, unemployment rolls soared, and homeowners defaulted on government-financed or -guaranteed mortgages. A greater number of risks were systemic and were functions of economic trends and conditions, asset bubbles, household and enterprise debt, and the volume and structure of derivatives.

Through changes in budgeting and accounting rules, some innovative governments have made their direct and contingent liabilities more transparent, and some have integrated them into budget statements and fiscal limits. Few countries, however, have made much progress in linking their fiscal fortunes to the types and magnitude of nongovernmental risks. Yet, these are the risks that have the potential to turn a mild recession into a crisis. The straightforward answer to the question heading this subsection is that the next crisis cannot be averted by fiscal action alone. New methods must be devised for identifying and containing private risk before it spills into the public arena.

1.7. CONCLUSION

Modern public financial management is a logical construct that links the three sets of ideas discussed in this chapter: core objectives, effective levers, and innovations. This architecture consolidates major PFM innovations and issues and reveals several salient clues about contemporary PFM reform.

First, innovation has occurred in pursuit of each PFM objective. PFM reform has advanced on all fronts, though not always with equal success. However, as has been discussed, the comprehensive sweep of reform does hazard overloading and confusing officials who manage PFM systems. Second, various reforms serve multiple PFM objectives. Third, the full array of levers has been deployed to advance each objective. Information alone does not ensure achievement of any of the objectives. Although all the levers have spurred adjustments in PFM processes—most the imposition of new rules—reliance on all three levers may congest the PFM reform agenda, especially in countries where additional requirements are not offset by elimination of old rules and procedures.

The aim of PFM reform is to change substantive outcomes by altering the behavior of those who allocate public resources and manage government programs and entities. PFM values sustainable public finances more than it values fiscal rules. The rules are merely means of changing the incentives, and actions, of politicians. The true test of MTBF is not the number of years covered by budget decisions, but the regard that policymakers have for the future. Performance budgeting emphasizes measurement, but the measures that really count are the substantive impacts of public services. It is fitting, therefore, to conclude this overview chapter by reflecting on whether the expectations of reformers are warranted.

Do new information and procedures suffice to change behavior in the ways intended by PFM reforms? Is it the case, for example, that having an MTBF will embolden short-sighted politicians to be heedful of the future? Will political and managerial leaders be more disciplined in managing fiscal aggregates and more mindful of the long-term sustainability of the government's fiscal position? Will they allocate incremental resources and reallocate existing resources on the basis of evidence of program effectiveness, and will they organize public services to optimize value for money? In a closed system, the answer might be "certainly," but PFM is an open system, exposed to cross-pressures from many sources, especially political and economic winds that blow policymakers off-course from PFM goals. There is no automatic transmission belt (or production function) that converts information and process into new incentives, new incentives into modified behavior, and modified behavior into different substantive outcomes.

Presented with projections that the current fiscal course is unsustainable, politicians and managers may opt to continue on it rather than take austere measures that would stir public outcry and retribution at the polls. Financial markets may deliver a much more powerful message than PFM-generated data, giving leaders incentive to be profligate when credit is easy and austere when it is not. If evaluative findings and performance indicators were strong enough, many governments would have a quite different roster of programs from those they now finance with public funds. If efficient service provision were the only objective, government leaders would boldly cut slack budgets, stand up to public workers when they get in the way of good performance, and repeatedly reengineer public services to get better value for money.

A small number of governments behave in the intended way and generally produce superior PFM outcomes. They have a strong civic tradition, an administrative culture that rewards performance and results rather than compliance and control, low levels of corruption, and a high-performing public service. Though almost all are parliamentary regimes, they have taken different routes to their current conditions, and differ in salient political characteristics. They have modern PFM systems and have adopted many of the innovations discussed in this book. Significantly, however, some modernized their PFM systems when they already were well managed, not before; others did so in response to fiscal shock. A reasonable conclusion is that a favorable political-administrative culture and the will to innovate may be necessary preconditions for effective PFM innovation.

Where does this leave the vast majority of countries that lack these favorable conditions but can benefit from PFM improvement? Two paths appear open: one is for leaders with the determination, commitment, and skill to modernize the country and to view PFM innovations as part of a far-reaching agenda to transform the public sector; the other is to redistribute power within government to support sturdy PFM modernization. Both paths point to the paramount importance of politics in PFM transformation. Political conditions are not the sole relevant factor, but they loom above others.

A government armed with the will to improve governance can make substantial headway without adopting the whole basket of contemporary reforms. It does not need formal fiscal constraints to live within its means or performance budgets to spend money wisely. Having these processes may make the task easier and enable government to improve faster and further. But PFM innovations are not substitutes for good governance. They will not banish corruption, motivate a demoralized or indifferent civil service, ensure that funds are spent only on authorized purposes, cancel white elephant projects, and cure government of other pathologies. In the current wave of PFM reform, quite a few middle- and low-income countries appear to have the will to improve public governance and finance. Many have introduced major PFM reforms. Their success will depend as much on political and managerial leadership as on formal systems.

REFERENCES

Alson, Lee, Marcos Melo, Bernardo Mueller, and Carlos Pereira, 2007, "Presidential Power, Fiscal Responsibility Laws, and the Allocation of Spending: The Case of Brazil," in *Who Decides the Budget?* ed. by Mark Hallerberg, Carlos Scartascini, and Ernesto Stein (Washington: Inter-American Development Bank), pp. 57–90.

Anderson, Barry, and Joseph Minarik, 2006, "Design Choices for Fiscal Policy Rules," *OECD Journal on Budgeting*, Vol. 5, No. 5, pp. 159–208.

Arizti, Pedro, Jim Brumby, Nick Manning, Roby Senderowitsch, and Theo Thomas, eds., 2010, *Results, Performance Budgeting and Trust in Government* (Washington: World Bank).

Blondal, Jon, 2004, "Issues in Accrual Budgeting," *OECD Journal on Budgeting,* Vol. 4, No. 1, pp. 103–19.

———, and Teresa Curristine, 2004, "Budgeting in Chile," *OECD Journal on Budgeting*, Vol. 4, No. 2, pp. 7–45.

Brixi, Hana Polackova, and Allen Schick, eds., 2002, *Government at Risk: Contingent Liabilities and Fiscal Risk* (New York: World Bank and Oxford University Press).

Caiden, Naomi, and Aaron Wildavsky, 1974, *Planning and Budgeting in Poor Countries* (New York: John Wiley & Sons).

Campos, Ed, and Sanjay Pradhan, 1996, "Budgetary Institutions and Expenditure Outcomes: Binding Governments to Fiscal Performance," World Bank Policy Research Working Paper No. 1646 (Washington: World Bank).

Cebotari, Aliona, Jeffrey Davis, Lusine Lusinyan, Amine Mati, and Paolo Mauro, 2009, *Fiscal Risks: Sources, Disclosure, and Management* (Washington: International Monetary Fund).

Commonwealth of Australia, 2010, *Australia to 2050: Future Challenges,* Treasurer of the Commonwealth (Canberra).

Dalton, Russell J., 2004, *Democratic Challenges, Democratic Choices* (Oxford and New York: Oxford University Press).

Heller, Peter, 2005, "Understanding Fiscal Space," IMF Policy Discussion Paper 05/04 (Washington: International Monetary Fund).

International Monetary Fund (IMF), 2009, *Fiscal Rules—Anchoring Expectations for Sustainable Public Finances,* Fiscal Affairs Department (Washington).

International Organization of Supreme Audit Institutions, 2004, *Implementation Guidelines for Performance Auditing* (Vienna).

Irwin, Timothy, 2007, *Government Guarantees: Allocating and Valuing Risk in Privately Financed Infrastructure Projects* (Washington: World Bank).

———, 2012, *Accounting Devices and Fiscal Illusions*, IMF Staff Discussion Note 12/02 (Washington: International Monetary Fund).

Joyce, Philip, 2011, *CBO: Honest Numbers, Power, and Policymaking* (Washington: Georgetown University Press).

Kelly, Jeanne, and Joan Wanna, 2004, "Crashing through with Accrual-Output Budgeting in Australia—Technical Adjustment or a New Way of Doing Business?" *American Review of Public Administration*, Vol. 34, No. 1, pp. 94–111.

Musgrave, Richard, 1959, *The Theory of Public Finance* (New York: McGraw-Hill).

Organisation for Economic Co-operation and Development (OECD), 2007, *Performance Budgeting in OECD Countries* (Paris).

Pharr, Susan J., and Robert D. Putnam, eds., 2000, *Disaffected Democracies: What's Troubling the Trilateral Countries?* (Princeton: Princeton University Press).

Pollitt, Christopher, 2000, *Public Management Reform: A Contemporary Analysis* (Oxford: Oxford University Press).

Schick, Allen, 1998, *A Contemporary Approach to Public Expenditure Management* (Washington: World Bank).

———, 2009a, "Budgeting for Fiscal Space," in *Evolutions in Budgetary Practice*, ed. by A. Schick and the OECD Senior Budget Officials (Paris: OECD).

———, 2009b, "Performance Budgeting and Accrual Budgeting: Decision Rules or Analytic Tools," in *Evolutions in Budgetary Practice*, ed. by A. Schick and the OECD Senior Budget Officials (Paris: OECD).

———, 2009c, "Sustainable Budget Policy: Concepts and Approaches," in *Evolutions in Budgetary Practice*, ed. by A. Schick and the OECD Senior Budget Officials (Paris: OECD).

———, 2010, "Postcrisis Fiscal Rules: Stabilizing Public Finance while Responding to Economic Aftershocks," *OECD Journal on Budgeting*, Vol. 10, No. 2, pp. 1–18.

Settergren, Ole, 2001, "The Automatic Balance Mechanism of the Swedish Pension System," The National Social Insurance Board (Stockholm).

Shah, Anwar, ed., 2005, *Public Service Delivery* (Washington: World Bank).

Talbot, Colin, 2010, *Theories of Performance: Organizational and Service Improvement in the Public Administration* (Oxford and New York: Oxford University Press).

Tanzi, Vito, and Ludger Schuknecht, 2000, *Public Spending in the 20th Century: A Global Perspective* (Cambridge: Cambridge University Press).

United States Congressional Budget Office (US CBO), 2011, *CBO's Long-Term Budget Outlook* (Washington).

United States General Accounting Office (US GAO), 2000, *Accrual Budgeting: Experiences of Other Nations and Implications for the United States* (Washington).

Valdes-Prieto, Salvador, 2000, "The Financial Stability of Notional Accounts Pensions," *Scandinavian Journal of Economics*, Vol. 102, No. 3, pp. 395–417.

Wehner, Joachim, 2006, "Legislative Institutions and Fiscal Policy," PSPE Working Paper 08-2006, Department of Government (London: London School of Economics and Political Science).

———, 2010, *Legislatures and the Budget Process: The Myth of Fiscal Control* (Basingstoke, UK: Palgrave Macmillan).

Wildavsky, Aaron, 1964, *Politics of the Budgetary Process* (Boston: Little, Brown & Company).

Wyplosz, C., 2012, "Fiscal Rules: Theoretical Issues and Historical Experiences," NBER Working Paper No. 17884 (Cambridge, Massachusetts: National Bureau of Economic Research).

PART II

Designing and Building: PFM Innovations and Reforms

CHAPTER 2

Developing Legal Frameworks to Promote Fiscal Responsibility: Design Matters

HOLGER VAN EDEN, POKAR KHEMANI, AND RICHARD P. EMERY JR.

One of the most pervasive problems in public finance is the upward drift of government expenditure, deficits, and debt over time (Rodrik, 1998; Mosley, 2005; Erauskin-Iurrita, 2008). The economic literature espouses various theories to explain the upward drift of expenditures as a percentage of GDP in the course of economic development.[1] The cause of debt and deficit levels becoming unsustainable is, however, more often attributed to political economy factors. Among the most commonly discussed theories is the deficit bias hypothesis, which contends that politicians increase public expenditures in excess of taxes for their own political gain, including by providing benefits to favored interest groups and increasing spending during election years.

Another factor, increasingly important in advanced economies, is that discretionary fiscal policy is often applied asymmetrically during the business cycle: government expenditures are raised in a recession but not sufficiently lowered in good economic times to balance the budget over the course of the business cycle. Although fiscal stimulus is strongly supported during recession, consolidation is pursued with great hesitancy. The fear of suppressing an emerging economic recovery, or the attempt to stimulate the economy out of structural problems, often leads to the postponement of fiscal consolidation efforts. Fiscal policy that is not applied symmetrically over the business cycle often leads to unsustainable growth in government expenditure and debt. A key lesson of the 2008–09 global economic and financial crisis may be that discretionary fiscal stimulus should be applied only if assurances are made that fiscal stimulus will be adequately compensated for down the road by fiscal retrenchment. In sum, cyclical fiscal policy measures should not impose permanent structural consequences on public finances.

[1]These include Wagner's Law, which argues that the demand for public goods and services in many countries seems to rise more than proportionately with income. Another theory is Baumol's disease, which contends that lower productivity growth of the public sector compared with the private sector leads to an increasing share of government in the overall economy to keep relative activity levels in both sectors equal.

Various public financial management (PFM) institutional innovations have appeared during the past 20 years in an effort to support more prudent and balanced fiscal policies. This chapter discusses the scope of legal frameworks, specifically fiscal responsibility legislation, to induce less biased and more sustainable and transparent fiscal policy. It looks at how the design of fiscal responsibility laws (FRLs) can improve fiscal outcomes, how the development of these laws over time affects their functioning, and what role the relative strengths and weaknesses of a country's PFM system should play in making choices about designing FRLs. It argues that, to some extent, FRLs can help solidify support for fiscal sustainability but cautions that they should not get too far ahead of societal acceptance of fiscal prudence. As the literature suggests, in many cases FRLs are more a consequence of changing societal views than a cause. FRLs can become more effective as they build positive reputational capital over time.

In general, and especially for developing countries, when designing FRLs it is better to start simple and develop complexity gradually, that is, to begin with more modest and flexible frameworks and slowly firm up the legislative prescription of fiscal policy. Under most circumstances, PFM capacity is an additional reason to develop FRLs gradually. Aligning PFM capacity with the complexity of the FRLs is important—the more complex the FRL the greater the PFM capacity required. An exception to this gradual approach might arise in times of fiscal crisis, when the opportunity for a more sustainable fiscal policy regime should be grasped.

The first section of this chapter defines FRLs and discusses three types of FRLs most commonly used by countries. The second section seeks to explain the sudden popularity of this innovation, including examining evidence of FRL effectiveness and the various rationales for introducing it. The third section explores the main design choices to consider when developing an FRL and then discusses how countries' choices have affected their relative success. This section also describes the progressive development of FRLs as countries enhanced their institutional frameworks. The fourth section reviews PFM capacities needed for implementing FRLs. The final section draws conclusions about how and under what conditions FRLs can play a positive role in strengthening fiscal outcomes.

2.1. FISCAL RESPONSIBILITY LAWS AS AN INSTITUTIONAL RESPONSE

2.1.1. What Are FRLs and What Makes Them Unique?

This chapter defines FRLs broadly as legal frameworks that embed in law an agreed-on set of policies, processes, or arrangements intended to improve fiscal outcomes, discipline, transparency, and accountability by requiring governments to commit to fiscal policy objectives and strategies that can be monitored. These legal frameworks can be part of budget system laws, but such laws frequently have a much wider scope encompassing the whole PFM process. In the past, however, budget laws have often neglected the fiscal policy process and have thus generated the need for many countries to develop separate FRLs.

As a policy tool, FRLs are unique for several reasons. First, they sacrifice discretion in making fiscal policy for the sake of rules. The issue of discretion versus rules makes the careful design of fiscal legal frameworks important. Rules can be blunt instruments and, if not designed properly, can limit the ability of governments to make crucial adjustments to fiscal policy when needed to adapt to changes in economic circumstances.

Second, FRLs evoke the issue of reputational investment and costs. The literature provides some evidence validating the hypothesis that FRLs' effectiveness in supporting fiscal discipline strengthens as the lifespan of their successful implementation lengthens, and conversely, the reputational costs of their disbandment increases in proportion to the length of their establishment.[2] Credible FRLs can help politicians be tougher on fiscal policy than they would otherwise be. A law, if it has a strong enough reputation, "forces the politician's hand." Thus, how to successfully build the reputational capital of such frameworks becomes critical.[3]

Third, to work effectively, a legal framework for fiscal responsibility requires adequate PFM systems aligned with the framework's level of sophistication. These three issues combined lead to a number of specific recommendations for the design and development of fiscal responsibility legislation. It should, however, be stressed that these recommended design and development characteristics are often not followed in practice, which may be one of the reasons for the positive but still limited impact of FRLs on fiscal outcomes.[4]

2.1.2. Three Types of FRLs

In the mid-1990s, only a few countries had FRLs; since 2000, these laws have become increasingly widespread, particularly in emerging market economies. These laws take various forms. This section focuses on three types of FRL commonly used. "Type I" FRLs focus on *fiscal responsibility principles* (transparency, accountability, and sustainability), but do not identify in detail how these principles are to be met. Frequently the law requires the government to state its fiscal policy objectives for the medium term, but not necessarily in numerical terms, and to report on whether these objectives have been achieved. These FRLs do not have much legal force because they do not require concrete fiscal policy actions.

[2] See, for example, Box 3 in IMF (2009). Countries that have maintained their FRLs for longer periods seem to have had greater success with fiscal consolidation. The direction of causality is, however, not completely clear.

[3] For a discussion of establishing credible policy commitments through institutional arrangements (including legislation), see North (1999). The issue of credibility of FRLs has parallels with that of establishing credibility for independent monetary policy.

[4] The impact of FRLs is broader and somewhat more positive than that of numerical fiscal rules for which the impact is mixed at best (Corbacho and Schwartz, 2007; Caceres, Corbacho, and Medina, 2010).

Type I FRLs were adopted in the 1990s in New Zealand and Australia. New Zealand began developing an informal fiscal framework in the 1980s and enacted a Fiscal Responsibility Act in 1994. The Australian Charter of Budget Honesty Act was passed in 1998. In advanced economies with a critical press and independent academia, such laws can still have a considerable impact, but in many less advanced economies such unspecific laws only present good intentions with little or no impetus for follow-through by the executive (Caceres, Corbacho, and Medina, 2010).

Type II FRLs focus much more concretely on *procedural rules*, both for fiscal transparency and for the fiscal process. These laws can, for example, prescribe requirements for reporting on fiscal outcomes both within and at the end of the budget year, or require that concrete fiscal policy targets be presented ahead of the budget submission.[5] This type of legislation can also prescribe development of a fiscal policy statement and, at a more advanced stage, a fully defined medium-term fiscal framework (MTFF) as a way to enforce appropriate decision making on fiscal aggregates. Type II FRLs can also prescribe how to achieve the fiscal targets, for example, by setting line ministry expenditure ceilings in line with those decisions at the start of the budget preparation process.[6] This process helps to ensure that the detailed preparation and negotiation of the budget is not "solved" by expanding the budget deficit. With regard to parliament, such types of FRL can legislate the discussion, review, and even approval of the fiscal strategy document ahead of the budget review process. Brazil, India, and Pakistan are emerging market economies with such process-focused FRLs.

Finally, a third type of FRL includes *rules for the stance of fiscal policy* or *places limitations on key fiscal policy aggregates*. Type III fiscal responsibility legislation is much more demanding with regard to the fiscal policy process than the previous two types of FRL. In 2012, some 76 countries worldwide had fiscal rules and of these approximately 70 had a legal basis either in national law or supranational treaty or agreement[7] and the remainder were based on coalition agreement or political commitment (see Chapter 3). In such laws, fiscal policy action is determined, at least in part, by numerical fiscal rules, or key fiscal aggregates are subject to quantitative limits, that is, fiscal policy has to be set within certain predetermined boundaries (which may or may not be effectively binding fiscal policy).

---

[5] Lienert (2010) reports that of 11 selected countries with FRLs, 8 required statement of multi-annual fiscal objectives and 5 had enhanced reporting requirements. These were not always the same countries.

[6] Sweden's Fiscal Budget Act of 1996, for example, requires parliament to set nominal expenditure limits for 27 central government expenditure areas.

[7] See Chapter 3. About two-thirds of the 76 countries with fiscal rules operate under national rules or a combination of national and supranational fiscal rules; one-third are governed only by supranational rules. In 2012, 34 countries had national fiscal rules and 47 had supranational fiscal rules (either in combination with national rules or separately).

As discussed in Chapter 3, more and more countries with fiscal rules have two or more such rules, indicating a willingness to give up a substantial amount of policy discretion.[8] Most common are debt and deficit rules, often in combination.[9]

Deficit rules usually have a more immediate impact on fiscal policy than do debt rules. Debt limits can be substantially higher than the actual debt level. In those cases, fiscal policy is still largely discretionary, and the debt ceiling mostly signals to markets the concrete translation of the government's sustainability objective. Deficit ceilings take away from the discretionary powers of government based on the assumption that temporarily high deficits may quickly turn to overshooting of the debt target. The level of discretion can be lowered even further by constraints on other fiscal aggregates such as government expenditure, current expenditure, or external (rather than total) debt financing.

The rules in type III laws have tended to become more complex over time, for example, imposing limits on the level of the structural deficit rather than the nominal deficit. The structural deficit is usually defined as a deficit from which the influence of the business cycle is removed on the basis of an econometric model of the economy's output gap.[10] Box 2.1 provides more background on the use of fiscal rules in anchoring fiscal policy. Type III legislation can either be focused only on the fiscal rules or be part of more comprehensive FRLs incorporating both type I and type II legislation, including fiscal policy principles and process and transparency procedures as described above.

The section on FRL design will address the issue of cumulative progression from type I to type II, and finally to type III legislation.[11] Type I and type II FRLs can, in principle, be integrated into the regular budget system law or public financial management act, or be part of a separate FRL. This chapter argues, however, that most countries will find significant benefit to keeping the FRL separate from the budget system law.[12]

Fiscal rules can also be integrated into other parts of the legal framework. For example, they can be part of fiscal decentralization legislation, specifying fiscal

[8] This willingness is often limited by escape clauses.

[9] See "Fiscal Rules Dataset 1985–2012" (IMF, 2012) and Chapter 3.

[10] Structural deficits can be defined in various ways. Other factors can be removed from the fiscal balance as well, such as the impact of fluctuations in asset prices, commodities, terms of trade, and so on. Because the output-gap method is fraught with uncertainties, especially in developing countries (in which the structural growth rate of the economy is uncertain), in some resource-rich economies structural balances are defined much more simply by structural resource revenues minus expenditures, with structural resource revenues defined by the "structural" (long-term or moving average) price of the main resource. Mongolia and, in the past, Chile are examples of countries with these simpler definitions of the structural balance. Chile presently uses a structural balance definition that combines an output-gap approach with a structural minerals-revenue approach.

[11] As noted by Lienert (2010), some advanced economies have chosen to adopt type III FRLs without elements of type I and II laws. The reasoning is often that the basic requirements for fiscal policy are supposedly adequately dealt with in those countries' regular budget system laws.

[12] New Zealand, however, which had a type I FRL beginning in 1994, integrated its FRL into its Public Finance Amendment Act of 2004.

BOX 2.1 The Rationale for Adopting Fiscal Rules in Fiscal Responsibility Laws

A significant weakness of fiscal principles and procedural rules is their lack of specificity about the actual fiscal policy stance a country should adopt. Numerical fiscal rules, however, provide a clear anchor for fiscal policy. Ideally, they determine, given the present economic and fiscal situation of the country, the levels at which fiscal aggregates should be set. Fiscal rules—in the ideal situation—provide automatic and objective answers that would otherwise require a great deal of economic analysis, judgment, and political compromise. They thus decrease policy transaction costs and provide better fiscal outcomes.

Since the late 1990s, many countries have adopted fiscal rules to guide their fiscal policy processes. Although these rules have been successful in certain circumstances, such as under relatively stable growth conditions, in controlling local government expenditure and, in some cases, during exit from fiscal crisis, they have been much less successful in dealing with large economic shocks or fundamental transformations of economies. In practice, designing fiscal rules that apply well to all economic circumstances has been difficult. Nominal deficit rules are procyclical, but structural deficit rules may not address long-term fiscal sustainability concerns (if the structural growth rate of an economy is decreasing). Debt rules may be too lax when overall public debt is low, but too restrictive when debt is high. Expenditure rules may be overly restrictive when extraordinary fiscal stimulus is called for, whereas fiscal consolidation processes are more likely to be guided by a consolidation timeline than a fixed numerical rule.

For the above reasons, the jury is still out on whether fiscal rules should be included in fiscal responsibility laws (FRLs) in all circumstances. Given the need to address multiple fiscal policy objectives (sustainability, stability, intergenerational equity) in a variety of economic circumstances, two discernible trends have emerged. The first, as discussed above, is to make fiscal rules more complex (e.g., in mineral-exporting economies structural fiscal balance rules are designed to incorporate both the domestic economic cycle and fluctuations of major mineral prices). This additional complexity enables them to be relevant under differing economic circumstances. Second, more countries are adopting two or more fiscal rules to define the anchor for fiscal policy, the idea being that different rules will address different policy objectives, and that at any one time only one rule will be the primary constraint under particular economic circumstances.

A more practical solution to these issues is perhaps the development of well-designed escape clauses in FRLs, allowing the fiscal rule framework to be inoperative during exceptional economic circumstances. A second solution, combining rules and discretion, would be for the FRL to define the fiscal rules that must be adhered to but leave the numerical values to be determined by government on a recurring basis.

limits for each of the layers of government. In their most "heavy" form, fiscal rules can be part of the constitution, providing a much stronger legal status than ordinary legislation, or they can even be part of international treaties.[13] The 1992 European Union (EU) Maastricht Treaty is the most prominent example of the

[13] Seven countries had constitutional FRL requirements in 2011: Comoros, France, Finland, Germany, Poland, Singapore, and Switzerland.

Forty-seven countries are subject to fiscal rules under currency unions and the EU. These are set forth, at least in part, by international treaties. The Eastern Caribbean Currency Union aims at reducing debt. The Central African Economic and Monetary Community limits deficits and debt. The West African Economic and Monetary Union requires both balanced budgets and a reduction in debt to 70 percent of GDP.

latter. It specifies for member governments a maximum deficit of 3 percent of GDP and limits debt to 60 percent of GDP. These ceilings were also included in the 1997 Stability and Growth Pact. The 2012 EU Fiscal Compact requires member countries to adopt, in either their constitutions or other durable legislation, a structural budget balance rule by 2014 (see Chapter 3 for details).

This chapter argues that choosing the most forceful legal instruments in formalizing FRLs is not always wise, especially if there is a risk that the fiscal requirements will not be met and the strong legal mechanism does not have enough support from the political establishment or society at large.

2.2. EVIDENCE AND RATIONALE FOR FRLs

2.2.1. Evidence of Impact of FRLs

Evidence that FRLs of the types discussed in the previous section have been successful in promoting better fiscal outcomes is mixed (Corbacho and Schwartz, 2007; EC, 2006; IMF, 2009; Lienert, 2010; OECD, 2002). Cross-country studies provide evidence of both success and failure, although results suggesting effectiveness seem to have been on the rise during the recent global crisis. A number of studies seem to indicate that countries with FRLs in place before the financial crisis were better placed going into it (IMF, 2009; Schick, 2010). Of course, many countries put their FRLs on hold during the crisis: in some cases this procedure was fully in line with their FRLs' escape clauses; in others, FRLs were breached and their reputation and future effectiveness suffered badly. The recent global crisis has made clear that many countries found it challenging to maintain fiscal rule requirements during a severe, once-in-a-generation economic downturn, or to return rapidly to fiscal sustainability after such a crisis.

FRLs, in the view of this chapter, should not be judged by how they manage such extreme circumstances. Arguably, they could play a role in returning fiscal circumstances to the precrisis situation, for example, by signaling postconsolidation fiscal targets. This chapter argues, however, that FRLs in general should deal with the "normal" structural and cyclical issues that countries face. The real disappointment of some FRLs was their failure to restrain fiscal parameters before the global financial crisis, and their inability to play a more decisive role in getting countries back on track toward fiscal sustainability after the crisis. This chapter argues that the reason for the varying degrees of success of fiscal responsibility legislation has had much to do with design choices. The choice of legislation has to fit the country's economic circumstances, the political will available to support fiscal discipline, and the level of PFM development.

2.2.2. Rationale for Adopting FRLs

Despite the relatively weak empirical basis, countries have "voted with their feet" to introduce FRLs. During the past 20 years, the number of countries with FRLs has increased significantly, especially since 2000 (see Chapter 3). The inherent logic and appeal of the FRL to policymakers have proved to be strong. The appeal rests on three propositions that have gradually received more acceptance in the literature and among policymakers. First, rules trump discretion in fiscal policymaking (see also Chapter 1). Second, the legal system can exert a powerful controlling influence on the actions of politicians, especially if higher-ranking legislation, such as "organic laws" and the constitution, is used. Third, the reputational capital of FRLs can build over time if they are appropriately designed and developed gradually.

Rules versus Discretion

The more fundamental discussion about whether a legal, rules-based framework for fiscal policy is really preferable to discretionary fiscal policy has slowly shifted. Twenty years ago, the prevailing view in policy circles was that if political will was present, no legislation was needed. Also, discretion, it was argued, if used appropriately, always provides the first-best response to economic circumstances while legal frameworks provide less flexibility. The FRL skeptics argued that political will cannot be legislated and that institutions by themselves cannot effect society's fiscal choices. Moreover, attempts by the executive, and especially the legislature, to bind themselves were misplaced, because any law could easily be superseded by a new law or a new budget (the budget is itself passed as a law). The prevailing argument was that an FRL could be revoked at any time. Moreover, FRLs may seem to function well in economic good times, but they invariably crumble during economic adversity—when they are most needed.

These arguments against FRLs have, in this chapter's view, proved to be overly pessimistic. This does not mean that political will cannot by itself suffice to steer fiscal policy. It clearly can. A number of emerging market and advanced economies have done so successfully for many years. These countries are, however, in the minority, and history has shown that the favorable political circumstances for discretionary policy can change and become less supportive. Westminster-system countries have until recently followed a tradition of not enshrining policy in law, but as pressures on government spending increased, countries such as Australia, New Zealand, and the United Kingdom have all promulgated FRLs of one type or another.

Recent developments in the rules-versus-discretion debate focus on the point that discretionary policy may be optimal if it is unaffected by political pressures and is implemented in a purely technocratic, "enlightened" way. However, even though enlightened discretion might lead to first-best solutions and rules-based policy only to second best, the biases and pressures on fiscal policy in reality often lead to third- or fourth-best outcomes for discretion. In those circumstances, a legal basis for fiscal policy might be preferable, even one that provides second-best solutions (Rodrik, 2008).

The Effectiveness of Legal Frameworks

The second rationale, the effectiveness-of-law argument, notes that FRLs in practice often have a higher status than normal legislation. In some countries—francophone countries are an example—FRLs are defined as organic laws, which have a higher formal status and cannot be overruled by new, "normal" legislation. In other countries, the most crucial elements of fiscal responsibility legislation are included in the constitution or in international treaties, also placing FRLs above other legislation and making reversal by the executive or legislature much more difficult.

More notably, FRLs can acquire their primacy over normal legislation through a process of reputation building somewhat akin to the development of independence by central banks. A central bank always remains, in principle, subject to reversal of its statutory legislation, but as its independent role in society earns approval, it becomes virtually impossible for politicians to attack the central bank's position. In a similar vein, there has been growing acceptance that fiscal legislation can attain reputational "capital" if designed and developed appropriately.

The Power of Reputation

A third objection to FRLs is that without adequate political will to reverse fiscal imbalances, FRLs are powerless, whereas with political will they are seen as irrelevant, more an expression of that political will than an effective factor in improving fiscal outcomes. This chapter proposes a more nuanced view. Although fiscal responsibility legislation needs a certain amount of political will to be enacted, it can strengthen political resolve by building up reputational capital. Also, by adjusting the amount of discretion allowed by the law, or by providing the opportunity for temporary suspension in exceptional circumstances, the law can be calibrated to the force of political will in society to sustain it. The government or the ministry of finance can gradually tighten the legislative framework as the law builds up reputational capital.

Such a dynamic view of the development of FRLs decreases the risk that effectiveness will be undermined by lack of political will. As noted, this view increases the importance of properly designing these laws so that they reflect the strength of political will in the society. In the authors' experience in advising countries, ministries of finance often err by proposing fiscal responsibility laws that are too strict and demanding, and that fail to reflect the actual political will in their countries. Such legislation often breaks down in the first few years (or weeks) of application. Modest FRL-type legislation often provides a better start to the process. Middle ground has to be sought though. A law that is continuously suspended during business cycle downturns will also fail to garner societal support and will fail to build up political capital. Some of the FRLs in South America and South Asia have suffered this fate. A perhaps unsurprising conclusion is that FRLs thus need to be neither too strict, nor too loose.

A Separate Law or Not?

The choice between enacting a new FRL or amending existing budget legislation to accommodate fiscal responsibility requirements is relevant in building up support and reputational capital for better fiscal outcomes. Many of the fiscal transparency and process requirements of an FRL could fit, from a legal and technical point of view, in existing organic budget laws or financial management acts.

The drawback to including such requirements in existing legislation is that a few amendments to such laws will have relatively little impact at the political or societal level. In many countries, proactive fiscal policy does not really exist, let alone a medium-term orientation to fiscal policy. Fiscal policy in such countries is an outcome, rather than a determinant, of the budget process. The concept of government proposing and deciding on fiscal policy for the medium term, ahead of the budget process, and determining the overall budget envelope thus represents a substantial change in the political economic process.

In many cases, the procedural rules introduced in FRLs explicitly limit the amendment rights of parliament, for example, by requiring adherence to fiscal limits decided on early in the budget process or just ahead of the budget review. This stricture usually implies that compensatory tax or expenditure measures have to be suggested when budgetary amendments are introduced. Introduction of fiscal rules will have an even larger impact on the budget process, further limiting the discretion of the executive and legislature. Such substantive changes to the fiscal-budgetary process need to be promoted and decided on in full recognition of what they mean. A new, separate law can promote such a new vision of the fiscal and budgetary process and thus be instrumental to building up reputational capital for disciplined fiscal policy.

2.3. DESIGN CHOICES

This section discusses a number of design issues important to the effectiveness of FRLs. Appendix 2.1 provides further details of the main features of fiscal responsibility legislation in selected countries.

Definitions

All laws need to be clear about the concepts they use. The macroeconomic and fiscal variables in FRLs should be defined according to, or aligned with, international standards on national accounts, and with government statistical reporting and accounting standards. Without use of such standards, FRLs can easily accommodate creative accounting, and fiscal limits can seemingly be met through definitional tricks.

Coverage

In principle, FRLs should encompass as much of general government activity as possible. The fiscal policy stance is determined by the impact of all government expenditures and revenues on macroeconomic activity. Ideally, the whole of general government should be covered, or even the wider public sector. The problem—from a fiscal management point of view—is that the central government often lacks the authority to regulate expenditure and revenue totals of the whole of general government, let alone the public sector. Local government and extrabudgetary funds frequently have their own budgetary autonomy.

A narrowly focused FRL can lead to shifting activities to those parts of the government, or even of the public sector, that are not captured by its rules or procedures. Including lower levels of government in the FRL can help ensure that fiscal policy is coordinated between levels of government. Extrabudgetary funds should be covered by the FRL if they are allowed to run a deficit or surplus. Tax expenditures and government guarantees are also common escape valves for FRLs—just as they are for medium-term fiscal and budgetary frameworks. Again, in principle, an FRL should cover these expenditures and quasi-expenditures.

Nevertheless, exceptions to the full-coverage rule can be acceptable. First, an exception can be acceptable when the fiscal impact of the part of government or public sector not included in the FRL is fiscally neutral—for instance, if that subsector is not allowed to borrow, or its borrowing is limited by regulation and not subject to political manipulation. Second, for many countries, including local government in the FRL as a means of achieving progress on fiscal sustainability might become too challenging politically. In practice, the full-coverage rule is often broken. FRLs cover local government only in roughly 54 percent of cases. Other examples are exempting social security spending or interest payments from the deficit rule and excluding government guarantees from public debt rules.

In such cases, the optimal should not be the enemy of the good. Central government can mitigate the impact of less than full coverage of the FRL by estimating the fiscal impact of the parts of government not under its control. It can then set its fiscal stance taking into account the position of parts of government, or even the public sector, not covered by the FRL. Another approach separately regulates, or eliminates, the borrowing powers of parts of government not covered by the FRL.

The full-coverage principle should be seen as a developmental objective. Most developing countries initially find it difficult to include local government in the FRL given that doing so requires a substantial amount of political and fiscal coordination between levels of government, especially if the country has a federal structure (see Chapter 12). Tracking tax expenditures can also be overly demanding for the PFM system and therefore is also often initially ignored in the coverage principle.

Statement of Fiscal Objectives and Targets

As countries develop more ambitious FRLs, fiscal objectives tend to become more detailed and specific. In a type I law, the fiscal objective could be framed as "maintaining debt levels consistent with fiscal sustainability," without being specific about what that means, but a type III law would actually state the debt limit as a percentage of GDP. Similarly on deficits, the fiscal objective for deficits could progress from "achieving a balanced budget over the economic cycle" to a specific balance, or structural balance target, as a percentage of GDP.

Objectives can differ significantly in whether they are planned objectives or objectives for actual realization. This is sometimes referred to as the *ex ante or ex post targeting* issue. Requiring a budget deficit to be balanced at the time of budget submission is, of course, quite different from, and much easier than, realizing a balanced budget at the end of the year. The German and Swiss debt-brake rules can be considered the most advanced form of targeting in that they introduce a form of fiscal accounting ensuring that any missed ex post fiscal targets are compensated for in later years (see Chapter 3 and Mayer and Staehler, 2009).

The decision to be specific about fiscal objectives needs to be aligned with the political will in society and the development of the PFM system. If fiscal objectives are more ambitious than society is willing to pursue, the FRL is likely to be breached earlier rather than later. It is thus important to accurately assess popular willingness to abide by fiscal objectives and to align the design of the FRL with the level of political will. The statement of fiscal objectives also has to be manageable by the country's PFM system. If in-year monitoring of fiscal aggregates is difficult, then obviously an ex post target will be hard to manage. Debt and deficit targets as percentages of GDP also assume that estimation of budget year GDP is accurate. In fact, the margin of error is often considerable. In many developing countries, GDP figures are also only available with a considerable time lag.[14]

Escape Clauses

Escape clauses in FRLs are perhaps the most important and difficult elements to design. As FRLs become more specific, clearly articulated escape clauses may be needed. The role of such clauses is to validate breaching of the FRL in times of severe economic crisis or when a natural catastrophe has occurred. Although an FRL should ensure fiscal discipline, expecting a highly specific legal framework to be appropriate even during a once-in-a-generation economic crisis is unrealistic. However, during the normal business cycle or when unexceptional economic shocks hit the country, the FRL should remain operational. For example, the fiscal framework of a resource exporter should be able to accommodate, and indeed stabilize, the impact of price fluctuations of the main export commodity.

The relative tightness and clarity of the escape clause is thus an essential design consideration. Who decides when the escape clause is to be activated is also important. Is executive decision sufficient, or is approval by parliament necessary? Other options include rules-based activation or decision by an independent fiscal council (see Chapter 6). The great benefit of escape clauses is that they can safeguard the institutional capital of the FRL. Invoking a realistic escape clause will cause much less damage to the long-term effectiveness of an FRL than will an unauthorized breach of its rules or procedures.

[14]This could result in only the numerator of a debt- or deficit-to-GDP ratio being targeted ex post.

Sanctions

To help prevent the executive or the legislature (or both) from not complying with the FRL, some FRLs incorporate sanctions as a design element. Ministries of finance are often particularly eager to include sanctions in FRLs on the grounds that sanctions increase the political cost of breaking the law and thus would make such occurrences less likely. Sanctions can be budgetary, procedural, or reputational, and they can be applied to government as a whole, to individual state entities, or to state officials.[15]

In the euro area, through early 2012, countries that did not adhere to the deficit ceiling of 3 percent of GDP could, if considerable efforts to rectify the situation were not effective (through the so-called excessive deficit procedure), be fined a maximum sanction of half a percent of GDP. This sizable fine was, however, not automatic but subject to political decision. Thus, in practice, despite repeated violations of the 3 percent rule (by almost all of the euro area membership), financial sanctions were never invoked under the Maastricht Treaty. The EU's new Fiscal Compact and Six Pack framework have changed these rules. The size of the sanctions has decreased, to 0.1 percent of GDP, and their application has become somewhat less political and more rules based. Chapter 3 provides further details of the new EU Fiscal Compact and the Six Pack.

Sanctions pertaining to the budget have also been attempted at the national level. Some countries have experimented with automatic expenditure cutbacks, for example, across-the-board spending cuts, withholding of transfers, and wage freezes for civil servants. These measures kick in if a certain rule in the FRL is violated. Borrowing limitations have also been imposed.

The success of actual monetary sanctions has been limited. In many cases those bearing the burden would not be the ones breaching the fiscal rules (often the previous government), making the instrument politically unattractive. The penalty in the Maastricht Treaty was so high that it became less credible and probably did not increase compliance as much as a less-onerous sanction might have. The design challenge is to develop a sanction that is painful and embarrassing for the executive but still credible.

Many countries have chosen the "name and shame," or reputational, approach to sanctions in FRLs. If a fiscal rule is breached or, even better, expected to be breached, the government is required to notify the legislature and report to it on the extent of the breach, the causes of the breach, and the measures the government is to take to reestablish compliance with the fiscal framework. The requirement can be toughened by stating the period within which compliance needs to be reestablished. The effectiveness of such "reporting and redress" sanctions depends on the political system, the power of an

[15]The most creative example of a procedural–state official sanction is perhaps Suriname, where the Minister of Finance is to be put in prison when the debt ceiling of 60 percent of GDP is exceeded. The Finance Minister who developed this law assumed that his fellow politicians would be too embarrassed to put him in jail and thus that the sanction would be highly effective.

independent press and academia, and possibly the existence of an independent evaluator of the government's actions, such as the supreme audit institution or a fiscal council. The German and Swiss debt-brake laws specify the redress period and even require government to compensate in future years for overspending in the year in question.

There is a fundamental discussion in the literature of whether sanctions, which are often not credible and are consequently ignored, are actually helpful in FRLs. Some argue that by opening up the possibility of sanctions (for events not covered by an escape clause) the possible breach of the FRL is actually facilitated. It is noteworthy in this context that fiscal rules that are enshrined in the constitution usually do not include sanctions.

The view of this chapter is that sanctions should be aligned with the political will in the country to enforce fiscal procedural or policy rules. Sanctions should be as painful as possible, but they should also remain credible. Again, ministries of finance are often overly optimistic about the fiscal pain that politicians will be willing to impose to avoid breaking the letter of the law. To protect the credibility of the legal framework the sanctions need to be discussed extensively with the political level. There is considerable room for creativity if monetary sanctions are combined with the name and shame approach. Automatic cutbacks and tax increases should be considered if the name and shame approach by itself proves ineffective.

The EU's new fiscal arrangement system is complex but still internally consistent. Several elements of the design, such as the new sanctions regime and placing enforcement in domestic law, should strengthen its enforceability. However, planning, monitoring, and enforcement of the framework will require substantial coordination and communication between the European Commission and the member countries. The complexity of the framework provides scope for differing interpretation and application. Maintaining the integrity of the new system from the start and building societal support will be crucial.

Transitional Requirements

Transitional requirements are often needed in FRLs, especially for countries that are outside a fiscal rules framework that they wish to enter. During a severe fiscal crisis when the political willingness to agree to an FRL is highest, it is at the same time often unrealistic to enter a long-term fiscal framework because fiscal aggregates may be considerably outside the intended fiscal limits. Transitional requirements can help specify the path to the long-term fiscal framework. The main design issue is the specificity of the transition path. Without any transitional requirements, countries often wait too long to begin consolidation efforts and fail to reach their fiscal targets in the first year. This will cause maximum damage to the reputation of the nascent FRL. Conversely, a strictly defined transition path may not provide enough policy discretion to exit the economic downturn at an optimal pace. Clearly, the relative uncertainty of the transition path will be influenced by the policy flexibility of the country, that is, what is the "maximum" speed of fiscal consolidation, and are short-term fiscal considerations more, or less, important than long-term ones.

Obviously, a country could delay adopting an FRL until it has brought its fiscal parameters back into the fiscal framework prescribed by the proposed FRL and returned to "normal" economic circumstances. This delay, however, could leave unexploited the opportunity to signal to markets that the government is attempting to return to fiscal sustainability. Such a signal, if credible, could help lower interest rates marginally and ease the transition process. Moreover, as discussed above, the political will to introduce an FRL may also have waned by the time the economy returns to normal.

2.3.1. Design of the Fiscal Policy Process

Although the design elements discussed above are important parts of FRLs, the more fundamental design elements in FRLs are those that underpin the fiscal policy process. These design elements are linked to the country's ambition to improve fiscal outcomes. Higher ambitions signal a need for more complexity in the FRL design, but also for more political will and a stronger PFM system to support implementation of the law.

Although improving fiscal outcomes is an overarching objective of an FRL, a number of intermediate objectives can also be identified (see Table 2.1). This chapter maintains that these intermediate objectives explain the gradual progression of FRLs from focusing on fiscal transparency, to fiscal process, and finally to fiscal rules.

The intermediate objectives described in Table 2.1 are important determinants of the final characteristics of an FRL. There is a clear progression in the described objectives with regard to the ambition level for improving fiscal outcomes. Requirements just to publish fiscal data accurately and timely both at the end of the year and in-year are not effective by themselves in controlling expenditure nor do they require excessive technical capacity. However, for developing countries timely publication of fiscal data can already pose substantial issues and require further development of fiscal reporting systems. Publishing medium-term fiscal forecasts, defining fiscal objectives, and reviewing past achievements relative to targets would have a stronger impact on fiscal discipline. Setting a fiscal framework including fiscal forecasts, objectives, and policy measures for the medium term is often a quite onerous requirement. Ensuring adherence to a set of fiscal rules within such a framework is usually complex, even for advanced economies.

As the progression is made through the described intermediate objectives, not only do the PFM requirements increase, but the government and legislature also constrain themselves more in the setting of fiscal policy. Thus, the political will needed to progress through these intermediate objectives also should increase. As stated before, in situations of limited PFM capacity or political will, a new FRL being drafted by a ministry of finance must not exceed by too much the realities of both PFM capacity and political will.

TABLE 2.1

Design Elements for Achieving Intermediate Fiscal Objectives

Intermediate fiscal objective	Examples of requirements in fiscal responsibility law
1. Improve fiscal transparency	• Publish accurate and timely midyear and end-of-year fiscal outcomes • Develop and publish fiscal forecasts for the medium term
2. Improve political accountability for fiscal and budgetary outcomes	• Publish fiscal policy objectives and strategy • Require government to report to legislature on achievements • Require the state auditor to independently report on fiscal policy achievements
3. Define a medium-term fiscal process	• Develop a fiscal strategy document presenting macro and fiscal forecasts, defining fiscal objectives for the medium term, and stating planned policy measures
4. Ensure that fiscal policy guides budgetary policy	• Require that fiscal policy decision making precede budgetary decision making • Present a formal medium-term fiscal framework at the start of budget preparation, including decision making on expenditure ceilings for the budget • Constrain the amendment rights of parliament within agreed-on fiscal policy parameters
5. Ensure fiscal discipline and sustainability	• Enact limits to key fiscal aggregates (debt- and deficit-to-GDP limits) • Require in-year rules on the use of revenue and expenditure windfalls, and on redress of overspending and lower-than-expected revenues
6. Ensure macrofiscal stability	• Ensure appropriate and symmetric fiscal policy responses through the use of fiscal rules aimed at stabilizing macroeconomic shocks (more complex rules, expenditure growth limits, cyclical deficit targets, rules-based stabilization funds)
7. Address intergenerational equity concerns	• Implement a rules-based framework that defines intergenerational equity and sets up a transfer rule from budget to sovereign wealth fund

Source: Authors' compilation.

An important part of enhancing fiscal policy processes is providing the ministry of finance the necessary authorization and powers. Presenting fiscal forecasts and calculating necessary policy measures to stay within the confines of MTFF or fiscal rules are tasks that must be given to the ministry of finance. In a number of developing countries, cabinet or parliamentary committees unilaterally change revenue forecasts, oil price assumptions, or other key elements of the fiscal or budgetary framework, undermining the credibility of fiscal policy setting. In calculating the impact of new policy measures on the ongoing costs of existing policies (the baseline), it is also extremely important that the ministry of finance have the final say on such estimates. If not, the estimates can be prone to political manipulation. Of course, this role of the ministry of finance does not preclude criticism by an independent evaluator such as the supreme audit institution or a fiscal council if these estimates are found to be systematically biased (see Chapter 6). Such criticism would strengthen the objectivity of the overall fiscal policymaking process.

2.3.2. FRL Development: A Gradual Process

Countries with the ambition to use legislation to improve fiscal outcomes need to view implementation of this legislation as a developmental process. Starting in a simple manner is vital for both developed and developing countries. In a first phase, only transparency and oversight requirements would be included in an FRL.

In a second phase, fiscal and budget process requirements would be added. The number of elements to be added in this second phase can be extensive. A basic requirement is the development of a medium-term fiscal outlook document that presents projections of fiscal aggregates under unchanged policy. A next step in this phase is expansion of the fiscal outlook document to a fiscal statement that includes fiscal objectives, strategy, and a rough indication of policy measures over the medium term. This fiscal statement presents the resource envelope available for the upcoming budget preparation process. It is a considerable step, however, to subsequently enforce in the FRL that the cabinet must set binding resource envelopes and sectoral expenditure ceilings according to a formal MTFF. This step could require that the MTFF be formally approved by the cabinet and approved, or perhaps even enshrined in law, by the legislature. Sending the MTFF to parliament for information is more common. In any case, FRLs that have progressed to this stage often formally include the requirement that the annual budget must fit into the fiscal limits set in the MTFF. Thus, parliament's amendment rights must be constrained, for example, by a requirement that any budget amendment should propose additional funding sources or compensatory spending cuts.

The third phase in the development of FRLs can be characterized by the setting of numerical rules for fiscal objectives. Numerical fiscal rules can have considerable benefits. If set appropriately, fiscal rules provide an anchor for fiscal policy that can help ensure fiscal sustainability. Depending on the type of rules and the extent to which they constrain decision making, they "objectify" fiscal policy, taking it out of the political debate. If limits to fiscal aggregates to ensure fiscal sustainability are distant from the actual parameters (for example, the debt limit is 60 percent of GDP, but the actual debt is 40 percent) some discretion to discuss fiscal policy remains. Countries take a further step when fiscal rules become the mechanism for stabilizing the effects of economic shocks or for addressing intergenerational equity concerns. In such countries, fiscal policy becomes largely rules based.

The use of fiscal rules requires substantial capacity for fiscal forecasting and monitoring. It also requires the capacity and political will to take required policy measures (and to adequately cost these measures over the medium term—a requirement that is often neglected). In general, using fiscal rules will require the ministry of finance to be able to identify baseline expenditure. In FRLs with more complex fiscal rules, flexibility in fiscal policy is seriously constrained. Still, for countries with sophisticated macroeconomic analysis and fiscal forecasting capacity, the benefits of, for example, structural deficit rules could enhance the countercyclicality of fiscal policy considerably.

This chapter does not discuss the appropriate rules for specific countries or specific economic circumstances. However, fiscal rules should reflect those circumstances. Numerical, strictly binding fiscal rules should be used only by countries with reasonable levels of economic stability that have the political will to follow through on the implied commitment and have PFM systems that ensure that fiscal parameters stay within accepted limits. Political will can be strengthened if less-restrictive FRLs function successfully for a number of years. More complex and constraining FRLs could be built upon initially less restrictive FRLs. Countries should see FRLs not as an unchanging element of the legal framework, but as an element that adapts to the fiscal policy challenges facing the country, society's commitment to fiscal discipline, the reputational capital built up by the existing legal framework, and the technical capacity to use complex fiscal policy rules.

Advanced economies enter the process of improving fiscal outcomes at a different point than developing countries. Their organic budget laws are often already quite strong; accordingly, some advanced economies have chosen to include accountability and process rules in their existing legal frameworks (Lienert, 2010). Consequently, fiscal rules have been left outside the legal framework, or integrated into more basic FRL legislation focusing only on fiscal rules. In advanced economies, the use of the constitution or international treaties is also more widespread. Again, such mechanisms are often rather narrowly focused.

2.4. PFM REQUIREMENTS FOR AN EFFECTIVE FRL

As discussed above, the ambitions of the FRL in containing and controlling fiscal aggregates should be aligned with the relative strengths of the PFM system. The experiences of a number of countries, including Australia, Brazil, and New Zealand, highlight the important role played by a well-developed PFM framework in assisting these countries to introduce the higher standards of transparency and accountability required by an FRL. In contrast, weak PFM systems and procedures limit government's ability to monitor and control fiscal outcomes and undermine the successful implementation of an FRL. Although it can be argued that a basic FRL can induce meaningful reforms just by promoting fiscal prudence despite a weak PFM system, a sufficiently developed PFM system is essential for the benefits of more sophisticated FRLs to be fully reaped. For example, an FRL that requires policymakers to determine the exact amount of fiscal adjustment obviously needs a PFM system with the requisite forecasting, costing, and monitoring tools.

A PFM system covers a broad range of processes and institutions. From a process point of view, the system starts with strategic planning, fiscal strategy, and budget preparation, then extends to budget execution, accounting, reporting, and external audit. On the institutional side, the ministry of finance is the main manager, supervisor, and standard setter for the PFM process. The basic elements of a good PFM system are a well-formulated medium-term fiscal strategy development process, clear and credible budget formulation, effective budget execution procedures, timely and accurate accounting and reporting, a strong independent audit institution, and transparent oversight by the legislature. These elements can improve an FRL's effectiveness and credibility by creating and facilitating a policy environment that binds government to sound fiscal criteria. A PFM system should, depending on the ambition level and complexity of the FRL (which are interrelated), be progressively capable of meeting requirements in the areas discussed in the following sections.

2.4.1. Monitoring and Reporting Fiscal Data

Fiscal reporting systems should be able to provide fiscal data that are accurate, reliable, and available on a timely basis, and include end-of-year financial reports and in-year budget execution reports. Information should also be available on outstanding debt, contingent liabilities, and other fiscal risks in line with the reporting requirements prescribed in an FRL. This information may be explicitly required by an FRL, but even an FRL that requires only a statement of fiscal policy objectives and reports on their achievement would benefit from this information.

The requirements of advanced, type III FRLs for monitoring fiscal policy and budget developments need to be supported by strong monitoring and reporting systems to provide a reliable basis for tracking implementation of the law. Budget monitoring and reporting should cover a comprehensive set of aggregates and should be sufficiently developed for gauging compliance with the fiscal rules to produce timely in-year and end-year reports. It is necessary to monitor and report regularly on fiscal developments and budget implementation against the objectives and targets of the fiscal strategy and approved budget.

Combining the various stages of the budget process into an integrated, or interlinked, financial management information system helps manage public monies better; allows greater financial control; and leads to better monitoring of the government cash position, better cash planning, and better fiscal reporting. Fiscal data should meet accepted quality standards. Systems integration is also important for establishing accountability for appropriate responses to changing economic or fiscal circumstances and is critical for fiscal transparency.

The reporting system will also help to ensure legislative and administrative compliance. The system should produce reports of commitments and payments that have been made against each legal and administrative control point, in any dimension, and report information on available budget balances at all points throughout the budget execution cycle. This level of detail will ensure that budget planners and managers are able to exercise control and allocate resources efficiently throughout the cycle. The recording of transactions against each budget line also provides a proper basis for assurance testing and reporting by internal and external audit. Another important requirement served by the financial reporting system is the control of compliance with other fiscal legislation, in particular, the statutory controls over spending from the consolidated fund, loan fund, capital fund, contingency fund, and all other special funds.

To enforce the aggregate control required by fiscal adjustment, the budget execution procedures must do more than simply ensure compliance with the approved budget; they must also be able to adjust to intervening changes and any within-year shocks and still enable operational efficiency. The budget system should ensure effective expenditure control and be supported by (1) a complete budgetary and appropriations accounting system that tracks transactions at each stage of the expenditure cycle; (2) effective controls at each stage of the expenditure cycle; (3) a system for managing multiyear contracts and forward commitments; (4) a personnel management system that controls staff levels and personnel costs; and (5) adequate and transparent procedures for managing procurement and outside contracting. The efficiency of the expenditure execution process also relies on an effective treasury and cash management system. An efficient cash management system would help in aggregate control of spending and efficient implementation of the budget, as well as minimizing the cost of government borrowing and optimizing the use of government cash balances with the help of a treasury single account (see Chapter 9).

Monitoring of fiscal policy developments and budget implementation should encompass government agencies such as the finance ministry, the external audit agency, and the parliamentary finance committee, as well as research organizations, think tanks, and international organizations such as the IMF.

2.4.2. Fiscal Forecasting

Countries that adopt FRLs with a requirement to present fiscal objectives should have reasonable capacity to forecast macroeconomic and fiscal aggregates to determine whether fiscal objectives are realistic and to estimate needed policy adjustments. Because FRLs usually require fiscal objectives to be set for the medium term, forecasting also needs to be extended to the medium term to assess fiscal parameters over a longer time horizon.

The framing of robust fiscal projections is an issue in a number of countries, as is having the necessary skill and capacity to produce accurate forecasts that provide a dependable basis for the fiscal framework, budgeting, and expenditure control for the medium term. Studies have shown an optimistic bias in the forecasts of economic growth and budgetary projections produced by government in some countries. This bias may arise because governments overestimate growth to avoid the political cost associated with the implementation of difficult fiscal correction measures.

Although corrective measures can be avoided ex ante, the ex post deficit may then turn out to be larger than forecasted because growth is lower than projected. In some countries, economic and budgetary forecasts prepared by independent institutions provide benchmarks against which the plausibility of government projections can be assessed and thus help limit or eliminate the source of optimistic bias. All possible efforts need to be made to produce reliable forecasts for a fiscal framework.

2.4.3. Fiscal Policymaking Capacity

If an FRL aims to ensure fiscal sustainability, the country should have the ability to assess sustainable limits for the public debt and deficit. If the FRL requires fiscal targets to be set to help stabilize the economy, policymakers should have an idea of the necessary fiscal policy stance. Many FRLs require production of a fiscal strategy note at the start of the budget process, providing a macroeconomic and fiscal forecast, fiscal policy targets, and policy measures to attain them.

The fiscal strategy has a vital role at the front end of the budget process and needs to be used for developing credible medium-term budget ceilings that reflect government policies and priorities. Discipline in the budget process is indispensable for achieving fiscal control, and budget comprehensiveness is a key ingredient in this. The budget needs to encompass all fiscal operations undertaken by government, including those of extrabudgetary funds and the quasi-fiscal activities of parastatal agencies and state-owned enterprises. It is important to ensure that fiscal policy decisions are based on a comprehensive framework of public activities.

2.4.4. Independent Review of Fiscal Policy

To give more credibility to the outcome of fiscal policy, and in more advanced FRLs, to assess if and for what reasons fiscal limits have been breached, state auditors have the task of reviewing fiscal policy objectives and outcomes. An independent assessment can provide assurance of the executive's compliance with the FRL, but most supreme audit institutions are presently not well placed to assess fiscal policy because this topic has been outside their core competency. This would mean that considerable capacity building would be required. As an alternative, countries sometimes assign this task to a fiscal council (as discussed in Chapter 6) or to a special support unit of the budget committee of parliament. Obviously, if these entities need to be set up, capacity building may be required for them, too. An advantage is that such entities are fully focused on assessing fiscal and budgetary policies.

External audit can be important in other ways for the effectiveness of an FRL. It can (1) detect weaknesses in management controls and bring out irregularities in the use of public funds, (2) determine the reliability of accounting and fiscal data, and (3) identify areas of waste and inefficiency and suggest ways of improving the efficiency of budgetary operations. These tasks will help support the transparency and control of government expenditure. The credibility of an external audit requires that the supreme audit institution and its staff be independent of the government units being audited and have unrestricted access to required information.

2.4.5. MTFF Development

As FRLs become more ambitious, they tend to prescribe development of full-blown MTFFs. An MTFF requires a more disciplined approach to fiscal policy-making by formalizing the development of a medium-term fiscal strategy and medium-term orientation within the budget process through a combination of (1) a medium-term macroeconomic framework that provides multiyear projections of macroeconomic variables such as GDP, inflation, exchange rates, and the balance of payments; (2) a framework that produces a set of multiyear targets or ceilings on fiscal aggregates, such as overall government expenditure, borrowing, and debt; and (3) identification of concrete policy measures that translate the projected overall resource envelope and the government's fiscal objectives into a set of credible and binding multiyear expenditure ceilings and policies.

An MTFF is a mechanism for setting multiyear fiscal objectives and having the cabinet make decisions that ensure that these objectives are met in budget formulation, approval, and execution. Hard budget constraints are needed to ensure that fiscal policy execution is consistent with macroeconomic stability objectives. Explicit medium-term expenditure ceilings consistent with overall fiscal objectives should be framed in the early stages of budget preparation. Therefore, expenditure allocations to sectors should be based on clear prioritization of policy objectives, guided by discussions between the ministry of finance and line ministries. Expenditure ceilings need to be based on separate assessments of the cost of current policies and of new measures. Ceilings derived from this process should be endorsed at the cabinet level to ensure that an adequate policy discussion governs the process.

Enhancing the top-down approach to preparing the budget also strengthens overall fiscal discipline. Expenditure ceilings should be applied as a means of controlling fiscal outcomes and compliance with fiscal rules. Expenditure control requires that expenditure ceilings for government as a whole and for individual ministries be firmly respected.

Although MTFFs strongly support fiscal discipline, extending the level of detail of budgetary planning would further enhance this discipline. Once an FRL begins prescribing medium-term budget frameworks (MTBFs), its capacity requirement again expands considerably. An MTBF requires development of a fully costed expenditure baseline, and costing of all new expenditure and revenue measures for the medium term (see Chapter 4). Such costing can be complicated if the budget is still structured by economic classifications. For better linkage between policy and the budget and for more accurate costing of program expenditure, countries often shift to program budgeting during the introduction of an MTBF. Thus, an FRL that requires a full MTBF will often require capacity in both baseline development and program budgeting. Capacity requirements to operate an MTBF extend to line ministries.

Both MTFFs and MTBFs require prudent risk management and contingency planning to ensure that government keeps sufficient capacity in reserve to meet reasonable risks from unforeseen and urgent events that emerge after the budget strategy has been approved. This could take the form of including planning or contingency reserves in the framework.

2.4.6. Intergovernmental Coordination

To establish overall fiscal control in countries with strongly decentralized expenditure assignments, it makes sense for FRLs to cover the whole of general government. Thus, additional PFM capacities, such as a well-designed system of intergovernmental fiscal relations supported by a functioning PFM system at the subnational level, are required. For fiscal adjustments to work for the country as a whole, subnational finances must be controlled in parallel to those of central government. In countries with large vertical imbalances arising from mismatches between expenditure and revenue responsibilities, an FRL would not be helpful unless these imbalances are accommodated by a rules-based system of transfers or borrowing rights. Similarly, if subnational governments have accumulated a large stock of debt, an FRL needs to be complemented by fiscal adjustment or debt-rescheduling programs with the national government.

2.4.7. A Strong Ministry of Finance

Fiscal policy does not materialize in a vacuum. A government cannot simply decide to adjust the fiscal deficit; public institutions need to put in place to support the decision. Without well-functioning fiscal institutions, even the best-designed fiscal measures risk failure. Key fiscal institutions for achieving and sustaining fiscal consolidation were discussed above and include those that forecast revenues; develop fiscal policy; plan, execute, and monitor the budget; and manage intergovernmental fiscal relations. These functions are primarily performed by the ministry of finance. A strong ministry of finance is critical to the success of an FRL. Again, as the ambition level of the FRL increases, so does the need for the ministry to develop additional capacities.

2.4.8. A Strong Institutional and Legal Framework

Implementing an FRL, even a basic one, will be greatly helped by a sound institutional and legal framework with strong transparency and accountability requirements, public oversight, and enforcement procedures. Of course, many FRLs themselves aim to increase transparency and accountability of the fiscal process. However, if general principles are already included in the budget system law, advancing to a more complex FRL will be easier.

A PFM system's effectiveness depends on its being well grounded in law and benefiting from supportive regulations and administrative practices. Many countries have public finance or organic budget laws that provide the legal framework for budget formulation, approval, and execution. Such laws are often supported by specific laws and regulations governing treasury operations, accounting, and reporting on management of the public debt. It is useful to have a comprehensive public finance law that establishes (1) clear roles and responsibilities for the key entities and offices involved in management of public finances; (2) an open and credible budget preparation process; (3) effective and disciplined budget execution; (4) reporting requirements that mirror the budget presentation; (5), transparency requirements and timing and audit requirements for financial accounts; and (6) accountability and compliance provisions. A budget system law is the foundation on which an effective FRL will be built. If a budget law is underdeveloped, the functioning of the FRL will be suboptimal. The development of adequate institutional and administrative capacity to enforce PFM laws and regulations is equally important.

Box 2.2 summarizes the main PFM requirements for progressively more sophisticated FRLs.

BOX 2.2 Key Public Financial Management Requirements to Support a Fiscal Responsibility Law

Depending on the scope and complexity of the fiscal responsibility law, a public financial management system should be progressively capable of meeting requirements in the following areas:

- Accurate, timely, and dependable fiscal monitoring and reporting
- Credible budget planning
- Effective and disciplined budget execution
- Reasonably reliable macroeconomic and fiscal forecasting
- Fiscal policy analysis and ability to set fiscal targets
- Independent review of fiscal policy outcomes (external audit, parliament, or fiscal council)
- A credible medium-term fiscal framework and a monitorable fiscal strategy describing the path of fiscal deficits and public debt resulting from government's revenue, expenditure, and financing policies
- Ability to cost new and existing policy measures over the medium term, that is, definition of the baseline
- Setting and executing fiscal policy in line with tightly defined numerical limits
- Well-structured cabinet decision making over the medium term
- As fiscal rules become more complex, sophisticated macroeconomic modeling to determine the structural growth rate, deficit, and resource revenues

2.5. CONCLUSION

FRLs can play a useful role in strengthening fiscal outcomes. Given the almost universal pressures to increase government spending, FRLs should be part of the institutional toolkit of any ministry of finance. However, adoption of an FRL is not a priority in all circumstances—if fiscal policy is under control and the political will is strong to keep it that way, this institutional innovation may not be a priority. Most countries are, however, not in that happy situation.

A legal framework that encompasses principles of transparent, accountable, and sustainable fiscal policy, a type I FRL, would seem desirable in any country. Whether that objective requires a separate law depends on the prominence fiscal policy has achieved in the political debate. Type II FRLs, focusing on fiscal process rules (concrete reporting guidelines, limitation of budget amendment rights, MTFF development), could also be adopted in most countries if tailored to the capacity of the local PFM system. For type III FRLs, which include numerical fiscal rules, economic and fiscal circumstances, the political appetite for fiscal discipline, and the capacity of the PFM system to operate the FRL are crucial factors. A common mistake is that ministries of finance are often too ambitious and overestimate what a type III FRL can achieve in a society that does not yet fully appreciate the importance of sustainable fiscal policy.

An FRL can gradually discipline the political debate, especially once it has built up reputational capital. The distance between the aspirations of the law and political reality should not become too large, otherwise the law will be breached. Sometimes compromise needs to be accepted, and FRLs may have to start with modest ambitions, encompassing, for example, only specification of principles of transparency, accountability, and sustainability. In such cases, FRLs are clearly not the whole answer to improving fiscal policy outcomes.

FRLs should not, however, be seen as static legislation. As economic circumstances change and as political acceptance grows, FRLs should adapt. As the reputational capital of these laws increases, the possibility of imposing tighter requirements arises, and the introduction of more sophisticated fiscal rules should be explored. Both emerging market economies and advanced economies have squandered opportunities to regularly strengthen their FRLs. A number of emerging market economies are now in a position to introduce FRLs with binding numerical rules without too much economic pain. Advanced economies have neglected to make their FRLs more sophisticated by, for example, introducing structural deficit limits.

Development of FRLs should be seen as a gradual process in which the requirements of the fiscal policy process gradually expand from following good practice principles, to transparency and process rules, and ultimately to numerical fiscal rules. During this process of becoming more sophisticated and prescriptive, it is important to define precisely a number of issues such as coverage, escape clauses, sanctions, and transition requirements. These elements can function as pressure valves that can serve countries well in times of extreme fiscal crisis. Again, the most strenuous FRL requirements will not always be the best and the longest lasting.

REFERENCES

Caceres, Carlos, Ana Corbacho, and Leandro Medina, 2010, "Structural Breaks in Fiscal Performance: Did Fiscal Responsibility Laws Have Anything to Do with Them?" IMF Working Paper 10/248 (Washington: International Monetary Fund).

Corbacho, A., and G. Schwartz, 2007, "Fiscal Responsibility Laws," in *Promoting Fiscal Discipline*, ed. by T. Ter-Minassian and M. Kumar (Washington: International Monetary Fund), pp. 58–77.

Erauskin-Iurrita, Iñaki, 2008, "Financial Openness and the Size of the Public Sector: A Portfolio Approach," Munich Personal RePEc Archive (MPRA) Paper No. 10564 (unpublished; Bilbao, Spain: University of Deusto).

European Commission (EC), 2006, "Part III: National Numerical Fiscal Rules and Institutions for Sound Public Finances," in *Public Finance Report in EMU—2006*. European Economy, No. 3/2006 (Brussels: European Commission).

International Monetary Fund (IMF), 2009, "Fiscal Rules: Anchoring Expectations for Sustainable Public Finances," Fiscal Affairs Department (Washington).

———, 2012, "Fiscal Rules Dataset 1985–2012," Fiscal Affairs Department, Fiscal Policy and Surveillance Division (Washington).

Lienert, Ian, 2010, "Should Advanced Countries Adopt a Fiscal Responsibility Law?" IMF Working Paper 10/254 (Washington: International Monetary Fund).

Mayer, Eric, and Nikolai Staehler, 2009, "The Debt Brake: Business Cycle and Welfare Consequences of Germany's New Fiscal Policy Rule," Deutsche Bundesbank Discussion Paper 24/2009 (Frankfurt).

Mosley, Layna, 2005, "Globalization and the State: Still Room to Move?" *New Political Economy*, Vol. 10, No. 3, pp. 355–62.

North, Douglass C., 1999, "Institutions and Credible Commitment" (unpublished; St. Louis, Missouri: Washington University).

Organisation for Economic Co-operation and Development (OECD), 2002, "Part IV: Fiscal Sustainability: The Contribution of Fiscal Rules," *OECD Economic Outlook*, No. 72, pp. 117–36.

Rodrik, Dani, 1998, "Why Do More Open Economies Have Bigger Governments?" *Journal of Political Economy*, Vol. 106, pp. 997–1032.

———, 2008, "Second-Best Institutions," *American Economic Review*, Vol. 98, No. 2, pp. 100–104.

Schick, Allen, 2010, "Postcrisis Fiscal Rules: Stabilizing Public Finance While Responding to Economic Aftershocks," *OECD Journal on Budgeting*, Vol. 10, No. 2, pp. 1–18.

APPENDIX 2.1. FISCAL RESPONSIBILITY LAWS IN SELECTED COUNTRIES: MAIN FEATURES

Country	Law (year)	Procedural rules	Numerical targets in FRL	Coverage	Escape clauses[1]	Sanctions
Argentina	Federal Regime of Fiscal Responsibility (2004)[2]	Yes	ER; DR	CG	No	Yes
Australia	Charter of Budget Honesty (1998)[3]	Yes	—	CG	No	No
Brazil	Fiscal Responsibility Law (2000)	Yes	ER; DR	PS	Yes	Yes
Chile	Fiscal Responsibility Act No. 20-128 (2006)	Yes	BBR	CG	No	No
Colombia	Original Law on Fiscal Transparency and Responsibility (2003)	Yes	BBR	NFPS	Yes	No
Ecuador	Fiscal Responsibility Law (2010)	Yes	ER	PS	No	No
Jamaica	Fiscal Responsibility Law (2010)	Yes	BBR; DR	CG —[4]	Yes	No
Mexico	Federal Law on Budget and Financial Responsibility (2006)	Yes	BBR	CG	Yes	Yes
Nigeria	Fiscal Responsibility Act (2007)		BBR	CG	No	No
New Zealand	Public Finance (State Sector Management) Bill (2005)[3]	Yes	—	GG	No	No
Pakistan	Fiscal Responsibility and Debt Limitation Act (2005)	Yes	BBR; DR	CG	Yes	No
Panama	New Fiscal Responsibility Law (2009)	Yes	BBR; DR	NFPS	Yes	No
Peru	Fiscal Responsibility and Transparency Law (2003)	Yes	BBR; ER	NFPS	Yes	Yes
Romania	Fiscal Responsibility Law (2010)	Yes	ER	GG	Yes	Yes
Serbia	FRL provisions introduced in the 2009 Budget System Law (2010)	Yes	BBR; DR	GG	No	No
Spain	Budget Stability Law (2007)	Yes	BBR	NFPS	Yes	Yes
Sri Lanka	Fiscal Management Responsibility Act (2003)	Yes	BBR; DR	CG	No	No
United Kingdom	Budget Responsibility and National Audit Act (2011)	Yes	BBR; DR	PS	No	No

Source: IMF staff and national authorities.

Note: BBR = budget balance rules; CG = central government; DR = debt rule; ER = expenditure rule; FRL = fiscal responsibility law; GG = general government; NFPS = nonfinancial public sector; PS = public sector.

[1] Includes only well-specified escape clauses.

[2] The FRL has de facto been suspended since 2009.

[3] These countries operate de facto rules that are not spelled out in an FRL.

[4] Also includes public bodies.

CHAPTER 3

Numerical Fiscal Rules: International Trends

NINA BUDINA, TIDIANE KINDA, ANDREA SCHAECHTER, AND ANKE WEBER

Strengthening fiscal frameworks, in particular through numerical fiscal rules, has emerged as a key response to the fiscal legacy of the 2008–09 global economic and financial crisis. In the euro area and in most other European Union (EU) member states, this strengthening is occurring through institutional reforms at the national and supranational levels, as agreed to in the Fiscal Compact and the Six Pack.[1] Outside the EU, many countries have started or are considering reforms to their existing fiscal rules and introducing new ones with a view to providing a medium-term anchor, supporting credible long-term adjustment efforts, and ensuring fiscal sustainability.

This chapter takes stock of the use of numerical fiscal rules around the world. It provides a systematic compilation and comparison of fiscal rules and their design elements.[2] Many countries put their fiscal rules into abeyance during the crisis; this chapter examines recent developments and the next generation of fiscal rules that is emerging from the crisis.

In particular, this chapter reviews trends—from the mid-1980s until early 2012—in the types and number of rules as well as their combinations and main characteristics, such as legal basis, enforcement, coverage, escape clauses, and provisions for cyclical adjustment. Information is provided for national rules that cover at least the central government, as well as for supranational rules. In addition, the chapter discusses key institutional arrangements and capacities that are important for monitoring and supporting rules. It does not, however, assess the implementation of fiscal rules or their role in fiscal performance.

The chapter is structured as follows: The first section defines fiscal rules, compares their objectives, and discusses supporting public financial management institutions and the different types of rules. The second section reviews trends in the types of rules used during the past two decades. The third section analyzes

---

This chapter draws from Schaechter and others (2012).

[1] These EU governance reforms include a requirement to adopt national structural budget balance rules, reduce debt annually until it reaches 60 percent of GDP, and strengthen national fiscal frameworks. These agreements are reviewed in the second section of this chapter and in Box 3.1.

[2] Country-by-country descriptions of the rules and their key features are provided in an IMF data set available at http://www.imf.org/external/datamapper/FiscalRules/map/map.htm.

rules' key features. The fourth section discusses how, in response to the crisis, existing rules have been adjusted, how new rules have been adopted, and how these "next generation" rules differ from earlier ones.

3.1. DEFINITION, INSTITUTIONAL CONTEXT, AND TYPES OF FISCAL RULES

3.1.1. Definition and Objectives

A fiscal rule is a long-lasting constraint on fiscal policy using numerical limits on budgetary aggregates.[3] Numerical limits on a particular budgetary aggregate set boundaries for fiscal policy that cannot be frequently changed and provide operational guidance. However, the demarcation lines of what constitutes a fiscal rule are not always clear. This chapter uses the following principles:

- In addition to covering rules with specific numerical targets fixed in legislation, those fiscal arrangements, in particular expenditure ceilings for which the targets can be revised, but only seldom (e.g., as part of the electoral cycle) are considered to be fiscal rules, as long as they are binding for a minimum of three years. Thus, medium-term budget frameworks (MTBFs) or expenditure ceilings that provide multiyear projections (see Chapter 4) but can be changed annually are not considered to be rules.
- Only those fiscal rules that set numerical targets on aggregates that capture a large share of public finances—deficit, debt, expenditure, or revenue—and at a minimum cover the central government level, are included. Thus, rules for subnational governments or fiscal subaggregates—for example, expenditure caps on particular spending items or those linked to the use of revenues from natural resources—are not included.[4]
- The focus is on de jure arrangements, not the extent to which rules have been adhered to in practice.

Unless indicated otherwise, this chapter covers only those rules that took effect by end-March 2012 or for which a specific transition regime was in place at that time (see Appendix 3.1 for a country list). Fiscal rules that were adopted but not yet implemented are described but not included in the figures and tables.

Like many of the public financial management innovations discussed in this book, rules aim to correct distorted incentives and contain pressures to overspend,

---

[3]This definition broadly follows Kopits and Symansky (1998), except that they include the element of "simplicity" in their definition. Although this is a desirable feature from a communication and monitoring point of view, in practice, fiscal rules have become increasingly complex. Thus, simplicity is not considered a defining feature of a fiscal rule in this chapter. In addition to numerical limits, fiscal rules can also establish procedures for the budgetary process (procedural rules) for the purpose of establishing good practices, raising predictability, and becoming more transparent (see Chapter 2). Many countries operate procedural and numerical rules in tandem, but this chapter reports only on the latter.

[4]See Baunsgaard and others (2012) for fiscal rules in resource-rich economies.

particularly in good times, to ensure fiscal responsibility and debt sustainability. As mentioned in the previous chapters, two main explanations have been put forward to account for deficit bias: governments' shortsightedness and the "common pool problem" that occurs because special interest groups or constituencies do not internalize the overall budgetary impact of their competing demands. The presence of many interest groups usually results in different entities competing and pushing for overspending of windfalls in good years, which leaves no room for a countercyclical response in bad years. In currency unions, supranational rules aim to internalize the regional costs of fiscal indiscipline and establish a framework for better coordination of the monetary-fiscal policy mix.

To mitigate deficit bias, a range of fiscal institutional innovations—including fiscal rules, fiscal responsibility legislation (see Chapter 2), and medium-term budget frameworks (see Chapter 4)—have been established during the past two decades around the world in support of more prudent and more balanced fiscal policies. Fiscal rules can also serve other objectives. Economic stabilization is inherent in fiscal rules that allow fiscal accounts to adjust to variations in economic activity. Fiscal rules have also been introduced to contain the size of government and support intergenerational equity. Providing a credible medium-term anchor has been the pervasive motive for adopting or strengthening fiscal rules policies after the Great Recession.

Still, the use of fiscal rules is not entirely without concerns, particularly when they are introduced in isolation. The potential concerns include leaving too little room to adjust to shocks, distracting from spending priorities, or undermining transparency as a result of incentives for creative accounting.

Recent efforts have focused on strengthening fiscal frameworks and the interaction among many of their main elements. The adoption of fiscal rules should thus be one of many components—some of which are discussed in the remainder of this chapter—that can enhance the probability of achieving established objectives. To be effective, fiscal rules need a set of institutional arrangements to convert the intent of the rules into the reality of budget policy and execution. Like all other public financial management innovations, rules introduced in isolation are not a panacea; in addition to political will, concrete institutional elements need to be in place.

3.1.2. Institutional Context: Rules as Part of a Public Financial Management Framework

Effective implementation and monitoring of fiscal rules presumes the existence of, and interaction with, a number of institutional arrangements and good institutional capacity. Many of these institutions and innovations are discussed in this book (see in particular Chapters 2, 4, and 6).

As part of a modern public financial management framework, fiscal rules have to be well integrated within the budget formulation and execution cycle. A top-down budgeting process, in which the aggregate expenditure limit is determined before the distribution of appropriations, helps reconcile the conflict between unlimited spending demands from line ministries and a finite budget constraint. An MTBF can reinforce fiscal rules and can, in turn, be strengthened by the adoption of a numerical fiscal rule. MTBFs enable governments to demonstrate the impact of current and proposed policies over the course of several years, set future budget priorities, and ultimately achieve better control over public expenditure. Presenting the budget for a multiyear horizon demonstrates ahead of time whether government policy is consistent with the fiscal rule and what policy actions are necessary to bring it in line if it is not, and increases the time frame available for making policy decisions that will meet the requirements of fiscal rules. What MTBFs cover differs widely across countries, thus affecting the link to fiscal rules (see Chapter 4).

Effective budget execution systems, such as commitment controls, arrears monitoring, and cash management systems, are essential to ensuring that budget outcomes correspond to budget appropriations. Reliable data and technical forecasting capacity are needed to ensure that projections of budgetary aggregates are sufficiently accurate to prevent large deviations from the announced fiscal policy stance from undermining the credibility of the rules. Budget reporting systems must cover the aggregates comprehensively, and must be sufficiently developed to produce timely in-year and end-year reports. Robust budget reporting systems allow internal monitoring of adherence to the rule, providing ample time for policymakers to make policy changes, if needed. Internal and external audit systems are also important for ensuring accountability. Fiscal data—consistent with the budget reporting system—should be publicly released in line with an announced calendar to allow external monitoring of the rule.

As discussed in detail in Chapter 2, numerical fiscal rules can be reflected in fiscal responsibility laws (FRLs). An increasing number of advanced and some emerging market economies are using independent bodies to enhance the credibility of their fiscal rules further. Independent fiscal councils—institutions with a specific mandate to assess and monitor the implementation and impacts of fiscal policy—also exist in some countries that do not have national fiscal rules in place (e.g., Belgium and Canada). Fiscal councils play a specific role in enforcing rules by providing an independent voice on their implementation. One example is the Swedish Fiscal Policy Council, which monitors compliance with the budget balance rule, assesses whether current fiscal policy is consistent with fiscal sustainability, and evaluates budget transparency and the quality of forecasts. Fiscal councils or independent committees can also provide key budgetary assumptions and methodologies which are critical inputs into the implementation of rules. Following the crisis, a number of countries have established, or are in the process of establishing, fiscal councils (see Chapter 6).

3.1.3. Types of Fiscal Rules

Four main types of fiscal rules can be discerned based on the type of budgetary aggregate they seek to constrain.

Debt rules set an explicit limit or target for public debt as a percentage of GDP. A debt rule, by definition, will most effectively ensure convergence to a debt target and is relatively easy to communicate. However, it takes time for debt levels to be affected by budgetary measures; therefore, debt rules do not provide clear short-term guidance for policymakers. Debt could also be affected by developments outside the control of government, such as changes in interest rates and the exchange rate, as well as "below-the-line" financing operations (such as financial sector support measures or the calling of guarantees), which could cause unrealistically large fiscal adjustments. Moreover, fiscal policy may become procyclical when the economy is hit by shocks and the debt target, defined as a percentage of GDP, is binding. Conversely, when debt is well below its ceiling such a rule would provide no binding guidance.

Budget balance rules constrain the variable that primarily influences the debt ratio, and these rules are largely under the control of policymakers. Such rules provide clear operational guidance and can help ensure debt sustainability. Budget balance rules can apply to the overall balance, structural balance, cyclically adjusted balance, and balance "over the cycle." An overall budget balance rule does not have economic stabilization features, but the other three explicitly account for economic shocks. However, estimating the adjustment, typically through the output gap, makes the rule more difficult to communicate and monitor. A balance "over the cycle" rule has the added disadvantage that remedial measures could be put off to the end of the cycle. Although interest payments are the only expenditure item not directly under the control of policymakers—even though spending rigidities may also complicate achieving short-term targets—excluding them from the rule weakens the link to debt sustainability. Similarly, a "golden rule," which targets the overall balance net of capital expenditure, is less linked to debt. "Pay-as-you-go" rules stipulate that any additional deficit-raising expenditure or revenue measures must be offset in a deficit-neutral way. Because pay-as-you-go rules do not set numerical limits on large budgetary aggregates, they are typically considered procedural rules and thus not included as numerical fiscal rules in this chapter.

Expenditure rules set limits on total, primary, or current spending. Such limits are typically established in absolute terms, apply to growth rates, or occasionally, are established as a percentage of GDP. The time horizon most often ranges between three and five years. These rules are not linked directly to the debt sustainability objective given that they do not constrain the revenue side. However, they can provide an operational tool for triggering the fiscal consolidation required for consistency with sustainability when they are accompanied by debt or budget balance rules. Furthermore, they can constrain spending during temporary absorption booms, when windfall revenue receipts are temporarily high and headline deficit limits easy to comply with. Moreover, expenditure rules do not restrict the economic stabilization function of fiscal policy in times of adverse shocks because they do not require adjustments to cyclical or discretionary reductions in tax revenues. Even greater countercyclicality can be achieved by excluding cycle-sensitive expenditure items, such as unemployment support, but at the expense of creating a larger gap with the sustainability target. Also, expenditure rules are not consistent with discretionary fiscal stimulus. However, expenditure ceilings directly define the amount of public resources used by government, and are in general relatively easy to communicate and monitor.[5]

Revenue rules set ceilings or floors on revenues and are aimed at boosting revenue collection or preventing an excessive tax burden (or both). Most of these rules are not directly linked to control of public debt because they do not constrain spending. Furthermore, setting ceilings or floors on revenues can be challenging because revenues can have a large cyclical component, fluctuating widely with the business cycle. Exceptions are those rules that restrict the use of windfall revenue for additional spending. Revenue rules alone could result in procyclical fiscal policy because floors and ceilings do not generally account for the operation of automatic stabilizers in a downturn or an upturn. However, like expenditure rules, they can directly target the size of government.

Given the trade-offs, many countries combine two or more fiscal rules—key features and the pros and cons of different rules are summarized in Table 3.1. Not all types of fiscal rules are equally apt to support the objectives of sustainability, economic stabilization, and possibly the size of government, even when the design features of a rule are fine-tuned. Using a combination of fiscal rules can help address the gaps. For example, a debt rule combined with an expenditure rule would provide a link to debt sustainability while assisting policymakers with short- to medium-term operational decisions, allowing for some countercyclicality, and explicitly targeting the size of government. This objective could similarly be achieved through a combination of a debt rule and a structural budget balance rule.

3.2 THE PAST TWO DECADES: FISCAL RULES ON THE RISE

3.2.1. Who Uses Fiscal Rules and How Many?

During the past two decades fiscal rules have spread worldwide. In 1990, only five countries—Germany, Indonesia, Japan, Luxembourg, and the United States—had fiscal rules in place that covered at least the central government level. In Japan and Germany, fiscal rules have a long tradition dating back to as early as 1947 and 1969, respectively, though adherence to the rules was weak for most years. From about 1990, the number of countries with national or supranational fiscal

[5] However, expenditure rules also can be manipulated by creative accounting, for example, by shifting toward more tax expenditure; this potentially calls for broad coverage under the rule. For a detailed analysis of various design features of expenditure rules, as well as experiences in Finland, the Netherlands, and Sweden, see Ljungman (2008).

TABLE 3.1

Properties of Different Types of Fiscal Rules

Rule	Pros	Cons
Debt rule	• Direct link to debt sustainability • Easy to communicate and monitor	• No clear operational guidance in the short term because policy impact on debt ratio is not immediate and is limited • No economic stabilization feature (can be procyclical) • Rule could be met via temporary measures (e.g., below-the-line transactions) • Debt could be affected by developments outside the control of government
Budget balance rule	• Clear operational guidance • Close link to debt sustainability • Easy to communicate and monitor	• No economic stabilization feature (can be procyclical) • Headline balance could be affected by developments outside the control of government (e.g., a major economic downturn)
Structural budget balance rule	• Relatively clear operational guidance • Close link to debt sustainability • Economic stabilization function (i.e., accounts for economic shocks) • Allows accounting for other one-off and temporary factors	• Correction for cycle is complicated, especially for countries undergoing structural changes • Need to define one-off and temporary factors to avoid their discretionary use • Complexity makes it more difficult to communicate and monitor
Expenditure rule	• Clear operational guidance • Allows for economic stabilization • Steers the size of government • Relatively easy to communicate and monitor	• Not directly linked to debt sustainability because no constraint on revenue side • Could lead to unwanted changes in the distribution of spending if, to meet the ceiling, shift occurs to spending categories that are not covered by the rule
Revenue rule	• Steers the size of government • Can improve revenue policy and administration • Can prevent procyclical spending (rules constraining use of windfall revenue)	• Not directly linked to debt sustainability because no constraint on expenditure side (except rules constraining use of windfall revenue) • No economic stabilization feature (can be procyclical)

Source: IMF staff assessment.

rules surged to 76 by end-March 2012 (Figures 3.1 and 3.2).[6] This increase includes responses to the recent global financial and economic crisis, aiming to provide credible commitment to long-term fiscal discipline.

The more prevalent use of national fiscal rules reflects responses to different pressures on public finances. National rules are now in effect in 45 economies

[6]The database covers 81 countries, five of which no longer had a fiscal rule in effect at end-March 2012 (Argentina, Canada, Iceland, India, and the Russian Federation).

Figure 3.1 Countries with Fiscal Rules (National and Supranational), 2012

Sources: National authorities; and IMF staff assessment.

Note: Based on fiscal rules in effect by end-March 2012. Rules that cover the same budgetary aggregate and are at the same level (either only national or only supranational) are not counted as separate rules because they constrain the same variable only in different ways. However, national and supranational rules are counted separately because the enforcement mechanisms vary.

(Figure 3.2, panel a). Advanced economies were the front-runners, but rules were later adopted in a number of emerging market economies, although they are used by only a few low-income countries (Figure 3.2, panel b). Factors that motivated the adoption of national fiscal rules range from reining in debt excesses that resulted from banking and economic crises in the early 1990s (e.g., Finland, Sweden) and debt crises in Latin American countries (e.g., Brazil, Peru); consolidation needs to qualify for the euro area (e.g., Belgium); and more generally, attempts to reduce trends of rising deficits and debts (e.g., the Netherlands, Switzerland). In some cases, the introduction of rules coincided with large fiscal adjustments (e.g., in Finland); in others it followed an improvement in fiscal position to ensure continued fiscal discipline after the global crisis (Kumar and others, 2009).

At the same time, supranational fiscal rules were introduced in currency unions and the EU, covering 47 economies. Limits to fiscal aggregates were adopted with the objective of preventing individual countries from running fiscal policies inconsistent with the needs of a monetary union.

- In EU member states, the rules are set at the 3 percent of GDP deficit and 60 percent of GDP debt ceilings included in the Maastricht Treaty in 1992 and the Stability and Growth Pact (SGP) in 1997. The SGP also includes a provision that countries should pursue country-specific medium-term budgetary objectives, defined in structural budget balance terms. The Six Pack governance reform of November 2011 introduced a new debt reduction rule and expenditure growth benchmarks (see Box 3.1).[7]

[7]The tables and figures in this chapter include only the rules that have already taken effect in the EU, that is, the overall budget balance rule, the medium-term objective, and the debt rule. Because the first two both cover the budget balance they are not counted as two separate rules.

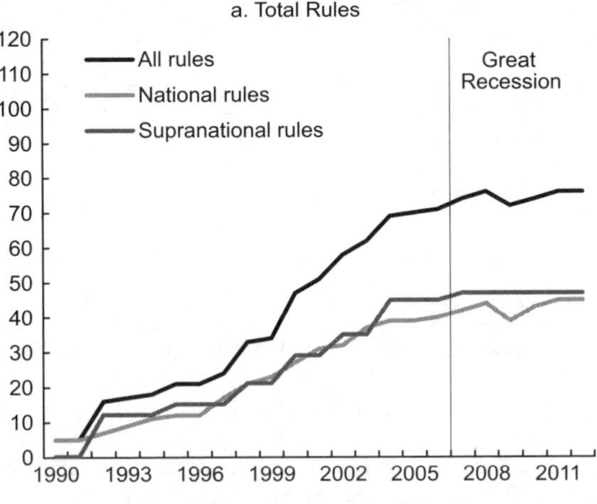

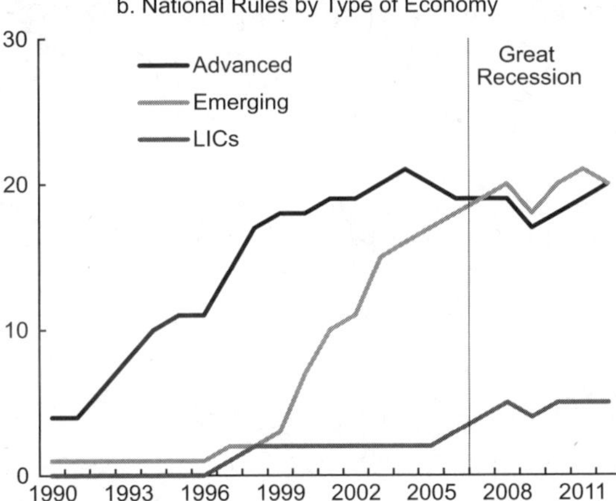

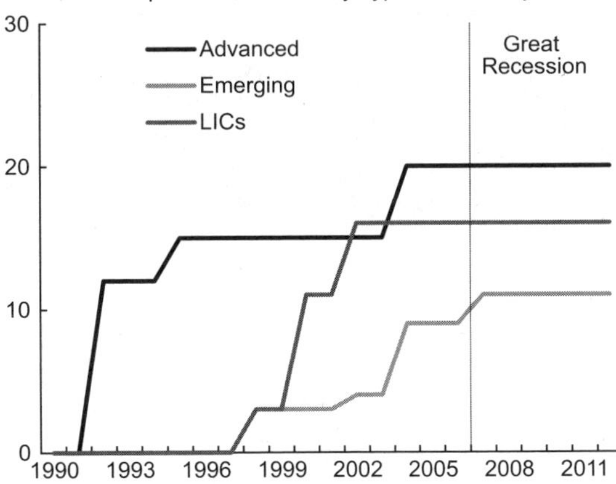

Figure 3.2 Number of Countries with Fiscal Rules

Sources: National authorities; and IMF staff assessment.

Note: Based on fiscal rules in effect by end-March 2012. LIC: Low-income country.

BOX 3.1 The EU Fiscal Compact and the Six Pack

In March 2012, members of the European Council (with the exception of the Czech Republic and the United Kingdom) signed an intergovernmental treaty, the so-called Fiscal Compact (formally, the Treaty on Stability, Coordination and Governance in the Economic and Monetary Union) to help ensure fiscal sustainability. The Fiscal Compact introduces several new elements for fiscal rules at the national level and reinforces the fiscal governance framework included in the 1997 Stability and Growth Pact (SGP) and in the 1992 Maastricht Treaty. The SGP had earlier been strengthened through a Six Pack of five new EU regulations and one EU directive, which took effect in December 2011. Countries are expected to adopt the newest provisions by 2014.

- *National structural budget balance rule.* The main new element of the Fiscal Compact is the requirement to adopt in legislation national rules that limit annual structural deficits to a maximum of 0.5 percent of GDP (1 percent of GDP for countries with debt levels of less than 60 percent of GDP and low sustainability risks). If a country is not in compliance, the European Commission can issue sanctions and fines. The issuance of both is to be more automatic than under the previous set of requirements.
- *Stronger enforcement of national rules.* To ensure enforceability, countries need to establish automatic correction mechanisms at the national level, to be triggered in the event of deviation from the rule. The European Court of Justice will verify the transposition of structural balanced budget rules to national legislation; it will not, however, verify compliance with the rules.
- *New debt rule at the supranational level.* The Fiscal Compact and the Six Pack also include a commitment to reduce the public debt-to-GDP ratio to the 60 percent of GDP threshold. The annual benchmark for the pace of debt reduction is one-twentieth of the distance between the observed level and the target, starting three years after a country has left the current Excessive Deficit Procedure (EDP). This will ensure asymptotic convergence to the 60 percent debt threshold.
- *New expenditure benchmark at the supranational level.* The annual growth of primary expenditure, excluding unemployment benefits and discretionary revenue increases, should not exceed long-term nominal GDP growth. This benchmark applies only when a country is not in EDP (i.e., if the overall deficit is less than 3 percent of GDP).
- *Broader criteria to open an EDP.* In addition to noncompliance with the deficit rule, countries can now also be placed in an EDP—by a qualified majority of the Economic and Financial Affairs Council—when they are not in compliance with the debt rule.
- *Budgetary procedures and independent fiscal councils.* To ensure effective implementation of these fiscal rules, the Six Pack sets out a number of broad recommendations to make medium-term budget frameworks more binding; prepare budgets in a more top-down sequence; report more frequently, timely, and comprehensively on fiscal developments and risks; and give a bigger role to independent councils for formulating budget assumptions and assessing compliance with the rules.

- The fiscal rules of the members of the Eastern Caribbean Currency Union (ECCU) aim to reduce the public debt-to-GDP ratios to 60 percent by 2020. Members also had in place for some time an overall deficit target of 3 percent of GDP, for which compliance was weak because of various shocks. This overall deficit target was dropped in 2006, and the primary balance level consistent with the 2020 debt target has been used to guide fiscal policy.

- In the West African Economic and Monetary Union (WAEMU), the two "first order" fiscal convergence criteria put in place in 2000 and covering large fiscal aggregates are a balanced budget (excluding foreign-financed capital expenditures) and a public debt-to-GDP ratio no higher than 70 percent. So far, compliance, in particular with the budget balance, has been weak (Ruggiero, forthcoming).
- The Central African Economic and Monetary Community (CEMAC) has a debt rule and a balanced budget rule in place. The specification of the latter was changed in 2008 from at least a balanced "basic fiscal balance," defined as total revenue net of grants minus total expenditure net of foreign-financed capital spending, to at least a balanced "basic structural fiscal balance"—replacing actual oil revenue with its three-year moving average. A rule was also added that the non-oil basic fiscal balance as a percentage of non-oil GDP should at least be in balance. These changes were made to provide greater flexibility in dealing with volatility in oil prices, while also ensuring sustainability of expenditure.

For the majority of currency union members, supranational rules are not yet complemented by national fiscal rules. By end-March 2012, of the 47 members of monetary unions and the EU, only 19 were also guided by national fiscal rules. Because enforcement and compliance with supranational fiscal rules has been mixed at best, the lack of national fiscal rules in most EU member states is now being addressed by the Fiscal Compact, which requires the adoption of a structural budget balance rule (see Box 3.1). So far, members of the three other currency unions operate only under supranational numerical fiscal limits, but implementation has also been uneven. Overall, about two-thirds of the 76 countries with fiscal rules in 2012 operate under national rules or a combination of national and supranational fiscal rules; one-third are governed only by supranational rules. The latter group includes mostly low-income countries (Figure 3.2, panel c).

In general, as of March 2012, most countries had more than one fiscal rule in place. The trend to multiple fiscal rules is, in part, the result of the introduction of supranational fiscal rules (which comprise two rules except for CEMAC members), but also reflects decisions to broaden national fiscal rules arrangements, particularly in emerging market economies. Lessons learned about the shortcomings or trade-offs of operating with a single rule played a role in these choices. For example, debt rules alone, although closely tied to sustainability objectives, do not provide sufficient operational guidance. Thus, for example, Lithuania, Namibia, and Poland reinforced their debt rules with expenditure or budget balance rules (Figure 3.3). The average number of national fiscal rules increased from 1.5 to 1.7 from 1997 to end-March 2012 (Figure 3.4). Moreover, about 40 percent of those that adopted national fiscal rules after 2000 chose a combination of national rules.

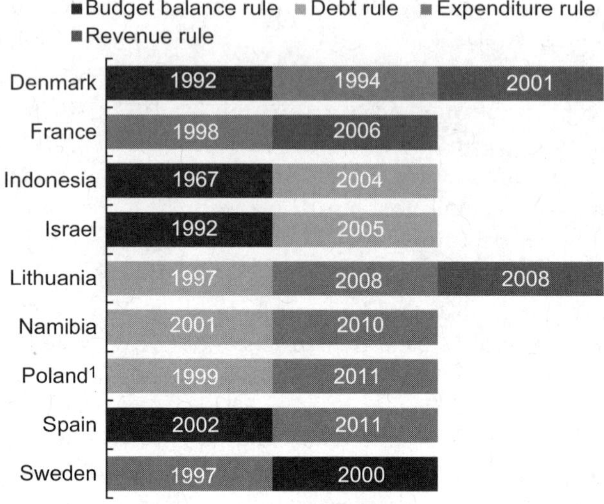

Figure 3.3 Selected Economies: Moving to Multiple Fiscal Rules

Sources: National authorities; and IMF staff assessment.

Note: Dates show when rules took effect or a transition regime started.

[1] From 2006–07 Poland also had a balanced budget rule in place.

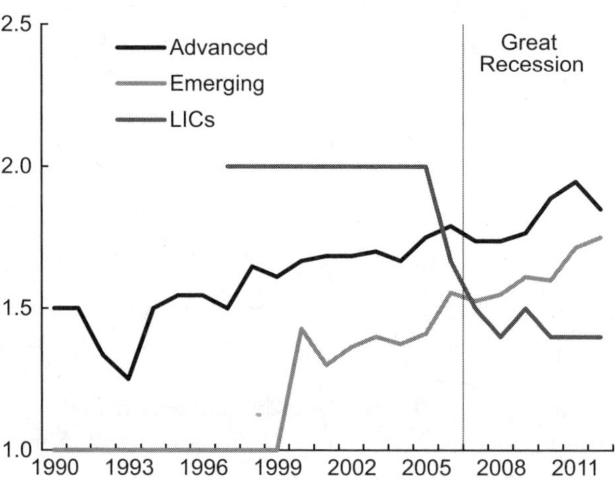

Figure 3.4 Average Number of National Fiscal Rules

Sources: National authorities; and IMF staff assessment.

Note: LIC: Low-income country.

3.2.2. What Types and Combinations of Rules?

The most frequently used rules constrain debt and the budget balance, often in combination. In part, the national rules mirror the supranational rules for members of monetary unions and the EU, except in the ECCU, which has only a budget balance rule (Figure 3.5, panel a). Across national fiscal rules, expenditure rules are also prevalent (Figure 3.5, panel b), but mostly in advanced economies.

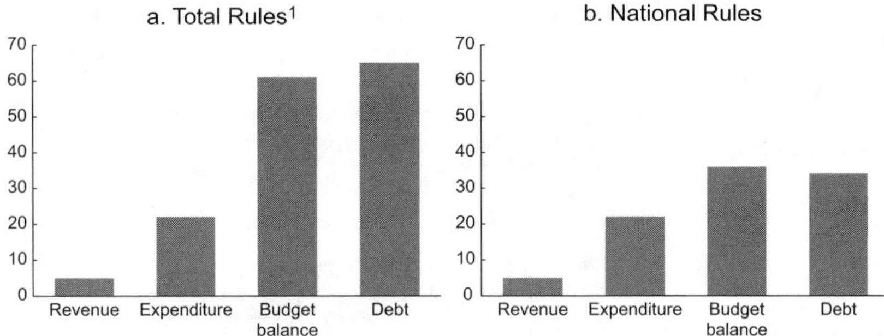

Figure 3.5 Types of Fiscal Rules, 2012 (Number of Countries with at Least One Fiscal Rule)

Sources: National authorities; and IMF staff assessment.

[1] Includes national and supranational rules.

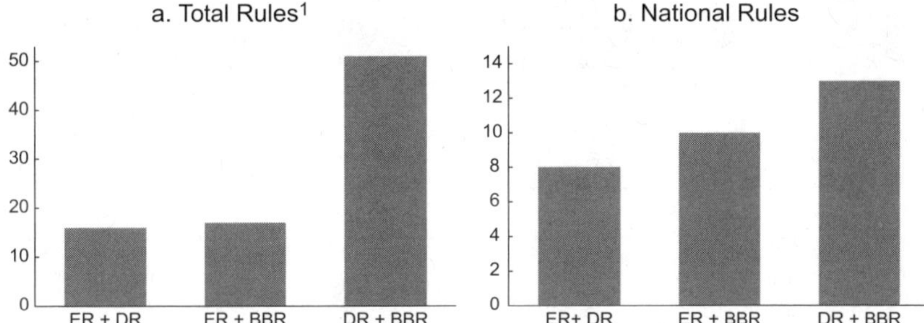

Figure 3.6 Widespread Combinations of Fiscal Rules in Use, 2012 (Number of Countries Combining Two Rules)

Sources: National authorities; and IMF staff assessment.

Note: BBR = budget balance rule; DR = debt rule; ER = expenditure rule.

[1] Includes national and supranational rules.

The expenditure rules are often combined with budget balance or debt rules to provide a greater anchor for debt sustainability (Figure 3.6). Revenue rules play a much more limited role, probably because they are less well suited to ensuring the sustainability of public finances.

Some regional differences in the types of fiscal rules persist. In particular, national debt rules predominate in low-income countries (Figure 3.7),[8] possibly reflecting institutional weaknesses that would complicate the implementation of expenditure rules. Budget balance rules that account for the economic cycle are still more prevalent in advanced than in emerging market economies. Pinpointing the output gap is challenging for the former group, but even more so for economies that are still undergoing structural changes. Thus, emerging market economies with budget balance rules that account for the cycle tend to use thresholds of actual economic activity rather than an output gap concept.

[8] However, the sample is small and comprises only four low-income countries with national fiscal rules. Other low-income countries operate under supranational rules.

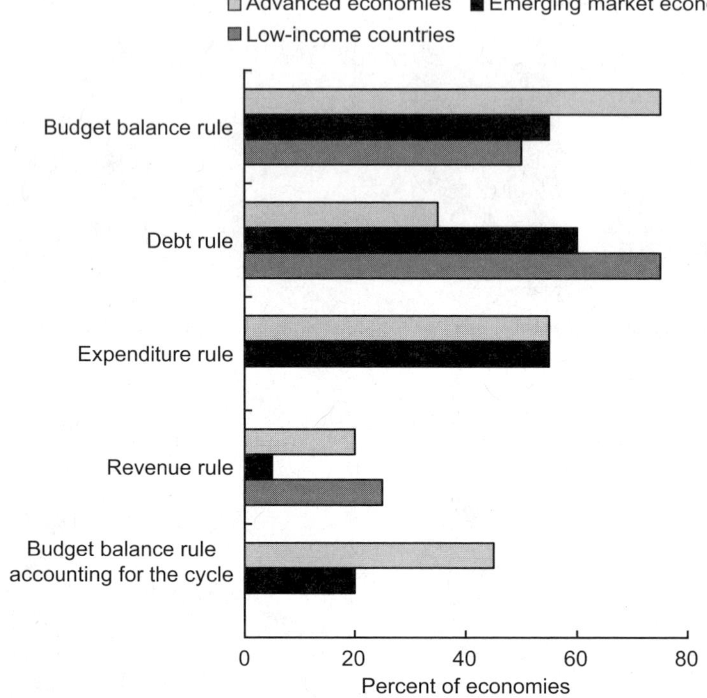

Figure 3.7 Regional Differences Regarding the Type of National Fiscal Rules (Share of Countries with Specific Type of Rule)

Source: IMF staff assessment.
Note: Includes countries with at least one national fiscal rule.

3.3. OTHER DESIGN FEATURES

3.3.1. Legislative Framework

The legislative basis differs by type of rule and country. The bulk of national expenditure, balance, and debt rules are embedded in statutory norms. The fewer existing revenue rules are implemented through a mix of political commitments, coalition agreements, and statutory norms (Table 3.2). Overall, a majority of budget balance and debt rules are supranational rules established by international treaties. Legislative support for national fiscal rules in advanced economies differs from that in emerging market economies and low-income countries (Figure 3.8). Expenditure rules are more commonly established through statutory norms in emerging market economies and low-income countries than in advanced economies. More limited medium-term planning capacity in the former group of countries has led to relatively simple forms of legislated expenditure rules (e.g., expenditure growth cannot exceed trend GDP growth). In advanced economies, however, expenditure rules tend to be more closely integrated into the MTBFs (see Chapter 4), which are sometimes part of coalition agreements. In advanced

TABLE 3.2

Statutory Basis of Fiscal Rules

	Type of Fiscal Rule			
Basis	**Expenditure**	**Revenue**	**Budget balance**	**Debt**
Political commitment	4	2	3	4
Coalition agreement	4	1	3	4
Statutory	12	2	21	14
International treaty[1]			41	47
Constitutional	0	1	2	1
Total	20	6	70	70

Sources: National authorities; and IMF staff assessment.
Note: Based on fiscal rules in effect by end-March 2012. The sum across columns can yield a higher number than the countries with rules because multiple rules are in place in many countries. All rules are national fiscal rules unless otherwise noted.
[1]These are all supranational fiscal rules.

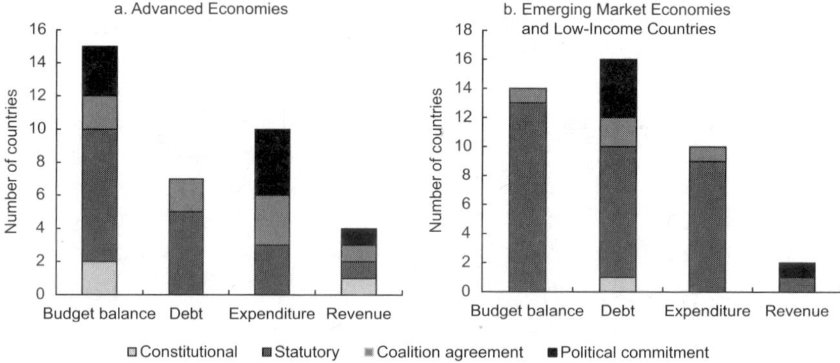

Figure 3.8 Statutory Basis of Fiscal Rules by Type of Rule and Economy, 2012

Sources: National authorities; and IMF staff assessment and calculations.
Note: Based on fiscal rules in effect by end-March 2012.

economies, more diverse legislative support of fiscal rules is observed. Only a few countries have enshrined fiscal rules in their constitutions, most of which were adopted after 2000 (Table 3.3).

The desirable legislative framework depends on country-specific circumstances. Rules enshrined in higher-level legislation are more difficult to reverse and therefore tend to be longer lasting because they are more difficult to modify even with a change of government. Although higher-level legislation thus tends to confer more stability to the framework, it may not necessarily enhance the effectiveness of the fiscal rules if enforcement mechanisms and accountability procedures are weak. For some countries with weak institutions, the simplicity of adoption and rapid implementation may also be key factors in deciding which legislative framework to use.

TABLE 3.3

Countries with Constitutional Legal Basis

Country	Type of rule	Year of adoption
France	Revenue	2006
Germany	Budget balance	1969, 2009
Poland	Debt	2004
Spain	Budget balance, debt, expenditure	2011
Switzerland	Budget balance	2003

Sources: National authorities; and IMF staff assessment.

Note: Includes only rules that took effect by end-March 2012. Other countries that have adopted fiscal rules in their constitutions but operational details are still being determined or include a long transition path until implementation are Hungary, Italy, and Spain. For the latter, the expenditure rule has already taken effect, while the structural budget balance rule takes effect in 2020.

3.3.2. Institutional and Economic Coverage

Although the majority of supranational budget balance and debt rules cover general government aggregates, less than half of the national rules do so. In monetary unions the importance of constraining general government arises from the potential moral hazard problems that could lead small countries to engage in fiscal neglect. Moreover, the higher legislative status of supranational rules makes it more likely for them to extend to the general government. Coverage of national expenditure rules and budget balance rules often does not extend beyond the central government, likely in response to autonomy and coordination issues with subnationals. For national revenue and debt rules, coverage of the general government is about as frequent as coverage of the central government alone (Figure 3.9).

About 20 percent of countries with fiscal rules in place by end-March 2012 exclude certain revenue or expenditure items from the target variable. Among these countries, the item most frequently excluded from targeted fiscal aggregates is capital expenditure. A rule that allows net lending only for investment purposes is termed a "golden rule" (Table 3.4). A few countries also exclude interest payments and cyclically sensitive expenditure from target variables.

Fiscal sustainability considerations argue for more comprehensive coverage, but other objectives and controllability arguments are put forward to exclude certain items. Broad coverage aims to manage total revenue and expenditure, and makes the target more transparent and easier to monitor. Nevertheless, excluding capital expenditure, for example, is sometimes seen as desirable because it is generally expected to contribute positively to long-term growth. However, this exclusion weakens the link with gross debt; not all capital expenditure is necessarily productive and other items such as health care and education expenditure may raise potential growth even more. Excluding interest payments and cyclically sensitive expenditure from target variables is also often discussed because they are not under government control in the short run and require short-term adjustments in other expenditure categories, with capital spending often the easiest to cut.

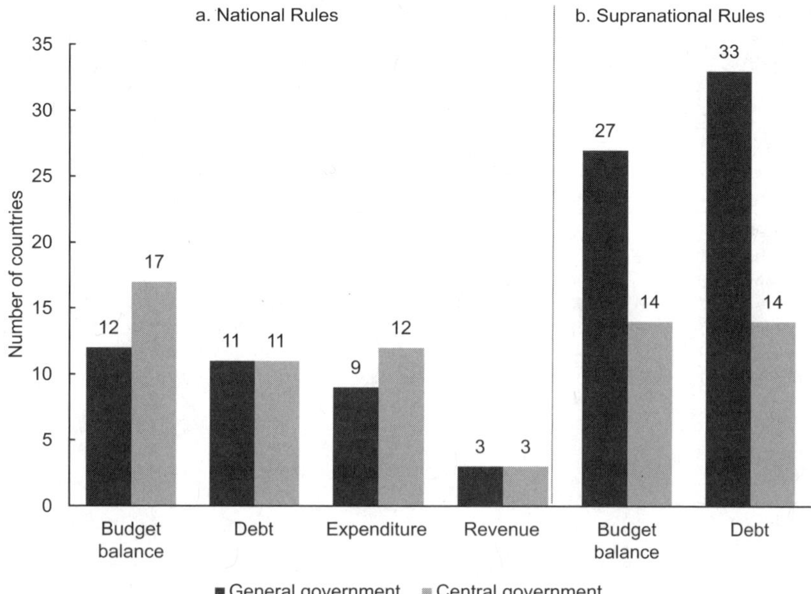

Figure 3.9 Coverage of Fiscal Rules, 2012

Sources: National authorities; and IMF staff assessment and calculations.

Note: Based on fiscal rules in effect by end-March 2012. "General government" also comprises those rules that cover the nonfinancial public sector.

TABLE 3.4

Coverage of Aggregate

Item most frequently excluded	Countries where exclusions apply (type of rule)
Interest payments	Finland (ER), France (ER), Spain (ER), Sweden (ER)
Cyclically sensitive expenditure	Denmark (ER), Finland (ER), Switzerland (BBR)
Capital expenditure	National: Brazil (ER, DR), Ecuador (ER), Hong Kong SAR (BBR), Japan (BBR)
	Supranational: WAEMU and CEMAC (BBR, DR, foreign-financed capital spending excluded)

Sources: National authorities; and IMF staff assessment.

Note: Based on fiscal rules in effect by end-March 2012. BBR = budget balance rule; CEMAC = Central African Economic and Monetary Community; DR = debt rule; ER = expenditure rule; WAEMU = West African Economic and Monetary Union.

3.3.3. Escape Clauses

Escape clauses can provide the rules with the flexibility to deal with rare events. The parallel with escape clauses within fiscal responsibility laws discussed in Chapter 2 is evident. They should include (1) a very limited range of factors that allow the clauses to be triggered in legislation, (2) clear guidelines on the interpretation and determination of events (including voting rules), and (3) a specific path back to the rule and treatment of accumulated deviations.

Formal escape clause provisions are primarily found in more recently introduced rules, and trigger events differ. Escape clauses exist for budget balance rules and debt rules in Brazil, Colombia, Germany, Mauritius, Mexico, Jamaica,

TABLE 3.5

Fiscal Rules with Escape Clauses

Country (year)	Natural disaster	Economic recession	Banking system bailout, guarantee schemes	Change in government	Change in budget coverage	Other events outside government control	Voting mechanism defined	Transition path defined
Brazil (2000)	X	X	—	—	—	—	X	—
Colombia (2011)	—	X	—	—	—	X	—	—
Germany (2010)	X	X	—	—	—	X	X	X
Jamaica (2010)	X	X	—	—	—	X	—	—
Mauritius (2008)	X	X	—	—	—	X	—	—
Mexico (2006)	—	X	—	—	—	—	—	—
Panama (2008)	X	X	—	—	—	X	—	X
Peru (2000)	X	X	—	—	—	X	—	X
Romania (2010)	—	X	—	X	X	X	—	X
Slovak Republic (2012)	X	X	X	—	—	X	—	—
Spain (2002)	X	X	—	—	—	X	X	X
Switzerland (2003)	X	X	—	—	—	X	X	X
EU member states (2005)	—	X	—	—	—	—	—	X
WAEMU (2000)	—	X	—	—	—	—	—	—

Sources: National authorities; and IMF staff assessment.

Note: For more details about the escape clauses, see Appendix 3.2. X = escape clause present. WAEMU = West African Economic and Monetary Union.

Panama, Peru, Romania, the Slovak Republic, Spain, and Switzerland (Table 3.5 and Appendix 3.2). In all cases, the escape clauses allow for temporary deviations from the rules in the event of a recession or a significant growth slowdown. Other triggers include natural disasters (Brazil, Germany, Jamaica, Mauritius, Panama, Peru, the Slovak Republic, Spain, and Switzerland), and banking system bailout (the Slovak Republic).[9]

Escape clauses have not always been well specified. Although it is difficult for rules to be both comprehensive and specific about potential trigger events, escape clauses in the past have occasionally left too much scope for interpretation. For example, until the constitutional change in 2009, the German rule allowed for deviations for "a disturbance of the macroeconomic equilibrium," which was frequently used to justify exceeding the deficit ceiling. In India, the escape clause allowed the government to deviate from the targets in exceptional circumstances "as the central government may specify." The Swiss and the Spanish fiscal rules also include rather broad "exceptional circumstances" provisions, although they do need to be justified by certain events (such as natural disaster, severe recession, and the like). In Switzerland, the escape clause can be invoked only by a supermajority in parliament, and in both countries, it must be accompanied by a medium-term correction plan.

[9] Denmark provides an example of an escape clause for a revenue rule, which aims to limit the size of government rather than ensure sustainability. Derogation from the rule is allowed if a tax rate is raised for environmental reasons or to fulfill Denmark's EU obligations and if extra revenue is used to reduce other taxes.

Escape clauses are embedded to some extent in the EU and WAEMU supranational fiscal rules. The escape clause introduced in the EU with the 2005 reform of the SGP provides that an excessive deficit procedure may not be opened if the deficit is close to its ceiling and the breach is temporary (both conditions have to be fulfilled simultaneously). It also allows for an extension of deadlines for the correction of the excessive deficit in case of adverse economic developments. In WAEMU, the escape clause is triggered by a large and temporary negative shock to real GDP and revenues, but the clause does not specify a transition path back to the rule (Table 3.5).

3.3.4. Automatic Correction Mechanisms

In addition to the sanction devices discussed in Chapter 2, automatic corrections of ex post deviations from the rule can raise enforceability, but to date they have been built into very few rules. As with other elements of rules, specifying the mechanism clearly and anchoring it in legislation can help adherence, but ultimately political will matters most. Some examples are summarized below:

- The Swiss and German structural budget balance rules contain automatic correction mechanisms known as "debt brakes" (see German Federal Ministry of Finance, 2011, and Bodmer, 2006). In both countries, deviations from the structural budget balance rule (positive or negative) are stored in a notional account. When the accumulated deviation exceeds a threshold, improvements in the structural balance are required within a defined time frame to reverse the deviation. The main differences between the two countries are the thresholds (1.0 percent of GDP in Germany per ordinary law and 1.5 percent per constitution; and 6 percent of expenditure in Switzerland) and the type of deviation that needs to be corrected. In Germany, only those deviations that did not result from errors in real GDP growth projections enter the notional account, whereas in Switzerland all misses are tallied. The latter course is more transparent but provides less flexibility to accommodate errors outside the control of government. In Switzerland, the excess amount must be eliminated within the next three annual budgets. In Germany, overruns only need to be reduced during an economic recovery to avoid procyclical tightening and can be corrected via expenditure and revenue measures.
- Poland's and the Slovak Republic's debt rules, which set a 60 percent debt-to-GDP ceiling, include thresholds that trigger actions to prevent the rule from being missed. In the Slovak Republic, when the debt-to-GDP ratio reaches 50 percent, the minister of finance is obliged to explain the increase to parliament and suggest measures to reverse its growth. At 53 percent of GDP, the cabinet is required to pass a package of measures to trim the debt and freeze wages. At 55 percent, expenditures are to be cut automatically by 3 percent and the next year's budgetary expenditures would be frozen, except for cofinancing of EU funds. At 57 percent of GDP, the cabinet must

submit a balanced budget.[10] Ideally, the later trigger points would not be needed if effective action is taken earlier.

- So-called sequesters are another form of automatic correction. In the United States, as a result of the failure of the Joint Select Committee on Debt Reduction to reach agreement on deficit-reduction proposals, automatic spending cuts (sequesters) are scheduled to take effect in March 2013 if Congress does not take legislative action. In this case, the sequestration is intended to be a one-time adjustment to the expenditure path rather than a recurrent mechanism embedded in a fiscal rules framework. Sequesters also tend to have the disadvantage of creating a bias against capital spending, which is the easiest item to cut quickly, as experienced in the United States in the 1990s.

Under the Fiscal Compact, EU countries' national structural budget balance rules will need to include an automatic correction mechanism. In light of the role that such mechanisms can play in avoiding a ratcheting up of debt from target misses, the 25 EU members that signed the treaty have committed to creating appropriate mechanisms, in line with guidelines to be issued by the European Commission.

3.4. THE "NEXT-GENERATION" FISCAL RULES: RESPONSES TO THE CRISIS

During the recent economic crisis, many countries put their fiscal rules into abeyance. The extreme output shock led many economies to stray from the limits imposed by rules. Moreover, countercyclical stimulus measures in most cases pushed aggregates beyond the constraints for normal times. Because few countries had escape clauses in place, rules either were not enforced or were altered by loosening the original ceilings while also defining adjustment paths that provided some flexibility given the high level of economic uncertainty. Table 3.6 provides some country examples.

A few countries were able to build on their precrisis reforms to anchor their exits from the crisis. For example, Germany has enshrined a structural budget balance rule in its constitution (deficit ceiling of 0.35 percent of GDP for the federal government and structurally balanced budgets for the Länder). After a transition period, which started in 2011, this rule will take full effect in 2016 for the federal government and 2020 for the states.

Many other countries established new rules or overhauled existing ones (Table 3.7). A variety of motivations led to these decisions—to reassure markets about the sustainability of fiscal policy and public finances, to commit to and lock in sustained adjustment efforts, and to guide expectations about the medium-term fiscal stance.

[10] After 2017, the debt limit will be lowered to 50 percent of GDP, and the correction mechanism will start to operate when the debt-to-GDP ratio approaches 40 percent of GDP.

TABLE 3.6

Fiscal Rules during the Crisis: Examples of Adjustments

Country	Description of revisions to rule
Bulgaria	The expenditure rule (ceiling on the expenditure-to-GDP ratio of 40 percent) was discontinued in 2010 and 2011, after its breach in 2009. The rule was reintroduced in 2012. The budget balance rule was adjusted from a balanced budget or surplus (2006–08) to reducing the overall balance continuously to less than 3 percent of GDP; from 2012 the deficit limit is 2 percent of GDP. Both the expenditure and budget balance rules were recently strengthened with an amendment in the Organic Budget Law, which came into force in January 2012.
Chile	The ceiling under the structural budget balance rule was widened from a surplus of 1 percent of GDP (2001–07) to a surplus of 0.5 percent of GDP in 2008, and a structural budget balance of zero in 2009. After using a de facto escape clause to accommodate countercyclical measures and a widening of the deficit, the current administration (2010–14) specified a target path to converge to a 1 percent of GDP structural deficit by 2014.
Denmark	In 2009 the expenditure rule related to public consumption was revised to reduce its share as a proportion of cyclically adjusted GDP to 26.5 percent by 2015. The structural budget balance target was revised from a surplus target by 2010 (set in 2001), to at least balance in 2011 to 2015 (set in 2007), to a structural deficit of less than 0.5 percent in 2015 and a balanced structural budget by 2020 (set in 2009).
Finland	In 2007 the government targeted a structural surplus of 1 percent of potential GDP but decided in February 2009 that it can temporarily deviate from the target if structural reforms are undertaken to improve general government finances in the medium or longer term. Since 2011, a target for central government balance of 1 percent deficit has been followed. The debt reduction rule was abandoned in 2008 and adjusted in 2011 with a view to achieve a substantial reduction in the central government debt-to-GDP ratio by the end of the parliamentary term (2015).
Israel	The ceilings of the Deficit Reduction Law were relaxed in the biannual budget adopted in July 2009 to allow a budget deficit of 6 percent and 5.5 percent of GDP for 2009 and 2010, respectively, and real growth of expenditure of 3 percent for 2009. The Deficit Reduction and Budgetary Expenditure Limitation Laws (2010) set a transition path to 2014 (1 percent of GDP deficit).
Panama	Budget balance and debt rules were revised in 2009. The law limits the deficit of the nonfinancial public sector to 1 percent of GDP and sets a target for public debt at 40 percent of GDP by 2015. The former was adjusted in June 2009 to a deficit ceiling of 2–2.5 percent of GDP, with the gradual transition period extended to four years. Under the new rules, the nonfinancial public sector ceiling can be relaxed depending on when real GDP growth in the United States and Panama falls below specified thresholds. The debt target was extended to 2017.
United Kingdom	From Nov. 2008 to Dec. 2009, the government departed from its budget balance and debt rules and adopted a temporary operating rule: "to set policies to improve the cyclically adjusted current budget each year, once the economy emerges from the downturn, so it reaches balance and debt is falling as a proportion of GDP once the global shocks have worked their way through the economy in full."

Sources: National authorities; and IMF staff assessment.

TABLE 3.7

National Fiscal Rules Adopted since 2010

Type of rule	Countries
Budget balance rule[1]	Austria, Colombia, Italy, Portugal, Serbia, Spain, United Kingdom
Pay-as-you-go rule[2]	Japan, United States
Debt rule	Hungary,[3] Serbia, Slovak Republic, Spain, United Kingdom
Expenditure rule	Ecuador, Israel, Japan,[4] Namibia, Poland, Romania, Spain, United States[5]

Sources: National authorities; and IMF staff assessment.
Note: The table also includes rules that were adopted but have not yet taken effect.
[1] All of these budget balance rules account for the economic cycle.
[2] The pay-as-you-go rules are considered procedural rather than numerical rules and thus are not counted in the data set.
[3] Constitutional requirement to cut the government debt-to-GDP ratio annually until it falls below 50 percent of GDP, starting in 2016.
[4] Limits on expenditure as part of the medium-term fiscal framework introduced in 2010.
[5] Discretionary spending caps enacted in August 2011 and automatic spending cuts (sequesters) scheduled to take effect in March 2013 if Congress does not take legislative action.

Although many reforms concern the European countries hardest hit by the crisis, the trend is broader as the examples below show.

- Most EU member states for which new rules have already taken effect are transition economies (e.g., Poland, Romania, and the Slovak Republic), while others are gradually adopting rules (Austria, Hungary, and Spain) (see Appendix 3.3). The process in the EU will speed up with the Fiscal Compact, under which countries are required to adopt, either in their constitutions or in other durable legislation, a structural budget balance rule by 2014 (see Box 3.1).
- In Spain, the constitutional amendment of September 2011 and its corresponding organic legislation (2012) require that the structural deficit for all levels of government stay within the limits set by the EU, and set debt limits for each level of government. The rule will enter into force in 2020.
- Portugal's new budgetary framework law (May 2011) establishes that the structural budget balance cannot be less than the medium-term objective in the SGP.
- Austria passed an amendment to its federal budget law stipulating that, from 2017 onward, the structural deficit at the federal level (including social insurance) must not exceed 0.35 percent of GDP.
- Italy approved a constitutional amendment (April 2012) that introduces the principle of a balanced budget in structural terms with details and implementation principles to be specified in secondary legislation by end-February 2013.
- Outside the EU, Colombia adopted a structural budget balance rule with a 1 percent of GDP deficit limit, taking effect in 2022. Serbia introduced in late 2012 a balanced budget rule that corrects for past deficit deviations and allows partial operation of automatic fiscal stabilizers, and establishes a debt ceiling.

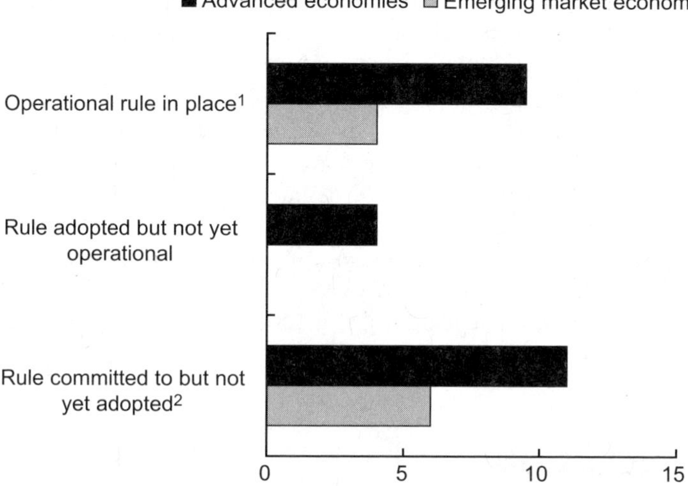

Figure 3.10 Number of Countries with Structural Budget Balance Rules

Sources: National authorities; and IMF staff assessment.

[1] Includes those with a clearly specified transition path.

[2] Includes those EU member states that have signed the Fiscal Compact but have not yet adopted a structural budget balance rule.

These next-generation fiscal rules explicitly combine sustainability objectives with more flexibility to accommodate economic shocks. Following the examples of rules adopted earlier in Chile,[11] Germany, and Switzerland, many of the new rules set budget targets in cyclically adjusted terms (e.g., those in Austria, Colombia, Portugal, Spain, and the United Kingdom) or account for the cycle in other ways (e.g., those in Panama and Serbia) (Figure 3.10). Some also correct automatically for past deviations with a view to avoiding the "ratcheting up" effects of debt (e.g., that in Serbia, and the debt brakes in Germany and Switzerland). Others combine new expenditure rules with new or existing debt rules, thereby providing operational guidance as well as a link to debt sustainability—if the rules were to operate separately, one of these criteria would be missing (e.g., Poland's rule).

At the same time, the design features of fiscal rules have become more comprehensive, and supporting arrangements have been strengthened—for example, by enshrining rules in legislation (away from political agreements), by adopting explicit escape clauses, and by providing for a path back to compliance if deviations occur.[12]

But the greater complexity of the rules frameworks also creates new challenges. The increased number of rules, their interaction, and their sophistication can

[11] The fiscal rule in Chile accounts not only for the economic cycle but also for deviations of copper and molybdenum prices from their long-term trends.

[12] Schaechter and others (2012) develop a summary fiscal rules index, which also accounts for the number of rules per country.

complicate implementation and make compliance more difficult to explain and monitor. To address the first challenge, several countries are reforming their budgetary procedures and MTBFs (e.g., Austria, Greece, Ireland, and Portugal). Fiscal councils can also play an important role (see Chapter 6). In a number of countries, governance reforms have set up, or adopted plans for, independent fiscal councils. Such bodies can raise voters' awareness of the consequences of certain policy paths, helping them reward desirable options and sanction poorer ones. Although the mere existence of fiscal councils and their ability to increase public awareness may not be sufficient to achieve good outcomes (see Debrun, Gérard, and Harris, 2012), combined with fiscal rules, councils can potentially raise, for governments, the reputational risk associated with noncompliance and serve as an additional enforcement tool.

3.5. CONCLUSION

The use of fiscal rules has become more widespread, especially as a means to anchor the fiscal exit from the recent global economic and financial crisis. Three waves can be observed. The first surge occurred in the early and mid-1990s, in part in response to bank and debt crises, but also to effect the consolidation required to qualify for the euro area. The second wave was driven largely by emerging market economies in the early 2000s; many adopted more than one rule and reformed fiscal and budgetary frameworks in response to experience with fiscal excesses. The third wave can be attributed to the recent crisis. A number of countries, especially in the euro area, are complementing supranational rules with national ones while other economies are upgrading their existing fiscal frameworks and rules. Most countries now have several rules in place, often combining the objective of sustainability with the need for flexibility to account for economic shocks (via budget balance rules that correct for the cycle).

The next-generation fiscal rules are designed to strike a better balance between discipline and sustainability and flexibility goals—they tend to account for economic shocks, and are often complemented by a battery of other institutional arrangements necessary to support the implementation and monitoring of these rules. These next-generation rules, however, are inclined to be more complex, creating new challenges for design, implementation, and monitoring. So far, communication policies seem slow to catch up, but a number of countries have started to put greater emphasis on the use of independent fiscal councils as monitoring and assessment devices to fill this gap.

Although design features of fiscal rules continue to differ across countries, convergence has started in some areas. Most fiscal rules have at a minimum a statutory basis, and anchoring national fiscal rules in the constitution (or other durable legislation) is part of the commitment under the EU Fiscal Compact. Until recently, few fiscal rules included well-specified escape clauses, but countries adopting or changing rules in recent years have defined clearer trigger points. Automatic correction mechanisms and sanctions are not yet widespread, but the former is another required feature of the Fiscal Compact. Although empirical evidence suggests that fiscal rules have generally been a factor in the success of fiscal adjustment, causality is difficult to assess (Debrun and others, 2008). Time will tell whether the next-generation rules provide the envisaged contribution to fiscal discipline. Given their relatively high degree of complexity, their effectiveness will also depend on country-specific institutional capacity.

REFERENCES

Baunsgaard, T., M. Villafuerte, M. Poplawski-Ribeiro, and C. Richmond, 2012, "Fiscal Frameworks for Resource Rich Developing Countries," IMF Staff Discussion Note 12/04 (Washington: International Monetary Fund).

Bodmer, F., 2006, "The Swiss Debt Brake: How It Works and What Can Go Wrong," *Schweizerische Zeitschrift für Volkswirtschaft und Statistik*, Vol. 142, No. 3, pp. 307–30.

Debrun, X., M. Gérard, and J. Harris, 2012, "Fiscal Policies in Crisis Mode: Has the Time for Fiscal Councils Come at Last?" paper prepared for the 4th Annual Meeting of OECD Parliamentary Budget Officials and Independent Fiscal Institutions, Paris, February 23–24.

Debrun, X., L. Moulin, A. Turrini, J. Ayuso-i-Casals, and M.S. Kumar, 2008, "Tied to the Mast? National Fiscal Rules in the European Union," *Economic Policy*, Vol. 23, No. 4, pp. 297–362.

German Federal Ministry of Finance, 2011, "Compendium on the Federation's Budget Rule as set out in Article 115 of the Basic Law." Available via the Internet: http://www.bundesfinanzministerium.de/Content/DE/Standardartikel/Themen/Oeffentliche_Finanzen/Schuldenbremse/2012-06-14-kompendium-en.html.

Kopits, G., and S. Symansky, 1998, *Fiscal Rules*, IMF Occasional Paper No. 162 (Washington: International Monetary Fund).

Kumar, M., E. Baldacci, A. Schaechter, C. Caceres, D. Kim, X. Debrun, J. Escolano, J. Jonas, P. Karam, I. Yakadina, and R. Zymek, 2009, "Fiscal Rules—Anchoring Expectations for Sustainable Public Finances," IMF Staff Paper (Washington: International Monetary Fund). Available via the Internet: http://www.imf.org/external/np/pp/eng/2009/121609.pdf.

Ljungman, G., 2008, "Expenditure Ceilings—A Survey," IMF Working Paper 08/282 (Washington: International Monetary Fund).

Ruggiero, E., forthcoming, "Togo: A Framework for Growth-Supporting Fiscal Rules" (Washington: International Monetary Fund).

Schaechter, A., T. Kinda, N. Budina, and A. Weber, 2012, "Fiscal Rules in Response to the Crisis—Toward the 'Next-Generation' Rules. A New Dataset," IMF Working Paper 12/187 (Washington: International Monetary Fund). Available via the Internet: http://www.imf.org/external/datamapper/FiscalRules/map/map.htm.

APPENDIX 3.1. COUNTRY COVERAGE

List of countries that had national or supranational (or both) fiscal rules in effect during the period from 1985 to end-March 2012 (or with clearly specified transition regimes).

Advanced economies	Emerging market economies	Low-income countries
Australia	Antigua and Barbuda[1]	Armenia
Austria	Argentina[2]	Benin[1]
Belgium[1]	Botswana	Burkina Faso[1]
Canada[2]	Brazil	Cameroon[1]
Cyprus[1]	Bulgaria	Cape Verde
Czech Republic	Chile	Central African Republic[1]
Denmark	Colombia	Chad[1]
Estonia	Costa Rica	Congo[1]
Finland	Ecuador	Côte d'Ivoire[1]
France	Equatorial Guinea[1]	Dominica[1]
Germany	Hungary	Gabon[1]
Greece[1]	India[2]	Grenada[1]
Hong Kong SAR	Indonesia	Guinea Bissau[1]
Iceland[2]	Jamaica	Kenya
Ireland[1]	Latvia[1]	Kosovo
Israel	Lithuania	Mali[1]
Italy[1]	Malta[1]	Niger[1]
Japan	Mauritius	Nigeria
Luxembourg	Mexico	Senegal[1]
Netherlands	Namibia	Togo[1]
New Zealand	Pakistan	
Norway	Panama	
Portugal[1]	Peru	
Russia[2]	Poland	
Slovak Republic[1]	Romania	
Slovenia[1]	Serbia	
Spain	Sri Lanka	
Sweden	St. Kitts and Nevis[1]	
Switzerland	St. Lucia[1]	
United Kingdom	St. Vincent and the Grenadines[1]	
United States		

Sources: Schaechter and others (2012).

[1] Countries with only supranational rules in effect by end-March 2012.

[2] Countries that had rules in effect at some point between 1985 and end-March 2012 but no longer did at end-March 2012.

APPENDIX 3.2. ESCAPE CLAUSES: COUNTRY EXAMPLES

Country	Description of escape clauses
Brazil (2000)	Real GDP growth of less than 1 percent for four quarters, and natural disaster but can only be invoked with congressional approval.
Colombia (2011)	In case of extraordinary events threatening the macroeconomic stability of the country, enforcement of the fiscal rule may be temporarily suspended, subject to the favorable opinion of CONFIS (an internal fiscal council headed by the finance minister).
Germany (2010)	Natural disasters or unusual emergency situations that are outside government control and have major impact on the financial position of the government. Absolute majority of parliament is needed to trigger the escape clause. Parliament must approve an amortization plan with a specified time frame for reducing the accumulated deviation. Until 2010, escape clause in case of a "distortion of the macroeconomic equilibrium."
Jamaica (2010)	The targets may be exceeded on the grounds of national security, national emergency, or such other exceptional grounds as the minister may specify in an order subject to affirmative resolution.
Mauritius (2008)	Temporary deviations in case of emergencies and large public investment projects.
Mexico (2006)	If non-oil revenues are below their potential because of a negative output gap, there can be a deficit equivalent to the shortfall.
Panama (2008)	If real GDP grows by less than 1 percent, the nonfinancial public sector deficit ceiling can be relaxed to 3 percent of GDP in the first year, followed by a gradual transition to the original ceiling (1 percent of GDP) within three years.
Peru (2000)	If real GDP declines, or in case of other emergencies declared by the congress at the request of the executive, the deficit ceiling can be relaxed to 2.5 percent of GDP. The executive must specify deficit and expenditure ceilings to be applied during the exception period. In both cases, a minimum adjustment of 0.5 percent of GDP is required until the 1 percent deficit ceiling is reached.
Romania (2010)	In case of a government change, the new government will announce whether its program is consistent with the medium-term budgetary framework (MTBF) and if not the ministry of finance will prepare a revised MTBF, to be approved by parliament and subject to the review and opinion of the fiscal council.
Slovak Republic (2012)	Escape clauses for a major recession, banking system bailout, natural disaster, and international guarantee schemes.
Spain (2002)	In case of natural disasters or an exceptional slowdown, exceptional budget deficits are to be accompanied by a medium-term financial plan to correct this situation within the next three years (to be approved by a majority vote by the parliament).
Switzerland (2003)	The government can approve by supermajority a budget deviating from the budget balance rule in "exceptional circumstances," which are defined in Budget Law as natural disaster, severe recession, and changes in accounting methods.
EU member states (2005)	An excessive deficit procedure may not be opened when the 3 percent deficit limit is exceeded only temporarily and exceptionally, and the deficit is close to the deficit limit (both conditions need to apply). Deadlines for excessive deficit correction can be extended in case of adverse economic developments.
WAEMU (2000)	Temporary and pronounced shortfall of real GDP (at least 3 percentage points below the average of the previous three years) and budget revenue (at least 10 percentage points below the average of the previous three years).

Sources: National authorities; and IMF staff assessment.

Note: WAEMU = West African Economic and Monetary Union.

APPENDIX 3.3. NEW FISCAL RULES ADOPTED SINCE 2010

Country	Description of rules
Austria	Parliament passed on December 7, 2011, an amendment to the federal budget law stipulating that, from 2017 onward, the structural deficit at the federal level (including social insurance) shall not exceed 0.35 percent of GDP. The amendment is conceptually similar to the German debt-brake rule but has so far not been able to be anchored in the constitution. Operational details are still being prepared in separate laws and regulations.
Colombia	A structural budget balance rule for the central government was approved by congress in June 2011. It sets a path that lowers the structural deficit to 2.3 percent of GDP by 2014 and provides a ceiling of 1 percent of GDP effective in 2022. The rule allows for fiscal expansion when the expected output growth rate is at least 2 percentage points lower than the long-term rate and creates a sovereign wealth fund.
Ecuador	A new expenditure rule was adopted in 2010 and took effect in 2011, but the existing budget balance and debt rules were dropped. The expenditure rule states that current expenditure cannot be higher than permanent income including oil revenue. External financing and oil revenues are to be used only to finance public investment.
France	The Multi-Year Public Finance Planning Act sets binding minimum targets for the net impact of new revenue measures.
Hungary	A debt rule, included in the constitution, will come into effect in 2016 and require cutting the government debt-to-GDP ratio annually until it falls to less than 50 percent of GDP. Debt reduction can be suspended when real GDP contracts.
Italy	A constitutional amendment was approved in April 2012 that introduces the principle of a structural balanced budget with details and implementation principles to be specified in secondary legislation by end-February 2013.
Japan	The Fiscal Management Strategy, which includes a pay-as-you-go rule, was adopted in 2010 (by cabinet decision). The rule implies that any measure that involves increases in expenditure or decreases in revenue needs to be compensated for by permanent reductions in expenditures or permanent revenue-raising measures. A medium-term fiscal framework, including a limit on expenditure, was also introduced.[1]
Namibia	An expenditure rule took effect in 2010 that caps the ratio of expenditures to GDP at 30 percent.
Poland	A new expenditure rule (beginning in 2011) limits the increase in central government discretionary spending and all newly enacted spending to 1 percent in real terms (based on consumer price index inflation) (defined in 2011 budget law).
Portugal	The new budgetary framework law (May 2011) approved a fiscal rule establishing that the general government structural balance cannot be less than the medium-term objective in the Stability and Growth Pact. It also includes requirements for a correction of the multiannual plan whenever deviations from the target occurs. The rule will come into effect in 2015.
Romania	Beginning in 2010 general government expenditure growth should not exceed projected nominal GDP for three years until the budget balance is in surplus. Moreover, personnel expenditure limits are binding for two years.
Serbia	In October 2010, fiscal responsibility provisions were introduced in the budget system law of 2009. These include numerical fiscal rules and the adoption of a fiscal council. The fiscal rules comprise a budget balance rule that corrects for past deficit deviations and allows a partial operation of automatic fiscal stabilizers. A debt rule provides a ceiling on general government debt of 45 percent of GDP.
Slovak Republic	In December 2011, a constitutional bill was adopted, taking effect March 1, 2012, that caps public debt at 60 percent of GDP. Automatic adjustment mechanisms take effect when the debt-to-GDP ratio reaches 50 percent. The bill also calls for setting up a fiscal council to monitor and evaluate fiscal performance.

Country	Description of rules
Spain	A constitutional amendment (2011) and its corresponding organic legislation (2012) require that the structural deficit for all levels of government stay within the limits set by the EU, and set debt limits for each level of government. The rules will enter into force in 2020, with transition rules in effect until then. The amendment also introduces expenditure ceilings and constrains growth in expenditure for all levels of government.
United Kingdom	The new cyclically adjusted budget balance rule, beginning in 2010, aims to achieve cyclically adjusted current balance by the end of the rolling five-year forecast period (currently by FY2016/17). The new debt rule (from 2010) targets a falling public sector net-debt-to-GDP ratio by FY2015/16.
United States	Statutory pay-as-you-go rules for revenue and mandatory spending were reinstated in February 2010 but are subject to important exemptions. In August 2011, Congress enacted discretionary spending caps, saving about $900 billion over the next decade. If Congress does not take legislative action, additional automatic spending cuts (sequesters) are scheduled to take effect in March 2013 to produce savings of US$1.2 trillion over a decade, with one-half coming from defense spending and the other half from domestic programs, excluding Social Security, Medicaid, parts of Medicare, and certain other entitlement programs.[1]

Sources: National authorities; and IMF staff assessment.

[1]The pay-as-you go rules are not counted in the data set of this report because they are considered to be procedural rather than numerical rules.

CHAPTER 4

Medium-Term Budget Frameworks in Advanced Economies: Objectives, Design, and Performance

JASON HARRIS, RICHARD HUGHES, GÖSTA LJUNGMAN, AND CARLA SATERIALE

Budgeting in most countries focuses on preparing an annual plan for revenue and expenditure, but an understanding of fiscal developments beyond this relatively short time horizon is important for the ability to make the right choices. Budget decisions made today generally have consequences for several years to come, and events expected to occur in two or three years time may call for action today. This realization has prompted many countries to introduce medium-term budget frameworks (MTBFs).

An MTBF is a set of institutional arrangements for prioritizing, presenting, and managing revenue and expenditure in a multiyear perspective. Such a framework enables governments to demonstrate the impact of current and proposed policies over the course of several years, signal or set future budget priorities, and ultimately achieve better control of public expenditure. An MTBF, therefore, does not refer solely to the actual numerical multiyear revenue and expenditure projections and restrictions presented alongside a given budget. Rather, an MTBF comprises all the systems, rules, and procedures that ensure the government's fiscal plans are drawn up with a view to their impact over several years.

MTBFs typically constitute part of a wider set of frameworks for medium-term fiscal policy planning, which are described in Box 4.1. Although an MTBF is not the same as a multiannual budget in which appropriations are authorized for a period longer than one year, in its most binding form it does provide a set of constraints on future budgets, against which any changes are reconciled. However, an MTBF is consistent with maintaining annual budgets. Therefore, even though MTBFs provide an administrative mechanism for multiyear planning of expenditure, the time horizon for the legislative appropriation of expenditure remains strictly annual in all countries considered in this chapter.

There is no single MTBF model, but rather a range of country approaches to extending the budget horizon beyond the year ahead. Indeed, any country

BOX 4.1 MTBF Terms and Concepts

Medium-term budget framework (MTBF)—institutional arrangements in the budget process governing the requirement to present certain medium-term financial information at specific times, procedures for making multiyear forecasts and plans for revenue and expenditure, and obligations to set numerical expenditure limits beyond the annual budget horizon.

Medium-term fiscal framework—standing requirements to commit to, report against, and be held accountable for medium-term aggregate fiscal objectives, such as debt limits, surplus targets or deficit ceilings, or broad expenditure limits. For the purpose of this chapter, expenditure ceilings are considered part of the MTBF if they cover all or a subset of *central* government.

Binding framework—a framework that holds government accountable for the multiyear expenditure parameters (estimates or ceilings) set in year $t-1$ or earlier, when, in year t, the budget for $t+1$ and new medium-term estimates for $t+2$ and $t+3$ are set. Accountability means that some active measure or action is required if there is evidence that the previously set expenditure parameter is going to be exceeded. A *fixed framework* is a subset of binding frameworks in which medium-term expenditure limits are set, but are not subsequently revised.

Indicative framework—a framework in which updates of medium-term estimates can be made without reference to the same estimate set in the previous year, and in which the appropriations in government's annual budget proposal for $t+1$ are not reconciled against the medium-term estimates for $t+2$ made in the previous year (or previous budget update, e.g., prebudget report).

Appropriation—maximum limits for individual expenditure items as defined in the budget. In this chapter, appropriations refer both to the expenditure limits set in the budget as adopted by parliament and to any sublimits imposed by government on ministries and agencies.

Estimate—an assessment of the expected outturn of a revenue or expenditure item. In the chapter, "estimate" is used as a collective term for *forecasts* and *no-policy-change assessments*, for which the distinction between these concepts is unimportant. (In some countries, the term "estimate" is used to refer to the legislated appropriations in the budget.)

Forecast or *projection*—an assessment of the most likely outturn, taking into account all available information. "Forecast" and "projection" are used interchangeably, with no conceptual difference between the two.

No-policy-change assessment—extrapolation into the future of a revenue or expenditure item under the assumption that today's policies are kept unchanged. The definition of current policy differs between countries, with some countries emphasizing an extrapolation of *existing legislation* whereas others also incorporate policies that have been proposed to parliament but that have not yet been formally adopted.

Expenditure ceiling—a maximum limit on an aggregate of expenditure that is broader than an individual appropriation. A *fixed ceiling* refers to a limit that is not revised upward once it has been set, and applies to the ex post expenditure outturn. A *flexible ceiling* is a limit that can be revised upward after it has been set.

that produces some kind of revenue and expenditure projections alongside its annual budgets can be said to practice a simple form of medium-term budgeting. At the same time, as more and more countries introduce a multiyear orientation to budget planning, some approaches have proved to be more successful than others.

This chapter, therefore, not only examines whether MTBFs in general improve a government's financial performance, but also assesses the relative performance of different kinds of MTBFs to identify the key characteristics of successful frameworks. It concentrates on advanced economies, which have similar levels of financial management capacity and relatively extensive experience with medium-term budget planning.

The first section explores the objectives of MTBFs. The second section identifies the main models found in advanced economies. The third section discusses the preconditions for developing a successful MTBF. The fourth section discusses common key features and design elements of advanced frameworks. The fifth section evaluates the performance of different MTBF models since the early 2000s, including how they were adjusted during and after the 2008–09 economic and fiscal crisis to help implement both fiscal stimulus and consolidation. The conclusion provides a set of lessons for countries looking to introduce or strengthen medium-term budget planning.

4.1. OBJECTIVES OF A MEDIUM-TERM BUDGET FRAMEWORK

Countries introduce MTBFs for a number of reasons. Looking beyond the annual budget cycle can improve public financial management outcomes by

- ensuring better control over the evolution of the aggregate fiscal position,
- promoting a more effective allocation of expenditure between sectors and priorities, and
- encouraging more efficient use of resources by budget managers.

These objectives are, to some extent, mutually reinforcing. Strengthening the emphasis on achieving sustainable public finances creates incentives to prioritize policies so that the most important ones receive funding. Producing detailed multiannual budget scenarios improves the administration's understanding of the cost drivers in different sectors and of the resource requirements of different policies, enabling government to set more credible multiyear ministerial expenditure plans, which, in turn, enable ministries to plan their activities in a more efficient way. The remainder of this section examines how effective MTBFs contribute to the realization of each of these objectives.

4.1.1. Strengthening the Sustainability of Public Finances

The principal motivation for adopting an MTBF in most advanced economies has been the desire to strengthen multiyear fiscal discipline. MTBFs accomplish this strengthening by combating tendencies for the expenditure level to rise incrementally over time and the fiscal balance to come in lower than government intended.[1] An MTBF can help improve fiscal discipline in three ways:

- by exposing to government and parliament the full multiyear fiscal impact of *a new policy* before it has been adopted, thereby avoiding unpleasant surprises down the road;
- by giving government an early warning about the sustainability of *existing policies* and encouraging it to take corrective action in advance where necessary; and
- by establishing binding *multiyear expenditure limits* that contain the total room for expenditure in subsequent budgets.

Projecting medium-term expenditure dynamics allows government to take into account both the short- and medium-term fiscal impacts when deciding on new policies. In many cases, the budget impact of revenue or expenditure policies does not follow a smooth pattern from year to year. For example, the number of eligible individuals for a new entitlement program increases over time, the largest construction costs of an infrastructure investment project start a few years into the project, or an increase in civil servants' wages is introduced halfway through the fiscal year. Presenting decision makers with a multiyear profile provides a better chance that only affordable policies will be approved.[2] Conversely, within a strictly annual budgeting horizon, policy changes that generate significant savings over time might be ignored, simply because their short-term impact is small. For example, closing down a redundant agency often generates limited savings in the first year because existing contracts have to be honored and redundancy payments have to be made. However, the savings over several years can be significant.

A well-designed MTBF can also alert government to adverse developments related to ongoing policies, allowing it to initiate adjustment well in advance. For example, medium-term projections can expose how an indexation mechanism for public sector wages, pensions, or unemployment benefits that might appear affordable today is actually unsustainable over the medium to long term. By identifying the problem and providing incentives to make policy changes today, MTBFs can help policymakers initiate early adjustments that have large impacts over time, rather than waiting until the policy becomes unaffordable, forcing large and disruptive changes later.

---

[1] These phenomena are often referred to as *deficit bias* or *fiscal illusion*, as discussed elsewhere in this book. This can be traced to incomplete knowledge about the full costs of spending and taxation, as well as the asymmetric nature of this incompleteness. The channels through which these deficiencies translate into public decision making have been thoroughly studied in the academic literature (Buchanan and Wagner, 1977; Weingast, Shepsle, and Johnsen, 1981; Roubini and Sachs, 1989; Alesina and Perotti, 1994; von Hagen and Hallerberg, 1999).

[2] Several studies have found that time horizons in public decision making are inherently short, either because of uncertainties of being reelected (Nordhaus, 1975; Persson and Svensson, 1989; Alesina and Tabellini, 1990) or because of a lack of information about medium- to long-term effects (Rogoff, 1990; Coate and Morris, 1999).

The sustainability of public finances can also be further enhanced if binding limits are placed on expenditure in the medium term. Such expenditure limits establish benchmarks against which multiyear estimates can be compared, thereby providing information on whether government's current policies are consistent with its aggregate fiscal objectives. Having an established limit on expenditure going into the preparation of the next budget also helps to contain bottom-up pressures for unaffordable increases in allocations. Finally, reaching agreement on stringent spending limits a few years before the budget is negotiated is typically easier than attempting to set such limits in conjunction with the prioritization of expenditure between different policy objectives.

4.1.2. Promoting More Effective Allocation of Resources

An MTBF can also help promote more effective allocation of resources by facilitating reallocations of expenditure from lower priority to higher priority areas. An MTBF opens up several channels for reallocation:

- A medium-term outlook in budgeting gives government an instrument for ensuring that policies are implemented *at the right time*. Improving timing also involves the ability to identify problems around the corner and to take timely action so that the impact comes when needed, not a year or two afterward.
- A medium-term perspective enables *more ambitious reallocation* of resources by removing many of the administrative and legal rigidities that apply in a one-year perspective but that are more malleable over a two- or three-year horizon.
- A medium-term budget framework allows government to *announce policy changes now that will be implemented later*. Doing so helps to set expectations and avoid the strong bias for the status quo that tends to otherwise prevail.

By identifying future policy issues early, MTBFs can take into account the time lags that characterize many policy changes. Significant policies often take a number of years to design, legislate, and implement before rendering the desired effect. A one-year horizon poses the risk that the impact of the policy changes will be felt only several years after the time intended by government. In contrast, an MTBF encourages government to anticipate policy lags and to initiate reforms that will come into effect only after two or three years.

In many cases, however, the problem is not so much identification and implementation lags as short-term rigidities preventing expenditure from being reduced. This occurrence is sometimes reflected in the distinction between discretionary and nondiscretionary expenditure that some countries have institutionalized in their budget systems. Although the vast majority of expenditure—through legal contracts, existing legislation, or simple administrative or political inertia—cannot be reduced in the short term, a planning period of two or three years opens up substantially more opportunities for reducing, or even shutting down, programs that have become obsolete or downgraded in the list of government priorities, and using those resources to fund new or higher priorities.

Giving advance warning of a future change in a ministry's resources budget can also help to manage expectations and help budget managers to prepare for the forthcoming increase or cut in resources. Advance warning can alleviate some of the resistance typically met when a budget reduction is proposed. The added time dimensions in the budget negotiations can also help government deal with excessive proposals for new spending. With a strictly annual budget horizon, a particular proposal can be met only with a binary yes or no. A medium-term horizon provides the option of committing to introducing the proposal in a future budget if sufficient fiscal space is available. The flip side, of course, is the temptation to fill all the years in the planning horizon with new policies, leaving no room for launching new initiatives at a later stage.

4.1.3. Encouraging More Efficient Use of Resources

A well-functioning MTBF can promote more efficient use of resources by creating more stable and predictable conditions under which ministries and agencies can plan their expenditures. These efficiency improvements arise through three different channels:

- More-predictable future budget allocations *promote multiyear planning* and create opportunities to negotiate better contracts, mitigate risks, and exploit synergies.
- Relaxing the strict annularity of budget authorizations allows budget managers to *spend resources as needed* or when they are most effective rather than rushing spending through at the end of the financial year using arrangements for carryover of unspent appropriations.
- Greater certainty about future allocations creates incentives for budget managers to *identify and exploit efficiency savings.*

Although official spending authorizations remain annual, an MTBF can enable governments to give clearer commitments to ministries and agencies about their budget allocations for the medium term. Budget actors are therefore in a better position to plan their activities. As discussed in Chapter 10, the efficiency of infrastructure investment can be increased by providing budget actors with more time to design projects, negotiate contracts, identify and manage risks, and exploit synergies between different interventions. However, efficiency gains can also be made on the current side of the budget through recruitment of skilled professionals, training of existing staff, execution of long-term procurement contracts, and administrative reorganization if budget actors are in a position to commit resources for more than one year.

A multiyear planning horizon also allows government to relax some of the strict annual limits on ministerial and agency expenditure, which can otherwise encourage inefficient use of resources. The combination of multiyear budget planning and carryover arrangements, whereby unused budget authorizations are automatically shifted to top up the next year's budget, can improve cost efficiency by removing the incentive for end-of-year spending surges.

Providing budget managers with greater multiyear budgetary certainty can also encourage them to identify and implement measures that yield efficiency savings without fear of having those savings revoked from their budgets in the next budget round. Of course, a trade-off arises between encouraging these kinds of operational efficiencies within a sector and exploiting opportunities to reallocate those savings to higher-priority sectors.

4.2. MEDIUM-TERM BUDGET FRAMEWORK MODELS

A country does not have an entirely free hand in designing a coherent MTBF. Rather, in choosing an MTBF model, countries face tension between the three objectives of medium-term budget planning discussed in the first section of this chapter:

- Maintaining *aggregate expenditure discipline* requires that the medium-term restrictions have the broadest possible *coverage* of government expenditure.
- Promoting more *effective allocation of resources* requires that decision makers be provided with *detail* about the future allocation of resources between sectoral, administrative, or program categories.
- Encouraging the *efficient use of resources* requires that budget managers be provided with *certainty* about their future allocations.

The tension between these objectives arises because the future demands on government are inherently uncertain. All governments find it difficult to commit themselves credibly to a comprehensive and detailed multiyear expenditure plan. Although a well-designed MTBF reduces uncertainty about future spending requirements, unforeseen pressures will inevitably arise. These pressures will have to be accommodated by increasing total expenditure, revising the allocation of expenditure, or leaving a large proportion of expenditure unallocated over the plan period, or through a combination of these measures.

This tension between competing objectives is reflected in the design of different MTBF models. Across the 24 advanced economies considered in this chapter, three broad approaches to medium-term budget planning can be identified.

Six countries can be described as having *no MTBF*. No multiyear expenditure and revenue estimates are presented alongside and on the same basis as the annual budget. These countries may produce aggregate fiscal or budgetary projections (such as required by stability or convergence programs); however, these documents are not integral to the budget documentation and do not constitute an ex ante framework for budget preparation.

An *indicative MTBF* is used by 11 countries. The multiyear expenditure and revenue estimates presented with the annual budget are intended to reflect the future costs of current policies and decisions but are not intended to bind future policies and decisions. These medium-term revenue and expenditure estimates are reset every year, without any reconciliation with the estimates presented in the previous year. Because they can be revised without any consequence, indicative frameworks are often comprehensive in their coverage and provide considerable detail about the composition of expenditure by economic, administrative, or program category. However, they provide relatively little certainty about future expenditure at either the aggregate or the detailed level.

Seven countries can be described as having a *binding MTBF.* The multiyear expenditure and revenue estimates presented with the annual budget are intended to both reflect the future costs of current policies and bind future policy changes. However, as discussed below, the nature, categorization, level of detail, coverage, and frequency of policy revisions of the medium-term commitment vary substantially across countries.

Binding MTBFs can be further subdivided into three distinct models based on the point at which they strike the balance between the three objectives highlighted above.

The *fixed aggregate ceiling* approach currently used by Austria, Finland, the Netherlands, and Sweden fixes a binding limit on all or most central government expenditure for two or more years, and is not revised during that period. Given the primacy attached to ensuring that this aggregate ceiling is respected, these models do not set binding multiyear limits on expenditure categories within the overall ceiling but leave this to the discretion of the annual budgeting process.[3] As such, this type of model is characterized by a higher degree of comprehensiveness and control at the aggregate level, but maintaining flexibility to revise and reallocate at the more detailed level.

The *fixed ministerial ceiling* approach currently employed by France and the United Kingdom fixes binding multiyear expenditure limits for each of the 25–30 central government line ministries. Given the challenges and risks associated with fixing expenditure allocation at this more detailed level, these models tend to revise the ceilings more frequently and cover less central government expenditure. Thus, this type of model is characterized by a high degree of fixity and specificity but a lower degree of comprehensiveness.

The *forward estimates* approach employed by Australia sets multiyear expenditure estimates for each of the central government's 217 programs (or outcomes, as they are described in the budget). Unlike in the fixed ministerial ceiling model, these estimates are subject to revision twice a year. However, revisions are permitted only (1) to realign budget allocations to recognized changes in external parameters, such as a change in inflation or a change in underlying program volumes, or (2) to reflect discretionary policy decisions approved by the cabinet. In the absence of any approved changes, the previous years' estimates remain and eventually become the budget appropriation. Thus, this type of model allows for a high degree of comprehensiveness and specificity, focuses on policy delivery, and

[3]This is not to say that countries with aggregate expenditure ceilings do not place any emphasis on policymaking, forecasting, and control of expenditure at a more detailed level. As discussed in the last section of this chapter, the integrity of the aggregate ceiling depends upon these countries having well-developed procedures for prioritizing and monitoring expenditure at the ministerial and program levels in a medium-term horizon.

TABLE 4.1

Categorization of MTBF Models in OECD Countries

Highest Tier of Multiyear Planning	Status of Multiyear Estimates: Binding	Indicative	None
Aggregate expenditure	Austria (post-2010) Finland (post-2003) Netherlands Sweden	France (pre-2009) Italy Czech Republic	Greece Iceland Ireland Poland Portugal Spain
Economic category		Belgium Germany Hungary Japan Turkey	
Ministry	France (post-2009) United Kingdom	Austria (pre-2010) Canada Denmark Slovak Republic Finland (pre-2003)	
Program	Australia	New Zealand	

Source: Authors' illustration.
Note: MTBF = medium-term budget framework; OECD = Organisation for Economic Co-operation and Development.

opens up the possibility for revisions and reallocations within both expenditure areas and the aggregate amount. However, the lack of a fixed ceiling leads to a lower degree of certainty about total expenditure.

See Table 4.1 for an illustration of how MTBF models are used in the Organisation for Economic Co-operation and Development (OECD) countries. Indicative MTBFs remain the most common model, but a growing number of advanced economies are adopting more binding approaches. Although Australia has been refining its forward estimates model since the 1980s, most other binding MTBF models were adopted within the last two decades: in the Netherlands in 1994, in Sweden in 1997, in Finland in 2003, in France in 2008, and in Austria in 2009. The United Kingdom has experimented with three different approaches to medium-term budget planning during the past three decades, as discussed in Box 4.2.[4]

4.3. PRECONDITIONS FOR A SUCCESSFUL MEDIUM-TERM BUDGET FRAMEWORK

Although more and more countries have adopted MTBFs, their performance against the various objectives set for them has been mixed. One reason for this mixed performance record is that medium-term budgeting is demanding and

---

[4] See Ahnert, Hughes, and Takahashi (2011) for a more detailed description of the United Kingdom's various approaches to medium-term budget planning since the 1960s.

BOX 4.2 MTBFs in the United Kingdom

The experience in the United Kingdom provides an interesting test of medium-term budget frameworks (MTBFs). The country has operated three distinct models over the past three decades, within the same broad institutional structure:

- From 1967 to 1993, the government had an indicative MTBF based on a rolling three-year aggregate expenditure ceiling known as "Planning Total." Planning Total covered all general government expenditure other than debt interest and was revised on an annual basis.
- From 1994 to 1998, the government moved to a binding MTBF based upon a fixed aggregate expenditure ceiling known as "Control Total." Unlike Planning Total, Control Total was fixed for periods of three years and was not revisited. This additional degree of discipline came at the expense of coverage because working-age benefits were added to the list of items excluded from the ceiling.
- From 1999 to the present, the government has operated a system of fixed ministerial ceilings known as "Departmental Expenditure Limits." Under this approach, multiyear ceilings are fixed for each of 25 central government ministries and are not revised for a period of two to three years. This additional degree of specificity came at the expense of a further reduction in coverage because local authority self-financed expenditure and all social security benefits were excluded from the ceiling.

Securing Medium-Term Sustainability of Public Finances

The evidence from the U.K. experience with different MTBF models confirms the finding that binding MTBFs can be more effective in promoting fiscal discipline than indicative MTBFs (see Figure 4.2.1). The move from an indicative aggregate to a fixed aggregate ceiling was associated with a major improvement in aggregate expenditure discipline as measured by the average error in forecasting general government expenditure three years ahead, which fell from 5.9 percent to 0.8 percent of GDP. The move from a fixed aggregate ceiling to fixed ministerial ceilings was associated with a further improvement in expenditure discipline with the average three-year-ahead forecasting error falling to 0.05 percent of GDP.

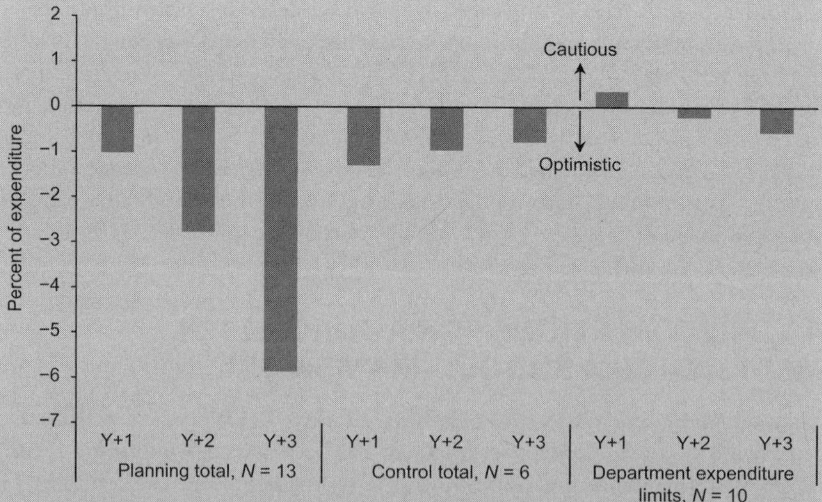

Figure 4.2.1 U.K. General Government Expenditure Forecast Errors, 1981–2009

Source: U.K. *Financial Statement and Budget Report*.

Note: N = number of observations; Y = budget year. "Cautious" means that actual expenditure was lower than forecast. "Optimistic" means that actual expenditure was higher than forecast.

requires a level of stability and predictability that typically develops only over time. Specifically, four preconditions are critical to the successful introduction of an MTBF:

- a credible and predictable annual budget;
- accurate medium-term macroeconomic and demographic projections;
- established fiscal objectives and rules; and
- a comprehensive, unified, top-down budget process.

4.3.1. Credible and Predictable Annual Budget

The foundation for the medium-term revenue and expenditure projections is the annual budget. Unless the short term is sufficiently predictable, the forecasting error for the medium term will be too large for the framework to serve as a basis for decision making. Figure 4.1 shows the average difference—expressed as a percentage of total expenditure—between projected general government expenditure (where possible, or central government expenditure otherwise) at the start of

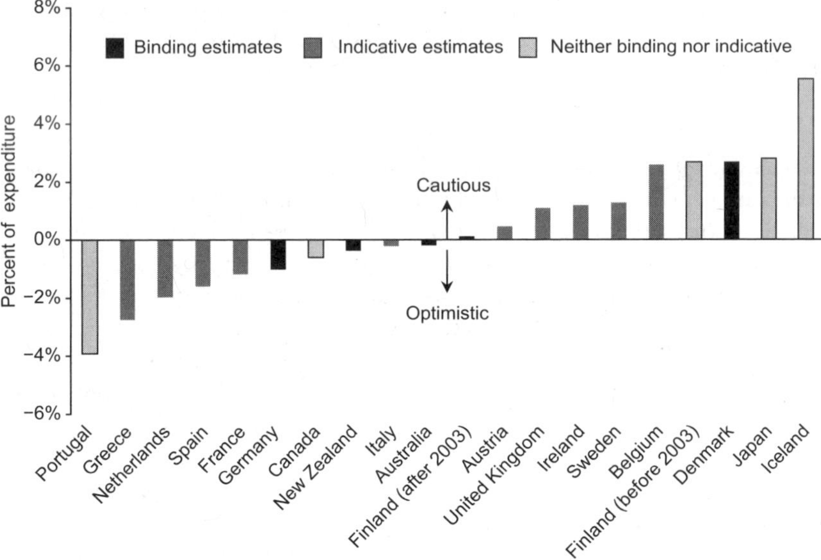

Figure 4.1 Average Difference between Planned and Actual General Government Expenditure for Forecasts Made in Previous Year, 1998–2007

Sources: EU countries: stability and convergence programs. Australia, Canada, Iceland, Japan, New Zealand: year-end budget reconciliation documents.

Note: For non-EU countries, central government figures were substituted for general government figures. "Cautious" means that actual expenditure was lower than forecast. "Optimistic" means that actual expenditure was higher than forecast.

the budget year and the final outturn for a set of OECD members in 1997–2007.[5] For example, in Portugal, expenditure was on average around 4 percent higher than forecast, whereas in Iceland, it was approximately 5.5 percent lower, on average, than forecast. The figure shows that for a large number of countries, substantial changes to total expenditure occur during the course of the fiscal year. It also shows that binding MTBFs tend to be in place in countries with relatively credible annual budgets. This credibility derives from a number of factors.

The first aspect of the credibility of the annual budget is that budget allocations need to be sufficient to fund the policy outcomes that budget actors are expected to deliver. Only when the ministry of finance and the responsible spending ministry or agency broadly agree that the budget allocation is appropriate for its purpose can a meaningful discussion of the medium-term financial requirements be held. Divergence between expectations and actual resource allocations can occur for several reasons, including a lack of clarity in the instructions given to spending ministries, unrealistic or uncosted policy expectations, insufficient understanding of production costs, or simple reluctance on the part of spending ministries and agencies to accept the restrictions imposed by the ministry of finance. Regardless of the reason, realistic allocations are necessary for the MTBF.

The second aspect is that expenditure dynamics for existing government programs and activities have to be understood. Producing accurate medium-term expenditure projections is difficult. However, standardized methods for determining future budget appropriations make it possible to remove a great deal of uncertainty. The most obvious example is entitlement schemes intended to compensate for a temporary loss of income, for example, sickness benefits, parental benefits, or unemployment benefits. The benefit levels are often indexed to inflation to maintain them in real terms. If this indexation mechanism is made explicit, medium-term forecasting is a matter of predicting volumes and inflation. Stability and predictability of the calculation of administrative appropriations, which is predominantly affected by price inflation, is also important.

A third aspect is firm control over budget execution, and an expectation that government will respect the allocations approved by the legislature. If the budget is not well prepared, if external conditions are unstable, or if control over in-year expenditure commitments is insufficient, government may have to regularly make major adjustments during the execution of the budget. In such a situation, in which the administration cannot deliver the approved annual budget, it is not feasible to expect that any medium-term planning will be taken seriously. Planning for the medium term makes sense only if the short term is stable.

[5] Countries discussed in this chapter but excluded from Figure 4.1 are the Czech Republic, Hungary, Poland, the Slovak Republic, and Turkey, because there were only four years of data or fewer for these countries. This sample was classified according to the stringency of multiyear planning that each country was implementing in 2007, except in the case of Finland, which changed its medium-term expenditure framework in 2003.

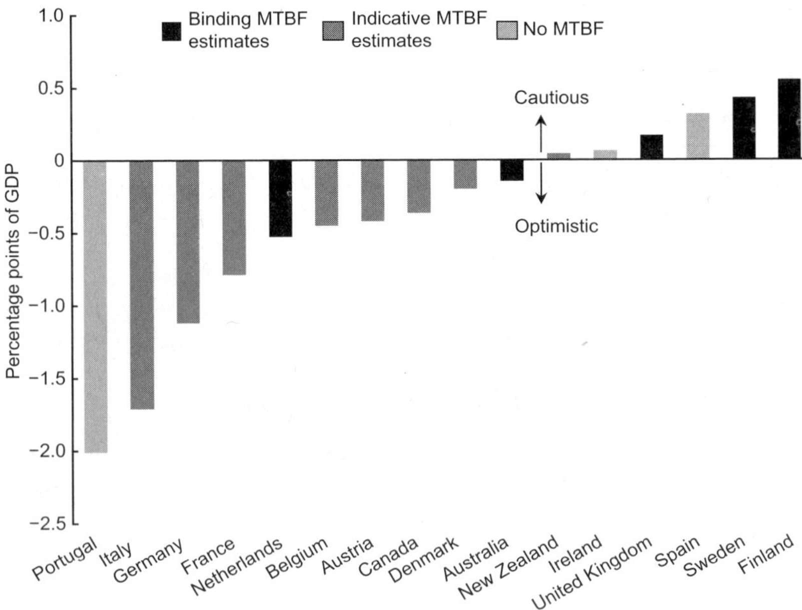

Figure 4.2 Average Error in Forecasting Real GDP Growth for Two Years Ahead, 2000–07

Sources: EU countries: stability and convergence programs. Australia, New Zealand, Canada: annually produced budget update documents.

Note: "Cautious" means that actual GDP growth was higher than forecast. "Optimistic" means that actual GDP growth was lower than forecast. MTBF = medium-term budget framework.

4.3.2. Accurate Medium-Term Macroeconomic and Demographic Projections

Government's multiyear projections of revenue and expenditure are only as credible as the economic and demographic assumptions on which they are based. Just about every revenue and expenditure item in the budget is driven by some exogenous factor. Personal income tax is affected by household income and employment levels, value-added tax by consumption, unemployment benefits by the number of individuals looking for work, and the cost of completing a building project by the inflation rate for construction materials and labor costs. The precision of the MTBF can be only as high as the forecasting accuracy of these economic and noneconomic determinants. Figure 4.2 shows the average error for GDP forecasted two years in advance for a selection of OECD countries for 2000–07.[6] For example, in Finland, actual GDP was on average about 0.5 percent higher than forecast. The figure shows that those countries that have adopted more binding MTBFs have tended to have more cautious medium-term economic growth forecasts than those without an MTBF.

As indicated in the previous section, a very unstable macroeconomic environment—as can occur following a major economic or other shock—can make forecasting

[6] Countries discussed in this chapter but excluded from Figure 4.2 are the Czech Republic, Greece, Hungary, Iceland, Japan, Poland, the Slovak Republic, and Turkey, because there were insufficient years of data. This sample has been classified according to the stringency of multiyear planning that each country was implementing in 2007.

too daunting a task to realistically apply a medium-term budget framework. In many cases, however, sufficiently accurate forecasting assumptions can be established. A central factor is the use of a comprehensive macroeconomic forecasting model that ensures that inflation, exchange rates, consumption, unemployment, and the output gap are consistent with one another.

As discussed in Chapter 6, countries have improved the accuracy and prudence of their macroeconomic forecasts by seeking independent input into their formulations.[7] By voluntarily agreeing to independently produced forecasts, governments put pressure on themselves to eliminate possible biases and improve their internal capacity. The use of independent forecasts has been a critical input into the MTBF in several countries, although it has taken very different forms.

4.3.3. Medium-Term Fiscal Objectives and Rules

A fixed objective for one or more aggregate fiscal variables in the medium term provides an anchor for the formulation of medium-term ceilings or projections. Although a majority of advanced economies set some form of fiscal objective or rule, the comprehensiveness, transparency, and strictness of these rules or objectives vary (see Chapter 3).[8] To guide the setting of medium-term budget parameters effectively, a good fiscal policy objective needs to be

- clear so that it can be readily translated into the level of expenditure,
- medium term in orientation to define a path for expenditure over time, and
- consistent over time to avoid disruptive changes that undermine the credibility of the framework.

The aggregate fiscal objectives and rules on the one hand, and the MTBF on the other hand, are mutually interdependent. Objectives for the balance or aggregate expenditure in the medium term are credible only if government has at its disposal the instruments that enable it to ensure that proposed policies are consistent with those objectives. However, taking the time and effort to build up an MTBF requires the discipline created by a standing fiscal framework. It is no coincidence that decision makers start to request information about how the cost of policies will evolve only when government has committed not to exceed a particular aggregate expenditure level or a particular deficit.

4.3.4. Comprehensive, Unified, Top-Down Budget Process

If the MTBF is to have an impact on fiscal outcomes, the annual budget process must be able to resolve conflicting pressures and priorities and translate them into

---

[7] As discussed in Chapters 1 and 2, several studies have found a positive bias in macroeconomic forecasts (Strauch, Hallerberg, and von Hagen, 2004; Jonung and Larch, 2006). Efforts have been made to address this positive bias by setting up independent forecasting agencies (Austria, Denmark, Germany, the Netherlands, Sweden, the United Kingdom, and the United States), or by committing to using private sector forecasts (Canada). See Calmfors and Wren-Lewis (2011) for a survey.

[8] See Kumar and others (2009) for a survey and discussion of fiscal rules.

a set of agreed-on expenditure allocations. Budget preparation can often fall short of this goal because of expenditure rigidities and fragmented decision making. If previous medium-term plans are discarded when the annual budget is prepared, the control that should be instilled by the MTBF is lost. To ensure that medium-term ceilings or estimates shape the annual budget, three elements need to be in place.

First, budget preparation should follow a top-down sequence to help the government preserve aggregate expenditure discipline throughout the process of prioritizing limited resources.[9] A top-down budget process is defined as a decision-making sequence in which a limit on total expenditure is adopted before expenditure is allocated to specific sectors or ministries, and ministerial expenditure ceilings are fixed before individual appropriations are debated. A top-down budget preparation process has been shown to be effective in addressing the tendency for incremental expenditure drift that would otherwise undo the restraint engendered by the MTBF.

Second, both the budget and the budget process should be comprehensive so that all major expenditure decisions are made at one time. Ideally, the budget should include all central government revenue and expenditure and should be adopted as a single document—this is often referred to as the principle of unity. If the budget is fragmented into separate budgets for social security, pensions, public investment funds, and extrabudgetary agencies, government's and parliament's understanding of government's consolidated revenue and expenditure position is clouded, complicating aggregate fiscal control. Furthermore, a budget process that allows policy initiatives with fiscal implications to be introduced after the budget has been adopted undermines the integrity and discipline of the budget process.

Third, the budget needs to be relatively unencumbered by extensive earmarking or standing expenditure commitments. In a situation in which certain revenue has been assigned to a specific objective (e.g., fuel excise to a road maintenance fund) or in which explicit objectives require the allocation of a certain percentage of total expenditure or GDP to particular sectors (e.g., education, health care, or agricultural support), the government can find it difficult to enforce multiyear expenditure restrictions. These expenditure rigidities reduce the scope for government to absorb new policies and pressures through reallocation of resources, which increases the pressure to expand the total expenditure envelope to accommodate them.

4.4. KEY FEATURES AND DESIGN ELEMENTS

Countries that have introduced medium-term budgeting have done so in different institutional contexts, facing different challenges, and pursuing different budget objectives. Accordingly, successful MTBFs differ in many respects. However, successful models have four key features in common:

[9] See Ljungman (2009) for a discussion of how a top-down budget process can help strengthen fiscal discipline.

- multiyear expenditure limits that define the nature, level, and terms of the restrictions being placed on future budget decisions;
- expenditure prioritization mechanisms that ensure that expenditure is allocated within those multiyear restrictions in a manner that reflects government policy priorities;
- forward-looking expenditure controls through which the consistency of updated medium-term expenditure projections with approved medium-term expenditure plans is monitored and enforced; and
- dynamic accountability arrangements through which adherence to stated medium-term objectives can be assessed by parliament and the general public over time.

4.4.1. Multiyear Spending Limits

One of the main challenges with adopting a medium-term horizon in budgeting is ensuring that decision makers remain committed to revenue and expenditure estimates for years beyond the legislated budget. As time goes by, government is often tempted to move away from what it had said it would do in the future. This straying can result from changes in the external environment (such as higher inflation or unemployment or more people eligible for maternity and paternity benefits), the introduction of new policies, or simply a lack of attention to formulation of the original medium-term plans. In all of these instances, a case can be made for allowing for some upward revision to the original multiyear estimate. However, accommodating these pressures calls into question the credibility and value of the medium-term planning process—with the concomitant risk that decision makers cease to invest time and effort in the production of accurate and updated fiscal projections.

Resolving this tension between the need for a firm commitment to medium-term estimates and the need to ensure that previously made plans are still relevant and legitimate when the time comes to implement them is a key issue in designing an MTBF. Four main questions arise in defining the multiyear expenditure limits that define that framework:

- What should the *nature* of those multiyear limits be—a nominal figure, a real level of expenditure, or a commitment to deliver a specific volume of output?
- What should the *level of detail* and the *categorization* of those multiyear limits be—aggregate expenditure, ministerial expenditure allocations, government programs, or economic expenditure categories?
- What should the *coverage* of those multiyear limits be—should certain categories of government expenditure not be subjected to any medium-term restrictions?
- How often should those multiyear limits be *revised* to allow for discretionary changes?

An effective set of multiyear spending limits should support all three objectives of the medium-term budget framework discussed in the previous section: spending is kept within available resources, the budget allocates money to the right policies, and the administration is efficient in delivering those policies. However, as discussed in detail below, a trade-off must be made between these objectives, and the trade-off manifests itself in the design of multiyear expenditure limits.

The nature of the multiyear spending limits concerns both what kind of restriction the government puts on itself in the medium term and what it takes upon itself to deliver. In its most simple and straightforward form, the government sets a nominal ceiling on expenditure, and commits itself not to exceed this level. This type of commitment is simple to interpret and monitor. A nominal expenditure ceiling lends itself to ensuring fiscal discipline, but can come into conflict with government's policy priorities if conditions change.

A second approach is to set a restriction on the real expenditure level and allow the nominal level to vary as inflation projections are updated. Setting ceilings in real terms avoids squeezing or expanding resource allocations simply because the price and wage levels in the economy vary, but comes at the cost of less transparency and predictability of expenditure.

Finally, the medium-term commitment can be defined as a particular level of policy output, allowing the expenditure allocations to vary with both price and volume parameters that affect the cost of delivering that policy. The most obvious example of such a commitment would be a legislated entitlement for which allocations vary with the number of eligible beneficiaries. This commitment mechanism protects the delivery of government goods and services, but requires sophisticated mechanisms for costing, forecasting, and revising expenditure estimates.

A second design feature of medium-term expenditure limits is the category of expenditure for which the limits are set and at what level of aggregation. Three broad approaches can be discerned.

- Government can commit to a future *aggregate level of expenditure.* In doing so, government emphasizes its commitment to maintaining an overall fiscal position for any particular composition of spending in the medium term.
- Government can commit to a future *allocation of expenditure between administrative or policy units* at the level of ministries, agencies, policy areas, or individual programs.
- Government can commit to a future *composition of expenditure* in economic categories such as consumption, investment, and transfers. Such a presentation can be useful for analyzing the impact of fiscal policy on the macroeconomy and making cross-country comparisons, but does not typically support the objectives of maintaining a sustainable fiscal position, allocative efficiency, and operational efficiency because the link to annual budget appropriations is weak.

A third design feature of medium-term expenditure limits concerns their coverage. Many countries decide either to exclude certain expenditure items from multiyear expenditure limits on the grounds that they are volatile, fiscally neutral, nondiscretionary, or countercyclical in nature, or to define alternative medium-term expenditure restrictions for specific types of expenditure. The items of expenditure excluded or treated separately can include interest payments, expenditure financed by demand-driven user fees, expenditure financed by external grants, formula-driven transfers, and unemployment benefits and other entitlements.

As shown in Table 4.2, the coverage of medium-term expenditure limits varies substantially across countries, reflecting differences in both the types of commitments and control arrangements. The widest coverage is seen in the more flexible forward estimate commitments in Australia and the aggregate ceilings of Finland, the Netherlands, and Sweden. Where ministerial ceilings in nominal terms have been chosen, as in the United Kingdom and France, numerous items have been excluded to enable compliance at the ministerial level.

TABLE 4.2

Expenditures Excluded from Multiyear Commitments

		MTBF Model					
		Aggregate ceilings			Ministerial ceilings		Program estimates
Criteria for Exclusion	Example	Sweden	Netherlands	Finland	United Kingdom	France	Australia
External obligations	Debt interest	Yes	Yes	Yes	Yes		
	International subscriptions				To EU		
Automatic stabilizer	Unemployment benefits		Yes	Yes	Yes	Yes	
Fiscally neutral	Spending of external grants			From EU	From EU		
	Spending of earmarked revenue		Gas		Lottery		
	Taxes on public bodies			VAT			
	Accounting adjustments				Noncash		
Formula-driven	Social security			Some	Yes	Yes	
	Health insurance			Some		Yes	
	Transfers from central government to local government			Yes		Yes	
Unpredictable	Spending of privatization windfalls		Yes				
	Military operations				Yes		
Coverage of multiyear restrictions (Percent of central government)		97	80	78	59	39	100

Source: National authorities.
Note: MTBF= medium-term budget framework; VAT= value-added tax.

The fourth design feature of multiyear spending limits concerns the frequency with which revisions to those limits are made to allow for discretionary changes in policy. Such revisions are distinct from the updates to existing medium-term plans allowed under commitments to real expenditure levels and output levels, which are intended to ensure that resources remain adequate for government policies. Government may change its policy priorities, either by reallocating between policy areas, or by increasing or reducing the total volume of public goods and services. There are two broad approaches to revisions.

An annual review cycle opens up the multiannual limits for revision every time the budget itself is discussed, which can be once—or sometimes twice—per year. These reviews of medium-term spending limits will reflect both changes to the annual budget, projected into the medium term, and changes introduced for years beyond the annual budget horizon.

A multiannual review cycle locks in the multiyear limits for a period of two, three, or four years. Between review cycles, the limits are not reopened to allow for changes in discretionary policy.

These four aspects of medium-term expenditure limits can be combined in several ways in the MTBF, as seen in the variety of country practices.

In Sweden,[10] the key political commitment to aggregate fiscal discipline is to remain below the three-year nominal ceiling on central government expenditure. The aggregate ceiling covers all primary central government expenditure. The ceiling is not revised once set, and an additional year is added to the ceiling each autumn alongside the budget. With regard to policies, nominal medium-term estimates are set for 27 expenditure areas, which are updated twice a year to reflect changes in macroeconomic factors, volumes in transfer systems, and policy changes. In addition, each of the 500 appropriations in the budget is defined in the medium term to remain constant in nominal terms, to be updated with inflation, or to be determined by volume. Depending on its definition, the medium-term estimate for each appropriation is updated twice per year together with the budget.

In the United Kingdom and France, the MTBF comprises a set of 25 to 30 ministerial spending ceilings, set for a two- or three-year period in nominal terms. Ministerial ceilings cover administrative expenditure, investments, and some program expenditure. However, a broader range of items, including interest expenditure, social security entitlements, and unemployment benefits, are not covered by any medium-term expenditure commitments. Ministerial expenditure ceilings are used both to enforce aggregate spending control and to define broad ministerial priorities.

In Finland, the government decides, at the beginning of its four-year term, on a binding ceiling for budget expenditure for the whole term in its Government Program.[11] The ceiling is set in real terms, and the annual central government

[10] See Ljungman (2007) for a description of the MTBF in Sweden.

[11] See Finland, Ministry of Finance (2011) for a discussion of the Finnish budget system.

spending limit decisions are revised only for changes in the price and cost level and for adjustments in the budget structure. The parliamentary term spending limits set a ceiling on about three-fourths of total budgetary expenditure. Expenditures affected by cyclical fluctuations and automatic stabilizers, such as unemployment security expenditure, are outside the scope of the spending limits (however, expenditure effects resulting from changes to the criteria for these items are included in the spending limits). The Netherlands operates a similar system of a fixed four-year aggregate ceiling expressed in real terms.

In Australia, the forward estimates model is based on the government's commitment to delivering approved policies and absorbing any changes in external conditions that affect the cost of producing those policies.[12] In practice, parameter-driven updates of medium-term estimates are made twice a year, allowing the total expenditure levels to change. Discretionary changes to policies and estimates can be introduced in either the annual budget or midyear update processes.

4.4.2. Expenditure Prioritization Mechanisms

The credibility of and respect for the government's medium-term expenditure plans require that they both reflect the government's policy priorities and are, at the same time, consistent with the multiyear spending limits defined by the framework. Achieving these dual objectives requires institutional mechanisms that allow competing policies to be prioritized in a manner that takes into account their medium-term budgetary impact. The key elements of an effective multiyear expenditure prioritization mechanism are

- an *integrated medium-term expenditure planning and budgeting* process;
- a clear separation between the cost of *maintaining existing policies* and the cost of *new policy initiatives* in budget documents, based on an unambiguous and widely accepted methodology; and
- a *forum for discussing and deciding on expenditure priorities* that is perceived to be comprehensive, politically legitimate, evidence based, and binding.

Three approaches to integrating medium-term expenditure planning in the budgeting process can be found across countries. First, the most well-developed MTBFs are fully integrated with the budget process, and all discussions of revenue and expenditure policies consider their impact in a multiyear horizon. A second and less ambitious approach is to maintain an annual perspective at the most detailed budget level. Medium-term projections are produced for specific parts of the budget, and often at a more aggregated level than for the annual budget. A third group of countries have opted for organizing medium-term planning as a separate process, following a different timetable from that for the preparation and approval of the annual budget. In general, the latter two approaches have been shown to have a very limited impact on actual policy prioritization.

[12] See Blöndal and others (2008) for a description of the Australian budget system.

To assess the affordability of existing policies and understand the fiscal implications of policy changes, decision makers have to be presented with a decomposition of the medium-term estimates into *ongoing policies* and *new discretionary initiatives*. In advanced MTBFs, new and existing policies are separated comprehensively and consistently, and presented both at a summary level and for individual allocations in the budget. In other cases, the medium-term fiscal impact is presented only for a few selected policies deemed sufficiently important to justify such a breakdown. A key decision in enabling a decomposition of expenditure projections is establishing the basis for the no-policy-change assessment. Approaches differ across countries and across different categories of expenditure within countries.

In its most restrictive form, unchanged policy is defined as a nominally unchanged allocation in the medium term. This definition is used as the basis for expenditure covered by the multiannual ministerial ceilings in the United Kingdom and for most subsidy programs in Sweden.

In a more accommodating approach, the projected medium-term allocations for unchanged policy are adjusted for parameters such as projected wage and price inflation and demographic factors that affect both the costs and recipient volumes of policies, possibly with a deduction of an efficiency dividend. This approach is used for expenditure in Australia and Sweden. It provides greater certainty to budget actors that policies will be delivered, and puts the onus on policymakers to make explicit policy changes if those policies are becoming too costly, or in Sweden's case, if they are jeopardizing the aggregate expenditure ceiling.

The final element of medium-term policy prioritization is the existence of an *institutional forum within government for discussing and deciding between competing expenditure pressures and proposals*. Although the nature of these decision-making mechanisms depends on the institutional and political context, the most effective of these forums tend to (1) cover all government activities, (2) engage high-level political decision makers, (3) make use of evidence about expenditure performance, and (4) represent the sole and final decision-making authority. Otherwise, the precise configuration of these forums varies, as in the examples below:

- In Finland and the Netherlands, the focal point for the determination of medium-term expenditure priorities is the Coalition Agreement, which is negotiated between the political parties that form the governing coalition at the start of each parliament. The Coalition Agreement itself sets the real expenditure ceilings for the four years of the parliamentary session.
- In the United Kingdom, the principal forum for discussing and determining multiyear expenditure limits for each department is the Comprehensive Spending Review conducted once every two to three years by the treasury with the final outcome negotiated between ministers, the chancellor of the exchequer (minister of finance), and the prime minister.

- In Australia, the task of arbitrating between competing new expenditure proposals for each annual budget is delegated by the cabinet to the Expenditure Review Committee, a cabinet subcommittee.
- In Sweden, the cabinet's annual budget retreat in the spring is the focal point for all major expenditure decisions, the outcome of which is an agreement on the level of expenditure for each of the 27 expenditure areas.

4.4.3. Forward-Looking Expenditure Controls

Having formulated its medium-term commitments and determined the priorities underpinning those commitments, government needs to have forward-looking expenditure controls in place that ensure compliance with the medium-term plans even as external conditions change. Four types of forward-looking control mechanisms are important to ensuring that expenditure decisions are consistent with those commitments and priorities:

- regular *updates of medium-term expenditure projections*,
- sufficient *margins between expenditure commitments and expenditure plans* to absorb unexpected events without requiring reprioritization of policies,
- firm controls on ministries' and agencies' ability to enter into *multiyear expenditure commitments,* and
- controls over the accumulation, stock, or drawdown of *carryovers*.

Frequent overshooting of expenditure limits set in the MTBF will quickly reduce its credibility. Safeguarding the integrity of the framework requires that initial plans be accurate and that decision makers be quickly informed of any emerging pressures so that they can take action if necessary. To ensure this level of accuracy and timeliness of information, high-quality expenditure projections, updated on a regular basis, are needed. Three approaches are found in countries with medium-term budget frameworks: (1) a complete reassessment of the expected expenditure in the government's medium-term plans on two or more occasions during the year; (2) a partial update of the medium-term projections halfway through the year; and (3) no update of medium-term expenditure projections outside preparation of the medium-term budget plans.

Even those countries with well-developed forecasting capacity will face uncertainty about future expenditure developments. Therefore, countries with effective MTBFs tend to set aside an unallocated margin or reserve between their medium-term expenditure limits and the sum of all projected expenditures. The function of this margin is to absorb the unexpected expenditure pressures that inevitably emerge. Such margins can take a number of forms (see Table 4.3): explicit prudency factors in GDP projections (as used in the United Kingdom), a conservative bias in expenditure forecasts (as in Australia), and provision of headroom under aggregate fiscal restrictions (as in Sweden). The size of margins or reserves varies across countries, but they tend to be relatively small in the budget year (about 1 percent of total expenditure) and increase in size in the out

TABLE 4.3

Reserves and Margins in MTBFs

	Implicit Margins		Explicit Margins		Total Contingency
Country	**GDP forecast**	**Other economic assumptions**	**Within expenditure estimate**	**Within budget balance**	**Percent of total spending**
Canada	MoF uses average of indicative forecasts	MoF adds 0.5% to 1.0% to interest rates and runs through model	Contingency reserve of 1.5% to 2.0% of total spending	MoF targets a surplus of 0.1% of GDP despite balance rule	3.5% to 4.0%
United Kingdom	MoF uses GDP forecast 0.25% below trend	7 other economic assumptions explicitly cautious	Reserves and margins equal to 0.75% to 1.0% of total spending	MoF targets average surplus of 0.2% of GDP despite golden rule	2.5% to 3.0%
Sweden	Budget based on central assumptions for GDP and other macro variables[1]		Budget margin within expenditure ceiling rising from 1.5% to 3.0% of total spending	None	1.0% to 3.0%
Netherlands	Deficit target and expenditure ceiling based on cautious economic scenario in which GDP is 0.5% to 1.0% below outturn		Central contingency reserve of 0.1% of total spending	Most recent CA targets structural surplus of 1.0% of GDP	1.1% to 2.0%
Australia	Budget is based on central economic assumptions[1]	Conservative bias in forward estimates of 0.5% to 1.5% of spending	No central contingency reserve	None	0.5% to 1.5%

Source: Annual budget documents.

Note: CA = cyclically adjusted; MoF = Ministry of Finance; MTBF = medium-term budget framework.

[1] "Central" refers to taking the forecast that is neither cautious nor optimistic but refers to the most likely perceived ex ante outcome.

years (to between 1.5 and 3 percent of total expenditure) as the range of uncertainty of expenditure and revenue outcomes increases.

However, overly generous contingency reserves also introduce a risk of creating expectations that more resources will become available as time progresses, thereby reducing the focus on policies during the budget prioritization process. One way to prevent this expectation is to put in place explicit rules governing how such reserves can be accessed. For example, in the United Kingdom claims on the central contingency reserves are permitted only for expenditure pressures deemed to be unforeseeable, unavoidable, and unabsorbable within ministerial budgets. Australia has even more stringent restrictions on its reserve, which can be used only to deal with unexpected variations in forecast parameters and not to fund new policies.

Another set of control elements prevents ministries or agencies from entering into multiannual expenditure commitments that are inconsistent with the agreed-on multiyear expenditure plans for their sectors. To be effective, these multiyear commitment controls must apply to all manner of expenditure commitments from political promises, to legal obligations, to contractual undertakings. In the United Kingdom, these controls take the form of a nominal delegated limit for each ministry, above which the ministry must seek treasury approval before entering into a multiyear commitment. Finland and Sweden have even more restrictive regimes that require all multiyear expenditure commitments to be approved by parliament as part of the budget.

The introduction of a medium-term perspective to budgeting also creates opportunities to promote intertemporal efficiency by allowing ministries to carry over unspent appropriations from one financial year to the next. At the same time, the unfettered accumulation of carryovers by ministries can create a risk to the credibility of the budget. To counter these problems, countries tend to adopt rules or numerical limits governing the amount of unspent appropriations that can be carried over. These limits can take the following forms:

- Limiting the *type of appropriations* that can be carried over; for example, Australia allows full carryover of administrative costs within departments but requires cabinet approval and reappropriation for any carryover of program expenditure.
- Limiting the *accumulation of carryovers* from one year to the next; for instance, as a default position, France and Sweden allow only 3 percent of expenditure to be carried over from one year to the next.
- Limiting the *drawdown of carryovers* in a given budget year; for example, until 2010, the United Kingdom allowed unlimited accumulation of carryover entitlements by ministries but required treasury approval before those carryovers could be spent in a given budget year.

4.4.4. Accountability Mechanisms

Ultimately, the credibility of a government's MTBF depends on its ability to demonstrate how today's assessment of the current and future budgetary position is consistent with previously formulated medium-term plans. Demonstrating this consistency between previous multiyear budget plans and current budgetary outturns and forecasts requires a set of accountability mechanisms that ensure that

- multiyear plans, annual budgets, and final accounts are presented on a comparable basis,
- any deviations between multiyear plans and expenditure outcomes are comprehensively and transparently reconciled, and
- governments and budget actors are held to account for any unjustified deviations from multiyear plans.

Ensuring comparability between plans and outcomes requires governments to harmonize the presentation of different kinds of financial reports. Countries with the most firmly established and effective MTBFs have typically adopted a single, harmonized classification system for multiyear projections, annual budgets, and final accounts.

- In the United Kingdom, multiyear departmental expenditure limits, annual ministerial budget estimates, and final departmental accounts are all presented in accrual terms.
- In Sweden, aggregate expenditure ceilings, the 27 expenditure areas, multiyear expenditure estimates, the annual budget, and final budget outturn are all presented in cash terms.
- In Finland, the multiannual spending limits, the annual budget, and final budget outturn are presented mainly in cash terms.
- In Australia, multiyear estimates, annual portfolio budget statements, and final budget outturn are presented in both cash and accrual terms.

By contrast, one of many reasons that the stability and convergence programs and targets required of all European Union member states have not been effective in constraining fiscal policy is that they are not presented on the same basis or do not have the same coverage as the main instrument of policy, the national budget. Although the three-year revenue and expenditure projections and targets in the Stability and Growth Pact are presented according to the European System of Accounts 1995, which is on an accrual basis and covers general government, these projections and targets are only tenuously linked to national budgets and accounts, which largely continue to be presented on a cash basis and cover only budgetary central government.

Although successive vintages of a government's multiyear expenditure plans will always deviate from one another and from the final expenditure outturns, the credibility of a government's medium-term plans can be further supported by providing a systematic account of the reasons for those differences—primarily between those changes that have occurred owing to discretionary policy changes and those that have occurred owing to factors outside government control. The level of detail differs across countries, but the most sophisticated of these reconciliations breaks down any differences between forecasts and outturn for each ministry, policy area, or program into

- macroeconomic determinants, such as GDP growth, inflation, or unemployment;
- operational parameters specific to the particular ministry, program, or policy area, such as lower than expected birthrate (for maternity benefits) or lower than expected level of enrollment (for school expenditure);
- accounting changes, such as changes in the accounting treatment of particular transactions within ministries or reclassification of a particular budget line from one ministry to another; and
- policy measures showing the gross impact of all major discretionary increases or reductions in expenditure on a particular ministry, policy area, or program.

This decomposition should be explained according to

- expected and actual carryovers showing the net drawdown or accumulation of unspent appropriations, and
- net over- or underspend, which should largely be accounted for by claims on the aforementioned contingency reserve and authorized or unauthorized overspending.

Once the size and source of any unjustified deviation from the government's multiyear expenditure limits has been identified, some mechanism for holding those responsible to account must be in place. Placement of responsibility requires that both ministries of finance and parliaments treat seriously deviations from multiyear expenditure plans that threaten compliance with government commitments, though typically not as seriously as overspends against annual appropriations. For example, in the United Kingdom, ministries that forecast a breach in their three-year expenditure limit in a future year are subject to the same administrative sanctions as those that exceed their budgets in the current year. Responsible ministries are required to have that forecast overspend regularized through a claim on the central contingency reserve or to accept an offsetting reduction in their expenditure ceilings in one of the other years. In Australia, where parameter-driven deviations from expenditure estimates are allowed, any overspends are subject to scrutiny by parliament under the parliamentary committee system, in which departmental heads report against their outcomes and are asked to explain any revisions.

Independent fiscal agencies can also play an important role in holding governments to account for performance against their multiyear expenditure plans. See Chapter 6 for a more detailed discussion.

4.5. EVALUATING THE PERFORMANCE OF DIFFERENT MTBF MODELS

This section evaluates the relative performance of different MTBF models (binding, indicative, and variants) in delivering the benefits discussed in the first section. By looking at both the contemporaneous performance of different models across countries and changes in an MTBF model within the same country over time, this section identifies which model or models most effectively achieve key public financial management objectives of ensuring better control over the aggregate fiscal position, promoting more effective allocation of expenditure between sectors and priorities, and encouraging more efficient use of resources by budget managers. (See Chapter 1 for a detailed discussion on public financial management objectives.)

4.5.1. Cross-Country Analysis of MTBF Approaches and Models

This subsection reviews the performance of the three broad approaches to medium-term budget planning (binding, indicative, and no MTBF) in meeting the above objectives. It goes on to examine the relative performance of the three binding models (fixed aggregate ceilings, fixed ministerial ceilings, and forward estimates). This analysis is based on a sample of 23 countries, which are grouped according to their MTBF approaches and models, as summarized in Table 4.1.

Securing and Maintaining a Sustainable Fiscal Position

The effectiveness of different MTBF models in securing aggregate fiscal discipline is assessed by looking at the accuracy of the countries' multiyear fiscal forecasts. Forecasting accuracy is measured by the average difference between three-year-ahead forecasts and outturns for government expenditure, revenue, and balance after base effects are controlled for.[13]

A comparison of relative forecast performance suggests that countries with binding MTBFs are better at meeting their medium-term fiscal objectives. Whereas all countries tended to overestimate the balance three years ahead, those with binding MTBFs did so by less than 0.1 percent of GDP, compared with 0.8 percent for those with indicative MTBFs, and 1.0 percent for countries with no MTBFs (Figure 4.3). This strong fiscal forecasting performance is attributable primarily to the success of binding MTBFs in constraining the medium-term evolution of expenditure. Although most countries tended to underestimate the level of expenditure three years ahead, those with binding MTBFs did so by only 0.3 percent of GDP on average compared with 1.6 percent of GDP for those with indicative or no MTBFs. Countries with binding MTBFs also tend to be more cautious in forecasting revenues. The general tendency is to underestimate revenues three years ahead, but those with binding MTBFs did so by 0.9 percent of GDP on average compared with 0.5 percent for those with indicative frameworks and 0.6 percent for those with no MTBFs.

Among the different binding MTBF models, fixed aggregate ceilings are most effective at controlling future expenditure (Figure 4.4). Countries with fixed aggregate ceilings tended to stick to their three-year-ahead forecasts for expenditure, whereas countries with fixed ministerial ceilings or forward estimates tended to overspend by between 0.8 percent and 1.0 percent of GDP. The success of MTBFs with fixed aggregate ceilings can be attributed to both the broad coverage of aggregate ceilings and government commitment to ensuring these ceilings are respected regardless of macroeconomic or fiscal developments in the interim.

However, Australia, with its forward estimates approach on a program basis (program estimates updated annually), displayed the best overall fiscal performance.

---

[13] Ratios to GDP are used to control for both size of government and levels of inflation, which can otherwise bias the results in favor of countries with smaller governments and lower inflation. Averages over 1997 to 2007 are used to control for cyclical effects while preventing the findings from being distorted by the onset of the global financial crisis in 2008.

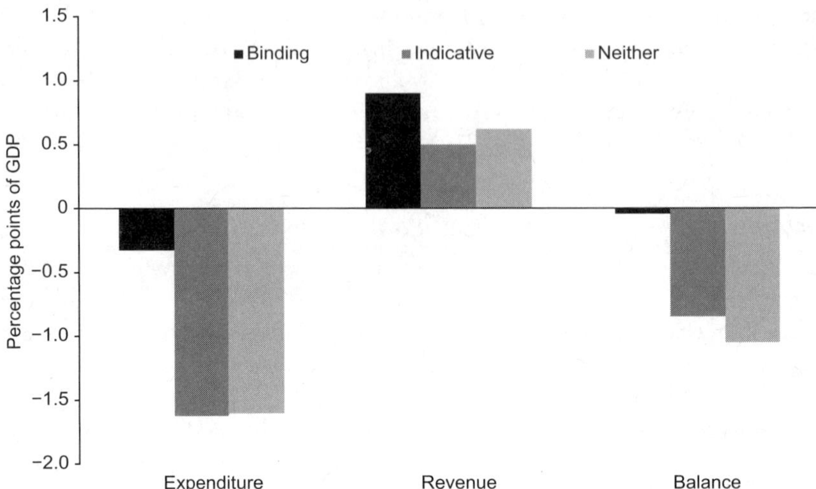

Figure 4.3 Average Three-Year-Ahead Forecast Error for Expenditure, Revenue, and Balance, 1998–2007

Sources: EU countries: stability and convergence programs. All other countries: year-end budget reconciliation documents.

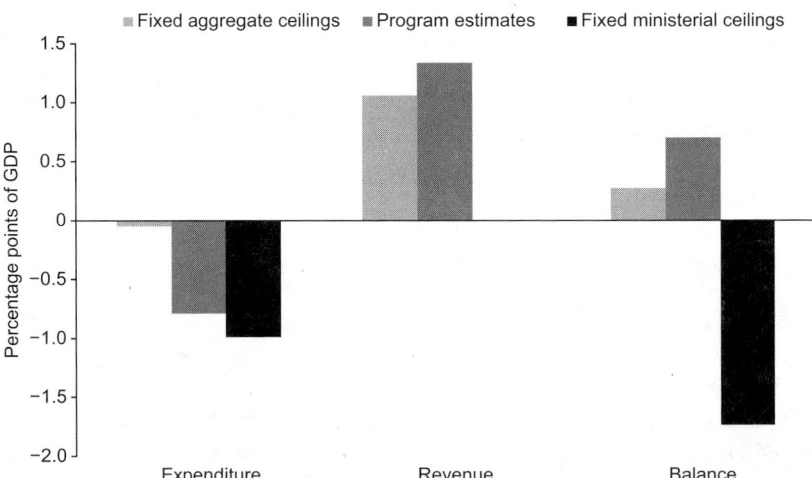

Figure 4.4 Average Three-Year-Ahead Forecast Error for Expenditure, Revenue, and Balance for Different Types of Binding Medium-Term Budget Framework, 1998–2007

Sources: Finland, the Netherlands, Sweden, United Kingdom: stability and convergence programs. Australia: year-end budget reconciliation documents.

For the period under examination, Australia tended to underestimate revenue three years ahead by 1.4 percent of GDP.[14] About 0.8 percentage point of this resulting revenue windfall was, on average, used to increase expenditure. However, this still left 0.6 percentage point of GDP overperformance against the government's initial

[14] To some degree, this overperformance on revenue was the result of positive terms-of-trade shocks from the upswing in prices of commodities—a key export in Australia, which boosted tax revenues.

forecast for the fiscal balance, the most cautious forecast for the fiscal balance of any country in the sample.

Although these results point to the effectiveness of the binding MTBFs, given the complex interactions that occur through the budget process, conclusively drawing out causality between the MTBFs and fiscal outcomes from the data alone is difficult. Relatively few data points are available and a large number of external factors are at play—such as exogenous economic shocks to individual countries that could lead to forecast errors even with the best system. Furthermore, well-functioning MTBFs and good fiscal outcomes may both be the result of strong underlying budget formulation and policymaking. However, discussion with key officials involved in the introduction and development of MTBFs indicates that the introduction of these frameworks did, in fact, change behavior and contribute to better fiscal outcomes. For example, as described in Box 4.2, the United Kingdom experimented with three different MTBF approaches in 30 years and found that the progressive introduction of more binding MTBF models coincided with a steady increase in the accuracy of the government's medium-term expenditure forecasts.

Enabling Medium-Term Expenditure Planning

The effectiveness of different MTBF models in enabling medium-term expenditure planning is assessed by examining the average volatility of general government expenditure. The average year-on-year volatility in the real growth rate of government expenditure is used as a proxy for the overall predictability of expenditure developments over time and, therefore, the extent to which ministries can expect some stability in their own allocations.[15] Once again, averages for 1998 through 2007 are used for the reasons already discussed.

Countries with binding MTBFs also seem to promote medium-term expenditure planning more effectively than do those with indicative MTBFs or no MTBF. Countries with binding MTBFs have an average annual volatility in real expenditure growth of about 2½ percent, which is less than half the 5.4 percent volatility of real expenditure in countries with indicative MTBFs (Table 4.4). Surprisingly, countries with no MTBF actually experience lower average volatility in real expenditure than those with indicative MTBFs.

Among countries with binding MTBFs, the forward estimates approach seems to promote medium-term expenditure planning most effectively. Australia's forward estimates resulted in average annual expenditure volatility of 1.8 percent compared with 2.7 percent for the United Kingdom's fixed ministerial ceilings and 3.0 percent for fixed aggregate ceilings. This somewhat counterintuitive finding could be attributed to the detailed understanding of expenditure dynamics engendered by Australia's forward estimates process, which serves to stabilize the year-on-year allocation of resources. It may also be attributable to the fact that under the fixed frameworks operated by Finland, the Netherlands, and the

[15]The volatility of total expenditure also depends on the structure of government spending. Countries with a large proportion of social security and unemployment transfers will typically experience higher volatility than countries with larger proportions of government consumption and investment.

TABLE 4.4

Predictability and Dispersion of Spending by MTBF Classification

	Average volatility of real government spending, 1998–2007 (Percent)	Real growth rate dispersion in government spending by function, 1998–2007 (Percent)
None	4.1	9.1
Indicative	5.4	9.5
Binding	2.4	6.7
of which		
Fixed aggregate	3.1	6.3
Fixed ministry	2.7	6.8
Program estimates	1.8	8.0

Sources: IMF, *World Economic Outlook*, October 2010; United Nations Statistics Division, Classification of the Functions of Government Database; Australian Bureau of Statistics, Commonwealth General Government Expenses by Purpose.

United Kingdom, major discontinuities in expenditure growth rates can occur when one multiyear expenditure plan runs into the next.

Promoting Effective Allocation of Resources

Measuring the effectiveness of different MTBF models in promoting efficiency is complicated by the lack of consensus on what constitutes an effective allocation of resources, which depends on the political preference of the government in office.

Therefore, two proxy measures of efficiency are used. The first is the extent to which nonfinancial performance information is used in setting ministerial budgets, which measures whether efficiency of expenditure is a formal consideration in the determination of its allocation. The second is the average standard deviation in real growth rates between different sectors during the 10 years from 1998 to 2008, which measures how closely the allocation of expenditure to different sectors moves with the overall growth of expenditure (low dispersion) or with some other idiosyncratic sense of sectoral priorities (high dispersion).

Countries with binding MTBFs tend to make more extensive use of nonfinancial performance information. All countries with binding MTBFs use nonfinancial performance information when setting ministerial budgets, as compared with 45 percent of countries with indicative MTBFs and 29 percent of countries with no MTBF. The universal use of nonfinancial performance information among binding MTBF countries makes it impossible to say which binding MTBF models are most effective in integrating performance information into budget decision making.

However, no correlation can be discerned between the type of MTBF in place and the dispersion of real growth rates in different sectors. As shown in Table 4.4, if anything, countries with binding MTBFs seem to have lower standard deviations in growth rates between sectors (6.7 percent) than do countries with indicative (9.5 percent) or no MTBF (9.1 percent). This outcome may be attributable to the fact that most countries with binding MTBFs are advanced economies with inherently more stable allocations of expenditure between sectors. It may also illustrate that although binding MTBFs may promote more active discussion of the efficiency and effectiveness of expenditure, this discussion does not necessarily result in a substantially different allocation of expenditure.

4.5.2. Operation of MTBFs Following the Financial Crisis

The global financial crisis proved to be a major test of many countries' fiscal positions, budgeting systems, and medium-term budget frameworks. In most instances, the medium-term budget frameworks helped governments respond to the crisis by providing a more sophisticated platform to plan, explain, and deliver both fiscal stimulus packages and subsequent fiscal consolidation programs. The analysis presented so far in this chapter has focused on the precrisis period. However, the period in the wake of the 2008–09 crisis also provides a number of examples of the use of MTBFs to adjust fiscal policy in a credible way following a large, unexpected shock that changes the state of the world.

Evidence of the role that MTBFs can play in supporting the credibility of a country's fiscal policy can be found in the relationship between government indebtedness and market perceptions of sovereign default risks in the aftermath of the crisis. Figure 4.5 illustrates the relationship between general government debt levels and credit default swap spreads for a group of 23 advanced economies at end-2011. It shows that the relationship between government indebtedness and market perceptions of sovereign default risk (as measured by credit default

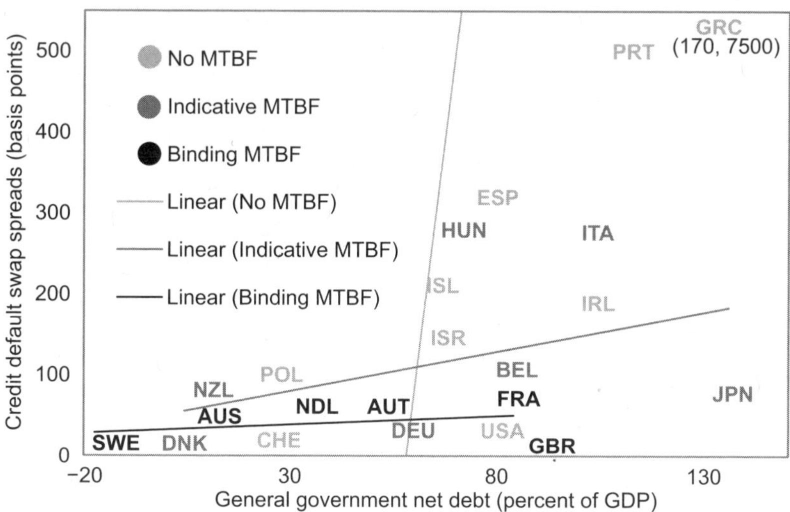

Figure 4.5 Perception of Default Risk versus Government Debt Levels, End-2011

Source: Credit default swaps from Thomson Reuters Datastream; net debt from IMF, *Fiscal Monitor* (October 2012).
Note: MTBF = medium-term budget framework. For expansion of three-letter country abbreviations, see, for example, the UN Statistical Division's list at http://unstats.un.org/unsd/methods/m49/m49alpha.htm.

swap spreads) was strongest for those countries without MTBFs and weakest for those countries with binding MTBFs. One interpretation is that, regardless of their debt levels in 2011, governments with binding MTBFs in place were able to convince markets that they would be able to deliver on their medium-term fiscal consolidation plans. Thus, having a binding MTBF in place provided these countries additional fiscal credibility.

The remainder of this section examines in more detail how the U.K. and Australian MTBFs responded to large reductions in both output and fiscal revenues in the wake of the crisis, initially through stimulus and then through fiscal consolidation.

The output shock accompanying the financial crisis led to a sharp and unexpected reduction in fiscal revenues (Figure 4.6). In the United Kingdom, before the crisis, total revenues were projected to be about 42 percent of GDP in 2010. After the crisis, revenues were revised downward 7 percentage points of GDP, to 35.1 percent of GDP. In Australia, the downward revision was slightly smaller, from a projected 25.5 percent of GDP to 22 percent of GDP following the crisis. These large shocks turned the fiscal outlook in each country on its head, and required policy responses to adjust to the new state of the world. The responses came in two parts.

The first was temporary fiscal stimulus. Unlike in a number of other countries where stimulus plans were laid out in broad terms and only for the year ahead and without requisite consideration of the evolution of public finances thereafter, the U.K. and Australian MTBFs provided platforms for the design and articulation of each government's fiscal plans in detail and over the medium term. An important part of an MTBF is the ability to estimate the economic impacts of fiscal policy changes, then feed them back into the public finance and macroeconomic projections, providing an integrated analysis of the shock and the policy response. Thus, the stimulus could be calibrated to provide optimal timing, composition, and size.

The second was a medium-term fiscal consolidation. Simultaneously with enunciating the full phasing of the stimulus, medium-term budget frameworks provided a platform for demonstrating when and how the stimulus was to be withdrawn and public finances returned to sustainability. This communication was important for managing market expectations. Rather than building increased spending into the expenditure base, which is the tendency under annual budgeting, medium-term budget frameworks were used to demonstrate how fiscal stimulus measures would be withdrawn and what the impact would be on economic growth and public finances.

In Australia, the consolidation path was announced at the time of the stimulus and was anchored by a fully specified deficit exit strategy. The exit strategy committed to keeping real expenditure growth to less than 2 percent a year until the budget returned to surplus and required that all new spending be offset (a pay-as-you-go rule) and that any revenue revisions be banked. Meeting these requirements for the entire forward estimates period became the focus of

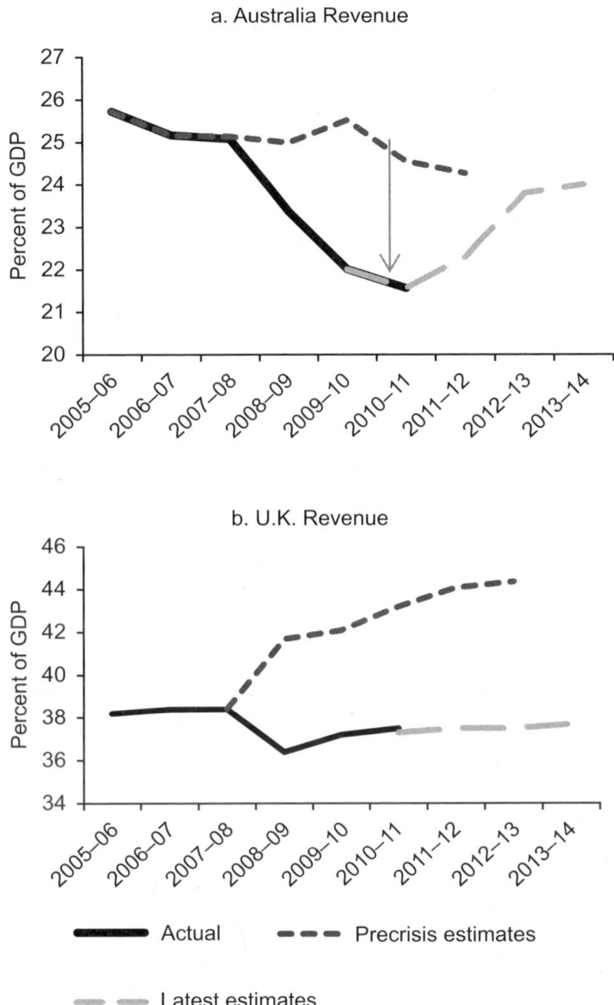

Figure 4.6 Adjustment of Revenue Forecasts after Crisis

Sources: Australia: 2008–09 and 2012–13 Budget Papers; United Kingdom: 2008 and 2012 Budgets.

decision making for the four subsequent budgets, ensuring that the strategy met expectations.

In the United Kingdom, the fiscal stimulus announced by the incumbent Labour government in the autumn of 2008 was delivered through a combination of temporary reductions in value-added taxes and a reprofiling of the three-year expenditure plans set out a year earlier in the 2007 Spending Review. This reprofiling of expenditure brought forward £3 billion (US$5.6 billion) of investment expenditure planned for 2010 into 2008 and 2009. Following the general election, the new Conservative–Liberal Democrat Coalition government used the 2010 Spending Review to set out detailed plans for eliminating the deficit and arresting the increase in government debt. The 2010 Spending Review set out five-year budgets for each line ministry for 2010–14 and assumed a reduction in government expenditure from 47 to 42 percent of GDP over the period.

In setting out the fiscal stimulus and consolidation plans, both countries' MTBFs obliged them to detail precisely how and when taxes and expenditures would rise and fall. This contrasts with the stimulus and consolidation plans of countries with no MTBF, which were general policy statements or commitments to meet particular spending rules or targets. The obligation to set out detailed expenditure plans at the outset of the crisis also enabled ministries and agencies to prepare for the consolidation phase by implementing the legislative, administrative, and operational measures needed to realize savings. For example, in the United Kingdom, the Department of Work and Pensions initiated a major reform to the system of disability benefits aimed at reducing its growing costs.

The real test of whether these countries' MTBFs were effective is whether the expenditure adjustment paths outlined initially were adhered to. Figure 4.7 suggests that this has been the case so far. In the United Kingdom, the spending reductions laid out in the 2010 spending review have been delivered, with expenditure actually coming in below the initial paths so far, and projected to remain in line with the initial commitment. Similarly, in Australia, the initial stimulus and exit path have been delivered, and although some variation in the 2011–12 outcome is expected as a result of reprofiling various expenditures (primarily defense), the expenditure share of GDP is projected to be in line with the initial path in 2012–13.

4.6. CONCLUSION

There is no single MTBF model. Countries establish MTBFs to achieve the public financial management objectives of maintaining a sustainable fiscal position, promoting more effective allocation of expenditure between sectors and priorities, and encouraging more efficient use of resources by budget managers.

The most appropriate model for a particular country or context depends on the point at which policymakers strike the balance between the competing objectives of multiyear budget planning. Aggregate expenditure ceilings tend to promote multiyear expenditure discipline more effectively, ministerial ceilings are more effective at facilitating multiyear expenditure planning, and forward estimates provide increased certainty that specific policy outcomes will be achieved.

This chapter underscores the following lessons from advanced-economy experience with MTBFs, which could help countries looking to embark on or progress down this path:

Successful multiyear budget planning requires sound basic fiscal institutions. Medium-term estimates need to be built upon a credible annual budget, based on prudent macroeconomic assumptions, guided by stable and transparent fiscal objectives, and implemented through a comprehensive and unified top-down

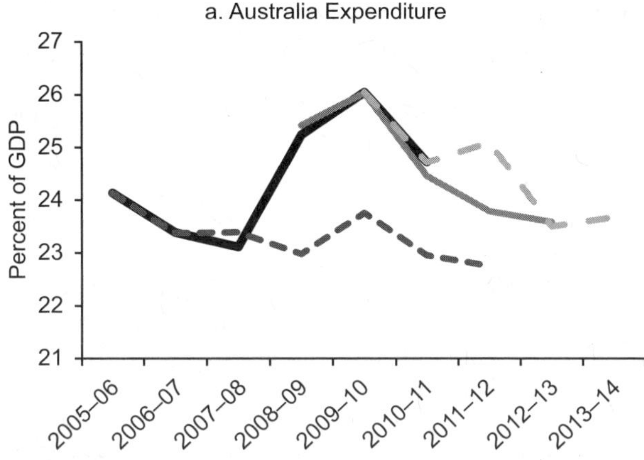

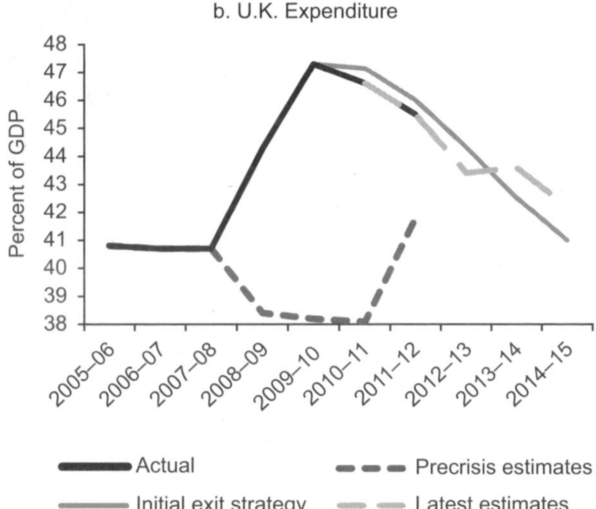

Figure 4.7 Adjustment of Expenditure Forecasts after Crisis

Sources: Australia: 2008–09 and 2012–13 Budget Papers; United Kingdom: 2008 and 2012 Budgets.

budget process. Countries face trade-offs, however, between coverage, specificity, and certainty in designing the multiyear expenditure restrictions upon which their medium-term plans are based.

In addition to mechanisms through which government can credibly commit to medium-term expenditure restrictions, effective MTBFs require institutional arrangements that enable government to prioritize expenditure within those restrictions, contain expenditure pressures, and demonstrate consistency between restrictions and the current budgetary position. Effective prioritization of expenditure within restrictions requires a clear separation of the cost of new and existing policies and an institutional forum for discussing and choosing between priorities.

Enforcing the credibility of the MTBF requires regularly updated multiyear expenditure projections, inclusion of adequate safety margins, firm control over multiyear expenditure commitments, and clear rules about the carryover of unspent appropriations.

The credibility of a country's medium-term budget plans depends on government's ability to present its annual budget and final accounts in a manner consistent with those plans, transparently account for any deviations, and hold budget actors responsible for any unjustified deviations.

Binding MTBF models are more effective than indicative MTBFs in promoting aggregate fiscal discipline and enabling multiyear expenditure planning. Some indirect evidence suggests that binding MTBFs also induce greater focus on the effectiveness of expenditure. There is less evidence that the adoption of an MTBF facilitates the reallocation of expenditure between sectors.

Finally, binding MTBFs also appear to provide a more effective platform for planning, communicating, and delivering both fiscal stimulus and fiscal consolidation plans. Anecdotal evidence suggests that, in the wake of the 2008 global economic crisis, countries with binding MTBFs were better able to convince markets of the credibility of their fiscal consolidation plans.

REFERENCES

Ahnert, T., R. Hughes, and K. Takahashi, 2011, "United Kingdom: Four Chancellors Facing Challenges," in *Chipping Away at Public Debt*, ed. by P. Mauro (New York: John Wiley & Sons).

Alesina, A., and R. Perotti, 1994, "The Political Economy of Budget Deficits," NBER Working Paper No. 4637 (Cambridge, Massachusetts: National Bureau of Economic Research).

Alesina, A., and G. Tabellini, 1990, "A Positive Theory of Budget Deficits and Government Debt," *Review of Economic Studies,* Vol. 57, pp. 403–14.

Blöndal, J., D. Bergvall, I. Hawkesworth, and R. Deighton-Smith, 2008, "Budgeting in Australia," *OECD Journal on Budgeting*, Vol. 8, No. 2 (Sept.), pp. 1–64.

Buchanan, J., and R. Wagner, 1977, *Democracy in Deficit: The Political Legacy of Lord Keynes* (New York: Academic Press).

Calmfors, L., and S. Wren-Lewis, 2011, "What Should Fiscal Councils Do?" CESifo Working Paper No. 3382 (Munich: Center for Economic Studies).

Coate, S., and S. Morris, 1999, "Policy Persistence," *Public Choice,* Vol. 50, pp. 5–25.

Finland, Ministry of Finance, 2011, *Developing the Spending Limits System*, Budget Issues 17b/2011 (Helsinki).

Jonung, L., and M. Larch, 2006, "Improving Fiscal Policy in the EU: The Case for Independent Forecasts," *Economic Policy*, Vol. 21, No. 47, pp. 491–534.

Kumar, M.S., E. Baldacci, A. Schaechter, C. Caceres, D. Kim, X. Debrun, J. Escolano, and others, 2009, "Fiscal Rules—Anchoring Expectations for Sustainable Public Finances," IMF Staff Paper 09/274 (Washington: International Monetary Fund).

Ljungman, G., 2007, "The Swedish Medium-Term Fiscal Framework," *OECD Journal on Budgeting*, Vol. 6, No. 3 (March), pp. 1–17.

———, 2009, "Top-Down Budgeting—An Instrument to Strengthen Budget Management," IMF Working Paper 09/243 (Washington: International Monetary Fund).

Nordhaus, W.D., 1975, "The Political Business Cycle," *Review of Economic Studies,* Vol. 42 (April), pp. 169–82.

Persson, T., and L.E.O. Svensson, 1989, "Why a Stubborn Conservative Would Run a Deficit: Policy with Time-Inconsistent Preferences," *Quarterly Journal of Economics,* Vol. 104, No. 2 (May), pp. 325–45.

Rogoff, K., 1990, "Equilibrium Political Business Cycles," *American Economic Review*, Vol. 80, No. 1 (March), pp. 21–36.

Roubini, N., and J.D. Sachs, 1989, "Political and Economic Determinants of Budget Deficits in Industrial Democracies," *European Economic Review,* Vol. 33, No. 5 (May), pp. 903–38.

Strauch, R., M. Hallerberg, and J. von Hagen, 2004, "Budgetary Forecasts in Europe—The Track Record of Stability and Convergence Programmes," European Central Bank Working Paper No. 307 (Frankfurt: European Central Bank).

von Hagen, J., and M. Hallerberg, 1999, "Electoral Institutions, Cabinet Negotiations and Budget Deficits in the European Union," in *Fiscal Institutions and Fiscal Performance*, National Bureau of Economic Research Conference Report, ed. by J. Poterba and J. von Hagen (Chicago: University of Chicago Press).

Weingast, B.R., K.A. Shepsle, and C. Johnsen, 1981, "The Political Economy of Benefits and Costs: A Neoclassical Approach to Distributive Politics," *Journal of Political Economy*, Vol. 89, No. 4, pp. 642–64.

CHAPTER 5

Managing and Controlling Fiscal Risks

NINA BUDINA AND MURRAY PETRIE

Since the early 1990s, the management of fiscal risk has become an increasingly prominent topic in public finance. New sources of risk and unexpected shocks to government finances have highlighted the importance of managing fiscal risks. The 2008–09 global economic and financial crisis provides a dramatic illustration of the magnitude of the risks to which public finances can be exposed, while at the same time underscoring the role of fiscal policy in managing the economic impact of those risks.

Fiscal risk is defined as the possibility of short- to medium-term deviations in fiscal variables compared with what was anticipated in the government budget or other fiscal forecasts (IMF, 2008). For the purpose of this chapter, fiscal risk is defined as the exposure of the government to short- to medium-term variability in the overall levels of revenues, spending, the fiscal balance, and the value of assets and liabilities.[1] Such a definition of risk calls for the application of a balance sheet approach to fiscal risk management, incorporating both flows and stocks of fiscal variables and their interactions.

Fiscal risks are classified as general economic risks, (e.g., lower economic growth than predicated resulting in loss of government revenues) or specific risks (e.g., potential cost of natural disasters). Fiscal risks from contingent and other opaque liabilities (e.g., government guarantees) can cause serious fiscal instability if left unchecked. But under conventional cash-basis government budgeting and accounting, the treatment of contingent liabilities is often inadequate and their fiscal consequences frequently overlooked in the standard fiscal analysis (for instance, see Schick, 1998, pp. 78–83, and Brixi and Schick, 2002). In recognition of these shortcomings, a number of international initiatives have been taken in the past two decades to improve information on fiscal risks and the effectiveness of fiscal risk management.[2]

Portions of this chapter draw extensively from Petrie (2002, 2008).

[1] Note that exposure to predictable, longer-term adverse trends (such as projected increases in spending on public pensions or health) is, from this perspective, viewed more as a known threat to long-term fiscal sustainability rather than as a source of fiscal risk.

[2] On risk disclosure, see IMF (2007a, 2007b, 2009a); on risk management and mitigation, see Brixi and Schick (2002), Hemming (2006), and IMF (2008).

This chapter assesses the international trend toward more active disclosure and management of fiscal risks since the early 1990s. The first section describes the main approaches used to classify different sources of fiscal risk; the second section puts forward a generic fiscal risk management cycle and discusses the context for fiscal risk management. The subsequent sections address, in turn, key aspects of risk assessment and management, including identifying risks; analyzing risks; incorporating risks in the budget; disclosing fiscal risks; mitigating risks; and monitoring and reviewing risks. The final section discusses the challenges that have emerged, and considers lessons learned and priorities for strengthening fiscal risk management.

5.1. SOURCES OF FISCAL RISK

Fiscal risks come from many sources and in many forms. This chapter classifies fiscal risks into general macroeconomic or specific risks. A further category of fiscal risk is also sometimes identified: structural or institutional weaknesses that constrain the effectiveness of fiscal risk management (Hemming and Petrie, 2002).

5.1.1. Types of Fiscal Risk

General economic risks refer to the exposure of public finances to variations in key economic and other parameters from the levels of those parameters assumed in the forecasts. Fiscal deficit targets may be missed owing to macroeconomic shocks. For example, a slowdown in economic activity could cause revenue losses and lead to increased spending on unemployment benefits and other elements of the social safety net. Public debt may shoot up if the exchange rate suddenly depreciates. Countries with relatively high debt levels may be vulnerable to interest rate shocks, low-income countries to aid shortfalls, and commodity-producing countries to sharp swings in commodity prices (through their impact on revenues).

In contrast, *specific fiscal risks* are not related to general forecasting parameters. They are narrower and arise from specific sources, such as the potential costs of guarantees or natural disasters;[3] the possible need to provide fiscal support to a state-owned enterprise (SOE) or private bank; the risk of tax noncompliance; variance in volume levels, for example, in natural resource production; and take-up rates for demand-driven (open-ended) subsidy schemes and social assistance programs.

Specific risks from contingent liabilities are particularly important; many governments have faced serious fiscal instability as a result of hidden fiscal risks from contingent liabilities. A contingent liability is generally defined as an obligation

[3] The fiscal implications of large-scale natural disasters could be significant, owing to weak revenues associated with large output losses and in some cases to significant reconstruction costs (e.g., Japan in 2011 and New Zealand in 2010–11).

to make a payment if, and only if, a specific event occurs or a specific condition arises in the future. A contingent liability can be explicit or implicit. Risks from explicit contingent obligations come into play when the government has a clear and firm legal obligation, or a declared policy, to provide fiscal support should a particular event occur. Government guarantees and other contingent liabilities complicate fiscal management, and have received ample attention in the literature (Brixi and Schick, 2002; Irwin, 2003; Hemming, 2006). Box 5.1 discusses some of the associated fiscal management issues.

In contrast, risks from implicit contingent obligations arise if no explicit obligation or policy to provide fiscal support is in place, but the government is

BOX 5.1 Government Guarantees and Other Contingent Liabilities Pose Problems for Fiscal Management

The main types of contingent liabilities are as follows:

- government guarantees, such as loan guarantees or minimum revenue guarantees in public-private partnerships;
- warranties and indemnities, such as assurances of protection from specified losses, for example, an indemnity against future site restoration costs that governments sometimes issue when privatizing state assets;
- underfinanced public insurance schemes for which the premiums do not cover expected claims, and payments are financed partly (or entirely) from general taxation, for example, a deposit insurance scheme or a disaster insurance scheme in the early years of establishment while reserves are being accumulated;
- legal action against the state that may result in a cost to the government; and
- uncalled capital, that is, an unpaid portion of shareholder equity, such as the uncalled capital many governments have in international financial institutions.

For a number of reasons a certain class of contingent liability—government guarantees—poses particular problems for fiscal management. First, government guarantees may be provided instead of lending or direct subsidies mainly because the latter are reflected immediately in the government's accounts, whereas guarantees have traditionally not been reported at all until, if ever, they have to be paid. Second, although government guarantees can be legitimate policy instruments in some circumstances (see Irwin, 2003; OECD, 2005), they complicate fiscal management because of the uncertainty about their fiscal impact, the undesirable incentives they can create, the lumpiness of their impact, and the fact that they have traditionally not been subject to the discipline of the budget process. Guarantees have proliferated in some countries resulting in shocks to the fiscal position when they are called (see Brixi and Schick, 2002, for a discussion of country examples). In addition, guarantees tend to be called just when the fiscal position is deteriorating for other reasons, because the same developments that trigger calls on guarantees often also negatively affect government revenues and other expenditures.

Uncertainty about the fiscal impact of guarantees has been illustrated in the current financial sector crisis. As of mid-2010, the uptake of guarantees was markedly lower than the protection offered, with several liquidity support and guarantee programs in Canada, the United Kingdom, and the United States expiring in 2010 without any guarantees being called. However, implicit contingent liabilities from banking system losses remain high in some countries, in particular in Ireland, where they totaled 10.8 percent of 2011 GDP (IMF, 2012b).

expected to, or pressured to, provide support should a particular event occur. Examples include expectations that the central government "stands behind" SOEs or subnational governments should they fall into financial difficulty; that government will provide assistance in the event of failure, for example, to depositors in a private bank failure; or that government will provide relief following natural disasters (in the absence of, or over and above the level covered by, a disaster insurance scheme). An implicit risk may still exist even when (sometimes especially when) governments have announced that they will not provide assistance in such an event or beyond a certain level—a good example being the "no bailout" clause in the policy framework for the European Monetary Union before the introduction in 2010 of the European Financial Stabilization Mechanism.

A feature of implicit fiscal risks is that their hidden and uncertain nature tempts governments to avoid dealing with them. In the meantime, the underlying risks can accumulate and may reach massive proportions. The classic example has been regulatory forbearance in banking supervision, that is, the failure to deal with insolvent banks in the hope that they will recover or that the cost of rescuing them will not have to be met until after the term of the present government.

Structural or institutional weaknesses can also constrain the effectiveness of fiscal risk management. Such weaknesses can increase the probability of a negative event occurring or the cost to government if it does occur. For example, if revenues are dominated by one or two sources, they are likely to be more volatile, especially if they are derived from natural resources. Other structural weaknesses include a high ratio of statutory and other nondiscretionary spending to total government spending, excessive earmarking of revenues to specific expenditure programs, and difficulties in coordinating fiscal policy among different levels of government. These weaknesses restrict government's ability to tighten fiscal policy in response to a shock, potentially amplifying the impact of a given shock.

Weak capacity to identify and manage fiscal risks is itself a source of risk. When decision makers lack good information, for example, because of poor macroeconomic forecasting or inadequate information on specific risks, fiscal management becomes a bit like "flying blind." This situation can be compounded if the institutions and actors responsible for specific risk management functions are not clearly identified, if those responsible lack the necessary authority, or if budgeting systems—such as separate current and development budgets, or annual rather than medium-term fiscal frameworks—frustrate effective management.

5.1.2. Evidence of the Magnitude of Different Sources of Fiscal Risk

The 2008–09 financial crisis and its aftermath have compellingly illustrated the range and magnitude of the different fiscal risks to which advanced economies especially are exposed. Over 2007–09, the fiscal-deficit-to-GDP ratio increased 12-fold, from 0.6 to 7.2 percent, on average, and in 2011, the deficit ratio was still seven times higher than its precrisis (2007) levels, despite its steady decline from peak levels in 2009. Advanced economies, in particular, are experiencing large—and likely long-lasting—fiscal deterioration (IMF, 2011, 2012a). Substantial discretionary fiscal support, provided by governments and central banks in response to the crisis, has contributed to the fiscal deterioration.

But the bulk of this deterioration results from significant exposures of government revenues and spending to the slowdown in economic activity, through its impact on revenue collections and increased spending on unemployment benefits and social safety nets. Underlying spending pressures—especially increased social security outlays and higher health and pension spending—are expected to further increase pressures on deficits. The large fiscal deterioration is forecast to result in a sizable public debt buildup, particularly in the Group of Twenty (G-20) advanced economies, where public debt is forecast to swell by 38.6 percent of GDP, on average, during 2008–15 (see Figure 5.1).

The output collapse and related revenue loss are the main contributors to large public debt buildups in the G-20 economies. Of the forecasted 38.6 percentage points of GDP increase in the general government debt ratio from 2008 through 2015, about half is explained by revenue weaknesses associated with the recession—including lower asset prices and financial sector profits—and the direct effect on the debt ratio of the fall in GDP. The decline in GDP has led to an unfavorable interest rate–growth differential despite falling interest rates. Fiscal stimulus explains an additional one-sixth of this forecast debt accumulation during 2008–15.

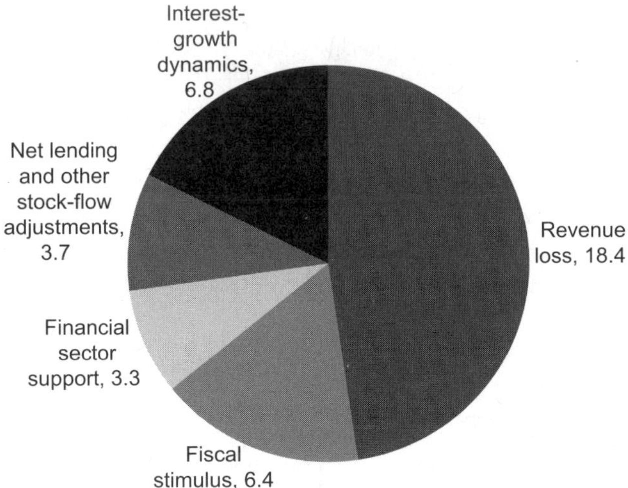

Figure 5.1 Group of Twenty Advanced Economies: Decomposition of Change in Debt-to-GDP Ratio, 2008–15 (Total Increase 38.6 Percentage Points of GDP; 2009 PPP-GDP Weighted)

Source: IMF (2011).
Note: PPP = purchasing-power parity.

5.2. FISCAL RISK MANAGEMENT CYCLE

Although management of fiscal risks is an ongoing process, breaking it down into discrete stages that constitute a generic risk management cycle, as described in Figure 5.2, can be useful.

One outcome of a well-functioning fiscal risk management cycle can be summarized as "the right information being made available to the right people at the right time." The information required to manage fiscal risks needs to be collocated with the responsibility for risk management, and those responsible should have the necessary authority to enable them to manage fiscal risks and to be accountable for doing so. This requirement emphasizes that risk management should be part of the standard operating procedures and culture of all ministries, departments, and agencies in government.

The fiscal risk management cycle starts with establishing the external and internal context within which the government operates. The external context should include the political and public financial management environment, for example, the relationship with the legislature, the fiscal relationship with subnational

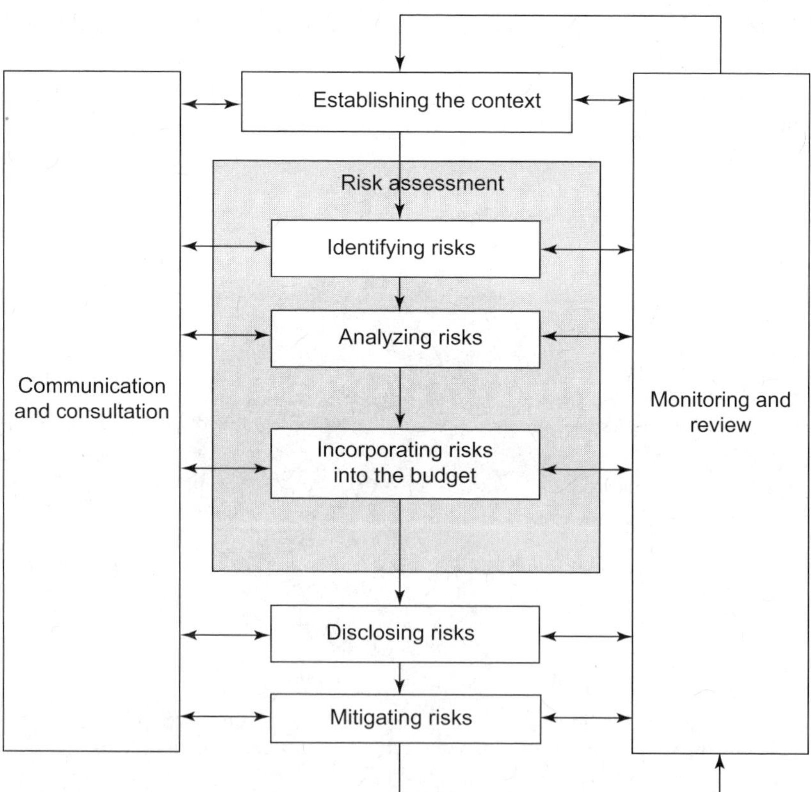

Figure 5.2 The Fiscal Risk Management Cycle

Source: Adapted from ISO (2009, p. 14).

governments, and the size of the SOE sector and of public financial institutions. It should also consider the exposure of the economy to external or internal shocks and natural disasters, and recent trends in key fiscal risks. The internal context should include government's objectives for fiscal risk management, the scope of the risk management function, the allocation of responsibilities within the executive, and the current capacity for managing fiscal risks.

In general, the objective of financial risk management for any entity is to improve the entity's financial position and performance while protecting the entity from unacceptable variance in returns. In government, however, the overall objective is national welfare maximization rather than a narrower focus on government's financial position. Government's fiscal position is both a bearer of risks emanating from other parts of the economy and a source of risks to the rest of the economy. Sound risk management by government is essential for effective risk management by the rest of the economy. National welfare maximization may properly lead government to absorb a portion of some financial risks (such as the risk of unemployment or old-age poverty, or the risk of government policy change).

The government's objective, therefore, is not to minimize fiscal risk, but to carry those risks that it is able to bear efficiently and at lower economic and social cost than other actors in the economy. Although active use of fiscal policy to try to smooth the economic cycle has been out of favor in the past two decades, the global financial crisis is a powerful reminder that fiscal policy can help to support demand during a major recession. This circumstance suggests the need to ensure there is enough "powder in the fiscal cannon" to spark a fiscal expansion when appropriate.[4] Governments should particularly try to avoid cutting spending during a recession—as some governments facing a loss of market confidence have had to do (e.g., Greece, Ireland, Portugal, and Spain) and the United Kingdom has done in an attempt to preempt a possible loss of confidence.

Public finance theory also suggests that governments should raise revenues in a way that is consistent with stable tax rates.[5] Volatility in tax rates and government spending imposes welfare costs in comparison with smoother and more predictable paths. Tax smoothing is also consistent with countercyclical fiscal policy.

A degree of risk aversion and prudence is appropriate given asymmetries in the impacts of unfavorable versus favorable outcomes, and the optimism bias and short time horizons of decision makers and officials. The degree of risk aversion should depend on a range of country-specific factors that determine government's ability to absorb financial pressures. These factors include the country's initial fiscal position, the nature and extent of fiscal risks, the structure of public finances, the degree of fiscal flexibility (e.g., how much fiscal space exists within a mandated deficit or expenditure ceiling; or the ability to draw on financial assets,

---

[4] The evidence indicates that the fiscal stimulus by country during 2008–10 was inversely related to the level of public debt, at least in large countries (IMF, 2009b).

[5] Leaving principal-agent costs aside, tax rate stability minimizes deadweight losses from taxation because of the shape of the deadweight loss function. Hence, a certain tax rate of 30 percent is preferable to a 50:50 chance of a tax rate of 28 percent or 32 percent.

or to borrow), and the capacity to respond to risks that may occur (which includes the legal framework, institutional capability, information availability, and technical capacity).

5.3. IDENTIFYING FISCAL RISKS

Responsibilities for identification of fiscal risks—a prerequisite for risk management—need to be allocated clearly and are often centralized in one institution. Information on existing risk exposures needs to be centralized within the government to account for potential interactions and portfolio effects. For instance, some risks offset each other (e.g., in some countries oil price changes have caused partially offsetting effects on government revenues and expenditures) whereas others can have magnifying effects (e.g., when government guarantees issued by diverse entities result in a bunching of exposure). These possibilities suggest a clear role for the ministry of finance or similar central agency (referred to in this chapter as the central fiscal institution, or CFI) to aggregate information on fiscal risks to which individual government agencies and the government as a whole are exposed.

However, institutional arrangements vary across countries. In some, a single ministry of finance is responsible for most or nearly all the core functions relevant to the management of fiscal risks—macrofiscal policy, macroeconomic forecasting, revenue and expenditure forecasting, revenue and expenditure policy, budget management, asset and liability management, aid management, revenue administration, oversight of SOEs and subnational governments, and financial sector regulation. This centralization facilitates the aggregation of information on risks, although clear assignment of roles and operating procedures within a unified ministry is still needed, as is intraministry coordination and information sharing.

In other countries, budget management is the responsibility of a separate agency, or functions such as macroeconomic forecasting, revenue forecasting, aid management, oversight of SOEs and subnational governments, and financial sector regulation are led by separate agencies or shared between separate agencies and the finance ministry. The more fragmented the assignment of functions across agencies, and the more autonomy granted to individual agencies, the more challenging the task of coordination and centralization of information on fiscal risks. Some countries may find it desirable to establish a high-level interagency committee on fiscal risk, chaired by the CFI, to oversee and coordinate activities and to ensure their proper integration with processes such as the annual budget, public investment planning, and financial market regulation.

Although governments generally have a specialist unit responsible for debt management (see Chapter 9), often within the ministry of finance (and several have extended the remit of their debt management offices to cover contingent liabilities) (Currie, 2002), many countries do not appear to clearly task a unit (or units) in the CFI with responsibility for risk identification and overall monitoring and analysis of fiscal risk. Specialized units for managing certain types of fiscal risk have recently been established in a number of countries—the chief example being public-private partnership (PPP) units—but only a few have established units for fiscal risk management more generally (e.g., Indonesia).[6] Among advanced economies, New Zealand provides an example of a comprehensive framework and clear accountabilities for fiscal risk management.[7]

Centralization of information on fiscal risks requires a clear definition of fiscal risks and the obligation of ministries and agencies to submit information on risks to the CFI regularly and routinely. Ministries could be required to submit information on fiscal risks to the CFI in their annual budget returns. Fiscal risks could also be incorporated in the government's accounting standards—for example, all individual ministries and agencies could be required to record and report their contingent liabilities.

The choice of cash or accrual accounting standards has important implications for the identification and management of fiscal risks. Accrual accounting entails the recognition of transactions or events at the time the transaction or event occurs rather than at the time a cash payment is made (provided that recognition criteria, such as reliable cost estimation, are met). Accrual accounting also entails the production of a full balance sheet, which provides significant additional information about the future implications of current policies (see Chapter 8). For example, under accrual accounting, information is provided on the full cost of current civil service pension policies and the variability in the value of the liability from year to year. The choice between defined-contribution and defined-benefit pension schemes, for instance, involves significant differences in the amount of fiscal risk borne by the government. Under a defined-benefit scheme, the government bears the risk of a mismatch between the return on any assets held by the scheme and the defined pension obligation. Under a defined-contribution scheme, the individual contributor bears the risk of uncertain return on pension fund assets.

The leading international accounting standards are moving toward more accurate accounting for risk. However, some types of risks—for example, risks from PPPs—still may not be reflected under accrual accounting standards.[8] Most important, future government revenues are not recognized as an asset under current accrual accounting standards, and many contingent obligations, such as guarantees, are not recognized as liabilities. Moreover, adopting accrual accounting standards is a demanding and protracted process. Therefore, countries can improve their management and disclosure of fiscal risks within a predominantly cash-based accounting system by recording and reporting supplementary information. Much of the information on fiscal risks, such as contingent liabilities, is in any case provided through supplementary reporting, even in those countries that have adopted the accrual basis for both budgeting and reporting (e.g., Australia and New Zealand).

---

[6] A Risk Management Unit was established in the Indonesian Ministry of Finance in 2006.The Risk Management Unit includes units responsible for analyzing fiscal risks in SOEs and in government support to infrastructure, as well as global economic risks.

[7] See Appendix 2 of IMF (2008).

[8] See Budina, Brixi, and Irwin (2007) for a discussion of the accounting for risks from PPPs in the European Union.

Governments lacking comprehensive centralized information on existing fiscal risks could start by preparing a Fiscal Risk Matrix as presented in Brixi and Mody (2002, p. 23).[9] This tool, which classifies risks in a two-by-two matrix according to whether they are direct or contingent, and explicit or implicit, has reportedly been used by a number of countries, including China, the Czech Republic, India, and the United States, to help identify the potential sources of fiscal risks and to promote risk awareness.[10]

5.4. ANALYZING FISCAL RISKS

In addition to information on risks, the CFI also needs the capacity to analyze these risks for incorporation into overall fiscal analysis.

5.4.1. Incorporating General Macroeconomic Risks in Fiscal Analysis

Governments can assess their fiscal exposure to macroeconomic risks by means of sensitivity analysis, scenario analysis, and, ultimately, stochastic analysis. Sensitivity analysis shows the impact of small changes in the forecast values of key macroeconomic variables (such as GDP, exchange rates, oil prices), taken one at a time, on government revenues and expenditures. It is the least demanding of these techniques and has become widespread in the two past decades.

Scenario analysis entails the design of alternative plausible combinations of macroeconomic variables to illustrate the fiscal impact of possible adverse developments in key macroeconomic parameters (e.g., a "low-growth" scenario).[11] This approach involves checking the robustness of the fiscal and debt positions to large adverse shocks to key macroeconomic variables (e.g., the real cost of domestic and foreign borrowing, real output growth, the primary balance, the real exchange rate, or a large commodity price shock in a commodity-producing country). In addition to analyzing the impact of general economic shocks, a scenario analysis can incorporate possible realization of contingent liabilities.

Risks stemming from macroeconomic uncertainty can also be assessed by means of stochastic analysis. This approach derives the probability distribution of future debt stocks based on stochastic simulations of key risk variables, explicitly capturing the volatility and comovements of key macroeconomic variables to assess fiscal vulnerability to shocks. Natural resource revenue volatility—a key source of risk in natural resource–exporting economies—can also be incorporated into a stochastic analysis. Box 5.2 presents an example of a framework that uses stochastic simulation methods to forecast the distribution and evolution of

[9] See also the Fiscal Risk Questionnaire (Brixi and Mody, 2002, pp. 46–50).

[10] Note that the Fiscal Risk Matrix is based on a broad definition of fiscal risk that includes long-term adverse trends such as future pension obligations.

[11] See IMF (2010b) for a recent example of scenario analysis for advanced and emerging market economies in the aftermath of the global economic crisis.

BOX 5.2 Framework for Fiscal Sustainability under Uncertainty in Indonesia

The first step is to create a baseline scenario of the likely future time path of the public debt, using the flow budget constraint equation. This equation updates future debt as a share of GDP, based on macroeconomic projections of key determinants of public debt dynamics, which in Indonesia are (1) non-oil primary deficit; (2) oil and gas fiscal revenues, which involve projections of the oil and gas extraction profile, prices, and taxation regimes; (3) growth-adjusted real interest payments on public debt; (4) capital gains or losses on net external debt due to changes in the real exchange rate; and (5) other factors that can lead to debt accumulation:

$$\dot{\boldsymbol{d}} = nopd - R_{oil} + (r - g)d + \hat{e}\alpha d + OF$$

where $\dot{\boldsymbol{d}}$ is the public debt-to-GDP ratio, *nopd* is the non-oil primary deficit as a share of GDP, g is the real GDP growth rate, r is the real interest rate on public debt, $\hat{e}$ is the change in the (bilateral, local currency units per US$1) real exchange rate where $e > 0$ denotes a real exchange rate depreciation, and R_{oil} denotes oil and gas fiscal revenues. Other factors (*OF*) include off-budget liabilities leading to debt increases (e.g., implicit contingent liabilities [bank bailouts] and called guarantees).

To deal with vulnerability to specific shocks and assess robustness to extreme events, the framework provides a variety of stress tests (IMF, 2003). To provide a broader view of the riskiness of the basic projections, the framework incorporates stochastic simulation methods (Celasun, Debrun, and Ostry, 2006; IMF, 2008; Budina and van Wijnbergen, 2009). These methods involve simulating the entire distribution of future debt stocks, based on stochastic realizations of key debt determinants (real growth rate, real interest rate, real exchange rate, oil prices). The probability density of the outcomes of the debt ratio in each year can be plotted from the stochastic simulations, generating a fan chart for the debt-to-GDP ratio. An example, prepared in early 2010, is included for Indonesia's public debt-to-GDP ratio (see Figure 5.2.1). The evolution of debt was forecast for 2010 and beyond using the identity equation that relates debt in year t to debt in the previous year, the primary non-oil balance in year t, projected oil and gas fiscal revenues, and other stock-flow adjustments in year t. In addition to key macroeconomic risks (shocks to real economic growth, the real exchange rate, and interest rates), the risk assessment also incorporated oil and gas production and price risks. An endogenous fiscal policy reaction was also incorporated in the stochastic analysis to assess its impact on fiscal risks (see right panel of figure).

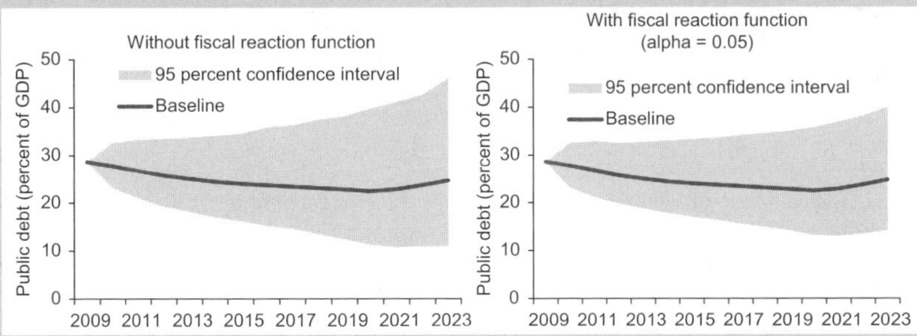

Figure 5.2.1 Public Debt-to-GDP Ratio—The Impact of a Fiscal Reaction Rule

Source: IMF staff calculations.

Source: Based on IMF (2010a).

(net) public debt and assets, explicitly accounting for oil and gas revenue volatility and expenditure policy (IMF, 2010a). This type of analysis also requires forecasts of oil and gas production and a revenue profile. The analysis can generate simulations based on various assumptions and rules for the intertemporal allocation of oil income. For example, fiscal policy in countries with limited proven oil reserves (e.g., Mexico) should be very different from the fiscal strategy in countries with vast oil and gas reserves (e.g., Kazakhstan and the Russian Federation) where price volatility is a more important challenge. The stochastic analysis can be expanded to include an endogenous fiscal policy reaction rule, whereby the primary balance is partially adjusted to deviations from baseline levels.[12]

5.4.2. Asset-Liability Management and the Government Balance Sheet

Another possibly complementary approach can be used to analyze fiscal risks from the perspective of asset-liability management and government net worth. This approach allows for analyzing fiscal risks arising from government direct and contingent liabilities in the context of an extended government balance sheet that includes future revenues as well as contingent liabilities, long-term obligations, assets, and direct liabilities.[13] Thus, fiscal sustainability analysis would be expanded to reflect off-budget factors and complemented by an analysis of government net worth and of future financial pressures and financing options.[14]

By recording both assets and liabilities, the extended balance sheet enables analysts to assess the impact of fiscal policies on net worth and to evaluate trends in net worth over time as a basis for determining the sustainability of fiscal policies. A number of studies use the public sector balance sheet approach to assess sustainability.[15] The overall exposure to risk will depend on correlations of different types of risks to the individual items in such an extended balance sheet. An extended assets and liabilities management framework would provide a useful context for the government's debt strategy—for instance, the selection of debt instruments and debt portfolio decisions to offset government risk exposures arising from contingent liabilities—as well as for fiscal planning (Brixi and Mody, 2002; IMF, 2009a).

[12] For a detailed discussion and estimation of such a reaction function for the United States, see Bohn (1998); and see Celasun, Debrun, and Ostry (2006) for a panel of emerging markets.

[13] This is an "economic balance sheet" incorporating all future cash inflows and outflows, not an accounting balance sheet, as discussed earlier in this chapter.

[14] For example, by relating fiscal performance to developments in the government's entire extended balance sheet (including the Fiscal Risk Matrix, containing various off-budget accounts, commitments, and contingent liabilities; and a Fiscal Hedge Matrix, which contains sources of government financial safety). See the Fiscal Risk Matrix, along with a Fiscal Hedge Matrix, presented for several countries in Brixi and Schick (2002).

[15] See Bohn (1998) for the United States, and Easterly and Yuravlivker (2002) for Colombia and Venezuela.

Another development in analyzing public sector net worth is the value-at-risk (VAR) approach. Specifically, VAR uses Monte Carlo simulations to derive the distribution of future stocks of the main categories of assets and liabilities, and hence net worth, based on stochastic realization of key risk variables used to value these stocks. The critical ingredient for VAR is the determination of the underlying variance and covariance structure of key risk variables (Barnhill and Kopits, 2003). This approach allows computation of the probability that the public sector net worth will become negative—which would signal a lack of fiscal sustainability and the possible need for policy changes to maintain sustainability.

5.4.3. Valuation of Contingent Liabilities and Guarantees

A number of possible qualitative and quantitative approaches can be applied to estimating the cost of specific risks from contingent liabilities and guarantees, depending on the nature of the risk, data availability, the significance of risk exposures, and institutional capacity. To the extent feasible, an estimate should be made of fiscal impact—both the range of potential costs and the expected (most likely) cost. Estimating the cost (or revenue loss from a revenue risk) of a more extreme outcome using VAR analysis may also be possible.

Quantification will not be feasible in a number of cases because of a lack of information, such as historical data on loss. Lack of capacity also constrains risk quantification in many countries, particularly lack of capacity for the use of sophisticated techniques for estimating the fiscal impacts of guarantees and other contingent or long-term obligations.[16] In such cases, a simple classification of guarantees into high, medium, low, or very low default risks, based on available information or educated guesses, should be employed to assess expected losses.

However, where there is a pooled program of risks, such as an ongoing program providing bank lending guarantees (e.g., to small businesses, or to farmers), historical loss data may allow a reasonably reliable estimate to be made for the expected annual costs of loan guarantees. Methods for estimating expected costs of a guarantee range from educated guesses, to market or historical data, to quantitative models such as options pricing[17] and stochastic simulations (Cebotari, 2008). Valuations based on market data are used when the borrower issues debt traded in the market or when finding comparable companies that do so is relatively easy. If market data are difficult to find, simulation methods are frequently used, but simulations may be cost effective only if the guaranteed amounts are large.

Countries that price guarantees and other contingent liabilities generally use all of the above methods. Sweden, for example, uses market data, options pricing,

---

[16] See Hemming and others (2006, pp. 37–40 and Appendix 4) for a discussion of techniques for estimating the fiscal cost of contingent liabilities.

[17] See Claessens and van Wijnbergen (1989) for pricing a guaranteed Brady bond.

and simulations to price guarantees. Chile, Colombia, and Peru use simulations to estimate contingent liabilities associated with any minimum revenue guarantees under PPP arrangements. The Federal Deposit Insurance Corporation in the United States uses expected loss estimates derived from historical and institution-specific loss data. The Republic of Korea uses investment rating agencies to assess the likelihood of payments on explicit contingent debts. The present value of government commitments (e.g., credit or minimum revenue guarantees under PPP contracts) can be calculated and tracked over time. As with debt, the present value of commitments can be expressed as a share of GDP or of government revenue to provide a sense of their significance. Governments could monitor the combined value of debt and other contingent government commitments, tracking their combined value as a share of GDP over time.

The stock of contingent liabilities should then be consolidated into a single portfolio, along with state debt and other public liabilities, to evaluate correlations, sensitivity to macroeconomic and policy scenarios, and overall risk exposure. A single portfolio allows government to relate its contingent liabilities to its comprehensive risk strategy and its guidelines regarding risk exposure, asset and liability management, hedging, and benchmarking.

5.5. INCORPORATING RISKS IN THE BUDGET

The impact of large, specific risks on the budget can be managed through various mechanisms. For example, one approach to mitigating the budgetary impact of potential losses related to contingent liabilities (e.g., calling of a guarantee) is to allocate sufficient resources to a contingency appropriation to meet such expenditure during the budget year. The appropriation should be under control of the CFI, with stringent conditions for access to resources, and with ex post reporting of actual spending against the relevant budget heads. Country practices suggest that this contingency reserve seldom exceeds 3 percent of total expenditure.

Decisions to extend explicit contingent liabilities, such as guarantees, need to be considered alongside other spending proposals. Under traditional cash-based accounting and budgeting systems, governments have to reflect the full cash impact of subsidies and loans, whereas the impact of guarantees and other contingent obligations is reflected only when and if they are called. This difference in treatment often provides incentives for substituting "risk expenditures" for immediate cash spending, even if immediate cash spending would be more cost effective.

Governments can correct this bias in favor of guarantees by reflecting the full likely fiscal cost of contingent support in the budget when such a scheme is approved. In countries with cash-based budgets, this cost can be expressed through a contingency appropriation of the expected annual cash outflow to meet calls on guarantees in any given year. The appropriation could be a general contingency appropriation, or a separate guarantee appropriation (e.g., for a large program of related guarantees, such as guarantees of loans to small businesses). Charging the sponsoring ministries and agencies a guarantee fee could also help to strengthen discipline over the use of guarantees.

Alternatively, governments can appropriate the full expected cost (net present value of all the expected future annual cash outflows) of guarantees, as is done in Canada, the Netherlands, Sweden, and the United States. This accrual-based approach is powerful in aligning incentives, but it requires reliable estimates of expected cost. The chosen approach, therefore, needs to balance these two issues: (1) decision making is best informed, and incentives are best aligned, if governments recognize the costs of commitments at the time they are made and (2) budget appropriations should be based on information generated by accepted and reliable budgeting practices and accounting policies.

Introducing an annual quantitative limit on the face value of guarantees is another, simpler approach if proliferating guarantees are a problem. The limit may apply to the total stock or the annual flow of new guarantees; it should be set on the basis of a sustainability assessment. The total guarantees limit may then be allocated among various agencies.

The governments of a number of oil-producing countries attempt to manage the impact of oil price volatility on the budget by establishing revenue stabilization funds, in which excess resource revenue during windfalls is set aside, thereby stabilizing recurrent resources available to the budget during downturns.[18] Such an arrangement can prevent the need to borrow during downturns, thus lowering the risk of accumulating a debt overhang. Political economy considerations could be another reason for establishing a stabilization fund—to ring-fence assets to ensure that resources will not be diverted elsewhere. Norway and Botswana provide the most-cited examples of the effective and transparent management of natural resource revenues, but some other (low-income) countries have also recently put in place sound public finance frameworks to manage the impacts of resource revenue volatility on the budget.

However, to ensure prudent management of oil windfalls, fiscal frameworks in oil-producing countries should also limit spending and non-oil deficits. An oil stabilization fund rule, which sets aside windfall oil revenues in a fund, is not sufficient to stabilize spending, because additional spending can be financed by borrowing, without yielding any net savings. In addition, having cash in a fund may be costly, because the cash could otherwise be used to repay higher-cost-yielding debt. Finally, the existence of cash in a fund may also tempt the government to use the money for other purposes. Therefore, having a fiscal framework or rule that limits the non-oil primary deficit to the "structural oil revenue,"

[18] Reserve funds are also common in subnational governments in some countries, in part owing to restrictions on their autonomy to raise revenues or to borrow. For instance, in the United States, 49 out of the 50 states have self-imposed legal prohibitions on borrowing to finance operational deficits in an attempt to reduce borrowing costs. In the absence of sufficient reserves in rainy-day funds, this inflexibility increases required spending cuts during economic recessions.

evaluated at a conservatively chosen oil reference price, is also necessary to stabilize spending and to yield overall surpluses during windfalls, deposited in a stabilization fund. Finally, effective public financial management and high levels of fiscal transparency and accountability are also needed to ensure prudent oil revenue management (see Chapter 13).

Governments are also taking a variety of steps to acknowledge the medium-term fiscal implications of their risk exposures. Many governments now conduct medium-term fiscal planning that considers not just next year's expenditure and revenues but those in the following two, three, or four years (see Chapter 4). A few governments (e.g., those in Australia, New Zealand, the United Kingdom, and the United States) have begun to publish long-term fiscal reports extending 30, 40, or more years into the future; risks from loan guarantees and PPPs may span 20–30 years into the future. Some governments conduct fiscal sustainability analyses that test whether their policies can be sustained in the long term without the government becoming insolvent, or whether they will eventually be obliged to raise taxes or cut spending.

5.6. DISCLOSING FISCAL RISKS

Although nondisclosure of fiscal risks has traditionally been the norm, the trend to greater disclosure among countries at all levels of development is increasing. In general, more developed economies have higher levels of disclosure. Disclosure is often, however, more a political economy issue than a technical challenge. In many countries, information on some fiscal risks is available within government, and with political will it could be published with relatively little effort. Some countries have mandated disclosure of fiscal risks in law (e.g., Australia, Brazil, Chile, the Czech Republic, New Zealand, and Pakistan).

An emerging view holds that a presumption should be made in favor of disclosure of information on all material fiscal risks, with exceptions narrowly and clearly defined. The case for publishing information on fiscal risks is that disclosure can create stronger incentives to ensure that all risks are identified, quantified, and carefully managed. Disclosure can help promote earlier and smoother policy responses to changing circumstances and can also increase confidence among stakeholders in the quality of fiscal management. Disclosure also reduces uncertainty for investors and taxpayers and can help improve a country's access to international capital markets.

Some empirical evidence indicates a positive impact of risk disclosure on capital market access. Research by IMF staff suggests that fiscal transparency, particularly fiscal risk disclosure, is associated with better sovereign bond ratings and greater access to international capital markets (IMF, 2008, pp. 14–15, and IMF, 2012c). The estimated coefficients on fiscal risk disclosure suggest that countries moving from no disclosure of macrofiscal risks, contingent liabilities, and quasi-fiscal activities to providing even partial information on all these areas would improve their credit ratings on average by a full notch (e.g., from Baa1 to 3A on Moody's ratings).

Circumstances potentially justifying nondisclosure include the following:

- if disclosure could create "moral hazard," that is, behavioral responses by private agents that increase the likelihood of the risk eventuating or the cost if it does eventuate—for example, disclosing the potential need to provide fiscal support to a bank could trigger a "run on the bank"; and
- if disclosure could prejudice the government's negotiating position—for example, with respect to public sector wages.

However, exceptions should not be broader than necessary: for example, it is possible to disclose the existence of a risk but not the amount.

Disclosure of fiscal risks from macroeconomic shocks has become increasingly common, including by all EU countries, most members of the Organisation for Economic Co-operation and Development (OECD), and some emerging market economies (e.g., Brazil, Chile, and Indonesia). In Indonesia, for example, an annual fiscal risk statement includes a sensitivity analysis of the state budget to variations in key macroeconomic assumptions. Uncertainty surrounding baseline projections is sometimes illustrated by the use of a fan chart (e.g., in the United States).

With respect to economic risks, half the member countries of the OECD publish a fiscal sensitivity analysis. Periodic assessments should also be published assessing the reliability of budget macroeconomic and fiscal forecasts compared with the outturn.

In addition to disclosing the sensitivity of the annual budget to small changes in key macroeconomic variables, the publication of alternative medium-term macrofiscal scenarios, as is done in New Zealand, is also desirable. A government might go a step further and discuss its fiscal strategy in the event that the economic and fiscal outlook turns out to be less favorable than that contained in the budget forecasts. Providing markets with a broad indication of the sorts of fiscal adjustments that will be made in response to possible negative developments—for example, spending cuts, tax increases, a bigger deficit, or some combination—may reduce the risk of abrupt market reactions to adverse market developments. This advance notice would be particularly important if the deficit and debt are already high or if the structure of public finances or features of the national economy create additional vulnerability.

With respect to contingent liabilities, comprehensive information should be published with the annual budget, with in-year fiscal reports, and with end-of-year financial statements, including

- a list of all individual guarantees and other contingent liabilities;[19]
- where feasible, the gross exposure of each contingent liability, its duration, and public policy purpose;
- where possible, an indication of likely expenditure; and
- details of past calls on guarantees.

---

[19] Above some materiality threshold; below the threshold, individual contingent liabilities may be aggregated into similar categories.

In addition, comprehensive estimated fiscal impacts of tax expenditures should be disclosed, both on the introduction of the tax expenditures and each year they remain in force.[20]

The IMF's *Manual on Fiscal Transparency* suggests that disclosure of fiscal risks can usefully be gathered into a single statement presented with the budget (IMF, 2007b).[21] Some countries are doing so, for example, Brazil, Indonesia (for the first time in 2007), and Pakistan. These statements present macroeconomic risks and details of specific risks such as public debt, contingent liabilities, and risks arising from PPPs, SOEs, and subnational governments, as relevant.[22] Whether this practice will become institutionalized in these countries and become more widespread remains to be seen. However, this initiative appears likely to promote the more centralized, systematic, and transparent approach to managing fiscal risks that is now widely regarded as desirable.

Presenting information on general economic risks in the context of the macroeconomic outlook, with details of specific fiscal risks in other parts of the budget documents, is a good practice and is done, for example, in Australia, New Zealand, the United Kingdom, and the United States.

A comprehensive statement of fiscal risks would also be an effective vehicle for reporting on the costs and risks of recent government interventions to support financial markets. Because of the range of instruments used (guarantees, liquidity support, asset purchases, and recapitalization), and the range of entities outside the government sector used to provide support (e.g., central banks, deposit insurance agencies, sovereign wealth funds, and state-owned banks), a comprehensive "sovereign balance sheet" approach is desirable for disclosure. Although the terms of individual interventions have often been reported transparently by governments and the other public sector entities concerned, the ensuing risks have seldom been reported in a systematic and integrated way, and it is difficult for the public to see the overall fiscal impacts and implications of the financial sector interventions across the whole country.

An initial fiscal risk statement—or any information on fiscal risks—needs to be presented carefully, so as not to cause an unnecessary adverse reaction. The government should state clearly the measures it is taking to reduce and manage the risks that are being disclosed. Particular care must be taken about whether, and how, to disclose implicit fiscal risks. Those countries that publish information on fiscal risks have, in general, gradually increased the coverage of risks and the quality and depth of information reported.

---

[20] See IMF (2007a, pp. 64–65) for a discussion of tax expenditure reporting. Tax expenditures are not often classified as fiscal risks, but their very nature typically creates uncertainty about their fiscal impacts. Furthermore, a proliferation of tax expenditures can create a risk of growing and hidden holes in the tax base.

[21] The IMF's *Manual on Fiscal Transparency* and Report on the Observance of Standards and Codes (ROSC) are being revised and updated in 2013.

[22] See IMF (2008) for a further discussion of country examples of fiscal risk statements.

5.7. MITIGATING FISCAL RISKS

Risk mitigation can be used to reduce potential fiscal risks before they are taken on or materialize, or to minimize the cost once a risk has materialized. Risks include both those that can be influenced by an entity and those beyond the entity's influence. In the latter case, the risk management objective is to minimize losses should the risk materialize.

Cost-effective risk mitigation starts with sound macroeconomic policies and appropriate debt management strategies, which reduce countries' vulnerability to crisis and also lessen the demand for guarantees. Similarly, well-regulated capital markets permit investors to spread risks and to allocate them to those most willing to bear them, so that private investors may be more willing to forgo government guarantees on new investments, and less likely to suffer catastrophic losses that might result in calls for government support.

5.7.1. Principles for Risk Allocation

Beyond these general considerations, some high-level principles for allocating risks between the government and other entities can be considered.[23] These principles are derived from insurance theory, finance theory, and microeconomics. They suggest the following:

- Risk should be allocated to the entity best able and with best incentives to control and manage it, or to the entity best placed to bear risk, for example, in PPPs governments are increasingly transferring project-specific risks (such as construction, operating, and design and technical risks) to the private sector, while accepting some economy-wide risks (for example, regulatory and political risks).
- Those able to influence the likelihood of an event occurring, or the cost if the event occurs, should bear some risk at the margin (e.g., coinsurance and deductibles in government insurance programs, in which the insured must meet the first specific amount or percentage of any claim).
- There may be justification for government compelling the purchase of insurance if there is moral hazard (e.g., deposit insurance or disaster insurance).
- When government intervenes to absorb losses of other entities, it should do so as far as possible in a way that preserves incentives for future risk mitigation, for example, by ensuring the entities bear some loss or by imposing new restrictions on their future activities.

In applying these principles governments have a number of generic choices about their level of risk exposure, including avoiding risk, transferring it, sharing it, or reducing it. Box 5.3 outlines some of the generic approaches and techniques

[23] These principles are drawn from IMF (2008, pp. 36–40).

BOX 5.3 Generic Approaches to Mitigating Fiscal Risks

A number of approaches government can use to mitigate risk are listed below, along with examples of each approach.

Avoid risk, by deciding not to undertake a risky commercial investment, or reducing the extent of government ownership of commercial activities; removing regulatory or tax impediments to the development of private insurance markets and reducing government provision of insurance.

Transfer risk to other entities by purchasing insurance and reinsurance; issuing catastrophe bonds; shifting from defined-benefit pension schemes for civil servants to defined-contribution schemes; securitizing and selling financial assets, such as student loans.

Share risk, by issuing partial guarantees (as in Canada, Chile, and the United States); charging risk-related guarantee fees and insurance premiums; offering partial consumer subsidies.

Diversify risk, through tax reform to diversify revenue sources; financial asset investment strategies.

Hedge risk, through currency swaps and commodity futures to counterbalance foreign exchange and commodity price risks (as used by many debt management offices, and as used in Mexico for oil price risks).

Reduce risk, by strengthening financial sector regulation; making membership in a deposit insurance scheme compulsory for all eligible members to avoid adverse selection; subjecting fiscal estimates to independent review; acting to reduce tax base erosion; reducing balance sheet leverage by using government financial assets to repay foreign currency debt; clarifying institutional responsibilities for fiscal risk management; introducing a comprehensive, medium-term budget; reducing operational risks through strengthening internal control, for example, separating risk analysis and monitoring from risk-taking entities.

Cap risk, by placing a ceiling on a consumer subsidy; by changing a vague implicit contingent liability into an explicit contingent liability, for example, by creating a disaster insurance or deposit insurance scheme with fixed upper limits on the amount of assistance per claim.

Create a buffer against risk, by creating additional fiscal space to meet the costs of risks if they arise; setting aside financial assets to meet costs if specific risks materialize; negotiating contingent financing support.

available to governments to mitigate fiscal risks. These approaches are not mutually exclusive, and they are often used in combination.

All countries mitigate risk by protecting their tax bases from erosion. Revenue losses from tax avoidance and tax evasion are a constant threat, sometimes exacerbated by growth in cross-border economic activity. Managing risks to tax bases requires close and constant monitoring of emerging areas of noncompliance and proactive changes to tax administration and tax policy. In some countries, specific features of the tax system, such as the extent and transparency of tax expenditures, present additional risks to the revenue base. The global financial crisis has created growing compliance risks in many countries from issues such as tax arrears, loss-reporting businesses, and the cash economy. It has been suggested that tax authorities should develop a tax compliance strategy for the crisis, focusing on the areas of highest risk, in an attempt to prevent an increase in the tax gap between the revenues that should be collected and those that are actually collected (Brondolo, 2009).

Aside from deposit insurance, which is common,[24] few governments have used insurance instruments to mitigate the potential impacts of fiscal shocks. However, in recent years some governments have purchased disaster or weather risk reinsurance instruments from large international reinsurers. Increasing integration and liberalization in the market for insurance has made it easier to pool risk across countries and, increasingly, to insure risks that were previously considered uninsurable. For example, Mexico issued an earthquake bond in 2006, and international institutions have designed insurance facilities to manage risks from natural disasters, for example, the Caribbean Catastrophe Risk Insurance Facility (World Bank, 2008).

Box 5.4 describes the potential for national drought insurance. The earthquakes in New Zealand caused the largest damage to existing capital stock as a share of national output of all countries experiencing recent natural disasters;

BOX 5.4 National Drought Insurance

New instruments are being developed to insure governments against the financial risks of national disasters. For instance, Mexico (since 2003), Ethiopia (in 2005), and Malawi (in 2008) have all entered into contracts with international risk markets to transfer some of their exposure to fiscal risk from drought (Syroka and Nucifora, 2010). The instruments are index-based derivative contracts that use a specified rainfall index to protect the government from the fiscal costs of drought-relief operations. When actual rainfall (often closely correlated with crop yields) is below a specified level, a payout is automatically triggered without the need to assess the actual level of losses, as required for traditional insurance products. This automatic payment helps the government to finance food relief and other fiscal support. In return for paying an up-front premium, the government is provided with a timely and predictable supplementary source of funds. These funds smooth the impact of droughts on government finances by reducing the need to cut spending on other programs to respond to the drought, to make allowance in a budget contingency fund, to resort to additional borrowing, or to rely on traditional humanitarian aid.

As an example, in 2007 Mexico's government-owned reinsurance company insured approximately 1,900,000 hectares against drought on the international market, for a sum insured of US$90 million at a premium of US$9.7 million. Technically, such contracts require the availability of a high-quality and long-time data series on which to construct the index. The weather risk market has grown to more than US$130 billion of risk transferred since its inception in 1997. Syroka and Nucifora (2010) note that the contracts are intended to enable countries "to manage risks, rather than managing crises," but that piloting the contracts over several seasons in any particular country is necessary to understand their scope, limitations, and role in the government's strategy.

[24] See Hoelscher, Taylor, and Klueh (2006) for a review of issues and country experiences in the design of deposit insurance schemes.

most of the country's reconstruction costs will be covered by the Earthquake Commission, offshore reinsurance, and commercial insurance.[25]

A variety of approaches can be used to reduce fiscal risks in large infrastructure projects, including the risk of "white elephant" projects, and of "optimism bias" on the part of agencies preparing and appraising public investment projects. Both risks result from the tendency for project proposals to systematically overestimate project benefits and to underestimate costs (see Box 10.3).[26] Systematically subjecting projects to independent review of their feasibility is considered a key safeguard (Rajaram and others, 2010). The Korea Development Institute is an example of institutionalized independent ex ante review of project feasibility. Subjecting projects to independent peer review at key gateways during the whole project cycle and using risk adjusters when reviewing project proposals to help improve the average accuracy of cost estimates are also good practices.

With respect to PPPs, a sound framework should be in place establishing the policy reasons for considering a PPP (e.g., more efficient design and construction, asset management, or service delivery). All projects should be subject to careful appraisal of their public policy justification before considering financing alternatives, and guidelines for appraising and managing PPPs should be established for the responsible agencies. Unsolicited PPPs should be treated with particular caution because of their potential to undermine competitive tendering.[27]

Another option for managing risks is to use surplus cash to reduce debt, with borrowing in the future if needed. Using cash to repay debt may be cheaper, but does leave open the question of whether the government will be able to borrow or raise taxes when liabilities fall due—possibly at a time of crisis.

These options are not mutually exclusive and their use would depend upon the likelihood and significance of the potential impact of fiscal risks. In particular, the mix of various mechanisms for risk mitigation should be based on the likelihood that a particular risk could materialize and the significance of the fiscal impact of the particular risk. Figure 5.3 sets out a simple matrix using these parameters that can be used to prioritize risk mitigation efforts.

The final step in risk mitigation is to check that retained (residual) risks are tolerable. This step is likely to require presenting decision makers and key stakeholders with detailed information on the level of residual risk exposure and

---

[25] The remaining reconstruction costs will be financed by central government borrowing (2¼ percent of 2011 GDP). Despite the earthquakes, the government aims to return to surpluses in 2014/15, one year ahead of its earlier plan. The Earthquake Commission is a government entity that provides compulsory earthquake insurance for homeowners, funded by a levy on house and contents insurance. There is a ceiling on the amount covered, backed by a sizable fund, reinsurance, and a residual government guarantee.

[26] For example, in a review of 258 transport projects in 20 countries, Flyvberg, Holm, and Buhl (2002) found that nine out of ten projects underestimated costs and that actual costs exceeded estimates by an average of 28 percent.

[27] South Africa has a comprehensive framework for the management of PPPs, including guidelines for the management of unsolicited proposals (Petrie, 2002).

		Consequence if risk eventuates	
		High	Low
Likelihood of risk	High	Urgent mitigation (explore all options)	Budget for
	Low	Insure Self-insure Research and analyze further	Tolerate

Figure 5.3 Simple Matrix for Prioritizing Risk Mitigation Efforts

Source: Authors' illustration.

exploring the costs and impacts of additional measures to reduce risks. This information is most easily conveyed by considering the risk-return trade-off in specific contexts. For instance, risk-return curves in debt management and financial asset portfolio investment are well established. At the aggregate level, analysis is required to check the sustainability of the fiscal position under different possible shocks.

5.7.2. Institutions for Risk Mitigation

The allocation of risk management roles and responsibilities must be guided by a clear legal and administrative framework. This framework needs to cover the allocation of roles between the central government and other public sector entities, and between the CFI and line ministries. Line ministries should have clearly specified responsibilities for managing the fiscal risks to which their activities expose the government, such as guarantees, legal action against the government, the implementation of public investment projects, SOEs under their policy supervision, and PPPs for which they are the sponsoring entity. To the extent that ministries and agencies are allowed to take on risks, the head of each such entity should be held responsible for the prudent management of the risks, and should be required to have a risk management strategy and monitoring and reporting arrangements in place.

Risk mitigation costs may be lower if actions are centralized. For example, the risk characteristics of the public debt portfolio can be relatively easily adjusted by changing the strategy for new issuance, through buybacks, or through the use of derivatives. Changes to debt management may therefore be an efficient way to adjust government's overall risk exposure (see Chapter 9). At a more sophisticated level, government's risk exposure can be managed by considering the risk characteristics of assets and liabilities and constructing portfolios in which asset and liability characteristics are matched—the so-called asset-liability management approach being adopted in some advanced economies.[28]

[28] See IMF and World Bank (2003), and the discussion in Section 5.4.

Finally, the CFI needs to be provided with the incentives to manage risks effectively—incentives that are supported by adequate accounting, budgeting, and disclosure rules, and by independent review or oversight institutions such as the supreme audit institution.

The CFI should have significant control over risk taking by spending ministries that might have weak incentives to manage their portfolios prudently or if their actions can impose costs on others. At the same time, the desirable degree of centralization in risk management depends on country characteristics. More advanced economies tend to operate more decentralized systems in which line ministries have responsibilities for monitoring SOEs, autonomous agencies, and PPPs. Depending on the constitutional arrangements for subnational governments, the central governments in some countries impose rules on their borrowing operations.

5.8. MONITORING AND REVIEWING RISKS

Having identified, analyzed, and budgeted for the impact of risks, and then disclosed and taken action to mitigate them, the central government must monitor retained risks. To this end, central government should routinely monitor

- the potential impact of key macroeconomic risks and vulnerabilities on the budget and public debt;
- emerging and potential areas of tax noncompliance;
- the finances of SOEs, public financial institutions, and the central bank;
- the financial positions of subnational governments if they can generate fiscal liabilities for central government;
- the financial position of all recipients of explicit government guarantees and of government on-lending; and
- the financial system and potential shocks from other implicit contingent liabilities.

Monitoring should focus on the areas of greatest risk, and include both interactions between risks and possible extreme (or "tail") risks. A wide range of views from official and nonofficial sources should be incorporated, to help avoid optimism bias and "group think."

Monitoring fiscal risks requires a mix of centralized and decentralized responsibilities, depending on the relative role of central agencies and line ministries in the public management system. Comprehensive and routine procedures should be established for ministries and agencies to report on areas of fiscal risk to the CFI. Systematic requirements for fiscal risk reporting should be set up, rather than relying on authority to obtain information on request or in an ad hoc manner. Finally, areas that expose the government to fiscal risk should be subject to internal audit, and the supreme audit institution should have a mandate to review any areas of fiscal risk and should initiate audits of high-risk areas.

The CFI needs to consolidate data across the public sector and regularly advise government on the overall level of risk and on cost-effective actions to reduce it. For example, a regular report could be made on the overall financial performance and position of the SOE sector, focusing on individual SOEs if there are concerns, and the finances of subnational governments could be reported on in countries where they can create fiscal risk for the central government. Where relevant, more research, information gathering, or analysis should be advised. The CFI should also develop contingency plans for managing specific risks if they should occur. (For implicit risks at least, such as possible bank rescues, such contingency plans should probably remain confidential within government.)

A proactive approach to risk monitoring is important. First, internal monitoring reports to decision makers should be routine and regular. Second, reports should contain information, analysis, and recommended actions to reduce risk. Third, monitoring reports should be submitted to officials who are sufficiently senior and have the authority to initiate the actions required to reduce risks. If decision makers have not taken action to mitigate a significant risk, the monitoring reports should continue to highlight the risk and its possible escalation.

Finally, the overall fiscal risk management system should be reviewed regularly to check the extent to which mitigation efforts are effective in achieving the objectives established at the outset. Monitoring and reviewing agents should also be alert to changes in context and environment and actively identify newly emerging sources of risk.

5.9. LESSONS LEARNED FOR STRENGTHENING FISCAL RISK MANAGEMENT

A basic weakness in many countries is the absence of a systematic and centralized approach to identifying fiscal risks. Many governments still lack basic information on the range and potential magnitude of the fiscal risks to which they are exposed. Some progress has been made as reflected in increasing analysis of the sensitivity of public finances to macroeconomic and commodity price risks, increased attention in a number of countries to managing guarantees, better governance of risk from resource revenue volatility and financial asset portfolios, and a trend to disclosure of information on fiscal risks among countries at all levels of development. However, CFIs in many countries lack sufficient authority, information, or capacity to provide comprehensive, relevant, and timely information to decision makers about risks to public finances and how they can be mitigated.

The global financial crisis has shown that the exposure of government revenues and expenditures to large negative macroeconomic shocks can have a significant fiscal impact. All countries need the capability for reliable macroeconomic and fiscal forecasting, free from political interference, including at least the capacity to estimate budget sensitivity to deviations from forecast levels of key macroeconomic variables (see Chapter 6). Fully developed alternative scenarios, stress tests, and stochastic analysis should also be used, as capacity allows, to assess fiscal sustainability and to support prudent risk management decisions.

A glaring international weakness is the inability of governments—for political economy and moral hazard reasons—to manage implicit fiscal risks. Key generic areas of potential exposure to implicit fiscal risks have long included the activities of state-owned financial institutions and corporations, subnational governments, and private banks. This weakness holds in countries at all levels of development, but the difficulty of managing implicit fiscal risks has been illustrated most clearly by some of the leading industrial countries in the global financial crisis. Postcrisis, these governments' exposures to implicit fiscal risks has increased owing to the extension for the first time of the "too big to fail" test to nonbank institutions, as well as owing to the potential increased moral hazard created by the sheer scope and scale of the bailouts.[29] Looking ahead, a new approach is required that provides a better trade-off between the social benefits of a dynamic financial sector and the social costs of periodic financial crises. This approach may require more effective prudential regulation, taxation, and supervision of the financial sector, and better-designed deposit insurance schemes.

Meanwhile, the eventual costs of the recent financial crisis will depend in part on how well the governments and public sector entities concerned manage the expanded on– and off–balance sheet explicit risks to which they are now exposed. As of mid-2012, the utilization rate of pledged support was about 70 percent and recovery of utilized support was about 30 percent (IMF, 2012a). Historically, the unwinding of fiscal support after a financial crisis has typically taken five to seven years. A systematic ex post assessment of the final costs of the financial sector interventions and how these varied by instrument type and design, institutional arrangement, and other parameters will be important for drawing lessons for future risk management.

The financial crisis has also illustrated another ongoing challenge to fiscal risk management: the difficulty of reflecting the cost of contingent obligations in budgets at the time the obligations are entered into. Similar issues arise with respect to PPPs—which are a growing source of fiscal risk as many governments look to address infrastructure gaps using nontraditional modes of public investment. Given the fundamental budgeting and accounting challenges PPPs present, governments must have sound policy frameworks and effective controls in place to guide the initial decisions to issue guarantees or enter new PPPs.

What policy priorities for fiscal risk management can be identified, drawing on the fiscal risk management cycle?

- Although a demanding exercise, all governments should develop an understanding of the main sources of fiscal risk, focusing on the largest such sources.

[29] Large financial institutions whose failure threatens financial stability may now have heightened incentives to take on excessive risk—the implicit government guarantee of their status enables them to borrow more cheaply than smaller institutions. The value of this cost advantage has been estimated at 0.2 percent of borrowing costs (IMF, 2010b, p. 75).

- Efforts should then focus on assessing the broad order of magnitude of the most significant risks, how they affect different elements of government finances, and how they interact (particularly under a shock). As noted, macroeconomic risk analysis is fundamental. Strengthening the capacity of the CFI for risk analysis could be a good starting point in many countries.
- Publishing information on the sensitivity of the fiscal position and on specific fiscal risks, such as public debt and government guarantees, should be an early part of a risk management strategy. These initial efforts should be progressively expanded into a comprehensive fiscal risk statement.
- Action should be taken to mitigate risks progressively by applying the principles for risk allocation and the generic approaches to reducing fiscal risks and prioritizing risk mitigation efforts, discussed above. In particular, clear responsibilities must be assigned for the management of fiscal risks and for ensuring effective controls are in place for taking on new specific fiscal risks, such as guarantees and PPPs.[30]
- Contingency plans must be developed and budgetary contingency mechanisms must be put in place.
- Major gains might be made in many countries through a reexamination of some basic policies from the perspective of fiscal risk management, for example, the tax mix, tax compliance, the framework for intergovernmental fiscal relations, or the quality of financial sector regulation.
- Proactive monitoring and reporting of fiscal risks must be ensured.
- Other institutional improvements must be implemented to better manage risks as capacity allows, for example, medium-term expenditure frameworks, and more independent scrutiny, together with more robust contingency arrangements.[31]

What can be done to promote better management of fiscal risks? The publication of the IMF's *Fiscal Risks: Sources, Disclosure, and Management* (2008) is a useful step that could help to promote improved risk management. Further attention needs to be given to accounting and budgeting for contingent liabilities and PPPs, including accounting standards and practical methodologies for estimating costs. Technical assistance could be provided to strengthen the capacity of CFIs to identify, analyze, budget for, disclose, and monitor fiscal risks. Peer-to-peer practitioner networks in different areas of fiscal risk could be established or extended. Further research and case studies would also be helpful to illustrate lessons emerging from successful and unsuccessful attempts to strengthen risk man-

[30] See Schick (2002, pp. 463–47) and Hemming (2006) for comprehensive sets of suggested standards and practices for the management of guarantees (the latter also covers PPPs).

[31] The 2010 initiative in the United Kingdom to establish the independent Office for Budget Responsibility illustrates that strengthening macroeconomic risk analysis is a never-ending process, even in a setting as institutionally advanced as the United Kingdom.

agement by countries at different levels of development, and from the introduction of new risk management techniques. New techniques include, for example, independent review of macroeconomic and fiscal forecasts, management frameworks for guarantees and PPPs, accrual budgeting, state-contingent debt instruments, deposit insurance and disaster insurance, and approaches to assigning responsibility for managing fiscal risks.

In addition, further efforts to disseminate and promote the IMF guidelines could pay dividends. It might stimulate some CFIs to assess their own country practices against the guidelines. Independent agencies, such as the supreme audit institution or a public sector "think tank," could have a role in assessing the country's fiscal risk management practices. Domestic or international nongovernmental organizations could help to promote better practices, especially with regard to monitoring disclosure practices against the guidelines. The international financial institutions might play a role in assessing member government practices against the guidelines and identifying priorities for strengthening risk management. These assessments might be made on a relatively ad hoc basis in response to requests for technical assistance,[32] or more systematically and proactively.

5.10. CONCLUSION

As illustrated dramatically by the global financial crisis, much remains to be done to improve the management of fiscal risks. A wide range of country circumstances in exposure to risks and management of risks has also been revealed. Examples of good practices can be found at all levels of development, but for many countries the management of fiscal risks remains fairly basic.

Some important advances, however, have been made since 1990. Whereas in 2002 Schick concluded that no generally accepted risk management principles could be discerned and that no model practices could be found to guide governments with respect to contingent liabilities and other fiscal risks, the period since then has seen the publication of the IMF Guidelines, further development and spread of good practices, and focused attention on strengthening fiscal risk management in many countries.

Great scope for improvement in fiscal performance through better management of fiscal risks remains in many countries at all levels of development. Beyond the measures noted in this chapter, priorities for strengthening risk management will depend very much on individual country circumstances and initial conditions, such as the degree of exposure of the economy to external shocks; the extent to which a country depends on natural resources; the size and structure of the country's public debt; and the size, level of concentration, and financial condition of its financial sector, SOEs, and subnational governments. The risk management cycle may be a useful tool for identifying potential areas of fiscal risk

[32] For example, a fiscal risk assessment could be conducted as part of a fiscal transparency Report on the Observance of Standards and Codes mission (as occurred in Switzerland) or as a stand-alone IMF technical assistance mission (as has occurred in Indonesia and Thailand).

management that could be strengthened, but successful reform will always depend on the careful recognition of capacity constraints and political economy considerations. Finally, although the global financial crisis has illustrated that fiscal risk management is an ongoing function, vigilance in recognizing the emergence of new sources of risk and of unexpected shocks to public finances must be maintained.

REFERENCES

Barnhill, Theodore, and George Kopits, 2003, "Assessing Fiscal Sustainability under Uncertainty," IMF Working Paper 03/79 (Washington: International Monetary Fund).

Bohn, Henning, 1998, "The Behavior of U.S. Debt and Deficits," *Quarterly Journal of Economics,* Vol. 113, No. 3, pp. 949–63.

Brixi, Hana Polackova, and Ashoka Mody, 2002, "Dealing with Government Fiscal Risk: An Overview," in *Government at Risk: Contingent Liabilities and Fiscal Risk*, ed. by Hana Polackova Brixi and Allen Schick (New York: Oxford University Press), pp. 21–58.

Brixi, Hana Polackova, and Allen Schick, eds., 2002, *Government at Risk: Contingent Liabilities and Fiscal Risk* (New York: Oxford University Press).

Brondolo, John, 2009, *Collecting Taxes during an Economic Recession: Challenges and Policy Options*, IMF Staff Position Note 09/17 (Washington: International Monetary Fund).

Budina, Nina, Hana Polackova Brixi, and Timothy Irwin, 2007, *Public-Private Partnerships in the New EU Member States: Managing Fiscal Risks* (Washington: World Bank).

Budina, Nina, and Sweder van Wijnbergen, 2009, "Quantitative Approaches to Fiscal Sustainability Analysis: A Case Study of Turkey since the Crisis of 2001," *World Bank Economic Review*, Vol. 23, No. 1. pp. 199–40.

Cebotari, Aliona, 2008, "Contingent Liabilities: Issues and Practice," IMF Working Paper 08/245 (Washington: International Monetary Fund).

Celasun, Oya, Xavier Debrun, and Jonathan Ostry, 2006, "Primary Surplus Behavior and Risks to Fiscal Sustainability in Emerging Market Countries: A 'Fan-Chart' Approach," *IMF Staff Papers*, Vol. 53, No. 3, pp. 401–25.

Claessens, Stijn, and Sweder van Wijnbergen, 1989, "Secondary Market Prices and Mexico's Brady Deal," *Quarterly Journal of Economics*, Vol. 108, No. 4, pp. 967–82.

Currie, Elizabeth, 2002, *The Potential Role of Government Debt Management Offices in Monitoring and Managing Contingent Liabilities* (Washington: World Bank).

Easterly, William, and David Yuravlivker, 2002, "Evaluating Government Net Worth in Colombia and Republica Bolivariana de Venezuela," in *Government at Risk: Contingent Liabilities and Fiscal Risk*, ed. by Hana Polackova Brixi and Allen Schick (Washington: World Bank).

Flyvberg, Bent, Mette Skamris Holm, and Søren Buhl, 2002, "Underestimating Costs in Public Works Projects: Error or Lie?" *Journal of the American Planning Association,* Vol. 68, No. 3, pp. 279–95.

Hemming, Richard, 2006, *Public-Private Partnerships, Government Guarantees, and Fiscal Risk* (Washington: International Monetary Fund).

———, and Murray Petrie, 2002, "A Framework for Assessing Fiscal Vulnerability," in *Government at Risk: Contingent Liabilities and Fiscal Risk*, ed. by H. Polackova Brixi and A. Schick (Washington: World Bank), pp. 159–78.

Hoelscher, David, Michael Taylor, and Ulrich Klueh, 2006, *The Design and Implementation of Deposit Insurance Systems,* IMF Occasional Paper No. 251 (Washington: International Monetary Fund).

International Monetary Fund (IMF), 2003, "Sustainability Assessments—Review of Application and Methodological Refinements" (Washington). Available via the Internet: https://www.imf.org/external/np/pdr/sustain/2003/061003.pdf.

———, 2007a, *Guide on Resource Revenue Transparency* (Washington). Available via the Internet: http://www.imf.org/external/np/fad/trans/guide.htm.

———, 2007b, *Manual on Fiscal Transparency* (Washington). Available via the Internet: http://www.imf.org/external/np/pp/2007/eng/101907m.pdf.

———, 2008, *Fiscal Risks: Sources, Disclosure, and Management* (Washington). Available via the Internet: http://www.imf.org/external/pp/longres.aspx?id=4265.

———, 2009a, *Crisis-Related Measures in the Financial System and Sovereign Balance Sheet Risk* (Washington).

———, 2009b, "The Size of the Fiscal Expansion: An Analysis for the Largest Countries" (Washington). Available via the Internet: www.imf.org/external/np/pp/eng/2009/020109.pdf.

———, 2010a, *Indonesia: Selected Issues,* IMF Country Report 10/285 (Washington: International Monetary Fund).

———, 2010b, *Fiscal Monitor: Fiscal Exit—From Strategy to Implementation,* November (Washington).

———, 2011, *Fiscal Monitor: Addressing Fiscal Challenges to Reduce Economic Risks*, September (Washington: International Monetary Fund).

———, 2012a, *Fiscal Monitor: Balancing Fiscal Policy Risks,* April (Washington).

———, 2012b, *Ireland—Sixth Review under the Extended Arrangement,* May (Washington: International Monetary Fund).

———, 2012c, "Fiscal Transparency, Accountability, and Risk," IMF Policy Paper (Washington). Available via the Internet: http://www.imf.org/external/np/pp/eng/2012/080712.pdf.

———, and World Bank, 2003, *Guidelines for Public Debt Management* (Washington).

International Organization for Standardization (ISO), 2009, *Risk Management—Principles and Guidelines* (Geneva).

Irwin, Timothy, 2003, "Public Money for Private Infrastructure—Deciding When to Offer Guarantees, Output-Based Subsidies, and Other Fiscal Support," Working Paper No. 10 (Washington: World Bank).

Organisation for Economic Co-operation and Development (OECD), 2005, "Explicit Contingent Liabilities in Debt Management," in *Advances in Risk Management of Government Debt* (Paris).

Petrie, Murray, 2002, "Accounting and Financial Accountability to Capture Risk," in *Government at Risk: Contingent Liabilities and Fiscal Risk*, ed. by H. Polackova Brixi and A. Schick (Washington: World Bank), pp. 59–97.

———, 2008, "Controlling Fiscal Risks," paper presented to the East-West Center/Korea Development Institute Conference "Sustainability and Efficiency in Managing Public Expenditures," Honolulu, Hawaii, July 24–25.

Rajaram, Anand, Tuan Minh Le, Nataliya Biletska, and Jim Brumby, 2010, "A Diagnostic Framework for Assessing Public Investment Management," Policy Research Working Paper No. 5397 (Washington: World Bank).

Schick, Allen, 1998, *A Contemporary Approach to Public Expenditure Management* (Washington: World Bank Institute).

———, 2002, "Toward a Code of Good Practice on Managing Fiscal Risk," in *Government at Risk: Contingent Liabilities and Fiscal Risk*, ed. by Hana Polackova Brixi and Allen Schick (Washington: World Bank), pp. 461–71.

Syroka, Joanna, and Antonio Nucifora, 2010, "National Drought Insurance for Malawi," Policy Research Working Paper No. 5169 (Washington: World Bank).

World Bank, 2008, *The Caribbean Catastrophe Risk Insurance Facility: Providing Immediate Funding after Natural Disasters* (Washington: World Bank).

CHAPTER 6

The Role of Fiscal Councils in Promoting Fiscal Responsibility

RICHARD HEMMING AND PHILIP JOYCE

Effective fiscal management depends on the availability of good information about the objectives, design, and impact of fiscal policy and requires appropriate incentives to achieve good fiscal outcomes. Setting up independent fiscal councils is increasingly viewed as a way to combat a bias toward spending and deficits, to promote fiscal responsibility more generally, and to improve the quality of the fiscal policy debate, all by providing independent scrutiny of fiscal policies, plans, and performance.

This chapter reviews the justification for and experience with fiscal councils, covering the background to calls for independent scrutiny; the functions that can be performed by fiscal councils; what fiscal councils actually do; factors determining the impact of fiscal councils; a comparison of two fiscal councils—the 35-year-old Congressional Budget Office in the United States and the Swedish Fiscal Policy Council, created in 2007; and a discussion of some important issues to consider in thinking about fiscal councils, especially in light of the recent global economic crisis.[1]

It is argued that fiscal councils can, in principle, play a useful role in disciplining fiscal policy and strengthening government finances, but their benefits should not be oversold, especially for developing countries in which the fiscal policy reform agenda is long and institutional capacity is limited.[2] Moreover, along with many other good fiscal policy practices and innovations, the decision to create a fiscal council, and its role should a council be set up, has to be appropriate to country circumstances.

Fiscal councils are typically executive or legislative agencies, and as such they should be distinguished from fiscal authorities, which have been proposed by some as the fiscal counterpart to independent central banks. The idea is that giving a fiscal authority the power to set fiscal targets or adjust taxes and spending within specified limits should depoliticize fiscal policy decisions and thereby improve fiscal outcomes. However, the analogy with independent central banks is flawed. Fiscal policy decision making is more complicated than formulating monetary

[1] For other discussions of fiscal councils, see Calmfors (2010a) and Hagemann (2010).

[2] This conclusion contrasts with that in a contribution by Giugale (2010), which sees the spread of fiscal councils or similar agencies from advanced economies to developing countries as both inevitable and desirable.

policy, in particular because tax, expenditure, and borrowing decisions can have complex and often contentious distributional consequences. It is widely acknowledged that such decisions should be made only by those democratically accountable for their consequences, thus, fiscal authorities have gained no traction at all. For this reason, fiscal authorities are not considered in this chapter.[3]

The first section of this chapter discusses why countries establish fiscal councils, their role and functions, and the requirements for a successful fiscal council. The second section compares two fiscal councils, and the third considers issues and challenges.

6.1. WHY SET UP A FISCAL COUNCIL?

Macrofiscal management is often characterized by a lack of fiscal discipline, with three related consequences: rising deficits and debt because the costs of spending increases are disguised or delayed, procyclicality in good times when revenue increases are spent rather than saved so that they can be used to support the economy in bad times, and spending inefficiency leading to poor service delivery and government waste. The resulting adverse implications for macroeconomic stability and growth explain why so much emphasis is placed on restoring and maintaining sound fiscal positions.

Why are fiscal positions allowed to deteriorate to a point that threatens default or the need for a bailout, and large, disruptive, and often externally imposed fiscal adjustments? Although well-known political economy explanations underpin government profligacy (time inconsistency, the common pool problem, rent seeking, and the political business cycle), financial markets and voters should be capable of punishing serious fiscal mismanagement. However, market discipline is not particularly forward looking in the sense that pressure on governments is ratcheted up commensurately with the worsening of fiscal positions. Rather, when markets react it is often a case of "too much, too late," and the response tends to be indiscriminate (as when a crisis in one or a few countries leads to a downturn in market sentiment more generally). At the same time, informational asymmetries mean that politicians can relatively easily conceal what they are doing from voters, which makes it difficult for voters to attach electoral penalties to bad policies.

Furthermore, the institutional innovations put in place to fill the gap have also been found wanting. Transparency initiatives (such as the IMF's fiscal transparency code and assessments)[4] have led to improved disclosure of fiscal information and the implementation of other good transparency practices, and generally put pressure on governments to be more open about their policies, plans, and performance. At the same time, fiscal rules, by placing limits on the use of fiscal policy discretion, have been used by governments to signal their commitment to fiscal

[3] See Debrun, Hauner, and Kumar (2009) for a discussion of proposals to set up fiscal authorities.

[4] This code is being updated in 2013.

discipline (see Chapter 3). However, little persuasive evidence indicates that either transparency or rules have a systematic and lasting positive effect on government finances.[5] Unless market discipline is effective or poor fiscal performance has a political cost, both transparency and rules lack any real enforcement mechanism. Governments are simply not capable of sanctioning themselves for poor fiscal performance, even as members of a club with regulations and penalties intended to promote fiscal discipline, like the euro area. Indeed, given that simple (i.e., balanced budget) rules lack flexibility and credibility, in practice, rules have become quite complex, which undermines transparency, makes compliance difficult to monitor, and creates wiggle room for countries to get around their restrictions.[6]

The 2008–09 global financial and economic crisis and its aftermath have drawn attention to shortcomings of current approaches to promoting fiscal discipline. The fiscal costs of bailouts and stimulus measures, combined with the impact of collapses in asset prices and economic activity, have exposed the inability of governments to create the fiscal space needed to manage not just extreme events, but even normal fiscal risks. Doubts have also arisen about whether the unprecedented fiscal adjustment programs now required of many advanced and some emerging market economies can be reliably delivered without better fiscal institutions. Naturally, much of the attention in this connection is focused on putting in place rules that are more effective in containing short-term fiscal excesses and at encouraging proper medium-term fiscal planning, as discussed in Chapter 4. However, even though committing to better rules is likely to increase the chances that large fiscal adjustments will succeed, this commitment alone is probably not enough.

The presumption is that better rules must go hand in hand with good transparency practices to limit opportunities for game playing. This is where the idea of setting up fiscal councils comes in, because increasing independent scrutiny of fiscal policy design and oversight of fiscal policy implementation is a good fiscal transparency practice that can help to keep governments honest. This scrutiny, in turn, can bolster rules-based commitments to fiscal discipline.[7] Some cross-country evidence suggests that fiscal councils create positive perceptions about a

---

[5]The emphasis here is on "a systematic and lasting effect." There is evidence that transparency scores and the strength of rules are correlated with fiscal performance, but establishing causality is difficult if only committed governments make use of them. There is also little evidence that they are effective over the business cycle.

[6]This wiggle room derives from the imprecise specification of rules (e.g., when rules have to apply on average over the medium term or the business cycle), from a lack of clarity about underlying assumptions, and from lax accounting and statistical standards that are open to creative manipulation. Thus, the United Kingdom created room for additional spending under its golden rule by revising its view on when the business cycle started and would end; the United States got around the Gramm-Rudman-Hollings rules created in an attempt to battle large 1980s deficits through optimistic economic assumptions (Schick, 2007); and Greece and other countries have exploited accounting and statistical loopholes in the Stability and Growth Pact to understate deficits and debt.

[7]Although the IMF fiscal transparency code (IMF, 2007) does not formally advocate setting up independent oversight agencies, it emphasizes the importance of external scrutiny of fiscal information (pillar IV), including by subjecting macroeconomic and fiscal forecasts to independent assessment (good practice 4.3.3).

government's ability to secure and safeguard fiscal discipline, especially if provisions are in place to formalize their influence and guarantee their independence (Debrun and Kumar, 2008). However, although Belgium's High Council of Finance scores well on both counts, and studies suggest that it was particularly effective during the 1990s when euro adoption motivated fiscal adjustment, its influence has subsequently waned.[8] Therefore, even fiscal councils cannot guarantee fiscal discipline.

Much of the discussion of fiscal councils addresses their potential contribution to fiscal discipline. It is also important to remember that governments lack incentives to allocate and manage resources in an efficient manner, with the result that they do not necessarily use public money effectively. Reforms that seek to bring more information on costs and performance to bear on resource allocation decisions frequently have a goal of providing the incentives necessary to foster spending efficiency (see Chapter 7). Whether fiscal council scrutiny also contributes to spending efficiency is discussed later in this chapter.

6.1.1. Role and Functions of Fiscal Councils

The independence of fiscal councils relates mainly to the responsibility that they are given to provide independent input into fiscal policy decisions and to provide an independent view on the conduct of fiscal policy. Thus, fiscal councils influence government policy not through formal rules and powers, but by providing information that can push policymakers in the direction of implementing more responsible and efficient policies. Therefore, in many countries, fiscal councils exist as a formal or informal "check" on executive fiscal agencies.

The belief in independent scrutiny as a good fiscal transparency practice that can enhance fiscal discipline is spreading. The case for fiscal transparency rests, in part, on the idea that governments should declare their fiscal policy intentions, announce outcomes, and explain deviations from plans, so that they are more accountable to legislatures and the public. Moreover, legislatures and the public will also have more faith in their own ability to judge the quality of fiscal policy decisions if they know that fiscal policies, plans, and performance have been subject to independent scrutiny. To this end, fiscal councils can perform two important functions: advising on fiscal policies and plans and auditing fiscal plans and performance.

As an advisory body, a fiscal council could review and comment on many aspects of fiscal policy, including

- the government's medium-term fiscal policy objectives, which would typically be specified as a debt or deficit path, including the debt sustainability analysis on which it is based;
- unfunded and contingent liabilities, and other prospective developments and sources of fiscal risk, that determine the need for future fiscal space;
- whether short-term fiscal targets are appropriate, given medium-term objectives;

[8] Hagemann (2010) discusses the evidence on the impact of fiscal councils.

- the cyclical position of the economy, commodity price changes, and other economic developments that might warrant a fiscal policy response;
- the size and impact of automatic stabilizers and the design and timing of discretionary tax and spending measures;
- the impact and cost of proposed policies, with a view to providing a check on the natural tendency of those proposing policies to overstate their benefits and understate their costs; and
- any other aspects of fiscal policy related to the fiscal council's mandate or that are the subject of a request from government.

As an auditing body, a fiscal council could verify that the government is providing reliable information on its finances. This verification could cover, for example, whether fiscal reports on both plans and performance (or budgets and outturns) are comprehensive in their coverage of fiscal activities and respect internationally accepted government accounting and statistical standards.[9] Fiscal councils could also analyze and explain whether plans can achieve their objectives, and deviations between plans and performance, paying particular attention to the contribution of errors in macroeconomic and fiscal forecasts, including the misjudged costs of new programs.

A fiscal council could be assigned either advisory or auditing functions, but a case can be made for having them do both. There are strong synergies between the two functions. Providing good advice is difficult without knowing that the information on which it is based is reliable, or without being able to tailor auditing activities to advisory activities. Thus, many fiscal councils have both advisory and auditing functions.

A common auditing function of fiscal councils is reviewing government forecasts. Poor forecasts have been a persistent source of unplanned deficits and debt, and a high priority is often attached to improving the quality of government forecasts. However, some fiscal councils go further, and actually provide independent forecasts for use by the government. As discussed in Chapters 3 and 4, macroeconomic and fiscal forecasts are often biased (they tend to be optimistic or pessimistic) or inefficient (they do not use all available information).[10] A specific concern is the tendency to commit to too much spending based on optimistic revenue forecasts, which leads to additional borrowing when revenue collections underperform and spending is not adjusted.

---

[9]There may appear to be some overlap here with the responsibility of an external audit office to sign off on the government's final financial statements. Although there is merit in having reports on budgets and outturns use the same accounting and reporting conventions as financial statements, as a practical matter financial statements take longer to produce. The fiscal council should focus on producing fiscal reports that are timely enough that they can be used for short-term fiscal decision making, but it should at the same time be alert to the possibility of misrepresentation caused by obvious violations of accepted accounting and statistical practices.

[10]Bayoumi, Klyuev, and Mülheisen (2007) include a detailed analysis of fiscal forecasting in industrial countries.

Three different responses are usually made to the problem of bias in forecasts. The first is to work with pessimistic forecasts, the second is to take a cautious approach to fiscal targeting, and the third is to build in contingency reserves (see Section 4.4). The problem with pessimism in forecasting is that it can result in a buildup of unbudgeted resources, which can be spent on whatever is politically most expedient or used to reduce debt without proper scrutiny of alternatives. A cautious approach to fiscal targeting—aiming for a more ambitious fiscal target than necessary to allow for potential revenue shortfalls—would rob headline fiscal targets of their true meaning and undermine fiscal transparency. It would be best to produce unbiased forecasts, and also to aim at hitting meaningful headline fiscal targets, and then rely on contingency reserves to handle forecast errors (and other deviations of actual expenditure from targets). However, given the inevitability of such errors, and the serious fiscal and macroeconomic implications of revenue shortfalls, erring on the side of caution is understandable.

In any event, governments should always use the best available forecasts. Although private macroeconomic forecasts can either be used directly or to benchmark government forecasts, private forecasters do not routinely produce revenue and expenditure forecasts. This being the case, there are three ways of improving the quality of fiscal and, if necessary, macroeconomic forecasts: (1) building forecasting expertise in government; (2) having a body like a fiscal council review government forecasts (which would be part of the fiscal council's auditing function); and (3) making such a body responsible for preparing macroeconomic or fiscal forecasts used by government. The first two are obviously complementary, while the third is an alternative adopted by some countries, such as Chile, the Netherlands, and the United Kingdom. All are likely to improve forecast quality.

However, the third option presents a problem—it is unclear whether governments, or more specifically the ministries of finance, are willing to truly relinquish responsibility for forecasting. On the one hand, forecasting is inherently judgmental, and the government might feel that it should make forecasts if it is to be held accountable for forecast errors. The government may also value the room for fiscal policy maneuver that judgment in forecasting provides, even though this benefit usually turns out to be illusory. On the other hand, if the fiscal council is the sole forecaster, the government can use the council as a scapegoat for poor fiscal performance, which may be an attractive option. In practice, however, it is possible that, even if the government concedes formal responsibility for forecasting, the fiscal council and the ministry of finance could end up cooperating on the forecasts, which would inevitably lead to questions about the independence of the fiscal council.[11]

[11] This concern is voiced by some commentators about the U.K.'s new Office for Budget Responsibility (OBR), which has taken over from the treasury responsibility for macroeconomic and fiscal forecasting. Because the OBR plans to maintain a constant dialogue with the treasury on the forecasts, which the latter uses as a basis for budget preparation, the concern is that the forecasts will end up being negotiated.

Forecasting has not only a macrofiscal dimension, but also a microbudgetary dimension. When governments are making frequent changes to taxes and spending programs, and especially when major tax and spending reform is being undertaken, judging the aggregate fiscal implications of those changes is critically important to both formulating fiscal plans and performing according to plan. In the face of a natural tendency to underestimate the costs of new spending programs and the revenue loss from tax cuts, and to overestimate the savings from spending cuts and tax increases, a fiscal council could cost (or "score") tax and spending changes. The Congressional Budget Office (CBO) in the United States has built part of its reputation on its costing function, which gained great importance in the 1990s when budget rules required new tax and spending measures to be self-financing. Some fiscal councils also verify the costs of existing spending programs.

Box 6.1 provides a list of fiscal councils and similar arrangements, including their functions (advisory, auditing, forecasting, and costing).[12] It covers both fiscal councils that have existed for a long time and those in their infancy. Among the most recent countries to establish fiscal councils are Portugal and the Slovak Republic. As part of efforts to reinforce fiscal governance and discipline at a national level, the European Union (EU) has recommended that member governments establish independent fiscal councils to monitor fiscal policy and assess compliance with fiscal rules. The EU is currently considering making this recommendation a requirement (see Chapter 3).

Box 6.1 does not report on the full range of fiscal council activities undertaken in countries. National audit offices in a number of countries, including those in countries such as Sweden and the United Kingdom, which also have fiscal councils, perform some fiscal council functions. In other countries, research institutes perform such functions; examples include the Institute of Economic Research and the Institute for Advanced Studies in Austria and the Institute for Fiscal Studies in the United Kingdom. In addition to those mentioned in Box 6.1, some other emerging market economies, and even some developing countries, are formalizing arrangements for independent input into fiscal policy (e.g., Indonesia, Jordan, and Nigeria).

6.1.2. Requirements for Successful Fiscal Councils

Although formal influence and guaranteed independence have been mentioned as factors that determine the impact of a fiscal council, no comprehensive investigation has yet been made of what determines the success of a fiscal council in promoting fiscal discipline. However, relevant factors might include the following:

- *Political support.* The chances of a fiscal council being successful are better if politicians inside and outside government are open to providing full

[12] For a fuller description of fiscal councils and other independent institutions in Europe, see European Commission (2006).

BOX 6.1 Fiscal Councils and Similar Arrangements

Australia, Parliamentary Budget Office (Established initially in 2011, to be fully established over four years.) Provides independent, nonpartisan, and policy-neutral analysis on the full budget cycle, fiscal policy, and the financial implications of proposals, including the costs of political parties' pre-election commitments. (Responsibilities: advisory, auditing, costing.)

Austria, Government Debt Committee (Established in1970 with a focus on deficit financing, mandate extended in 2002; 16 members.) Broad mandate to analyze and comment on fiscal policy. The Austrian Institute of Economic Research and the Institute of Advanced Studies provide independent forecasts. (Responsibilities: advisory, auditing.)

Belgium, High Council of Finance (Established in 1936, reformed in 1989 and 2006; 14 staff.) Chaired and staffed by the ministry of finance. Focuses on the government borrowing requirement, fiscal policy over the cycle, and debt sustainability. Coordinates fiscal policy across all levels of government to ensure compliance with EU fiscal rules. The Federal Planning Bureau prepares macroeconomic forecasts used for budget preparation. Played an important role in the run-up to euro adoption, but its influence has since waned. (Responsibilities: advisory, auditing.)

Canada, Parliamentary Budget Office (Established in 2008; 14 staff.) Provides advice on all aspects of public finances, prepares forecasts, and scores new policies on request. Does not undertake ex post analysis of fiscal performance. (Responsibilities: advisory, forecasting, costing.)

Chile, Two Expert Panels (Established in 2001; Advisory Committee on Trend GDP has 16 members; Advisory Committee for the Reference Copper Price has 12 members.) Produce forecasts of trend GDP and copper prices as a basis for determining deviations from the medium-term structural surplus target. (Responsibility: forecasting.)

Denmark, Economic Council (Established in 1962; 35 staff.) Independent of the ministry of finance. Monitors compliance with fiscal rules. Mandate also covers tax, expenditure, and other structural fiscal policies. (Responsibilities: advisory, auditing.)

Germany, Advisory Board to the Federal Ministry of Finance and Joint Economic Forecast Project Group (Established in 1950.) Assess compliance with fiscal rules and debt sustainability, and make fiscal policy recommendations. Provide independent macroeconomic and fiscal forecasts. The Working Group on Tax Revenue Forecasts provides independent revenue forecasts based on the government's macroeconomic projections. (Responsibilities: advisory, auditing, forecasting.)

Hungary, Fiscal Council of the Republic of Hungary (Established in 2009; 30 or more staff.) Concerned with credibility in fiscal policymaking, transparency in public finances, and public debt sustainability. Surveillance functions include evaluation at aggregate and disaggregate level, and compliance with standards, procedures, and fiscal rules. Prepares nonbinding forecasts. Emphasis on dissemination to the public. (Responsibilities: auditing, forecasting.) Significantly weakened following 2011 reorganization, which eliminated its dedicated staff and reduced its budget to near zero.

Ireland, Irish Fiscal Advisory Council (Established in 2011; 5 members.) Monitors government's adherence to its own fiscal targets. Concerned with the appropriateness and soundness of the government's macroeconomic projections, budgetary projections, and fiscal stance. Had significant input to the 2012 Fiscal Responsibility Bill defining and establishing national fiscal rules. (Responsibilities: advisory, auditing.)

Japan, Fiscal System Council. Comprises academics. Advises across a wide range of fiscal policy issues. Council on Economic and Fiscal Policy provides macroeconomic and fiscal forecasts, while Council on Policy Evaluation evaluates fiscal performance—both are run by the ministry of finance but comprise outside experts. (Responsibilities: advisory.)

BOX 6.1 (*continued*)

Mexico, Center for the Study of Public Finances (Established in 1998; 150 staff.) Modeled on the U.S. Congressional Budget Office, but with a more limited mandate. Scrutinizes fiscal plans, formally presents its own estimates to congress, and reviews performance against fiscal rule. (Responsibilities: auditing, costing).

Netherlands, Central Planning Bureau (Established in 1945; 170 or more staff.) Formally part of the ministry of economic affairs. Produces official government forecasts, reviews economic policies of parties contending elections, and reconciles budget policy positions of coalition partners. (Responsibilities: auditing, forecasting.)

Portugal, Council on Public Finances (Established 2012; 5 members.) Monitors fiscal developments to assess progress toward targets; assesses budget forecasts and government measures taken to achieve fiscal targets; analyzes the sustainability of existing commitments such as pensions, health systems, public-private partnerships, and the like. Does not advise on alternative policy paths. (Responsibilities: auditing, forecasting.)

Republic of Korea, National Assembly Budget Office (Established in 2003.) Covers any aspect of fiscal policy of interest to parliament. Reviews fiscal plans, prepares alternative macrofiscal projections, and appraises major projects. There is no independent review of fiscal performance. (Responsibilities: advisory, forecasting, costing.)

Romania, Romanian Fiscal Council (Established in 2010; 5 members, 6 staff.) Reviews economic and fiscal forecasts, monitors budget implementation, comments on fiscal policy. (Responsibilities: advisory, auditing.)

Serbia, Fiscal Council (Established 2011; 3 members.) Assesses credibility of the fiscal policy, compliance with fiscal rules, and fiscal impact of draft laws. Reviews macroeconomic forecasts that underpin the budget, assesses fiscal risk and economic policy, and prepares an opinion on the draft Fiscal Strategy Report. (Responsibilities: Auditing, forecasting, advisory.)

Slovak Republic, Council for Budgetary Responsibility (To be established; created by law in 2011.) Will publish reports on fiscal sustainability; submit to parliament an evaluation of fiscal policy in relation to fiscal rules and transparency rules; and publish costings of draft legislation. (Responsibilities: auditing, advisory, costing.)

Slovenia, Fiscal Council of the Republic of Slovenia (Established in 2010; 7 members.) Mandate includes short-term fiscal policy, trends in public finance, sustainability of longer-term government finances, effectiveness of structural policies, efficiency in the use of public money (including EU funds), and monitoring of guarantees. (Responsibilities: advisory, auditing.)

Sweden, Fiscal Policy Council (Established in 2007; 8 members, 4 staff.) Monitors compliance with medium-term fiscal surplus target and expenditure ceilings. The National Audit Office assesses forecast quality. (Responsibilities: advisory, auditing.)

United Kingdom, Office for Budget Responsibility (Established in 2010; 3 executives and 15 staff, all civil servants.) Core mandate is to prepare macroeconomic and fiscal forecasts and to assess progress toward fiscal sustainability. Will also cost budget measures. (Responsibilities: auditing, forecasting, costing.)

United States, Congressional Budget Office (Established in 1975; 250 staff.) Analyzes president's budget based on its own assumptions and forecasts, considers alternative paths for fiscal policy, and scores new policies. Produces in-depth studies and reports on a variety of topics. Has a reputation for political independence and the quality of its analytical work. (Responsibilities: advisory, auditing, forecasting, costing.)

Sources: Debrun, Hauner, and Kumar (2009); European Commission (2006); Hemming and Kell (2001); Hagemann (2010); IMF (forthcoming); and national websites.

information on fiscal plans and performance to outsiders, and if they are willing to listen to, resist influencing, and act upon independent views based on that information. They also have to be prepared to give the fiscal council permanent legal status as an independent entity, commit to its multiyear funding, and allow its staff to work without interference or fear of reprisal (e.g., seconded civil servants or academics who may want future government funding for their research). If politicians are not prepared to subordinate their own self-interests to the cause of fiscal discipline, fiscal councils will be ineffective and possibly short lived. This was the fate of the Hungarian fiscal council. As a consequence of critical comments made in 2010 on the new government's fiscal program, the council's 2011 budget was cut to near zero and its dedicated staff eliminated. It was replaced by a much smaller and more compliant alternative.[13]

- *An appropriate fiscal framework.* Commitment to fiscal discipline requires more than setting up a fiscal council; if that is all that happens, it will probably have little impact on turning around a weak fiscal position or safeguarding a strong one. Governments that truly want to strengthen government finances will address weaknesses in the entire fiscal framework by improving fiscal transparency, possibly putting in place fiscal rules, and reforming the budget process. These steps would ideally include moving toward a medium-term budget framework, but not before basic budget procedures are brought up to the necessary level (see Chapter 4 for a more detailed discussion), and addressing other systemic obstacles to sound fiscal policy formulation and implementation.
- *A well-defined mandate.* Even though a fiscal council could have an auditing function or advisory function alone, it will be most effective when it performs both advisory and auditing functions, with the reviewing of forecasts and cost estimates part of the latter. Whether a fiscal council provides macroeconomic or fiscal forecasts and costs new policies for official use depends on the quality of government forecasts and costing, and on the resources and priorities of the fiscal council. Resources will invariably be limited, which may constrain the ability of a fiscal council to undertake some tasks. Once the role of a fiscal council is determined, it should be given a formal mandate specifying the scope and limits of its responsibilities.
- *Clear legal backing.* Legislation should set up the fiscal council; describe its role and responsibilities; and specify the relationship between the legislature, the executive, and the fiscal council. The role of the fiscal council should also be included in formal descriptions of the budget process (e.g., in the budget law), with the timing of its input reflected in the budget timetable.
- *The right location.* In the United States, with its presidential system and separation of powers, the CBO is a legislative office, formally independent

[13] Kopits (2011) describes and discusses the short history of the Hungarian fiscal council.

from the executive and, in practice, independent from the legislature by virtue of the nonpartisan nature of it judgment. The CBO counterparts in Mexico and the Republic of Korea are in the same position. In a parliamentary system, the fiscal council is usually an independent executive office, as in Belgium, Denmark, the Netherlands, and Sweden. In a few cases in which specialist committees perform some fiscal council functions, these committees are in effect part of government, as in Germany. In general, there is no right or wrong location, especially if the fiscal council is truly independent. The case may be stronger for a legislative or parliamentary office if the legislature or parliament is an effective counterbalance to a spendthrift executive. By the same token, the case for an executive office is stronger if the legislature is a source of deficit bias because it interferes with what might otherwise be the sound policies of the government. An executive office may also be appropriate if the legislature is adequately supported by budget, public accounts, and other specialized committees.

- *Technically qualified staff.* Some fiscal councils are quite small while others are large; size will ultimately reflect the mandate.[14] The mandate will also determine whether staffing is temporary or part-time—in which case a committee of experts might suffice—or whether a fiscal council has permanent staff with a skill mix appropriate to its tasks. One issue that arises in staffing a fiscal council is finding technically competent staff, especially in countries where the necessary skills are in limited supply. For example, it clearly makes little sense for a fiscal council to hire talented forecasters from the ministry of finance to review the forecasts made by the less talented forecasters who remain behind. It makes more sense to hire them to make independent forecasts that the government will use (and then redeploy the less talented forecasters). That said, a fiscal council is not a substitute for an effective government, and especially for a strong ministry of finance. It may be beneficial to transfer some ministry of finance functions to an independent body and to subject other functions to oversight by that body, but the ministry of finance still has to perform its core functions well. If it does, a fiscal council will help it perform them even better.
- *Clear reporting requirements.* To be effective, a fiscal council must work in the open, with its reports made public. Government should also be required to respond to the fiscal council's reports, indicating where it has followed the advice of the fiscal council, used its forecasts, agreed with its analysis, and so forth, and where this is not the case. When disagreeing, government should explain why it is ignoring all or part of what the fiscal council says.[15] Such

[14]The U.S. CBO has by far the broadest mandate among fiscal councils and has a correspondingly large staff of approximately 250. Most fiscal councils are much smaller, with 3 to 12 core members and a technical secretariat of 10–30.

[15]However, this does not imply that the minutes of discussions between the ministry of finance and the fiscal council should be published. It is far from clear that reporting the detailed, often technical discussions of fiscal sustainability, fiscal targeting, forecasts, and the like would add much to transparency; it may even detract from it.

requirements play an important part in ensuring that the fiscal council is truly independent and that its work assists governments seeking to make better fiscal policy decisions, both by constraining their ability to make poor choices and helping them resist the poor choices of others. They also make governments more accountable by ensuring that information is available that can result in bad fiscal policy decisions having a financial or political cost.

- *Accountability*. Finally, whether the fiscal council is doing work of good quality could be an issue. Although the usefulness of the fiscal council's work will be reflected in the way the government responds to its views and ultimately in fiscal outcomes, perhaps an appropriate model is national audit offices, which are guided in their work by an international body, the International Organization of Supreme Audit Institutions, the aim of which is to promote the adoption of good audit practices. A similar entity could be put in place for fiscal councils. However, with the limited, albeit growing, number of fiscal councils in place to date, perhaps membership in a more informal knowledge-sharing group would provide necessary assurances.

6.2. THE U.S. CONGRESSIONAL BUDGET OFFICE AND THE SWEDISH FISCAL POLICY COUNCIL

In addition to the more general discussion of fiscal councils above, reviewing the experiences of specific institutions can illuminate them as a whole. This section reviews the U.S. Congressional Budget Office (CBO) and the Swedish Fiscal Policy Council (FPC). They have been chosen because, although both institutions are fiscal councils with good reputations, they have substantial differences. The CBO has been in place for more than 35 years, whereas the FPC was established relatively recently, in 2007. The CBO has a broader mandate, and a much larger staff, than the FPC. Finally, the CBO exists within a presidential system of government, and the FPC exists within a parliamentary system.

6.2.1. The Congressional Budget Office

The CBO was created in 1974, and came into existence in 1975, as part of an effort to support an increased role for the U.S. Congress in the budget process.[16] This occurred at the end of a period of intense budgetary warfare between President Richard Nixon and the congress, primarily exemplified by the refusal of the president to spend money for various programs that he opposed, but that had received legal appropriations. As a part of the congressional budget reform codified in the Congressional Budget and Impoundment Control Act of 1974, new committees (called Budget Committees) were created in the congress. These committees were

[16] This discussion relies exclusively on Joyce (2011).

responsible for developing a budget resolution, which was an annual statement of overall fiscal policy.

As a part of this new process, the CBO was given the responsibility to

- assist the congress in putting together the budget resolution through the development of a budget baseline, which in practice represents an alternative fiscal outlook to that presented by the president in his annual budget proposal and requires the CBO to develop an independent macroeconomic forecast;
- provide cost estimates for (or "score") legislation considered by the congress, relative to the baseline; and
- conduct studies of issues related to the economy and the budget, as needed and requested.

Two design features were most important to the CBO's development. First, it was to be *independent*, in the sense that the CBO not only was a legislative branch agency (and thus not controlled by the president) but also did not report directly to any congressional committee. Second, it was to be *nonpartisan*, which was explicit for the director, and implicit for other CBO staff, who serve at the pleasure of the director. In 2012, the CBO had approximately 250 staff, about one-third of which sat in the Budget Analysis Division, which is responsible for cost estimating and the spending portion of the budget baseline. Other CBO staff work on macroeconomic forecasting, revenue estimation and analysis, and policy analysis of other issues facing the congress. The agency is heavily staffed by economists with PhDs.

Over time, the CBO has developed a reputation as a highly objective and credible source of information on the economy and the budget. This did not occur by accident, but rather through a combination of managerial decisions and policy analyses that established and cemented that reputation. Its first director, Alice Rivlin, fostered a culture of nonpartisanship that has been maintained through seven subsequent directors. At a number of times in its history—most notably in response to energy legislation proposed by President Jimmy Carter in 1977, President Ronald Reagan's economic program in 1981, and health reform proposals of Presidents Bill Clinton in 1994 and Barack Obama in 2009—the CBO has been in the middle of policy debates in which its analytical responses were viewed as nonpartisan and credible, often in the face of substantial pressure from the majority party in the congress to reach a different conclusion.

The following observations can be made concerning the experience of the CBO during its history:

- Its greatest influence has come through its cost estimating function. By all accounts, much greater attention has been paid to the cost of legislation since the creation of the CBO. Many bills are changed in response to—or in anticipation of—CBO scoring.
- It plays a much greater role in public education than was originally anticipated—both directly (all CBO estimates and studies are available free of

charge on the CBO website) and through the media, which rely on the CBO as the main source of credible information on the budget.

- The existence of the CBO has had profound influences on the relationship between the president and the congress. It has tended to moderate the inclination on the part of the executive to "game" the budget by, for example, painting a rosy scenario of future economic growth. Furthermore, because in the U.S. system the president tends to initiate policy, the CBO's most high-profile analyses have involved responding to presidential proposals. A recent example was the Obama health care reform in 2009. The CBO has been more influential as an independent agency than it would have been as simply a staff arm of one of the congressional committees. It would not have been possible in the latter arrangement for the CBO to remain nonpartisan, given the highly partisan environment of the U.S. Congress.
- Despite its influence at the level of individual policies, it has had little effect on constraining deficits, which by 2010 were at record post–World War II levels. Its efforts to remain nonpartisan have led to some reluctance at times to prod policymakers into action, even in the face of large budget deficits. Although it has not typically been hesitant to offer opinions about the dangers of deficits, it has little direct or persuasive power to make politicians act to rein them in.

Two of the factors that are most important to the CBO's success—its size and expertise—would be difficult to replicate in most other countries. Limited resources might prevent an organization of similar size from being created in other countries (even with country size adjusted for). The establishment of forecasting expertise within the legislature might have the effect of taking this expertise away from the ministry of finance, which would be unlikely to lead to improvements at the macroeconomic or microeconomic level. In addition, the U.S. Congress, according to one study, exercises the strongest independent budgetary powers out of 28 countries examined.[17] In countries with weaker legislatures, a fiscal council like the CBO would not be expected to be as influential.

6.2.2. The Swedish Fiscal Policy Council

The FPC was established much more recently than the CBO, in 2007.[18] It was created, in part, to help prevent a recurrence of the extreme financial crisis that gripped Sweden in the 1990s. The FPC is an agency of the government, and consists of eight members—six academic economists and two ex-politicians. FPC members perform their duties, in addition to their normal jobs, for a nominal monthly stipend. A small full-time staff of four persons assists the members. The FPC supplements this staff by turning to consultants to work on its reports. FPC members are also expected to contribute to the writing of the reports.

[17] For more details see Lienert (2005, p. 23).

[18] The following discussion is based on Calmfors (2010b).

The FPC has a relatively broad mandate, with the following components (Calmfors, 2010b, pp. 7–8):

- To assess the extent to which the government's fiscal policy objectives are being achieved. These objectives include long-term sustainability, the surplus target, the ceiling on central government expenditure, and fiscal policy that is consistent with the cyclical situation of the economy.
- To evaluate whether economic developments are in line with healthy long-term growth and sustainable high employment.
- To examine the clarity of the government's budget bill and spring fiscal policy bill, in particular with respect to the grounds given for the economic policy stance and the motivation for policy proposals.
- To monitor and evaluate the quality of the government's economic forecasts as well as the underlying models.

The only formal reporting requirement for the FPC is the production of an annual report, which it has published since 2008. These reports have included a number of criticisms of government policies by the council, related to issues such as fiscal stimulus and the reform of unemployment insurance. They have also criticized some of the government's economic reporting practices. Aside from this formal reporting, the Swedish news media have routinely reported the results of council analyses and have interviewed FPC members as economic and budgetary issues are considered throughout the year. The opposition also makes use of FPC analyses when formulating alternative economic policies.

A few observations can be made based on the brief experience of the Swedish FPC:

- Given its broad mandate, the FPC really has very limited resources, with a total budget of approximately 700,000 euros (US$875,000). Thus, it is well positioned to comment on the analyses of other institutions, but does not have sufficient resources to do much independent research. It cannot, for example, make an independent macroeconomic forecast.
- Unlike the CBO, the FPC is heavily dependent on academics for both overall policy direction and the writing of its reports. Because the FPC members have full-time jobs independent of their council positions, the activities and opinions of an individual member can be taken to be positions of the council when this may or may not be true. The presence of ex-politicians on the council has increased its legitimacy and improved the readability of its reports.
- Although it was originally thought (and the arguments for fiscal councils would suggest) that the FPC would embrace a more restrictive fiscal policy stance than that of the government, the FPC has at times advocated a more fiscally activist position than the government. The fact that the FPC comments are critical of government policy has been a source of tension with the ministry of finance, which has threatened the FPC with budget cuts. The FPC, in turn, has claimed that its independence would be more secure if it were a parliamentary office.

- The FPC has clearly had some influence on fiscal policy in Sweden, but it is perhaps too early to judge its impact. Whether the FPC's limited size and budget will restrict its ability to be fully effective remains an open issue. But there seems to be little question that over its short life the FPC has quickly gained a reputation, both inside and outside Sweden, for independent, high-quality analysis, and it is often mentioned as an example of a fiscal council that other countries should emulate.

6.2.3. The CBO and FPC Compared

The CBO and FPC are similar in some respects and quite different in others. Both institutions clearly have in common the goal of maintaining an independent voice. For the CBO, this means independent of political influence, which is evidenced by the fact that many of its most controversial and highest-profile analyses have been in response to presidential policy proposals. For the FPC, it means independence from the party or coalition in power. Also, both institutions seem to have developed reputations for sound, nonpartisan analysis, but neither has necessarily promoted a more aggressive stance on government deficits than would have occurred absent their existence.

A number of differences between these agencies can be discerned. The CBO's mandate to provide alternate macroeconomic forecasts, budget baselines, and cost estimates requires that it have far more in-house technical analytical capacity. In fact, the CBO's heavy emphasis on cost estimates, which has arguably been where its greatest impact has been felt, represents the biggest difference in the mandates of the two institutions. This, along with the difference in the size of the two countries and the complexity of their fiscal systems, carries with it the need for the CBO to have a much larger staff. Moreover, the approach to staffing the two institutions is substantially different, with the FPC relying more on part-time consultants and the CBO relying almost exclusively on full-time staff.

6.3. ISSUES AND CHALLENGES

Discussions of fiscal councils have not directly addressed certain questions, but these questions are relevant if fiscal councils are to be part of concerted policy responses to the large fiscal imbalances that are the legacy of the global financial and economic crisis.

Is it necessary to combine fiscal councils and fiscal rules? Fiscal councils, simply by virtue of monitoring and reporting on fiscal performance, have the potential to make well-functioning rules more effective in containing the inappropriate use of discretion and thereby improve fiscal outcomes. By the same token, fiscal rules, by providing a benchmark against which fiscal performance can be assessed, should enable a fiscal council to make more definitive judgments. It is too early to say whether fiscal councils and rules work well together, in part because the evidence to date is unclear on the effect of rules on fiscal performance given that causality is difficult to assess. Moreover, if government will always try to circumvent rules, ultimately financial markets and the electoral system must be relied on to discipline government. The issue then is how fiscal councils can contribute to fiscal discipline other than by making rules more effective. This depends on the answer to the following question:

Can fiscal councils help to make financial markets and the electorate more effective constraints on fiscal policy? Market discipline does not work well because it is not sufficiently forward looking. It works eventually, as it did in Greece, but light needs to be shed on why financial markets have in the past responded slowly and abruptly to an accumulated record of bad policies and outcomes rather than reacting more quickly and in a more measured way as policies and outcomes deteriorate. One reason may be that the costs of monitoring fiscal developments on a continuous and timely basis in a large number of countries are too high, even for organizations that have surveillance mandates like the Organisation for Economic Co-operation and Development, the IMF, and the European Commission. Thus, fiscal councils can contribute to making market discipline more effective by providing regular updates on fiscal performance. These updates could make transparency more effective in providing relevant fiscal policy information because, instead of monitoring fiscal developments, financial markets would monitor the fiscal policy reports of the monitors, which are the fiscal councils.[19]

By the same token, the availability of better information will allow voters to educate themselves about fiscal policy matters, and politicians will understand that voters are well placed to use the ballot box to penalize bad and reward good fiscal performance. In this way, fiscal councils can help to reinforce democratic accountability. If financial markets and the electorate become more effective because timely, independent analyses of fiscal policy are the norm, then rules are probably best thought of not as an independent source of fiscal discipline, but rather as a clear statement of fiscal policy intent against which fiscal performance can be judged. In other words, the role of rules (with an assist from fiscal councils) is to help transparency, financial markets, and voters do their jobs.

Should fiscal councils play a stabilization role? Although fiscal councils could make judgments as to whether the stance of fiscal policy is appropriate given the cyclical position of the economy, they are not directly involved in stabilization as envisaged under some fiscal authority proposals. This leaves unaddressed the well-known problems with discretionary stabilization, particularly its procyclicality in good times. However, making the short-term management of rainy-day or stabilization funds part of the fiscal council's mandate is something to consider. For example, the fiscal council could advise on using such funds to launch quick, reversible changes to a key tax rate or spending program in response to stabilization

[19] Even without fiscal councils, the IMF and the European Commission are publishing much more information about fiscal policies in the crisis countries in Europe than in the past, and markets are responding quickly to news about fiscal developments (some might say that they are overreacting). Fiscal councils can ensure that as much information remains available after the crises are over and for many more countries.

needs. Such an approach could blend independent input and democratic accountability in a way that provides a practical means of helping discretionary stabilization work in a more timely, temporary, and targeted manner. However, although final decisions on stabilization measures must inevitably rest with government, routinely involving a fiscal council in even limited tax and spending decisions may make it appear to be too much like a fiscal authority.

What impact can a fiscal council have on expenditure efficiency? When focusing on fiscal discipline, it is easy to lose sight of expenditure efficiency, yet improving efficiency is a key objective of most governments. Although fiscal councils do not have expenditure efficiency as part of their mandates, their actions can be efficiency enhancing because fiscal discipline and spending efficiency are closely related.[20] Governments that are not preoccupied with having to address fiscal imbalances and their wider macroeconomic consequences can pay more attention to the microeconomic aspects of fiscal policy, including the efficiency of spending.[21] Moreover, fiscal stability provides an appropriate background for making sound decisions about spending with medium-term implications, especially in the context of a medium-term budget framework. One reason that spending efficiency has proved to be such an elusive objective is that fiscal discipline has itself proved to be elusive. Therefore, even though the role of spending watchdog should be left to others, most notably national audit offices and relevant parliamentary committees, fiscal councils can make contributions to both fiscal discipline and expenditure efficiency.

Could other institutions play the fiscal council's role? Clearly, other institutions often perform some fiscal council functions. National audit offices, research institutes, international organizations, and even central banks do so, often quite well. However, specialization provides benefits, as is often the case in connection with national audit offices, for which fiscal council functions have been a sideline, but which are frequently not well suited in their analytical perspective or staffing to perform these functions. National audit offices are probably better left to concentrate on their traditional financial and performance audit functions. Moreover, political legitimacy and impact will be greater if fiscal council functions are the responsibility of one exclusively focused organization, and if that organization is inside government so that it can play a formal role in fiscal policy formulation and implementation, especially in the budget process. This issue, however, has to be placed in a country-specific context.

Advanced and emerging market economies with well-functioning fiscal institutions and good technical capacity can afford the luxury of considering which modern public financial management practices are appropriate for them and how

[20] Although some fiscal councils are responsible for costing new policies, that does not mean they are assessing efficiency. Their concern is that underestimated program costs will have consequences for fiscal discipline.

[21] It is sometimes argued that fiscal distress prompts the search for efficiency gains, but the record suggests that the burden of fiscal adjustment can fall heavily on productive spending, especially public investment.

best to implement those practices. But many developing countries do not have this luxury. Although they can certainly benefit from independent scrutiny of fiscal policy, this may not be their highest priority, and they might not have access to high-quality local input even if they were interested in it. Under these circumstances, involving outsiders should be considered when and where it can make a more significant difference than other reforms. The precise response to the need for an outside view should also be tailored to country requirements and opportunities, and could fall well short of setting up a fiscal council.[22]

6.4. CONCLUSION

The most persuasive justification for the creation of independent fiscal institutions is that the objectivity they bring to the budget process acts as a check on the tendency of government to pursue fiscally unsustainable policies, make optimistic assumptions about the effects of those policies, or both. These cases can be moderated by the existence of an objective voice, such as a fiscal council. It is important, however, not to either oversell the benefits of independent agencies, or have them dilute government economic policy expertise. It is too early to disentangle the impact of fiscal councils on fiscal outcomes, and evidence of this type can be difficult to uncover. Furthermore, particularly in developing countries, where economic and budgetary expertise may already be at a premium, it is important not to create fiscal councils by taking from the ministries of finance key skilled staff who are essential for the successful implementation of fiscal policy.

REFERENCES

Bayoumi, Tamim, Vladimir Klyuev, and Martin Mülheisen, eds., 2007, *Northern Star: Canada's Path to Economic Prosperity*, IMF Occasional Paper No. 258 (Washington: International Monetary Fund).

Calmfors, Lars, 2010a, "The Role of Independent Fiscal Policy Institutions," report to the Finnish Prime Minister's Office (Helsinki).

———, 2010b, "The Swedish Fiscal Policy Council—Experience and Lessons," paper prepared for Conference on Independent Fiscal Institutions, Budapest, Hungary, March.

Debrun, Xavier, David Hauner, and Manmohan S. Kumar, 2009, "Independent Fiscal Agencies," *Journal of Economic Surveys,* Vol. 23, No. 1, pp. 44–81.

Debrun, Xavier, and Manmohan S. Kumar, 2008, "Fiscal Rules, Fiscal Councils and All That: Commitment Devices, Signaling Tools, or Smokescreens?" *Proceedings of the Ninth Banca d'Italia Workshop on Public Finance* (Rome: Banca d'Italia).

European Commission, 2006, "National Independent Institutions," in *Public Finances in EMU* (Brussels).

[22] Thus, if increasing budget realism is a priority and poor forecasts result in large deviations between budgets and outcomes, an advisory panel on forecasting can provide an independent view on the economic and fiscal outlook. This approach can be gradually extended as new fiscal priorities emerge, until a point is reached at which consolidating the responsibility for independent scrutiny of fiscal policy under a fiscal council is the logical next step.

Giugale, Marcelo, 2010, "Fiscal Quality: A Developing Country Perspective," in *The Day after Tomorrow: A Handbook on the Future of Economic Policy in the Developing World*, ed. by Otaviano Canuto and Marcelo Giugale (Washington: World Bank).

Hagemann, Robert, 2010, "Improving Fiscal Performance through Fiscal Councils," Economics Department Working Paper No. 829 (Paris: Organisation for Economic Co-operation and Development).

Hemming, Richard, and Michael Kell, 2001, "Promoting Fiscal Responsibility: Transparency, Rules and Independent Fiscal Authorities," in *Fiscal Rules*, papers presented at the Banca D'Italia Research Department Workshop, Perugia.

International Monetary Fund (IMF), 2007, "Code of Good Practices on Fiscal Transparency" (Washington). Available via the Internet: http://www.imf.org/external/np/fad/trans/code.htm.

———, forthcoming, "The Functions and Impact of Fiscal Councils" (Washington).

Joyce, Philip, 2011, *The Congressional Budget Office: Honest Numbers, Power and Policymaking* (Washington: Georgetown University Press).

Kopits, George, 2011, "Independent Fiscal Institutions: Developing Good Practices," *OECD Journal on Budgeting*, Vol. 11, No. 3, pp. 1–18.

Lienert, Ian, 2005, "Who Controls the Budget: The Legislature or the Executive?" IMF Working Paper 05/115 (Washington: International Monetary Fund).

Schick, Allen, 2007, *The Federal Budget: Process, Politics, Policy*, 3rd ed. (Washington: Brookings Institution Press).

CHAPTER 7

In Search of Results: Strengthening Public Sector Performance

TERESA CURRISTINE AND SUZANNE FLYNN

During the past two decades, governments have tried to improve public sector performance by introducing numerous reforms, including performance measurement, management, and budgeting. These reforms depend on performance information (PI), which is essential to measure, monitor, and enhance performance. Governments in advanced economies now produce more PI (performance measures and evaluations) than ever before. Many have also sought to incorporate PI in budgeting, planning, and accountability processes. Yet information can only improve performance if it is used in decision making—it is not an end in itself. The initial assumption that more and better information would provide the right incentives to change behavior has not proved true in all cases. Ensuring the routine use of PI in budgeting has been more challenging than in management.

Nevertheless, both demand and supply factors are pressuring governments to do more to monitor and improve performance. Most countries have more educated electorates than 40 years ago, with higher expectations about the quality of services and government accountability. Private sector service delivery has improved along with communication and information technology, often creating 24-hour access to information and services. Citizens are also expecting higher-quality service provision from the public sector, requiring that governments not only improve the quality of services but also provide more individually tailored services. In addition, in many countries, citizens are demanding that governments be more accountable for what they achieve with taxpayers' money. This is combined with the perception, magnified by the global economic and financial crisis, that citizens increasingly distrust politicians and governments (Dalton, 2004). Politicians have felt compelled to produce visible results and to demonstrate to the public that they are accountable.

Budgetary constraints have created strains on the supply side. Since the end of the post–World War II boom, many advanced economies have faced fiscal deficits and weaker economic growth combined with the burden of rising health care and pension expenditures. Governments confronting these financial stresses have been under pressure to improve public sector efficiency and to achieve more with less funding. Previous economic crises motivated governments to introduce performance reforms, for example, in Sweden and Denmark in the 1980s and in the Republic of Korea in the late 1990s. The recent crisis may do the same.

This chapter considers how governments—especially those in advanced economies, where the experience is longest—have sought to improve public sector performance, and how those efforts can be made more effective in the future. It concentrates on reforms that use the budget and other public financial management (PFM) processes. The first section briefly discusses approaches to improving performance in a wider context. The second section examines the links between performance reforms and PFM systems and provides an overview of the PFM tools and trends for improving efficiency and effectiveness in advanced economies. The third section discusses key issues and challenges emerging from country experiences with implementing these initiatives. The fourth section seeks to frame the ongoing debate about the benefits of performance budgeting (PB) and in doing so to dispel some myths surrounding these initiatives. The final section discusses the use of PI during the recent fiscal stimulus and how PI can be used in fiscal consolidation by those countries adopting this approach.

7.1. IMPROVING PERFORMANCE IN A WIDER CONTEXT

The "performance movement" has a long history with several previous incarnations (Redburn, Shea, and Buss, 2007). The current wave of performance reforms began more than 25 years ago with the advent of "new public management." Under this label, countries embraced a plethora of reforms, including performance measurement; performance management;[1] PB; performance auditing; performance contracting; and performance-related pay, policy and program evaluations, strategic and spending reviews, and benchmarking. The central theme is on shifting the emphasis of government management, budgeting, and accountability from controlling inputs and compliance with procedural rules toward substantive results. Advocates claim these reforms have enhanced public sector efficiency, accountability, and transparency.

The current wave of reforms differs from previous incarnations in its extensive duration, wide reach, and use of computer-based communication and information technologies. Performance reforms, especially performance measurement and management, and to a lesser extent PB, are ubiquitous. They extend not only to most advanced economies, but also to numerous emerging market economies and to some low-income countries. These reforms have also been introduced to varying degrees at the subnational level in many advanced and emerging market economies.

[1] Performance management can be broadly defined as the use of PI to improve public sector performance, including in strategic planning, human resources management, and budgeting. OECD (1996) defines performance management more tightly as a management cycle under which program or organizational performance objectives and targets are established, managers are given flexibility to achieve them, actual performance is measured and reported, and this information feeds into decisions on operations, design, funding, and rewards or penalties.

Advanced economies have embraced a wide variety of reforms to enhance performance and service delivery. There has been no single approach because countries have adapted reforms to their individual historical, political, and institutional contexts. Government initiatives have included reorganization (merging departments, creating agencies and shared services), reforming the nature of service provision (one-stop shops, e-government), decentralizing responsibilities and service delivery to lower levels of government, streamlining government services, introducing market-type competition and mechanisms (contracting out, internal markets, privatization, public-private partnerships), and providing more information and choice to citizens in the provision of public services.[2]

More than other aspects of PFM, performance reforms are related to the wider system of public administration. Improving performance is not solely concerned with the management of public finances. Performance is affected by the personnel, organizational, and accountability systems and cultures within which agencies and civil servants operate. Improving efficiency or effectiveness is difficult without taking into account wider public sector influences.

7.2. PERFORMANCE REFORMS AND PUBLIC FINANCIAL MANAGEMENT

While acknowledging the importance of the initiatives discussed above, this chapter concentrates on reforms that aim specifically to improve performance through the budget and related PFM processes. A number of reasons arise for linking performance reforms to financial management. The budget process is one in which all agencies must participate. Including PI in budget preparation pressures agencies to develop and improve this information and to use it in planning, reporting, and funding decisions. The central budget authority (CBA) can potentially use PI in making budgetary decisions and to monitor spending ministries' and agencies' progress and to hold them accountable for results. In sum, having budgetary decision makers focus on program results can motivate agency heads and managers to take action to improve performance. The risk, however, is that the budget process and other PFM systems tend to be dominated by issues of money and financial control, and performance issues can be sidelined or crowded out, especially given the time constraints imposed by the annual budget process.

Within the PFM framework, governments have adopted a range of tools as part of their efforts to improve efficiency and effectiveness. These tools include performance measures (outputs and outcomes measures), PB, program and policy evaluations, and expenditure reviews. This section examines the trends across Organisation for Economic Co-operation and Development (OECD) countries in using these tools.

---

[2] See OECD (2005) for public sector reform trends across OECD countries.

7.2.1. Performance Measurement

Performance measurement is a process for monitoring and reporting organizational or program performance, in particular measuring progress toward achieving preestablished goals. Performance measurement frameworks that monitor and report on agencies' performance can be either part of the budget process or outside of it. Governments have developed different types of information to assess performance, including performance measures, performance targets, and benchmarking.

Performance measures are produced by 80 percent of OECD countries and can be used to measure processes, outputs (goods and services produced or provided), and outcomes (the ultimate achievements of an activity). The majority of countries develop both output (90 percent) and outcome (73 percent) measures (OECD, 2007a). The actual number of output and outcome measures produced varies widely across OECD countries. For example, Finland produced about 300 output and 50 outcome measures. Nearly three-quarters of OECD countries include performance data in their budget documentation. The degree to which expenditure is linked to specific performance targets, however, varies extensively. France reported including 600 performance targets in the budget and linking more than 90 percent of expenditure to specific targets. Mexico included 350 performance targets in the budget and linked less than 31 percent of expenditure to performance targets (OECD, 2007a).

Some 30 percent of governments have used benchmarking to measure relative performance of public sector entities (e.g., hospitals or schools) or states. For example, the United Kingdom uses league tables to rank the performance of schools and hospitals.[3] Benchmarking has been used in Australia's Review of Government Service Provision to compare states' performance and efficiency in delivering 14 public services. It has also been used in Denmark and Norway to compare the performance and efficiency of local governments and municipalities, and in Sweden to compare the quality and efficiency of health care provision.

7.2.2. Performance Budgeting

PB is concerned with the inclusion and use of PI (performance measures and evaluations) in budget preparation and decision making. In the 2000s, more OECD countries began developing PB systems (e.g., Austria, France, Poland, and the Republic of Korea) or revamping and revising their existing systems (e.g., Canada, the United Kingdom, and the United States). By 2011, nearly 70 percent of OECD countries had in place standard PB frameworks for their spending ministries.[4]

---

[3]These league tables have been controversial because they fail to explain the causes of poor or good performance. It is important that raw data be supplemented with more detailed explanations.
[4]This is according to a 2011 OECD survey on performance budgeting completed by 31 out of the 34 member countries and the Russian Federation (OECD, 2012).

There is no one model of performance budgeting. Definitions in the literature concentrate on three types: presentational, performance-informed, and direct performance budgeting (see Box 7.1). The most common form of PB applied in OECD countries is performance-informed budgeting. This model has no mechanical or automatic link between performance (either planned or actual results) and funding. PI is used along with other information on economic, political, and policy priorities to inform but not determine budget allocations. The weight given to PI depends on the policy area, the information available, and the political and economic context.

Requirements for performance-informed budgeting include establishing strategic goals and objectives for government expenditure, developing PI to measure and evaluate results, and formally integrating PI into the budget preparation process and budget funding decisions. Nearly all OECD countries develop PI, and many have sought to integrate it into the budget process by adjusting or adding new procedures and by changing to program or output-outcome budget classifications. Countries that have adopted an output or outcome budget classification include Australia, New Zealand, Sweden, and the United Kingdom. Many governments have changed procedures to include PI in budget negotiations between the CBA and spending ministries and in negotiations between ministries and their agencies.

Some 77 percent of OECD countries indicated that evaluation reports are used as part of the budget discussions and negotiations between the CBA and the

BOX 7.1 Definitions of Performance Budgeting

Different models and approaches to performance budgeting (PB)—presentational, performance-informed, and direct performance budgeting—are discussed below.

Presentational performance budgeting. Performance information (PI) is presented in budget documents or other government documents. The information can refer to targets, or results, or both, and is included as background information for accountability and dialogue with legislators and citizens on public policy issues. The PI does not have a formal role in decision making.

Performance-informed budgeting. In this form of PB, resources are indirectly related to proposed future performance or to past performance. The PI is important in the budget decision-making process, but does not determine the amount of resources allocated and does not have a predefined weight in the decision. PI is used along with other information to inform the decision-making process. The majority of Organisation for Economic Co-operation and Development (OECD) countries that use PI in the budget process engage in performance-informed budgeting.

Direct performance budgeting. Direct linkage involves allocating of resources directly and explicitly according to units of performance achieved, generally outputs. This form of PB is used only in specific sectors and in a limited number of OECD countries. It is not recommended that a direct or tight linkage between funding and performance results be applied on a systematic government-wide scale.

Source: OECD (2007b).

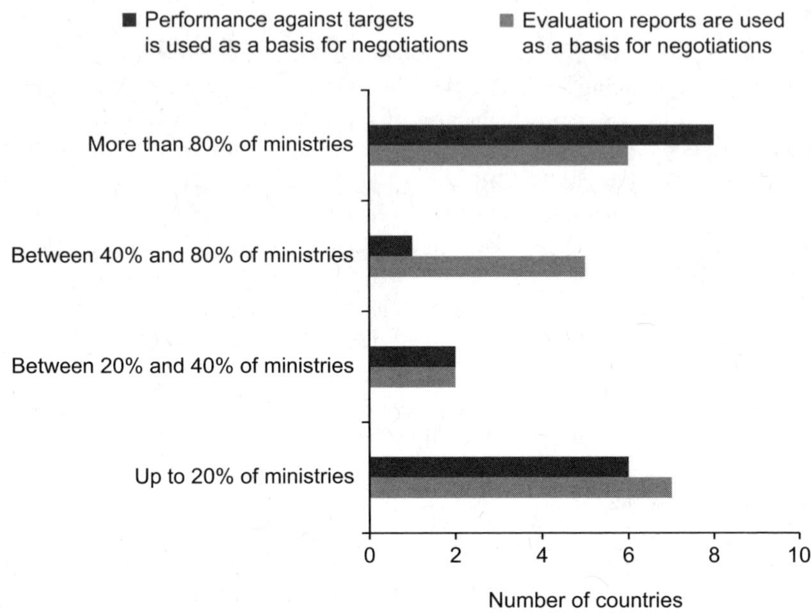

Figure 7.1 Proportion of Spending Ministries with Which Performance Information Is Used in Budget Negotiations with the Central Budget Authority

Source: OECD (2007a).

spending ministries, and 67 percent of countries used performance against targets.[5] Still, a formal requirement to include PI in budget negotiations does not mean that it will be used in all cases and for all ministries and agencies. As Figure 7.1 demonstrates, coverage varies extensively. For example, eight countries reported that they use performance against targets in discussion with more than 80 percent of their ministries, and six reported using it with 20 percent or fewer of ministries.

Figure 7.2 shows the different ways, including for monitoring, planning, and allocative purposes, in which PI is generally used in decision making by the CBA and the line ministries.

The most common use of PI by CBAs is to push for change in programs, followed by cutting expenditure and allocating resources between ministries and agencies. In 2007 spending ministries used PI less, and for justifying existing allocations to specific programs and activities; for planning purposes, that is, setting targets for the next year; and for managing programs and agencies and compelling change in programs. In 2011, spending ministries used PI for setting allocations for programs, proposing new areas for spending and strategic planning and prioritization (OECD, 2012). Research indicates that PI is more often used by spending ministries in their negotiations with their agencies than by the CBA (OECD, 2007a). A common approach to integrating PI into the budget preparation process is through discussions of agencies' performance agreements and contracts. This approach is used in countries with executive agencies, for example, New Zealand.

[5] Question 83 of OECD (2007a).

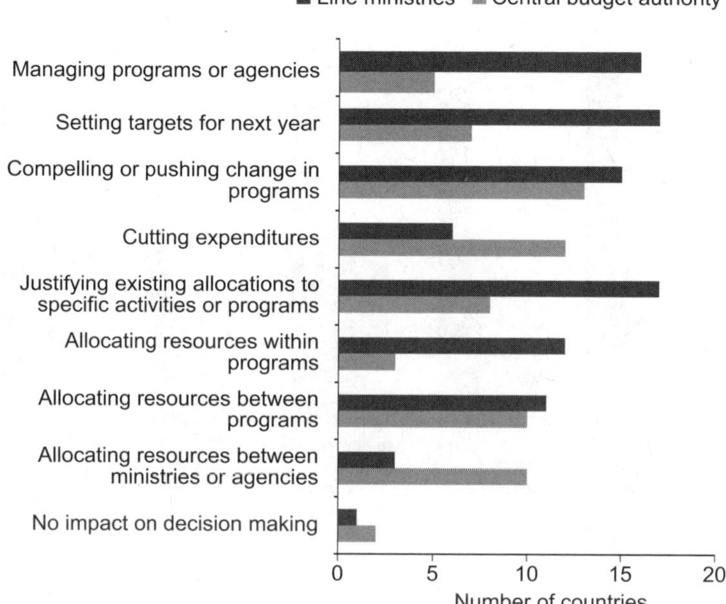

Figure 7.2 Usage of Performance Information by Central Budget Authority, Line Ministries

Source: OECD (2007a).

7.2.3. Program and Policy Evaluations and Expenditure Reviews

OECD countries have a long history of conducting program and policy evaluations. In 2007–08, more than 80 percent of OECD countries reported conducting evaluations. Figure 7.3 provides details on the types of evaluations developed by the CBA, the ministry of finance, and spending ministries. Spending ministries conduct more evaluations than other entities. Most frequently, they produce reviews of ongoing programs. These evaluations can be used either during the budget preparation process or outside the budget process.

Countries have also developed spending or expenditure reviews. These reviews differ from traditional program and policy evaluations in a number of ways. They are led by the central agencies (CBA, ministry of finance or prime minister's office); have a wider, generally cross-government focus; and tend to concentrate not only on improving efficiency and effectiveness, but also on expenditure prioritization, reallocation, and cutbacks. In 2011, 15 OECD countries reported conducting spending reviews.

Expenditure reviews can be ad hoc or systematic and can focus on all government ministries or selected strategic policies, functions, or areas. Ad hoc reviews include the Canadian 1994 program review that covered all government ministries and focused on spending cuts. Since the late 1990s, the United Kingdom has systematically conducted comprehensive spending reviews. The first, in 1998,

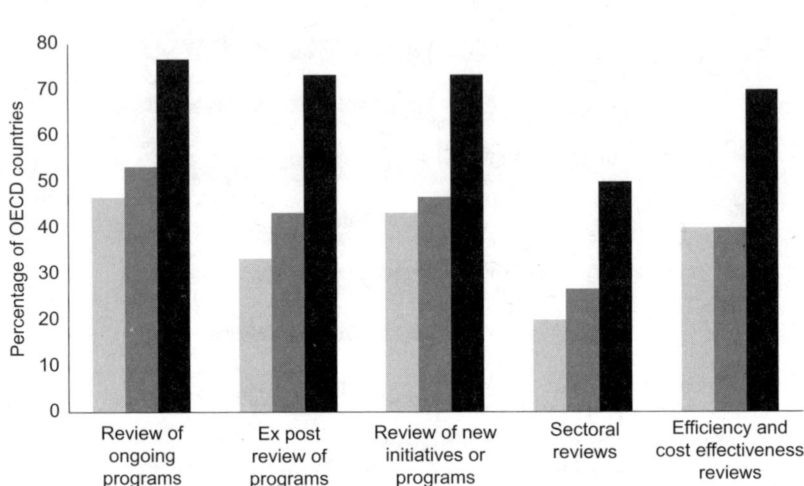

Figure 7.3 Types of Evaluations Commissioned and/or Conducted by Central Budget Authority, Ministry of Finance, and Spending Ministries

Source: OECD (2007a).

Note: OECD = Organisation for Economic Co-operation and Development.

covered all government ministries and focused on reallocating resources to key priorities and improving efficiency. Subsequent reviews have taken place every two to three years. Expenditure reviews can also focus on selective policies or functions. For example, the Dutch interdepartmental policy reviews looked at specific policy areas, including social benefits and labor policies.

The motivations for conducting reviews vary, including installation of a new government with different political priorities, new policies requiring reallocations, conditions of fiscal stress requiring savings, or as part of wider reform efforts seeking to improve efficiency and effectiveness. Reviews do not necessarily focus primarily on spending cuts. The Australian strategic reviews concentrate on selected policy areas or programs (e.g., the climate change program) with a focus on improving their performance and effectiveness. The U.S. Program Assessment Rating Tool, which was overseen by the Office of Management and Budget, during a four-year cycle aimed to assess all federal programs, concentrating on their effectiveness through evaluating program purpose, design, planning, management, results, and accountability. In times of fiscal stress, however, expenditure reviews tend to concentrate on budgetary savings. These issues are discussed in more detail in Section 7.5.

7.3. KEY ISSUES AND CHALLENGES

If there is widespread agreement on the need to improve public sector efficiency and effectiveness and the tools to do so are extensively available, why is it so difficult to get there? Many countries have announced reforms or passed legislation but face challenges with implementing and integrating them into budget, managerial, and accountability systems. Implementing reforms implies not only developing their technical aspects but also changing the behavior and culture of key actors to induce them to focus on results. These challenges have been discussed at length elsewhere (OECD, 2007a, 2007b). This section concentrates on three issues: (1) improving PI, (2) developing incentive structures to motivate spending ministries and agencies to improve results, and (3) engaging politicians in reforms and motivating them to use PI.

7.3.1. Improving Performance Information

Many governments struggle with designing measures (of outputs and outcomes) and improving the quality, credibility, relevance, and timeliness of PI. Since at least 1995, 40 percent of OECD countries have been producing output measures, and these measures are well developed in education, health, and transport. Many countries, however, still grapple with accurately measuring government's diversity of activities, especially intangible tasks—for example, foreign policy advice. Although the majority of OECD countries develop outcomes, they are more complicated to measure than outputs. External factors, which are not within the control of the service provider, influence results, and there are difficulties in attributing outcomes to specific programs and activities. Thus, holding service providers accountable for results can be problematic. For both outputs and outcomes, developing baseline information and maintaining data systems that produce sufficient high-quality data in a timely manner can also be challenging.

Countries have also encountered issues with the quality and timeliness of program and policy evaluations. A frequent complaint from ministries of finance is that evaluations by spending ministries are of poor quality, usually support rather than question the relevant program, rarely address value-for-money issues, and are produced too late for budgetary decision making. It is a difficult balancing act, as spending ministries have the information needed to produce meaningful evaluations, yet they can also have a vested interest in ensuring that the evaluation is favorable.

Although a large volume of PI is produced, improving its quality remains challenging. International and national guidelines on producing good-quality PI are in generous supply. Establishing central guidelines, however, does not automatically improve quality. Monitoring if and how these guidelines are implemented by spending ministries and agencies and comparing the quality of reporting across agencies are essential.

A 2009 study highlighted the variability of the quality of performance reporting across selected countries and spending ministries (Boyle, 2009). For example, in Australia, in the three sectors (agriculture, health, and transportation) examined, fewer than 40 percent of the indicators were quantitative, only 30 percent established a target, and only 20 percent had baseline data associated with them. Without targets and baseline data, it is difficult to assess changes and progress in performance. Other advanced economies have noted similar problems with improving the quality of reporting among their spending ministries.

Countries have sought to enhance quality through independent reviews of indicators and of monitoring and reporting systems. In some countries, the supreme audit institution has tried to improve the validity and quality of PI. For example, the New Zealand Audit Office undertook a review of the quality and use of PI. In the United States, a private-sector body has played a role in reviewing government performance reporting.[6] Other efforts have been mounted to include independent experts in the evaluation process so as not to leave evaluation only to spending ministries. Users of PI should understand its limitations and that, as the experience of advanced economies and of state and local governments underscores, developing useful PI generally takes several years.

7.3.2. Developing the Right Mix of Incentives

Among the most protracted of problems facing reformers is the creation of incentives to change behavior and improve public sector performance. The fundamental assumption of any incentive system is that individuals, groups, or organizations are motivated by receiving rewards and avoiding sanctions. Various instruments can be used to generate incentives in the public sector, including pay and career prospects, budgets, naming and shaming, managerial or financial flexibility, legal incentives, and competitive and market pressures.[7] Incentives created under these instruments can be explicit, implicit, positive, or negative. This section discusses how three instruments (budgets, managerial flexibility, and naming and shaming) can be used by central agencies (and by spending agencies themselves) to motivate spending ministries and agencies improve performance.

Using Budgets to Motivate Performance

As discussed previously, PI is most often used by CBAs and spending ministries in budget negotiations for planning, budget allocations, and monitoring purposes. Traditional budget negotiations included discussion of what ministries were expected to achieve with their allocations. PB systems have formalized this discussion by making these expectations more explicit through performance measures or targets. This strategy has created incentives for ministries to use PI in their own budget preparation. Most often, ministries use PI to set allocations for programs and to justify to the CBA both new and existing spending. In turn, the CBA seeks to obtain value for money from increased spending and new programs. CBAs' use of PI for monitoring and accountability can create implicit incentives for ministries and agencies to focus on performance results and on problem areas. More intensive monitoring of a program and pushing for change are among the common actions taken by CBAs if a performance target is unmet or a program has received a poor evaluation.

In theory, budgets could automatically be increased or reduced based on performance against agreed-on targets or ex post evaluations. In practice,

---

[6] From fiscal year 1999 to 2009, the Mercatus Center, based at George Mason University, assessed all federal agency performance reports to see how well they were informing congress and the public.

[7] See Boyne and Hood (2010) for a detailed discussion of the different types of incentives and instruments.

countries tend not to mechanically reduce or increase agency or program budgets based solely on performance results. In most countries at a government-wide level, PI is used to inform but not determine budget allocations. PI is rarely used by CBAs to eliminate programs or determine pay. Although CBAs and spending ministries do use PI to cut expenditure on poorly performing programs, they do so infrequently. Only five OECD countries reported that their CBA took this action more than 40 percent of the time.[8] This low proportion reflects a number of factors, including the difficulty of obtaining good-quality information. Automatically linking budgets to results can create incentives to manipulate data. Priority programs, even those performing poorly, are unlikely to see funding reduced. Indeed, in some cases lack of funding could be a contributing factor to poor performance.

Direct Performance Budget and Performance Bonus Systems

Governments are also exploring explicit positive financial incentives to motivate improved performance. Direct or formula performance budgeting (see Box 7.1) is the exception to the discussion above. This type of budgeting uses a formula to automatically link funding to outputs. It is not applied at a government-wide level and is used only in certain sectors, mostly education and health, especially in diagnosis-related groups. These direct or formula PB systems require detailed and high-quality performance and cost information, which is difficult to obtain. Their results in both education and health are widely debated. Although they have been known to increase volume of production and in some cases improve efficiency, depending on the program design,[9] there are concerns about their impact on the quality of service and on cost controls.

Another area in which governments are applying positive financial incentives is through performance bonuses or top-up schemes. In these cases, organizations or states are given financial bonuses for meeting performance targets, achieving performance improvements, or implementing institutional capacity building within selective areas and programs. Although no detailed cross-country comparative research on these schemes is available, there are a number of country examples (see Box 7.2).

Creating financial incentives for improving performance explicitly linked to funding generates risks of perverse incentives. These risks are more pronounced for direct PB systems, in which all funding is determined by performance results, than for bonus schemes. Perverse incentives can lead to, among other things, cheating, goal displacement (focusing only on what is measured), and gaming,[10] that is, misrepresentation of performance targets or data.

---

[8] Question 85 of OECD (2007a).

[9] See Smith (2007) for details of schemes in health.

[10] "Gaming" is defined by Bevan and Hood (2006) as reactive subversion, such as "hitting the target and missing the point" or reducing performance where targets do not apply. Well-known gaming problems include ratchet effects, threshold effects, and output distortions.

BOX 7.2 Examples of Performance Bonus Schemes

Schemes that link achievement of a performance target to a performance bonus include the U.S. Department of Transportation's highway safety belt scheme, which rewarded states that achieved targets in improving safety belt use, and the United Kingdom's local government public service performance agreements, which provided grants for capacity building and additional funding from the central government if at least 60 percent of local authorities' targets were met. Australia's national partnership system linked achievement of performance targets to federal grants and bonus funding for states. In the early and mid-2000s, the U.K.'s National Health Service paid a bonus to hospitals that reduced waiting times and increased the percentage of patients treated in emergency rooms within four hours (Kelman and Friedman, 2009).

Bonuses are also linked to the implementation of administrative modernization and institutional capacity-building reforms. Examples include the European Union Structural Fund's 4 percent performance reserve, Italy's regional development policy grants (2000–06), and in the United States, the Obama administration's Race to the Top educational program.

Increased or Decreased Managerial Flexibility to Motivate Performance

In theory, performance management and budgeting systems hold agencies or managers accountable for results, and in return, agencies or managers receive greater managerial flexibility and a relaxation of input controls (budget and staff) to achieve these results. There are competing theories about how this should operate. The first argues that managerial flexibility should be part of reforms introducing performance budgeting and management systems. The second claims managerial flexibility should be "earned" through demonstrated performance improvements. The third contends that decisions about relaxation of input controls should be separated from performance and determined on a case-by-case basis, depending on financial and managerial controls that are in place within an agency. The capacity and willingness of government to honor its side of the bargain are influenced by institutional context and the widely varying systems of public administration.

In practice, regardless of the approach taken, no clear pattern emerges across OECD countries of increasing managerial flexibility and relaxing input controls. Research indicates that in selected countries PB reforms have been accompanied by a relaxation of input controls, although not a significant reduction (Andrews, 2010). Comparative research on the experience of U.S. states, however, indicates that not only has managerial flexibility not been enhanced, but new reporting requirements and information technology systems have increased controls (Moynihan, 2006).

Initiatives that reward good performance by reducing input controls and increasing managerial flexibility are not common—although one example is in the United Kingdom under the Blair and Brown administrations, which rewarded improved performance by local authorities with freedom from inspections and central regulations. Punishing poor performance with increased monitoring or control is among the more frequent courses of action by the CBA when a program is performing poorly. Stronger actions may also be taken against continuous poor performers. For example, in the United States under the No Child Left Behind program, schools that continuously underperform can face a range of sanctions, including removal of staff and closure of the school. In this particular case, early sanctions came with technical assistance or targeted funding to help poor performers build institutional capacity.

Public Naming and Shaming

Since the early 2000s, the volume of PI released to the public, either as part of budget documents or in separate performance plans and reports, has increased significantly. Public information has enhanced transparency, even if the information's quality has varied. In theory, publicizing the performance of agencies, programs, states, individual schools, and hospitals can highlight good performers and pressure poor performers to improve. It can also generate competition among providers to improve performance, especially if the public has the option to exit or choose among different service providers.

The underlying assumption is that citizens, external bodies, and interest groups are interested in PI and will use it to monitor organizations and push for improvements.[11] Although this topic is underresearched, in most countries the public clearly has only limited interest in government-wide plans and performance reports (Pollitt, 2006a). Citizens are more interested in the performance of services that affect them directly, such as health and education, but how citizens evaluate these services is more related to their individual experience of the relevant service than to reported PI. Partially in realization of this, many countries are seeking to improve the quality of customer service and the interaction between citizens and frontline employees.

Among civil servants, public recognition of good performance (e.g., a reward ceremony, or a letter from or meeting with the minister) can also serve to motivate. In a cooperative environment, recognized performance leaders (individuals, groups, or agencies) can exchange ideas, experiences, and best practices with others.

For each country, the right instrument and incentive mix will depend on the wider institutional structure of public administration and governance within which its public servants operate. These systems have more than one objective; for example, government-wide personnel systems are concerned not only with performance, but also with preventing corruption and promoting diversity and equality.

7.3.3. Political Economy Challenges

Two main challenges confront reformers. First, politicians must be induced to set clear objectives for policies and programs. Politicians have frequently been accused of setting vague and unattainable goals—either intentionally because the

[11] See World Bank (2010) for a discussion of whether public sector performance affects citizens' trust in government.

goals are a product of political compromise or unintentionally because the politicians lack experience with goal setting. Vague goals are difficult to measure and achieve, and unattainable goals weaken the support of civil servants and ultimately create unrealistic expectations. Second, politicians must be induced to use PI in decision making. Their capacity to use PI is influenced by the wider political system, that is, whether it is a presidential, semipresidential, or parliamentary system; whether it is a minority or majority government; and whether the prevailing political culture is adversarial or strives for consensus.

Engaging Politicians in the Legislature

Legislators tend to make only limited use of PI, especially in budgetary allocation decisions. This limited use occurs even in countries in which the legislature has been the main initiator of PB reforms, as in, for example, France and the United States.[12] Informational and institutional factors limit the incentives for legislatures to use PI. These factors include too much information and poor-quality or poorly presented information. Legislators often lack the time, resources, and expertise to examine PI. Furthermore, their priorities are influenced by political, ideological, and constituency interests.

Legislative authority in the budget process varies widely. Failure to use PI in budgetary allocation decisions is a larger issue in countries in which the legislature has a strong role in budget allocation, for example, in the U.S. federal and state governments. The experience of U.S. states, however, paints a more complex picture. Although PI is not used directly in allocative decisions, it has been used to inform the budget debate. A survey highlights how in some states, PI changed the nature of budget discussions and the questions asked by legislatures. PI produced a greater focus in budget deliberations on outcomes and what could be achieved with public funds (Willoughby, 2004).

In other countries, there are signs that legislatures use PI for accountability purposes. Parliamentarians informed by performance reports ask questions about agencies' or ministries' performance, or lack thereof. This type of questioning tends to be selective rather than systematic and to concentrate on more high-profile topics. Differences among individual legislators also occur: new members are more open to using PI than those who have been in office for a number of years (Bourdeaux, 2006; Bourdeaux and Chikoto, 2008).

Engaging Politicians in the Executive Branch

Evidence shows more widespread use of PI by executive branch politicians in several countries. Case studies provide examples of executive branch politicians and their appointees using PI in national, state, city, and local governments. At a national level, some politicians use PI to inform budgetary decisions. For example, in Canada, as part of its strategic review exercises (see Box 7.3), the treasury

[12] The 2001 *loi organique n°2001-692 du 1er août 2001 relative aux lois de finances* (generally known as the LOLF) in France and the 1993 Government Performance and Results Act in the United States.

cabinet committee reviews and decides on the cutback proposals contained in departmental strategic reviews. In Australia, the expenditure review committee examines proposals for new funding, all of which include planned performance and cost-benefit analysis.

States in Australia and Brazil and local governments as diverse as China's Guangdong Province and Bogota city in Colombia have all reported using PI in budgeting. In the United States, PI has been used to varying degrees by governors, chief executives, and political appointees in a number of states for budgeting, monitoring, and management purposes.[13] In the United States, 38 states have introduced performance budgeting legislation and 50 have initiated performance budgeting mandates. The Government Performance Project highlighted Delaware, Maryland, Oregon, Texas, Utah, and Washington as leaders in performance budgeting.

It is possible to argue that PI is most often employed by politicians for monitoring and control purposes. In Chile, Colombia, and Mexico, presidents have developed performance systems to monitor progress toward achieving high-priority goals and targets.[14] These systems have often been developed alongside those used by the ministry of finance in the budget process.[15] Creating too many monitoring and reporting systems, and failing to link them, can cause problems.

The U.K. system, under the Blair and Brown administrations, was arguably the most comprehensive and long-lasting performance monitoring system. PI was discussed alongside the spending review process. Ministers were held accountable for the delivery of targets in public service agreements. The chancellor of the exchequer chaired a subcommittee of the cabinet on public services and expenditure to discuss and monitor progress toward achieving key performance indicators. A minister even publicly offered to resign for failure to achieve a key performance target. Ultimately, the success of the U.K. system is subject to debate, especially the use of hard targets for control. In parliamentary regimes with a limited number of political appointees and career civil servants, performance systems can potentially be used by politicians to obtain more information and control over senior career civil servants, who traditionally have an information advantage.

Despite the examples discussed above, motivating politicians to use PI in budget decisions remains challenging. Politicians do not necessarily use PI in the manner reformers intend. A larger volume of PI is produced than is ever used. The interest in, and use of, PI waxes and wanes with the political salience or sensitivity of an issue, with changes in political regimes, and with individual political leaders. Recognition appears to be growing, however, of the value of performance systems as governing and monitoring tools. When regimes change, it is important for reformers to engage with new politicians and to present PI in a manner that is useful to them, given their interests and time constraints.

---

[13] For discussions of PB in U.S. states and cities see Lu, Willoughby, and Arnett (2009) and Folz, Abdelrazek, and Chung (2009).

[14] In Chile and Colombia, this took place under previous presidential regimes.

[15] See World Bank (2010) for a discussion of Latin American countries.

Changing accountability structures can create motivational incentives. If top leaders establish systems to hold their ministers and political appointees accountable for performance, incentives are created for ministers, in turn, to monitor progress within their departments and to set expectations for civil servants and agencies to improve performance.

7.4. DISPELLING THE MYTHS AND FRAMING THE DEBATE—EMERGING LESSONS

The previous section addressed some of the issues facing countries implementing performance tools. After a decade of accelerated performance reforms, the benefits of performance initiatives, specifically performance measurement and PB systems, continue to be debated. Even though performance reforms are portrayed in technical and neutral terms, they have attracted equally passionate proponents and opponents.

On the one hand, the literature abounds with scholars' and practitioners' depictions of successful case studies (Pollitt, 2006b; Osborne and Gaebler, 1992; Kamensky and Morales, 2005).[16] The reported benefits of PB reforms include improved mechanisms for planning, setting objectives, and monitoring progress; greater transparency; more information on policies and programs that work, and those that do not work and why they do not; and improved efficiency and improved expenditure allocations. On the other hand, an equally prolific number of articles highlight the shortcomings, obstacles, and unintended consequences of performance measurement and budgeting systems. These criticisms claim that the reforms propose generic measurement standards that ignore the uniqueness of programs and sectors, distort goals, create counterproductive incentives and gaming, impose heavy reporting requirements, and turn into extensive compliance exercises. In addition, the reforms are purported to centralize control, distract from more fundamental budget reforms, and generate unrealistic expectations about the feasibility of directly linking performance results to funding (Radin, 2006, 2009; Schick, 2009a).

Reaching firm conclusions is difficult, because, as with most PFM reforms, the impact of performance measurement and PB resists easy determination.[17] This uncertainty reflects the lack of agreed-on definitions of terms, the diverse objectives and implementation approaches of these reforms across countries and sectors, and the paucity of systematic evaluations. Isolating from external influences the effects of specific institutional reforms on performance and evaluating the differences between short-term and long-term impacts are also fraught with problems (Curristine, Lonti, and Joumard, 2007). Conflicting assessments of these initiatives not only make reaching concrete conclusions about their impact

[16] See Pollitt (2006b) for more comparative experiences with performance management and measurement in four European Union member states: Finland, the Netherlands, Sweden, and the United Kingdom.

[17] See Chapter 5 of Pollitt and Bouckaert (2004) for a discussion of these issues.

difficult but have also given rise to numerous myths.[18] This section seeks to frame the ongoing debate by discussing and dispelling some of these myths, illustrated below.

Performance reforms will lead to rational decision making and an end to politics in budgeting. An underlying assumption of earlier PB initiatives was that the provision of "objective" information on policy and program performance would override political factors in funding decisions. Experience has proved this is rarely the case, especially in politically competitive environments with strong ideological and partisan divides. This assumption ignores the messiness of decision making in most governments. It is rare that one decision maker makes a decision based on one piece of information. Rather, a mix of information (political, financial, economic, performance) and many decision makers and decision-making stages are involved. More recent approaches to PB, mainly performance-informed budgeting, acknowledge that PI is one among many pieces of information in the budgetary decision-making process and that politics still plays a key role.

PI is only performance targets. The tendency in both the literature and in the public domain is to concentrate only on performance targets. The U.K. performance system became synonymous with centrally driven performance targets. Much of the criticism of performance measurement concentrates on the distorting effects of such targets. In reality, governments produce a mix of PI and develop extensive evaluations because performance measures and targets provide only a snapshot of performance. Evaluations and other forms of PI are needed to comprehend the underlying causes of poor and good performance.

More information is always better. The extensive volume of PI produced by governments is not matched by corresponding use. When establishing performance measurement systems, countries tend to develop a large volume of indicators or targets in an effort to measure everything. More is not better. Requiring that spending ministries and agencies develop volumes of information is time consuming and distracts from other work. Overloading decision makers with information makes it difficult for them to discern what is relevant and useful. Awareness is growing that too many indicators make it difficult to focus on key priorities and are costly to monitor.

Performance budgeting automatically or mechanically links funds and performance results. Performance-informed budgeting is the most common form of PB adopted in OECD countries. This approach has no automatic or mechanical link between resources and results. Direct links exist only in selected sectors and in bonus schemes; they are generally avoided at a government-wide level. Efforts to automatically link results to funding require detailed information on outputs and costs, which are difficult to obtain at a government-wide level. Furthermore, financially rewarding good performance and punishing bad does not take account of government priorities or the underlying cause of poor performance, which

[18] Hood and Jackson (1991) have taken a loosely similar approach to discussing administrative doctrines.

could be underfunding, poor management, or bad program design. Financial rewards can also generate incentives to manipulate data.

Performance systems inevitably fail when gaming occurs. In most systems that link funding to performance, there will be incentives to game, especially as key actors learn how the rules operate and how to manipulate the system to their own advantage. Gaming, however, does not preclude improved performance. The key question is whether a performance system, even with gaming behavior, produces a better level of performance than no performance system at all.[19] The other issue is whether improvements under such a system can be sustained. This highlights the importance of performance regimes being dynamic systems that change rules and incentives as reforms evolve. All budgeting systems involve gaming to some extent, as agencies and program supporters seek to obtain more money for their interests. Performance systems are no different.

Performance budgeting stands alone. PB goes hand in hand with performance management. PB seeks to create incentives to motivate agencies to improve performance; therefore, it is concerned with setting objectives, monitoring performance, and inducing line ministries and managers to use PI to improve operations, management, and allocation of resources. Contemporary PB reforms are more closely related to performance management initiatives than were older reforms, which concentrated more on expenditure prioritization. Countries with well-developed planning systems must ensure that planning is integrated with the performance system to prevent the creation of two separate systems for monitoring and reporting.

Performance budgeting is always accompanied by increased managerial flexibility and relaxation of input controls. The capacity and willingness of governments to increase managerial flexibility and to relax input controls are influenced by the institutional context and the wide variety of systems of public administration. The impulse to relax controls and the speed at which such relaxation is accomplished also depend on the context. The fundamental question is whether the current system of control restricts managers' capacity to improve efficiency and effectiveness. It is important to assess the risks when relaxing input controls and to take into account not only efficiency but also concerns about avoiding corruption and failure to comply with regulations. The issue is how to balance these objectives.

Performance budgeting inevitably turns into a compliance exercise. Performance reforms with extensive and detailed reporting requirements can degenerate and have degenerated into little more than reporting and compliance exercises. This is more likely when the reforms increase reporting requirements and controls and reduce managerial flexibility. This outcome is also an issue when the government entity responsible for delivering the service has little ownership of the performance objectives or measures and its sole role is reporting performance to the center. Performance reforms, however, do not inevitably become compliance

---

[19] See Kelman and Friedman (2009) for a discussion on this point in relation to the controversial U.K. National Health Service performance target for improving emergency room waiting times.

exercises. This development can be avoided if reform design reduces and minimizes reporting requirements and removes a rule for each rule added, if managers see PI as useful for their jobs, and if incentives to use PI are related to the wider management and accountability systems. These systems need to be reoriented to a performance—as opposed to a traditional compliance—approach. Performance systems must be changed and adjusted over time to ensure that they do not become routine but rather renew their focus on performance.

Performance reforms are a failure if the whole government is not using PI to produce large-scale improvements. Perhaps because of the high expectations generated by reformers or the high standard for success imposed by critics, performance initiatives are sometimes labeled failures if PI is not uniformly used to demonstrate large-scale performance improvement. Expectations of uniform application of reforms across the entire government are not realistic. For most PFM reforms, progress is mixed. Some agencies and programs are reform leaders, some are laggards, and some never engage. Although there are instances of quick transformations of agency and organizational performance, progress can equally be incremental or confined to particular sectors and areas.

Reformers often believe that once the law has been passed or the internal rules are changed the desired behavior will ensue. However, just as important as the rules are the existing structures and incentives in which key actors operate. For performance reforms, changing the behavior of civil servants and politicians to focus on results is complex and requires persuasion and incentives to motivate actors to move away from the traditional means of making budgetary decisions.

7.5. USING PERFORMANCE INFORMATION FOR FISCAL STIMULUS AND CONSOLIDATION

Most research on the use of PI in budgeting has taken place during good fiscal times. In less than three years since the 2008–09 global economic and financial crisis, many advanced economies went from implementing large stimulus packages to facing fiscal consolidation measures. The rapidly changed situation raises two questions: What role, if any, did PI play in the selection and monitoring of programs and projects for the fiscal stimulus packages? What role can PI play in fiscal consolidation? Advocates argue that PI underpins budgetary decisions in good times, and in bad times, helps decision makers make more intelligent and informed expenditure reductions. Critics claim that in crises, PI will be ignored in favor of more direct means of cutting expenditure.

7.5.1. Fiscal Stimulus

The primary objective of the internationally coordinated fiscal stimulus effort was to stop the global financial and economic tailspin and to stimulate economic growth. Countries' budget systems went into crisis mode to implement fiscal stimulus packages, in many cases straining standard budgeting processes (see Chapter 1 and Schick, 2009b). Politics determined the overall size and structure of the packages, but what role did PI play in allocating money to programs and projects that were part of these packages?

A key challenge facing countries was balancing the urgent need to increase demand in the economy by spending money quickly with ensuring money was well spent. Given the urgency and time constraints, limited attention seems to have been paid to ex ante use of PI in the traditional sense. Instead, the "three Ts" criteria (timely, targeted, and temporary) were applied to decide on allocations of funds. Countries applied these criteria in many ways, including, for example, bringing forward approved payments, increasing spending on infrastructure projects, and maintaining roads and buildings.

Ex post there has been greater use of PI in monitoring and reporting on stimulus packages in general and on specific projects. A number of countries, including Canada, Chile, France, and the United States, have used indicators to monitor their stimulus spending. The measures of performance concentrated on how much has been spent, how quickly, how many jobs have been created, and the impact on economic growth. Some countries, including Australia and Chile, have conducted ex post evaluations of individual programs and policies. There have been international and country-specific evaluations of the impact of the stimulus packages on economic growth and job creation.[20] Indeed, the attention given by some governments, and by the media in particular, to monitoring and the impact of stimulus money is much greater than that normally paid to the performance of traditional government spending.[21] It is generally agreed that the internationally coordinated effort achieved its primary objective and prevented a global financial and economic meltdown, but the impact of stimulus on individual countries' economic growth and job creation is a hotly debated topic.

7.5.2. Fiscal Consolidation

In advanced economics, gross government debt in 2012 is expected to surpass 110 percent of GDP. In addition, by 2030 pensions and health care spending are expected to add more than 4 percent of GDP to fiscal deficits in advanced economies (IMF, 2012). For many advanced economies, given the size of predicted debt and increases in age-related spending, it appears additional measures will be needed in the future to enhance the sustainability of public finances.

For those countries that are currently undergoing consolidation, the size, pace, and content of the fiscal adjustment vary.[22] Generally, fiscal adjustment has been broad based, including both expenditure and revenue measures. In advanced economies, about 60 percent of the adjustment has come from the expenditure side. (See Appendix 7.1 for details of measures introduced by selected individual countries from 2009 to 2012.) Most countries have introduced reforms to age-

---

[20] For example, the U.S. Congressional Budget Office produced regular reports on its estimate of the number of jobs created by the American Recovery and Reinvestment Act of 2009.

[21] For example, CNN Money reported regularly on aspects of federal stimulus, including results.

[22] See IMF (2011a, 2011b, 2012) for details on the size and pace of the consolidation for individual countries.

related spending, including increasing the retirement age and tightening pension eligibility requirements. Reforms in health care systems include efforts to contain pharmaceutical spending and increasing cost sharing in health care expenses.

Proposals for expenditure cuts have also included reducing operational and program expenditures, such as wage freezes, wage cuts, and staff reductions. Examples have included a two-year pay freeze for U.S. federal government employees and the U.K. proposal to cut 330,000 public sector jobs. In addition, some governments have adopted requirements for across-the-board efficiency savings or spending caps or cuts.

Can Performance Information Play a Role in Consolidation? If So, How?

In three respects the situation in the wake of the 2008–09 financial and economic crisis could favor the use of PI. First, unlike in previous recessions, OECD countries now have in place systems of performance indicators, evaluations, and performance budgeting that they have been developing for many years. Second, if the current predictions hold, it is likely that for most advanced economies consolidation will not be a one-off exercise, but will take place over a number of years. This could provide time, which was not available when the stimulus packages were implemented, for developing processes to use PI in making consolidation decisions. Third, given the scale of expenditure reductions required there is an interest and incentive for governments to demand and use information on program and agency performance. Initial stages of consolidation tend to concentrate on "low-hanging fruit," those reductions easiest to identify and quickest to implement. As consolidation moves beyond the initial stage it can become more difficult to find reductions and harder choices have to be made.[23] Governments may need to address fundamental questions not only about how they provide services but about what services they provide and what the role of the state should be.

Countries will need strategic tools to help reduce expenditures in a manner supportive of longer-term sustainability. Using PI, including expenditure and strategic reviews and evaluations, in this process could help countries to make more informed choices. Countries with advanced PB systems have established organizational objectives, goals, and measures. Many countries also have efficiency indicators. Even before the crisis, some OECD countries required efficiency savings from public sector organizations.[24] Although it is important to note the difficulty in measuring efficiency and the problems with quality, these indicator systems could provide information to feed into reviews of internal efficiency. A few countries, Canada and the United Kingdom, for example, have developed operational efficiency reviews to find savings.

---

[23]The exception is countries that, because of market pressures, are forced to produce front-loaded consolidation plans and announce or make extensive reductions quickly.

[24]The 10 OECD countries surveyed (Austria, Canada, Finland, France, Germany, Italy, the Netherlands, Norway, Sweden, and the United Kingdom) reported requiring productivity and efficiency improvements for public sector organizations (Lonti and Woods, 2008).

PI cannot help with macro-level decisions, which are based on political and societal choices. These include decisions on the composition of the consolidation package—whether it concentrates more on increasing taxes or reducing expenditures; whether expenditure cuts will be across the board or reductions will focus on selected sectors or ministries; and which areas, if any, will be protected from cuts. In theory, however, PB can help by providing a tool or process that facilitates implementation of these choices at the micro level. Decisions will need to be made within sectors, among ministers, and between and within programs on operational and program expenditures. In practice, consolidation exercises tend to be centralized processes led by central agencies, mainly the ministry of finance. The challenge for these entities is to obtain detailed information on spending ministries' performance and costs. PI, if it is available and of good quality, can help to fill the gap and assist with the following:

- Making strategic assessments of spending ministries' proposed budget cuts or reallocations.
- Developing options for reductions and alternative funding scenarios through the use of expenditure reviews. Among other things, reviews highlight mission creep and overlapping programs. Operational reviews also bring to light potential agency efficiency savings.
- Facilitating strategic reallocations from low- to high-priority and to high-performing programs and areas.

If spending ministries or agencies are required to develop or implement spending cuts or spending is capped, in theory, PI could fill a similar role by assisting with the following:

- Reviewing the mission and objectives of the ministry and identifying the programs and functions that are still relevant or necessary to realize the key objectives. If required, PI can facilitate more strategic decisions about staff reductions.
- Providing information on the performance of different programs seeking to fulfill similar objectives and tasks, and in general, on all programs' performance to facilitate reductions or reallocations.
- Producing options for saving by providing efficiency information on the performance and costs of similar services provided by all agencies within the ministry.
- Identifying changes in operations, structures, or procedures that would allow the mission of the organization or program to be carried out more effectively.

In Practice, What Has Happened to Date?

Most countries are still either developing or implementing their fiscal consolidation plans and procedures. Since the process is still in its early days, only limited research and information are available. The emerging, albeit skeletal, picture is mixed. Figure 7.4 shows the results of a 2011 OECD survey that asked

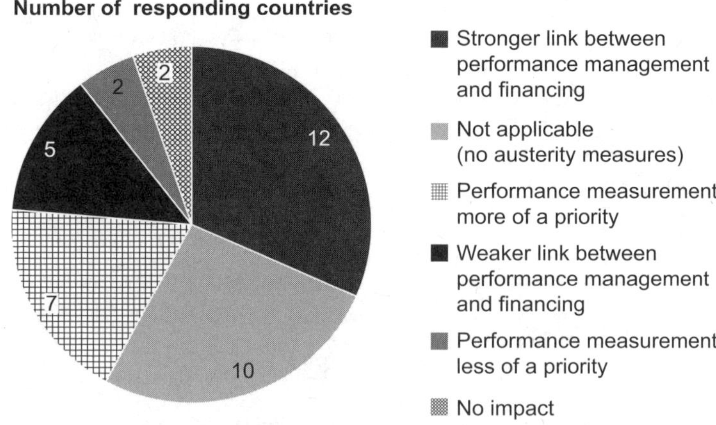

Figure 7.4 How Have Recent Austerity Measures Affected Performance Budgeting Practices?

respondents how recent austerity measures had affected performance budgeting practices in their countries. On the one hand, for more than one-third of respondents, there was a stronger link between performance management and financing, and for more than one-fifth, performance management had become more of a priority. On the other hand, for another one-third of respondents, there were no austerity measures; for five countries, there was a weaker link between performance management and financing; and for two, performance measurement had become less of a priority.

The use of expenditure reviews for consolidation is varied, and to date countries appear not to be exploiting the full potential of this mechanism; only 15 OECD countries surveyed conduct spending reviews. The saving measures adopted from the latest round of spending review included operational efficiency measures and adjustments to programs (OECD, 2012). The next subsection discusses some examples of countries that are using expenditure reviews.

Rules and Reviews

At a national level, some countries are adapting or revising their current PB systems or are developing new procedures to assist in consolidation efforts. Expenditure reviews that take a rules-and-reviews approach are among the tools countries have adopted. Rules establish, at the outset of the exercise, the amount or percentage of expenditure reduction. Rules are there to press for savings and to ensure the initiatives are taken seriously. The review aspect is vital to promoting strategic choices reflecting priorities and performance. Data from performance indicator systems and evaluations are necessary components of expenditure reviews.

Box 7.3 discusses three countries that have adopted the combined rules-and-reviews approach but in different ways—the Republic of Korea, Canada, and the

BOX 7.3 Rules-and-Reviews Approach: Country Examples

Republic of Korea. In 2005, building on its existing performance budgeting system, the Korean government introduced self-assessment of budgetary programs by line ministries. It was modeled after the U.S. Program Assessment Rating Tool. This tool uses a rules-and-reviews approach. The Ministry of Strategy and Finance (MOSF) reviewed the spending ministries' and agencies' assessments of programs. Approximately one-third of major budgetary programs were reviewed each year. All assessed programs were ranked. Those ranked as ineffective were subject to a 10 percent budget cut. In 2005, the first year of the reform, 15 percent of programs were ranked as ineffective; by the third year this number had fallen to 5 percent. Many factors could explain this change, not excluding agencies' learning how to manipulate data to game the system and a reduction in the engagement of the MOSF. In reaction to demands for fiscal consolidation, the MOSF raised the threshold for program ratings, and a higher proportion of programs were ranked ineffective. By 2010, 24 percent of programs were ranked as ineffective and the link between budget allocations and evaluations, which had weakened by year three, began to restrengthen. In this case, the government adjusted an existing performance budgeting tool to help achieve fiscal consolidation.

Canada. The strategic review process, which started in 2007, assessed all direct program spending over a four-year period with the aim of promoting value for money from existing spending. These reviews evaluated whether programs were aligned with government priorities as well as program efficiency and effectiveness. Ministries were required to identify reallocation and reinvestment opportunities. This consisted of identifying the lowest-priority and the lowest-performing 5 percent of programs for reallocations and the higher-priority, higher-performing programs for reinvestment. The proposed 5 percent reductions were presented to a treasury board committee, which accepted or rejected the proposals. After the first year, the savings, if accepted, were returned to the center. This exercise applied both a rule and a review. Moving ahead, the government is conducting reviews with a more operational focus and concentrating on improving efficiency and effectiveness of government operations. The 2011 budget introduced a one-time strategic and operational review covering CAN$75 billion in direct spending that emphasized operational costs but also used PI. Administrative services reviews were also conducted to examine government-wide solutions to improving service delivery, including reengineering the way government does business and looking at back-office operations.

The Netherlands. In 2009/10, the Dutch government launched Fundamental Policy Reviews, based on a similar exercise known as interdepartmental reviews in the 1980s and 1990s. These reviews established independent, nonpolitical working groups to review expenditure in 20 policy areas. This was an official exercise order by the cabinet, which itself chose the policy areas. These included what in many countries would traditionally be regarded as untouchable areas (child benefits and income support, public safety and terrorism, development aid, defense, transportation and water management, higher education, and energy and climate change). The working groups included civil servants and independent experts. The chairperson of each group was a senior official with no responsibility for the area under review. No proposed ideas could be blocked or vetoed. For each policy area, options had to be produced for a compulsory 20 percent reduction in expenditure, which had to be presented to a council of ministers. The final decision was left to the politicians and the reports were sent to parliament. The results of the spending reviews formed part of the coalition agreement for the new government and some options were implemented.

Netherlands. These examples show how countries are building on existing systems and using PI to assist in consolidation.

A number of lessons have emerged from countries' experiences with these reviews. These lessons include the importance of having an established rule or budgetary goal for the review and obtaining high-level political support. Other lessons are the need for transparent procedures and regulations in conducting reviews, establishing clear institutional roles, specifying the responsibilities of key actors, and including an independent element in the review process.

Challenges

A number of challenges arise with using PI to inform budgetary decisions during difficult fiscal times. Many, but not all, are similar to those facing countries in good times. Challenges include issues with the quality of PI and receiving relevant information in a timely manner. There is a clear danger that PI will be ignored by politicians and budget officials as governments continue to operate in crisis mode and adopt a "slash-and-burn" approach to expenditure reduction.

Research by Hou and others (2011) highlights that, with a few exceptions, PI is not being used in U.S. states to the same extent as before the crisis even though many states have well-developed PB systems. The research concludes that PI is used more often in good fiscal times than in bad. One explanation is that states have experienced an unprecedented drop in output and revenues and their budgeting systems are in crisis mode, requiring rapid action. The emphasis has been on protecting priority areas, leaving little time to consider PI. In addition to economic and market factors, two other issues are forcing the states to act rapidly. First, the states received only temporary additional funding from the federal government to help during the crisis. Second, nearly all U.S. operate on a balanced-budget fiscal rule, which forces them to make the cutbacks during the budget year. The procedures are not in place for a medium-term approach to consolidation, nor does there appear to be time for a more considered approach.

The primary difference between using PI in good and in bad fiscal times can be viewed as an incentive paradox. In bad times, the incentives increase for the center to demand and use PI in budgeting, whereas the incentives for spending entities to provide this information decreases. More than ever, the ministry of finance and politicians are searching for information and processes that will assist in the review of old spending and will help find cost-reduction options.

In difficult times, the incentives structure for spending ministries shifts from the carrot to the stick. In good times, ministries and agencies provide PI to support and justify new or existing spending. Once spending ministries know that this information will be used to reduce expenditure, they are motivated to game the system and manipulate data. However, a few examples can be found of countries using financial incentives to engage ministries even when requiring reductions. For example, in Canada, in the first round of strategic reviews, ministries were allowed to bid to have their savings reallocated to higher priorities within the ministry. In some countries, ministries have been allowed to keep a portion of efficiency savings; for example, in Finland spending ministries could keep up to 50 percent of efficiency gains.

In the current crisis situation, it is not clear whether countries will be able to use financial incentives to motivate agencies to provide information. Other types of incentives may be needed. Nonfinancial and more implicit incentives may play a role. For example, if the need for fiscal consolidation is widely recognized and accepted among political leaders and the general public, and a plan has been developed, all ministries will feel pressure to cooperate. The pressure is especially strong when all programs and expenditures are being reviewed as part of consolidation plans, and pain is shared as even old spending, traditionally protected by interest groups, is in peril of being axed.

If across-the-board or even organization-specific cuts are contemplated, a ministry may have incentives to use PI to develop its own proposals rather than waiting for external bodies to determine its reductions. Ministries may also have an interest in conducting or participating in strategic reviews as a means to rethink how they can continue to provide existing services with reduced funding scenarios. Incentives such as increasing managerial flexibility and allowing ministries freedom to redesign work processes and structures could help promote participation. Alternatively, countries have included an independent element in the reviews either by establishing independent commissions or, as in the Netherlands, by including independent members in the review process. The danger, however, beyond the consolidation period is that performance budgeting and management initiatives may become associated with cutbacks and reductions, rather than being considered tools that provide information to support better decision making and improved performance.

Any conclusion about PB in this period of consolidation would be premature. The approach that countries take will depend on many factors, including the required speed of consolidation; their existing PB and management systems; the volume, quality, and type of PI produced; and the political willingness to use it. It is important for policymakers and reformers to present PI to decision makers in the form and at the time it is needed. Although slash-and-burn approaches may produce results quickly, which for some countries is essential, for others more strategic choices could help mitigate the impact on the state's long-term governance and service delivery capacities.

7.6. CONCLUSION

Across OECD countries, performance tools have become an integral part of how governments do business. Nearly all OECD governments have developed PI (evaluations and performance measures) and have sought with varying degrees of success over the past decade to integrate it into management, accountability, and budgeting processes. Although countries have taken diverse approaches to developing and implementing these reforms, some common trends have emerged. PI is more often used for management and monitoring purposes by both spending ministries and agencies and by politicians in the executive. For countries that use PI in the budgeting process, the most common approach taken is the performance-informed budgeting approach. Although PI is used in some countries in budget negotiation between central budget authority and spending ministries, it appears to be more frequently used within spending ministries in negotiations with their agencies and in state and local governments.

Despite this, it has proven more challenging to ensure the use of PI in budgeting than in management. This is because of difficulties in aligning incentives, issues of political economy, time pressures of budgeting, and informational and institutional constraints. Most countries continue to struggle with changing the culture and behavior of key actors to focus on results. Country experiences have highlighted a number of lessons. These include the importance of leadership at both a political and an institutional level to support the reforms and to place pressure to improve performance; the importance of ownership and engaging those in the front line delivering services; the need to evolve and adopt performance systems as political and economic circumstances change; and finally, the importance of changing and evolving incentive structures to avoid gaming, and performance reforms becoming a compliance exercise.

The need for fiscal consolidation following the Great Recession has altered the incentive structure. The pursuit of fiscal consolidation has generated greater incentives for both ministries of finance and politicians to demand and use information on programs that are working and those that are not. Countries' experiences highlight how performance tools can be used with a rules-and-reviews approach to facilitate more strategic choices and a more fundamental review of government objectives and spending. Performance tools can provide information about options for expenditure reduction and, most important, how to improve performance. Ultimately, however, politicians make the choices. Past crises have presented opportunities for reform and have motivated the introduction of fundamental changes in public financial management and public administration more widely. This crisis again presents an opportunity for countries to improve their systems and to seek to transform the culture as they continue on their performance journey.

REFERENCES

Andrews, Matt, 2010, "Good Government Means Different Things in Different Countries," *Governance: An International Journal of Policy, Public Administration, and Institutions*, Vol. 23, No. 1, pp. 7–35.

Bevan, Gwyn, and Christopher Hood, 2006, "What's Measured Is What Matters: Targets and Gaming in the English Public Health Care System," *Public Administration*, Vol. 84, No. 3, pp. 517–38.

Bourdeaux, Carolyn, 2006, "Do Legislatures Matter in Budgetary Reform?" *Public Budgeting and Finance*, Vol. 26, No. 1, pp. 120–42.

———, and Grace Chikoto, 2008, "Legislative Influences on Performance Management Reform," *Public Administration Review,* Vol. 68, No. 2, pp. 253–65.

Boyle, Richard, 2009, "Performance Reporting: Insights from International Practice," Managing for Performance and Results Series (Washington: IBM Center for the Business of Government).

Boyne, George, and Christopher Hood, 2010, "Incentives: New Research on an Old Problem," *Journal of Public Administration Research and Theory,* Vol. 20, Suppl. 2, pp. i177–i180.

Curristine, Teresa, Zsuzsanna Lonti, and Isabelle Joumard, 2007, "Improving Public Sector Efficiency: Challenges and Opportunities," *OECD Journal on Budgeting,* Vol. 7, No. 1, pp. 1–41.

Dalton, Russell J., 2004, *Democratic Challenges, Democratic Choices: The Erosion of Political Support in Advanced Industrial Democracies* (Oxford: Oxford University Press).

Folz, David A., Reem Abdelrazek, and Yeonsoo Chung, 2009, "The Adoption, Use and Impacts of Performance Measures in Medium-Size Cities: Progress toward Performance Management," *Public Performance & Management Review,* Vol. 33, No. 1 (September), pp. 63–87.

Hood, Christopher, and Michael Jackson, 1991, *Administrative Argument* (Aldershot, U.K.: Dartmouth).

Hou, Yilin, Robin S. Lunsford, Katy C. Sides, and Kelsey A. Jones, 2011, "State Performance-Based Budgeting in Boom and Bust Years: An Analytical Framework and Survey of the States," *Public Administration Review,* Vol. 71, No. 3, pp. 370–88.

International Monetary Fund (IMF), 2011a, *Fiscal Monitor: Addressing Fiscal Challenges to Reduce Economic Risks,* September (Washington).

———, 2011b, *Fiscal Monitor: Shifting Gears—Tackling Challenges on the Road to Fiscal Adjustment,* April (Washington).

———, 2012, *Fiscal Monitor: Balancing Fiscal Policy Risks,* April (Washington).

Kamensky, John M., and Albert Morales, 2005, *Management for Results 2005* (Lanham, Maryland: Rowman and Littlefield).

Kelman, Steve, and John N. Friedman, 2009, "Performance Improvement and Performance Dysfunction: An Empirical Examination of Distortionary Impacts of the Emergency Room Wait-Time Target in the English National Health Service," *Journal of Public Administration Research and Theory,* Vol. 19, No. 4, pp. 917–46.

Lonti, Zsuzsanna, and Matt Woods, 2008, "Towards Government at a Glance: Identification of Core Data and Issues Related to Public Sector Efficiency," Working Paper on Public Governance No. 7 (Paris: Organisation for Economic Co-operation and Development).

Lu, Yi, Katherine Willoughby, and Sarah Arnett, 2009, "Legislating Results: Examining the Legal Foundations of PBB Systems in the States," *Public Performance and Management Review,* Vol. 33, No. 2, pp. 266–87.

Moynihan, Donald P., 2006, "Managing for Results in State Government: Evaluating a Decade of Reform," *Public Administration Review,* Vol. 66, No. 1, pp. 78–90.

Organisation for Economic Co-operation and Development (OECD), 1996, *Performance Management in Government: Contemporary Illustrations* (Paris).

———, 2005, *Modernising Government: The Way Forward,* Directorate for Public Governance and Territorial Development (Paris).

———, 2007a, International Budget Practices and Procedures Database, 2007/8 (Paris).

———, 2007b, *Performance Budgeting in OECD Countries* (Paris).

———, 2012, Budgeting Levers, Strategic Agility and the Use of Performance Budgeting in 2011/12: 8th Annual Meeting on Performace and Results, GOV/PGC/SBO (2012)10 (unclassified; Paris).

Osborne, David, and Ted Gaebler, 1992, *Reinventing Government* (New York: Basic Books).

Pollitt, Christopher, 2006a, "Performance Information for Democracy: The Missing Link," *Evaluation,* Vol. 12, No. 1, pp. 38–55.

———, 2006b, "Performance Management in Practice: A Comparative Study of Executive Agencies," *Journal of Public Administration Research and Theory,* Vol. 16, pp. 25–44.

———, and Geert Bouckaert, 2004, *Public Management Reform: A Comparative Analysis—New Public Management, Governance, and the New-Weberian State* (Oxford: Oxford University Press).

Radin, Beryl A., 2006, *Challenging the Performance Movement: Accountability, Complexity and Democratic Values* (Washington: Georgetown University Press).

———, 2009, "What Can We Expect from Performance Measurement Activities?" *Journal of Policy Analysis and Management,* Vol. 28, No. 3, pp. 505–12.

Redburn, F. Stevens, Robert J. Shea, and Terry F. Buss, 2007, *Performance Management and Budgeting: How Governments Can Learn from Experience* (Armonk, New York: M.E. Sharpe).

Schick, Allen, 2009a, "Performance Budgeting and Accrual Budgeting: Decision Rules or Analytic Tools," in *Evolutions in Budgetary Practice*, ed. by Allen Schick and the OECD Senior Budget Officials (Paris: Organisation for Economic Co-operation and Development).

———, 2009b, "Crisis Budgeting," *OECD Journal on Budgeting,* Vol. 9, No. 3.

Smith, Peter, 2007, "Formula Funding and Performance Budgeting," in *Performance Budgeting: Linking Funding and Results*, ed. by Marc Robinson (Basingstoke, UK, and New York: Palgrave Macmillan).

Willoughby, Katherine G., 2004, "Performance Measurement and Budget Balancing: State Government Perspective," *Public Budgeting and Finance,* Vol. 24, No. 2, pp. 21–39.

World Bank, 2010, *Results, Performance Budgeting and Trust in Government* (Washington).

APPENDIX 7.1. REVENUE AND EXPENDITURE MEASURES IN SELECTED COUNTRIES SINCE 2009

	Expenditure Measures							Revenue Measures							
	Public wage freeze or reduction	Control of the size of civil service	Savings from pension-related spending	Savings from health care–related spending	Reduction in social benefits[1]	Reduction in public investment	Other expenditure measures	Increase in personal income tax	Increase in corporate income tax	Increase in capital gains tax	Increase in social security contribution rates	Increase in value-added or sales tax	Increase in excises	Increase in property tax	Improvement in tax compliance
Advanced economies															
Australia		✓	✓	✓		✓	✓[2]	✓[3]	✓[4]				✓		✓
Canada	✓	✓	✓			✓	✓[2]	✓			✓		✓		
France		✓	✓	✓			✓	✓	✓		✓	✓	✓		
Germany					✓				✓						
Greece	✓	✓	✓	✓	✓	✓	✓[2]	✓			✓	✓	✓	✓	✓
Ireland	✓	✓	✓	✓	✓	✓		✓		✓		✓	✓	✓	✓
Italy	✓	✓	✓	✓	✓	✓	✓[2]	✓	✓	✓	✓	✓	✓	✓	✓
Japan	✓	✓				✓	✓	✓			✓		✓		✓
Korea															✓
Portugal	✓	✓	✓	✓	✓	✓	✓	✓	✓	✓		✓	✓	✓	✓
Spain	✓	✓	✓	✓	✓	✓	✓	✓	✓	✓	✓	✓	✓	✓	✓
United Kingdom	✓	✓	✓	✓	✓	✓	✓[2]	✓		✓	✓	✓	✓		✓
United States[5]	✓			✓			✓[6]			✓	✓		✓		
Emerging market economies															
Argentina							✓[7]					✓		✓	
Brazil			✓									✓			
China													✓	✓	✓
Hungary	✓	✓	✓	✓	✓		✓				✓	✓	✓		✓
India							✓[8]						✓		
Indonesia															✓
Latvia	✓	✓		✓	✓	✓	✓[7]	✓		✓	✓	✓	✓	✓	✓
Lithuania	✓	✓	✓	✓	✓	✓	✓[7,9]					✓	✓	✓	✓
Mexico	✓	✓				✓	✓[7]	✓	✓			✓	✓		✓

Poland	✓	✓	✓		✓			✓		✓	✓	✓	✓		
Romania	✓	✓	✓	✓	✓	✓	✓				✓	✓	✓		✓
Russian Federation	✓	✓				✓	✓				✓		✓		✓
Saudi Arabia															
South Africa															✓
Turkey	✓			✓									✓		

Sources: European Commission Working Papers; IMF Staff Reports; and IMF staff estimates.

[1] Excluding pension and health care benefits.

[2] Savings from spending efficiencies.

[3] Includes flood levy, reduction in the private health insurance rebate, and changes to fringe benefits tax on cars.

[4] Includes minerals resource rent tax and carbon tax.

[5] All adjustments refer to the federal government only. Social Security contributions refer to "payroll tax."

[6] Discretionary spending caps and automatic cuts.

[7] Subsidies.

[8] Gasoline prices liberalized in 2010/11.

[9] Reduction in local government transfers.

PART III

Strengthening the Foundations: Modernizing the PFM Infrastructure

CHAPTER 8

The Role of Fiscal Reporting in Public Financial Management

GUILHEM BLONDY, JULIE COOPER, TIMOTHY IRWIN, KRIS KAUFFMANN, AND ABDUL KHAN

Without good information, governments cannot make good decisions about public finances. Moreover, unless information is published, they are unlikely to be held accountable for those decisions. Fiscal reporting—whether in audited accounts, fiscal statistics, or other documents—is thus central to public financial management.

Because of the importance of information, even seemingly technical choices about fiscal reporting can have important effects. Suppose, for example, that the cost of employing civil servants is measured in cash disbursed and the government wants both to contain the budget deficit and to win favor with civil servants. Then it may well choose to grant those employees more generous pensions but no increase in their wages. By contrast, if an estimate of the change in the cost of future pensions is included in this year's budget deficit, as it sometimes is, the government is more likely to offer an increase in wages or no increase in remuneration at all. Thus, reporting choices can influence important decisions with major fiscal impacts.

Because reporting is important, it has long been controversial. Although the royalist political theorist Robert Filmer (1588–1653) argued that the public should have "an implicit faith" in the government and respect its "profound secrets," the philosopher and social reformer Jeremy Bentham (1748–1832) believed that "the eye of the public" made "the statesman virtuous." Bentham also hated the idea that the British government might adopt commercial accounting, because he believed that its terminology would make public finances obscure. If it were introduced, he said, "Exit public opinion: enter darkness: such as that which forms the characteristic of absolute government."[1] Similar concerns are sometimes expressed today.

Despite these concerns, fiscal reporting has in many respects grown more like financial reporting in the private sector. Many governments that once reported only cash flows and debt now also report accrual flows and full balance sheets. Others have extended the scope of financial reports to cover not just government

[1]The quotations are from Filmer (1680/1991, pp. 3–4) and Bentham (1843, vol. 10, p. 145, and vol. 5, p. 383).

departments but a broader range of public entities. These changes have prompted, and have in turn been guided by, the development of new standards for preparing accounts and fiscal statistics.

Among the causes of these changes has been a desire to uncover problems hidden by traditional fiscal reporting. Thus, one reason for the adoption of accrual reporting was that cash reporting was not revealing costs in a timely manner. Increases in the coverage of financial reports were motivated by the use of new kinds of public entities to carry out spending "off budget." Fiscal problems were building up but were not being reported.

The 2008–09 global financial and economic crisis and its prolonged aftermath show that more needs to be done to improve fiscal reporting. The crisis has devastated public finances in many countries, but reporting before the crisis gave few warnings of the looming problems. In Greece, government reporting hid public spending and debt, partly because earlier efforts to improve its comprehensiveness and coverage met, as they often do, with redoubled efforts to keep spending and debt out of the accounts. In other countries, troublesome developments in the financial sector, which ultimately became fiscal problems, received no attention in fiscal reporting, even in statements of fiscal risk. In most countries, the cost of future pensions and health care—which, though not a cause of the crisis, has complicated the response to it—was known, but not reflected in any measures of the debt or deficit.

Fiscal reporting has many aspects. This chapter looks at four that have changed significantly in the two decades since the early 1990s and are likely to change further in the next. The first section considers the comprehensiveness of reports, that is, the range of assets and liabilities they recognize. The second considers the coverage of reports, that is, the variety of public institutions they encompass. The third considers the influence on reporting of accounting and statistical standards. The fourth considers possible enhancements of traditional reporting, especially in light of the crisis.

8.1. COMPREHENSIVENESS OF REPORTING

Increases in the comprehensiveness of reporting, as defined here, are closely related to the transition from cash to accrual reporting, because the recording of flows on an accrual basis is naturally associated with the recording of a full range of assets and liabilities, not just cash.

8.1.1. Differences between Cash and Accrual Reporting

Fiscal reporting has long been a core element of fiscal stewardship. Governments of all designs have enacted constitutions, laws, or decrees that govern the use of money. In parliamentary democracies, governance has generally been exercised through a rule that funds held by the government cannot be spent without an appropriation approved by the parliament. Enforcing these rules requires both control mechanisms that govern the release of cash against appropriations and detailed reporting of revenue and expenditure so that compliance with the rules can be checked and variances scrutinized. Cash accounting, which records physical movements of cash in and out of the government treasury, has historically been associated with this focus on compliance. Figure 8.1, panel a, illustrates the logical framework of cash accounting, in which net inflows during the reporting period equal the increase in the bank balance during the period.

However, cash reporting has weaknesses. Some economic events important to governments do not involve an immediate exchange of cash. For example, purchasing goods and services on payments terms involves having the use of goods before they are paid for. Similarly, the deterioration of an asset over time indicates that the asset is losing its effectiveness in service delivery, and funds will need to be spent on its refurbishment or replacement, yet there is no reference to this in cash accounts. These weaknesses also allow governments to use accounting devices to minimize their deficits by deferring cash disbursements or bringing forward cash receipts (Box 8.1).

Governments using cash accounting have often addressed some of these problems, for example, by monitoring and controlling commitments as well as cash disbursements. Accrual accounting attempts to solve the problems of cash

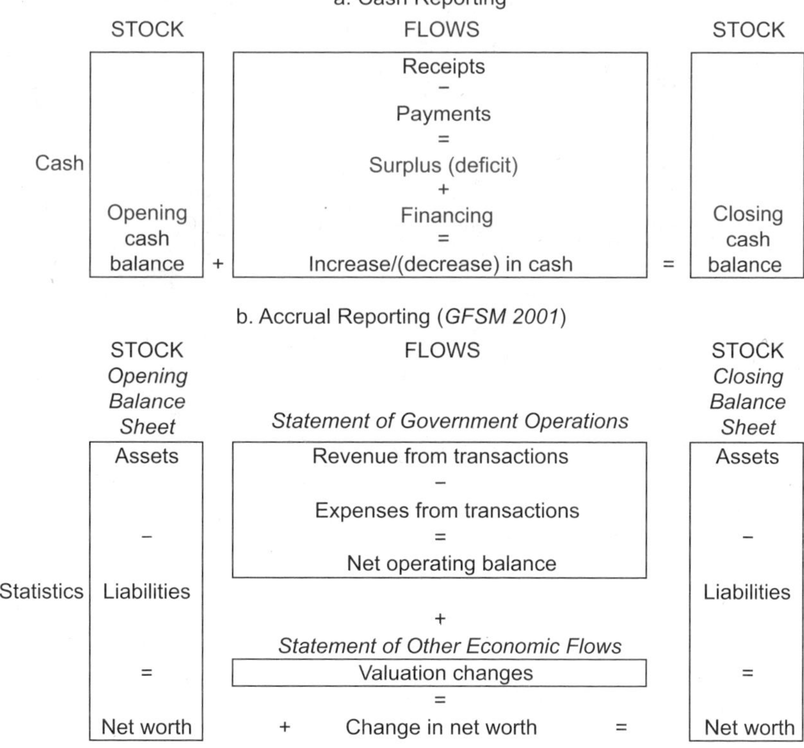

Figure 8.1 The Structure of Cash and Accrual Reporting

Sources: Authors; and IMF (2001).

Note: Each box in panel b encloses a financial statement whose name is given in italics. The *Government Finance Statistics Manual (GFSM) 2001* also generates a measure of the surplus called "net lending/borrowing" equal to the net operating balance plus the net acquisition of nonfinancial assets.

BOX 8.1 Deficit Devices and Fiscal Illusions

The essence of a deficit device is to reduce the deficit without actually improving public finances, or without improving them to the extent suggested by the reduction in the deficit. To do this, the device must initially either increase reported revenue or decrease reported spending and, in later years, either decrease reported revenue or increase reported spending. Four kinds of device can thus be distinguished. Accrual accounts can be distorted by accounting devices, but cash accounts are particularly vulnerable because they record transactions when cash is transferred: the time of the recording can be manipulated simply by changing the time of this cash transfer.

Deferred spending reduces spending now but increases it later. Many governments have met cash-based deficit targets by building up arrears to their suppliers. The U.S. government once met a target by delaying a military payday from the last day of one financial year to the first day of the next. Such delays reduce this year's deficit, but only by increasing future deficits.

Hidden borrowing increases reported revenue now but increases reported spending later. An example is a sale-and-leaseback contract, in which a government sells a building it is using and simultaneously signs a long-term lease with the new owner. Simple accounting treats the sales proceeds as revenue that reduces this year's deficit. But the sale proceeds are like the proceeds of a loan and the lease payments resemble debt service, so it is misleading to treat the sale proceeds as ordinary revenue.

Disinvestment increases reported revenue now and reduces reported revenue in the future. Under simple cash accounting, the proceeds of privatization are revenues that reduce the deficit. But if the sale deprives the government of future dividends, its true fiscal benefit may be much smaller than its reported effect. Under other rules for measuring the deficit, the proceeds of the sale of financial assets, such as shares in a public enterprise, do not reduce the deficit, but the proceeds of the sale of nonfinancial assets do.

Forgone investment reduces reported spending now but reduces reported revenue later. An example is the use of concessions instead of publicly financed investments in user-fee-funded infrastructure. Concessions, like many other policies with helpful accounting effects, can sometimes be good policy, but they can also appeal to governments simply because they reduce deficits in the short term, even if (compared with the case of public finance) they also increase future deficits.

Source: Irwin (2012).

accounting more fundamentally by recording transactions not when cash changes hands but when the critical economic events occur: expenses are recognized at the time goods or services are used or consumed, and revenues are recognized when the relevant underlying economic event (e.g., tax assessment) occurs.[2] Events that change the value of assets and liabilities are recorded, irrespective of the timing of associated cash flows. So, if the government defers a payment it has to make, a liability is revealed on its balance sheet and the accrual measure of the deficit is unchanged.

Whereas net inflows in cash accounts equal the increase in the stock of cash, net inflows in accrual accounts equal the increase in the value of government

[2] Both expenses and revenues are also subject to the recognition criteria that it should be probable that the government will spend or receive money and that the amounts should be capable of being reliably measured.

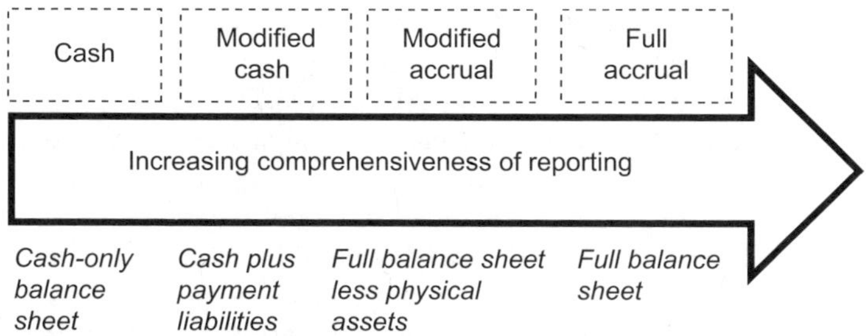

Figure 8.2 A Spectrum of Accounting Methods

Source: Authors.

assets net of liabilities. For this reason, accrual accounting involves production of a full balance sheet as well as an income statement[3]—and typically also a cash flow statement.[4] Figure 8.1, panel b, illustrates the logical framework of accrual accounting, using the IMF's *Government Finance Statistics Manual 2001* (*GFSM 2001*) as an example.

Some accounting practices fall in between cash and full accrual accounting. Figure 8.2 shows a spectrum over which the scope of the assets and liabilities in the balance sheet and the associated flows become more complete (and more complex) as one moves to the right. Although not embedded in standards, names have been developed for various points along this pathway, with "modified cash" accounting often being used to describe cash accounts in which some expenses are recorded when they are incurred (not when they are paid) and "modified accrual" used to describe accounts based on accrual principles with some exceptions, such as not recognizing nonfinancial assets like land and buildings (Schiavo-Campo and Tommasi, 1999, pp. 226–27).

8.1.2. Trends in Adoption of Accrual Reporting

Governments and others have long been aware of the potential value of reporting on an accrual basis. For example, reformers in the first decade of the twentieth century campaigned for accrual reporting by local governments in the United States, and the Hoover Commission reports of 1949 and 1955 recommended that the U.S. federal government adopt accrual accounting (Chan, 2008). But it was only in the 1990s that governments started to adopt accrual accounting.

Whether governments have switched from cash to accrual reporting can be measured in several ways. If the adoption of accrual reporting is interpreted to mean that central government publishes audited government-wide accounts on a

[3]In accounts, the income statement is also called the *profit and loss* or the *statement of financial performance*. In fiscal statistics, the main accrual flow statement is called the *statement of government operations*.

[4]Although it is normal to refer to a transition from cash to accrual reporting, it would often be more accurate to refer to a transition from cash-only to accrual-and-cash reporting.

full accrual basis, including an income statement, a cash flow statement, and a balance sheet in which both financial and nonfinancial assets are recognized, then perhaps only a dozen or so countries qualify (Table 8.1).

But there is often a long delay between the announcement of the adoption of accrual accounting and its full implementation, and many governments have moved away from cash accounting without fully implementing accrual accounting. For example, although the U.K. government did not meet all the criteria for inclusion in Table 8.1 until 2011, it proposed accrual accounting in a consultation paper in 1994, and departments began presenting accrual financial statements in 2001. Many other governments currently meet all but one of the criteria for inclusion in Table 8.1 and may soon meet all. Brazil and Denmark do everything except publish cash flow statements. Iceland does everything except recognize nonfinancial assets. In Japan and the Republic of Korea, the accrual accounts are produced but not audited.

The IMF's *Government Finance Statistics Yearbooks* provide another basis on which to measure the spread of accrual reporting and also allow identification of countries that have moved away from cash reporting without adopting full accrual reporting. Table 8.2 shows changes in the comprehensiveness of the reporting of assets and liabilities from the 2004 to the 2011 yearbook. The row totals show reporting in 2004, the column totals reporting in 2011. In 2004, 9 countries supplied data on financial and nonfinancial assets, a rough indicator of full accrual reporting; by 2011, 14 did. Another 27 countries, including many in the European Union, reported financial but not nonfinancial assets—an approach that roughly corresponds to the "modified accrual" category in Figure 8.2. A further 17 at least

TABLE 8.1

Year in Which Central Governments Began to Publish Audited Government-Wide Accounts on a Full Accrual Basis

Country	Year
New Zealand	1992
Sweden	1995
Australia	1998
Finland	1999
United States	2002
Canada	2003
Philippines	2003
Estonia	2006
Russian Federation	2006
France	2007
Switzerland	2009
United Kingdom	2011
Chile	2012

Source: Authors, using financial statements of the governments of the named countries.

Note: The table shows when each of the named central governments began to publish audited financial statements that include an income statement, a cash flow statement, and a balance sheet in which financial and nonfinancial assets are recognized. Reports produced by audit institutions are counted as audited. Only governments that have continued to publish each of those statements since the initial year are included in the table.

TABLE 8.2

Comprehensiveness of Reporting of Assets and Liabilities to the IMF

Assets and Liabilities on Balance Sheet in 2004 Yearbook	Assets and Liabilities on Balance Sheet in 2011 Yearbook: None	Liabilities only	Liabilities and financial assets	Liabilities and financial and nonfinancial assets	2004 Totals
None	113	6	14	3	**136**
Liabilities only	12	9	3	3	**27**
Liabilities and financial assets	0	2	10	0	**12**
Liabilities and financial and nonfinancial assets	1	0	0	8	**9**
2011 totals	**126**	**17**	**27**	**14**	**184**

Sources: *Government Finance Statistics Yearbooks* for 2004 and 2011 (IMF, 2004, 2012b).

Note: The data are for either of the two years before the year of the yearbook, whichever is more comprehensive. The countries included are those that were members of the IMF in both 2002 and 2009. Reporting for any definition of government is counted. Kazakhstan, which reported nonfinancial assets in the 2004 yearbook without reporting financial assets, is treated as having reported no assets for that year.

reported liabilities. The yearbooks also provide a flow-based indicator of the move away from cash accounting: in 2011, 64 countries reported flow data on some form of noncash basis, up from 38 in 2004 (IMF, 2012a).

A traditional feature of fiscal stewardship is the use of financial reports to hold the government accountable for the execution of the approved budget. This task is simpler when budgeting and reporting are done on the same basis. When accrual reporting is introduced, achieving the otherwise-desirable outcome of budgeting and reporting on the same basis creates a further dimension of complexity that challenges the capacity of not just accountants but also budgeters, policymakers, parliamentarians, and their stakeholders (see Chapter 11). To ensure comparability with budgets and to preserve the benefits of familiarity, some governments have chosen to introduce accrual financial statements, but to keep producing other fiscal reports (statistics or budget execution reports) on other bases of accounting. For example, the U.S. government produces both an accrual-based annual financial report and a mainly cash-based budget execution report called the Combined Statement of Receipts, Outlays, and Balances.

Adoption of accrual reporting in some countries has been associated with changes in fiscal management—such as a move to medium-term budgeting (see Chapter 4) and the adoption of fiscal responsibility legislation or new fiscal rules (see Chapters 2 and 3). One reason is that accrual reporting offers a broader range of fiscal indicators than does cash accounting. In introducing its first public sector balance sheet, for example, the U.K. government noted that the "inclusion of public sector assets means that the balance sheet offers a richer indication of the health of the public finances over time than public debt alone" (U.K. Chancellor of the Exchequer, n.d. p. 1). With respect to flows, Table 8.3 shows four standard indicators available in accrual accounts, only one of which—cash balance—is

TABLE 8.3

Fiscal Indicators Available in Accrual Statistics, Russian Federation, 2010

Indicator	General government (percent of GDP)
Net operating balance	1.6
Change in net worth	0.9
Net lending/borrowing	−1.5
Cash balance	−2.6

Sources: IMF (2012b); and IMF, World Economic Outlook database.

available in cash reporting. The additional indicators offer a broader perspective on the sustainability of fiscal policy than any single indicator on its own.

In some countries, such as Australia and New Zealand, the adoption of accrual accounting was associated with a broader set of economic reforms aimed at improving efficiency by embracing market-based competition in a range of sectors traditionally closely regulated or owned by government (see Chapter 1). These two countries embarked on a drive toward closer engagement of the private sector in what were previously traditional areas of government (by contracting out, privatization, or public-private partnerships) and toward an explicitly performance-based approach to managing government resources that provided greater financial flexibility to public sector managers (see Chapter 7). Accrual accounting was seen as supportive of these endeavors.

Accountants and auditors in the public sector also had a natural interest in the improvements being made in private sector accounting standards. And the adoption of accrual accounting was facilitated by the formulation and implementation of accrual accounting standards for government that were based on private sector standards but modified to reflect the specific circumstances of government.[5] The development of computerized accounting systems that enabled the more complex accrual approach also aided the application of accrual accounting to government. With the development of various accrual-based international standards for both statistics and accounting—including the United Nations' System of National Accounts 1993 (SNA 1993) and the European Commission's European System of Accounts 1995 (ESA 95), and later International Public Sector Accounting Standards (IPSAS) and the IMF's *GFSM 2001*—accrual accounting became an international benchmark to which many countries aspired.

Practical impediments to adoption of full accrual accounting can be encountered, including the absence of trained accounting professionals within government, the absence of technical and political leadership, the lack of change agents (to overcome barriers to reform embedded in organizational culture), the cost of capacity building, and the cost of implementing new systems. A particular challenge in moving to full accrual accounting is the need to develop a full database of physical assets and to value those assets as required by accrual accounting standards. Some of the valuation methods—such as the market-based valuations required by *GFSM 2001*—require, in the absence of an active market for the

[5]As an example, it had previously been argued that the differences in the operations of government and enterprises were a reason for retaining cash-based accounting (IMF, 1986, p. 2).

assets, technical accounting capacity and difficult judgments. In developing countries, achieving robust cash accounting—supplemented by information on financial liabilities—is usually the priority and is typically sequenced before adoption of full accrual accounting.

The cost of overcoming these impediments to implementation of accrual reporting is not insignificant. For example, in 2010 the Dutch Minister of Finance informed parliament that the costs of implementing an accrual reporting regime in central government would be at least €129 million initially and at least €13 million a year thereafter.[6] By comparison, total spending of central government was €269 billion in 2010 (IMF, 2012b, p. 349). No complete cost-benefit analysis of accrual reporting has been done, probably because of the difficulty of placing a financial value on the hoped-for benefits, such as transparency and accountability.

Despite the costs, growing fiscal problems in advanced economies may well encourage more governments to adopt accrual reporting or, when accrual reporting is already used, to recognize a more comprehensive range of assets and liabilities. Many of the interventions made by governments in response to the global financial crisis, including the purchase of nonperforming assets and issuance of guarantees, are better reflected in accrual than in cash accounts. But even under most accrual reporting standards, guarantees are frequently not recognized on government balance sheets, and under some standards contractual pensions and obligations related to public-private partnerships are not recognized. These omissions create the same kinds of problems that led many governments to move from cash to accrual accounting in the first place and may create further pressure, both within governments and from external stakeholders, to enhance the comprehensiveness of fiscal reporting.

8.2. COVERAGE OF REPORTING

Traditionally, central governments' financial reports were closely tied to the budget, and thus showed the spending and revenue of government departments—an approach that was simple and allowed governments, the legislature, and the public to see how most taxes were spent and to check whether the budget was executed as planned. Transfers made in the budget to the central bank, state-owned enterprises (SOEs), and other extrabudgetary entities were reported, but not the total spending or total revenue of these entities. If the government reported debt, it probably recorded only its direct debt, and not the debt of other public entities.

Despite their appeal, budget reports have widely recognized limitations. Extrabudgetary funds can perform ordinary public functions, so budget reports can underestimate the impact of government on the economy. Similarly, the debts of SOEs may be implicitly or explicitly government guaranteed, so a measure of debt that includes only direct debt may underestimate the government's debt-related

[6]Letter by Mr. drs. J.C. de Jager, Minister of Finance of the Netherlands, to the Chairman of the House of Representatives of the Netherlands, dated June 10, 2010. Original in Dutch.

problems. And, if spending is being devolved from the central government to subnational governments (see Chapter 12), budget reports can give a misleading picture of changes in total public spending.

Over time, these limitations have grown. The importance of public bodies other than government departments expanded after World War II, as public welfare systems developed, private businesses were nationalized, and independent regulatory agencies were created. Later, many governments sought to move the market-based activities of their ministries and departments into public corporations, only some of which were eventually privatized. Governments under pressure to reduce their reported deficit or debts also found it convenient to transfer responsibilities for spending and borrowing to these entities because they were outside the scope of the budget report. In the developing world especially, governments set up government-controlled and government-guaranteed development banks that could be used to channel resources to favored projects. Almost everywhere, governments encouraged their SOEs to pursue social as well as commercial goals. The problem was that the costs to the central government's budget were often not avoided, just deferred: at some point the development banks and SOEs needed government bailouts. As the limitations of reports with narrow coverage became more obvious, the coverage of reports was often extended beyond the budget—though in divergent directions in accounts and statistics.

Government finance statistics are part of a broader system of national accounts in which the national economy is divided into five sectors: households, nonprofits, financial corporations, nonfinancial corporations, and governments (ISGWNA, 1993). Statisticians have therefore produced reports for government as a sector (*general government*), as well as for subsectors of general government such as *local government* and *central government* (which is broader than *budgetary central government*). State-owned banks and other enterprises are typically classified as financial or nonfinancial corporations and therefore excluded from statistics on government finances, though they can be included in reports on the *public sector*, a category that combines general government with government-controlled financial and nonfinancial corporations.

The extension in the coverage of statistics has been clearest in the European Union, where fiscal statistics are used as the basis of fiscal rules in a set of countries that differ greatly in the allocation of public responsibilities among the tiers of government—central, provincial, and local. Because of these differences, European rule makers and statisticians have emphasized the importance of data on general government, not just central government. As early as 1990, all members of the European Union, except Italy and Portugal, reported fiscal data to the IMF for general government (IMF, 1990, pp. 44, 96). Now all do. In the face of governments' efforts to keep spending out of the accounts by having it undertaken by SOEs, European statisticians have also tried hard to include in general government all public entities that carry out noncommercial government functions, irrespective of their legal form.

Extensions of coverage have not been confined to Europe. Table 8.4, which has the same structure as Table 8.2, shows changes in the coverage of fiscal statistics reported to the IMF and published in its yearbooks of fiscal data. It reveals that

TABLE 8.4

Broadest Coverage of Fiscal Statistics Reported to IMF

	Coverage of Fiscal Statistics in 2011 Yearbook				
Coverage of Fiscal Statistics in 2004 Yearbook	**None**	**Budgetary central**	**Central government**	**General government**	**2004 Totals**
None	53	17	5	23	**98**
Budgetary central	3	9	0	4	**16**
Central government	5	4	3	10	**22**
General government	2	3	2	41	**48**
2011 totals	**63**	**33**	**10**	**78**	**184**

Sources: IMF (2004, 2012b).
Note: For concreteness, reporting is proxied by reporting of revenue. See also note to Table 8.2.

from 2004 to 2011, the coverage of fiscal statistics increased in 59 countries, remained constant in 106, and declined in 19. Four countries that previously reported only for budgetary central government and ten that reported only for central government now report for general government.

The coverage of accounts has also been extended, but generally not in the same way. Modern business accounting requires companies to consolidate in their accounts all the entities that they control (typically own), even if those entities are legally separate. The underlying principle is that these are the entities for whose financial performance they can reasonably be held accountable. Several governments have fully or partially followed this principle. In Australia, New Zealand, and the United Kingdom, for example, the central governments' accounts consolidate SOEs. But in countries in which central government does not control local governments, accounts have not been extended to combine the operations of different levels of government.

Accounts and statistics thus divide up the public sector in different ways. Figure 8.3 illustrates this by showing a hypothetical public sector made up of seven institutions: a central government that controls an SOE and a central bank, and two local governments, independent of central government, each of which controls a municipal enterprise. The dotted lines show common statistical groupings (others are possible), and the solid lines show the coverage of consolidated accounts that follow the rule that all controlled entities must be consolidated.

Considerable diversity remains in the coverage of both statistics and accounts, however. Many countries do not yet report statistics for general government (Table 8.4), while some in Latin America report them for the nonfinancial public sector. Australia reports them for the entire public sector. The coverage of the accounts of central governments is also diverse (Table 8.5); the idea that control should determine which entities are consolidated in government accounts is not universally accepted or, if accepted, is interpreted in different ways. The United States, for example, uses the control criterion but does not consolidate the central bank on the basis of its independence in conducting monetary policy. In contrast, Australia does consolidate the central bank, considering that independence in monetary policy does not imply a loss of control for the purposes of applying the control criterion.

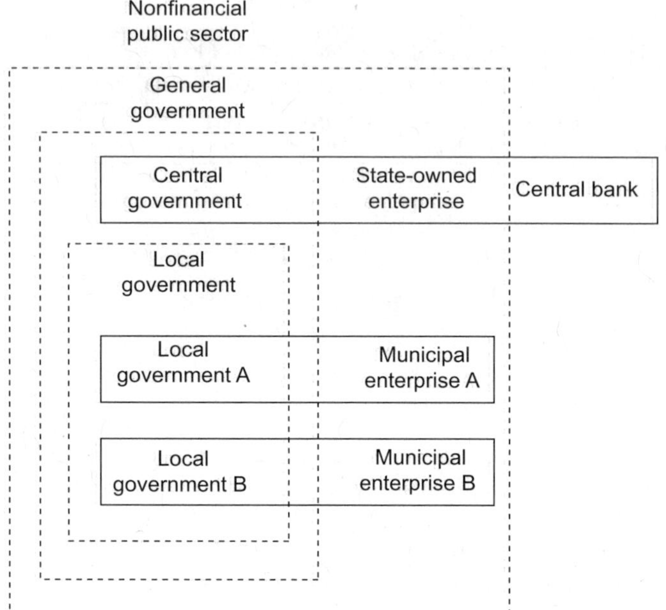

Figure 8.3 How Accounts and Statistics Divide Up the Public Sector

Source: Authors.

As the diversity of practices suggests, the choice of coverage is controversial. On the one hand, increasing coverage helps reveal governments' attempts to reduce their reported deficits and debts by pushing spending and debts outside the boundary of existing reports. And, with the crisis, governments have acquired large new banks and other financial institutions, while central banks have taken on new assets and liabilities and engaged in activities that arguably have fiscal implications. On the other hand, there is a good reason for continuing to consider reports that cover only the government's noncommercial, tax-funded activities. Public enterprises, for example, are quite different from government departments, and combining their operations with those of government departments leads to a loss of information on the size and performance of the distinctive part of government.

A simple way out of the reporting dilemma is to present information for the entire public sector and its main subsectors. Table 8.6 provides an illustration drawn from Australia's fiscal statistics. It shows total assets, total liabilities, and net worth of general government, the nonfinancial public sector, and the entire public sector. Such a balance sheet—especially if it is comprehensive in its inclusion of assets and liabilities—is sometimes called a "sovereign balance sheet."[7] In accounts, the reporting of segments of government allows a similar breakdown of controlled entities (see IPSAS 18, Segment Reporting).

[7]See IMF (2009), including, in particular, Appendix II.

TABLE 8.5

Coverage of Recent Accounts of Selected Central Governments

Country	Principal	Legislature	State-owned enterprises	Central bank	Subnational government	Selected other exclusions
Australia	Central government and entities it controls	Yes	Yes	Yes	No	
Canada	Central government and financially dependent controlled entities	Yes	Some[a]	No	No	
Finland	Central government	Yes	No	No	No	
France	The state	Yes	No	No	No	
New Zealand	Central government and entities it controls	Yes	Yes	Yes	No	
Sweden	Central government	Yes	No	No	No	
Switzerland	Central government	Yes	No	No	No	
United Kingdom	Public sector bodies that exercise public functions or are substantially funded from public money	No	Yes	No[b]	Yes	Rescued financial institutions
United States	Central government	Yes[c]	Some[d]	No	No	Rescued financial institutions

Sources: Financial statements of governments.

Note: The selected governments are the advanced economies in Table 8.1.

[a] Largely self-financing state-owned enterprises such as Canada Post are not consolidated.

[b] The U.K. government has said it will consolidate the central bank in future accounts.

[c] The accounts provide only cash-based data on the finances of congress.

[d] For instance, the postal service is consolidated but Amtrak and many financial enterprises are not.

TABLE 8.6

Summary Balance Sheet of Public Sector, Illustration from Australia's Fiscal Statistics, 2010–11 (*percent of GDP*)

	General government	Nonfinancial public sector	Public sector
Assets	111	119	129
Liabilities	48	56	67
Net worth	63	63	63

Sources: Australian Bureau of Statistics; and IMF, *World Economic Outlook*, April 2012.

Note: Liabilities include shares and other contributed capital.

8.3. STANDARDIZATION OF REPORTING

The past two or three decades have also seen the rise of standards for government accounts and statistics, notably the IMF's manuals on government finance statistics and IPSAS.

The IMF's first manual (IMF, 1986) prescribed a cash-based standard for reporting spending and revenue, in part because that was how governments prepared their accounts, but also because that was the approach taken by the United Nations' cash-based system of national accounts. The 1986 manual was thoroughly updated by *GFSM 2001*, which prescribed an accrual framework that incorporated stocks as well as flows (Figure 8.1, panel b). The change reflected concerns about the limitations of cash accounting mentioned in the first section of this chapter, as well as the adoption in 1993 of the accrual concept in the United Nations' system of national accounts (ISWGNA, 1993). Although the adoption of accrual accounting by some governments had made the practical problems created by the new framework somewhat less daunting, it was recognized that full adoption of the new system would take many years. Indeed, 10 years after its publication, only El Salvador, Hong Kong Special Administrative Region, the Russian Federation, and the Slovak Republic submitted for the 2011 yearbook of statistics the four main statements envisaged by *GFSM 2001* for general government (see IMF, 2012b).

The IPSAS Board is a private entity with no official standing, but over time its standards have become more influential. The first bodies to adopt IPSAS were international bodies such as the North Atlantic Treaty Organization and the Organisation for Economic Co-operation and Development (OECD). More recently, governments have either begun to adopt IPSAS or harmonize their standards with them. The French government's reporting refers to IPSAS alongside other standards, while the Swiss government's refers primarily to IPSAS (with some modifications). Many other governments have announced plans to adopt IPSAS (IFAC, 2008).

The rise of IPSAS and *GFSM 2001* has raised the issue of whether these two sets of standards should be further harmonized. Accounts and statistics serve overlapping but not identical purposes, so there is reason to assume that they should be similar, but not identical. Both allow assessment of a government's finances, but accounts are mainly concerned with the accountability of a given entity, whereas statistics are designed to aggregate the finances of groups of entities, such as all governments in a given region (national or supranational). Harmonization of accounts and statistics is also constrained by the need to avoid inconsistencies between statistics for different sectors (one sector's liability is another's asset) and the desire not to introduce unnecessary differences between accounts for governments and accounts for other entities. In addition, analysis can be aided by the existence of reports prepared from different perspectives: if nothing else, having two maps helps in resisting the temptation to mistake either for the terrain.

But some of the differences between statistical and accounting standards are reflections of inessential differences in their origins, not of fundamental differences in their purposes. Moreover, accounts and statistics are often prepared using the same source data generated by financial management information systems, so the avoidance of unnecessary differences can simplify reporting. A task force set up in the mid-2000s discussed harmonization and, among other things, produced work that led to a standard for the disclosure in a government's accounts of information about the part of the consolidated government that lies within general government (see IPSAS 22, Disclosure of Financial Information about the General Government Sector) (Dupuis, Laliberté, and Sutcliffe, 2006).

Several arguably inessential differences remain. Figures 8.1, panel b, and 8.4 show that the structures of the main statements of *GFSM 2001* and IPSAS are similar, but each system uses its own terminology and classifies the flows between opening and closing stocks in its own way. Unlike IPSAS, *GFSM 2001* distinguishes the relatively predictable changes in net worth caused by transactions from those caused by volatile and typically unpredictable changes in market values. Unlike *GFSM 2001*, IPSAS includes a single statement whose bottom line is the total change in net worth.

Also, although many assets and liabilities appear on the balance sheets of both IPSAS and *GFSM 2001*, there are some differences. Obligations to make payments in only certain circumstances are more likely to be recognized by IPSAS than by *GFSM 2001*. One reason is that in statistics the presence of a contingent liability on the government sector's balance sheet implies the presence of a contingent asset on another sector's. Last, assets and liabilities are not always valued

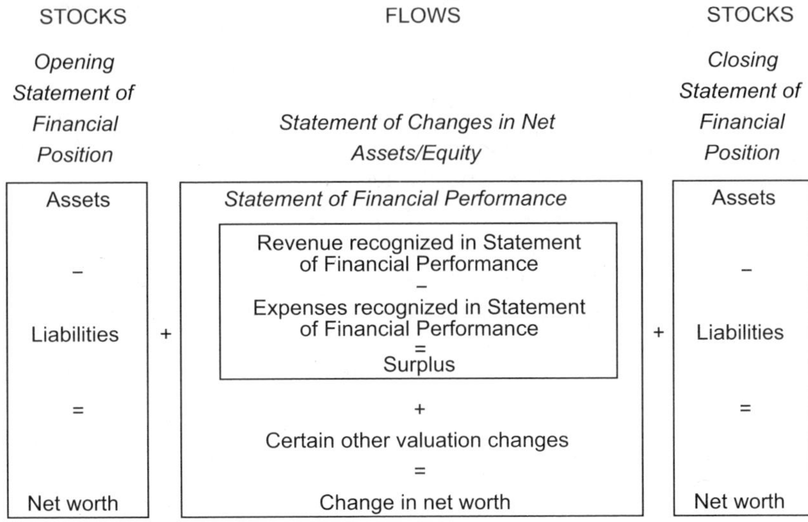

Figure 8.4 The Structure of IPSAS Reports

Source: Authors, using information from IPSAS 1.

Note: IPSAS = International Public Sector Accounting Standards.

TABLE 8.7

Use of GFS Surplus Measures in Accounts: Extracts from the Commonwealth of Australia's Government Financial Statements, 2009–10

	Percent of GDP
Net operating balance	−3.8
+ Other economic flows normally recognized in statement of financial performance	−0.6
= Operating result	−4.4
+ Certain other economic flows normally recognized in statement of change in net assets/equity	−0.1
= Change in net worth	−4.5
Other measures available in accounts	
Net lending/borrowing	−4.4
GFS cash surplus	−1.7

Sources: Australian government financial statements for 2009–10; and IMF, *World Economic Outlook*, for Australian GDP.

in the same way: *GFSM 2001* favors market (fair) values and IPSAS sometimes allows other values, such as depreciated historical cost.

An interesting attempt to integrate statistics and accounting can be found in Australia, where the central government produces a single accrual-based flow statement in its IPSAS-like accounts that incorporates concepts from *GFSM 2001* (Table 8.7).

8.4. ENHANCING FISCAL REPORTING

Accounts and statistics prepared according to IPSAS, *GFSM 2001*, or similar standards still exclude much important information on public finances. This section briefly reviews some of the new fiscal reports provided by governments and considers how such reporting might evolve in the future.

8.4.1. Future Spending and Taxes

The primary focus of fiscal reporting—from the viewpoint of setting standards—has been retrospective, with a particular focus on preparation of financial statements and associated statistics for the previous financial year. These backward-looking reports support the goals of transparency and are fundamental to accountability as it relates to stewardship in the execution of the budget. For example, fiscal reporting allows public accounts committees to conduct hearings examining issues arising in audited financial statements.

Since the early 1990s, a trend has emerged of governments producing more forward-looking data to enhance financial reports. Budgeting in many countries now involves preparation of medium-term budget frameworks, for which specific forward-looking financial reports are produced—typically for a period of three or four years (see Chapter 4). In response to new challenges in fiscal sustainability, many countries have chosen to project their forward-looking reports well beyond the three to four years covered by a typical medium-term budget framework. Such reports are intended to support analysis of the longer-term impact of existing policies given factors such as aging populations and increasing health care costs (see also Chapter 1). Specific examples of this type of analysis include the following:

- *Long-term fiscal projections*, which seek to project the long-term impacts of existing policy. Table 8.8 lists some of the countries undertaking such reporting.
- *Debt sustainability reports*, in which debt and debt service, normally as a percentage of GDP, are projected over the long term. Sensitivity analysis is often performed to see how the projected level of debt changes with changes in the assumptions for the cost of borrowing, the primary fiscal balance, and economic growth.
- *Generational accounts*, which show the present value of the taxes that people in each of several age cohorts can expect to pay over their remaining lifetimes, less the transfer payments they can expect to receive—all under current policy (Kotlikoff and Raffelhuschen, 1999).

TABLE 8.8

Stand-Alone Reports on Long-Term Sustainability of Public Finances in the Group of Seven Countries

Country	Recent report	Coverage	Periodicity	Mandatory
Canada	Parliamentary Budgetary Office, Fiscal sustainability report, 2011	General government	One-off	No
France	Ministry of Economy, Finance and Industry, Stability program, 2011	General government	Annual	Yes
Germany	Ministry of Finance, Report on the sustainability of public finances, 2008 Ministry of Finance, Stability program, 2011	General government	At least every four years Annual	Yes
Italy	Ministry of Economy and Finance, Mid-long term trends for the pension health and long-term care system, 2011 Ministry of Economy and Finance, Stability program, 2011	General government	Annual	Yes
Japan	—	—	—	No
United Kingdom	Office for Budget Responsibility, Fiscal sustainability report, 2011 Office for Budget Responsibility, Convergence program, 2011	General government	Annual	Yes
United States	Office of Management and Budget, Analytical perspectives, 2011 Congressional Budget Office, Long-term budget outlook, 2011 General Audit Office, Federal fiscal outlook, 2011 General Audit Office, States' and local governments' fiscal outlook, 2011	Central government State and local governments	Annual	No

Sources: Reports of named governments.

- *Sector-specific analysis*, in which the long-term impacts of specific policies are analyzed, such as the U.S. Congressional Budget Office's long-term projections for social security.

The IPSAS Board has issued an exposure draft of a recommended practice guideline on the reporting of the long-term sustainability of public finances (IPSASB, 2011). The guideline, which would not be mandatory, envisages a variety of options, among them the presentation of measures based on the present values of projected future flows. In this regard, the U.S. government's reporting is particularly interesting. As well as presenting projected future flows, it also shows estimates of their present values (Table 8.9). The present values inherit the uncertainty of the projections and, in the discount rate, introduce a new source of uncertainty, so should not be considered at all precise. The value of this approach lies in summarizing the implications of cash flow projections in a way that helps draw attention to the projections and the sustainability of current policies. In particular, the bottom line of the table (the net present value of primary receipts less spending) serves as an estimate of the sustainability of current fiscal policy.

It would also be possible to develop the kind of disclosure made by the U.S. government by showing the present values of future spending and revenue alongside a traditional balance sheet, to produce what might be called an enhanced balance sheet, as illustrated in Table 8.10. The kinds of future spending and revenue that could be shown are, more specifically, those whose present values are not reflected in the values of assets and liabilities that are already recognized on the traditional balance sheet; otherwise there would be double-counting. Like a table of present values of primary spending and revenue (such as Table 8.9), the enhanced balance sheet would summarize projections of future cash flows; unlike such a table, it would also put the values in a familiar context.

TABLE 8.9

U.S. Federal Government's Summary of Long-Term Fiscal Projections, 2010
(*present values of 75-year long-range projections*)

	US$ trillions	Percentage of 75-year GDP
Receipts	*175*	*20.2*
Social security payroll taxes	38	4.4
Medicare payroll taxes	12	1.4
Individual income taxes	91	10.5
Other	34	4.0
Primary spending	*192*	*22.1*
Defense discretionary	31	3.6
Nondefense discretionary	31	3.6
Social security	49	5.7
Medicare A	17	2.0
Medicare B and D	20	2.4
Medicaid	24	2.8
Other mandatory	19	2.2
Receipts less primary spending	−16.3	−1.9

Source: Financial report of the U.S. government, for year ending September 30, 2010.

TABLE 8.10

Possible Form of Enhanced Balance Sheet

	Assets	Liabilities	Net assets
Financial	Cash Bonds Other financial assets ...	Debts Short term Long term ...	
	Total financial assets	Total financial liabilities	Net financial worth
Nonfinancial	Land Buildings ...	Contractual pensions Insurance liabilities ...	
	Total existing assets	Total existing liabilities	Net worth
Future	Present value of future tax revenues (based on existing policy)	Present value of future expenditure (based on existing programs and entitlements policy)	
	Total extended assets	Total extended liabilities	Extended net worth

Source: Authors' illustration.

The present values of future taxes and of spending on public pensions, health care, and other services are not assets and liabilities according to IPSAS and *GFSM 2001* (until, for example, the tax is collectible or the pension is payable). Yet, they represent potential economic benefits and costs that can be valued, at least approximately. The enhanced balance sheet in Table 8.10 would acknowledge the differences between these rights and obligations and those that are currently recognized as assets and liabilities by showing the two sets of values in different categories. It would acknowledge the similarities by presenting a measure of net worth that combines the two sets of values.

Whether this kind of enhanced balance sheet would prove useful would need to be considered carefully. At a practical level, avoiding double-counting might prove difficult. Moreover, the difficulties of accurately projecting future flows and of selecting an appropriate discount rate mean that the uncertainty surrounding the present values of future taxes and spending is much greater than the uncertainty surrounding the valuations of conventional assets and liabilities. At a conceptual level, the present values of future flows are fundamentally different from the assets and liabilities recognized on a standard balance sheet. Therefore, whether it is appropriate and useful to present the different items on the same statement and to call that statement any kind of balance sheet are open questions.

8.4.2. Risks

Enhanced reporting directed at improving the understanding of the future implications of past and existing policy choices and associated risks is particularly important in the current global economic environment. The crisis has increased concerns about fiscal sustainability, not simply owing to awareness of the sizable current fiscal deficits, but also because of the greater understanding of exposure to fiscal risks and future costs, including, for example, the impact of aging populations on pensions. Properly analyzing and transparently addressing these issues are strongly supported by the use of enhanced forward-looking fiscal reporting.

Some governments now include information on risks—factors that could cause fiscal outcomes to differ from forecasts—in their forward-looking financial reports. Risks associated with macroeconomic shocks are disclosed by many countries. All European Union countries, most OECD members, and some emerging market economies (e.g., Brazil, Chile, and Indonesia) disclose risks associated with macroeconomic assumptions such as growth, inflation, interest rates, exchange rates, and international oil prices—through sensitivity analyses, alternative macroeconomic scenarios, or stress tests for fiscal aggregates (see Chapter 5) (IMF, 2009). Information on some contingent liabilities is also frequently disclosed in financial reports, though the extent of disclosure varies. Countries disclosing some such information include most advanced economies, the majority of states acceding to the European Union, a third of the remaining emerging market and transition economies, and a handful of developing countries (OECD, 2007; IMF, 2009).

The response to the recent crisis—caused in no small part by government guarantees of certain liabilities of the financial sector—has highlighted differences in the degree of disclosure of contingent liabilities by government. Some countries, such as Japan, disclose their guarantees and contingent liabilities but do not make any estimation or provision for the amount expected to be paid against these potential obligations. Other countries, such as Switzerland and the United Kingdom, also report contingent liabilities and also recognize a liability when it is probable that a payment will have to be made and the amount can be estimated. Similarly, in the cases in which credit reform accounting applies in the United States, reports recognize the present value of estimated future payments from loan guarantees as a liability.

8.4.3. Other Issues

Many fiscal reports are produced on an annual or quarterly basis. However, the recent crisis demonstrated that significant changes in fiscal and monetary conditions, particularly those driven by financial markets, can happen very quickly. Suggestions have been made that governments should operate a system of continuous disclosure, wherein key changes in fiscal conditions are made public as they become known to government, not in the next scheduled report:

> Stable economic policy is not served by sudden jumps in revenue or expenses throwing out the Budget bottom line between key economic statements. This is made worse when markets and commentators are caught out by the size of the fluctuations. The private sector operates under rules of continuous disclosure. Why shouldn't the public sector? (Australian Government, 2008, p. 10)

In 2010, the New Zealand government imposed a requirement of continuous disclosure on its SOEs, and the Australian government now requires the treasury and finance departments to publish on their websites material changes in revenue and expenditure forecasts as they occur.

Reforms directed at improving performance, including enhanced accountability for performance in an environment of greater managerial flexibility and performance budgeting, have generated a desire for more reporting of nonfinancial data. These reports seek to complement strictly financial reporting with specific information on the outputs and outcomes produced by programs (see Chapter 7). If budgets are explicitly prepared on the basis of agreed-upon outputs—as in so-called purchaser-provider arrangements in which there is an explicit link between funding of a program and outputs—demonstrating that agreed-upon output targets have been met is a core element of public sector accountability.

Achieving transparency in revenue policy in financial reports is a particular challenge. Many countries have taken to offering various tax incentives (reduced rates and exemptions) to achieve specific policy goals. Yet the impact of these revenue initiatives is not transparent in financial statements: even though revenue in income and cash flow statements will be lower than the maximum potentially available as a result of these measures, this lost revenue potential cannot be seen in the reports. Many OECD countries report tax expenditures annually but mostly in separate reports (or annexes to the budget) and thus tax expenditures are not presented alongside direct expenditure initiatives contained in the budget and are generally projected forward only for a few years (OECD, 2010).

Many countries, aided by computerized accounting systems, have designed their charts of accounts to enable reporting on a range of information not required by international standards—including, for example, information about the performance of a program (for managerial purposes), geographic location of expenditure (to support analysis of development policy), proportion of the benefit that each gender gains from program outputs, or the origin of goods purchased (to inform economic analysis).

There is growing global interest in reporting on the state of the natural environment. Conventional accounting practices simply do not provide adequate information for environmental management purposes. However, interest is emerging in including environmental information in enhanced reporting—aspects of the natural environment that are controlled by the government would be treated as a public asset and degradation of the environment is thus akin to an expense. Already countries are imposing carbon taxes and devising emissions trading schemes in an effort to address concerns about global warming, and in this context, the trend toward enhanced environmental reporting is likely to gain importance for governments.

One issue currently under discussion is whether any of the above reporting on enhanced financial information should become the norm and, if so, whether international standards should be further developed for its preparation. As an example of movement in this direction, the United Nations Statistical Commission has initiated an updating of the System of Environmental-Economic Accounts.

8.5. CONCLUSION

Fiscal reporting has developed significantly in the recent past. The comprehensiveness and coverage of reports have increased as governments have sought to solve fiscal problems and make better use of their resources. New accrual-based international statistical and accounting standards have been developed. And many governments have chosen to prepare additional reports on risks, the long-term sustainability of public finances, and other issues.

Yet many issues remain unresolved. Although the governments of many advanced economies have either moved to full accrual accounting or plan to do so soon, some doubt that its benefits are worth its implementation costs. Others believe that accrual reporting is essential but needs to be made more comprehensive, for example, to ensure recognition of more contingent liabilities. Questions also remain about the appropriate coverage of fiscal reports. In statistics, the need for reports on general government is widely accepted, but there is also a case for reports on the entire public sector, which today are rare. In accounting, a similar debate is occurring about whether governments' accounts should consolidate the central bank and SOEs. Though many governments report risks and long-term projections, there is no consensus on how such reports should be prepared. One unresolved question is how to summarize long-term fiscal projections in a way that makes clear their implications and their relationship to the government's main financial statements; the enhanced balance sheet presented in the previous section is an attempt at such a summary.

The global financial and economic crisis has sharpened the focus on these issues. The absence of warnings of possible fiscal problems from the financial sector may lead to a renewed focus on the reporting of fiscal risks, and the speed with which many governments' finances deteriorated may lead to more frequent reporting or even requirements for continuous disclosure. Furthermore, fiscal spillovers may spur further harmonization of fiscal reporting based on international standards. The problems revealed or created by the crisis should generate pressure for fiscal reporting that is more comprehensive; broader in coverage; more standardized; and more revealing of fiscal risks, long-term fiscal problems, and other issues important for public financial management.

REFERENCES

Australian Government, 2008, *Operation Sunlight: Enhancing Budget Transparency,* Ministry for Finance and Deregulation (Canberra).

Bentham, Jeremy, 1843, *The Works of Jeremy Bentham,* ed. by John Browning, Vols. 5 and 10 (Edinburgh: William Tate).

Chan, James L., 2008, "American Government Accounting Standards" (unpublished). Available via the Internet: http://jameslchan.com/papers/ChanAmGASCh3Sept08.pdf.

Dupuis, Jean-Pierre, Lucie Laliberté, and Paul Sutcliffe, 2006, "Task Force on Harmonization of Public Sector Accounting—Final Report," paper presented at the fifth meeting of the Task Force on Harmonization of Public Sector Accounting, Paris, March 8–10.

Filmer, Robert, (1680) 1991, '*Patriarcha' and Other Writings*, Cambridge Texts in the History of Political Thought, ed. by Johann P. Somerville (Cambridge: Cambridge University Press).

International Federation of Accountants (IFAC), 2008, "IPSAS Adoption by Governments" (New York).

International Monetary Fund (IMF), 1986, *A Manual on Government Finance Statistics* (Washington).

———, 1990, *Government Finance Statistics Yearbook 1990* (Washington).

———, 2001, *Government Finance Statistics Manual* (Washington).

———, 2004, *Government Finance Statistics Yearbook 2004* (Washington).

———, 2009, "Crisis-Related Measures in the Financial System and Sovereign Balance Sheet Risks" (Washington).

———, 2012a, "Fiscal Transparency, Accountability, and Risk" (Washington).

———, 2012b, *Government Finance Statistics Yearbook 2011* (Washington).

International Public Sector Accounting Standards Board (IPSASB), 2011, "Reporting Service Performance Information," consultation paper prepared for the International Federation of Accountants (New York: IFAC).

Intersecretariat Working Group on National Accounts (ISWGNA), 1993, *System of National Accounts* (New York: UN Statistical Commission).

Irwin, Timothy, 2012, "Accounting Devices and Fiscal Illusions," IMF Staff Discussion Note No. 12/2 (Washington).

Kotlikoff, Laurence J., and Bernd Raffelhuschen, 1999, "Generational Accounting around the Globe," *American Economic Review*, Vol. 89, No. 2, pp. 161–66.

Organisation for Economic Co-operation and Development (OECD), 2007, *Budget and Procedures Survey* (Paris).

———, 2010, *Tax Expenditures in OECD Countries* (Paris).

Schiavo-Campo, Salvatore, and Daniel Tommasi, 1999, *Managing Government Expenditure* (Manila: Asian Development Bank).

United Kingdom Chancellor of the Exchequer, n.d., "The Public Sector Balance Sheet" (London).

CHAPTER 9

Cash Management and Debt Management: Two Sides of the Same Coin?

JOHN GARDNER AND BRIAN OLDEN

The past 20 years have been a period of profound change in how government financial assets and liabilities are viewed and managed. This change has been driven by many factors, including the increase in volume and complexity of financial markets as more countries, especially in Latin America and Eastern Europe, gained access to the capital markets and financing instruments became more sophisticated and complex. Significant innovation has also occurred in information and communication technologies, institutional design, and capacity building—largely in advanced economies, but also in emerging market economies and developing countries. The increased complexity of markets and portfolios requires a greater degree of professionalism and development of strategies to build capacity and retain critical staff with skills that also happen to be highly attractive to the private sector.

Since the early 1990s, awareness has been increasing of the need to integrate the management of all government financial assets and liabilities. Cash and debt management appear at first glance to be quite distinct in their objectives and functions and, indeed, they have developed separately over time in many countries. Cash management has a relatively short-term outlook whereas debt management has a medium- to long-term horizon. Cash management's key objective is having the right amount of money in the right place at the right time to meet government obligations in the most cost-effective way (Storkey, 2003). The main goal of debt management is to ensure that the government's financing needs and its payment obligations are met at the lowest possible cost over the medium to long term, consistent with a prudent degree of risk (IMF and World Bank, 2001).

Despite the differences, they intersect at many points. Consequently, the number of debt management offices (DMOs) that have been assigned responsibility for cash management operations has increased significantly, including in New Zealand, Sweden, and the United Kingdom, among others.

This chapter argues that an integrated approach to cash and debt management makes sense for a variety of reasons. Joint responsibility for cash and debt management increases the incentives to manage all government financial resources as a single portfolio; it helps ensure that confusing signals are not sent to the market regarding government's financial management strategy, and it ensures that debt issuance decisions are made in the context of the government's overall cash flows. Combining cash and debt management functions in one unit consolidates scarce financial sector resources, reducing the difficulties in recruiting professional staff who are in short supply and streamlining the use of information technology (IT) systems and back-office facilities such as settlement and clearing operations.

Efficient and effective cash and debt management are extremely important for governments during normal times, but become critical during financial crises. In normal times, good cash management practices can produce considerable savings for governments through accurate understanding and management of liquid financial assets and shortages. During periods of financial crisis, these same functions can mean the avoidance of withdrawing government support from vital sectors of the economy just at the worst possible time. Similarly, effective public debt management permits fiscal policy to operate efficiently while minimizing financial portfolio risks relating to market movements and debt rollovers. In contrast, a debt management strategy that is poorly designed, implemented, and communicated can induce adverse investor sentiment, raise debt-servicing costs, damage government reputation, and exacerbate market instability. In periods of serious financial instability, countries can put their entire economic well-being in jeopardy if their debt management operation has been unable to foresee and mitigate risks.

The 2008–09 global financial and economic crisis had and will continue to have severe consequences for cash and debt management operations in advanced and less-advanced economies. Countries that had proficient systems in place before the crisis clearly benefited from them during the crisis.

The professionalization of government cash and debt management operations makes vital contributions to the overall public financial management objectives described in this book. This chapter focuses on the innovations witnessed in recent years in both cash and debt management operations and on why an integrated approach to management of government financial resources is preferable when seeking to optimize efficiency and effectiveness of these operations. The first section describes developing trends and innovations in public cash and debt management. The second section discusses current issues and challenges, including the need to improve coordination between cash and debt management. The third section examines specific issues for emerging market economies and developing countries. The fourth section briefly addresses the implications of the crisis for cash and debt management before drawing some general conclusions.

9.1. DEVELOPING TRENDS AND INNOVATIONS IN CASH AND DEBT MANAGEMENT

9.1.1. Public Cash Management

The advantages of successful active cash management are clear. Government is sure that its public policy priorities can be implemented without the risk of cash shortages restricting or rationing expenditures leading to payment arrears. Net short-term borrowing costs are reduced to a minimum, and surplus cash is invested to earn a market-related interest rate. Fiscal risks are contained to the extent possible by contingency buffer reserves of cash, and monetary policy is not adversely affected by government's financial market activities.

Cash planning is the process by which a government forecasts its cash availability and cash needs for a future time span—often the fiscal year, and in more detail over shorter periods. Its objective is to understand the expected trends in aggregated liquid financial resources over the chosen time horizon, or, put simply, the overall expected balance in its bank account. *Cash management* defines those activities undertaken by the government cash manager to ensure that financing is in place to meet the government's spending obligations and that identified cash surpluses are put to the most efficient use consistent with the defined risk parameters.

In the past 20 years, developments in the availability of government cash planning information have transformed its performance. Changes have been driven by technological advances both in computerized information databases and in telecommunications. These advances have allowed every aspect of central and subnational public cash management to be improved. Technological advances have facilitated government banking arrangements such that commercial banks can readily cope with high volumes of electronic revenue and expenditure transactions across large geographical regions. In addition, zero-balancing of accounts can occur on a daily basis and in some cases more frequently, committed amounts for future payment can be automatically included within cash plans, and spreadsheet analysis of actual versus forecast errors is performed for thousands of line items that comprise annual budget law appropriations. Government cash managers also rely heavily on the availability of complete databases of historical revenues and expenditures to enable better cash planning through the use of trend analysis, often using interfaces with government financial management information systems (FMISs) (Khan and Pessoa, 2010).

9.1.2. Government Banking Arrangements and Payments Systems

Maintaining a treasury single account (TSA) is now considered a prerequisite for effective cash planning. Today many governments automatically stream their revenues and expenditure payments through a TSA (see Box 9.1). The concept is simple although hardly new. It dates from the British colonial era when it was originally devised as a single actual bank account (because most government payments and revenues were made in cash) rather than the accounting ledger it is considered to be today.

Although the concept may not be new, the introduction and implementation of a TSA is certainly an innovative and often challenging process, especially in emerging market economies and developing countries. For example, creation of a TSA in Indonesia involved consolidating in excess of 24,000 individual government-controlled bank accounts, a task that required that everyone from head

BOX 9.1 Treasury Single Account Foundational Principles

A treasury single account (TSA) is a unified structure of government bank accounts enabling consolidation and optimum use of government cash resources. It separates transaction-level control from overall cash management. In other words, a TSA is a bank account or a set of linked bank accounts through which the government transacts all its receipts and payments and gets a consolidated view of its cash position during each day. This banking arrangement for government transactions is based on the principle of fungibility of all cash irrespective of its end use. Although it is necessary to distinguish individual cash transactions (e.g., a typical revenue or expenditure transaction of a government unit) for control and reporting purposes, these objectives are achieved through the accounting system and not by holding or depositing cash in transaction-specific individual bank accounts. This enables the ministry of finance and treasury to delink management of cash from control at a transaction level.

An effective TSA system is founded on three key principles:

- The government banking arrangement should be unified to enable the ministry of finance and treasury to oversee cash flows in and out of these bank accounts and allow complete fungibility of all cash resources, including on a real-time basis if electronic banking is in place. Although a TSA structure can contain ledger subaccounts in a single banking institution (not necessarily a central bank) and can accommodate external zero-balance accounts in a number of commercial banks, these separate accounts should be integrated with a top account (called the TSA main account), usually at the central bank, for consolidating balances (usually at the end of each day) to determine the aggregate cash position.
- No other government agency should operate bank accounts outside the oversight of the treasury. Institutional structures and transaction processing arrangements determine how a TSA is accessed and operated. The treasury, as the chief financial agent of the government, should manage the government's cash (and debt) positions to ensure that sufficient funds are available to meet financial obligations, idle cash is efficiently invested, and debt is optimally issued according to the appropriate statutes. In some cases, debt and cash management is performed by a debt management office.
- The TSA should have comprehensive coverage, that is, it should ideally include cash balances of all government entities, both budgetary and extrabudgetary, to ensure full consolidation of government cash resources.

Source: This box is largely extracted from Pattanayak and Fainboim (2010).

teachers to the education ministry be informed that their bank accounts and check books would be removed.

The rules underlying the operation of a TSA are straightforward, and many countries have moved away from using multiple bank accounts in parallel with rolling out an FMIS. Once it is clearly understood that the payments process—usually centralized through a TSA—is independent of the expenditure decision-making role of government agencies, the need for agencies to handle actual payments disappears. This business process is often so changed when the FMIS is implemented at the agency level. The agency undertakes the procurement process through the FMIS, which automatically checks that budget execution conforms to appropriation rules before approving the expenditure. The agency confirms in the FMIS that goods and services have been delivered according to the contract.

Centrally (at the treasury), an automatic payment is generated to the supplier from the TSA. Daily bank account reconciliation of the TSA is also performed automatically within the FMIS using electronic links with the TSA and reported centrally by the treasury.

The rules for government banking arrangements are also changing as technology develops. Many countries are moving toward greater diversity, competition, and transparency in their banking operations. For example, in developing countries standard commercial banking facilities can be rare in remote regions and now banking through mobile telephone networks is emerging. Governments are actively considering this means for making a range of payments to suppliers, for salaries of civil servants, and for benefits to the public. Such an innovation can sharply reduce the use of cash as a means of transactions. It can ensure that payments to suppliers are made on time without incurring arrears or late payment charges. It also radically reduces the opportunities for corrupt practices. Revenue payments to the government can also be made efficiently using this technology.

Technological changes have pressured central banks to modernize their roles. In the days when revenues and payments in cash were the norm, control of monetary policy was enhanced by the central bank undertaking all transactions on behalf of the government, often the largest generator of cash movement in the country. In many cases, the central bank built and maintained a network of branches across the country with significant levels of staff and resources to service its single client.

With the advent of fast and efficient electronic commercial banking networks covering most of a country's regions, the effectiveness of some central banks' banking operations have become questionable. In today's environment, a central bank may be unable to develop, or justify the cost of, its own computerized network for its only customer—the government. While private sector businesses were instantaneously accessing and moving financial resources around the country, governments were still taking a week or even a month to make payments or transfer revenues to a central account with bank account reconciliations taking even longer (if occurring at all).

Many governments are now concluding that the central bank ought not to play the role of the government's retail banker. Although resisted by some central banks, it is becoming generally accepted as more efficient from a public cash management perspective to use commercial banks and their electronic networks to perform as many government revenue and expenditure transactions as possible. This change is feasible because government account balances at the commercial banks can be electronically swept into the TSA at the central bank each night.

Governments, particularly those with effective FMISs, can now tender their retail banking business to those commercial banks that maintain electronic networks throughout the country. Assuming that the banks can provide the services efficiently, they are remunerated through transaction fees. This setup is an extremely attractive business for banking groups because they can persuade government employees, suppliers, contractors, and institutions to maintain bank accounts at their branches to receive or make government payments efficiently. The banks can then sell additional profitable services to these new customers. Indeed, so attractive is this potential business that the first tender of this kind for government banking business in a large Asian country produced a negative winning bid—the bank offered to pay the government a small fee for every transaction made.

Governments can realize many benefits by using these modern banking and payments systems. The operation of a TSA can potentially allow the government to save money in three ways by avoiding the following situations:

- pools of cash being held in commercial bank accounts earning little or no interest;
- despite these pools of cash, undertaking expensive borrowing to finance expenditures;
- the central bank, to operate effective monetary policy, draining this government liquidity from the banking system at a significant cost, reducing its dividend to the government.[1]

The TSA clearly provides a more efficient method of accounting for and reconciling government transactions. It also assists the cash manager in cash planning because the necessary aggregation of government cash resources is already accomplished, and it aids active cash management because individual financing or investment operations can be performed directly as and when required.

In summary, a centralized payments system can provide benefits to accounting, recording, and reconciling bank statements. Government use of commercial banks to provide retail banking services can make transactions more effective and efficient; reduce the use of cash for government transactions; reduce opportunities for corruption; and allow rapid, regular computerized bank statement reconciliations. It also releases the central bank from a role that it cannot perform competitively—having only one customer and little incentive to account transparently for its profit and loss on such business.

With the central bank still operating wholesale banking services for the government, that is, the TSA, government credit exposure to the commercial banks is avoided owing to daily sweeping of unused cash balances in these accounts; the performance of monetary policy operations is aided; and full control over the account subledgers is retained as required for agency and donor accounts.

9.1.3. Cash Planning

Many countries are now following the lead of developed governments by establishing a cash management unit (CMU), sometimes attached to the DMO, which has the responsibility to perform cash planning and active cash management. Technological advances in computerized budget management have greatly assisted the cash manager in forecasting available government cash resources. Whether

[1] There is a report (perhaps apocryphal) that one Asian government was able to reduce all its expenditure arrears, its total borrowings, and its budget deficit (totaling about 5 percent of GDP) at a single stroke when it fully implemented the TSA, so great were its "unknown" funds lying idle in central and commercial bank accounts around the country.

a fully fledged FMIS or a spreadsheet budget model is used, a transferable database containing all annual budget allocations can be employed to perform aggregated projections of the TSA balance for the current fiscal year. The degree of complexity that these projections entail may be chosen by the cash planner. Often the basis is a daily projection over the nearest month, weekly for the following two months, and monthly for the rest of the fiscal year.

The modern government cash planner uses computerized records of expenditures to calculate seasonality patterns for individual line items, or aggregated groups of items if appropriate.[2] The power of modern computerized spreadsheets allows the planner to populate the model with historical line item data downloaded from the accounting records. The model can then determine whether trends exist during the year that can be used to predict future expenditure demands. Again, the complexity of these calculations depends on planning needs and available technical capacity. In many developing countries, simple historical averages are being used effectively to provide this analysis.[3] The most accurate forecasts are frequently produced through the development of a network of contacts with the most active revenue and spending agencies. These agency officials should be able to provide updated plans that can override purely seasonal factors within the cash plan.

Modern debt-recording databases can be linked to the CMU spreadsheet so that debt-servicing requirements during the fiscal year are directly incorporated when available cash resources are projected. Also particularly important is the availability of commitment planning and budgeting. Commitment controls allow the FMIS to establish expected dates of payments for committed expenditures in advance of requirements, and the CMU can readily access this information to include it in the planning model.

The cash planning model can also be used to simulate short-term cash consequences of fiscal risks that might occur during the year. Senior officials of the ministry of finance or the government can request the cash planner to provide estimates of the liquidity constraints that would arise under certain defined circumstances, such as significant changes to revenue projections, increased expenditures through public policy changes, crystallization of contingent risks such as guarantees, moral hazard expectations (particularly relevant in the current crisis, especially in relation to banking sector bailouts), and changes in debt-servicing costs through movements in interest rates and foreign exchange values.

The cash planner should normally provide the central bank with detailed information about forecast government revenue and expenditure cash movements through the banking system. These movements are often the most significant (and difficult to predict) of the autonomous influences on monetary conditions, and this information can greatly assist in the operation of monetary policy. If a developing country does not have credible cash planning and forecasting, the

[2] In-year revenue projections are normally the responsibility of the specialist revenue agencies.

[3] Cambodia and Lebanon are starting to use basic trend extrapolation from historical averages, whereas Australia, for instance, has very sophisticated mathematical forecasting models.

central bank needs to develop the capacity to estimate government cash movements in the banking system. If the ministry of finance can perform this task more accurately for its own purposes, this additional cost to the central bank can be eliminated, again to the benefit of the government budget if doing so increases the central bank dividend.

9.1.4. Active Cash Management

A prerequisite for active cash management is that the CMU's cash plans and forecasts be credible. Credibility is gained when forecasts have compared favorably to actual expenditure outcomes over a significant period. At the stage when such credibility is evident, the committee or body controlling the CMU is in a position to give the CMU authority through regulations enacted for this specific purpose to perform active cash management operations and transactions.

In developed countries, cash management activities have, since 2000 or so, become very sophisticated and normally need to be closely coordinated with the actions of the DMO. The primary objective of the CMU's cash planning exercise is to estimate the expected balance in the TSA during the period ahead *before any cash management activity takes place*. This bank balance profile, covering as it must the whole of government cash resources available for budgetary purposes, normally shows large swings between positive and negative territory. The secondary objective of the CMU is to make this profile *after cash management operations* as stable and close to a target level as possible.

Because borrowing almost always costs significantly more than deposit interest, owing both to market interest rate spreads and to credit rating effects, experienced cash managers first focus on periods of anticipated cash shortages. Developed countries usually have no difficulty raising short-term cash in the government treasury bill (T-bill) market. Cash managers have agreements with the central bank, which may act as fiscal agent for the treasury in the domestic market, to borrow as necessary without conflicting with open market monetary operations or confusing market participants. It is important that the marketplace understand that fiscal policy, cash management activity, and monetary policy are separate and independent. Thus, expected cash shortages are covered either by a regular calendar of T-bill issuance or by individually announced auctions. These announcements sometimes specifically state that the borrowings are for cash management purposes; for example, the U.S. federal government issues "cash management bills" as necessary. The maturity of these T-bills is designed to match the expected period of shortage until revenues are predicted to exceed expenditures.

Modern cash managers often operate a cash buffer system in the TSA. This targeted cash surplus acts as a contingency reserve for errors in the cash planning forecasts. Clearly, if the T-bill market is so efficient that the government can borrow within a 24-hour period to cover almost any contingency, the buffer level can

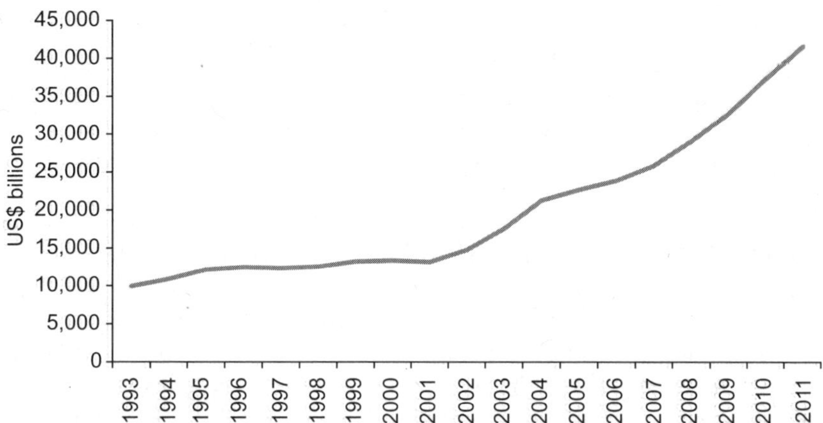

Figure 9.1 Sum of All Countries' Public Domestic Debt Securities

Source: Bank for International Settlements.

be set at or close to zero, as for example in Sweden. Many other countries, however, believe that the buffer reserve[4] should be calculated taking into account the probability of error in their forecasts. To have a certain confidence level that this variance is covered (95 percent, for instance), a minimum cash buffer level must be held in the TSA.

9.1.5. Public Debt Management

Debt management is the framework, system, or process that allows the required amount of government funding to be raised in a manner consistent with government's risk and cost objectives and any other debt management goals. The increased borrowing levels in advanced economies in the 1980s, as well as the large infrastructure and financing needs of emerging market economies following the breakup of the Soviet Union in the early 1990s, were undoubtedly catalysts for a greater focus on debt management. Figure 9.1 shows the significant growth in the sum of all countries' public domestic debt securities since the early 1990s.

The large financing requirements created awareness of the importance of debt management operations to long-term fiscal sustainability and efficiency of the public financial management system. The increased complexity of financial markets and the instruments that were developed also led to awareness of the need to professionalize the debt management function because general civil service skills were no longer sufficient to manage such complex portfolios.

[4] Overnight credit lines from commercial banks are another, similar, option.

Improving the Understanding of Risk in Debt Management Operations

One of the key areas in which debt management has improved is in risk management. The centralization of debt management operations into single institutional units and the implementation of debt databases that include all government debt liabilities have facilitated the introduction of a portfolio-based approach to debt management, something that was not possible under a fragmented structure. The centralized availability of data has also enabled the use of risk management techniques, such as probability and scenario analyses (see Chapter 5), to estimate exposures to market risks. Market risk can include the impact of interest rates, exchange rates, and the maturity structure of the debt portfolio on debt-servicing costs.

Sophisticated modeling techniques are now being used by advanced DMOs, which have invested heavily in risk management specialists and systems. DMOs have also been at the forefront in refining risk models to suit public sector requirements. One example is the development of cost-at-risk models (derived from the value-at-risk models used by private sector financial institutions and asset managers) to estimate the fiscal and budgetary risks associated with debt portfolios. Less-sophisticated debt managers have also begun to develop simplistic risk management capacity, often using scenario analysis and other basic modeling techniques to analyze the structure of their debt portfolios as an input to their debt management decision-making and strategy formulation processes. Generic models have been produced by the IMF and the World Bank to assist DMOs in analyzing their portfolios.

As debt managers have become more sophisticated, and with the introduction of instruments such as derivatives,[5] repo agreements,[6] and increased use of bank deposits to invest surplus government cash, the need to develop credit risk management capacity has assumed greater importance. This importance was heightened by the problems facing the banking industry following the crisis. Advanced economies have steadily refined their credit risk models using a variety of techniques first employed by the private sector. Unfortunately, the recent crisis has shown that some of the models used in the financial services industry did not provide the supposed protection because a number of erroneous assumptions were used as inputs. The consequence of these shortcomings was a false sense of security and an absence of more subjective inputs into the risk management process. The lessons from the recent crisis need to be learned, and government risk

[5] Derivatives are agreements that shift risk from one party to another. The value of a derivative is derived from the value of an underlying price, rate, index, or financial instrument. Derivatives allow specific financial risks to be traded in financial markets in their own right. There are two broad classes of financial derivatives: forward-type contracts, including swaps (e.g., interest rate swaps), and option contracts.

[6] Repo or repurchase agreements are the sale of securities with an agreement to buy back the security at a later date at an agreed-on price. One party receives a cash loan while the counterparty receives securities for an agreed-on period of time.

management practices need to be overhauled (as in the private sector) if such a crisis is not to recur.

Emerging market economies and developing countries have traditionally had less need for sophisticated credit risk management procedures because their portfolios tend to be simpler and concentrated on the liability side (credit risk is not a major issue if the entire portfolio is made up of borrowings and derivatives are not used). Therefore, their credit risk modeling has been more rudimentary. However, as capacity and access to markets improve, the demand for more sophisticated credit risk modeling is likely to grow. Building human capacity is a considerable problem given that risk management specialists are highly attractive to the private sector, and skill shortages in the public sector plague virtually all countries.

Many of the advances in risk management capacity development in DMOs have resulted from a greater awareness of the fiscal risks inherent in debt and government guarantee portfolios and the need to minimize the volatility of budget performance resulting from fluctuations in debt-servicing costs. Unlike most other budgetary expenditures, debt-servicing costs are difficult to influence internally because much of the volatility associated with these costs is determined exogenously through movements in international interest and exchange rates or in changes in international perceptions of the creditworthiness of individual sovereign borrowers; this latter factor has been spectacularly in evidence during the crisis.

Debt managers need to account for a variety of risks and to put procedures in place to minimize and monitor the risks in the portfolio. Box 9.2 identifies key risks that need to be taken into account in debt management operations.

A good risk management framework requires a set of guidelines or rules for risk identification, monitoring, and reporting (see Chapter 5). Most advanced DMOs have procedures that apply to each stage of the risk management process. Clear rules on how risks should be analyzed need to be approved by senior management, and good international practice would dictate that a specialized unit be established to monitor and report on risk to DMO senior management.

Typically, exposure to market risk should be monitored frequently: advanced economies monitor market exposure on a real-time or, at the very least, a daily basis. With modern IT systems, senior managers and controllers should have online access to market exposures, and clear limits on the level of acceptable exposure should be established by senior management. Breaches of these limits should require immediate explanation and correction.

In a world in which many countries still operate cash-based budgeting and accounting systems, risk management requires a two-pronged approach. In a cash-based environment, policymakers' primary concern is to ensure that annual budget estimates are not jeopardized through excessive risk. Cost-at-risk models were developed by public sector debt managers for this purpose. These models show the extra cost that would need to be borne by the budget if certain defined risks were to materialize. However, to ensure that annual budget figures are not being manipulated at the expense of the long-term economic portfolio value, guidelines must be in place for analyzing market risk, which will identify longer-term

BOX 9.2 Key Risks Inherent in Government Debt Portfolios

Market risk. In less-advanced debt management offices, simple deterministic models of the impact of the interest rate and exchange rate on debt-service costs are often used in addition to other basic scenario analysis. Advanced economies use value-at-risk or cost-at-risk and other techniques such as risk-adjusted performance measurement to measure the market risks inherent in the portfolio.

Credit risk. If government is in the position of being a creditor to another body (usually a bank), it bears a risk that it will not have its asset paid back in full should that body fail. This risk is readily seen if government deposits cash in a bank, but derivative instruments can also embody significant credit exposure of the government to the counterparty. This exposure is often difficult to detect and to quantify. Thus, credit risk assumes greater importance the more complex the portfolio becomes. The use of derivatives and other instruments with asset characteristics requires considerably more attention, and the need to monitor counterparty exposures is now an essential part of risk management operations.

Regulatory and legal risk. The increasing complexity and volume of financial instruments has led to a wide range of regulatory and legal risks. For example, many contracts for instruments currently being used by advanced and emerging market economies have not been tested in national courts. This type of risk is of particular concern for instruments that require collateralization, such as repo agreements and securitized instruments for which ownership of collateral may be disputed in the event of default on contractual obligations.

Operational risk. Operational risk refers to the risk of loss resulting from inadequate or failed internal processes, people, and systems or from external events (Storkey, 2011). A key advance in debt management, in both developed and developing countries, has been the increased focus on the operational risks inherent in the debt management function. Failure to control operational risk adequately may not only have adverse financial consequences, it can also affect the country's international reputation. Improvements in internal control and audit, business continuity planning, or disaster recovery, and a move toward "straight-through processing" of transactions through advances in information technology systems have also helped with the evolution of operational risk management practices.

portfolio exposures. As a consequence, risk managers in the most advanced DMOs analyze both cash- and market-based risk exposures.

Less-sophisticated DMOs may not have high risk management capacity, but simple analyses of the underlying exposures of the portfolio should be carried out to inform strategic decision making. For example, a basic prerequisite should be the requirement to report on the currency, interest rate, and maturity structure of the portfolio. Credit risk should similarly be monitored (see Box 9.2).

As DMOs have become more professional, the pressure to measure debt manager performance has increased. Most if not all advanced DMOs are measured against a set of quantitative and nonquantitative criteria to determine the "value added" by the debt managers in achieving budgetary savings as opposed to the impact of exogenous factors, such as falling interest rates or favorable currency movements. Some countries, including Ireland and Sweden, use a benchmark portfolio as a yardstick against which actual performance is measured, whereas others, including the United Kingdom, make greater use of nonquantitative performance measures owing to the difficulty of creating a benchmark in a market in which the government is the largest player.

Need for Medium-Term Debt Strategies

Many countries now consider a medium-term debt management strategy (MTDS) to be an essential tool for guiding debt management operations. In the 1980s, access to capital markets, both domestic and international, was largely limited to the Organisation for Economic Co-operation and Development (OECD) countries and a few other large economies; most emerging market economies and developing countries were primarily relegated to concessional financing from international financial institutions. Consequently, developing countries' borrowing strategies were, in reality, determined by how much funding was available from international financial institutions. Until the 1990s, the ability to influence currency or interest rate composition was a luxury that only a few countries could claim.

This situation has changed significantly. The increase in the number of countries developing and implementing an MTDS is attributable, to a large degree, to the increased access that emerging market economies (precrisis) had to international and domestic capital markets and hence greater choice in shaping their borrowing needs and portfolio compositions. Developing nations (e.g., Ghana) also succeeded in accessing international capital markets. The range of debt instruments has also greatly expanded, with international financial institutions offering greater flexibility in the choice of currency, maturity, and interest rate (particularly for nonconcessional loans). Access to hedging instruments has expanded, and institutions such as the World Bank now offer hedging advice and instruments.

However, these developments have also complicated the decision-making process. In the past the question was whether to borrow, but the current availability of broader choices now dictates that debt managers seek guidance on structuring their debt portfolios to meet underlying debt management objectives. An MTDS examines the alternative options and assesses the risks and costs associated with different policy choices.

An MTDS must be realistic and implementable. Too many debt strategies have been fatally weakened by failing to take into account the macroeconomic and debt sustainability assumptions underlying fiscal policy (see Chapter 5). Many early attempts at an MTDS resulted in wish lists of desired portfolio outcomes, with little relationship to what was achievable based on the instruments available to the debt manager. A concerted effort by donors, including the IMF and the World Bank, to educate debt managers in emerging market economies and developing countries is now resulting in the development of more realistic strategies (IMF and World Bank 2007, 2009).

An MTDS should reflect government's planning horizon, typically a three- to five-year period, and should reflect the key linkages between its inputs. These inputs include cost and risk analysis, the macroeconomic framework, the annual borrowing requirement, the timing of government cash requirements and the sources of financing, and risk hedging. Domestic capital market development concerns may also be an important element of the MTDS. The MTDS should be approved by government (in some cases, by parliament) to ensure that it has political legitimacy and that it offers the debt manager a blueprint for operations in the medium term. The MTDS should also be reviewed frequently (at least semiannually), and regular monitoring of progress in implementing the strategy is essential to ensure that it remains relevant and reflects any changes in macroeconomic or macrofiscal policy.

Clear incentives must be in place to ensure that a realistic MTDS guides debt managers. In the absence of an MTDS, debt management operations run the risk of diverging from other fiscal policy objectives or may lack consistency with other macro objectives. A well-prepared, realistic MTDS guides the debt manager. Essentially, it becomes a reference point by which to justify performance.[7]

Developing Domestic Government Debt Markets

Since the early 1990s, domestic government securities markets in advanced economies have changed significantly. A trend toward introducing primary dealer systems[8] and increasing the size of benchmark bond issues (see Box 9.3) has helped significantly in developing secondary market trading activity in domestic bonds. Better and more integrated settlement and clearance systems have also encouraged foreign investors to enter domestic markets, further contributing to liquidity. The advent of the euro has had a profound impact on European bond markets. Euro-area-wide trading and clearance platforms have been created, and the smaller countries in the euro area now have access to hedging instruments such as liquid futures and options that may not have been available in smaller-currency domestic markets. These developments have increased the international market profiles of domestic bond markets in smaller countries.

Domestic markets in many of the larger emerging market economies in Latin America and Eastern Europe have grown considerably (see Figure 9.2), to a point that liquid trading in government securities now exists, covering most points of the yield curve, and liquidity has largely been maintained (e.g., Brazil, Colombia, the Czech Republic, and Poland), notwithstanding varying degrees of disruption during the global financial and economic crisis. In Eastern Europe, new pools of domestic investors with longer-term investment horizons were also created by reforms to the pension and insurance industries; these pools will continue to grow and create natural demand for longer-dated government securities.

Foreign investor appetite has also been a feature of the most successful market developments. Foreign investors bring international expertise to domestic markets and impose discipline on issuers to ensure that the domestic market complies

---

[7] In Ireland (precrisis), a benchmark portfolio approved by the government, against which the performance of the debt manager was measured, was deemed to be the de facto debt strategy. The benchmark was reviewed annually to ensure it met the guidelines laid down by the minister of finance and other fiscal policy objectives.

[8] In many countries, governments have designated a group of financial firms as the principal intermediaries in the government securities market; these intermediaries are referred to as "primary dealers" or a "primary dealer system."

BOX 9.3 Prerequisites for Developing Bond Markets and Attracting Foreign Investment

Technical characteristics of government securities. To attract foreign investors and to encourage secondary market trading, the conventions used in designing domestic securities should comply with international standards. Compliance with international conventions on settlement periods should also be ensured. Foreign investors should not be penalized for investing, that is, taxes should not be withheld for nonresidents.

Liquidity. Market liquidity (ready and willing buyers and sellers at all times) is essential to attract foreign investment and to encourage secondary market trading. Strategies to achieve liquidity have included issuing benchmark bonds that can be tapped on an ongoing basis to create sufficient size to promote liquidity, and using bond buyback and switching programs. However, even these policies may not be adequate in smaller countries where the market in its entirety may be too small for a liquid bond market to develop.

Price transparency. Many countries have established primary dealer systems offering selected market makers (typically banks) rights and obligations to promote price transparency and improve liquidity in the market. Typical obligations of primary dealers, in return for concessions during bond auctions, include the need to quote prices on benchmark stocks and to maintain narrow bid-offer spreads. Promotion of electronic trading and the posting of trading prices and volumes also help to improve price transparency.

Marketing and investor relations strategies. Marketing and investor relations strategies are increasingly seen as vital to developing domestic bond markets. Some countries have gone so far as to establish investor relations offices (Mexico and Turkey). In a time of increased competition for foreign capital, a comprehensive marketing strategy will assume ever-increasing importance. Countries need to differentiate their products from those of similarly rated entities.

Market infrastructure and regulatory environment. Ensuring that clearing and settlement systems comply with international standards and, if possible, that domestic systems can connect to international payments systems is essential. The development of market infrastructure in emerging market economies and developing countries has been heavily emphasized in recent years, often with donor assistance. Most countries now have at least a rudimentary system in place and many have a fully functioning, internationally recognized clearing and settlement architecture.

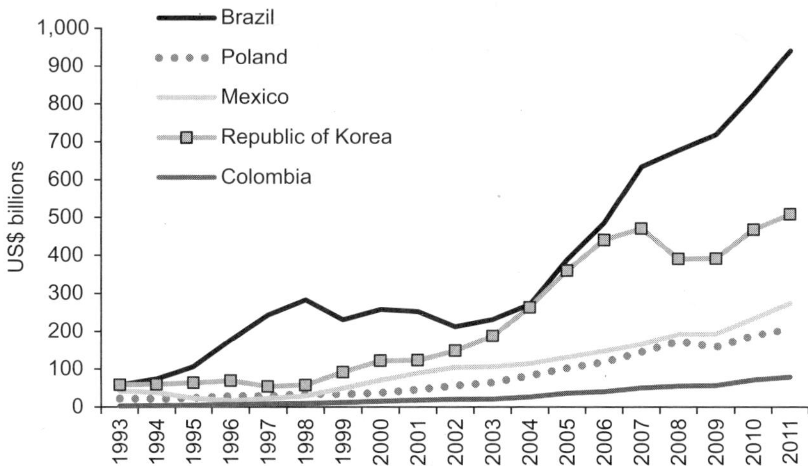

Figure 9.2 Government-Issued Domestic Debt Securities in Selected Countries

Source: Bank for International Settlements.

with international standards. These advantages, however, are tempered by the knowledge that foreign investors tend to be less attached to domestic markets and are quicker to exit during market turbulence, as experienced in the early days of the Asian financial crisis in the late 1990s and the global financial and economic crisis. However, on balance, the presence of foreign investors is beneficial to efforts to develop domestic markets.

The situation for some of the smaller emerging market economies and developing countries has not been as encouraging. Smaller countries face problems in attracting capital to domestic markets owing to lack of scale, which affects liquidity, and this difficulty is often exacerbated by the absence of a well-developed domestic investor base. As a result, many smaller economies are finding it difficult to establish liquid markets, particularly at the longer end of the maturity spectrum. Some prerequisites for developing domestic bond markets are outlined in Box 9.3.

For most emerging market economies and developing countries, the existence of a domestic government debt market is an important precondition for the growth of a broader domestic capital market. Therefore, although the primary objective may be to open up a new source of medium- to long-term government funding, the wider objective of helping to develop the broader financial sector infrastructure is a highly desirable coproduct. This is also important from the monetary authorities' perspective because well-functioning money and capital markets are essential transmission mechanisms for monetary policy.

9.2. ISSUES AND CHALLENGES IN CASH AND DEBT MANAGEMENT

9.2.1. Cash Management Challenges: Full Government Coverage, Buffer Levels, and Management of Credit Risks

Since the late 1980s, governments in a number of developed countries appeared to have resolved many of their cash planning difficulties. They can ensure that expenditures are accurately and realistically projected. They have complex revenue forecasting models that produce high-quality estimates of cash inflows. These improvements permit governments to predict their available cash balances with only marginal errors. The remaining challenges in cash planning for these countries are in commitment controls, budget and TSA coverage, and uncharted fiscal risks.

However, the recent financial crisis has uncovered some serious weaknesses in cash planning and management in several developed countries, particularly in the periphery of the euro area. Although central government cash requirements can be forecasted reasonably effectively, if the whole of general government is not covered, sudden unexpected cash demands and shortages can arise. These fiscal risks often relate to the activities of unmonitored entities, such as subnational governments and state-owned enterprises and agencies, or to contingent liabilities such as public-private partnerships and government guarantees of various other types (see Chapters 5 and 10). Without full coverage, cash managers are unaware of all potential demands on cash resources, and cannot readily calculate the required cash buffer to hold in the TSA to meet unexpected variations in expenditures or revenues. Thus, at some point the government cannot fulfill the short-term expenditure needs demanded by government policy priorities, resulting in the buildup of expenditure arrears.

Cash buffer calculations can be extremely complex mathematical exercises, often with probabilistic confidence levels derived from the statistical distribution of cash flow forecasting errors. However, such precise buffer calculations are not always necessary. The cash planning model can be used to perform "what-if" simulations to determine appropriate buffer levels under a variety of scenarios. Even in unusual situations, the calculation can be fairly straightforward. In Iceland, for example, following the onset of its banking crisis in late 2008, some large domestic bond auctions failed. The size of these immediate borrowing requirements was far greater than regular fluctuations in the TSA balance and might have caused severe problems in government business and debt servicing if the TSA had not already held a large cash reserve. This reserve was at risk of being depleted by expenditure requirements during the crisis. It was recommended that the minimum cash buffer level be kept slightly above the size of the normal benchmark bond issue until the government securities market had stabilized and risk of further auction failure became insignificant.

Times of expected cash surpluses (greater than the requisite buffer) are often more difficult for the cash manager than shortages. A simple solution is for the CMU to deposit the surplus with commercial banks for the expected surplus period. This solution, however, ignores the monetary policy implications for the central bank or the credit risk to the government if the commercial bank were to fail. Taking a large amount of money from the TSA at the central bank and depositing it in the banking system spurs credit growth and, depending on other changes in liquidity, may require costly draining operations[9] through the central bank's open market operations. The CMU needs to coordinate such actions carefully with the central bank.

To ensure that government does not shoulder credit risk when placing deposits with commercial banks, CMUs often operate in the repo market. This market has developed to provide collateral to depositors in case of bank failure. The repo market allows short-term deposits to be made by one party (e.g., the government) to another (e.g., a commercial bank), which provides a pledge on high-quality collateral (such as government securities) to secure against credit risk. In many countries, repo markets have become very large and efficient, and governments can place large amounts of cash into the markets at good rates while taking little or no credit risk during the term of the deposit.

[9] Central banks sell debt instruments to the banking system if liquidity levels are considered to be too high, and it must pay market interest on these instruments. This is a simplistic description because in certain instances the central bank may want money to return to the banking system, for example, if tax revenue collections have been unexpectedly large.

Efficient repo markets provide a seemingly ideal instrument for government deposits. During the recent crisis, however, several developed countries had great difficulty obtaining repo rates for their surplus cash. The credit crunch had so tightly restricted the supply of very high-quality collateral, such as government securities, that none was available against repo transactions. CMUs, such as that in France, either provided deposits to the commercial banks against no collateral or against much lower-quality bonds (like mortgage-backed securities). These activities were met with accusations that unofficial liquidity support had been provided to the banking system and came under intense scrutiny because such nontransparent actions were not considered to be part of the function of the CMU or of the government.

Normally, the CMU will operate only in the domestic currency because the government has the highest domestic credit quality—being able to print money if necessary. If, however, foreign currency is maintained by the CMU, other securities might be available for short-term investment. If the government holds surplus balances of certain liquid currencies (U.S. dollars, yen, euros, pounds sterling), short-term high-credit securities are available for attracting a market return without the tension described above. These securities have no effect on domestic monetary policy or on the foreign exchange rate if the deposits are kept in their original currency. Many commodity-producing countries use this method of obtaining an adequate return on their surplus cash while maintaining sufficient liquidity for budgetary needs.

Another alternative for active management of surplus cash is to buy back already-issued government securities on the secondary market. This option is often less favored because it may affect monetary policy in the same way that deposits in commercial banks do. It also requires close coordination with government debt managers because the DMO may be reluctant to have its securities bought by the CMU, potentially causing market confusion or disrupting its planned bond auction calendar.

In developing countries, the CMU normally is advised to negotiate with the central bank for interest to be paid on deposits of its surplus cash resources. These negotiations center on the tension between the extra costs to the central bank of draining monies deposited by the CMU in the banking system and the credit risk taken by the government when depositing with commercial banks. In several countries, for instance, Indonesia, the central bank has agreed to pay a market-related interest rate on specified surplus time deposits from the CMU. Although this rate is slightly lower than the actual market rate available from commercial banks, this compromise adequately resolves the monetary policy–credit exposure tension.

9.2.2. Debt Management Challenges: Reducing Fragmentation and Improving Coordination and Professionalism

In the early 1990s, fragmentation of government debt portfolios across a number of institutions was relatively common, and domestic and external debt were often managed by different institutions. Foreign and domestic debt portfolios were also frequently shared between the central bank and the ministry of finance, and in some cases, individual budget units borrowed on their own behalf.[10]

This fragmented approach to debt management had many negative consequences, including the absence of a coordinated borrowing and debt management strategy and inefficient costing and management of risks. The problem also extended to the approval and monitoring of contingent liabilities, such as government guarantees, because sectoral ministries frequently managed their own portfolios, leading to the creation of many unquantified and unmonitored fiscal risks. As a result, reporting and monitoring were often extremely complex, delayed, and prone to error.

This fragmentation was one of the reasons for the emergence of DMOs. Other reasons included the need to improve professionalism owing to the increased complexity of financial markets and the need to separate debt management from monetary policy.

Although the concept of a dedicated DMO is not new—Sweden has had a debt agency for more than 200 years—the number of specialized DMOs has increased significantly since the early 1990s. The centralization of authority to borrow, monitor, and report on government debt portfolios has increased transparency, led to greater efficiency in debt management operations, and allowed countries to adopt portfolio-based techniques for debt management similar to those used by private sector institutional asset management companies.

Early examples of countries with independent DMOs include Ireland, Portugal, and Sweden; their institutional models were the most radical, with the DMO completely independent of the ministry of finance.[11] In Ireland (as in other countries), earlier efforts to develop debt management units within the rigid structures of the civil service had failed—the units were unable to attract and retain staff with financial market expertise because of pay constraints, and personnel policies tended to favor general administrative skills over the highly specialized skills required to establish a dedicated DMO. The institutional model favored by these "early adopters" was significant in that these independent institutions enjoyed a high degree of delegated authority, a comprehensive legal framework regulating their operations, and, crucially, the ability to recruit and retain staff outside the constraints imposed by public sector pay guidelines.

[10]This was a common problem in countries that relied heavily on project financing from international financial institutions for sector-specific projects. Frequently, the central fiscal authorities were only marginally involved (if at all).

[11]The Swedish National Debt Office has been in existence for more than 200 years. The Irish National Treasury Management Agency and the Portuguese Instituto de Gestão da Tesouraria e do Crédito Público have been in operation since the early to mid-1990s. The New Zealand Debt Management Office was established in the 1980s but is not institutionally independent of the ministry of finance.

The independent DMO was not the only model being considered as efforts to professionalize debt management operations gathered momentum in the late 1990s and early 2000s. Although some countries, such as Hungary, followed the separate independent DMO route, others, including Colombia, France, Thailand, and Turkey, elected to develop the DMO as a division or directorate within the ministry of finance or treasury, similar to the early New Zealand model. Still others decided to establish separate DMOs reporting directly to the ministry of finance, and a small number of countries decided to retain the central bank as the primary debt manager. The latter model has become uncommon as countries increasingly attempt to separate monetary and fiscal policy operations. Table 9.1 offers examples of the institutional structures used by different countries for debt management operations.

The precise institutional model, although important, was a secondary concern. Of far greater importance was political awareness of the need to professionalize debt management operations within a single organizational unit and the commitment to meet the challenges that this would entail. Political commitment was not easily forthcoming because many other fiscal issues concerned policymakers in an era of radical economic change. This was, and continues to be, particularly so in emerging market economies, especially those directly affected by the breakup of the Soviet Union. In advanced economies, securing political commitment was also difficult for this relatively small area of fiscal policy,

TABLE 9.1

Examples of Central Government Debt Management Institutional Arrangements

Separate and independent DMO	Separate DMO as agency of ministry of finance	DMO within treasury or ministry of finance	DMO within central bank
Germany	Australia	Argentina	Denmark
Hungary	Belgium	Brazil	India[1]
Ireland	Netherlands	Canada (shared with Bank of Canada)	
Portugal	New Zealand	Chile	
Sweden	Nigeria	China	
	United Kingdom	Colombia	
		France	
		Indonesia	
		Italy	
		Japan	
		Korea	
		Mexico	
		Russia	
		Spain	
		Thailand	
		Turkey	
		United States	

Source: IMF.
Note: DMO = debt management office.
[1] External debt is managed by the ministry of finance. Legislation to establish an independent DMO was considered by the government in 2012.

particularly if the scale of the debt portfolio was not at the forefront of the political agenda.[12]

As the role of the public debt manager became more refined during the course of the 1990s, a number of rules and best practices emerged that have been followed by the more advanced DMOs. The early innovations of DMOs, such as those in Austria, Ireland, New Zealand, and Sweden, resulted from recasting standard practices found in the private sector financial services industry to conform to the realities of public financial management. Many of these refinements were documented in publications such as the IMF and World Bank *Debt Management Guidelines* (IMF and World Bank, 2001). Key rules include identification of debt management objectives, transparency and accountability of debt management operations, institutional frameworks that meet international standards, and a framework for medium-term strategic debt and risk management.

In emerging market economies and developing countries, the primary objective is to ensure that government financing needs and payment obligations are "met at the lowest possible cost over the medium to long run, consistent with a prudent degree of risk" (IMF and World Bank, 2001, p. 6). This objective is often accompanied by a secondary objective of developing the domestic debt market to widen the pool of financing opportunities and to facilitate the development of domestic nongovernment capital markets.

The internal organizational structures of DMOs have been predicated on the principle of separation of responsibilities. Most advanced and emerging market DMOs pursue an organizational model that differentiates between transaction originators and transaction processors. This system is crucial to implementation of modern operational risk control processes and procedures. Box 9.4 highlights good international practice in structuring modern DMO operations.

Advances in IT systems have played a major role in minimizing operational risk. IT systems reduce the need for human intervention (thereby reducing human error) in transaction and settlement processing. Improvements in IT have also increased the transparency of debt management operations and greatly enhanced monitoring and analysis of government financial operations, thereby enhancing risk management capacity, particularly in advanced economies. Emerging market economies and developing countries still need to develop their IT systems further; nevertheless, significant advances have been made since the early 2000s.

The establishment of specialized DMOs has had a profound effect on capacity. Offices that were able to circumvent public sector pay guidelines (e.g., those in Austria, Ireland, New Zealand, and Sweden) managed to retain key specialized

[12] Some of the earliest proponents of professionalization of the debt management function, including Ireland and New Zealand, were faced with critical economic challenges in the 1980s and with unsustainable sovereign debt levels. Many other advanced economies started to look at this issue only in the late 1990s or early 2000s when their debt problems became more acute (e.g., France, Germany, and the United Kingdom).

BOX 9.4 Good International Practice for Separation of Responsibilities in Debt Management Offices

- *Senior management.* Supported by internal audit and compliance.
- *Front office.* Responsible for primary issuance and execution of both domestic and external securities, and all other funding and portfolio management operations, including secondary market and derivative transactions.
- *Middle office 1.* Responsible for policy and portfolio strategy development and accountability reporting.
- *Middle office 2.* Responsible for internal risk management: policies, processes, and controls.
- *Middle office 3.* Responsible for liaison and coordination with internal and external institutions; fiscal policy, monetary policy, and credit rating agencies.
- *Back office.* Responsible for transaction recording, reconciliation, confirmation, and settlement; maintenance of financial and accounting records and database management; coordination with ministry of finance budget execution and accounting functions.

staff. However, those that did not have the same flexibility (e.g., the United Kingdom) found that the more professional environment offered by independent DMOs was an incentive for staff even if levels of remuneration did not match those in the private sector. The experience to be gained in working in DMOs was also an attraction and could help to retain staff, at least while they built up their marketability.

These developments have been driven by incentives to generate budgetary savings and reduce fiscal risks through greater centralization of the debt management function. Benefits also accrued from the perception in the capital markets of a more professional approach to debt management in those countries that had provided the necessary resources and political commitment. The risk premiums associated with the sovereign market debt issued by these countries were significantly reduced.[13] A vivid precrisis example was Brazil during the 2000s.

9.2.3. Coordination of Cash Management and Debt Management

This chapter contends that coordinating cash and debt management is important to avoid conflict and achieve compatibility. Initial strategies to develop a professional approach to debt management focused almost exclusively on the liability side of the balance sheet. Cash management was often neglected or carried out by other units in the treasury or ministry of finance, and in some cases by the central bank. This secondary status frequently led to suboptimal outcomes because cash and debt management operations were not coordinated or the objectives being

[13]The global crisis had an impact on certain sovereigns' credit spreads, in particular, Greece, Ireland, and Portugal, but the crisis was a catastrophic event that no amount of professionalization could have countered.

pursued were not necessarily in line with fiscal and monetary policies. For example, tensions arise if the government debt manager is issuing debt in the market (for market-development purposes) at the same time that the cash manager is striving to place surplus funds into the market at a considerably lower deposit interest rate.

During the last 10–15 years, however, awareness has increased of the need to integrate the management of all government financial resources, especially cash management with debt management operations. This awareness has coincided with a greater understanding of the need to manage government assets and liabilities more professionally.

As a consequence, the number of DMOs that have been assigned responsibility for cash management operations has increased significantly, including those in a number of euro area countries, and those in New Zealand, Sweden, and the United Kingdom. DMOs are increasingly regarded as government's financial portfolio manager given that those scarce skills developed in managing the debt portfolio can also be used for other purposes.

A more integrated approach to cash and debt management makes sense for many reasons:

- *Issuance strategies are coordinated across the full range of the ministry of finance's instruments.* The short end of the yield curve is frequently reserved for issuance of instruments connected with cash management operations whereas the longer end is reserved for debt management operations. Integrating cash and debt management operations can ensure that strategies at different points in the yield curve do not conflict.
- *Joint responsibility increases incentives to manage government financial resources as a portfolio.* Charging a single entity with managing all government financial activities ensures that confusing signals are not sent to the market about government's financial management strategy and that assets or liabilities are not being managed suboptimally.
- *Debt issuance decisions are made in the context of government's overall cash flows.* Integration allows for better information flow and coordination of strategic debt issuance decisions, ensuring that such decisions are made with full knowledge of government's net cash flow position.
- *Scarce financial sector resources are consolidated in one unit.* Skilled professionals with financial market experience are in short supply in the public sector in most if not all countries. Therefore, establishing separate units to deal with market-related activities (as has been the case in a few countries) dilutes these already scarce resources.
- *Information systems and transaction processing procedures are integrated.* Many of the procedures and processes associated with managing transactions connected to financial assets and liabilities are similar. Combining the functions allows the use of IT systems and back-office facilities, such as settlement and clearing operations, to be streamlined.

On balance, an integrated approach to cash and debt management is the optimum institutional arrangement, although some countries have chosen to maintain separate units for cash and debt management (e.g., Indonesia and Serbia). This separated institutional arrangement can work, although it requires close coordination and communication. However, this level of coordination is normally difficult to achieve.

9.3. CHALLENGES OF CASH AND DEBT MANAGEMENT IN EMERGING MARKET ECONOMIES AND DEVELOPING COUNTRIES

Emerging market economies and developing countries trying to implement effective cash planning and active cash management techniques face a number of challenges not evident in more advanced economies. A TSA structure and centralized payments system are often vehemently opposed by powerful figures and institutions within government, simply as a result of their not understanding the technicalities of the business process change. Spending agencies often do not grasp that centralizing payments does not mean loss of control over execution of their approved budget during the fiscal year. Resistance to such changes is natural and can be overcome by education and training by the treasury or CMU. However, negative reactions sometimes suggest that ulterior motives such as corrupt practices lie behind the unwillingness to cede control over cash resources.

Developing countries face an enormous undertaking in determining the number of government bank accounts in existence and then convincing the owners of the accounts to close them and pay the balances to the TSA. Nevertheless, it is achievable and has been successful to varying degrees in many countries. As with implementation of many innovations, political will and support at the highest levels of government are necessary either to win over those with opposing viewpoints or to enact rules and regulations forcing government institutions to comply.

Central banks in developing countries might also resist moving government retail banking operations to the commercial banking sector. If the central bank has built a network of provincial branches specifically to serve the government, its reluctance to concede that its commercial bank competitors are more efficient is natural. Modern communications and data processing technology can greatly assist the treasury in its cash management and accounting and reporting objectives. The CMU must make a detailed case to the minister of finance about the efficiencies to be gained from using modern methods.

Accurate cash planning can also be a difficult task in developing countries. Although the implementation of cash plans across line items of the budget is relatively simple and a model can be readily provided through technical assistance, a more substantive issue is the inability of the cash manager to obtain accurate, timely, and updated revenue and spending plans. The CMU is rarely provided with sufficient authority to demand these projections and improvements in their accuracy. This problem relates both to rules and regulations that can be issued by the government and to the network of data providers in government agencies. The cash manager must be able to communicate directly with individuals in spending agencies that make cash flow estimates and those individuals must be held responsible for determining why errors in forecasts occur and how they can be rectified. Difficult institutional and cultural changes may be required for this to happen.

In many developing countries, certain preconditions for accurate cash planning do not exist. These preconditions can be related to efficient debt-recording databases, commitment controls, or coverage. As in developed countries, the cash plan must incorporate as many areas of fiscal risk as possible.

Public debt management in developing economies was rudimentary before the late 1990s. Public sector borrowing mainly consisted of concessional debt from international financial institutions and bilateral credits from export credit agencies. Debt management-related "decisions" were dominated by the terms and conditions imposed by the lenders. Loan conditions tended to be inflexible and very little input from country authorities was permitted.

Repayment problems in developing countries emerged in the late 1970s and were soon followed by the growing awareness that debt relief would become a cornerstone of any strategy to kick-start economic growth in the developing world. A series of debt-relief initiatives, ranging from bilateral agreements to formal Paris Club restructuring negotiations, culminated in the 1996 Heavily Indebted Poor Countries (HIPC) Initiative championed by the IMF and the World Bank. The Multilateral Debt Relief Initiative, a product of the Group of Eight Gleneagles meeting in July 2005, offered 100 percent cancellation of multilateral debts owed by HIPC-eligible countries to the IMF, the World Bank, and the African Development Bank.

The debt-relief initiatives were accompanied by access to a more diverse range of funding as international financial institutions such as the World Bank increased the range of instruments and terms and conditions associated with their loans. Improved macroeconomic fundamentals resulting from debt-relief initiatives also resulted in improved credit standings, which attracted private sector investors, and for some countries, access to international capital markets became a reality in the 2000s.

The need for developing countries to provide analyses of their debt portfolios to ensure compliance with the conditions of the HIPC Initiative and subsequent debt-relief initiatives led to a more widespread acknowledgment of the importance of consolidated debt recording and reporting. The many donor-financed projects to introduce debt-recording systems have greatly increased capacity in this area.[14] More recent initiatives such as the *Debt Management Guidelines*

---

[14] Both the United Nations Conference on Trade and Development–Debt Management and Financial Analysis System and the Commonwealth Secretariat's Debt Recording and Management System were specifically developed to help low- and middle-income countries develop their debt management capacity. Implementation of these systems is often funded by donors.

published by the IMF and World Bank (2001) and recent joint IMF/World Bank initiatives to strengthen debt management in developing countries and emerging market economies, including the implementation of debt management strategies using MTDS modeling techniques, have also increased awareness and debt management capacity in developing countries.

Some emerging market economies faced specific problems. For example, the need to fund large-scale infrastructure improvements required newly independent states to develop their debt management capacity quickly. Again, donors were very active in assisting emerging market economies to implement debt management solutions and to develop debt management capacity. These initiatives have had mixed results, although it is safe to say that debt management capacity in general is now significantly greater in most emerging market economies.

Problems remain, however. Legal frameworks for debt management, although improving, still require further strengthening, particularly in developing countries. The appropriate institutional setting for debt management operations, and training and retention of staff, remain major issues in both developing countries and emerging market economies. Although debt management systems have improved in many countries, further work is required. In addition, many of the debt management systems implemented since 2000 still need to be integrated with other public financial management systems, and integration of debt management operations with cash management remains an issue in many countries, despite the obvious advantages outlined earlier.

Development of domestic government debt markets is still at an early stage except in the larger emerging market economies, and in many cases continuing reforms to the pension and insurance industries are required to create stable domestic demand for longer-maturity government securities. In addition, moves to develop medium-term debt management strategies have not always been realistic, nor have they been accompanied by a sense of what is achievable at different stages of development.

Further improvements in debt management operations in both emerging market economies and developing countries will require technical assistance and absorbing the lessons learned by advanced economies. Recent initiatives such as that launched by the IMF and World Bank on strengthening debt management can help, although more is needed (IMF and World Bank, 2007). Continued investment in systems and people will be necessary to build on progress achieved to date.

9.4. CRISIS IMPLICATIONS

The consequences of the crisis for advanced economies will likely include a repricing of risk, especially for countries that experienced the worst of the crisis (Greece, Ireland, Portugal, and Spain, among others), leading to higher borrowing costs in the medium term. The funding requirements of some

OECD countries, coupled with deteriorating macroeconomic conditions, are likely to lead to greater credit spreads for the foreseeable future. Debt managers will need to work harder to convince investors of the merits of investing in their bonds, and competition for capital is likely to exacerbate the spread differentials.

The crises will also have long-lasting effects on emerging market economies and developing countries. The volume of debt to be issued by advanced economies in the short to medium term will reduce the availability of international capital for countries with lower credit ratings and will likely result in higher borrowing costs for those who need to fund internationally. An impact will also likely be felt on the development of domestic markets, with foreign investors demanding higher yields. Access to international markets will also depend on stronger marketing and more-intense investor relations strategies to differentiate credits and attract international demand.

These implications increase the importance of the role of debt and cash managers as countries struggle to shake off the effects of the crisis. Efficient and effective management of public financial assets and liabilities will be a crucial element of country strategies to achieve fiscal sustainability and return to normal growth paths in the medium term. The improvements made in the past 20 years must be built upon to ensure government debt and cash managers are sufficiently equipped to carry out their functions.

9.5. CONCLUSION

The range of technological innovations and instruments available to cash and debt managers has increased considerably, but not without creating greater challenges. These include ensuring that proper controls and risk management processes are in place to allow for the achievement of specific debt and cash management strategies within wider fiscal policy objectives. Advanced economies have actively pursued proper processes. Further capacity building will be required in developing countries as their interactions with market-based instruments increases.

The argument that an integrated approach to cash and debt management, in most institutional settings, is preferable to a more fragmented approach is difficult to refute except for reasons of institutional or political expediency. Most private sector treasury operations manage their financial assets and liabilities on an integrated basis and the public sector environment should be no different.

The proper institutional setting for a debt management office, however, is very country specific and depends on, among other factors, the political environment, the legal framework, and the achievable level of sophistication of debt and cash management operations.

It is difficult to foresee how profoundly the aftermath of the global financial and economic crisis will affect the future roles of the debt and cash manager. Debt and cash managers are likely to increase in importance as they grapple with high levels of indebtedness, a more risk-averse investor base, and increased competition for access to the capital markets as they seek to ensure that government liquidity is maintained. These daunting challenges in countries across the development spectrum argue even more forcefully for an integrated and professional approach to financial asset and liability management.

REFERENCES

International Monetary Fund (IMF) and World Bank, 2001, *Debt Management Guidelines* (Washington, amended 2003).

———, 2007, "Strengthening Debt Management Practices: Lessons from Country Experiences and Issues Going Forward," Joint IMF and World Bank paper (Washington).

———, 2009, "Managing Public Debt: Formulating Strategies and Strengthening Institutional Capacity," Joint IMF and World Bank paper (Washington).

Khan, Abdul, and Mario Pessoa, 2010, *Conceptual Design: A Critical Element of a Government Financial Management Information System Project,* Technical Notes and Manuals No. 2010/07 (Washington: International Monetary Fund).

Pattanayak, Sailendra, and Israel Fainboim, 2010, "Treasury Single Account: Concept, Design and Implementation Issues," IMF Working Paper 10/143 (Washington: International Monetary Fund). Available via the Internet: http://www.imf.org/external/pubs/cat/longres.cfm?sk=23927.0.

Storkey, Ian, 2003, "Government Cash and Treasury Management Reform," *Asian Development Bank Governance Brief,* Issue 7 (Manila).

———, 2011, *Operational Risk Management and Business Continuity Planning for Modern State Treasuries,* Technical Notes and Manuals No. 2011/05 (Washington: International Monetary Fund).

CHAPTER 10

Managing Public Investment

ISRAEL FAINBOIM, DUNCAN LAST, AND EIVIND TANDBERG

During the last few decades, the management of public investment has kept pace with broader changes in public financial management (PFM). The old approach of dual budgeting was abandoned in favor of a more integrated approach in which investment became increasingly delegated to spending ministries. Although initially successful, this response ended up downplaying the strategic importance of public investment to the economy, exposing long-term and costly decisions—characteristic of many large infrastructure projects—to shorter-term political whims and ultimately threatening economic prosperity. Realization of this danger has led to the resurgence of a more strategic approach to the management of public investment in which long-term priorities are more systematically identified.

The creation or renovation of physical assets is the ultimate output of government infrastructure projects and the main area of public investment considered in this chapter. Sound public investment management should follow PFM's three well-established goals: (1) fiscal sustainability, and its consistency with total public investment spending over the long term; (2) allocative efficiency, requiring that selected projects be consistent with the government's sectoral priorities, and resources be shifted to more productive sectors; and (3) operational efficiency, with projects and programs delivering outputs and outcomes in a cost-efficient manner.

In recent years, PFM reforms have come a long way toward meeting these objectives. For example, medium-term budget frameworks (see Chapter 4) bring with them greater assurance of funding over the medium term, and performance budgeting (see Chapter 7) improves the link between government policy objectives and desired outcomes while encouraging more efficient spending. Moreover, a growing number of countries have introduced longer-term fiscal projections.

This chapter examines the changing nature of public investment management and draws practical lessons for the way it should evolve in the future. It is divided into three sections. The first section discusses the challenges of traditional public investment management and its compatibility with new PFM innovations and asks what impact the new PFM innovations have had on the way governments manage their public investments. The second section looks at whether specialized processes for managing public investment spending are still needed, and how the traditional public investment management tools have adjusted to complement the broader PFM reforms. The third section discusses the different approaches to financing public investments by focusing on how governments can make effective use of new contracting and funding arrangements for public investment (such as public-private partnerships). The chapter concludes by briefly examining emerging issues arising from the 2008–09 global economic and financial crisis and its aftermath and summarizing lessons for public investment management.

10.1. PUBLIC INVESTMENT AND THE NEW PUBLIC FINANCIAL MANAGEMENT TOOLS

Public investment management has over time become a technical function, often decentralized to sector ministries, with, at best, a residual regulatory and coordination role retained at the center. In parallel, its share as a percentage of GDP shrank between 1965 and 1990 globally from about 17 percent to 4 percent, a level it has more or less maintained since. Even in middle- and low-income countries, where the case for public investment would seem to be particularly strong, the share of GDP declined from 32 percent in 1965 to less than 10 percent in 2000.

Since 2000 and in the last few years in particular, there has been a reemergence of interest in public investment. What has driven this change? One concern has been the deleterious effects of the decline in public investment. In some advanced economies, the abundance of European Union (EU) Structural Funds has sparked renewed interest in public investment. In other countries, new forms of financing, such as public-private partnerships, have provided an attractive way to fund projects with apparently little or no impact on budgets and taxation. Finally, the 2008–09 global financial crisis triggered renewed interest in countercyclical fiscal policies, with a number of countries adopting economic stimulus packages that included accelerated infrastructure maintenance and increased investment in ready-to-go public projects.

10.1.1. Characteristics of Public Investment and Challenges of Traditional Public Investment Management

Unlike most other spending, public investment is generally lumpy. Large infrastructure projects in particular have long lead times for both the design and implementation phases, and because they are generally site specific, they have significant sunk costs. These characteristics have created a number of needs: a medium- to long-term planning framework; a carefully defined project cycle; and specialized skills, tools, and institutional and funding arrangements.

The traditional approach to public investment management, which concentrates on national development plans generally produced by a separate ministry of planning, has several weaknesses. These weaknesses include the tendency to become disconnected from fiscal constraints; a mismatch between required funding in the plan and budgetary allocation; procyclical spending; dual budgeting in which investment spending is handled separately from the rest of the budget; and ineffective sequencing and prioritization of projects, and inadequate planning, design, and monitoring of projects.

To address some of these weaknesses, the public investment program (PIP) approach introduced in the 1980s attempted to create a pipeline of well-prepared projects ready for selection in the annual budget process. The PIP approach aimed to strengthen the planning process by rigorously applying a systematic and standardized project cycle to all projects. In practice, however, many countries used the PIP to create long wish lists with no clear prioritization and sequencing; funding would then be sought for the projects on these lists.[1] In other countries, the PIP approach was simply superseded by the more holistic medium-term budget framework discussed in the next section.

Traditional arrangements for public investment do not always keep a spotlight on operating costs throughout the full project cycle, particularly if dual budgeting is still practiced, if budgets retain a purely annual focus, and if projects are centrally planned and managed. As a result, funding for operating costs or the skilled staff needed to run the new facility may not be available when construction is completed, leading to delayed operation. To address this issue, some countries have resorted to devolving investment management to line ministries, making them responsible for harmonizing their investment and recurrent spending programs within their medium-term sector strategies. However, because spending ministries are often over-optimistic about the funding they are likely to get from the budget, and finance ministries are generally unable to meet their full expectations, devolution alone has generally been unable to resolve the mismatch between project investment and the recurrent costs arising from the investment.

The traditional ministry of planning still exists in many middle- and low-income countries, where investment is often donor funded and capacity in spending ministries to plan and implement projects remains weak. In most Organisation for Economic Co-operation and Development (OECD) countries, where these constraints usually do not exist, the traditional ministry of planning has been dismantled and its functions either merged into the ministry of finance or fully devolved to spending ministries.

10.1.2. Impact of the New PFM Innovations on Public Investment Management

The significant developments in PFM since the early 2000s have positively influenced the management of public investment, bringing it more into the mainstream of fiscal management and budgeting. Although this influence is to be welcomed, the new PFM tools do not completely meet the more specialized needs of public investment management. Understanding the benefits and the shortcomings of these new PFM tools is a prerequisite to understanding the way that public investment management has evolved and should continue to progress. This section discusses the most relevant developments, those that have had a clear

[1] In the 1990s, PIPs were the instrument of choice for low-income countries, which used them to present wish lists of projects at donor round tables, and projects were selected according to donor preferences.

impact on public investment: medium-term fiscal frameworks, medium-term budget frameworks or expenditure ceilings, performance budgeting, and accrual accounting.

10.1.3. Public Investment Focusing on the Medium Term

Fiscal frameworks can create a more realistic and sustainable environment for public investment, as long as their coverage is comprehensive, their time horizon is adequately long, and they accurately reflect public investment costs. However, the practice in many countries often diverges, sometimes to a significant degree, from these requirements.

Furthermore, in times of crisis and consolidation, or uncertainty due to funding volatility, public investment is generally the first casualty. When fiscal policy is tightened, investment and maintenance tend to bear most of the adjustment and conversely tend to expand more than other expenditures in times of fiscal expansion. This gives rise to procyclical fiscal policy and a stop-and-go approach to public investment. The cost of this behavior can be significant when unfinished projects are left to deteriorate before they even start to yield economic benefits and capital stock is inadequately maintained, risking significant future rehabilitation costs.

The provision of adequate fiscal space for public investment has long been a concern in the budgetary planning process. Nowadays, investment spending must be accommodated within medium-term macroeconomic and budgetary frameworks and associated fiscal targets, as discussed in Chapter 4. These fiscal targets can affect the level of public investment spending in the following ways:

- An overall fiscal balance places a cap on total public investment spending given that such spending is generally included under "discretionary" spending. The budget available for investment is often determined as a residual, after all "nondiscretionary" recurrent spending (salaries, transfers, debt service, operating costs) has been considered.
- Restrictions on gross public debt further limit the scope for such spending because large capital projects are often funded from borrowing.
- Goals for structural balances can reduce procyclicality in spending, including public investment spending.

However, such clear-cut impacts on public investment cannot be taken for granted. For example, researchers remain divided about the impact of the EU's Stability and Growth Pact on public investment (Galí and Perotti, 2003; Blanchard and Giavazzi, 2004; Mehrotra and Välilä, 2006; Dahan and Strawczynski, 2010).

Medium-term fiscal targets, and the underlying medium-term budget frameworks (MTBFs), assume that public investment projects, particularly infrastructure projects, will pay for themselves over the longer term either through fees or tariffs, or through increased revenues resulting from the higher growth generated by the investment. Although revenue generation may be achieved quickly for certain types of infrastructure investment (roads, ports, airports), other projects (social sector investments) may take significantly longer to deliver results (and the impact will be indirect), and others still (government buildings, prisons) are unlikely to deliver any additional revenues.

Moreover, many large-scale public investment projects suffer from significant cost overruns during construction as well as an overestimation of benefits to be expected once the project is completed. Flyvbjerg, Skamris Holm, and Buhl's (2004) study of 258 major transport infrastructure projects completed between 1927 and 1998 in 20 nations across five continents found that the majority had cost overruns or benefit shortfalls. For example, 90 percent of projects with cost overruns ended up with completion problems, and rail passenger traffic turned out to be 51.4 percent lower than estimated (see Box 10.3).

Decisions on investment spending may also be externally driven, complicating a country's overall fiscal policy management, as with the EU Structural Funds and Cohesion Funds and aid-receiving low- and middle-income countries. The external funding organization generally has its own focus and priorities, which may be at odds with the country's own policy priorities. Furthermore, many countries treat such funding as extrabudgetary for fiscal balance purposes. Under such conditions, the task of maintaining a coherent fiscal policy framework requires close coordination with the external organizations and access to information on their expected disbursements. If these conditions are not met, or the external flows are volatile, the fiscal policy framework can become ineffective.

10.1.4. Medium-Term Budget Frameworks

By the 1990s, national development plans and public investment programs were being overtaken in advanced economies by the more integrated medium-term budget framework. MTBFs have been effective in bringing public investment within budgeting constraints, in countering the tendency toward dual budgeting, and in focusing budgetary decisions beyond the traditional and often misleading first-year effect of an investment project. The more effective MTBFs have generally been accompanied by decentralizing the responsibility for detailed budgetary management to sector ministries, making them responsible for aligning their investment and recurrent spending needs with their medium-term sector strategies and their program objectives, within budget ceilings set in the MTBF.

For a while the MTBF approach appeared to provide the right balance of medium-term integrated budgetary planning linked to policy priorities, a focus on deliverables and outcomes, and fiscal sustainability. Its medium-term horizon facilitated inclusion of operating and maintenance costs for projects nearing completion, and provided assurance of funding, at least over the MTBF period, for approved investments. As the MTBF became the main vehicle for resource allocation, the traditional central planning function lost its funding allocation role, leaving it with project design and monitoring tasks that many countries have since delegated to line ministries.

However, as noted in Chapter 4, only binding MTBFs provide tangible certainty of funding over the medium term. Most MTBFs provide only indicative ceilings for outer years, which many countries can find difficult to respect, particularly in times of uncertainty or when there are changes in government. Therefore, many MTBFs have merely inherited the optimism bias—overestimation of benefits and underestimation of costs—endemic to traditional planning frameworks without soberly addressing the problems of funding certainty. Furthermore, the short time horizon of MTBFs—3–5 years compared to 10–20 years for major capital investment projects—may further compound the problem, putting a project's priority status at risk during its implementation lifetime, leading to possible abandonment or cutback before completion.

This partly explains why some countries have been unwilling to abandon the traditional planning framework, even after the advent of the MTBF. Starting in the mid-1990s, a few countries (such as Ireland) began to give the national development plan a new lease on life, followed in the early 2000s by several others. From there, renewed interest in investment planning processes and institutional arrangements became more widespread. Although approaches varied (see Box 10.1), all aimed to promote realism by keeping the plans focused and fully coordinated with fiscal planning processes. Some countries, such as Ireland and the United Kingdom, have further opted to strengthen the link between MTBFs and longer-term planning by introducing the concept of long-term budget commitments for large investment projects, often combined with carryover mechanisms that facilitate investment planning and execution.[2]

10.1.5. Performance Budgeting

Objectives, outputs, and outcomes have long been familiar concepts in the context of public investment. Project proposals are normally justified by the specific demands for public goods and services that they will address—patients or students not being adequately serviced, congested roads, inadequate office accommodation for staff. Justifying large projects is often costly and time consuming. It requires significant efforts in project specification and outline design; feasibility studies with cost-benefit or cost-effectiveness analyses; and fully costed, detailed design with specific deliverables and expected outputs before the go-ahead is finally given.

Performance budgeting applies the techniques used in public investment planning across the whole budget, creating a more comprehensive environment for budgetary planning encompassing a broader set of service delivery objectives (see Chapter 7). Performance budgeting presupposes a medium-term context, and therefore is a natural fit with the MTBF approach. This ideal combination ensures that planning and budgeting processes are harmonized at both the strategic (MTBF) and the operational levels, equally providing justification for investment spending and assurance of funding over the project's lifetime.

---

[2] These and other cases are discussed in Laursen and Myers (2009).

BOX 10.1 Recent Progress in National Development Planning

Ireland provides one of the first examples of a modern national development plan (NDP). Its first NDP, covering the period 1993–2000, coincided with the planning cycle for EU Structural Funds, although more than 90 percent of the NDP's financing came from the regular budget. The Irish NDP is a strategic investment plan for the government, broadly defined to include capital spending as well as current spending that enhances human and social capital (e.g., education). The Irish NDP, managed by the ministry of finance and fully costed and coordinated with the budget process, provides financing indications consistent with long-term fiscal projections, regularly updated and revised during both medium-term and annual budget reviews. (For more information, see the most recent NDP covering 2007–2013 at http://www2.ul.ie/pdf/932500843.pdf.)

Denmark published its Investing in Denmark's Future plan in 2001. The plan describes recent developments in public investment, identifies the priority needs for the next 10 years, sets out a financial framework for the period, and specifies the investment projects that will be implemented. (See http://www.fm.dk/db/filarkiv/3749/future2001.pdf.)

In late 2008, the *United Kingdom* passed legislation that established a new, independent Infrastructure Planning Commission (IPC) with the aim of fast-tracking infrastructure schemes of national importance. Each national ministry (in areas such as energy, aviation, road and rail transport, and water and sanitation) was asked to set out a national policy statement detailing its national infrastructure priorities. The decision to go ahead with a project would then be made independently by the IPC, operating within a framework established by the ministers. (See http://infrastructure.independent.gov.uk/.)

In 2008, *Australia* established Infrastructure Australia to depoliticize public investment assessment and decision-making processes. Its four objectives are (1) to provide an independent assessment of a project's value for money; (2) to establish a pipeline of priority projects for implementation, subject to financing availability; (3) to provide a national perspective on infrastructure priorities; and (4) to create an ability to "overcome any tendency of spending ministries to consider only a limited set of investment options." (See http://www.infrastructureaustralia.gov.au/index.aspx.)

Performance budgeting in theory involves devolution of responsibility for delivering agreed-on outputs and outcomes to program managers. This devolved responsibility includes investments, avoiding the isolation often associated with project implementation units. Program managers are given some budgetary flexibility to adjust spending, within limits set by the MTBF, and to address emerging issues, including those related to project implementation—such as cost overruns, savings, delays, and design changes.

Thus, the trend toward devolving project management responsibility to spending ministries is fully compatible with performance budgeting.

10.1.6. Relevance of the Accrual Approach to Public Investment

From an economic perspective, the primary difference between physical assets and current spending is the productive life of the asset once it is delivered for use. The useful life of infrastructure can be several decades. The accounting basis will determine the way in which that asset is presented in the accounts. Under cash accounting, the asset is expensed when stage payments are made during its construction. Under accrual accounting, it is expensed as it is being "consumed" over the years of its productive life, whereas the payments made during construction are reflected as the acquisition of the asset in the books of government—the "consumption" under accrual reflects the progressive depreciation in the value of the asset.

The progressive adoption of accrual accounting (see Chapter 8), which provides a more accurate picture of a government's capital assets, promotes integration between capital and current budget decisions and more rational choices about when to initiate new investment projects. More explicit trade-offs between maintenance and new investment are an important element of this type of accounting.

The spread of accrual accounting is changing the way that governments view public investment. The accrual approach takes a more comprehensive view of assets, allowing government to report systematically on the use of resources from the moment of asset creation through the life of the asset. Recording information on the age of the asset, its useful life, and its utilization rate gives some indication of how much should be spent on maintaining the stock of capital, and enables more effective planning and better use of resources for maintenance.

Table 10.1 summarizes how the new PFM tools fit with and have affected public investment management. The table stresses both the advantages of these tools and their shortcomings in addressing the challenges of traditional public investment management.

10.2. RECENT DEVELOPMENTS IN PUBLIC INVESTMENT MANAGEMENT TOOLS

This section examines how the management of public investment itself is evolving through revisions to existing, and development of new, public investment tools. Even with the new public financial management innovations discussed in the previous section, public investment management still requires some specialized tools of its own. In particular, this section looks at the broad characteristics of a new framework for managing public investment, focused on (1) the appraisal stage; (2) the project selection stage; and (3) the project management, monitoring, and ex post evaluation stages.

10.2.1. Changing the Framework for Managing Public Investment

The new PFM innovations have helped to address some, although not all, of the weaknesses of the traditional planning frameworks and public investment management discussed in the previous section. Public investment planning and man-

TABLE 10.1

Public Investment and the New Public Financial Management Tools

	Fit with Public Investment		
New Tool	**Advantages**	**Shortcomings**	**Good practices and challenges**
Medium-term budget frameworks (MTBFs)	Facilitates effective integration of public investment within the budget process, avoids dual budgeting, and provides assurance of funding over the medium term (3–5 years).	Time horizon is too short for large infrastructure projects, which may have life spans of 10 years or more. Still need a robust investment planning process to ensure quality projects are selected.	Separate investment budget should be discontinued. However, the need for a longer-term public investment planning framework remains and must be linked to the rolling MTBF.
Performance budgeting	Provides a common performance focus for the whole budget instead of just the public investment budget. Useful for integrating investment with operating costs.	Requires enhanced capacity and systems to monitor performance.	Need to align the public investment performance framework with the new performance budgeting framework. Requires more diligent attention to operating costs throughout the investment period and beyond.
Accrual accounting	Enhances asset management transparency and public investment decisions in particular, emphasizing maintenance costs.	Requires capacity and significant building of awareness in concerned stakeholders.	Need to manage the change process as accrual accounting is introduced.

Source: Authors' compilation.

agement have adjusted to be compatible with, and benefit from, these PFM innovations and to change their own overall framework.

The first prerequisite for the new planning framework is to become fully integrated into the overall fiscal management and budgeting processes, while maintaining the means to monitor and report effectively on each project. This integration implies the following:

- The macro framework for public investment should be the same as, or at least consistent with, the overall macro framework. This alignment would ensure common macroeconomic goals for government spending as a whole and encourage greater realism in setting fiscal space for investment, at least over the medium term.
- Public investment should be fully aligned with policy priorities, including long-term strategic objectives (if defined), and should not crowd out funding for ongoing projects unless they have been formally suspended or abandoned.

- Public investment should be funded through the MTBF, approved as part of new budget initiatives, justified as integral to the expansion of government services, and aligned with overall budgetary performance management.

MTBFs and performance budgeting effectively address most of these requirements by integrating investment spending within a more comprehensive resource use framework. Nevertheless, certain specific needs of public investment management extend beyond these general PFM reforms. These needs include keeping track of, and ensuring funding for, investment projects with implementation cycles significantly longer than the typical MTBF and the average political cycle. To address this issue, the new planning frameworks should have the following characteristics in addition to those listed in the bullet points: a strategic framework setting out long-term development objectives and priorities with a time horizon of 10 to 15 years, the ability to track projects from inception to ex post evaluation, and the capacity to keep decision makers informed of the longer-term implications of public investment decisions.

Some recent developments aim to extend the fiscal and budgetary horizons beyond the three to five years of the MTBF; for instance, long-term fiscal projections are becoming more widely used (see Chapter 1). However, these efforts have generally been produced at fairly aggregated levels of spending, often with a focus on demographic changes. A few countries have introduced longer-term commitments in certain sectors—for example, the transport sectors in Ireland and the United Kingdom.[3] These are sector-specific envelopes, aimed at providing sufficient funding to cover sector needs rather than to cover specific projects.

The phases for managing a project from inception to ex post evaluation—the project cycle—have not changed, and include

- the *inception phase*, comprising project specification and preliminary cost estimates for different options;
- the *evaluation phase*, which ensures that each project proposal is subjected to rigorous, consultative, and wide-ranging evaluation;
- the *selection phase*, which delivers a pipeline of fully appraised and costed projects for decision makers to select from;
- the *design phase*, which delivers detailed design plans for the project;
- the *execution phase*, which provides ongoing assessments of project status, including continued relevance, potential cost overruns, and risks; and

[3] Ireland's Transport 21 represented a major policy commitment by the Irish government to address a perceived transport infrastructure deficit. The program, which extends to 2016, covers national roads, public transportation, and regional airports under a 10-year envelope agreed to with the department of finance—a period twice as long as that used for other areas of investment (Laursen and Myers, 2009). In the United Kingdom as well, long-range planning for transport investment has been guided in the past by a seven-year budget guideline provided to the department for transport by the treasury (Laursen and Myers, 2009).

- the *ex post evaluation phase*, which establishes lessons to be learned for future project formulation and management.

Public investment management initiatives taken since the early 1990s all emphasize the need for an effective project cycle. They differ only in the specific tools and procedures used at key decision points in the cycle. A number of countries have adopted the "gateway" model first introduced in the United Kingdom, which combines strategic reviews at key points throughout the project cycle with risk assessment, to determine whether a project may pass from one phase to the next. The reviews can be centralized or decentralized, with a growing tendency toward the latter. New Zealand's application of the gateway model puts the burden of responsibility on line ministries and agency managers, within established procedures and expectations (Table 10.2).

Other initiatives have focused primarily on developing the processes leading up to the financing decision point, with less emphasis on implementation and traditional ex post evaluation. This model is more widespread among emerging market economies and low-income countries, in which "development" remains a priority policy agenda and securing funding is the critical issue for public investment. Among the better examples are the National Investment Systems (known as SNIs) developed in Latin American countries, of which the Chilean model (outlined in Box 10.2) is the oldest and most developed (and includes ex post evaluations). Like the gateway model, the SNI model tasks central agencies mainly with defining procedures for line ministries and implementing agencies.

10.2.2. The Appraisal Process

Effective assessment processes require thorough reviews of the expected costs and benefits of each project, including comparisons among alternative projects. In countries in which investment appraisal is not constrained by fiscal considerations, the resulting approved pipeline of projects may exceed by several times the size of available resources. Furthermore, project appraisals in these countries tend to focus on whether each project is consistent with the country's broadly defined "development needs" rather than on cost-benefit or cost-effectiveness analysis.

While project appraisals may differ, the core objective is to ensure that the project proposals put forward are subject to detailed scrutiny and analysis, and that the portfolio of investment projects is compatible with the available resource envelope. Detailed guidance on substantive issues related to the preparation and assessment of projects is also commonly provided, such as how to conduct cost-benefit analysis and which shadow prices and discount rates to use in project assessments.[4]

However, few of the new initiatives have been particularly successful in addressing the optimism bias that can be found in many significant investment proposals. Box 10.3 outlines two types of measures to address optimism bias. The

---

[4] For a good example, see the U.K. Green Book, which can be found at http://www.hm-treasury.gov.uk/data_greenbook_index.htm.

TABLE 10.2

New Zealand's Gateway Review Process

Review	Objective	Description
Strategic assessment	Confirm the need for the project or program. Check that it is likely to achieve the desired outcomes.	This review is for programs and for projects in early stages of development. It investigates the direction and planned outcomes of the project or program, together with the progress of constituent projects. It is repeated over the life of the program or project at key decision points.
Business justification and options: Indicative business case	Determine how the business requirement can be delivered, and how affordability, achievability, and value for money can be established.	This project review comes after the draft indicative business case has been prepared. It focuses on the project's business justification, before the key decision on approval for a development proposal.
Delivery strategy: Detailed business case	Determine whether acquisition and delivery strategy are appropriate for the desired business change. Implementation plans are in place.	This review investigates the draft detailed business case and the delivery strategy before any formal approaches are made to prospective suppliers or delivery partners. The review may be repeated in long or complex procurement situations.
Investment decision	Determine whether project is still required, affordable, and achievable. Implementation plans are robust; investment decision is appropriate.	This review investigates the updated detailed business case and the governance arrangements for the investment decision. The review takes place before a work order is placed with a supplier and funding and resources are committed.
Readiness for service	Organization is ready to make the transition to implementation. Ownership and governance are in place for operation.	This review focuses on the readiness of the organization to go "live" with the necessary business changes and the arrangements for operational services.
Operational review and benefits realization	Confirm smooth operation, delivery of outputs, and achievement of benefits.	This review confirms that the desired benefits of the project are being achieved and the business changes are operating smoothly. The review is repeated at regular intervals during the lifetime of the new service or facility.

Source: New Zealand Government (2010).

first is to improve the forecasting of project costs; the second relies on incentives, including financial and criminal penalties, independent peer reviews, and public hearings. Some countries in which line ministries are responsible for project preparation and assessment have set up mechanisms to strengthen the quality of project preparation and appraisal without establishing centralized institutions for coordination and scrutiny.

BOX 10.2 Chile's National Investment System

The Chilean National Investment System (SNI), created in 1973, has a deeply rooted legal base in the constitution and in several laws and numerous regulations. Over the years, the system has built up significant capacity to appraise projects and to train others in investment planning and management.

The main objective of the SNI is to increase the quality of public investment by providing the government with a portfolio of viable and socially relevant investment projects. The SNI tries to eliminate "white elephant" projects during the preinvestment stages.

The purpose of the SNI is to force any investment initiative to abide by project life cycle analysis at both the preinvestment stage (idea or concept, definition or profile preparation, prefeasibility study, feasibility study, financing, and approval) and the investment stage (detailed design, investment, operation, and ex post evaluation). The SNI ensures that all public investment projects (including defense) comply with quality standards and norms for identification, formulation, evaluation, and analysis, enabling their transformation from investment ideas into investment project proposals and thereafter into investment decisions. Typical activities during key pre-execution stages of the SNI project cycle include the following:

- *Idea:* Identification of benefits, geographic locale, and objectives.
- *Profile:* Examination of technical and institutional alternatives; establishment of first-cost assessments for investment, operation, project life, and other requirements; delivery of a preliminary evaluation.
- *Prefeasibility:* Elimination of nonviable alternatives. Early assessment of financing. Study of all aspects: marketing, demand, technical, environmental, human resources, institutional. Delivery of financial, economic, and distributional appraisals, and sensitivity and risk analysis. Identification of the best alternative.
- *Feasibility*: Definition of key risk parameters. Arrangement of final financing scheme. More in-depth study of modules with highest risks, check of all assumptions.
- *Design*: Detailed engineering design, blueprints, and specifications; definition of all logistics; final adjustments before execution stage; drafting of bidding proposal.
- *Ex post evaluation*: Comprehensive approach focused on program and institutional performance, rather than traditional ex post evaluation of the investment.

The Social Development Ministry (termed the Planning Ministry before 2011) and the Budget Directorate manage the SNI, with the former responsible for analysis (including cost-benefit or cost-effectiveness analysis) and approval during the preinvestment stage as well as ex post evaluation, and the latter responsible for overseeing the investment stage. The sponsoring line ministry or agency initiates the idea, follows each step of the project cycle, and then takes over operations once the project is completed. The SNI approach emphasizes ex post evaluation to determine the efficiency and effectiveness of each investment through a feedback process that includes measurements of short-, medium-, and long-term results and compares predicted with actual performance of projects. Guidance materials and manuals, and a regularly updated bank of projects, underpin the SNI process and facilitate wide-ranging investment analysis.

Sources: Ley (2006); Mimica (2008). See also http://sni.ministeriodesarrollosocial.gob.cl/.

BOX 10.3 Addressing Optimism Bias in Investment Projects

Two types of reform measures were recommended by Flyvbjerg, Skamris Holm, and Buhl (2004) to correct for the optimism bias found in their study of large infrastructure projects: better forecasting methods and improved incentive structures.

To improve forecasting methods, the authors suggested using "reference class forecasting" to reduce inaccuracy and bias, particularly for nonroutine projects—stadiums, museums, exhibition centers, and other unique projects. Forecasts should be benchmarked against comparable (reference class) forecasts; costs and benefits should be made subject to reference class forecasting. The objective is not to forecast the specific uncertain events that will affect the particular project, but to place the project in a statistical distribution of outcomes from their class of reference projects. It requires three steps for each project:

1. *Identifying a relevant reference class of past projects.* The class must be broad enough to be statistically meaningful but narrow enough to be truly comparable with the specific project.
2. *Establishing a probability distribution for the selected reference class.* This requires access to credible empirical data for a sufficient number of projects within the reference class to make statistically meaningful conclusions.
3. *Comparing the specific project with the reference class distribution* to establish the most likely outcome for the specific project.

Reference class forecasting provides a better anchor for sensitivity analysis by introducing a historical basis for establishing the range of variations of costs and benefits. The initial large and costly compilation of historical information would be recovered after a few years through the benefits of more realistic assessments.

With regard to incentives, the authors propose the following institutional checks and balances to address optimism bias: (1) enhanced financial, professional, or even criminal penalties for repeated and unjustifiable biases in estimates of costs, benefits, and risks; (2) independent peer reviews, made available to the public; and (3) public hearings, citizens' juries, scientific conferences, and review panels that allow stakeholders and civil society to provide input or voice criticism. Budgetary incentives that discourage optimism bias can also be useful. If the private sector is involved, sovereign guarantees should be avoided to ensure risk is appropriately borne.

Sources: Flyvbjerg (2004, 2007).

10.2.3. Project Selection Mechanisms

As part of updating their budget procedures, many countries have introduced steps to ensure that key budget decisions for different sectors are made at the same time. Most advanced economies now have highly structured budget processes, with key decisions concentrated in specific cabinet or cabinet subcommittee meetings at predetermined steps of the process.

The same circumstances apply to public investment. Because project development progresses over long periods and projects reach key decision points at different times, there is a natural tendency for countries to approve investment projects on a continuous basis. However, many countries now make public investment decisions at cabinet meetings set aside for this purpose as an integral part of the budget process. Figure 10.1, taken from the U.K. Green Book, illustrates the integrated decision-making process for budgets and public investments used in

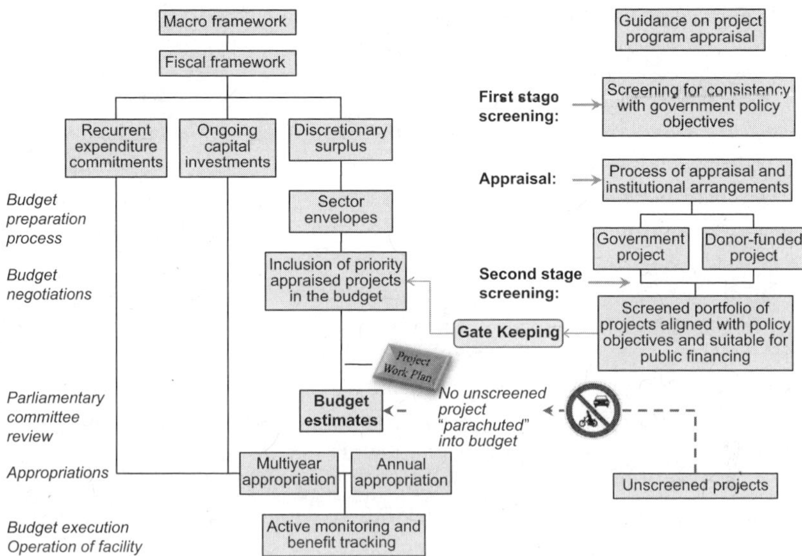

Figure 10.1 U.K. Integrated Budget and Investment Process

Source: U.K. Green Book.

Note: The U.K.'s Gateway function, managed by the Office of Government Commerce (OGC—an independent office of the treasury), examines public investment programs and projects at key decision points in their life cycles, ensuring that they can progress successfully through all stages from idea to implementation. The process is mandatory for procurement, information-technology-enabled and construction programs, and central government projects, and complements, rather than replaces, existing spending ministry internal processes.

An OGC review involves a thorough examination of the project, including its management structures, at initiation and then at key decision points in its development. There are five review stages in the process: three before the contract is awarded (business justification, delivery strategy, and investment decision) and two that appraise service implementation and confirm the operational benefits. The process includes an additional step, parallel to the five stages, to deliver strategic assessments at key decision points (such as program adjustments and resources reallocation). The OGC's brief is to ensure the delivery of value for money in public spending by providing policy standards and guidance on best practice in procurement and projects and estate management, and by monitoring and challenging departments' performance against these standards, grounded in an evidence base of information and assurance.

the United Kingdom. The traffic sign image in the figure indicates that there should be a prohibition against "parachuting" new investment projects into the budget outside the regular procedure and timeframe.

The specific decision rules for new investments may vary considerably across countries. Under binding MTBFs, line ministries are required to finance new investment proposals within their overall budget envelopes, which in some cases are further divided into separate envelopes for current and capital spending. This approach forces each line ministry to prioritize its spending internally. In countries that require special reviews for new initiatives, such as Australia, the decision to fund a new project follows the same review process as any other new policy initiative.

In environments in which MTBF ceilings are indicative only, final decisions on which projects to fund are generally left to the cabinet or one of its committees. A public investment planning framework, if in place, should ensure that only those projects that have been properly appraised and that are aligned with government priorities are considered for funding.

10.2.4. Managing Risks in Public Investment

The risks associated with public investment include construction cost and time overruns, higher-than-planned operating costs, and lower-than-expected revenues or benefits. These risks can affect the completion of the project or its operations once completed.

The identification and management of fiscal risks are particularly critical for projects funded through borrowing. The decision to borrow for a particular project is usually made after an in-depth cost-benefit analysis has been carried out as part of the project appraisal stage. The expected rate of return from the project may, however, be undermined by two potential fiscal risks most likely to surface only after completion of the project: the expected increase in future revenues may not materialize, and operating costs may be higher than anticipated.

Additional fiscal risks to the central government may also arise from guarantees provided to third-party borrowing, mainly borrowing by local governments and state-owned enterprises (see Chapter 5). The potential risks for central government are, first, that the third party has not undertaken an adequate cost-benefit analysis, and second, that the guarantee will be called if the third party's fiscal situation becomes unsustainable. Although central government may have performed due diligence at the time the guarantee was granted, because the third party is likely to have some degree of autonomy, the risk will always be present until the loan has been paid in full.

The new financing instruments available to public investment projects add a further layer of fiscal risk. In public-private partnerships in particular (see the third section of this chapter), risk sharing is built into often complex project agreements that few governments can adequately assess and monitor.

Linking a project's monitoring plan to the project's risks has been suggested by many analysts (CABRI, 2010). Such a contract management plan should identify and estimate the main project risks, and the individuals and institutions responsible for monitoring and managing each risk. The CABRI report groups risk indicators that should be monitored during project implementation as follows:

- early warning indicators that raise awareness before a risk translates into a major problem;
- indicators related to the technical and operational aspects of the project; and
- output indicators, which measure the different project dimensions (quantity, quality, cost, and on-time completion of a particular stage).

Financial measures are often used to address and mitigate risks, particularly if risks concern the typical implementation challenges that many projects face. Normally these financial measures include a mix of incentives that induce more effective project management behavior and more flexible budgetary procedures that account for the lumpy nature of public investments. Box 10.4 describes these measures.

10.3. FINANCING PUBLIC INVESTMENT

Public investment projects can be funded from a variety of sources—budget revenues, earmarked revenues, borrowing, external grants, and more recently, public-

BOX 10.4 Using Incentives and Carryovers to Foster Effective Project Implementation

Incentives. If investment cost increases are absorbed into annual budget revisions during the year, line ministries have an incentive to underestimate the costs in the original budget submission. One way to counter this is to make the line ministries responsible for ensuring that project costs stay within initial estimates by requiring them to cover, fully or partially, any cost overrun within their existing budget envelope. An incentive for efficient project implementation would be to allow the ministry or agency to retain cost savings from their investment projects, with the flexibility to reallocate the savings to other activities. However, this could also lead ministries and agencies to overestimate initial project costs. Although it is difficult to eliminate this kind of behavioral tendency, some countries have tried to mitigate it by, for example, allowing ministries and agencies to retain and reallocate only part of cost savings, or by limiting the alternatives to which the savings can be reallocated.

Carryovers. Increases and reductions in annual investment needs for a particular project are usually related to changes in the pace of project implementation, for a variety of reasons including weather, land disputes, contract or labor disputes, and so forth. Project costs may be reduced one year then expanded the following year in comparison with the original plan. To deal with unplanned project implementation issues, many countries have provisions in their legal frameworks that empower the ministry of finance to authorize line ministries and agencies to carry over unused appropriations for certain categories of spending, usually including investment spending, from one year to the next. Some countries also allow ministries to "borrow" forward from the following year's appropriation, if warranted for project implementation efficiency reasons. Carryover and borrow-forward authority is usually restricted to specific budget appropriations and purposes, and the amount is generally limited in the legal framework, typically up to 5 percent of annual appropriations.[a]

[a] For a more detailed discussion of carryovers, see Lienert and Ljungman (2009).

private partnerships. The preferred, and least onerous, methods of funding line ministries' investments projects are to use direct budget funding or earmarked taxes. However, only a few countries (mostly OECD members) can use these methods for any sizable portion of their public investment funding requirements. Most resort to a combination of funding using several, if not all, of the methods listed above, and often with different sources of funding for different stages of the investment process. This section briefly examines the challenges and risks with three of these funding methods, placing most emphasis on the more recent innovation in public investment funding—public-private partnerships.

10.3.1. Funding Investment through the Budget

In many advanced economies, capital spending is usually financed like any other budget spending: the net borrowing requirement is financed through a portfolio approach that minimizes the financing cost at a predetermined acceptable risk profile. Implementing agencies receive the necessary funds from the budget with no special, project-specific financing arrangements. General budget financing is particularly common in countries with high credit ratings and effective governments. The ministry of finance is able to borrow at a lower rate than any government agency or public corporation would be able to on its own, and no major incentive problems warrant moving the investment out of the government sector. This is still the predominant approach to public investment financing in European OECD members. Even in the United Kingdom, a leader in developing nontraditional approaches to financing public investment, regular budget financing still covers about 75 percent of the government's capital spending. The main risk in this approach comes from severe economic downturns, such as the global economic crisis, in which the cost of borrowing or the size of public debt becomes a significant fiscal concern. Public investment spending is often among the first areas targeted when fiscal consolidation is required.

Some countries adhere to a strong tradition of earmarking government revenues for particular purposes as part of the political decision-making process. The United States provides the clearest example of this approach, which has many different variations. The financing might be completely on-budget, as when a new tax or a tax increase is used to fund a new investment project. Financing might also be channeled through an extrabudgetary mechanism, a public-private partnership, or some combination of approaches.

10.3.2. External Financing

Some countries have access to concessional financing for investments or policy measures in specific sectors. In advanced economies, the clearest examples are the EU mechanisms that give grants and concessional loans for purposes such as science, the environment, and regional integration. The availability of low-cost financing improves the outcomes of cost-benefit and cost-effectiveness analyses and therefore contributes to somewhat higher investment in these priority sectors. Research suggests that EU regional support has had a significant and positive impact on the growth performance of European regions, particularly since the Structural Funds reform of 1988. However, the results also indicate that the economic effects of such support are stronger in developed countries, emphasizing the importance of accompanying policies aimed at strengthening country capacity (Cappelen and others, 2003).

In most low-income countries, financing limitations are perceived as a major obstacle to sufficient and efficient public investment. Even if governments have access to capital markets, that access is generally limited and borrowing costs are high. Governance and public administration weaknesses tend to undermine the quality of investment project preparation, assessment, and implementation. Often the only option for low-income countries is project-specific donor financing—grants or loans from bilateral donors or concessional loans from the World Bank and other development banks—which paradoxically requires more effective preparation, selection, and implementation of projects. The funding donor will generally insist on extensive oversight mechanisms that may undermine government ownership of the investment project and its integration within the country's budget and development processes. Box 10.5 highlights issues of public investment in donor-dependent countries.

BOX 10.5 Challenges of Managing Public Investment in Aid-Dependent Countries

Donor funding may introduce the following complexities into the management of public investment:

- projects selected according to donor preferences, with limited alignment with country priorities and limited coordination with similar projects funded by other donors, leading to potential duplications and overlaps;
- cofinancing arrangements that countries find difficult to meet, affecting timely receipt of external funds;
- volatility of donor disbursements due to factors outside the country's control;
- country difficulties in meeting general conditions required by donors, often not connected to the project;
- donors' preference for managing the projects outside the country's budget process with consequent failure to adequately budget for recurrent costs, undermining the value of the asset created;
- donors' introduction of their own procurement systems, undermining the existing public sector systems;
- donor funding not included in the government accounts, undermining transparency and accountability; and
- requirement to create separate project management units at the ministries responsible for implementation, staffed with personnel hired by donors at higher salaries, limiting the capacity-building opportunity and breeding discontent among the regular ministry staff.

Donors are addressing some of these challenges—by choosing budget or sector support instead of individual project support, or by accepting the use of government budgeting and accounting systems for their projects—which will gradually lead to the full inclusion of donor funds within government reporting frameworks.

10.3.3. Managing Public-Private Partnerships

The private sector can be involved in realizing public investments and providing public services in a number of ways. The most far-reaching approach is privatization, whereby the government divests itself of the responsibility to invest as well as to provide the public service. Many countries have privatized on a large-scale, selling their electricity, telecommunications, and water companies to private operators. At the other end of the scale, government may keep the ownership of an asset and the responsibility for operating it, but may employ private sector contractors to carry out some of the functions related to the asset, for instance, operations and maintenance of government buildings.

Public-private partnerships (PPPs) are intermediate arrangements between full privatization and full retention of the asset within the government. PPPs take many forms, but the term usually describes an arrangement in which a private sector entity designs, constructs, and operates an asset that provides a public service under a detailed contract with the government, and is compensated through government payments, user fees, or both. This mechanism has been used in many areas, but seems to be particularly popular for roads, bridges, office and school buildings, and prisons. PPP funding mechanisms are expanding and diversifying across both countries and sectors, particularly for economic and social infrastructure projects. Box 10.6 presents recent findings for EU countries.

BOX 10.6 Public-Private Partnership Investment in the European Union

Trends in number and value of EU public-private partnership (PPP) projects. According to the PPPs and public sector investments database (Blanc-Brude, Goldsmith, and Valila, 2007; Kappeler and Nemoz, 2010), in the EU, the total number of PPP projects with a capital value of €5 million or above steadily increased from 2 in 1990 to 144 in 2006, and then declined in 2009 to 118. The capital value of signed projects grew from €1.4 billion (US$1.9 billion) in 1990 to €29.6 billion (US$43.2 billion) in 2007, and then in 2009 declined to €15.7 billion (US$22.5 billion). Overall, some 1,340 contracts were signed between 1990 and 2009, with a total capital value of €253.7 billion (approximately US$358 billion). The number of PPPs signed fell from its peak in 2006 of 144 to 84 in 2011. Although the number of PPPs has continued to decline since 2009, the total value has been maintained or increased. In 2011, the total value was €17.9 billion (US$23.2 billion) owing to several contracts above the €1 billion (US$1.3 billion) mark, the largest being a high-speed rail link between Tours and Bordeaux in France—set at €5.4 billion (US$7 billion) (EPEC—the European PPP Expertise Centre).

EU PPPs by country and sector. Even though they are still limited, PPP markets have diversified by country and sector. The United Kingdom accounts for some two-thirds of all European PPP projects; Spain accounts for 10 percent; and France, Germany, Italy, and Portugal each account for between 2 and 5 percent. In project value, however, Portugal accounts for the third-largest share after Spain and the United Kingdom. Hungary is the largest in total value among new EU member states. Railways and motorways continue to dominate the high-value deals signed in 2011 (six of the seven highest-value projects in France, Italy, and the United Kingdom), but PPPs cover a wide variety of projects, including a €1.5 billion project for a new ministry of defense headquarters in France. In the United Kingdom education and health PPPs have increased over time, in both numbers and value (see below). Elsewhere, transport (mainly roads) still dominates, but countries are gradually diversifying their portfolios. For example, three countries (France, Germany, and Spain) have now developed and diversified their PPP contracts from the transport sector to social investments (schools, hospitals), prisons, and water and waste treatment and management.

PPPs and size of public investment. In all EU countries, PPP investment flows represent less than 1 percent of GDP, being significant only in Greece, Portugal, and the United Kingdom, and, to a lesser extent, in Ireland and Spain. Only in Portugal and the United Kingdom has PPP investment exceeded 10 percent of total annual public investment. At the sectoral level, on average, the results show that (1) in the transport sector, U.K. PPPs represented about 10 percent of total investment in 2000–07, and in the rest of the EU the figure has been increasing, reaching about 5 percent in 2005–08; (2) in the education sector, PPP investment in the United Kingdom has been increasing, reaching almost 20 percent in 2005–09, but in the rest of the EU it remains very small; (3) in the health sector, PPP investment has also increased rapidly in the last decade in the United Kingdom, reaching almost 40 percent of public sector investment, while remaining insignificant in the rest of the EU (Kappeler and Nemoz, 2010).

Effective use of PPPs requires the specialized knowledge and expertise often found only in private sector financial market environments, a reality that has led countries to establish dedicated units for this purpose. A dedicated PPP unit is an organization set up with full or partial aid of the government to ensure that the necessary capacity to create, support, and evaluate PPP agreements is made available to public sector contracting agencies. Some 17 OECD countries, at last count, have dedicated PPP units.

Proponents of PPPs argue that they provide better incentives for efficient construction and operation of capital projects. They argue that PPP contracts allocate risks between the public and private partners in accordance with their abilities to manage these risks. For instance, the public partner should carry the risk of political interference, whereas the private partner should take responsibility for ensuring that the asset is well maintained. Table 10.3 shows how the different risks in a PPP arrangement could be shared. Some research suggests that sizable cost savings can derive from PPP contracts compared with government implementation of major infrastructure investment projects, but this view is challenged by others.[5]

For a PPP contract to be worthwhile, the efficiency gains must be large enough to compensate for the increased financing and structuring costs. A PPP contract is usually based on commercial project financing, and the interest rate will generally be significantly higher than for centralized government borrowing. The contracting process involves considerable efforts from legal and financial experts, and the costs of their services tend to be high.

PPPs may allow a government to pursue public investments outside the regular budget. This is particularly true in a traditional, cash-based budgeting and accounting system, which will reflect only the annual payments made to the project entity over the lifetime of the project. This has been an important consideration for many cash-constrained governments and governments that for political reasons want to reduce the apparent size of the public sector. Some EU governments have indicated that the Maastricht Treaty limits on government deficits have been a driver in their pursuit of PPP-financed investment projects.[6]

However, the increasing use of accrual accounting, combined with developments in international accounting[7] and statistical standards, reduces the opportunities to use PPPs to distort fiscal realities (see Chapter 8). A ruling was issued by Eurostat in 2011 closing a loophole that allowed assets and liabilities to be excluded from the government's balance sheet; the new ruling states that if government revenues from tolls, for example, exceed 50 percent of the total value of

---

[5] For a discussion of different views on the impact of PPPs, see Connolly and Wall (2007). A comprehensive review of value-for-money assessments concludes that "individual PPP evaluations are still widely contestable and have a long way to go before claiming a strong degree of rigour" (Hodge, 2010, p. 105). Finally, Irwin (2012) suggests that the benefits of PPPs may be illusory.

[6] For a critical perspective on PPPs in general and the experience in Hungary in particular, see Stefanova (2006).

[7] See International Public Sector Accounting Standards (IPSAS) 32, "Service Concession Arrangements: Grantor," October 2011 (http://www.ifac.org/sites/default/files/publications/files/B8_IPSAS_32.pdf).

TABLE 10.3

Efficient Risk Sharing in a Public-Private Partnership Contract

Type of risk	Source of risk	Assumer of risk
Site-related risks: Site conditions; site preparation; land use	• Ground conditions, supporting structures • Site redemption, tenure, pollution or discharge, permits, community liaison • Preexisting liability • Native title, cultural heritage	• Construction contractor • Operating company or project company • Government • Government
Technical risks	• Fault in tender specifications • Contract design faults	• Government • Design contractor
Construction risks: Cost overrun; delay in completion; failure to meet performance criteria	• Inefficient work practices, materials wastage • Changes in law, delays in approval, and the like • Lack of coordination of contractors, failure to obtain standard planning approvals • Insured *force majeure* events • Quality shortfall or defects in construction, commissioning tests failure	• Construction contractor • Project company and investors • Construction contractor • Insurer • Construction contractor or project company
Operating risks: Operating cost overrun; delays or interruption in operation; shortfall in service quality	• Project company request for change in practice • Industrial relations, repairs, occupational health and safety, maintenance, other costs • Government change to output specifications • Operator fault • Government delays in granting or renewing approvals, providing contracted inputs • Project company fault	• Project company and investors • Operator • Government • Operator • Government • Project company and investors
Revenue risks: Increases in input prices; changes in taxes and tariffs; demand for output	• Contractual violations by government-owned support network • Contractual violations by private supplier • Other contractual violations • Decline in revenue • Decreased demand	• Government • Private supplier • Project company and investors • Project company and investors • Project company and investors
Financial risks: Interest rates; inflation	• Fluctuations with insufficient hedging • Payments eroded by inflation	• Project company and government • Project company and government
Force majeure risks	• Floods, earthquakes, riots, strikes	• Shared (or insurer)
Regulatory and political risks: Changes in law; political interference	• Construction period • Operating period • Breach or cancellation of license • Expropriation • Failure to renew approvals, discriminatory taxes, import restrictions	• Construction operator • Project company with government compensation per contract • Government • Insurer and project company • Government
Project default risks	• Combination of risks • Sponsor suitability risk	• Investors • Government
Asset risks	• Technical obsolescence • Termination • Residual value transfer	• Project company • Project company or operator • Government

Source: Grimsey and Lewis (2004).

BOX 10.7 Disclosure Requirements for Public-Private Partnerships

Information on public-private partnerships (PPPs) should be disclosed in government budget documents and end-year financial reports. In countries with significant PPP programs, disclosure could be in the form of a "Statement on PPPs." In addition to an outline of the objectives of the current and planned PPP program, and the capital value of PPP projects that are at an advanced stage of bidding, information for each PPP project or group of similar projects should include the following:

- future payment obligations for the following periods: 1–5 years; 5–10 years; 10–20 years; 20 years and longer;
- significant terms of each project that may affect the amount, timing, and certainty of future cash flows, valued to the extent feasible (e.g., contingent liabilities, the concession period, the basis upon which renegotiation is determined);
- the nature and extent of rights to use specified assets (e.g., quantity, time period, or amount as appropriate), obligations to provide or rights to expect provision of services, arrangements to receive specified assets at the end of the concession period, and renewal and termination options;
- whether the PPP assets (or any part thereof) are recognized as assets on the government balance sheet, and how the project affects the reported fiscal balance and public debt;
- whether the PPP assets (or any part thereof) are recognized as assets either on the balance sheet of any special-purpose vehicle, or in the private partner's financial statements;
- any preferential financing for PPPs provided through government on-lending or via public financial institutions;
- future expected or contingent government revenue, such as lease receipts, revenue or profit-sharing arrangements, or concession fees; and
- any project financing or off–balance sheet elements such as contingent liabilities provided by entities owned or controlled by government. Signed PPP contracts should be made publicly available. Within-year fiscal reports should indicate major new contracts that have a short-term fiscal impact.

Source: Hemming and others (2006).

government payments to the private partner in a PPP project, the project should remain on the balance sheet of government. The IMF recommends that, even for PPPs deemed primarily to be in the private sector, government should provide extensive disclosure of project risks and future payments in the budget documents (see Box 10.7).

10.4. IMPACT OF THE GLOBAL ECONOMIC AND FINANCIAL CRISIS ON PUBLIC INVESTMENT

During the crisis (2008–09) and subsequent recession, many OECD countries implemented stimulus packages. On the expenditure side, the packages tried to focus on timely, temporary, targeted investments that were ready to be implemented rapidly,[8] such as increasing spending on infrastructure projects and maintenance of roads and buildings.

[8]This section draws on OECD (2011).

Public investment programs amounted to 11.1 percent of total public spending in 2008 and 9.3 percent in 2009, equivalent to 4 percent of GDP in 2009 (compared with 3.3 percent in 2006). The countries most proactive in including public investment in their stimulus packages were Australia, Canada, France, Germany, Mexico, Poland, the Republic of Korea, Spain, and the United States. Given that subnational governments are responsible on average for two-thirds of OECD investment spending, these governments played a key role in several countries in executing the stimulus packages. By the end of 2010, most countries had allocated more than 90 percent of their stimulus funds.

Since this stimulus period, advanced economies have made large cuts in public investment, in many cases more than any other spending item (IMF, 2012). In emerging market economies, however, the increase in capital spending early in the crisis had not by 2012 been rolled back. Despite the possible negative consequences in the medium term on potential growth, many advanced economies have reverted to procyclicality. Although government financing of public investment through the budget has been hard hit by the crisis, so has financing through PPPs. The PPP markets in Europe have contracted, accompanied by changes in risk allocation and in finance instruments, as discussed in Box 10.6.

10.5. CONCLUSION

This chapter assesses the changing role for public investment as a specialized area of public financial management. It argues that public investment management and planning have evolved in line with the new PFM innovations discussed in the preceding chapters, mainly by becoming more integrated into the overall fiscal management and budgeting processes. However, certain specialized public investment management tools are still needed. New public investment management tools have been developed and existing ones revamped, with an emphasis on a more strategic approach to managing public investment within the wider PFM framework. The key conclusions about the impact of the new PFM tools on public investment are summarized below. Despite their benefits, these tools have shortcomings and do not address all of the weaknesses of traditional public investment management.

MTBFs have been effective in bringing the public investment component of spending into the budgeting mainstream and within fiscal constraints, and, along with performance budgeting, in countering the tendency toward dual budgeting. However, the time horizon of MTBFs is too short for large infrastructure projects in particular and investment planning in general, which partly explains why countries have been unwilling to abandon the planning framework, though some countries have adopted long-term investment commitment processes to address this problem.

Performance budgeting, along with the accrual approach, may create a more comprehensive environment for investment planning around a broader set of service delivery objectives, in which future operating costs can be kept under regular review throughout the investment period. Risk management should be an integral part of project management and should be practiced at every stage of the project cycle. Its objective is to identify, assess, and manage significant risks that could derail project execution. Once the risks have been identified and assessed, they should be monitored continuously until the end of the project.

The new generation of public investment planning systems create a commonly accepted framework, with clearly defined procedures, for making decisions at key stages of a project's life cycle, which is complementary to the new PFM tools of medium-term and performance budgeting.

Finally, although most countries would prefer to fund their public investment projects directly from the budget—as is done in advanced economies that have ready access to bond markets to fund their budget deficits—many have to seek external sources to fund individual projects, which requires additional effort, creates new risks, and potentially distorts policy priorities. Investment project funding (public-private partnership arrangements in particular) has opened up new opportunities that budget or borrowing constraints would otherwise have denied, but has also introduced new challenges and risks that most governments remain ill equipped to adequately address.

REFERENCES

Works Cited

Blanc-Brude, Frederic, Hugo Goldsmith, and Timo Valila, 2007, "Public-Private Partnerships in Europe: An Update," Economic and Financial Report No. 2007/3 (Luxembourg: European Investment Bank).

Blanchard, Olivier J., and Francesco Giavazzi, 2004, "Improving the SGP through a Proper Accounting of Public Investment," Discussion Paper No. 4220 (London: Centre for Economic Policy Research).

Cappelen, Aadne, Fulvio Castellacci, Jan Fagerberg, and Bart Verspagen, 2003, "The Impact of EU Regional Support on Growth and Convergence in the European Union," *Journal of Common Market Studies*, Vol. 41, No. 4, pp. 621–44.

Collaborative Africa Budget Reform Initiative (CABRI), 2010, "Ensuring Value for Money in Infrastructure Projects in Africa." Available via the Internet: http://www.cabri-sbo.org/en/programmes/infrastructuredialogue.

Connolly, Ciaran, and Tony Wall, 2007, "Public Private Partnerships: The Logic of Myths" (Belfast and Newtownabbey, Northern Ireland: Queen's University Belfast/University of Ulster).

Dahan, Momi, and Michel Strawczynski, 2010, "Fiscal Rules and Composition Bias in OECD Countries," CESifo Working Paper No. 3088 (Munich: CESifo Group).

Flyvbjerg, Holm, 2004, "Procedures for Dealing with Optimism Bias in Transport Planning: Guidance Document," paper prepared for the U.K. Department for Transport (London).

———, 2007, "Eliminating Bias in Early Project Development through Reference Class Forecasting and Good Governance," in *Decisions Based on Weak Information: Approaches and Challenges in the Early Phase of Projects*, ed. by Kjell J. Sunnevag (Trondheim: Norwegian University of Science and Technology [NTNU]), pp. 90–110.

———, Mette K. Skamris Holm, and Soren L. Buhl, 2004, "What Causes Cost Overrun in Transport Infrastructure Projects?" *Transport Reviews*, Vol. 24, No. 1, pp. 3–18.

Galí, Jordi, and Roberto Perotti, 2003, "Fiscal Policy and Monetary Integration in Europe," *Economic Policy*, Vol. 18, No. 37, pp. 533–72.

Grimsey, Darrin, and Mervin K. Lewis, 2004, *Public Private Partnerships—The Worldwide Revolution in Infrastructure Provision and Project Finance* (Cheltenham, UK: Edward Elgar).

Hemming, Richard, and others, 2006, "Public-Private Partnerships, Government Guarantees, and Fiscal Risk" (Washington: International Monetary Fund).

Hodge, Graeme, 2010, "Reviewing Public-Private Partnerships: Some Thoughts on Evaluation," in *International Handbook on Public-Private Partnerships*, ed. by G. Hodge, C. Greve, and A.E. Boardman (Northampton: Edward Elgar).

International Monetary Fund (IMF), 2012, *Fiscal Monitor: Taking Stock: A Progress Report on Fiscal Adjustment,* October (Washington).

Irwin, Timothy, 2012, "Accounting Devices and Fiscal Illusions," IMF Staff Discussion Note No. 12/02 (Washington: International Monetary Fund).

Kappeler, Andreas, and Mathieu Nemoz, 2010, "Public-Private Partnerships in Europe before and during the Recent Financial Crisis," Economic and Financial Report No. 2010/4 (Luxembourg: European Investment Bank).

Laursen, Thomas, and Bernard Myers, 2009, *Public Investment Management in the New EU Member States: Strengthening Planning and Implementation of Transport Infrastructure Investments* (Washington: World Bank).

Ley, Eduardo, 2006, "Appraisal of Public Investment: Chile" (Washington: World Bank).

Lienert, Ian, and Gösta Ljungman, 2009, "Carry-Over of Budget Authority," PFM Technical Guidance Note (Washington: International Monetary Fund).

Mehrotra, Aaron, and Timo Välilä, 2006, "Public Investment in Europe: Evolution and Determinants in Perspective," *Fiscal Studies,* Vol. 27, No. 4, pp. 443–71.

Mimica, Edgardo S., 2008, "Managing Project Appraisal: The Chilean Experience," presentation at Workshop on Experiences in Public Investment Management, Istanbul, Turkey, February 28–29.

New Zealand Government, 2010, "The Gateway Process: Manager's Checklist," State Services Commission.

Organisation for Economic Co-operation and Development (OECD), 2011, *Making the Most of Public Investment in a Tight Fiscal Environment: Multi-level Governance Lessons from the Crisis* (Paris).

Stefanova, Anelia, 2006, "The Role of the Public Banks in Financing Infrastructure Construction via the PPP Scheme: The Experience from Hungary" (Liben, Czech Republic: CEE Bankwatch Network).

Other Resources

Afonso, Antonio, and Miguel St. Aubyn, 2009, "Macroeconomic Rates of Return of Public and Private Investment: Crowding-In and Crowding-Out Effects," The Manchester School, Supplement 2009, pp. 21–39.

Denmark, Ministry of Finance, 2006, "Introducing a Cost-Based Appropriation System" (Copenhagen).

Eurostat, 2004, "Treatment of Public Private Partnerships," News Release No. 18, February 11.

Ferris, Tom, 2008, "Managing Public Investment: Overview of Ireland's Experience of Public Investment Management—with Particular Emphasis on Transport Projects," Public Investment Workshop, Istanbul, Turkey, February 29.

Handjiski, Borko, 2009, "Investment Matters: The Role and Patterns of Investment in Southeast Europe," World Bank Working Paper No. 159 (Washington: World Bank).

Hasnain, Zahid, 2011, "Incentive Compatible Reforms: The Political Economy of Public Investments in Mongolia," Poverty Reduction and Economic Management Unit (Washington: World Bank).

Jacobs, Davina F., 2009, *Capital Expenditure and the Budget,* IMF Technical Notes and Manuals Series (Washington: International Monetary Fund).

Jenkins, Glenn P., 2008, "Project Appraisal and Public Sector Investment Decision Making" (unpublished presentation).

Kamps, Christophe, 2004, "The Dynamic Effects of Public Capital: VAR Evidence for 22 OECD Countries," Kiel Working Paper No. 1224 (Kiel, Germany: Kiel Institute for the World Economy).

Kappeler, Andreas, and Timo Valila, 2007, "Composition of Public Investment and Fiscal Federalism: Panel Data Evidence from Europe," Economic and Financial Report 2007/02 (Luxembourg: European Investment Bank).

Klakegg, Ole Jonny, Knut Samset, and Ole Morten Magnussen, 2006, "Improving Success in Public Investment Projects: Lessons from a Government Initiative in Norway to Improve Quality at Entry" (Trondheim: National University of Science and Technology [NTNU]).

Lane, P., 2003, "The Cyclical Behaviour of Fiscal Policy: Evidence from the OECD," *Journal of Public Economics*, Vol. 87, No. 12, pp. 2661–75.

Naidoo, Kuben, 2007, "Capital Budgeting in South Africa," presentation at the Fourth Annual Seminar of the Collaborative Africa Budget Reform Initiative, "Are We Asking the Right Questions? Embedding a Medium-Term Perspective in Budgeting," December 13–15.

Peree, Eric, and Timo Valila, 2005, "Fiscal Rules and Public Investment," European Investment Bank, Economic and Financial Report 2005/02.

———, 2007, "A Primer on Public Investment in Europe, Old and New," European Investment Bank, Economic and Financial Report 2007/01.

Perotti, Roberto, 2004, "Public Investment: Another (Different) Look," IGIER.

Robinson, James, and Ragnar Torvik, 2002, "White Elephants," Centre for Economic Policy Research (CEPR) Discussion Paper No. 3459.

Scandizzo, Pasquale, and Mauro Napodano, 2011, "Public Investment Management: Linking Global Trends to National Experiences: The Evolution of International Best Practices."

Schwartz, Gerd, Anna Corbacho, and Katya Funk, 2008, *Public Investment and Public-Private Partnerships: Addressing Infrastructure Challenges and Managing Fiscal Risks* (Washington: International Monetary Fund).

Spackman, Michael, 2001, "Public Investment and Discounting in European Union Member States," *OECD Journal on Budgeting*, pp. 213–260.

———, 2002, "Multi-year Perspective in Budgeting and Public Investment Planning," National Economic Research Associates.

Toigo, Pietro, and Robert Woods, 2006, "Public Investment in the United Kingdom," *OECD Journal on Budgeting,* Vol. 6, No. 4.

Vizzio, Miguel Angel, 2000, *Los SIP en América Latina y el Caribe*, Serie Política Fiscal # 09, CEPAL, Marzo.

Wagenvoort, Rien, Carlo de Nicola, and Andreas Kappeler, 2010, "Infrastructure Finance in Europe: Composition, Evolution and Crisis Impact," EIB Paper 1/2010 (Luxembourg: European Investment Bank).

CHAPTER 11

Accrual Budgeting: Opportunities and Challenges

ABDUL KHAN

Governments are becoming increasingly familiar with accrual-based financial reporting, but to date only a few have implemented accrual budgeting. As a result, no widespread understanding of the underlying concepts and the practical implications of adopting this reform has yet developed. This lack of experience is perhaps one reason for the diverse views about what accrual budgeting is and how it affects various aspects of public finance, including fiscal policy, appropriations, funding of agencies, and cash management and control. This chapter provides an overview of the key concepts related to accrual budgeting with a view to clarifying some of these issues and underscoring both the opportunities and challenges presented by accrual budgeting.

More specifically, this chapter discusses the core characteristics of accrual budgeting that distinguish it from cash budgeting. It explains that there is no unique model of accrual budgeting, as illustrated by the different frameworks adopted by various governments, including those of Australia, Austria, Canada, Denmark, New Zealand, Switzerland, and the United Kingdom. In addition to these central governments, some state and local governments in these and other countries also use accrual budgets.

This chapter is divided into five sections. The first section defines accrual budgeting; the second discusses how accrual budgeting works in practice. The third and fourth sections examine the potential benefits of, and challenges in, adopting accrual budgeting. The last section reviews the prerequisites for successfully implementing accrual budgeting.

11.1. WHAT IS ACCRUAL BUDGETING?

The term "accrual" refers to a fundamental accounting concept concerning the timing of recognition of economic events in financial reports. Accrual accounting is a system of accounting in which transactions and other flows between institutional units are recognized when economic value is transferred, increased, or lost, regardless of the timing of the related cash receipts or payments. This contrasts with the cash basis under which transactions and other events are recognized only when the related cash is received or paid. "Accrual" when applied to accounting and reporting—as in accrual accounting—indicates the preparation of ex post financial statements on an accrual basis, in accordance with applicable accounting principles and standards. Trends in the development and use of accrual accounting are discussed in detail in Chapter 8.

The literature provides no single agreed-on definition of accrual budgeting. In this author's view, accrual budgeting means application of the accrual concept to the preparation and presentation of the budget. This is consistent with Lüder and Jones' (2003) definition. Accrual budgeting entails planning that includes revenues and expenses in the budget of the year in which the underlying economic events are expected to occur, not necessarily in the year in which the related cash is expected to be received or paid (Khan and Mayes, 2009). Accrual budgeting also means that the estimated impact of budget decisions will be planned for and included on the projected government balance sheet. A stricter definition requires that spending ministries be given budgets that are defined according to accrual concepts—and, in particular, that the budget set quantitative limits through appropriations in the annual budget law or by administrative directive on the expenses that they incur rather than on the cash payments they make (Blöndal, 2004; Robinson, 2009).

Accrual budgeting requires the application of generally accepted accounting principles (GAAP) in the preparation of the budget. Accrual is not an overriding concept in accrual budgeting or accounting; for example, understandability, relevance, reliability, and comparability are key considerations in the preparation of accrual-based financial information (IPSASB, 2000). Tensions between these concepts could naturally arise, and judgment may have to be exercised to strike an appropriate balance. For example, estimating budgeted tax revenue on an accrual basis could be subject to significant uncertainty; therefore, the estimate may be considered unreliable. In such a case, the accrual-based estimate may have to be revised and a measure that is closer to a cash-based estimate may have to be accepted. Thus, the reliability concept overrides the accrual concept in this example. Similarly, the lack of a reliable measure may lead to nonrecognition of specific expenses, assets, and liabilities both in budgets and in financial statements. This is not a departure from accrual budgeting and does not mean that the budget is based on "modified accrual." On the contrary, accrual-based standards would usually mandate such treatment in these circumstances.

Although allocative decisions are made in accrual terms under accrual budgeting, the accrual budget still recognizes the cash implications of budgetary decisions. Accrual budgeting implies the use of accrual operating statements and cash flow statements. Finally, although accrual appropriations can be a feature of accrual budgeting, as more fully discussed below, the concept is broader than appropriations alone because it also refers to the provision of the accompanying prospective financial information about the implications of the government's plans.

11.2. ACCRUAL BUDGETING IN PRACTICE

11.2.1. Application of the Concept

The specific features of the accrual budgeting frameworks countries have adopted vary widely. Countries may choose to emphasize different analytical measures of fiscal policy, their appropriations and funding arrangements may vary, and the ways they manage cash may differ. The common element in these otherwise disparate frameworks is the application of the accrual basis—in conjunction with other applicable accounting and budgeting principles and practices—to quantify and present the financial implications of the government's budgetary policies and programs (see Box 11.1).

Accrual and cash budgets are not mutually exclusive concepts. Under accrual budgeting, the cash flow implications of budget decisions should be measured and reported through a "budgeted" or prospective cash flow statement, as discussed

BOX 11.1 Definitions of Accrual Budgeting in Country Practice

The Australian National Commission of Audit (NCoA)[a] stressed the importance of accrual principles when recommending that the government adopt accrual budgeting:

> The Commonwealth government should formally adopt *accrual principles* [emphasis added] as the basis for an integrated budgeting, resource management and financial reporting framework both at the agency level and at the aggregate budget sector level. (Australia, NCoA, 1996)

The United Kingdom also uses a definition that emphasizes the use of the accrual (or resource) concept for planning and control purposes:

> Resource budgeting involves using *resource accounting information* [emphasis added] as the basis for planning and controlling public expenditure. It supports the fiscal framework by distinguishing between resource consumption and capital investment and requires departments to match their costs to the time of the service delivery. (United Kingdom, H. M. Treasury, 2001)

New Zealand stresses the importance of the independently determined generally accepted accounting practices, including the accrual concept, in the preparation of its budgeted and ex post financial statements.

The Swiss federal government also identifies the adoption of internationally recognized accounting concepts and standards as a key objective of its New Accounting Model, which incorporates accrual accounting and budgeting (Switzerland, Federal Finance Administration, 2008).

Canada stresses the importance of accrual principles in determining one of its key fiscal indicators at the macro level, although it does not apply accrual budgeting at the agency level:

> [T]he budgetary balance is presented on a full accrual basis of accounting, recording government liabilities and assets when they are incurred or acquired, regardless of when the cash is paid or received. (Canada, Government of, 2010)

[a] The NCoA was formed in 1996 by the then newly elected Commonwealth (federal) government in Australia to undertake a review of the government's finances and make recommendations on necessary improvements.

later. Therefore, accrual budgets should not lead to a loss of information or of the management benefits of cash budgeting. Loss of cash information or management benefits would arise only if one starts with a definition of accrual budgets that excludes cash flow budgeting. This chapter discourages the adoption of such a definition because of its practical disadvantages (such as loss of cash information and control) but also because it is inconsistent with an accrual framework as defined by internationally accepted standards,[1] which consider cash an integral part of such a framework. More specifically, standards (Financial Reporting Standards Board of the New Zealand Institute of Chartered Accountants, 2005) and guidance (Institute of Chartered Accountants in England and Wales, 2003) that deal with prospective financial statements for both the public and private sectors generally require forecast cash flow statements to be included.[2]

11.2.2 Accrual Budgeting and Appropriations

A widely held view is that accrual budgeting necessarily requires accrual appropriations, which would be consistent with the budget's focus on annual appropriations and authorization of expenditures. However, not all spending is authorized each year; for instance, demand-driven items, such as unemployment benefits, tend to be governed by separate legislation. Moreover, budgets and their related documentation are increasingly used to provide information about the full financial implications of government policies and programs for the medium to long term, in addition to being a mechanism for legislative approval. Finally, even the accounting basis used to measure and present budgetary information can be different from the basis used for legislative authorization of expenditure.[3]

In line with countries' experiences and the definition of accrual budgeting adopted by the author, accrual budgets can accommodate an appropriations framework based on either an accrual-based concept of expenses and capital expenditure, cash-based expenditure, commitments, or a combination thereof. Although accrual appropriations are commonly interpreted as legislative authorization to incur an expense, capital expenditure, or a liability, another interpretation is that

[1] Among these standards are the International Public Sector Accounting Standards (IPSAS), the International Financial Reporting Standards (IFRS), and the IMF's *Government Finance Statistics Manual (GFSM) 2001.*

[2] One of the shortfalls of the European Stability and Growth Pact is that its requirements focus on a deficit that is based on a selective application of accrual concepts (it excludes depreciation and civil and military pension costs, usually two of the largest adjustments required to move from cash to accrual) and does not require cash flow statements (budget or actual) to be produced. This is not consistent with internationally accepted accounting or statistical standards, and makes the reconciliation between predominantly cash-based budgeting and accounting and the European System of Regional and National Accounts (known as ESA95) national account basis a difficult exercise.

[3] For example, the U.S. federal government uses a combination of obligations (commitments), accrual, and cash appropriations. However, the budget deficit calculation after the end of the year does not recognize obligations as expenditure. Instead, the budget deficit is calculated on the basis of mainly cash expenditure and selected accrued costs.

the amount to be appropriated is determined on an accrual basis, but the authority conferred by the appropriations still relates to cash payments. For instance, Australia has the latter type of appropriations. Cash appropriations are generally defined as the legislative authorization accorded to the executive to spend cash. Furthermore, budgets and appropriations—even when formulated in accrual terms—may not recognize expenses in an identical manner. Thus, in New Zealand, losses arising from changes in the market value of assets and liabilities are not appropriated. Therefore, accrual budgets recognize these losses in the budgeted financial statements, but they are not reflected in the appropriations.

Accrual budgets offer various options for, but do not mandate, an appropriations model. Just as the preparation of accrual-based ex post financial statements does not force governments to adopt any particular approach to management or decision making, the adoption of accrual budgeting does not require governments to appropriate money in any particular way. Accrual appropriations can also take different forms. Contrary to commonly held views, there is no unique model of accrual appropriations. New Zealand's framework is probably the closest to the "pure" form of accrual appropriations, with most expenses being appropriated on an accrual basis. Yet under the New Zealand framework, appropriations for capital contributions[4] and repayment of debt are cash based. Switzerland appropriates accrual-based expenses and capital expenditure, but does not allow appropriations for depreciation to be used for cash expenditure. Denmark appropriates accrual-based expenses but does not appropriate capital expenditure, which is financed by internal borrowing[5] and repaid through depreciation funding over the life of the asset (Denmark, Ministry of Finance, 2006). Finally, Australia appropriates accrual-based expenses (excluding depreciation) and capital expenditure, but the government selected this approach after considering and trying various alternatives, as discussed in Box 11.2.

Accrual budgets can also accommodate cash appropriations. Several options are discussed below:

- *Appropriate cash requirements as per budgeted cash flow statement.* New South Wales—the largest state in Australia—produces full accrual-based budgeted financial statements but appropriates on a cash basis. Canada determines its macro-level budget deficit or surplus—a key measure of fiscal policy—on an accrual basis, but still uses cash appropriations.
- *Appropriate the same cash-based amounts as in the previous option, but recognize the difference between the accrual-based amounts and the appropriations as a payable or receivable.* The accrual budgeting model recommended by the

[4] Increases in government investment in a department or public corporation to increase its output capacity or improve its efficiency.

[5] The Folketing (parliament) approves a borrowing limit for each agency in the appropriations bill. This grants authority to the minister to borrow to make investments. Exceptions to these appropriations arrangements are investments in infrastructure (roads, bridges, railways) and in national property (palaces, gardens, monuments of special cultural worth).

BOX 11.2 Australia: Appropriations under Accrual Budgeting

The National Commission of Audit (NCoA) in Australia recommended cash appropriations within an accrual budgeting framework. The NCoA was set up by the incoming government in 1996 to undertake a review of the Commonwealth's finances and recommended, among other things, the adoption of an integrated accrual accountability framework including accrual budgeting. The NCoA considered accrual appropriations but decided in favor of cash appropriations. The difference between the accrual-based amounts and the cash appropriations would be recognized as a receivable or payable in the agency's and the ministry of finance's balance sheet. The NCoA noted that the main advantage of this model is that the benefits of accrual budgets are obtained without any major change to the existing appropriations arrangements under cash budgeting. The NCoA stressed that although appropriations would be on a cash basis, it would not be seen in isolation but as part of a comprehensive financial plan that the accrual budget represents.

The Commonwealth Budgeting, Reporting, and Accounting (COBRA) Scoping Study (Australia, Department of Finance, 1997), set up by the cabinet to consider the implementation issues related to the NCoA recommendations, considered four different options for implementing accrual budgeting:

- Option 1: Accrual budgets and estimates with appropriations representing cash flow implications of accrual budgets (the option recommended by the NCoA).
- Option 2: Accrual budgets and estimates with accrual appropriations subject to agreed-on cash limits.
- Option 3A: Outcome- and output-based accrual budgets and estimates with accrual appropriations subject to agreed-on cash limits (preferred option).
- Option 3B: Purchaser-provider model with outcome- and output-based accrual budgets and estimates and accrual appropriations subject to agreed-on cash limits.

It is interesting to note that the options included both cash and accrual appropriations, and all the accrual appropriations models explicitly mentioned cash limits. The actual model implemented in the 1999–2000 budget was based on option 3A.

Beginning with the 2010–11 budget, the appropriations framework was amended and depreciation, amortization, and "make good" expenses were no longer appropriated. Instead, a departmental capital budget provides the appropriations for capital expenditure. However, other accrual-based items, including employee entitlements and accounts payable, continue to be appropriated. A full set of accrual-based budgeted financial statements is still published.

National Commission of Audit (NCoA) to the Australian federal government was based on this option (see Box 11.2).

- *Obtain legislative approval for both the accrual- and cash-based requirements including capital expenditure.* The United Kingdom adopted such an approach. Austria also adopted a framework requiring parliamentary approval of, and legal control over, both accrual- and cash-based amounts.

Accrual budgets can also be combined with commitment appropriations. Just as commitment appropriations have been incorporated into a predominantly cash-based budgeting framework by countries such as the United States, it would be possible to have accrual budgets but exercise legislative control at the commitment stage, possibly in conjunction with cash- or accrual-based appropriations (see Box 11.3).

BOX 11.3 Expenditure Control and Basis of Appropriations

Neither cash nor accrual appropriations may be fully effective in controlling public expenditure. Controlling cash payments (the traditional objective of cash appropriations) after a liability has been incurred simply leads to a buildup of arrears. Accrual appropriations would be more effective because control would be exercised before a liability is incurred. However, fully effective control can be exercised only when binding commitments are entered into, for example, through the issuance of a purchase order or the signing of a contract. Once the contract has been established and the goods or services delivered in accordance with the contract, the government may no longer be in a position to avoid the liability. It follows that in relevant circumstances appropriations should cover authorization of commitments, not just liabilities or payments. France has separate legislative approvals for cash expenditures and commitments. The U.S. federal government uses a combination of commitment, accrual, and cash appropriations.[a]

A sound internal control system (of which expenditure control is a part) should require controls to be exercised at a number of stages of the expenditure process. Thus, controls should apply during requisition, ordering (commitment), receipt of goods and services and acceptance of a liability (accrual), cash payment, and where applicable, consumption. This does not mean that accounting, budgeting, and appropriations should be undertaken on five different bases; rather, the accounting and budgeting system should facilitate the effective functioning of such controls through appropriate accounting processes, internal control systems, and reporting facilities.

[a] The U.S. government defines appropriations as budget authority to incur obligations (i.e., commitments) and to make payments from the treasury for specified purposes (U.S. Government Accountability Office, 2006).

Even the assets and liabilities reflected in the budgeted balance sheet may be included as part of the legislative oversight mechanism. For example, New Zealand allows departments to use the proceeds of the sale of assets, together with any working capital it holds, to purchase or develop assets without the need for any further appropriations. However, the budgeted net assets are incorporated into the appropriations system and agencies cannot exceed that level of net assets without seeking further authorization.

The discussion above should not be viewed as implying that there are no arguments in favor of accrual appropriations within an accrual budgeting framework. Proponents of accrual appropriations argue that consistency between the budgeting and appropriations bases unmistakably signals the change in culture in public financial management. The NCoA in Australia acknowledged this argument, but still decided to recommend cash appropriations partly to simplify the move to accrual budgeting. The Canadian Auditor General also commented that departments were not using accrual information effectively because their budgets and appropriations continued to be on a largely cash basis.

11.2.3. Control over Cash under Accrual Budgeting

A commonly held view is that under an accrual appropriations system, the ministry of finance would have no option other than to make the amount appropriated available to agencies in cash, regardless of the agencies' cash requirements.

Agencies would be free to spend the cash in the budget year or subsequent years. The ministry of finance would thus lose control over aggregate cash expenditure, which could have an adverse impact on the conduct of fiscal policy. As discussed above, accrual budgeting does not mandate accrual appropriations. So continuing with cash appropriations would be one way to avoid these risks. The following discussion examines ways in which even under accrual appropriations these risks can be avoided or minimized.

Accrual appropriations do not necessarily mean that agencies have to be given cash equivalent to their appropriations. If a government considered it necessary to give agencies only the cash they needed, this could be accommodated within an accrual appropriations framework. Accrual appropriations can be combined with cash control arrangements in a number of ways:

- Accrual-based amounts could be appropriated but specific elements of the appropriation could be designated for which no cash would be provided. The Swiss federal government has adopted such an approach (see Box 11.4).
- Accrual-based amounts could be appropriated but cash could be made available to agencies only as required. The difference between the appropriations and agreed-on cash requirements could be recognized as receivables or payables by the ministry of finance and the agency. The Australian state of Victoria has adopted this approach.

BOX 11.4 Control over Cash: Country Practice

Swiss federal agencies are effectively subject to ex ante limits on both an accrual and a cash basis. Although accrual-based costs are used to monitor agency performance, the government's debt-brake rule is cash based. Appropriations are analyzed among cash, noncash, and intragovernment items. Depreciation and accrued liabilities are considered noncash, whereas accounts payable are treated as cash. The system prevents any appropriation for a noncash item—for example, depreciation—from being spent in cash. Agencies are also not allowed to change their expenditure mix to reduce, for example, accrued liabilities (which are noncash) and increase cash expenditure.

The U.K. Parliament approves both resource requirements and net cash requirements. Although cash is not controlled directly through the budgetary system, the net cash requirement for "supply expenditure" is controlled through the "supply estimates processes." The Alignment (Clear Line of Sight) Project proposed that net cash requirements should continue to be part of the parliamentary limits. The Comptroller and Auditor General reviews compliance with both the net cash requirement and the net resource requirement limits. According to the U.K. Treasury, the Resource Accounting and Budgeting System, as the accrual-based framework is known, has led to an improvement, not a deterioration, in cash management.

New Zealand maintains control over agency cash requirements even though it focuses mainly on accrual indicators for fiscal policy purposes. Agencies submit cash profiles for the whole year as well as more detailed cash payments schedules; these are approved by the treasury, as are all subsequent changes. Agencies are required to reconcile cash requests back to appropriations to ensure that cash requests do not exceed authorized levels (New Zealand, The Treasury, 2010).

Thus, neither accrual budgeting nor accrual appropriation has prevented governments from exercising centralized control over cash. The key issue is whether and to what extent a government wishes to exercise such controls, which, in turn, depends partly on the focus of fiscal policy and any fiscal rules of the government, and on considerations such as the degree of flexibility to be given to managers.

Accrual budgeting neither mandates nor prohibits fungibility of cash and noncash items. It is sometimes argued that if an entity saves on accrual-based expenses, for example, on depreciation or provisions, the entity should be entitled to spend the saving in cash. Regardless of whether such arrangements improve managerial performance, from a fiscal management perspective, automatic and full fungibility may not be prudent. The United Kingdom started in 2006 with full fungibility, but subsequently revised the framework. Switzerland disallows fungibility. In Australia, savings in depreciation cannot be spent in cash.

The absolute amount of aggregate cash payments is not necessarily controlled through the annual appropriations process, regardless of whether the appropriations are on a cash, commitment, or accrual basis. For example, in some jurisdictions, such as the United States, selected appropriations relate to commitments, not just cash payments. Once such appropriations are voted on by the legislature and the commitment is incurred, the related cash payments can be made in future periods. Furthermore, annual appropriations may control only part of the total cash payments in a budget year. Other expenditures may be subject to different forms of budget authority, as in the following examples:

- In the United States, the largest federal programs, including entitlements for health care and social security, are not subject to annual review. The outlays are based on statutory formulas that define eligibility, and benefits are often adjusted for changes in the cost of living or other economic factors. According to U.S. Office of Management and Budget estimates, discretionary items in 2010 accounted for less than 40 percent of the total outlays (U.S. Office of Management and Budget, 2010).
- In Australia, "special appropriations" account for some 75 percent of annual expenditure. Special appropriations are used mainly when cash-limited appropriations might not be viable, for example, for social security payments. Special appropriations may also be used for loan repayments and intergovernment payments made under other agreements or laws.

It is often argued that control can be exercised only over the cash expenditures or the accrual-based expenses, but not both. Therefore, under accrual budgeting, controls should be over accrual items and no limits or controls over cash can be applied. A variation of this theme is that even if dual controls could be exercised, doing so would be undesirable because it would detract from the additional flexibility that accrual budgeting is supposed to provide to managers. The discussion in this section demonstrates that, in practice, governments continue to exercise controls over both cash and accrual items in one form or another. The nature and extent of the controls can vary and reflect, among other things, the balance between control and flexibility that each government considers appropriate.[6]

Finally, it is useful to note that the U.S. Government Accountability Office in a 2007 study found that all countries following accrual budgeting considered cash information to be important, especially for monitoring the country's fiscal position, even if fiscal indicators are accrual based. This was also true regardless of the specific models of accrual budgeting adopted by various governments.

11.2.4. Budget Documentation under Accrual Budgeting

A typical accrual budget includes a set of ex ante or budgeted statements. These are also referred to as prospective, forecast, or estimated financial statements; this chapter uses the term "budgeted statements." This information is ideally produced at the aggregate and the agency levels. The documents supplement other information in a full set of budget documents, such as the budget speech, a discussion of macroeconomic issues, measures to achieve policy objectives, and information about expected and actual performance.

- The budgeted operating statement presents budgeted revenues, expenses, and operating results, or some variations thereof, for example, net lending/borrowing as defined in the IMF's *Government Finance Statistics Manual (GFSM) 2001.*
- The ex ante cash flow statement presents budgeted cash inflows and outflows—usually analyzed by operating, investing, and financing activities—and, if desired, cash deficit/surplus.
- The prospective balance sheet presents projected assets, liabilities, and net equity.[7]

Lüder and Jones (2003, p. 35) suggest that "complete and explicit systems of accrual budgeting" would require the projection and disclosure in the budget of these three core budget statements. However, international practice varies. Although Australia and New Zealand[8] produce full sets of budget statements in accordance with GAAP, Canada and the United Kingdom do not. In addition, separate capital budgets may be prepared by agencies to present their capital expenditure plans and seek necessary legislative approval. Australia, Switzerland, and the United Kingdom make use of such capital budgets.

[6] In the private sector, budgeting for and managing both profitability and liquidity are considered critical parts of financial management. As a result, controls are routinely applied to both accrual and cash items.

[7] The operating statement and the balance sheet are also referred to in the literature as, respectively, the statement of financial performance and the statement of financial position.

[8] New Zealand follows a specific standard—Financial Reporting Standard No. 42: Prospective Financial Statements—to prepare its budgeted financial statements.

11.3. ADVANTAGES OF ACCRUAL BUDGETING

11.3.1. Accrual Budgeting and Fiscal Policy

Along with accrual reporting, accrual budgeting facilitates a move away from a focus on a single indicator of fiscal policy toward an approach that uses different indicators for different purposes. Governments and analysts have the flexibility to choose the indicators that are most relevant to them (see Box 11.5). Thus, conventional accrual-based budgeted financial statements would provide key indicators, such as operating balance, cash surplus/deficit, and net worth. The *GFSM 2001* measure—net lending/borrowing—adjusts the operating balance by writing back depreciation and deducting capital expenditure. Variations of these measures include gross operating balance, overall fiscal balance, overall primary balance, net financial worth, and gross debt or net debt as discussed in Chapter 8.[9]

By contrast, cash budgets provide a more limited set of fiscal indicators for fiscal policy analysis. By definition, these measures are based on cash flows and exclude measures based on assets and liabilities or revenues and expenses that do not involve cash flows in the budget year, such as pension entitlements, depreciation, and provisions and accounts payable including arrears. Analysts sometimes attempt to rectify the limitations of exclusively cash-based measures by including accounts payable and receivable, including arrears, but pension entitlements, depreciation, and provisions are often neglected. However, in this author's view, without an accrual-based framework, such adjustments may be ad hoc, selective, and at times even subjective.

Internationally accepted standards recommend fiscal indicators that are based on the use of accrual accounting concepts. For example, *GFSM 2001* identifies net operating balance as a summary measure of the ongoing sustainability of government operations, and net lending/borrowing as an indicator of the impact of government activities on other sectors of the economy. Both of these measures are based on accrual accounting concepts. The EU Stability and Growth Pact also uses a variation of accrual-based net lending/borrowing.

Box 11.5 shows that accrual budgeting does not mandate any particular measures for analysis and monitoring of fiscal policy. New Zealand uses measures that are the most closely based on accrual-based GAAP. Switzerland focuses on cash-based measures, although it uses the International Public Sector Accounting Standards (IPSAS) to prepare both its ex post and budgeted financial statements. A jurisdiction's preference for fiscal indicators may also evolve over time. Thus, Australia previously focused more on the accrual-based fiscal balance, but the underlying cash balance appears to be given more prominence in recently published budget documents.

---

[9] For an explanation of these and other analytical measures for fiscal policy, see Box 4.1 in *GFSM 2001* (IMF, 2001).

BOX 11.5 Fiscal Policy Indicators

This box summarizes the key fiscal policy indicators adopted by the countries that have introduced accrual budgeting as defined in this chapter.

New Zealand uses a set of indicators that are accrual based and derived from the application of generally accepted accounting practice to budgets. The key indicators used by New Zealand are operating balance, debt, and net worth.

The United Kingdom used the golden rule and the sustainable investment rule to guide its fiscal policy,[a] until suspending them in response to the global financial crisis. The golden rule was based on a measure that is similar in concept to net lending/borrowing, but includes depreciation. The temporary operating rule makes use of two fiscal aggregates: surplus on current budget (SOCB) and public sector net debt (PSND). SOCB is the difference between revenues and expenditure, measured on an accrual basis. Depreciation is counted as an expense but provisions are not. PSND is a measure of the stock of debt and includes gilts (government securities) and national savings less liquid assets, finance leases and on–balance sheet public-private partnerships, and lending for policy reasons, such as lending to students. Liquid assets, such as cash in deposit accounts, offset gross debt.

Canada uses a combination of cash and accrual measures to monitor fiscal policy. The two main measures are budgetary balance and financial source/requirement. Budgetary balance is the difference between revenues and expenses determined on an accrual basis. The financial source/requirement measures the difference between cash inflows and outflows.

Denmark's budget balance is determined in accordance with the Stability and Growth Pact (SGP). Net financing requirement and debt balances are also regularly reported and monitored.

Austria's accrual budgeting model retains the focus of fiscal policy on the deficit calculated in accordance with the SGP requirements.

However, Australia and Switzerland have adopted cash-based fiscal policy indicators. Australia focuses primarily on a cash measure for fiscal policy purposes. It uses the underlying cash balance, which equals the net cash flows arising from operating and investing activities.[b] Fiscal balance—equivalent to *Government Finance Statistics Manual (GFSM) 2001* net lending/borrowing—is also published. Switzerland's fiscal policy is focused on controlling aggregate cash expenditure. It is expressed through the debt-brake rule that requires cash revenue and expenditure to be balanced over the business cycle.

---

[a] Golden rule: Over the economic cycle, the government will borrow only to invest and not to fund current spending. Sustainable investment rule: Borrowing to finance investment will be set so as to ensure that net public debt, as a proportion of GDP, will be held over the economic cycle at a stable and prudent level.

[b] Underlying cash balance is equivalent to *GFSM 2001* cash surplus/deficit less earnings of a fund to finance pension obligations of government employees (Future Fund) that are to be reinvested to meet future superannuation payments and are therefore not available for current spending. *GFSM 2001* cash surplus/deficit is calculated as net cash flows from operating and investment activities less net acquisitions of assets under finance lease and similar arrangements.

11.3.2. Accrual Budgeting and Long-Term Fiscal Sustainability

No budgeting or accounting system alone can provide complete information about the public finances. Accrual budgeting is an improvement over cash budgeting in that it provides more information on the longer-term implications of policy decisions. However, it is not sufficient for fully assessing the intergenerational implications and sustainability of existing policies. Under the existing accrual accounting principles and standards, certain rights and powers of a sovereign government are not treated as assets and certain obligations of governments are not regarded as liabilities. Thus, the sovereign power of taxation is not recognized as an asset, and government obligations, for example, in respect of old age pensions and health care, are not recognized as liabilities.

The information about assets and liabilities in the government balance sheet, therefore, needs to be supplemented by other information when assessing long-term fiscal sustainability. Several governments—regardless of whether they follow cash or accrual budgeting—currently publish such information, although reports vary in form and content, frequency, and the number of years into the future their projections cover. The IPSAS Board (IPSASB) is currently working on a project on this topic and has issued an exposure draft (IPSASB, 2011).

11.3.3. Consistency between Budgeting and Reporting

Fiscal transparency and accountability are greatly enhanced if both budgeting and reporting are done on the same accrual basis (for countries that already use accrual financial reporting; see Chapter 8 for details on these countries). Using the same basis for both budgeting and reporting enables comparability between the budget as authorized and the actual results. It is argued that budgeting and financial reporting are closely related parts of an integrated resource management framework; therefore, providing consistent information about the state of public finances in this form will help inform the public debate (IMF, 2012).

Accrual budgeting can provide a framework for measuring and presenting the full financial implications of policies and programs and allows comparison of the budget with the ex post financial statements. For example, if a new policy leads to additional hiring, the cash appropriations for the budget year would represent only a part of the cost of this decision. Pension and other employee entitlements that may not have immediate cash implications, but will have significant impact over the longer term, would be shown in accrual-based budgets, but not in cash budgets. Information about the impact of policies on assets and liabilities received through ex post financial statements can, in some cases, be too late to influence important decisions. The budget process is the appropriate time for such decisions, and the budget documentation prepared at this stage should provide information about the full financial implications of the proposed policies.

11.3.4. Improving Information on Costs and Liabilities

Accrual budgeting initiatives are often associated with efforts to improve public sector performance through a range of measures, including (1) focusing on outputs and outcomes, (2) granting more flexibility to managers, (3) using a purchaser-provider arrangement to fund agencies, and (4) raising awareness of the cost of capital and the full costs of government operations. The capacity of accrual budgets to provide information about the full costs of programs or services—regardless of the timing of the cash payments—is important in assessing performance.

Accrual budgets also recognize the full costs of employee entitlements. Both accrual and cash budgets show annual cash expenditures on employee pensions and other entitlements, but accrual budgets also include accrued entitlements as part of expenses and disclose the stock of liabilities as part of the projected balance sheet, whereas cash budgets do not include such information.

Accrued employee entitlements can be a significant burden on future taxpayers, over and above the annual cash costs of salaries and pensions. Recognition of such costs and liabilities in the budget improves transparency. For example, the U.S. federal government's accrued employee pensions significantly exceeded the corresponding cash outlays during the period 1997–2005 (Figure 11.1).The published financial statements of the U.K. government showed that as of March 31, 2010, the public service pension liability of £1.1 trillion (US$1.67 trillion; 79.8 percent of GDP) was the largest item on the balance sheet and significantly exceeded government securities of £803.8 billion (US$1.22 trillion).

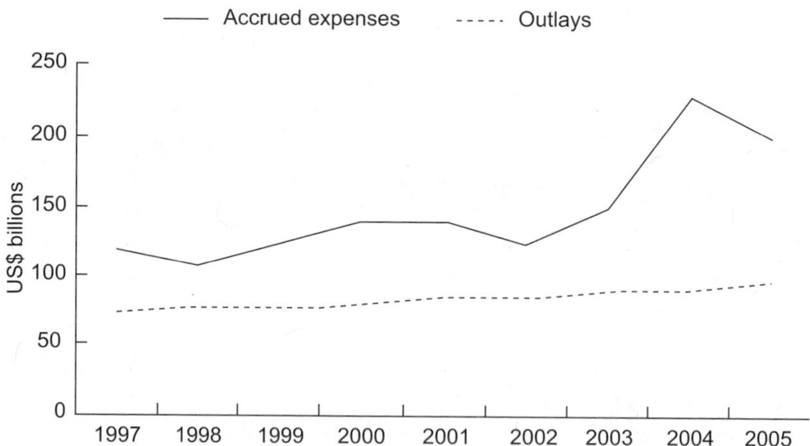

Figure 11.1 Accrued Expenses and Outlays for U.S. Federal Employee Pensions

Source: Congressional Budget Office (www.cbo.gov).

11.3.5. Managing Capital Assets

Capital expenditures are included in cash budgets if such expenditures are to be incurred in cash. Capital expenditures financed through arrangements such as public-private partnerships (PPPs), finance leases, or installment credits are not recognized in cash budgets except to the extent that they involve cash payments in the budget year. Liabilities incurred under such arrangements are also normally not recognized in cash budgets.

Accrual budgets, however, would recognize all budgeted acquisitions of fixed assets, regardless of whether they involve any cash payments in the budget year. If all budgeted capital expenditure is to be incurred in cash in the budget year, the estimated cash payments would appear in the budgeted cash flow statement. If part of the capital expenditure does not require cash payments in the budget year but involves the incurrence of liabilities,[10] the liabilities would be reflected in the projected balance sheet. The estimated increase in the stock of fixed assets is also reflected in the projected balance sheet.

Accrual budgets also recognize the depreciation of fixed assets as an expense in the budget year, whereas cash budgets do not. Accrual budgets include the consumption or usage of the assets, as approximated by depreciation, as an expense. A cash budget reflects only the cash expenditure to purchase assets in the budget year. An accrual-based budget will provide additional information on the depreciation of fixed assets as part of the full costs of government goods and services and the increase in stock of fixed assets and any liabilities (PPP or other) through the budgeted balance sheet.

This information can provide incentives to better manage capital assets, especially the acquisition, disposal, and maintenance of fixed assets. It facilitates better planning of investments and maintenance and also provides incentives for ministries and agencies to dispose of assets that are no longer used or needed. The allocation of capital asset acquisition costs, in the form of depreciation, over the course of the asset's useful life can help to eliminate the perceived bias against capital spending that occurs because it is recorded as one lump sum (see Chapter 10).

11.4. CHALLENGES IN IMPLEMENTING ACCRUAL BUDGETING

The challenges with adopting accrual accounting are discussed in Chapter 8. This section addresses the challenges in adopting accrual budgeting. Previous sections have addressed the risk of agencies shifting funds, if any, appropriated for noncash items to other operational uses. This section addresses three challenges in more

[10] Accounting standards and other pronouncements provide guidance on whether proposed arrangements constitute PPPs or finance leases and whether liabilities are incurred under such arrangements. This helps reduce the use of subjective criteria in determining whether to include or exclude relevant information from the budget.

detail: first the increased complexity, second the scope for manipulation, and third the costs and technical capacity required.

11.4.1. Greater Complexity

Accrual budgets are complex and may not be fully understood by politicians, civil servants, and the public at large. Planning for the impact of policies and programs in accrual terms is more difficult than simply forecasting expected cash flows. Assets and liabilities are affected not only by transactions, but also by the accounting and valuation policies adopted. Differences between cash and accrual deficits and the significance of each indicator may also be difficult to interpret. Presenting accrual budget information in a user-friendly manner can be challenging. Parliamentarians and the public may understand the budget less as a result of the technical nature of accruals.

Budgeting on a cash basis reduces the complexity of the budget presentation, but at the loss of the richer information provided by the accrual basis. Governments do not operate in a cash-only environment. They also incur liabilities and acquire assets. Preparing cash budgets does not mean that these complexities cease to exist. It simply means that the budgets do not provide complete information about the implications of proposed policies and programs.

11.4.2. Scope for Manipulation

Accrual budgeting, like cash budgeting, is susceptible to manipulation, especially given its complexity. For example, under accrual budgeting, governments can change fiscal estimates or results by changing assumptions about interest rates or tax arrears and other noncash items, adjusting discount rates, capitalizing expenses, and revaluing assets. Detecting manipulations in accrual budgets is also harder (Schick, 2007, and Chapter 1). Some of these issues are applicable to accrual accounting and reporting as well as accrual budgeting.

It is necessary to be aware of these risks and to take actions to mitigate them. Strict adherence to accounting standards is a key step in this direction. In particular, requirements about assumptions established in standards or guidance on prospective financial reporting should be followed. For example, standards usually require that assumptions be consistent among themselves and with the current plans, and be applied consistently. Standards also provide detailed guidance to enhance the reliability of assumptions, such as the use of an independent third party to review assumptions; the use of specialist skills to develop assumptions; consistency with an entity's documented strategies and plans; and documented analysis of related risks of future actions and events. In addition, all relevant information, including bases for assumptions, risks and uncertainties, and accounting policies, should be disclosed. Thus, the prerequisites for introducing accrual budgeting should not be underestimated.

The supreme audit institution could provide assurance to the legislature and the community about the assumptions, accounting policies, and other specific aspects of the budget. For example, the auditor general of the Australian state of

Victoria reviews the accrual budget and provides assurance that the budget is consistent with the target established for the key financial measure and has been properly prepared on the basis of the economic assumptions disclosed in the notes. The auditor general also comments on whether the methodologies used to determine the assumptions are reasonable. However, this kind of review of budget documentation is not standard practice and would have resource implications.

Cash budgeting, too, is subject to manipulation. Common techniques relate to timing issues, such as delaying expenses beyond the reporting period or accelerating revenue collection from the next reporting period. Other possible manipulations of cash budgeting include the following:

- reducing budget deficits by taking over pension funds and including the cash receipts from the funds as revenues but ignoring the more significant pension liabilities also assumed;[11]
- treating cash injections into public corporations as below-the-line items but—unlike in an accrual framework—not recognizing the loss in value of these investments; and
- entering into PPPs and finance lease or installment payment contracts under which only the budget year cash flows are recognized whereas the significant liabilities (and contingent liabilities) are ignored.

Some of these manipulations could, in a pure cash budgeting framework, fail to be categorized as manipulations. Manipulation of assumptions or asset valuations under an accrual budgeting framework would normally be regarded as departures from GAAP, and the necessary disclosure of assumptions and accounting policies would help users detect them.

11.4.3. Costs and Capacity Requirements

Some of the more significant costs of moving to accrual budgeting include developing a register of government assets; evaluating government assets; and recruiting and paying for staff with the technical know-how to inform and train the ministry of finance, spending ministries, and politicians on the new system. These costs would also be incurred to implement accrual accounting and reporting even if accrual budgeting is not adopted; however, accrual budgeting would probably require more skilled staff and more sophisticated information technology facilities.

Registering and valuing assets is a complex and time-consuming task. Many governments have not maintained up-to-date registers of assets. Asset valuation is difficult in the public sector because governments own public assets—such as monuments—that are unique and do not lend themselves to valuation. Assets can be valued according to historical cost or current value; each method has its pros

[11] For example, the Portuguese government took over the pension fund of private sector bank employees in 2011, and the United States in 1997 assumed the assets and liabilities of the pension system of the District of Columbia's teachers, police officers, and firefighters.

and cons, but valuation will be time consuming regardless of the method chosen. Again, these challenges would be faced when accrual accounting is implemented, even if accrual budgeting is not adopted.

Historically, the public sector has not employed many qualified accountants and financial managers, but it also has not engaged in overly complex financial transactions. With the growing importance of employee entitlements, including pensions, and financial instruments such as derivatives, leases, and PPP transactions, the skills of accountants and financial managers have had to improve. If accrual budgeting is considered necessary and useful, governments should realize that a substantial increase in accounting expertise and staffing is required, and these reforms should be timed accordingly.

11.5. PREREQUISITES

11.5.1. A Phased Approach to Implementation

A phased approach would help to manage the considerable challenges involved in implementing accrual budgeting. Different models of accrual budgeting are available and the degree of complexity can, at least to some degree, be contained by selecting a relatively simple model as a first phase of a progressive move to accrual budgeting. Thus, accrual budgeting could initially be applied to financial assets and liabilities but not nonfinancial assets. Another way of phasing may be to use accrual information in fiscal policymaking and budget planning while keeping appropriations on a cash basis. Accrual appropriations could be considered as part of a subsequent phase. Advanced reforms such as providing fungibility between cash and noncash items and other incentives could be considered when the more fundamental aspects of the accrual budgeting framework have been implemented and are operating satisfactorily.

Once the choice to introduce accrual budgeting is made, the steps to build up the capacity and infrastructure (e.g., systems) need to be properly analyzed. Based on experience to date, an advanced economy that can access the necessary skilled resources could probably implement accrual budgeting in two to five years.[12] Countries with only rudimentary systems and processes and limited access to skilled resources may need much longer to adopt such a framework.

11.5.2. Political Support

Political support at both the executive and the legislative levels is critical for successful implementation. The legislature should be supportive of such reforms to improve transparency and accountability. The executive should also be a supporter of the reform, particularly given its potential to improve management of

[12] In Australia, the decision to implement accrual budgeting was made in 1997, and the first accrual budget was submitted to parliament two years later for fiscal year 1999/2000.

costs and assets and liabilities. The reform process should start with clear and explicit decisions at the highest level of the executive, for example, the cabinet. The initial political support should be continuously reinforced through a concerted change management and communication program. In particular, proposed changes to the appropriations framework and to the form and content of budget documentation, including the new budgeted financial statements, should be explained to the legislature and agencies as they are developed and before they are formally adopted.

11.5.3. A Sound Cash Budgeting System

A sound cash-based budgeting framework is an essential foundation for initiating a reform program to implement accrual budgeting. A clear and transparent budget process; a history of reliability of cash estimates; and effective budget execution, accounting, and financial reporting systems should be in place before accrual budgeting reforms are contemplated.

11.5.4. Accrual Accounting

Whether accrual accounting must be implemented before accrual budgeting is a subject of debate. A phased approach may be helpful in managing the complexities and progressively developing the technical capacity and general understanding of accrual concepts and methods. Australia and the United Kingdom used phased approaches. Austria, New Zealand, and Switzerland, however, adopted accrual accounting and budgeting simultaneously.

11.5.5. Technical Capacity

An appropriate mix of skills is essential for the successful implementation of accrual budgeting. Building up adequate capacity to prepare the necessary accrual-based estimates and analyze and interpret the estimates is likely to be a major challenge. Officials in charge of budget preparation may not have the necessary expertise in accounting concepts and principles. Nevertheless, these officials are essential for successful implementation because they have important institutional knowledge about the budget process and policy issues. Therefore, it is important to supplement, not transplant or displace, these existing skills. Institutions such as a national professional accounting body, a supreme audit institution, and an active parliamentary public accounts committee will also facilitate the transition.

11.5.6. Information Technology System

Implementing an accrual budgeting system will be a major project requiring significant resources. If at all possible, accrual budgets would be generated through an automated system that is integrated with the financial management information system. However, if full integration is not practicable, a budgeting system that interfaces with the financial management information system may be an acceptable alternative.

11.6. CONCLUSION

Adoption of accrual budgeting remains a relatively new reform with different frameworks adopted by different countries. Despite the varying frameworks, presenting ex ante and ex post information on a consistent accrual basis can improve transparency and accountability and facilitate decision making. Accrual budgeting does not inevitably lead to accrual appropriations or any particular model of funding, and it does not necessarily imply any loss of control over cash. The degree of flexibility to be given to managers over cash and accrual items is a matter for governments to decide.

Nevertheless, governments contemplating a move to accrual budgeting should not underestimate the challenges. A systematic analysis of the current framework and the changes necessary to move to accrual budgeting should be undertaken. Strong political support and a good cash-based system are among the prerequisites for a successful move to accrual budgeting. If necessary, a phased approach could be adopted, under which different transactions are progressively brought within the purview of the accrual budgets as capacity and skills improve. Thus, it may be possible to apply accrual budgeting initially to financial assets and liabilities but continue to budget for nonfinancial assets on a cash basis. Similarly, the more ambitious reforms designed to improve incentives and performance, if desired, may be attempted only after the basic features of the accrual budgeting framework have been put in place. Countries could also decide to implement accrual accounting and reporting first and adopt accrual budgeting at a subsequent stage.

REFERENCES

Australia, Commonwealth of, Department of Finance, 1997, "Commonwealth Budgeting, Reporting and Accounting (COBRA) Scoping Study" (Canberra).

Australia, Commonwealth of, National Commission of Audit (NCoA), 1996, "Accounting Framework of the Commonwealth: Current and Proposed," in *Report to the Commonwealth Government* (Canberra).

Blöndal, Jón R., 2004, "Issues in Accrual Budgeting," *OECD Journal on Budgeting*, Vol. 4, No. 1, pp. 103–19.

Canada, Government of, 2010, "Canada's Economic Action Plan, Year 2, Budget 2010: Leading the Way on Jobs and Growth," Department of Finance Canada (Ottawa).

Denmark, Ministry of Finance, 2006, *Introduction to a Cost-Based Appropriations System* (Copenhagen).

Financial Reporting Standards Board of the New Zealand Institute of Chartered Accountants, 2005,"Financial Reporting Standard No. 42: Prospective Financial Statements" (Wellington).

Institute of Chartered Accountants in England and Wales, 2003, *Prospective Financial Information—Guidance for UK Directors* (London).

International Monetary Fund (IMF), 2001, *Government Finance Statistics Manual 2001* (Washington).

———, 2012, *Fiscal Transparency, Accountability, and Risk* (Washington). Available via the Internet: http://www.imf.org/external/np/pp/eng/2012/080712.pdf.

International Public Sector Accounting Standards Board (IPSASB), 2000, *IPSAS 1, Presentation of Financial Statements* (London).

———, 2011, *Reporting on the Long-Term Sustainability of a Public Sector Entity's Finances,* Exposure Draft 46 (Toronto: International Federation of Accountants). Available via the Internet: https://www.ifac.org/sites/default/files/publications/files/IPSASB_RepLong-Term_Sustainability_of_Public_Finances.pdf.

Khan, Abdul, and Stephen Mayes, 2009, *Transition to Accrual Accounting,* Technical Notes and Manuals No. 09/02 (Washington: International Monetary Fund).

Lüder, Klaus, and Rowan Jones, 2003, *Reforming Governmental Accounting and Budgeting in Europe* (Frankfurt am Main: Fachverlag Moderne Wirtschaft).

New Zealand, The Treasury, 2010, *Treasury Instructions* (Wellington). Available via the Internet: http://www.treasury.govt.nz/publications/guidance/instructions.

Robinson, Marc, 2009, "Accrual Budgeting and Fiscal Policy," *OECD Journal on Budgeting,* Vol. 1, No. 1, pp. 1–28.

Schick, Allen, 2007, "Performance Budgeting and Accrual Budgeting: Decision Rules or Analytic Tools?" *OECD Journal on Budgeting,* Vol. 7, No. 2, p. 109–38.

Switzerland, Federal Finance Administration, 2008, "The New Accounting Model of the Swiss Confederation," *OECD Journal on Budgeting,* Vol. 8, No. 1, pp. 1–31.

United Kingdom, H.M. Treasury, 2001, *Managing Resources: Full Implementation of Resource Accounting and Budgeting* (London).

United States Government Accountability Office, 2006, *A Glossary of Terms Used in the Federal Budget Process* (Washington).

———, 2007, *Accrual Budgeting Useful in Certain Areas but Does Not Provide Sufficient Information for Reporting on Our Nation's Longer-Term Fiscal Challenge* (Washington). Available via the Internet: http://www.gao.gov/products/GAO-08-206.

United States Office of Management and Budget, 2010, *Historical Tables and Analytical Perspectives, Budget of the U.S. Government, Fiscal Year 2011* (Washington: U.S. Government Printing Office).

PART IV

Adapting to the Environment: PFM Reform in Developing Countries

CHAPTER 12

Bridging Public Financial Management and Fiscal Decentralization Reforms in Developing Countries

ANNALISA FEDELINO AND PAUL SMOKE

Decentralization—the allocation and sharing of the responsibilities for managing public functions and resources across levels of government—has been a pervasive international trend since the early 1990s.This chapter explores the links between reforms to public financial management (PFM) and those to decentralization. Conceptually, a strong and potentially beneficial relationship exists between these two initiatives. In reality, in many countries, coordination and sequencing of decentralization and PFM reforms has proved to be elusive. This chapter examines how more integrated analysis and better coordination in the development and execution of PFM and decentralization reforms could potentially yield benefits for overall public sector performance.

PFM reforms are vital to attaining the expected benefits of decentralization because of their critical role in maintaining fiscal discipline, efficient provision of public services, and accountability of subnational governments to higher levels of government and local constituents. At the same time, subnational governments can be critical actors in the effective implementation of PFM reforms in countries where they have been fiscally empowered through decentralization reforms. Correctly balancing central control and local autonomy is important. PFM reform that is too lax creates the risk of enabling irresponsible local government fiscal behavior, whereas PFM reform that is excessively controlling can unduly constrain the local autonomy essential for effective decentralized systems.

The relationship between these reforms, however apparent in principle, is not well established in practice. The two reforms are often formulated through independent initiatives and managed by different national agencies with somewhat contradictory perspectives and objectives. In developing countries, the two reforms are typically supported by different international organizations with similarly conflicting priorities. Conflict between those responsible for PFM reform and those responsible for decentralization policy is not uncommon, and the two efforts may also start at different times. The resulting reforms can create mixed signals for actors and generate inconsistencies in government systems and operations. These types of conflicts occur in virtually all countries undertaking PFM and decentralization reforms, but are ubiquitous in developing countries where policy and management coordination failures are particularly risky and institutional capacity is often spread too thin, chasing too many and sometimes incompatible reform initiatives. These countries are thus the primary focus of this chapter.

This chapter neither advocates nor discourages decentralization but instead takes the position that different types and degrees of decentralization are appropriate in different circumstances.[1] In addition, it recognizes that once decentralization is undertaken, often for political reasons, backtracking to any substantial degree is difficult. One critical role of PFM reform is to help ensure that subnational governments conscientiously execute their new responsibilities as they evolve under decentralization, but how exactly this happens will differ from case to case. The analysis highlights that more robust contextual assessment than is normally undertaken can help analysts understand the implications of country context for links between decentralization and PFM.

Throughout, this chapter emphasizes the need to take political economy factors into account in developing and linking the two types of reform. Both PFM and decentralization have important technical dimensions. The design and implementation of these potentially complex and far-reaching reforms, however, is not a purely technical exercise, and treating them as such can lead to infeasible or problem-ridden reform programs that may even hinder the attainment of the results they seek to promote. Similarly, treating these reforms as purely political measures without sound commensurate technical underpinnings may also doom them to fail.

This chapter is organized as follows: The first section discusses the array of challenges to aligning PFM and decentralization reforms in practice and considers how context may influence starting points for PFM and decentralization and also affect the relationship between national and subnational PFM systems. The second section covers selected case studies that illustrate the diverse links between PFM and decentralization reform and how they play out in the reform process, and considers how they might be developed better to improve results in the future. The final section draws some preliminary general lessons from the case studies and other available information about how to more robustly analyze and effectively bridge PFM and fiscal decentralization reforms.

12.1. CHALLENGES TO BRIDGING PFM AND FISCAL DECENTRALIZATION

Trying to ensure that PFM and decentralization reforms are coordinated and not independently developed, as is typically the case, can yield potential benefits. Making this coordination happen, however, is not straightforward, even in the

[1]The literature analyzing the benefits and pitfalls of decentralization is well known, but its results are relatively weak and inconsistent. Ahmad and Tanzi (2002), Ahmad and Brosio (2006), Smoke (2006), Shah (2008), and Fedelino and Ter-Minassian (2010) provide literature reviews of conceptual and empirical arguments in favor of and against both fiscal and general decentralization.

best of circumstances. A number of factors complicate the coordination of PFM and decentralization reforms, including

- differences in the nature and objectives of the two reforms;
- contrasting institutional frameworks for developing reforms, and variations in the form of the intergovernmental system;
- diversity of starting points for reform;
- prioritizing, timing, and sequencing of reform processes as driven by political, technical, and other considerations;
- commonly excessive focus on normatively sound design of reforms relative to pragmatic implementation; and
- the role of international development and financial institutions, particularly in aid-dependent countries.

Each of these factors is explored in more detail below.

12.1.1. Differences in Nature and Objectives of PFM and Fiscal Decentralization Reforms

The commonly weak links between PFM and decentralization reform are not difficult to understand. First, the two reforms differ somewhat in their nature. The key elements of PFM are similar for all governments and concentrate on the management of public finances and the budget process (budget preparation, approval, and execution). PFM reforms are generally concentrated on financial management issues and are more technical and uniform than decentralization initiatives. Moreover, PFM reforms are, in many cases, adjusted to specific country contexts.

In contrast, decentralization involves a greater variety of diverse reforms related not only to fiscal, but also to political (subnational elections and accountability) and administrative (territorial, organizational, and nonfinancial procedural) concerns. Fiscal decentralization cannot be meaningfully divorced from these other dimensions because it cannot work effectively without them. In addition, these elements may collectively play out in highly diverse ways in different contexts, with varying degrees of functional empowerment, fiscal self-sufficiency, and autonomy across levels of government.[2]

For example, under decentralization more spending autonomy is often granted to subnational governments to improve service delivery. Fiscal federalism theory suggests that this initiative should result in improved (optimal) resource allocation if appropriate functions are decentralized. But without the mechanisms and conditions that create incentives for local administrators and politicians to perform (e.g., if local administrators are not following sound managerial practices, if local politicians are centrally appointed rather than elected, if local political

[2] Eaton and Schroeder (2010) provide a useful review of the literature on measuring and linking the various aspects of decentralization.

competition is limited), the lack of appropriate managerial practices and accountability to users of public services will hinder efficiency improvements.[3] A change in intergovernmental fiscal relations (in this case, spending autonomy) will not be meaningful unless it is appropriately linked to broader institutional and political contexts. Clearly, the nature of the intergovernmental system and the relative importance of various levels of government make obvious the need for different approaches to decentralization and for different types of related PFM and other systems and procedures.

Second, the objectives pursued through PFM and decentralization reforms may vary considerably in different circumstances. Although there are country variations and PFM reforms with diverse goals, ultimately PFM reforms tend to focus on achieving one or more of the core PFM objectives of maintaining a sustainable fiscal position, effective allocation of resources, and efficient provision of public services (see Chapter 1). Decentralization is often formally justified as a means to improve the performance of the public sector in meeting citizen needs, but the range of actual objectives is very broad, including improving democratic governance and promoting peace. Furthermore, particular objectives can have varying degrees of importance in different cases, requiring substantially different types of reform.

In some countries, decentralization is initially more focused on promoting democratic governance than on enhancing service delivery and fiscal accountability. For example, after decades of dictatorship and neglect of the poorest regions, Bolivia embraced decentralization in the late 1980s to strengthen democratic structures. Municipal elections were first held in 1987 (changes to regional governments came nearly two decades later). In postconflict or in-conflict countries, the primary objective of decentralization may be to maintain or promote peace and to develop greater political stability, as demonstrated by the experiences of Cambodia, the Democratic Republic of the Congo, Iraq, and Kosovo. Depending on governments' prioritization of the multiple objectives of decentralization, they may feel the need to pursue dramatically different sequences, trajectories, and paces of reform.

Third, a committed government may find it somewhat easier to start fresh with extensive PFM reforms than with an entirely new intergovernmental system. The obstacles to introducing PFM reforms may be lower partly because they are typically less political and visible to the public and thus attract less public debate and support or resistance than do decentralization reforms.

---

[3] Allocative efficiency can be undermined by devolution, however, if preferences are homogeneous (subnational governments have no informational advantage over the center), economies of scale are present (services cannot be provided efficiently by smaller jurisdictions), or externalities exist (subnationals do not take into account the effects of their decisions on other jurisdictions). Concerns have also been raised about subnational jurisdictions engaging in detrimental competition to attract mobile labor and capital (the "race to the bottom" via a reduction of taxes, among others) and about the risk of local elite capture and corruption once central oversight is removed. Conceptual thinking and empirical evidence on these latter issues, however, is far from conclusive. For more analysis of these points, see United Cities and Local Governments (2008, 2010).

12.1.2. Differences in Institutional Frameworks and Perspectives

Generally, different actors are involved in the design and implementation of the two types of reform. The institutional framework surrounding decentralization reform is usually more complex than that for PFM. PFM reform is normally (although not always and not exclusively) managed by the ministry of finance or national treasury. These agencies often have considerable authority over other state institutions by virtue of their control over national budgeting and financial management. Decentralization reforms are more typically, although again not always, managed by other agencies, such as the ministry of local government (e.g., Kosovo and Uganda), the ministry of interior (e.g., Cambodia), or the ministry of home affairs (e.g., Indonesia).

These national agencies responsible for local government oversight are commonly at odds with the ministry of finance, either because they are more pro-decentralization or because they are trying to take over some local government oversight functions that the ministry of finance may feel are under its jurisdiction. In addition, local government ministries rarely operate from a position of relative strength in the overall political and administrative landscape. They must rely on developing good working relationships with central agencies that define government-wide policies, such as the ministry of finance, civil service commission, and ministry of planning. They must also cooperate with those spending ministries and agencies that oversee and support delivery of public services, such as the ministry of education, the ministry of health, and the ministry of public works. Thus, for decentralization to work effectively, a broad range of actors with different perspectives and levels of influence must be accommodated. Effective coordination is critical but usually difficult to achieve owing to inherent and evolving tensions between the underlying roles and objectives of these actors.

Decentralization also involves the adoption of new systems and procedures, but it is rare for a national government to pursue aggressive comprehensive reform. Few governments, for example, seek a complete restructuring of territorial jurisdictions, even though there may be good fiscal, political, or administrative reasons to do so. Existing jurisdictions may be too small to be fiscally viable and to allow for economies of scale or the internalization of externalities in service delivery, or they may be too large to be well connected to citizens politically. However, the boundary changes needed to correct such problems are often strongly resisted. Thus, some institutional parameters that could improve the quality and impact of decentralization (and related PFM reform) may be difficult to modify substantially, at least initially.

12.1.3. Diversity of Context and Starting Points

Understanding the context in which PFM and decentralization reforms will be initiated is important for their design and implementation. In some cases in which reforms are being considered, a credible PFM system might already be in place, but is not being used properly. In other cases, some elements of a quality

PFM system may be in place, but others need to be developed. In still other cases, the current PFM system may be dysfunctional, nontransparent, and politically captured, and reformers face the challenge of building an entirely new system.

Decentralization may take various forms, including deconcentration, in which subnational administrative entities report primarily to higher levels of government; delegation, in which subnational entities are contracted to perform specific functions; and devolution, in which subnational administrative entities report primarily to locally elected councils. The latter type of reform has been the preferred practice in recent years, but many countries have or aspire to a mixed system that blends these various approaches, and different levels (intermediate versus local) can be given different roles.

In some cases, higher or intermediate subnational levels (states or provinces) have greater functions or more autonomy, such as in Ethiopia, India, and Vietnam. In other cases, lower levels (such as municipalities and districts) play a greater role or enjoy more autonomy than higher levels, as in Indonesia, Kenya (pre-2010 constitution), and South Africa. Sometimes such divisions of responsibility are primarily based on political consideration (e.g., empowering local levels to diffuse ethnic tensions associated with regional levels), but specific functional assignments are normally justified by the nature of specific services. Some services, such as garbage collection, street cleaning, and traffic and parking are naturally local, and the central government can relinquish control over them with little political or economic risk. Other services that have broader effects would be assigned to a higher level of government or shared among levels of government, and the center would likely retain some control over them.

In any of these cases, subnational administrative or government units may be at various stages of PFM development, and depending on the nature of the system, may have different relationships with national PFM systems. Normally, for example, deconcentrated levels are fully integrated into the national budget, whereas devolved levels are usually characterized by independent budgetary systems and norms.

Decentralization can also start from very different positions. In some cases, the term is used to refer to the reinventing or strengthening of subnational governments that already exist but have not been functioning well. Thus, reforms may target the improvement or replacement of existing systems and procedures, and may take place over varying periods of time and through different mechanisms. The Kenya Local Government Reform Program that began in the mid-1990s, for example, was intended to improve the performance of long-standing local governments by instituting new procedures and incentives and using innovative strategic reforms and learning-by-doing training.[4] The 1991 constitution of the former Yugoslav Republic of Macedonia, following independence from the Socialist Federal Republic of Yugoslavia, defined existing municipalities as the basic unit of local government. The center, however, continued to dominate

[4]This initiative is documented in Smoke (2003, 2008a, 2008b). The situation in Kenya changed with the adoption of a new constitution in 2010 that mandates substantial devolution.

public finances, and municipal elections were not held until 2005 as part of a new, multiethnic democratic order adopted in response to the ethnic Albanians' armed rebellion.

In other cases, decentralization means transforming existing local administrative units of the central government (deconcentrated system) into elected levels of more autonomous subnational governments, as occurred in Indonesia. Reforms thus attempt to realign accountability structures (usually changing the balance from primarily upward to a greater focus on horizontal and downward) with reformed or new systems and procedures supported by capacity building.

In extreme cases (usually postconflict or low-income countries), decentralization can involve the creation of subnational administrations or governments. In situations in which units of government are newly created or revamped, decisions must be made about which levels to create or empower, the nature of their relationships with other levels, and how to build appropriate new systems and procedures, including PFM systems, over time. This is the process under way in Cambodia as the country expands the decentralization reforms, initially limited to the commune level, to the district and provincial levels.

12.1.4. Reform Priorities and Sequencing

Another major concern in considering the relationship between PFM and decentralization reforms is the relative primacy of each from the perspective of the national government and external entities supporting reform programs. On the one hand, PFM is often seen as a building block or a precondition for fiscal decentralization, the contention being that PFM reform should lead fiscal decentralization reform. The argument is that as new (or expanded) responsibilities for managing public functions and resources are assigned and shared among various levels under decentralization reform, a sound PFM system ensures that these functions and resources can be properly managed and monitored—thus contributing to the success and sustainability of decentralization itself.

This approach, however, is more likely to be more feasible in countries where an orderly program of public sector reforms is being rolled out by a reform-minded government. But where decentralization was initially undertaken for broader and, from the government's perspective, more urgent, often political, objectives, it may not be feasible to postpone subnational reforms until sound PFM reforms and systems are substantially developed. Where some key decentralization parameters are already in place when PFM reform begins, the PFM agenda would ideally at least partially respond to the decentralization agenda rather than the adaptation being fully reversed.

Examples of such situations include countries in which subnational elections have been held as the result of perceived political urgency during a period of crisis or a major political turnover or in an immediate postconflict environment. Under such circumstances, it may be counterproductive for the new representative entities to be idle with no functional assignments, unable to show any results to the constituents who elected them, while state-of-the-art PFM reforms are being fully worked out and implemented. This was the experience in the newly created (Serbian-majority) municipalities in Kosovo. Following municipal elections in late 2009, new administrative structures were quickly established, but they were initially institutional shells preparing for the exercise of new functions, and the elements of the system, including PFM, to be phased in.

Although subnational governments should not be excessively empowered before basic PFM reforms are in place, they must perform some visible functions to validate their existence and begin to develop credibility with citizens, especially if the overall public sector is perceived to lack legitimacy. In such cases, PFM and decentralization reforms need to be built simultaneously rather then sequentially; PFM reforms are sometimes part of decentralization reforms even before an overarching PFM reform program begins.

In low-capacity, aid-dependent countries, decentralization may start as an externally funded parallel system intended to provide limited local services and to develop local governance ahead of formal decentralization or major PFM reforms. Such developments cannot be ignored when PFM reforms are being designed. In some cases, these parallel systems create better PFM processes at the subnational level than those being used by the central government. To automatically assume that they must be replaced by a normatively defined, comprehensive national approach could be counterproductive.

Cambodia's decentralization, for example, first emerged from an initially small donor-funded project that evolved into the creation of a modest local government (commune) system.[5] Local PFM procedures were piloted and revised as part of an integrated overall system, and they generally improved and reflected higher standards of reporting and monitoring than those of the central government's deficient PFM system. Although a major national PFM reform was later initiated, many of the old problems remain, and it is unclear which of these practices—commune, old national PFM, under-reform national PFM—will prevail subnationally as the central government empowers local governments above the commune level and the ongoing national PFM reforms are rolled out.

More generally, even if the subnational systems are less well conceived than best practices would require, PFM reformers may run the risk of creating more problems than they solve if they try to impose new normatively ideal reforms rapidly on nascent subnational systems. Thus, careful analysis and a strategic approach to reform are required.

12.1.5. Beyond Reform Design to Strategic Implementation

As noted above, best practice design has been a major thrust of public sector reform, especially when supported by international agencies. Inflexibly using demanding normative reform principles in developing countries often results in the proposal of systems that are far more advanced than what is in place in the country and will require massive changes to attain. The common approach of

---

[5] Smoke and Morrison (2011) review the Cambodia experience and the relevant literature.

building capacity by offering intensive training courses is rarely sufficient to build appropriate skills and modify the behavior of relevant actors. In addition, even when such systems are formally adopted, they may be partly neutralized by the continuation of business as usual by powerful actors.[6]

Given commonly experienced delays and diversions in bringing many well-designed reforms to life, more attention has been paid in recent years to implementation strategy.[7] The use of the platform approach to PFM reform is an example. This approach is discussed elsewhere (Chapters 1 and 14), so this subsection focuses on decentralization implementation.

Emphasizing implementation in no way minimizes the importance of using normative principles to envision and design the eventual intergovernmental system. It simply advocates framing the implementation of the desired system in the context of a well-considered process. So, for example, a key decentralization concern, such as obtaining an appropriate balance between legitimate national priorities and a degree of subnational autonomy that meets the basic requirements of decentralization, need not have a single, one-time resolution. Reformers may intend to allow significant subnational autonomy eventually, but in the early stages of reform, when subnational accountability and capacity are low, greater national control would be warranted. The issue, then, is how to prevent the system from stagnating in a centralized form that precludes subnational governments from exercising the autonomy associated with the potential benefits of decentralization.

One potential solution is to adopt an implementation process in which subnational governments are allowed to exercise greater fiscal autonomy or receive additional resources as they meet certain criteria. The implications for PFM reform, for example, might be to impose greater ex ante control on subnational fiscal decisions in the early stages of decentralization. As subnational governments demonstrate improved fiscal performance, the system can evolve toward greater reliance on ex post controls.

If capacity and readiness vary across jurisdictions at the same level, an asymmetric approach could be used, such that entities with demonstrated capacity are allowed to move faster toward greater autonomy than peers with less capacity. Asymmetric arrangements are often well suited to larger or more advanced urban centers, which are often better prepared to take on additional responsibilities. PFM-related triggers, such as complying with specific reporting and auditing requirements, could be used to guide such processes.

For example, the Public Debt Law of Kosovo allows municipalities to borrow if they have received an unqualified audit opinion from the auditor general for the previous two years. When the law came into effect in early 2010, only the capital, Pristina, was in a position to borrow.

---

[6] See, for example, de Renzio (2011) on PFM reforms and Eaton, Kaiser, and Smoke (2011) on decentralization reforms.

[7] Some attention to the implementation of decentralization may be found, for example, in Smoke and Lewis (1996); Bahl and Martinez-Vazquez (2006); Shah and Chaudhry (2004); and Smoke (2007, 2010).

Another type of strategic approach ties funding levels to compliance with certain financial or administrative requirements. Kenya's current Local Authority Transfer Fund, for example, is allocated by an objective formula, but the allocations can be reduced if local governments do not meet certain PFM requirements (Smoke, 2003). More broadly, performance-based grants have been used in countries such as Uganda to create various broader performance and capacity-building incentives for local governments.[8] None of these examples involves the adoption of an overall strategic approach, but the strategic elements inherent in each can provide guidance to reformers contemplating more comprehensive reforms.

12.1.6. Role of International Development Partners

International development partners have played a significant role in many public sector reform programs in developing countries, including those related to PFM and decentralization (Development Partners Working Group on Decentralisation and Local Governance, 2011). The development partner efforts have had two particularly pronounced effects. First, they have often been the driving force behind the imbalance discussed in the preceding subsection between attention to design and attention to implementation. Although more attention is now given to implementation, few countries seem able to create strategic implementation processes and use them effectively.

Second, international development partners are diverse and have their own objectives and priorities. In pursuing their respective objectives, it is not uncommon for them to generate new tensions or reinforce existing tensions between government agencies in charge of various aspects of public sector reform. Development partners have occasionally pursued PFM reform with little attention to decentralization reforms being supported by other development partners or different departments of the same agency (Uganda is one such example). Individual aspects of reform are difficult enough to deal with, and better coordination across reform areas is even more challenging. However, without improving coordination, the danger of wasting resources and placing reform programs on a collision course becomes even greater.

12.2. LEARNING FROM COUNTRY CASE STUDIES

This section reviews and compares three country cases. It illustrates how contextual factors, including political economy incentives, affect the nature and relative priority of the decentralization and PFM reforms being pursued. It also tries to document the positive and negative results to date in each country and their underlying causes and influences. Finally, suggestions are made for how the PFM–fiscal decentralization reform link might be improved in each case. These cases were selected because they illustrate different starting points and approaches

[8] See Steffensen (2010) for a detailed explanation and examples of performance-based grants used to date. Lewis and Smoke (2009, 2012) review the literature on other types of performance systems.

to decentralization and PFM reforms and because sufficient information is available to highlight details of useful issues. They are intended to provide a selective rather than an exhaustive illustration of the different approaches to decentralization.

The cases are

- *Indonesia*, which formerly had a deconcentrated system under strong central control that was rapidly and significantly devolved under a so-called big-bang reform in the wake of a major political and economic crisis;
- *Kosovo*, where significant PFM improvements took place ahead of an ambitious—and politically motivated—decentralization reform; and
- *Uganda*, where a major political shift allowed the development of a shared consensus and framework for strong local government, the support for which dissipated over time.

12.2.1. Indonesia

As in many ethnically diverse countries colonized by European powers, building national unity through centralization was a priority after independence, creating in Indonesia the foundation for the authoritarian Suharto regime. Attempts to decentralize in the 1970s and 1980s, often donor promoted, never gained political traction and largely involved deconcentration. In the aftermath of the 1997 Asian economic crisis, amid rising political tensions between the provinces and the center, the post-Suharto government pursued decentralization to hold a very diverse and weakly unified country together.[9] The government enacted a decentralization framework and adopted what has been called a big-bang implementation approach. Reform primarily empowered local governments in reaction to fears that strong provinces would generate regional conflicts, separatism, or federalism.

Indonesia has three levels of government—the central government, 33 provinces, and 510 local governments[10]—and a relatively advanced decentralization framework.[11] The legal framework introduced in 1999 and 2000 eliminated hierarchical relationships between local governments and higher levels and defined responsibilities of each level.[12] It devolved many functions, with only defense, foreign affairs, justice, monetary policy, finance, police, development

[9] Indonesia is the fourth-most-populous country in the world, comprising more than 17,000 islands, and more than 200 languages.

[10] There are two types of second-tier subnational governments, cities (*kota*) and districts (*kabupaten*). Since the 2001 reform, the number of subnational governments has increased, and it is expected to continue to do so (IMF, 2009).

[11] For more detailed discussion of fiscal decentralization in Indonesia, see Lewis (2003, 2005, 2006); Alm, Martinez-Vazquez, and Indrawati (2004); World Bank (2005); Kaiser, Pattinasarany, and Schulze (2007); Lewis and Oostermann (2008); Lewis and Smoke (2009); USAID (2009); and Lamont and Imansyah (2012).

[12] For details of the legal framework, see Laws 22 and 25 (1999) and Law 34 (2000); Law No. 28 (2009); and the constitutional amendment of 2000.

planning, and religion reserved for the center. Local governments must provide health, education, environmental services, and infrastructure, and may provide other services not legally reserved for higher levels. The provinces became responsible for services spanning multiple districts. As a result, subnational governments manage almost one-third of total public expenditures and carry out about half of total development expenditure.

Subnational revenue sharing is generous, but own-source revenues are weak relative to local government responsibilities.[13] The main source of subnational revenue is a general allocation grant fund based on a minimum of 26 percent of central government revenues, which accounts for about 60 percent of all transfers. The allocation of this grant to individual provinces and local governments is determined by a formula, with the latter receiving 90 percent of the pool. Even though the formula includes a redistributional component, it is not enough to affect the overall disequalizing impact of the system (IMF, 2009). Revenues from income taxes, the land and building tax, and natural resources receipts (oil, gas, mining, and so forth) are shared between the center and the subnational governments according to defined criteria that are primarily origin based. In addition, special allocation grants are allowed for earmarked transfers. Their share of total grants from central government is small but increasing.

Subnational own-source revenues were limited in the original decentralization law, but they are considerably more substantial for provinces than for local governments. The 2000 regional taxation law expanded the scope for own-revenue and allowed local governments to introduce new taxes. Local governments, however, adopted unsatisfactory revenue sources that were contested, and a new subnational revenue law in 2009 created a more prescriptive framework. This law did devolve the land and building tax, which is to be phased in through 2014, but local governments are not obligated to collect it. Some may not have the capacity to do so, and some may not need to do so given the generous revenue-sharing arrangements and lack of incentives for own-source revenue generation.

Local governments once borrowed extensively, mostly through mechanisms controlled by the ministry of finance. Although this was an improvement over the system it had replaced, it was still insufficient for robust local financing of much-needed infrastructure investment. Because local government borrowing performance deteriorated over time, with both poor loan allocation decisions from the centralized mechanisms and poor repayment, local borrowing remains limited.[14] Reform on this front has been slow, largely owing to internal disputes between ministry of finance departments over control of local government borrowing.

On the PFM front, Indonesia has not faced the same serious challenges to the subnational financial management system that have plagued a number of decentralizing countries. The PFM system was centralized in the Suharto era, and the systems and staff were initially transferred to the newly empowered local

---

[13] See Smoke and Sugana (2012) for a recent detailed review of the revenue system.

[14] According to the 2009 budget, outstanding loans of regional government at end-2007 (on-lent foreign loans and domestic loans from the central government) amounted to 0.02 percent of GDP.

governments, with modifications over time. Local governments keep their own budgets and bank accounts, subject to national regulation.

Overall, there has not been a major disconnect between PFM and decentralization, and many of the improvements adopted in the local government financial management system have attempted to move the system in a better direction. The immediate fiscal effects of decentralization were not disruptive because the basic PFM system remained in place, a substantial portion of local government staff was transferred from the deconcentrated bureaucracy, and as noted above, local governments had limited revenue autonomy. Thus, some historical factors and design features, regardless of whether intentional, constrained local fiscal autonomy, forestalling problems sometimes experienced with extensive and abrupt decentralization.

Despite the overall positive picture of a major rapid decentralization that avoided some of the fiscal challenges critics feared, issues remain. Beyond the challenges posed by weak local revenue autonomy and a nearly dysfunctional subnational borrowing system, a number of central government ministries continue to provide services that are supposed to be local functions, and subnational service performance delivery is highly uneven. Large aggregate local government surpluses (detailed figures for individual local governments are not available) suggest that some local governments do not have the capacity or incentives to meet their responsibilities effectively. In 2004, new laws weakened local government budgeting and civil service control, partly in reaction to lack of performance.

Although an established PFM system and diagnostics exist on paper, issues have also arisen on this front. Difficult debates between the ministry of finance and the ministry of home affairs have occurred over responsibility for the development and oversight of the subnational financial system. The capacity of local governments to operate that system effectively varies considerably, and the level of monitoring and reporting on outcomes is inadequate. Weak fiscal reporting capacity at the subnational level continues to limit fiscal policy management and coordination. State Finance Law 1/2003 prescribes that the consolidated central and local government budget deficits be limited to 3 percent of GDP, and that general government debt not exceed 60 percent of GDP. The central government has not established mechanisms for allocating fiscal objectives between central and local governments and ensuring compliance with the law. Moreover, the government is unable to monitor and report on its performance against these fiscal rules owing to the lack of timely general government financial statistics from subnational governments. Subnational governments are required by law to submit their budgets regularly and to report on budget execution to the central government, but long delays occur—sometimes as long as two years on the execution side—making it difficult for the ministry of finance to monitor local financial operations. In addition, development partners provide a variety of capacity-building activities for local PFM that differ somewhat in approach and geographic coverage, have not been comparatively evaluated, and are seen by some analysts as failing to support the development of a standardized national system.

Two broad issues underlie these weaknesses. First, Indonesia never established a coherent strategy or coordination mechanism to operationalize and implement its fiscal decentralization framework. A ministerial-level Regional Autonomy Review Board was empowered to design policy, but it is no longer influential. The ministry of home affairs has the strongest official role, but other central agencies, such as the ministry of finance, the national planning agency, and sectoral ministries, do not fully accept the ministry of home affairs' leadership. Overall, the coordination of decentralization policy remains weak and reform progress on some fronts is ad hoc and erratic rather than strategic and progressive.

Second, the development of subnational government accountability mechanisms is complex and difficult. Local civil servants accustomed to looking to their parent ministries are learning to pay more attention to elected local government councils. The councils are learning to deal with the civil servants who are supposed to report to them and the citizens who elected them, and citizens are learning how to hold councils and service providers accountable. Insufficient attention has been paid, however, to strategically fostering these accountability relationships critical to securing the potential benefits of decentralization and creating an environment conducive to further relaxation of central control over local government fiscal activities.

How Indonesia will deal with the need to develop decentralization more strategically, coordinate the central actors, improve horizontal and downward accountability, and further develop and institutionalize PFM and other technical capacity at the local level will determine how effective and fiscally responsible decentralization can be in the future. The government of Indonesia is starting to give more attention to the challenges of local governments and is considering a number of reforms and incentives to improve their performance, including experimenting with performance-based transfers, but none has yet gathered significant momentum.[15]

12.2.2. Kosovo

Fiscal decentralization in Kosovo is a political necessity. The Comprehensive Settlement Proposal[16] contains a blueprint for local self-government largely inspired by European models; by allowing municipalities significant autonomy, and even greater latitude to Serb-majority municipalities through asymmetric arrangements, the settlement seeks to promote democracy and mend ethnic tensions. Underpinning decentralization, territorial reorganization of municipalities—

[15]The papers from a conference marking a decade of big-bang decentralization in Indonesia and considering its future are presented in Lamont and Imansyah (2012).

[16]Since the end of the conflict in 1999, various attempts had been made to secure agreement with Serbia. The "Comprehensive Proposal for the Kosovo Status Settlement" (presented to the UN Security Council by Special Envoy Marti Ahtisaari in March 2007) failed to gain consensus and was subsequently withdrawn owing to a veto threat by Russia in the summer of 2007. The Kosovo government unilaterally declared independence in February 2008, and is implementing the proposal as its main political strategy.

the basic units of local self-governance—has proceeded rapidly. Political municipal elections for municipal assemblies and mayors were held in the 36 municipalities in November 2009, but were boycotted in three of the Serbian-majority municipalities in the country's north.

Although legislation grants municipalities significant competencies in key areas, most notably health care and education, their revenue autonomy has remained severely limited. Own-source revenues are scarce and poorly administered. The main local revenue handle, the property tax, is affected by low compliance rates and inadequate administration.

The move toward greater decentralization coincided with increasing macrofiscal pressures. Growth stagnated in 2009, and fiscal imbalances have grown. Following the enactment of municipal finance legislation in 2008, central grants to municipalities have increased by more than 50 percent, leading to a sharp rise in municipal spending (also driven by the political cycle);[17] at the same time, own-source revenues have remained virtually flat (the sharp increase in transfers may have weakened collection incentives). Thus, decentralization is creating tension between the need to ensure fiscal discipline (in a country that has adopted the euro and aspires to join the European Union) and the demands of and opportunities for greater autonomy for subnational governments.

PFM reforms preceded decentralization, and later came to support it. As Kosovo set out to rebuild its institutions following the conflict with Serbia, modern budget processes were introduced, including a comprehensive well-functioning centralized treasury system that enables production of timely and reasonable analytical reports (World Bank, 2007).

Local government budgets are executed through the central treasury system, and treasury control over local government spending levels has generally been effective. Municipalities are fully covered by the treasury single account (TSA) system (see Chapter 9 for a discussion of TSAs).[18] All municipal revenues are transferred to the TSA on a daily basis, and all expenditures are paid from the TSA. The treasury system is also the main source for reporting on municipal finances.

Central control, however, which has been viewed as the cornerstone of ensuring sustainable public finances and was welcome in the early days of decentralization, will need to adapt to the new reality of greater municipal autonomy. Municipalities have been resenting what they view as excessive interference by the central government in their own affairs; in turn, the central government has relied on tight execution through the central treasury to control municipal finances. The result is suboptimal consultation and limited joint coordination on fiscal policy among government levels. As political and fiscal decentralization deepen,

[17] Municipal expenditure as a share of GDP rose by almost 2 percent of GDP during the period 2007–09. See Fedelino and Ter-Minassian (2010) for further details.

[18] A standard TSA is a bank account or a set of linked bank accounts through which the government (and its entities and spending units) transacts all receipts and payments and consolidates its cash balances. See Box 9.1.

the central government will need to transform its PFM toolkit from heavy reliance on ex ante control to the development of ex post accountability mechanisms.

This transformation will not be easy. Although seemingly paradoxical, it is well accepted that effective fiscal decentralization requires strong central government institutions. Fiscal decentralization requires assigning more decisional and operational powers to municipalities. In this process, however, central government needs to ensure that national priorities are respected and needs to retool itself to adapt to its changing functions. Thus, the impact of decentralization must be assessed not only with regard to local governments, but also with regard to the critical need for capacity building in the central government to manage the post-decentralization environment.

Kosovo has not yet given these needs sufficient attention. Ministries affected by decentralization could approach the shift from policy implementation to monitoring and evaluation of the implementation of decentralized competencies by, for example, setting realistic service standards and supporting their monitoring and evaluation.[19] Comparative experience shows that in a run-up to decentralization, line ministries often focus solely on the preparation of transfer of competencies, and only later worry about their ability to manage the ensuing environment. The experience in Kosovo indicates that this transition will take much longer than the relatively compressed period that has been mandated to formulate and pass the complex body of legislation underpinning political and fiscal decentralization.

12.2.3. Uganda

Uganda has received a great deal of attention in the decentralization literature as a developing country that embraced genuine and significant decentralization with an unusual level of enthusiasm (Smoke, 2000; UNCHS, 2002; Onyach-Olaa, 2003; UNCDF, 2003; UNDP, 2003; World Bank, 2003; USAID, 2009; Muhumuza, 2006; Okidi and Guloba, 2006; Asiimwe and Musisi, 2007; Smoke, Muhumuza, and Ssewankambo, 2010). Following an extended period of internal conflict after gaining independence from Great Britain in 1962, Uganda began an era of greater stability with the rise to power of Yoweri Museveni and the National Resistance Movement in 1986. Museveni quickly moved to establish the foundation for a functioning state and adopted an extensive program of public sector reform.

Decentralization received more attention than PFM in the early stages of the National Resistance Movement period. From the beginning, citizen engagement and local capacities were emphasized as key drivers of economic development and political legitimacy.[20] Decentralization was portrayed as critical for democratization,

[19] See Government of Kosovo (2008), from page 26 onward.

[20] The role of local governments is highlighted in key government policy documents, including the *Poverty Reduction Strategy Paper*, *Fiscal Decentralization Strategy*, and *National Development Plan* (Government of Uganda, 2000, 2002, 2010).

service delivery, and poverty reduction. More fundamentally, the National Resistance Army, which prevailed in the 1980s conflict and brought the National Resistance Movement to power, built its base of support with village-level National Resistance Councils, which became the inspiration and model for local government. By the late 1990s, a strong legal framework for decentralization was in place, and local governments quickly became among the most empowered and best financed in Africa.

Although local governments were originally given substantial resources and autonomy, they always relied heavily on intergovernmental transfers. The transfer system was originally designed to cover the recurrent budget. A capital expenditure transfer was set up with donor funding as a somewhat parallel system closely linked to participatory planning and compliance or performance-based conditions. This transfer was later subsumed under a broader capital budgeting process when the government began to gradually decentralize the development budget in 1999–2000. Both recurrent and capital transfers occur as of 2012, and both can be conditional or unconditional. Over time, however, the balance has dramatically shifted toward conditional transfers (more than 90 percent in 2012), and grants have decreased as a share of total public expenditure (from more than 25 percent in 2004 to a projected 18 percent in 2013) and GDP. This rebalancing is only one indication of a broader pattern of recentralization that has been occurring in Uganda in recent years.

What accounts for this transformation?[21] First, after several years of reform, central agencies that originally supported (or did not overtly oppose) decentralization began to realize its implications for their control over resources, and some acted to protect their territory. Sectoral ministries under the mandates of the National Poverty Reduction Strategy and the Medium-Term Expenditure Framework began to develop Sector Wide Approaches that increased standards, monitoring, and central control (Jeppsson, 2002; Kasumba and Land, 2003; Wunsch and Ottemoeller, 2004; Ahmad, Brosio, and Gonzalez, 2006; Smoke, Muhumuza, and Ssewankambo, 2010). The ministry of finance, planning and economic development (MoFPED) also advanced PFM reforms, but they initially paid little attention to local governments or to the separate system of local PFM developed and implemented by the ministry of local government. The MoFPED finally focused on subnational PFM and made the contentious decision to replace the new system with one more consistent with national PFM reforms, which required the retraining of local government officials.

Second, emerging documentation of poor expenditure management processes and service outcomes in the late 1990s led to concerns that too many responsibilities and too much autonomy had been decentralized too quickly (Ablo and Reinikka, 1998; Jeppsson, 2001; Reinikka and Svensson, 2004). This empirical evidence reinforced the perceived need for various central ministries to take steps to recentralize and particularly caught the attention of the donor community,

[21] Smoke, Muhumuza, and Ssewankambo (2010) review these issues in more detail.

which was contributing heavily to many of the public sector reform and service delivery initiatives associated with the National Poverty Reduction Strategy. All of the new reforms, however, focused almost exclusively on reimposing upward accountability, with little attention to the equally or more important challenges of building the downward accountability to citizens required for effective decentralization.

Third, the political weakening of the National Resistance Movement and the emergence of multiparty elections led to a number of reforms to support electoral strategies and strengthen central controls that reinforced the effects of the technical reforms outlined above (Green, 2008; Muhumuza, 2008). These reforms included extensive creation of new local governments (districts) with little capacity, recentralization of procurement and recruitment of senior local government staff, and formal establishment of regional governments (albeit with limited action taken to set them up) that had been abolished to deal with perceived challenges to national unity posed by traditional kingdoms (regions) and to emphasize the empowerment of the local governments.

Finally, the behavior of some of the development partners created challenges for decentralization. Even when the donors supporting decentralization were working together, they focused their efforts on the relatively weak ministry of local government and did not sufficiently work with other ministries that needed to be on board. In some cases, different departments of the same development agencies supporting decentralization were pursuing PFM or sectoral reform efforts at odds with the legal framework for decentralization and the donor programs supporting it.

The Decentralization Development Partners Group commissioned a study to consider how to reintroduce discretion and improve performance. This study resulted in the 2002 Fiscal Decentralization Strategy, which introduced new budgeting and financial management processes. This strategy improved information and monitoring, but it also imposed a budget template that largely reinforced the limited budgetary discretion of local governments.[22] The Fiscal Decentralization Strategy formally provided for some flexibility that was substantially stifled in practice, and its stated intention to loosen restrictions after local government capacity was built was never implemented.

Ultimately, decentralization in Uganda was pursued initially for political reasons and in isolation from other public sector reforms, including PFM, that have now overwhelmed it. The nature, pace, and trajectory of reform was clearly too ambitious to take root and result in vigorous performance, owing to both insufficient capacity and inadequate accountability pressures. Excessive emphasis was probably placed on formal system development and insufficient attention given to building local capacity, accountability, and governance.

In short, PFM reforms in Uganda during the past decade, including the Fiscal Decentralization Strategy, have undeniably improved information, monitoring,

[22] Details of the budgeting process are outlined in Government of Uganda (2002).

and fiscal discipline. These achievements, however, have come at an unnecessarily heavy price—the considerable undermining of local governments' autonomy and ability to respond directly to the expressed needs of their constituents. Going forward, the benefits of PFM reforms can be maintained and the benefits of decentralization realized if the right actors can be engaged to develop a strategy for gradual reintroduction of local autonomy and performance incentives to retain and improve fiscal responsibility. Given the political situation in Uganda, however, and the discovery of oil, primarily in the more powerful and assertive traditional kingdoms, the challenges in the coming years will be considerable.

12.3. GENERAL LESSONS LEARNED

This section highlights strategic considerations that could help analysts understand the interconnections between PFM and fiscal decentralization and how they might be improved to yield better results. Generalizations are difficult, given the diversity of context discussed in the case studies and the limited empirical evidence about what works well in practice. Still, this section offers a few simple principles for consideration, with the caveat that they involve a certain amount of simplification and need to be used and developed as appropriate for specific cases. Some of these points may appear intuitive, but despite how obvious they may seem, they are rarely adequately considered in policy circles. Even though the recommendations are general, much can be gained from this type of analysis, and those responsible for decentralization and PFM reforms have a responsibility to undertake such efforts. Further work is needed to develop a more robust framework.

First, Pay More Attention to Context When Considering How to Frame and Implement Normatively Desirable PFM and Decentralization Reforms

PFM and decentralization reforms have frequently been pursued in a way that is too heavily based on purist principles or on borrowed approaches from other countries. Moreover, the reforms have often been undertaken without an assessment of broader international experience or an in-depth diagnosis of the prevailing country-specific political and institutional context and its implications for workable subnational PFM and decentralization reform options. This was clearly the case in Uganda. Gaining an understanding of the underlying motivations for and objectives of both types of reform is crucial, as is determining which entities (across and within levels of government) will be receptive to these reforms and have the capacity to bring them to fruition.

Equally valuable is assessing whether existing PFM and subnational government systems can be reformed or whether a completely new system needs to be developed. In either case, some positive features of the existing system may be working well, but are sometimes lost as reforms and new systems are developed. Although it may be easier—and tempting—to turn the page and start new, normatively inspired reforms from square one, in practice, using and adapting existing systems may secure more rapid, more robust, and ultimately more sustainable results.

Second, as Much as Possible, Embed Technical PFM Reforms in Broader Public Sector and Decentralization Reforms

Decentralization involves a broad array of roles and reforms beyond the fiscal arena—administrative, political, and regulatory, among others. PFM reformers commonly tend to perceive technical PFM reform as a prerequisite for other reforms. For decentralization, they may even argue that no functions and resources should be given to local governments until the necessary systems, procedures, and capacity to manage them effectively are fully in place. National agencies generally have stronger technical expertise and do need to ensure that the evolving intergovernmental system follows established procedures and standards. Developing sufficient local capacity requires resources and time, suggesting an inherent tension between this overarching PFM approach and the rapid adoption of decentralization.

The normative position that PFM reform should always precede decentralization will sometimes be at odds with political reality—countries with a strong political imperative for decentralization (for example, when emerging from conflict) do not have the luxury of waiting for an ideal PFM system to be developed before advancing decentralization (as the experience of Kosovo shows). Moreover, from a local government and citizen perspective, if local governments are going to be created, they need to be doing something, even if very basic, to establish their credentials in delivering services to meet the needs of the citizens they represent. A neat, orderly, sequenced comprehensive PFM reform process in advance of empowering local governments does not meet this need, and electing and paying local councils simply to learn how to budget and keep financial records is unlikely to be politically viable and may even undermine decentralization efforts.

However, linking PFM reform to broader decentralization reform should be possible, giving local governments simpler but visible functional responsibilities early and allowing them to learn commensurate basic PFM skills. Cambodia is an example in which initial piloted (and parallel) reforms at the local level were progressively formalized and rolled out. As the system develops and capacity is enhanced, a higher level of PFM skills can be built along with the devolution of additional service functions and resources. In short, the scope and pace of decentralization could proceed in tandem with the capacity of subnational governments to perform functions assigned to them, and new PFM initiatives could be aligned and embedded in broader decentralization reforms. This is a win-win approach in which local governments are not given functions without adequate PFM safeguards but are able to perform some functions that establish their legitimacy and create a foundation for further fiscally responsible reform. The failure to adopt such an approach was one of the critical factors that led to the recentralization in Uganda.

Third, Ensure That a Well-Grounded Strategy for Pursuing Reform Programs Is in Place

Building on the notion that PFM reforms can be linked to specific functions undertaken by local governments as decentralization proceeds, such as service delivery or revenue generation, identifying the appropriate steps becomes important. A good starting point would be reforms that can be executed with a high probability of success, which may be simpler types of functions and processes, although the decision ultimately depends on the systems and capacity in a particular country.

A second step would be to build on these initial functions strategically in successive rounds of reform, subsequent to careful monitoring and assessment of initial steps. Appropriate incentives for local governments to adopt new functions and more advanced PFM processes can be usefully employed. Creative ways of structuring reforms and partnerships that hold some promise for learning and results should be sought. An example is working with spending ministries to devise plans for the progressive functional devolution in a particular sector or partnering with nongovernmental organizations or private firms in ways that assist local governments to better meet their assigned functions.

Fourth, Build Capacity Necessary for the Specific Steps of the Implementation Strategy

Although only mentioned in passing in the preceding analysis, much capacity building in decentralization and local government PFM is generic, classroom-based training. Such training is often so different from what local government officials are used to and so poorly reinforced through subsequent support that concepts and skills taught in training courses are frequently lost or muddled when officials get back on the job. A more productive approach would be to target capacity building to the more limited functions and tasks that will be immediately used. Once these skills are mastered and institutionalized, additional skills can be developed as more significant and challenging functions and tasks are assumed. Providing periodic, on-site follow-up technical assistance can also help to keep learning on track and to deepen and reinforce skills and capacities.

In decentralization, two additional considerations must be recognized. First, as emphasized in the country cases, central government officials implementing decentralization and supporting or regulating local governments also require training to fulfill their new roles effectively.

Second, local capacity building needs to be both technical and governance oriented. Local governments must receive training to meet their functional responsibilities and maintain fiscal discipline. And citizens, elected officials, and local government staff must be trained to work with each other under new accountability relationships generated by decentralization. The best system and greatest technical capacity do not result in the expected advantages of decentralization unless the behavioral changes underpinning the attainment of these advantages occur. Local government staff, who may have previously looked to the center for direction, must learn to work effectively with elected local councils, who must be able to engage with budgeting and financial management processes and be responsive to their constituents. Similarly, citizens need to understand how local government resources are managed and accounted for. Citizens may even be involved in this process directly, through participatory planning, budgeting, or monitoring.[23] The experience in Uganda highlights how failure to establish adequate accountability channels and capacity at the local level can undermine decentralization reform and require later redressing.

Fifth, Consider Innovative Mechanisms and Approaches That May Help to Facilitate Successful Implementation of Reforms

Public sector reform tends toward standardization, but asymmetric approaches can sometimes be valuable. The possibility was noted above that decentralization and PFM reforms can be differentially targeted to specific types of local governments (e.g., large metropolitan areas versus small rural districts) or based on specific performance or capacity measurement (see Chapter 7). Local governments may also be allowed a degree of choice in defining and pursuing specific reform trajectories, so that they assume responsibility for what they agree to do rather than simply being told what to do by the center.[24]

Enforceable accountability mechanisms, such as central government contracts with local governments to undertake certain reforms, hold promise. Financial incentives for adoption of reforms and improvement in performance, for example, the emerging wave of compliance or performance-based grants being adopted in the developing countries referred to above, may also be used to increase the effectiveness of decentralization and subnational PFM reforms.

Sixth, Identify and Work With the Supporters and Opponents of Reform and Take Steps to Coordinate the Various Actors

PFM and decentralization reforms are staged in a crowded arena: multiple national agencies are typically at odds, pursuing disparate agendas (often with support from different external donors). The ministry of finance is positioned to play the leading role in ensuring that subnational PFM systems are robust and adhered to even where subnational levels have substantial fiscal autonomy, but many other actors are relevant. These significant players include ministries involved in local government oversight and support as well as those in charge of civil service regulations and those responsible for ensuring that standards are met in the delivery of specific public services with national significance (such as health, education, public works, or other sectors). All of these actors need to be keenly involved in the political discourse surrounding the development of decentralization and the process of reform itself.

---

[23] See Brinkerhoff and Azfar (2010) for a discussion of governance dimensions of decentralization.

[24] See Smoke (2007, 2008b) for more discussion and examples of asymmetric decentralization.

Given the large number of actors, the creation of effective coordination mechanisms for decentralization by itself is difficult enough and, of course, decentralization is seldom the only or most important driving force in public sector reform (Smoke, 2010). The problems caused by weak coordination of public sector reforms can be so significant, however, that the potential benefits of improving coordination mechanisms are great.

12.4. CONCLUSION

This chapter pushes the boundaries of conventional discourse on the links between PFM and decentralization reform, with a particular emphasis on developing and transition countries. In an ideal world, PFM reform and decentralization reform would have a strong conceptual and practical relationship. In such a world, PFM systems would be designed and implemented to support and enhance the allocation and sharing (whether immediate or eventual) of the responsibilities for managing public functions and resources across government levels.

In reality, this ideal relationship is generally not well established nor put into operation. Every major force that drives one of these reforms collectively challenges the realization of a seamless coordination between, and sequencing of, decentralization and PFM reforms. Even at a more pragmatic level, reformers cannot always afford the luxury of implementing normative principles in a well-sequenced and highly coordinated manner and over a long time span. Thus, decentralization and PFM often proceed separately, and at times in fundamentally inconsistent ways. This tendency is reinforced by the landscape of shifting political and economic conditions, reform objectives, and actors (domestic and external) involved in the reforms.

Although no single solution to this consequential policy dilemma is evident, this chapter highlights some key issues and strategic considerations that could help analysts to understand more systematically the PFM–fiscal decentralization linkages. It outlines some basic principles that use both old and new ways of contemplating how PFM and decentralization reform can work together more effectively. Recognizing the limitations of this analysis and the need for further work, this chapter is not naively suggesting that the generic approach outlined here is uniformly desirable, easy to accomplish, free of transaction costs, or fully attainable even in the most favorable circumstances. However, more formal, methodical analyses of these issues are clearly important. Much more effort in this direction is well within the reach of motivated policy analysts and reformers. Accepting the challenge to deal with these important reforms more systematically holds great promise for improving public sector performance.

REFERENCES

Ablo, Emmanuel, and Ritva Reinikka, 1998, "Do Budgets Really Matter? Evidence from Public Spending on Education and Health in Uganda," Policy Research Working Paper No. 1926 (Washington: World Bank).

Ahmad, Ehtisham, and Giorgio Brosio, eds., 2006, *Handbook of Fiscal Federalism* (Cheltenham, UK: Edward Elgar).

———, and Maria Gonzalez, 2006, "Uganda: Managing More Effective Decentralization," IMF Working Paper 06/279 (Washington: International Monetary Fund).

Ahmad, Ehtisham, and Vito Tanzi, 2002, *Managing Fiscal Decentralization* (Oxford, UK: Routledge).

Alm, James, Jorge Martinez-Vazquez, and Sri Mulyani Indrawati, 2004, *Reforming Intergovernmental Fiscal Relations and the Rebuilding of Indonesia* (Cheltenham, UK: Edward Elgar).

Asiimwe, Delius, and Nakanyike Musisi, 2007, *Decentralization and Transformation of Governance in Uganda* (Kampala: Fountain Publishers).

Bahl, Roy, and Jorge Martinez-Vazquez, 2006, "Sequencing Fiscal Decentralization," Policy Research Working Paper No. 3914 (Washington: World Bank).

Brinkerhoff, Derick, and Omar Azfar, 2010, "Decentralization and Community Empowerment," in *Making Decentralization Work: Democracy, Development and Security*, ed. by Ed Connerley, Kent Eaton, and Paul Smoke (Boulder, Colorado: Lynne Rienner Publishers), pp. 81–114.

de Renzio, Paolo, 2011, *Buying Better Governance: The Political Economy of Budget Reforms in Aid-Dependent Countries* (Oxford: Global Economic Development Program, Center for International Studies, Oxford University).

Development Partners Working Group on Decentralisation and Local Governance, 2011, *Busan and Beyond: Localizing Paris Principles for More Effective Support to Decentralisation and Local Governance Reforms* (Bonn: Gesellschaft für Internationale Zusammenarbeit [GIZ]).

Eaton, Kent, Kai Kaiser, and Paul Smoke, 2011, *Political Economy of Decentralization: Implications for Aid Effectiveness* (Washington: World Bank).

Eaton, Kent, and Larry Schroeder, 2010, "Measuring Decentralization," in *Making Decentralization Work: Democracy, Development and Security*, ed. by Ed Connerley, Kent Eaton, and Paul Smoke (Boulder, Colorado: Lynne Rienner Publishers), pp. 167–90.

Fedelino, Annalisa, and Teresa Ter-Minassian, 2010, *Making Fiscal Decentralization Work: Cross-Country Experiences*, IMF Occasional Paper No. 271 (Washington: International Monetary Fund).

Government of Kosovo, 2008, *Whole-of-Government Review* (Pristina: Functional Review and Institutional Design of Ministries—FRIDOM).

Government of Uganda, 2000, *Poverty Reduction Strategy Paper* (Kampala: Ministry of Finance, Planning and Economic Development).

———, 2002, *Fiscal Decentralization in Uganda: Draft Strategy Paper* (Kampala: Fiscal Decentralization Working Group).

———, 2010, *National Development Plan* (Kampala: Ministry of Finance, Planning and Economic Development).

Green, Elliot, 2008, "District Creation and Decentralization in Uganda," Working Paper No. 24 (London: Crisis States Research Center, London School of Economics).

International Monetary Fund (IMF), 2009, *Macro Policy Lessons for a Sound Design of Fiscal Decentralization* (Washington).

Jeppsson, Anders, 2001, "Financial Priorities under Decentralization in Uganda," *Health Policy and Planning*, Vol. 16, No. 2, pp. 187–92.

———, 2002, "SWAP Dynamics in a Decentralized Context: Experiences from Uganda," *Social Science and Medicine*, Vol. 55, No. 11, pp. 2053–60.

Kaiser, Kai, Daan Pattinasarany, and Günther Schulze, 2007, "Decentralization, Governance and Public Services in Indonesia," in *Decentralization in Asia and Latin America: Towards a Comparative Interdisciplinary Perspective*, ed. by Paul Smoke, Eduardo Gomez, and George Peterson (Cheltenham, UK: Edward Elgar).

Kasumba, George, and Anthony Land, 2003, "Sector-Wide Approaches and Decentralization: Strategies Pulling in Opposite Directions? A Case Study from Uganda" (Maastricht: European Centre for Development Policy Management).

Lamont, James, and Handry Imansyah, eds., 2012, *Ten Years after the Big Bang: The Future of Fiscal Decentralization in Indonesia* (Jakarta: University of Indonesia Press and Ministry of Finance).

Lewis, Blane, 2003, "Tax and Charge Creation by Regional Governments under Fiscal Decentralization: Estimates and Explanations," *Bulletin of Indonesian Economic Studies*, Vol. 39, No. 2, pp. 177–92.

———, 2005, "Indonesian Local Government Spending, Taxing and Saving: An Explanation of Pre- and Post-Decentralization Fiscal Outcomes," *Asian Economic Journal*, Vol. 19, No. 3, pp. 291–317.

———, 2006, "Local Government: An Analysis of Administrative Cost Inefficiency," *Bulletin of Indonesian Economic Studies*, Vol. 42, No. 2, pp. 213–33.

Lewis, Blane, and Andre Oostermann, 2008, "The Impact of Fiscal Decentralization on Subnational Government Fiscal Slack in Indonesia," Decentralization Support Facility Working Paper (Jakarta, Indonesia: World Bank).

Lewis, Blane, and Paul Smoke, 2009, "Incorporating Subnational Performance Incentives in the Indonesian Intergovernmental Fiscal Framework," in *National Tax Association Proceedings of the 101st Conference on Taxation* (Washington: National Tax Association), pp. 418–26.

———, 2012, "Incentives for Local Service Delivery: International Experience and Options for Indonesia," in *Ten Years after the Big Bang: The Future of Fiscal Decentralization in Indonesia*, ed. by James Lamont and Handry Imansyah (Jakarta: University of Indonesia Press and Ministry of Finance).

Muhumuza, William, 2006, *Decentralization and Rebuilding State Capacity under the NRM Government*, Sponsored by SIDA/SAREC and FSS Interdisciplinary Research Grant (Kampala: Makerere University).

———, 2008, "Pitfalls of Decentralization Reforms in Transitional Societies: The Case of Uganda," *Africa Development*, Vol. 33, No. 4, pp. 59–81.

Okidi, John, and Madina Guloba, 2006, *Decentralization and Development: Emerging Issues from Uganda's Experience* (Kampala: Economic Policy Research Center, Makerere University).

Onyach-Olaa, Martin, 2003, "The Challenges of Implementing Decentralization: Recent Experiences in Uganda," *Public Administration and Development*, Vol. 23, No. 1, pp. 105–13.

Reinikka, Ritva, and Jakob Svensson, 2004, "Local Capture: Evidence from a Central Government Transfer Program in Uganda," *Quarterly Journal of Economics*, Vol. 119, No. 2, pp. 679–705.

Shah, Anwar, 2008, *A Global Dialogue on Federalism*, Vol. 4 of *The Practice of Fiscal Federalism: Comparative Perspectives* (Montreal: McGill–Queen's University Press).

———, and Theresa Thompson Chaudhry, 2004, "Implementing Decentralized Local Governance: A Treacherous Road with Potholes, Detours, and Road Closures," Policy Research Working Paper No. 3353 (Washington: World Bank).

Smoke, Paul, 2000, "Fiscal Decentralization in East and Southern Africa: A Selective Review of Experience and Thoughts on Moving Forward," paper presented at the Conference on Fiscal Decentralization, Washington, November 20–21. Available via the Internet: http://www.imf.org/external/pubs/ft/seminar/2000/fiscal/smoke.pdf.

———, 2003, "Erosion and Reform from the Center in Kenya," in *Local Governance in Africa: The Challenge of Decentralization*, ed. by James Wunsch and Dele Olowu (Boulder, Colorado: Lynne Rienner Publishers).

———, 2006, "Fiscal Decentralization Policy in Developing Countries: Bridging Theory and Reality," in *Public Sector Reform in Developing Countries*, ed. by Yusuf Bangura and George Larbi (London: Palgrave Macmillan), pp. 195–227.

———, 2007, "Fiscal Decentralization and Intergovernmental Relations in Developing Countries: Navigating a Viable Path to Reform," in *Decentralized Governance: Emerging Concepts and Practice*, ed. by G. Shabbir Cheema and Dennis Rondinelli (Washington: Brookings Institution Press).

———, 2008a, "The Evolution of Subnational Planning under Decentralization Reforms in Kenya and Uganda," in *Decentralization and the Planning Process*, ed. by V. Beard, F. Miraftab, and C. Silver (Boulder, Colorado: Routledge).

———, 2008b, "Local Revenues under Fiscal Decentralization in Developing Countries: Linking Policy Reform, Governance and Capacity," in *Fiscal Decentralization and Land Policies*, ed. by Gregory Ingram and Yu-Hung Hong (Cambridge, Massachusetts: Lincoln Institute Press), pp. 38–69.

———, 2010, "Implementing Decentralization: Meeting Neglected Challenges," in *Making Decentralization Work: Democracy, Development and Security*, ed. by Ed Connerley, Kent Eaton, and Paul Smoke (Boulder, Colorado: Lynne Rienner Publishers), pp. 191–217.

Smoke, Paul, and Blane Lewis, 1996, "Fiscal Decentralization in Indonesia: A New Approach to an Old Idea," *World Development*, Vol. 24, No. 8, pp. 1281–99.

Smoke, Paul, and Joanne Morrison, 2011, "Decentralization in Cambodia: Consolidating Central Power or Building Accountability from Below?" in *Decentralization in Developing Countries: Global Perspectives on the Obstacles to Fiscal Devolution*, ed. by J. Martinez-Vazquez and F. Vaillancourt (Cheltenham, UK: Edward Elgar), pp. 313–42.

Smoke, Paul, William Muhumuza, and Emmanuel Ssewankambo, 2010, *Uganda Decentralization Assessment* (Washington: Associates in Rural Development for USAID).

Smoke, Paul, and Rubino Sugana, 2012, "Subnational Own Source Revenues and Shared Taxes in Indonesia: Taking Stock and Looking Forward," paper presented at the conference "Alternative Visions for Decentralization in Indonesia," sponsored by the Decentralization Support Facility, Jakarta, March.

Steffensen, Jesper, 2010, *Performance-Based Grant Systems: Concept and International Experience* (New York: United Nations Capital Development Fund).

United Cities and Local Governments, 2008, *Decentralization and Local Democracy in the World—First Global Report on Decentralization and Local Democracy* (Barcelona).

———, 2010, *Local Government Finance: The Challenges of the 21st Century—Second Global Report on Decentralization and Local Democracy* (Barcelona).

United Nations Capital Development Fund (UNCDF), 2003, *Local Government Initiative: Pro-poor Infrastructure and Service Delivery in Rural Sub-Saharan Africa* (New York).

United Nations Center for Human Settlements (UNCHS), 2002, *Local Democracy and Decentralization in East and Southern Africa* (Nairobi).

United Nations Development Program (UNDP), 2003, *Decentralization and Local Governance: Towards a "Home Grown" Solution in Uganda* (Pretoria).

United States Agency for International Development (USAID), 2009, *Democratic Decentralization Strategic Assessment: Indonesia* (Washington).

World Bank, 2003, *Decentralization Policies and Practices: Participants Manual* (Washington).

———, 2005, *East Asia Decentralizes* (Washington).

———, 2007, *Kosovo: Public Expenditure and Financial Accountability (PEFA) Public Financial Management Assessment* (Washington).

Wunsch, James, and Dan Ottemoeller, 2004, "Uganda: Multiple Levels of Local Governance," in *Local Governance in Africa: The Challenges of Democratic Decentralization*, ed. by James Wunsch and Dele Olowu (Boulder, Colorado: Lynne Rienner Publishers), pp. 181–210.

CHAPTER 13

Public Financial Management in Natural Resource-Rich Countries

TERESA DABÁN SÁNCHEZ AND JEAN-LUC HÉLIS

Richness in natural resources can be both a blessing and a curse. The revenues generated by natural resources present great economic opportunities but also pose significant challenges.[1] The endowment of natural resources, used wisely by countries, can promote growth, employment, and raise living standards. For many countries, however, the blessing has become a curse. This "resource curse" is a complex phenomenon through which abundant revenues from natural resources translate into economic stagnation, waste, corruption, and conflict.

To overcome these challenges, the large body of literature on the resource curse recommends implementing prudent macroeconomic policies and strengthening the institutional framework, in particular, the public financial management (PFM) system. However, the PFM literature offers little guidance on systematically and comprehensively identifying the most effective actions that natural resource-rich countries should take to strengthen their PFM systems.

Most PFM literature focuses on promoting transparency and adopting special operational mechanisms, such as natural resource funds, for managing resource revenues, sometimes as a way of bypassing existing weak PFM systems. When rigidly designed and implemented, however, these special mechanisms have sometimes reduced the efficiency of government spending, led to fragmentation and delay in the budget process, and eroded incentives for reforming existing budgetary institutions. This chapter argues that unfavorable preexisting institutional conditions combined with the adoption of poorly designed, opaque, and rigid special operation mechanisms have contributed to some countries' failures to avoid the resource curse. The few success stories mostly relate to countries that already had relatively strong institutional systems during their preresource period. These examples provide little guidance for the reform path that developing resource-rich countries should follow to avoid the curse.

This chapter proposes a PFM framework and reform path for natural resource-rich countries that aims at enhancing—instead of replacing or bypassing—existing budgetary institutions, while preserving the integrity of the budget process and taking account of the diversity of these countries. The first section identifies

[1]This chapter focuses on "nonrenewable natural resource revenues" and "nonrenewable resource–producing countries," which for the sake of simplicity will be referred to in the text as "resource revenues" and "resource-producing countries."

the specific advantages and challenges associated with managing revenues generated from natural resources and the mechanisms that can transmit the resource curse. The second section provides an overview of country experiences with managing natural resources and adopting special operational mechanisms. It also discusses successes and failures of these mechanisms. The third section outlines this chapter's proposed PFM measures to help natural resource-rich countries, especially developing countries, avoid the curse.

13.1. ADVANTAGES AND CHALLENGES OF RESOURCE REVENUES: THE RESOURCE CURSE

The current set of natural resource-rich countries differ widely in income per capita, resource dependence, human development, and transparency (Figure 13.1). These countries also vary considerably in their economic, political, and institutional development (Box 13.1). Despite this diversity, governments of these countries face similar advantages and challenges in managing revenues from natural resources, although their capacity to exploit opportunities and deal with challenges differs significantly.

Governments derive large amounts of revenues from natural resources in different ways, including through taxes, royalties, bonuses, and dividends from national resource companies. Resource revenues can provide important advantages over other types of government revenue. The most salient advantage is that resource revenues are generated from a subsoil asset—a "gift of nature"—whose discovery translates into expansion of the country's GDP and government's financial envelope. Resource revenues are not subject to conditions that donors and lenders usually impose on recipient countries. Another advantage resides in the "enclave" nature of resource revenues, which makes it possible for resource revenues to be generated even under extremely challenging circumstances, as shown in Angola and Colombia, where internal armed conflicts did not stop oil production.

However, many challenges are associated with managing resource revenues. The overarching trial is how to avoid the resource curse. The first and most commonly discussed transmission mechanism is *Dutch disease*,[2] a set of negative macroeconomic effects caused by a large increase in resource-funded spending. If mainly allocated to domestically produced goods, a large increase in spending can push up domestic prices, the nominal exchange rate, and eventually the real exchange rate. Capital and labor are shifted into the production of nontradable goods with an accompanying erosion of the competitiveness of the nonresource economy. This can reduce economic diversification and render the economy overly dependent on the natural resource sector. Two illustrative cases of Dutch

[2]The term was coined in 1977 by *The Economist* to describe the overvaluation of the Dutch guilder and the decline in the manufacturing sector in the Netherlands after the discovery of natural gas in the 1960s.

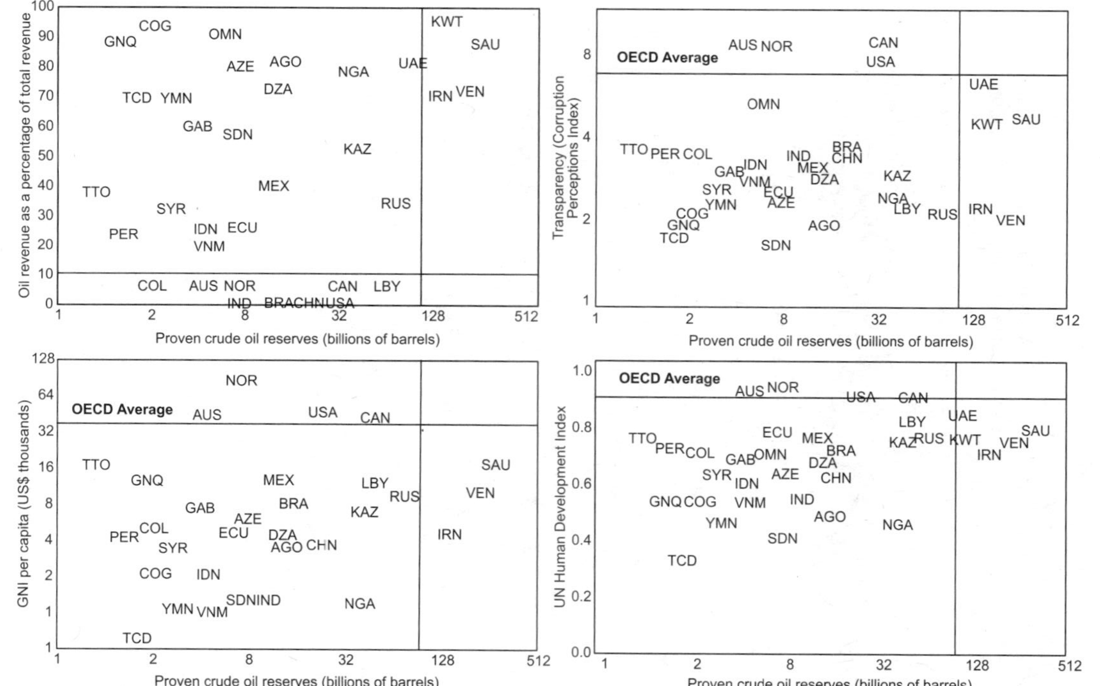

Figure 13.1 Overview of Selected Oil-Producing Countries, 2010

Sources: British Petroleum; IMF, *Fiscal Monitor* database; *Oil & Gas Journal*; Organization of the Petroleum Exporting Countries (OPEC), *Annual Statistical Bulletin*; Transparency International, Corruption Perceptions Index 2010; United Nations Development Programme, Human Development Index 2010; and other official and public-domain sources.

Note: Estimates have been compiled using a combination of the above-named sources. Estimate of Russian reserves is based on information in the public domain. Canadian reserves include an official estimate of 26.5 billion barrels for oil sands "under active development." Venezuelan reserves are from the OPEC *Annual Statistical Bulletin*, which noted in 2008 that the figure included "proven reserves of the Magna Reserve Project in the Orinoco Belt, which amounted to 94,168 mb." Reserves include gas condensate and natural gas liquids as well as crude oil. Annual changes and shares of total are calculated using thousand million barrels figures. Proved crude oil reserves are generally taken to be those quantities that geological and engineering information indicates with reasonable certainty can be recovered in the future from known reservoirs under existing economic and operating conditions. GNI = gross national income. For expansion of three-letter country abbreviations, see, for example, the United Nations Statistics Division's list at http://unstats.un.org/unsd/methods/m49/m49alpha.htm.

BOX 13.1 Overview of Resource-Rich Countries

The increase in exploration activity in the last few decades has resulted in the discovery and extraction of more natural resources in more countries. This increase in extraction has been spurred by growing demand for commodities, especially from emerging market economies, and the development of new technologies that facilitate the extraction of oil and other materials from previously inhospitable terrain. As a result, the current collection of natural resource-rich countries is quite diverse. Despite this diversity, these countries can be broadly categorized into four distinct groups.

Developed resource-producing countries. This group of countries is characterized by low resource dependence, high GDP per capita, high levels of both human development and transparency, and strong linkages between the resource sector and the rest of the economy. In most cases, resource production came on-stream once the country was at a relatively advanced stage of economic and institutional development. These countries also have political systems in which citizens have the opportunity—and the incentive—to hold government accountable. Bureaucracies are competent and insulated from political influence. Property rights are well defined, the rule of law prevails, and the judiciary system is independent. Policies are usually underpinned by broad social consensus, long-term perspectives, and prudent economic management.

Middle Eastern resource-producing countries. These countries specialize in oil production, with oil contributing about one-third of total GDP and three-fourths of annual government revenues. Government legitimacy is in many cases based on traditional and religious authority, bolstered in some cases by extensive welfare systems and large bureaucracies. This situation usually results in a high level of spending and inefficient non-oil sectors. Some of these countries, however, are making progress in diversifying their economies.

Resource-producing emerging market economies. These countries are characterized by high resource dependence and in some cases unequal income distribution. In some cases, the institutional framework is marked by limited accountability and transparency, incomplete separation of powers between the judiciary and the government, and unclear property rights.

Low-income resource-producing countries. These countries include large and small oil producers in low-income countries. Prevailing conditions are a rural economy, sometimes in extreme poverty; high resource dependence; and the absence of both an efficient bureaucracy and basic infrastructure. Some countries in this group are making progress toward more accountable forms of government, but the exploitation of resource revenues by the elite is still too often embedded in institutionalized practices and rent-seeking behavior. Overall, the rule of law is generally weak, and accountability and transparency mechanisms need substantive improvements.

disease are Nigeria, where, during 1970–2000, oil exports led to the rapid collapse of agricultural exports, and Equatorial Guinea, where cocoa and coffee production declined from approximately 60 percent of GDP in 1991 to less than 9 percent in 2001 (Gelb, 1988; McSherry, 2006).

A second transmission mechanism of the resource curse is through the *extreme volatility of resource revenues*,[3] which can lead to waste, boom-and-bust cycles, and

[3] Volatility in resource prices can include variation in the extraction rate and the calendar of payments by resource companies to governments. However, by far, world resource prices are the main source of volatility.

excessive borrowing. Waste can arise from the pressure that large and sudden increases in resource-funded public spending puts on the country's administrative capacity. It can also result from frequent upward and downward adjustments in expenditures and the ensuing poor quality of spending programs that are increased or downsized at the last minute, in line with fluctuating revenues. Excessive borrowing can arise from government difficulties in cutting the budget during busts or from a tendency to overborrow during booms. In Mexico, a policy of borrowing against future oil earnings during its small oil windfall in 1979–81 triggered a spiraling of growth in spending. In Angola, the practice of mortgaging future oil earnings to increase public spending has repeatedly led to budget and debt crises. During the oil boom of the 1970s, Nigeria borrowed heavily to finance public consumption, and in the mid-1980s suffered two shocks, notably a reduction in the oil price per barrel from US$30 to US$18 and a swing from borrowing to repaying.

A third transmission mechanism arises from the generation of resource revenues through the *depletion of a nonrenewable, nonfinancial asset.* Resource revenues are exhaustible and temporary. The nonrenewable nature of resource revenues means that, independently of their structure as taxes, royalties, fees, bonus, or dividends, resource revenues are derived from the consumption or sale of an existing asset, not from income. It also indicates that, if part of resource revenues are not saved or allocated to the production or acquisition of other forms of reproducible and productive (physical and financial) capital, the use of resource revenues can reduce the government's net worth for future generations.

A fourth mechanism for transmitting the resource curse is the risk that an excessive reliance on resource revenues will transform resource-rich countries into *rentier states.* The theory of rentier states (Moore, 2004) holds that countries that receive substantial and regular resource revenues from the outside world tend to become less accountable to their citizens. Moreover, rentier states may not feel compelled to promote wealth creation, which they could subsequently tax, and embody a higher probability that resource revenues may be captured by narrow elites or interest groups. Capture can undermine the development of an open and inclusive policy decision-making process and, in some cases, induce political instability and conflict. Under these circumstances, governments usually devote more attention to inefficient redistribution mechanisms, such as wasteful investment projects (white elephants), inefficient national resource companies, low-quality spending programs (including ill-targeted subsidies for failing industries), or overstaffed civil services.

In Nigeria, for instance, the Ajaokuta steel mill built in the 1970s absorbed more than US$3 billion and in 2012 is not yet fully operational on a commercial basis. In 1975 in Kuwait, the government employed 75 percent of the workforce, but most government employees were underqualified and underutilized (Eifert, Gelb, and Tallroth, 2003). In Saudi Arabia, with the oil windfall of the 1970s, the government eliminated several taxes and downsized the tax administration department, while at the same time increasing spending substantially. When oil prices dropped in the 1980s, and efforts to increase taxes and cut back spending failed, the government experienced a deficit of 10 percent of GDP (Tsalik, 2003). The Biafra war of secession in Nigeria in the late 1960s and conflicts in the Cabinda region of Angola seemed to be related to resource-revenue issues (Eifert, Gelb, and Tallroth, 2003).

13.2. COUNTRY EXPERIENCES WITH THE MANAGEMENT OF RESOURCE REVENUES

13.2.1. The Impact of Preexisting Economic and Institutional Conditions

To date, resource-producing countries' experiences with managing resource revenues and preventing the resource curse is, at best, mixed. Except for a few successful examples (see Box 13.2), the most common experience in resource-producing countries has been a cycle of high revenue (and revenue expectations) fueling high expenditure, followed by a resource market slump, a decline in resource revenues, and sharp budgetary adjustments. As a result, most resource-producing countries tend to fall behind non-resource-producing economies in economic development, rates of growth, GDP per capita, and human development.

Cross-country experience shows that success in preventing the resource curse depends on countries' conditions and institutions in place before resource revenues come on stream. Most resource-producing countries that have successfully overcome the curse had sound governance systems and competent public administrations before the resource era. These countries were equipped to encourage politicians and interest groups to use resource revenues in an efficient, transparent, and sustainable way and thereby to prevent the resource curse.

In contrast, in resource-producing countries that have failed to avoid the emergence of the resource curse, the institutions in place before the discovery and exploitation of the natural resource were weak or nonexistent. These countries usually lacked both PFM systems and public administrations competent to design and implement a sound fiscal strategy. They also lacked predictable legal frameworks and strict enforcement of the rule of law. Separation of powers was limited, which undermined the development of effective transparency and accountability mechanisms. In addition, experience shows that countries that have failed to prevent the resource curse have been more inclined to develop high and persistent "resource dependence" and a rentier mentality. This dependence usually reflects chronically low tax mobilization, lack of access to borrowing, and a poorly diversified nonresource economy, especially during the preresource era.

13.2.2. Use of Special Operational Mechanisms

Some resource-producing countries, especially developing countries, have resorted to special operational mechanisms to manage their resource revenues, in some cases to bypass ill-functioning PFM systems. The most frequently used mechanisms include special arrangements for the allocation and use of resource revenues,

BOX 13.2 Prevention of the Resource Curse: A Few Success Stories

The successes of Australia, Canada, Chile, Norway, and the United States in preventing the resource curse are attributable to institutional environments conducive to efficient government, robust political institutions, and strong positive spillover from the resource sector to nonresource sectors. Norway's notable economic performance since the 1960s is due to its reorientation of its traditional engineering skills from shipbuilding to the export of technology on deepwater drilling platforms. The expansion of Canada's manufacturing sector was driven by innovations introduced by the resource sector. Success stories in Latin America include mining-led industrial development in the cities of Monterrey (Mexico), Medellín (Colombia), and São Paulo (Brazil).

In Botswana, positive factors include sound precolonial tribal institutions, which encouraged broadly based participation and constrained political leaders. This framework was reinforced by strong and wise leadership by Botswana's earliest presidents, which helped to balance tribes' interests and build a "developmental state." Additional factors were a predictable legal environment and an effective medium-term hard budget constraint, defined in the parliament-approved National Development Plan, both of which were adopted before the diamond era.

The cornerstone of Chile's impressive fiscal performance is its structural balance rule. The rule has helped preserve fiscal discipline and insulate public spending from fluctuations in the price of copper. The rule is supported by solid and hierarchical institutional arrangements and a high level of transparency. Two independent panels of experts estimate the long-term copper price and potential output. However, in recent years, implementation of the rule has revealed challenges, mainly derived from the complexities of calculating the structural balance, the lack of explicit clauses to deal with unexpected shocks, and the absence of a long-term anchor. The rule was suspended in February 2010, following an earthquake. In May 2010, the authorities appointed a high-level commission to recommend reforms to strengthen the rule. The commission produced a report (Comité Asesor, 2010; Larraín and others, 2011) that identified the shortcomings and challenges and proposed a few improvements. The government adopted some of the commission's recommendations, including simplifying the calculation of the structural balance, strengthening transparency, and adopting escape clauses. In addition, the government decided to implement the commission's recommendation to create a Fiscal Council, although at the time of writing, it had yet to be established.

Ghana, Indonesia, Malaysia, Namibia, South Africa, and Trinidad and Tobago are also cited as success stories despite their relatively less-favorable institutional frameworks. For instance, in Indonesia, the lack of institutionalized transparency and accountability mechanisms allowed rent seeking and corruption to flourish. However, a technocratic bureaucracy that focused on improving the financial sector, preserving macroeconomic stability, and fostering infrastructure and agricultural activities partially compensated for those weaknesses. (For more details on Indonesia and Malaysia, see Gelb [2011].)

natural resource funds, parallel budgetary and treasury procedures, separate investment committees and oversight institutions, and special legal frameworks. Three rationales are usually put forward to justify the adoption of these special mechanisms: (1) to crystallize public support for the government's policies for managing resource revenues and for protecting revenues for future use (this is even the case in countries with strong institutional frameworks); (2) to overcome the weaknesses of the existing PFM system by quickly implementing certain "parallel" mechanisms; and (3) to carve out a space within the public sector in which the appropriate budgetary mechanisms and transparency standards can be put to work in a highly visible manner, given that PFM reforms are likely to take time. Some of these mechanisms are discussed in detail below.

Special Arrangements for the Allocation and Use of Resource Revenues

Some resource-rich countries have successfully designed and implemented special rules-based frameworks or operational arrangements for managing revenues from natural resources. For example, in Norway, the portion of resource revenues used to finance the nonresource deficit cannot be larger than 4 percent of the balance of the oil fund in the medium term. In Botswana, budgeted diamond revenues have to be equal to capital spending in the budget. In Chile's rule, expenditure is determined according to structural mining and nonmining revenues (Dabán, 2010).

In other cases, the adoption of special arrangements for the allocation and use of resource revenues has not been as effective as originally envisaged, especially in low-income countries. In Chad, the establishment of multiple and complex earmarking arrangements led to separate budget and cash management systems for oil-funded and non-oil-funded transactions. This system included a mechanism to save 10 percent of oil revenues in a Future Generation Fund. However, spending pressures in the country's non-oil budget resulted in arrears and costly borrowing, while low-yielding assets were being accumulated in the oil accounts (Dabán and Lacoche, 2007). Countries such as Nigeria and Venezuela have attempted to use a long-term oil price to determine the portion of oil revenues to be saved, but without much success, because of a lack of realism in the oil price projections. In Ecuador, the proliferation of earmarking arrangements led to liquidity problems and weakened expenditure quality (Thomas and others, 2008). In Algeria, the creation of specific oil accounts allocated to multiyear public investment projects has complicated cash management and undermined transparency and accountability (Humphreys and Sandbu, 2007).

Natural Resource Funds

Many resource-producing countries have created natural resource funds,[4] in most cases for stabilization and saving purposes. (See Box 13.3 for examples.) The funds are designed to be used in the event of a shortfall or depletion of resource revenues, as for example in Norway and Chile.[5] In some low-income resource-producing countries, the creation of natural resource funds has also been justified on the grounds of weaknesses in the existing PFM systems. For example, in Algeria, Chad, and Ecuador, the lack of well-defined budget classification systems

[4] Resource funds that are linked to fiscal resource revenues have many names depending on their specific objective, including stabilization funds, liquidity funds, savings funds, funds for future generations, or sovereign wealth funds (Baunsgaard and others, 2012).

[5] For a detailed discussion on Norway's sovereign wealth fund, see Ekeli and Sy (2011).

BOX 13.3 Natural Resource Funds in Resource-Rich Countries

Natural Resource Funds with Stabilization Objectives

Chile's Economic and Social Stability Fund (FEES, 2006) was created by the Fiscal Responsibility Law as part of reforms that institutionalized the operation of a structural balance rule for fiscal policy formulation and implementation. It replaced a price-contingent copper stabilization fund. The FEES receives as inflows the actual central government surplus (net of contributions to the Pension Reserve Fund and to the recapitalization of the central bank). Its funds can be drawn on if desired, according to needs defined in the annual budget law. Until 2008 the FEES accrued substantial financial assets. This was because Chile ran large fiscal surpluses due to a substantial increase in copper prices relative to the projected long-term copper prices used in the calculation of structural mineral revenue and in the determination of the structural balance. Chile has subsequently withdrawn resources from the FEES to finance fiscal deficits caused by a fall in actual copper prices and by fiscal stimulus packages introduced during the 2008–09 global economic crisis.

Russia's Reserve Fund (RF, 2008) was established from part of the resources of an oil stabilization fund. Oil and gas revenue in excess of the budget allocation is deposited in the RF until its balance reaches 10 percent of GDP (excesses are to be transferred to a savings fund). RF assets can be withdrawn to cover financing needs if there are oil and gas revenue shortfalls. Its assets can also be used for early debt repayments. Since its establishment, the RF has been gradually depleted (it amounted to less than 1 percent of GDP in mid-2012 compared with 10 percent of GDP in 2008) because the non-oil balance has been much higher than oil revenue.

Natural Resource Funds with Savings Objectives

Chile's Pension Reserve Fund (FRP) (2006) was established to meet future pension costs. For that purpose, it receives annual contributions from the budget of 0.2 percent of GDP irrespective of the fiscal balance, and up to 0.5 percent of GDP if fiscal surpluses exceed 0.2 percent of GDP. The government has had to borrow to make contributions to the FRP in recent years given overall fiscal deficits, but the mandatory contributions to the fund are low.

Alaska's Permanent Fund (1976) receives 50 percent of the state's mineral revenues (up from 25 percent in1980). It pays annual dividends to the population based on a fraction of the fund's realized earnings, as a safeguard against pressures to spend the oil revenue. In practice, the dividends have come to be seen as entitlements, and at times the government has borrowed substantially to finance increased spending. This debt accumulation runs against the intended intergenerational transfer of resources.

Funds for Future Generations (FFGs). Several countries, including Gabon and Kuwait, have created FFGs financed by a fraction of annual oil revenue (between 10 and 25 percent). The use of the funds' resources is relatively general, including (despite the funds' titles) for discretionary transfers to the budget. In Gabon, transfers to the budget can happen only when the fund's balance surpasses a certain threshold. The allocation of a large fraction of oil revenue to the fund in Kuwait has been smooth because the government has recorded very large overall surpluses. In Gabon, allocations have not been so smooth because fiscal surpluses have been much smaller than those in Kuwait.

and the absence of reliable internal controls and expenditure tracking systems were used to justify the creation of special funds for the execution and payment of resource-funded spending.

Countries have used different institutional arrangements to create their natural resource funds. In some cases, resource funds are created as separate treasury accounts that are managed in coordination with the budget process. Other countries have created natural resource funds as separate institutions with their own legal personalities, institutional independence, and authority to spend resource revenues for certain uses. These "separate" resource funds have their own boards, mandates, and regulations to make it more difficult to raid their assets. For example, in the United States, in the state of Alaska, the Permanent Fund is a separate public corporation, with a separate legal personality, and institutional and administrative independence. Its trustees are appointed by the government, and its rules can be changed only by referendum. In Azerbaijan and Kazakhstan, oil funds are managed off-budget through presidential directives, with the purpose of insulating oil revenues from spending pressures from the legislature. In Chad, oil revenues are earmarked to separate funds managed outside the budget and treasury processes to prevent the revenues from being allocated to nonpriority spending.

Countries' experiences with natural resource funds, however, have not always been positive. The effectiveness of resource funds can be undermined by the absence of liquidity constraints, political interference, and public pressure to spend the money (Stevens and Mitchell, 2008). For example, in Chad, the growing balances in the Future Generation Fund were largely offset by increased domestic borrowing and the accumulation of arrears (Dabán and Lacoche, 2007). In addition, the existence of resource-funded expenditures that are executed and paid for through separate funds usually complicates cash and asset management.

Political interference, which has occurred in both developed and developing countries, has in some cases undermined resource funds' effectiveness. For example, in the Canadian province of Alberta, provincial authorities frequently changed and circumvented the rules governing the management of the Albertan Heritage Fund to allow the government to raid the fund. Evidence also shows that resource funds have not always been successful in preventing the development of a rentier mentality. Alaska shows some indications that the Permanent Fund, which distributes a dividend directly to the people, is turning Alaskan public society into a rentier society (Stevens and Mitchell, 2008). The oil-funded annual dividend discourages entrepreneurship, erodes tax collections, and increases public debt.

Separate Investment Bodies

Some resource-producing countries have created separate bodies to carry out resource-funded capital spending or to invest the balance of the resource fund. Kuwait and Saudi Arabia have long-standing investment agencies—the Kuwait Investment Authority and the Public Investment Fund, respectively—that undertake capital spending that is not integrated into the budget process (see Chapter 10). In addition, some resource-producing countries have created separate investment committees to design and monitor the resource funds' investment strategies. For instance, in São Tomé and Príncipe, the Management and Investment Committee includes representatives of the ministry of finance and the central bank, a member appointed by the president, and two members appointed by the national assembly, one of whom must be from the opposition (Humphreys and Sandbu, 2007). The creation of separate investment bodies can strengthen decision-making processes, as long as they are perceived as independent and not subject to political pressures. However, separate investment committees have often resulted in dual budgeting and asset management practices, with poor outcomes at the strategic, budgetary, and operational levels. In addition, some low-income countries have difficulty finding enough qualified people to staff these committees, and independence can be difficult to guarantee.

Separate Oversight Bodies

Some resource-producing countries have attempted to add an extra layer of accountability to the standard mechanisms provided by the supreme audit institution. Some have made mandatory an annual audit of the resource fund by an external independent auditor, as in Azerbaijan and Kazakhstan. Other countries have created parallel oversight institutions. For instance, in Chad, the Collège is responsible for conducting ex post assessments of oil-funded expenditures. In Timor-Leste, the Petroleum Fund Consultative Council, made up of former government officials, provides opinions on major issues and acts as an intermediary for communication with the public (Kim, 2005). In Mauritania, the National Hydrocarbon Revenue Monitoring Committee, made up of public officials, is responsible for estimating and monitoring the transfers from the oil fund to the treasury single account. São Tomé and Príncipe has chosen to combine the two options. It has created a joint government–civil society organization, the Petroleum Oversight Commission, which enjoys investigative, administrative, and judicatory powers. In addition, the oil account is subject to mandatory annual audits by an international accounting firm. Finally, the National Assembly conducts yearly public plenary sessions on oil-sector issues.

The creation of separate oversight bodies poses several challenges in low-income countries. The deliberations of these bodies and their advice to legislators, even if they do not have the power of veto, inevitably carry great weight. In fact, in countries with weak institutions, separate oversight bodies can be perceived as a second "government" or "congress." Their existence may also undermine the morale of existing oversight institutions and create further conflicts. In addition, most low-income countries can have difficulty finding citizens with the appropriate skills, experience, and independence of action to place themselves in opposition to government decisions. For instance, in Chad, owing to the lack of human and technical capacity, the Collège has carried out its oversight function only sporadically and in overlap with the Cour de Comptes (State Audit Institution) (Dabán and Lacoche, 2007).

Special Legal Frameworks

In some resource-producing countries, the management of resource revenues is regulated by the general budget legislation, which is usually complemented by additional legislation, as in Norway and Alaska, or by including special provisions in the fiscal responsibility legislation, as in Mexico and Ecuador. To counter the dangers of patronage, some resource-producing countries have enshrined the management of resource revenues in the constitution, in an organic law, or in special legislation. Success stories include countries such as São Tomé and Príncipe, Timor-Leste, and Mauritania, which have enacted simple oil revenue management laws adapted to their needs and capacities. However, Chad's experience illustrates that excessive complexity and rigidity of the corresponding legal framework can jeopardize the success of an oil revenue management law (Dabán and Lacoche, 2007; Thomas and others, 2008).

13.3. PFM REFORMS FOR NATURAL RESOURCE-RICH COUNTRIES

The analysis so far shows that preventing the resource curse entails significant policy and institutional challenges. These challenges mainly pertain to the successful implementation of prudent fiscal policy and the development of robust institutional systems. The previous section discussed the experiences of those countries that have attempted to overcome institutional challenges, with varying degrees of success, by introducing special operational mechanisms, in some cases circumventing existing budget systems. When these mechanisms are poorly designed, very rigid, and opaque, they can result in, among other problems, fragmentation and delay in the budget process and inefficiency in government spending.

This section proposes a PFM framework for improving rather than replacing existing budgetary institutions. It proposes sequencing reforms over the short and medium terms. In the short term, reform would focus on better integrating resource revenues and special operational mechanisms into the existing budget processes. Over the medium term, reform would concentrate on strengthening existing budget institutions and convergence with more sophisticated, if not best, international practices. The sequence of proposed reforms aims to address the institutional and policy challenges posed by the management of resource revenues. These challenges pertain to developing a long-term strategy and a medium-term fiscal framework, integrating resource revenues into the treasury and budget processes, strengthening asset management, enhancing accountability and transparency, and adopting a special legal framework. Each of these elements is discussed in turn.

13.3.1. Planning for the Medium Term

Because of the temporal nature and high volatility of resource revenues, a resource-producing country would benefit from adopting a long-term strategy for the allocation of resource revenues among alternative uses. The monitoring and implementation of the long-term strategy would use the nonresource primary deficit (as a ratio of nonresource GDP) as the key fiscal indicator (Medas and Zakharova, 2009). The strategy might envisage a prudent path of expenditure, a strong political commitment that resource-related savings will be used to finance future nonresource deficits, and a comprehensive asset management strategy, including indicative targets for the government's net financial and physical (infrastructure) wealth. Strategy design requires assessing the government's overall net wealth, including estimates of the value of natural resources in the ground (an inherently complex task), and long-term projections of future resource revenues. This assessment should take into account the size of proven resource reserves, costs of production, realistic projections for world prices, extraction and depletion rates, and the fiscal regime of operators (including the national resource company), with all the uncertainties attached to each factor. In addition, the long-term strategy should assess the pros and cons of alternative uses of resource revenues, including increasing expenditures, cutting taxes, retiring outstanding debt, and building resource savings. Resource-producing countries would benefit from the adoption of medium-term fiscal and budget frameworks to underpin the implementation of the long-term strategy (see Box 13.4).

Medium-term budget frameworks (MTBFs) are discussed in detail in Chapter 4. The MTBF could include, for instance, three-year ceilings for both the level of spending and the nonresource deficit, consistent with the long-term fiscal strategy, in addition to medium-term projections for annual withdrawals of resource revenues from treasury accounts to finance the nonresource deficit. The MTBF can help resource-producing countries avoid implementing procyclical fiscal policies, which is important because volatile fiscal policies destabilize aggregate demand, exacerbate uncertainty, and induce macroeconomic instability. In addition, large swings in expenditure are likely to reduce its quality and efficiency.

The MTBF needs to be fully integrated into the budget process. It should be designed to handle unexpected shortfalls or windfalls in resource revenues, such as those stemming from a sudden drop or increase in world commodity prices. To avoid having to cut spending sharply if a shortfall occurs, the government needs to ensure sufficient financing capacity. Because many resource-producing countries are credit constrained (especially when resource prices are low), liquidity cushions are recommended. Fiscal policy responses to windfalls depend on country circumstances. For a country with a relatively strong financial position, a sustainable nonresource deficit, and reasonable public expenditure management, an expansion in the nonresource deficit may be appropriate, especially if resource revenues are expected to remain strong and the additional spending is productive (such as on key infrastructure and human capital). For other countries, much more of the resource windfall should be saved (in financial, rather than physical, assets held abroad) or used to reduce gross public debt. The more dependent on resource revenues the government is, the higher the risks associated with procyclical spending of those revenues. Hence, more guarded use of the windfall is advisable in highly resource-dependent countries.

BOX 13.4 Efforts toward Multiannual Budget Planning in Resource-Rich Countries

A number of resource-producing countries have been reorienting their budget processes to lengthen the period covered by their fiscal frameworks. Many reform initiatives have included a fiscal policy statement establishing a medium-term path for expenditure aggregates, medium-term macroeconomic forecasts, requirements for ministries to maintain budget estimates beyond the budget year and to explicitly cost new measures, and hard cash budget constraints for ministries.

In a number of cases, countries have introduced legislation on medium-term budget planning:

- In *Azerbaijan*, the organic budget law requires that a budget be prepared for the upcoming year as well as for the three following years. The government prepares medium-term economic forecasts that include government priorities and its public investment plan, which are updated annually.
- In *Russia*, since 2007, the parliament has approved full-fledged rolling three-year federal budgets. Russia's Budget Code mandates a target for the non-oil deficit of 4.7 percent of GDP (although the target was suspended from April 2009 through end-2013 as a result of the global financial crisis). To capture the full effect of spending decisions and to create stability in the budget process, Russia's rolling three-year budget explicitly links existing policy to parameters (inflation and volumes in transfer systems), and a specific fiscal space available for new policies is determined before the start of each budget preparation round. Russia also maintains two oil funds: the Reserve Fund (a rainy-day fund) and the National Wealth Fund, oriented toward long-term savings.

In *Norway*, a key concern is how to use oil reserves to cover future non-oil deficits caused not only by the depletion of reserves but also by pension liabilities. The authorities' fiscal policy is based on a fiscal guideline—over the cycle, the non-oil deficit should average 4 percent of the financial wealth accumulated in the oil fund (approximately equal to the average real rate of return on financial investments). This rule implies limited use of oil wealth in the short term, with increasing use over time. For Norway, the usual sustainability benchmarks indicate that the present fiscal stance is broadly sustainable, while implying some gradual decline in the non-oil deficit in the long term. The Norwegian fiscal guideline is also unusual because it isolates the annual budget from oil price volatility, but makes it sensitive to variations in the value of the financial wealth accumulated in the oil fund, for example, due to changes in the stock market.

Some countries have introduced fiscal responsibility laws (FRLs). In *Chile*, a structural balance guideline was institutionalized in the 2006 FRL (see Box 13.3). The framework is supported by two funds (stabilization and savings). *Mexico's* FRL, approved in March 2006, mandates the inclusion of five-year quantitative projections and costing for new fiscal measures in the budget documents. It also envisages a balance-or-surplus rule and the use of a reference oil price to smooth expenditures.

Sources: Thomas and others (2008); Dabán and Hélis (2010); Baunsgaard and others (2012).

13.3.2. Integrating Resource Revenues into Budget Processes

In principle, resource revenues could be managed in the same way as other government revenues and be deposited in the TSA. However, under certain circumstances, often arising from a weak treasury infrastructure and poor cash management practices, some resource-producing countries may consider it useful to set up a *resource revenue account* (RRA). The RRA can help solidify public support for building a resource buffer for the future and provide an easy and transparent way to present and manage the stocks and flows of resource revenues.

If created, it is advisable to establish the RRA as an account coherently integrated into the budget process. Integration with the budget is best achieved by ensuring that the account operates only as a government account rather than as a separate institution and that the account has no authority to spend. As discussed earlier, country experience shows that, in the absence of strong institutional frameworks, resource accounts created as separate institutions can lead to an excessive concentration of power and to fragmentation of the budget process, and may even discourage reform efforts in existing budgetary institutions. In addition, the rules and operations of the account should be transparent, with stringent mechanisms to ensure accountability and prevent misuse. A country could establish a system in which all resource revenues are deposited into the RRA, while annual withdrawals from the RRA are determined in the annual budget law and are intended to finance the nonresource deficit. The authorization of larger-than-budgeted withdrawals from the RRA should be subject to transparent and tightly controlled conditions, ideally similar to those contemplated in the organic budget law to alter budget appropriations.

Regarding budget execution, resource revenues should be handled in the same way as the rest of government revenues. However, the availability of resource revenues may create strong pressure either to increase spending above the annual budget appropriations or to shift the use of resource revenues to nonpriority spending. Therefore, resource-producing countries would benefit from enhancing expenditure controls to prevent budget overruns. The main challenge in resource-producing countries is combating pressure to increase annual withdrawals from the RRA above the levels originally budgeted. To curb these pressures, the annual budget law could clearly establish that annual withdrawals from the RRA should not exceed the amount explicitly authorized for this purpose. Enforcement of this provision can be greatly facilitated by the administration's strongly expressed political commitment to the approved budget and by entrusting the ministry of finance with the powers and responsibilities within the cabinet (or council of ministers) to enforce it.

Budget overruns can also be minimized with the formulation—and regular updating—of prudent and sound commitment plans, in coordination with spending ministries, and the enhancement of accounting, reporting, and internal-control systems. In addition, resource-producing countries can especially benefit from establishing a well-designed mechanism for the orderly amendment of the budget. The government should conduct a midyear review of budget execution. If either a material shortfall in resources (whether resource revenues, nonresource revenues, or donor funding) or an increase in expenditures beyond the authorities' control occurs, the government should assess a range of courses of action. These actions would include seeking additional financing while not undermining the sustainability of the government's net financial position, reducing or reallocating some budget allocations, increasing nonresource revenues, and requesting from the legislature the authorization for a higher-than-budgeted withdrawal from the RRA.

Given the usually high expectations triggered by resource revenues, resource-producing countries can benefit from the adoption of a system to track spending execution and to show as early as possible the positive impact of resource revenues. This requires putting in place sound budget and accounting classifications and a well-defined reporting system. The tracking system discourages the use of earmarking provisions, separate special accounts, and special budgetary bodies, which, as discussed earlier, have the potential to generate negative side effects.

13.3.3. Strengthening Asset Management

Resource-producing countries may accumulate large deposits in the RRA, especially at the start of their natural resource production horizon. The criteria for investing the balance of the RRA should be determined according to the volume, the expected use, and the time horizon of resource savings. If the resource deposits are small to moderate, and the authorities expect to use them in the short to medium term, there may be no need for an investment policy other than holding the RRA's balance in a domestic currency–denominated account at the central bank and conducting simple and limited investment operations. However, the accumulation of large resource deposits, which the authorities expect to use over the long term, calls for the design of a more sophisticated investment strategy.[6]

The investment strategy could be return driven, yet conservative, with prudent provisions for limiting risk and ensuring liquidity. Especially in low-income countries and small middle-income countries, it is advisable to invest the RRA abroad, in foreign currency–denominated instruments, because the domestic economy is unlikely to be able to absorb large investments. In general, the responsibility for designing and approving the investment strategy for government assets, including the RRA, should reside with the ministry of finance. However, as discussed earlier, under certain circumstances, resource-producing countries may create a separate investment committee to add a layer of independent management. Low-income countries often have difficulties finding enough appropriately skilled people to staff these committees, which consequently may not be able to provide the ministry of finance with an independent and nonpartisan opinion. Alternatively, the financial agent of the treasury could act as an investment advisor to the ministry of finance. The designation of the financial agent of the treasury depends on local capacity and the volume of financial assets to be invested and managed. For small-to-moderate resource deposits, the central bank could act as the financial agent, under a well-designed protocol. For large resource deposits, which are maintained in foreign currency–denominated offshore accounts, the treasury could contract for the services of a major international financial institution, selected through a competitive open tender.

---

[6] Under this scenario, the resource fund could qualify as a sovereign wealth fund (SWF). In this case, at a minimum, the government should adhere to the Santiago Principles on the management of SWFs, which have been adopted by the International Working Group of Sovereign Wealth Funds (see http://www.iwg-swf.org/pr.htm for more information).

Management of the RRA should be integrated into an overall government asset-liability strategy. The balance sheet of the RRA should be consolidated with other government financial operations into a statement of assets and liabilities that is audited and presented annually to the legislature. This statement should include information on public debt and the asset and liability positions of the national resource company, if one exists. A key objective of the statement is to present an estimate of government's net financial wealth, and to permit the legislature and the public at large to review the net saving resulting from the operations of the RRA when consolidated with other government financial operations.

13.3.4. Enhancing Accountability and Transparency

Citizens of resource-producing countries may find it easier to impose discipline on government and reduce the risk of mismanagement of resource revenue if they are well informed and can rely on well-defined accountability mechanisms. To that end, resource-producing countries should adopt institutional arrangements to ensure that citizens have access to information about the magnitude of resource revenues, the rate at which they are spent, the composition and impact of the spending, and management of the RRA balance.

To strengthen transparency of the use of resource revenues, the budget documents should make explicit the contribution of resource revenues to financing the budget deficit. In particular, the budget documents would present the calculation of the nonresource deficit as the difference between nonresource revenues and all budgeted expenditures, and identify the portion of resource revenues used to finance the nonresource deficit. In addition, the budget documents would establish the annual amounts of resource revenues to be deposited in and withdrawn from the treasury accounts. Transparency would also be strengthened by attaching to the budget documents the country's long-term fiscal strategy.

Transparency and oversight of the RRA's operations are also vital. In particular, the success of the RRA—both actual financial returns and public perception—depends in part on the transparency and accountability of its operations. Therefore, it is advisable to establish specific reporting mechanisms, including the production and dissemination of an audited annual report on the operations of the RRA.

To ensure accountability, resource-producing countries with weak institutional frameworks should have the RRA audited by an independent, internationally known external auditor, in addition to the usual audit conducted by the supreme audit institution. Given the significance of resource revenues, some countries may also find it useful to create special oversight boards, which can help broaden society's participation in the decision-making process (for example, by allowing for consultation with civil society organizations and eminent citizens). The special oversight board may also help counterbalance conflicting political interests, improve transparency, and promote public debate on resource issues. However, the creation of separate oversight bodies poses several challenges, especially in low-income countries, as discussed earlier.

BOX 13.5 The Extractive Industries Transparency Initiative Criteria

As soon as the Extractive Industries Transparency Initiative (EITI) Board considers that a country has met the five requirements listed below, the country becomes an EITI candidate country.

1. Regular publication of all material oil, gas, and mining payments by companies to governments ("payments") and all material revenues received by governments from oil, gas, and mining companies ("revenues") to a wide audience in a publicly accessible, comprehensive, and comprehensible manner.
2. Where such audits do not already exist, payments and revenues are the subject of a credible, independent audit, applying international auditing standards.
3. Payments and revenues are reconciled by a credible, independent administrator, applying international auditing standards and with publication of the administrator's opinion regarding that reconciliation, including discrepancies, should any be identified.
4. This approach is extended to all companies including state-owned enterprises.
5. Civil society is actively engaged as a participant in the design, monitoring, and evaluation of this process and contributes toward public debate.

A public, financially sustainable work plan for all the above is developed by the host government, with assistance from the international financial institutions where required, including measurable targets, a timetable for implementation, and an assessment of potential capacity constraints.

Source: EITI (2005), p. 9.

Since 2000, a number of international efforts to promote greater transparency in resource-rich countries have been attempted. One is the Extractive Industries Transparency Initiative (EITI), which is a globally developed standard that promotes revenue transparency. Its areas of interest include transparency over revenues of resource-rich countries and payments by oil and mining companies to governments and to government-linked entities. EITI has an established methodology and criteria that a country must be fully compliant with to become an EITI candidate country (see Box 13.5 for the criteria).

13.3.5. Adopting a Special Legal Framework

The implementation of the recommendations outlined earlier could be facilitated by adoption of a specific PFM legal framework for the management of resource revenues. It may suffice to reflect these provisions in high-ranking legislation, such as an organic budget law or other legislation of a quasi-constitutional character. The framework must be based on strong ownership and broad consensus; drafted in line with the parameters of the local legal system; and integrated with existing expenditure regulations, limitations, and laws that govern budget processes. In addition, the framework should be as simple as possible, particularly in low-income countries, and avoid duplications. It should not regulate subjects that are already addressed in other legislation and regulations, such as public procurement, public information, disclosure, conflicts of interest, and judicial review.

The legal framework should include a broad definition and coverage of resource revenues. The framework should cover all types of resource revenues, including royalties, taxes, bonuses, dividends of the national resource company, premiums, and in-kind revenues.

13.3.6. Sequencing of PFM Reforms

Resource-producing countries may need to adopt reforms to strengthen their PFM systems in line with the recommendations discussed in this section. In the short term, reforms should focus on adopting basic PFM tools (see Table 13.1). Budget formulation reforms should aim to expand the content of the budget

TABLE 13.1

Sequencing of Public Financial Management Reforms for Resource-Producing Countries

Step	Short term	Medium term
Budget presentation	Expand the content of budget documents to include a comprehensive definition and projections of resource revenues, and an estimate of the nonresource deficit and the contribution of resource revenues to financing it.	Reform the general budget law to make permanent the proposed expansions in the content of budget documents.
Planning and budgeting	Formulate rough long-term resource projections based on resource companies' inputs and an aggregate medium-term budget framework (MTBF). Adopt a code to monitor the execution of priority programs.	Build capacity to make long-term resource projections. Adopt a long-term fiscal strategy, an MTBF, and a well-defined budget classification system.
Resource revenue account (RRA)	Set up an RRA fully integrated into the budget process. If resource deposits are large, they should be managed by international financial institutions and deposited offshore.	Deposit all resource revenues in the treasury single account. Strengthen central bank capacity to manage resource deposits. Develop an integrated asset-liability strategy.
Budget execution	Formulate commitment plans and an interim reporting and tracking system. Secure political commitment to amend the budget in an orderly way.	Reform the general budget law to reinforce minister of finance's prerogatives within the cabinet (or council of ministers).
Asset management	Adopt an investment strategy for the RRA.	Develop a more sophisticated investment strategy for the portfolio that balances return and risk. Explore setting up an investment committee.
Oversight and transparency	Establish a special unit in the ministry of finance to reconcile and disseminate resource-revenue information. Strengthen the content of budget documents. Commission external audits of the RRA by an independent firm.	Reform the organic budget law to establish a special reporting mechanism for resource revenue–related operations. Explore setting up a special oversight institution. Strengthen the supreme audit institution.
Legal framework	Rely on the annual budget law and other pieces of legislation.	Adopt a resource-revenue-management law, based on broad consensus.

Source: Authors.

documents to include a comprehensive definition of resource revenues, as well as an estimate of the nonresource deficit. Countries should also begin to put together their MTBFs and long-term projections of resource revenues. A special unit could be created at the ministry of finance to be put in charge of reconciling and disseminating information on resource revenues. To strengthen budget execution, reforms should focus on introducing a simple regulatory code to track the execution of priority spending and on formulating commitment plans for main line ministries. Asset management can be enhanced by setting up a well-defined RRA and outlining a simple investment strategy to manage its balance. Any legal changes required by these reforms may be introduced in the short term in the annual budget law.

Over the medium term, reforms would target more profound changes aimed at adopting (or converging toward) best international practices. Some of these reforms may require amending the general budget law or adopting a special legal framework. Reforms could, for example, focus on building capacity in formulating long-term alternative scenarios and sensitivity analysis for resource revenues, adopting a long-term fiscal strategy, and expanding the MTFF to include medium-term budgets. In addition, actions could be taken to adopt a well-defined budget classification system. Reform efforts for asset management should aim to strengthen government capacity to manage the RRA balance and develop an integrated asset-liability strategy. A more sophisticated investment strategy that balances financial returns and risks for resource savings may be needed. Special reporting mechanisms for resource revenue–related operations may also be required. Accountability would be enhanced by strengthening the supreme audit institution's oversight capacity, or perhaps creating a special oversight institution.

13.4. CONCLUSION

The resource curse is not an iron law, but a preventable disease. However, to ensure the transparent and efficient management of resource revenues and avoid the resource curse, resource-producing countries need to strengthen their PFM systems substantially. This strengthening is important for two related reasons. First, the management of resource revenues poses important macroeconomic, intergenerational, political economy, and governance challenges when compared with other government revenues. These challenges derive from the difficulties of managing large, volatile, and (in some cases) temporary resource revenues and the way in which resource revenues are generated, without the direct scrutiny of taxpayers or donors. Second, resource-producing countries need to strengthen their PFM systems to be able to implement successfully the prudent fiscal policies and long-term fiscal strategy needed to avoid the resource curse.

Given that implementing PFM reforms takes time, some resource-rich countries have adopted special operational mechanisms, often to bypass existing ill-functioning PFM systems. The most used mechanisms include rules-based frameworks, resource funds, parallel budgetary and treasury procedures, separate investment committees and oversight institutions, and special legal frameworks. The adoption of these mechanisms is intended to quickly crystallize public support for government management of resource revenues and to start PFM reform in a separate stand-alone body or procedure, instead of reforming the entire PFM system.

Cross-country experience shows that in a few cases the adoption of special operational mechanisms for the management of resource revenue has been successful. When rigidly designed and implemented, however, these special mechanisms have sometimes eroded competition for resources within the budget, reduced the efficiency of government spending, and led to fragmentation and delay in the budget process. In other cases, the establishment of separate bodies has resulted in high administrative costs reflecting the sometimes privileged bureaucracy of these separate bodies, and eroded incentives for reforming existing budgetary institutions.

Against this background, a PFM framework and reform path for the management of resource revenues should aim to enhance, instead of replace, existing budgetary institutions, while preserving the integrity of the budget process, and taking into account the institutional diversity of resource-producing countries. Such a framework includes the following elements: (1) a transparent and comprehensive presentation of resource revenue in the budget—emphasizing the role of the nonresource deficit; (2) a set of sound long-term projections, a sustainable long-term fiscal strategy, realistic medium-term fiscal frameworks, and a well-defined budget classification system; (3) a system of flexible and transparent transfers from the treasury accounts to finance the nonresource deficit; (4) the development of a unified budget execution process, avoiding rigid earmarking mechanisms; (5) sound cash flow management, based on an integrated banking system and a treasury single account; (6) sound and integrated asset-liability management; and (7) enhanced accountability and transparency mechanisms.

Governments should adopt a sequenced path of PFM reforms. Some reforms can be implemented in the short term, even in countries where PFM arrangements are weak. Over the medium and long terms, reforms should aim to converge with more sophisticated international practices.

REFERENCES

Baunsgaard, T., M. Villafuerte, M. Poplawski-Ribeiro, and C. Richmond, 2012, "Fiscal Frameworks for Resource Rich Developing Countries," IMF Staff Discussion Note 12/04 (Washington: International Monetary Fund).

Comité Asesor para el Diseño de una Política Fiscal de Balance Estructural de Segunda Generación para Chile, 2010, *Propuestas para Perfeccionar la Regla Fiscal: Informe Final,* Dirección de Presupuestos, Gobierno de Chile, Santiago, Chile.

Dabán, T., 2010, "Strengthening Chile's Rule-Based Fiscal Framework," IMF Country Report 10/232 (Washington: International Monetary Fund).

———, and J.L. Hélis, 2010, "A Public Financial Management Framework for Resource-Producing Countries," IMF Working Paper 10/72 (Washington: International Monetary Fund).

Dabán, T., and S. Lacoche, 2007, "Fiscal Policy and Oil Revenue Management: The Case of Chad," in "Chad: Selected Issues and Statistical Appendix," IMF Country Report 07/28 (Washington: International Monetary Fund).
Eifert, B., A. Gelb, and N.B. Tallroth, 2003, "Managing Oil Wealth," *Finance & Development*, Vol. 40, No. 1. Available via the Internet: https://www.imf.org/external/pubs/ft/fandd/2003/03/eife.htm.
Ekeli, T., and Amadou Sy, 2011, "The Economics of Sovereign Wealth Funds: Lessons from Norway," in *Beyond the Curse: Policies to Harness the Power of Natural Resources*, ed. by Rabah Arezki, Thorvaldur Gylfason, and Amadou Sy (Washington: International Monetary Fund).
Extractive Industries Transparency Initiative (EITI), 2005, *Source Book* (London: EITI Secretariat at the U.K. Department for International Development).
Gelb, A., 1988, *Oil Windfalls: Blessing or Curse* (New York: Oxford University Press).
———, 2011, "Economic Diversification in Resource-Rich Countries," in *Beyond the Curse: Policies to Harness the Power of Natural Resources*, ed. by Rabah Arezki, Thorvaldur Gylfason, and Amadou Sy (Washington: International Monetary Fund).
Humphreys, M., and M.E. Sandbu, 2007, "The Political Economy of Natural Resource Funds," in *Escaping the Resource Curse*, ed. by M. Humphreys, J.D. Sachs, and J.E. Stiglitz (New York: Columbia University Press).
Kim, Y.K., 2005, "Managing Oil/Gas Wealth in Timor-Leste," in "Democratic Republic of Timor-Leste—Selected Issues and Statistical Appendix," IMF Country Report 05/150 (Washington: International Monetary Fund).
Larraín, F., R. Costa, R. Cerda, M. Villena, and A. Tomaselli, 2011, *Una política fiscal de balance estructural de segunda generación para Chile*, Estudios de Finanzas Publicas, Octubre, Santiago, Chile.
McSherry, B., 2006, "The Political Economy of Oil in Equatorial Guinea," *African Studies Quarterly*, Vol. 8, No. 3, pp. 23–45.
Medas, P., and D. Zakharova, 2009, "A Primer on Fiscal Analysis in Oil-Producing Countries," IMF Working Paper 09/56 (Washington: International Monetary Fund).
Moore, M., 2004, "Revenues, State Formation, and the Quality of Governance in Developing Countries," *International Political Science Review*, Vol. 25, No. 3, pp. 297–319.
Stevens, P., and J.V. Mitchell, 2008, *Resource Depletion, Dependence, and Development: Can Theory Help?* (London: Chatham House).
Thomas, T., P.A. Medas, R. Ossowski, and M. Villafuerte, 2008, *Managing the Oil Revenue Boom: The Role of Fiscal Institutions* (Washington: International Monetary Fund).
Tsalik, S., 2003, *Caspian Oil Windfalls: Who Will Benefit?* (New York: Open Society Institute).

CHAPTER 14

Challenges of Reforming Budgetary Institutions in Developing Countries

RICHARD ALLEN

Interest in strengthening budgetary institutions—defined as the laws, procedures, and rules that determine and regulate the behavior of public officials and organizations[1]—and public financial management (PFM) can be traced back at least 2,000 years. For example, Roman planners of the Claudian aqueducts considered eventual operational and maintenance costs in selecting alternative routes and designs. The fiscal traditions of Turkey date back to the Ottoman Empire. More modern times provide evidence of a stream of reforms, from the "tally sticks" used to record the budget in seventeenth-century England to the latest techniques of fiscal rules (Chapter 3), fiscal risk analysis (Chapter 5), expenditure ceilings, medium-term budget frameworks (Chapter 4), performance budgeting (Chapter 7), accrual accounting and budgeting (Chapters 8 and 11), and expenditure review. In Europe and the United States, a detailed history of the development of budget systems goes back 200 years or more. Yet the processes and determinants of this evolution, as societies move through varying stages of development, although critically important, are imperfectly understood.

The issues addressed in this chapter are these: First, what are the main factors that determine the development of budgetary institutions and systems over time? Second, what lessons can developing countries learn from the long experience of more advanced economies in improving their budgetary institutions, and for the prioritization and sequencing of reforms? Third, how can the international financial institutions (IFIs) and other providers of financial and technical support facilitate the process of reform in developing countries—what adjustments are required to the approaches and models currently applied? These issues are complex, and the conclusions reached by the chapter tentative. The chapter also identifies several areas in which further research would be helpful.

The chapter is structured as follows: The first section provides a conceptual framework for strengthening budgetary institutions and a historical perspective. Against this background, the second section outlines the challenges for developing countries in strengthening their budgetary institutions. The third section sets

This chapter is a substantially revised and updated version of an IMF working paper (Allen, 2009).

[1]This definition of budgetary institutions is based on North (1991).

out a possible framework for the design and sequencing of such reforms, and the fourth section provides concluding remarks.

14.1. HISTORICAL DEVELOPMENT OF BUDGET REFORMS

The quality of governance and public institutions is increasingly seen as fundamental in shaping the economic and social prospects of developing countries, including their efforts to strengthen budgetary institutions and PFM. North, Wallis, and Weingast (2006), for example, have postulated that societies pass through three essential stages—primitive societies; natural states (or "limited access orders") dominated by elites with primary access to power and resources, but vulnerable to violence and political conflict; and "open-access orders" characterized by competition in political and economic arenas.[2] They provide evidence that the transition to becoming an open-access society can take a long time, depending on the pace of adaptation of institutions, organizations, and behavior.

Other writers on public choice and rent seeking, although not embracing the full implications of North, Wallis, and Weingast's analysis, have nevertheless accepted the crucial role played by institutions and the "rules of the game" in determining the opportunities for and progress of reform in the public sector, including the budget arena (Schiavo-Campo, 1994; Campos and Pradhan, 1998; Tanzi, 2000).[3] This literature predicts, in general, that the development of political institutions is likely to precede that of economic institutions, which, in turn, precedes the development of budgetary institutions. However, there are exceptions to this pattern[4] and discontinuities in the development process. Another interesting model, little developed in the literature, is based on a possible relationship between the development of institutions and the process of evolution.[5]

Good fiscal outcomes (for example, maintaining a sustainable fiscal position and an economically efficient allocation of budgetary resources to priority sectors) depend upon having in place processes and procedures for preparing, executing,

---

[2] De Renzio (2011) provides a useful survey of the literature in this field. See also North (1991).

[3] Tanzi (2000) argues that in the real world, as opposed to the ideal world described in classic public finance literature in which the state plays a "normative" role, policymakers assign more weight to their own welfare and that of individuals close to them than they do to the general population. Policies are often greatly influenced by small groups who, in their privileged positions as relatives, close friends, or political associates, have easy access to top policymakers whom they can influence. The power of these "keepers of the gate" can be extraordinary and can distort policies in directions far removed from the ideal. Often such gatekeepers influence not so much general policies as how these policies are carried out and who benefits from them, for example, who is exempt from a tax or import duty.

[4] One exception is the People's Republic of China, where liberalization of economic and, to a lesser extent, budgetary institutions has preceded political liberalization.

[5] This idea was suggested by John Kay (*Financial Times*, October 1, 2009) in relation to the development of large business corporations. According to Kay, corporations develop more as a result of complex adaptation and incremental change than by applying a preexisting formula or model ("intelligent design"). There is thus a relationship with Darwinian evolutionary theory in the natural world.

and overseeing the budget. The budget, however, is both a central institution of the state and a key mechanism for determining the distribution of resources and economic rents to the elites that dominate natural states and to the wider groups and stakeholders that influence the development of open-access societies. Therefore, it can be predicted, first, that the incentive for politicians to fragment the budget (for example, by making important resource decisions outside of the budget and setting up extrabudgetary funds) in developing countries will be substantial and, second, that the budget is, almost by definition, hard to reform except arguably in circumstances that permit or facilitate rent-seeking behavior.

Evidence for the extremely gradual evolution of budgetary institutions can be found in the history of the three countries—France, the United Kingdom, and the United States—illustrated in Table 14.1. In all three countries, a similar pattern can be observed. First was a period during which basic systems of accounting, budgeting, and financial reporting were established according to a uniform set of standards and procedures. In France and the United Kingdom, these basic requirements were laid down broadly in the first half of the nineteenth century, when modern institutions of economic and political competition were also being established.[6] There followed a period of approximately 100 years in which these institutions were refined and consolidated. For example, although most funds were appropriated by the parliaments in the British system of the mid-nineteenth century, no single document reported all government expenditures, no comparison was made between budgeted expenditures and actual expenditures, and different accounting mechanisms were used by various departments and ministries.

By the end of the nineteenth century, many characteristics of a modern budgeting system (in particular, a comprehensive budget and robust accounting, reporting, and control systems) had emerged in Europe. In the United States, a broadly similar pattern can be discerned, but extending over a somewhat longer period. The establishment of basic budgetary institutions took place in the course of the nineteenth century, with further developments and modifications in the first half of the twentieth century (partly reflecting the periodic disputes between the president and congress over control of the budget).

The important point in the context of this chapter is that these developments were taking place at a time when France, the United Kingdom, and the United States were establishing the democratic and competitive economic and political institutions that mark the transition to an open-access society. It is reasonable to postulate that many developing countries will go through a similar set of stages in the evolution of their budgetary institutions as developed countries have done during the past two centuries, though the adjustment process may be faster.

---

[6] In the United Kingdom, important reforms of financial administration also took place in the seventeenth and eighteenth centuries, mainly to finance military campaigns. In his classic book, *The Sinews of Power* (1988), Brewer has shown that efforts to reduce corruption, for example, through the Commissioners of Accounts, and to strengthen the collection of customs and tax revenues contributed greatly to the effectiveness of U.K. state power relative to France and other countries. Parliament also developed an important role in the oversight of public accounts during this period.

TABLE 14.1

Selected Dates in the Development of Budget Systems: France, the United Kingdom, and the United States

France	United Kingdom	United States (Federal)
1791: Accounting Office reporting to parliament 1807: Independent "Cour des comptes" 1814–19: First Restoration—Baron Louis's reforms 1862: Imperial decree on rules for budgeting and treasury single account	1787: Consolidated Fund established 1866: Exchequer and Audit Departments Act (established modern budgeting and accounting system) 1866: Comptroller and Auditor General established	1776: Treasury Office of Accounts established 1809: Appropriations Act (modified in 1870 and 1874) 1887–89: Consolidated accounting, bookkeeping, reporting procedures (Cockrill Commission) 1894: Dockery Act established Comptroller of the Treasury; consolidated annual statement of revenues and expenditures 1921: Budgeting and Accounting Act established Bureau of the Budget and General Accounting Office 1940: Consolidation of uniform standards and procedures for accounting and reporting 1950: Accounting and Auditing Act
1959: Medium-term budget framework for investments 1968: *Rationalisation des choix budgetaires* (The Rationalization of Budget Decisions) 2001–06: Program budgeting From 2006: Accrual accounting 2008: Full medium-term budget framework	1960s: Public Expenditure Survey (PES) and Program Assessment Review (PAR) 1980s: Next Steps Program 1990s: Comprehensive multi-annual budgeting 1991: Citizen's Charter 1998: Public Service Agreements 2000–04: Resource (accrual) budgeting	1982: Federal Managers Financial Integrity Act 1990: Chief Financial Officers Act 1993: Government Performance and Results Act 1994: Government Management Reform Act 2010: Government Performance and Modernization Act

Source: Author's compilation.

Note: Measures that established the basic framework of accounting and budgeting are shown above the broken lines; items shown below the lines were introduced later, especially from the 1980s onward, in a "new wave" of reform.

14.2. CHALLENGES FACING REFORMERS IN DEVELOPING COUNTRIES

Recent research suggests that, in low-income countries, stronger budgetary institutions are associated with improved fiscal performance (Dabla-Norris and others, 2010). This relationship has already been established in the literature for more advanced economies, though the direction of causality has not been demonstrated beyond reasonable doubt.[7] However, as noted above, strengthening budgetary processes and systems in low- and middle-income countries is likely to be constrained

[7]The relevant literature is summarized in Dabla-Norris and others (2010).

by the poor quality of their public institutions: weak centers of government and cabinet systems that create problems of policy coordination and efficient planning, strong patronage systems in which leadership of public agencies is reserved to supporters and patrons of the president, and weak capacity in human resources and information systems. In addition, such countries have insufficient financial resources to spend on necessary technical systems and capacity building.

Systematic long-term data that would demonstrate the long periods required for budgetary improvements to take root in developing countries are lacking, but relevant and suggestive experience is summarized in Gupta and others (2008) and in evidence drawn from the rich experience of the IMF's technical assistance work in the field, especially in Africa. In some cases, isolated progress has been made—for example, in implementing a concrete provision such as a revised budget calendar, a commitment control system, or a simple cash accounting system. In general, however, the reform process has been frustratingly slow, even in narrow technical areas of the budget system, and in some cases after progress is made for a period of years, a reversal occurs. This conclusion is supported by a study of the World Bank's Independent Evaluation Group (2008) and work by de Renzio (2011) that shows a similarly mixed pattern of budget reform outcomes in 16 aid-dependent countries.[8] Recent evidence from the World Bank's Country Policy and Institutional Assessment (CPIA) database suggests that PFM systems have barely improved, according to their measures during the past 10 years.[9] Similar evidence is presented in Andrews (2013).

The thesis that the process of strengthening budgetary institutions is likely to be difficult and slow is given further support in a study that reviews the history of the United Nations as a pioneering provider of technical assistance to developing countries in the fiscal area (among others) (Kohnert, 2008). In the 1950s and 1960s, the United Nations provided assistance on such topics as program and performance budgeting, tax reform, budget classification, accounting methods, and treasury systems to many developing countries. It also acted as a standard setter in these fields, publishing manuals and running international conferences on the topics of budget classification, government finance statistics, and accounting issues.[10] During the same period, the World Bank was also providing advice to developing countries on economic and fiscal issues in a series of more than 20 *Economic Development Reports*. The analysis and recommendations in some of

[8] De Renzio (2011) used data from World Bank/IMF assessments carried out between 2001 and 2004 under the Heavily Indebted Poor Countries (HIPC) Initiative, and more recent PEFA assessments.

[9] Vani (2012) shows that the mean CPIA score for 127 countries increased only from 3.4 to 3.5 between 2001 and 2011.

[10] Kohnert (2008) refers to the following interesting example: The United Nations developed and published an economic classification of the budget (1958), a functional classification (1962), a manual on performance and program budgeting (1962), and a manual on government accounting (1964). In 1963, it encouraged member countries to adopt a multiannual approach to budgeting, and provided training on taxation issues in cooperation with the Harvard Business School. Eminent scholars who participated in these early missions include Richard Goode, Walter Heller, Richard Musgrave, Stanley Surrey, Robert Triffin, and William Vickrey.

these reports bear a strong resemblance to the advice being offered by the World Bank, the IMF, and bilateral donors to the same countries 50 years later.[11] The experience of financial reforms in earlier periods of history also supports this gradual, incremental view of development, as related to budgetary institutions.[12]

Of course, as noted above, development is not a linear process, and countries can be expected to advance at varying speeds. The budget systems of some countries—as well as their economic and political institutions—have clearly developed quite rapidly since 1990, especially among emerging market economies such as those found in Chile, some countries in Central and Eastern Europe, the Republic of Korea, South Africa, and also some low-income countries such as Ethiopia (Peterson, 2011). In some countries with colonial histories, many basic features of an efficient budget system (e.g., commitment controls, a single treasury account, a comprehensive budget, a regular budget calendar, end-of-year accounts, internal and external audit, and in-year reporting) existed at the point of independence, but have subsequently declined through the neglect of formal rules; loss of authority by the finance ministry; donor dependence; uncompetitive salaries in the civil service; and lack of human capacity in economics, finance, and accountancy.

Postconflict countries and fragile states are in a special category. Conditions for institution building may be more favorable, at least in the initial stages, because of the vacuum created by the decline of previous institutions, strong political leadership, and a powerful donor presence (World Bank and ODI, 2011). Schiavo-Campo (2007) argues that strengthening the budget process in postconflict countries is less likely to be impeded by ruling elites, some of which may have been destroyed or severely weakened by the conflict itself. In such countries, however, questions have been raised about the sustainability of the reforms, often both driven and implemented by donors and their international consultants, who devote limited efforts to building the capacity of the regular civil service.

It may be argued that budget reform should be much easier in the early part of the twenty-first century than it was 100 years ago because there is a significantly greater awareness of what constitutes good practice in this field; international standards have been established in areas such as accounting and audit (see Chapter 8); and vastly more efficient methods of transmitting information,

---

[11] See, for example, IBRD (1960). This study recommends the adoption of a single comprehensive budget, including data on both recurrent and capital expenditures; an administrative, economic, and functional classification of budgetary expenditures and revenues; strengthened financial control; control by the finance, ministry of budget, and civil service establishments; transparent budget documents and parliamentary debate; and independent external audit. Many of the weaknesses identified in the study persist to this day.

[12] See, for example, Normanton (1966), which describes the Exchequer and Audit Departments Act of 1866, which established a comprehensive framework of accounting and audit institutions in the United Kingdom that has survived to the present "in all its essentials," as "the greatest achievement of the classical budget movement." However, the framework was not adopted in Germany and the United States until the 1920s, during which time "it had become widely generalized in the West and was supported by a body of academic theory" (p. 21).

ideas, and cross-country experience have been developed and disseminated in an increasingly globalized environment. These advances may indeed facilitate a process of change, provided that the national authorities demonstrate the required degree of political will and leadership. However, there is little empirical evidence to support the view that reform has become easier and more rapid. The argument also misses the point that the fundamental constraint on improvement is not the absence of technical understanding or knowledge, or the lack of sufficient skills or capacity in the public service, or efficient information technology systems—though these issues certainly need to be addressed during reform—but the absence of a supporting environment of political leadership, business processes and procedures, and incentives for change that makes it *possible* to move forward in the first instance and to be sustained over time. Budgets are also much larger in relation to GDP, and more complex structurally, than they were 100 years ago. This is likely to complicate and delay the process of reform, regardless of improvements in technology and communications.

14.3. DEVELOPING A FRAMEWORK FOR REFORMING BUDGETARY INSTITUTIONS

As noted, the process of reforming budgetary institutions is difficult and slow largely because it is driven much more by institutional and political economy factors than by technical ones. A possible framework for analyzing these nontechnical factors is set out by Dressel and Brumby (2009), the World Bank (2011), and Allen and Grigoli (2012). The framework draws attention to five critical institutional interfaces that shape the budget process—formal political institutions, administrative institutions, the role of civil society, other external actors, and internal incentives and drivers within the government's budget office and ministry of finance (Figure 14.1). Equally important, the framework requires reformers to take account of the socio-structural context in which budgetary institutions are embedded. Structural constraints, such as climate, the level of development, the degree of ethnic fragmentation, and the availability of natural resources, constitute boundaries within which budgetary institutions work and evolve.

In practical terms, modernizing budget institutions requires strengthening the "production function" of a ministry of finance or the central budget office so that it can deliver more relevant and precise policy advice, as well as improved operational functions such as the reporting and control of budget execution. Improved budgeting involves several factors, some traditionally neglected, such as the culture, morale, and incentives of the organization; the quality and experience of its management and staff; the organizational structure; the business processes that support and underpin the organization; and the supporting information and human resource management systems. Strengthening relations with the other main actors shown in Figure 14.1 is also crucial. These factors interact, and solutions in one area (for example, an improved organizational chart or introduction

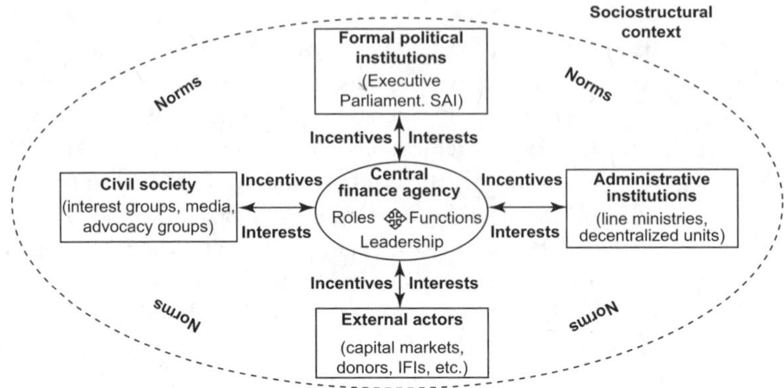

Figure 14.1 The Political Economy Environment of Budgetary Institutions

Source: Dressel and Brumby (2009).

Note: IFI = international financial institution; SAI = supreme audit institution.

of a new information technology system) will not necessarily deal with inefficiencies in another area, and are likely to have limited impact if progress is not made along several fronts simultaneously.

Conventional approaches and tools for analyzing budgetary institutions focus primarily on the formal, technical characteristics of these systems, and pay relatively little attention to analyzing the informal rules and incentives that shape the budget process and affect its operational efficiency or the complex network of relationships among the various players outlined in Figure 14.1. To evaluate the capabilities of a ministry of finance, or the budget process more generally, an assessment of these political economy influences on incentives and the behavior of key actors is not only desirable but essential.

Filling in the framework discussed above, Diamond (2012a, 2012b) provides another useful lens through which to view political economy factors, which he divides into three broad categories: first, *"conditioning" factors* determined by a country's political environment, its economic environment, its governance arrangements, and its technological and capacity environment; second, the *institutional design* of the PFM systems, including relationships within the executive branch, between the legislative and executive branches, and between the executive branch, civil society, and other stakeholders in the budget process; and third, factors that arise from the *internal organization* of the ministry of finance and other central finance agencies—the managerial culture, the limitations of leadership and skills, and other capacity constraints.

Unfortunately, the recommendations contained in most technical assistance reports prepared by the IFIs and other donor organizations, although thoroughly analyzed and justified at a technical level, almost invariably take little account of political economy factors. Consequently, they may be of only limited value in assisting the national authorities to develop a strategy for strengthening budgetary institutions. Many such recommendations fail to meet the test of political reality—they may be supported by the minister of finance but fail to achieve any support from the minister's political colleagues and other actors. This helps explain why many initiatives for reforming the budget process or reorganizing ministries of finance fail to be implemented fully, and why de jure reforms (i.e., changes in the legal framework or other formal rules) tend to be more successful than de facto reforms (Andrews, 2006, 2010, 2013). Through a more thorough analysis of the political economy factors, potential roadblocks to reform initiatives can be identified, recommendations that are nonstarters politically can be weeded out, and change management programs can be proposed to facilitate implementation of the proposed reforms and to ensure they are sustained.

Political economy analysis can highlight serious inefficiencies in the budget process that need to be addressed. For example, an independent revenue agency may share responsibilities for revenue forecasting with the finance ministry, or with the ministry of economy and planning. The revenue agency arguably has an incentive to underestimate the future path of government revenues to more easily hit the performance targets set by the ministry of finance. However, the planning ministry has an incentive to overestimate revenues, as well as the overall rate of economic growth, to demonstrate that the country's poverty reduction targets are being achieved, thus making the country attractive to foreign investors and donors that provide overseas development assistance. In this context, the ministry of finance is more likely to take a neutral position, because its incentive is to adopt a fiscal position sustainable to international creditors. Any reform that attempts to harmonize the forecasting function but fails to take account of the relationships and interactions between these players is unlikely to be successful.

Another relevant example concerns the relationship between the executive and legislative branches of government in the budget process. In more than half the Organisation for Economic Co-operation and Development countries, the legislature has unlimited freedom to make amendments to the annual budget put forward by the executive branch (Wehner, 2010). In such cases it may be difficult to ensure that fiscal rules, such as limits on the level of government borrowing and debt, are enforceable. These problems can be overcome if high levels of cooperation exist between the executive and legislative branches and mechanisms are in place for building consensus between the two branches on the need for fiscal discipline (and the application of a fiscal rule), but in many advanced economies such mechanisms are weak. Similar tensions between the two branches of government also arise in many low-income countries, as a note on the financial implications of the new constitution in Kenya highlights (Murray and Wehner, 2011). The important point is that, in these cases, the informal relationships among the parties can be critical in determining whether formal procedures set out in the legal framework (e.g., a fiscal rule that strengthens budget discipline) can be implemented and enforced.

Two further issues will be discussed in this section: the role of donors in influencing and in many cases driving the budget reform process, and the role of diagnostic instruments.

14.3.1. The Influence of Donors

In many countries, donors and their associated international consultants exert a strong influence on reform (Allen, 2008). Donors frequently provide a substantial proportion of the funding for such measures, in addition to supplying technical assistance. This activity may lead to a dependence on donors and the consultants they hire that inhibits the development of local capacity and channels finance into projects perhaps inappropriate or untimely for the country concerned. The national authorities may respond passively because they may benefit from lucrative rent-seeking opportunities. By extracting large fees for services without direct accountability for results, consultants can be viewed as complicit in the rent-seeking process. This is in contrast to models of PFM reform, such as the "strengthened approach" advocated by the Public Expenditure and Financial Accountability (PEFA) program,[13] in which countries are assumed to take the lead in setting priorities, with donors and IFIs playing a supporting role. Continued care is needed to ensure that the prescriptions of donors are actually relevant and appropriate to the needs of each particular country.

In many cases, donors have focused their financial and technical resources on big-ticket initiatives—such as the introduction of a medium-term expenditure framework (MTEF) and integrated financial management information systems—that are dependent upon large injections of external funding and technical assistance. The presumed idea behind this approach is that the programs may act as a centripetal force toward which other reforms would gravitate. However, a survey of MTEF and information systems projects in Ghana, Tanzania, and Uganda suggests that the approach has had mixed success (Wynne, 2005). Another study notes that some positive lessons have emerged from a decade of MTEF experiments in Africa, including greater awareness of the need to look beyond the annual budget horizon and to focus on the results of government spending. At the same time, "costly failures" have arisen from premature implementation of MTEFs: little or no local ownership; damaging distraction from basic PFM improvements; heavy stress on limited budget capacity; and little improvement in macroeconomic balances, financial control and predictability, or spending efficiency (Schiavo-Campo, 2009). Earlier flagship projects promoted by the World Bank in related areas—such as public investment programs

[13] Documents describing the strengthened approach can be found on the PEFA website (www.pefa.org). PEFA is a partnership comprising the World Bank, the IMF, the European Union, the U.K. Department for International Development, France, the Swiss Economic Cooperation and Development Division, and Norway established in 2002 and financed by a multidonor trust fund. The secretariat is housed in the World Bank.

in the 1980s (see Chapter 10) and cash budgeting—also largely failed to deliver their expected benefits (Lienert and Sarraf, 2001).

Government officials in many countries may have too uncritically accepted advice from the IFIs and donors as a condition of receiving much-needed international assistance and debt relief. Moreover, such improvement initiatives are frequently based on "best practices" exported from developed countries before the initiatives have been fully implemented and assessed, and without ensuring that they can be assimilated into the standard budget practices of the recipient country, or indeed, whether they are relevant to the country's development needs (Schick, 1998).

A related trend is for the IFIs and donors to support—and, in many cases, to take a lead role in drafting—action plans for strengthening budgetary institutions that take a much too optimistic view of the time needed for such measures to be planned and implemented. Little account is taken of the institutional barriers and constraints noted above, or to reach out to all stakeholders whose participation and cooperation is essential to the effective implementation of the reforms concerned (Andrew, 2013). This bias toward underestimating the time required to plan and implement reform initiatives can partly be explained by the electoral cycle and the consequent short time horizon of most finance ministers, who are likely to lose interest if told that reforms will take many years to complete. Moreover, the trend toward providing a larger share of aid in the form of "general budget support" rather than project financing has also raised donors' fiduciary concerns and compressed the time frame of support operations.

In addition to having overoptimistic time horizons, many plans are overloaded with hundreds of activities and actions. The IFIs and donors—and their advisors—are in many cases to blame, for this enables them to package together measures into a "public sector reform" grant or loan that gains approval from the IFI management board and gives the donor increased leverage in the country. However, these packages often prove unmanageable and ineffective, raise unrealistic expectations about what can be achieved, and fall into disarray with only a small fraction of the measures implemented. More nuanced approaches have been tried, for example, the "hurdle" approach in Thailand (Shah and Shen, 2007),[14] that attempt to create an incentive for spending agencies to improve financial management in return for greater flexibility in managing their resources, but these have met with mixed success.

[14]Thailand embarked on a process of "conditional devolution" of performance budgeting reforms. The Bureau of the Budget offered to reduce line itemization for spending agencies, provided they met core financial management standards in seven areas: budget planning, output costing, financial and performance reporting, internal control, procurement management, and internal audit. The hurdles, however, were set at such a high level that hardly any agencies cleared them. As a result, "progress all but stalled, and when the Thaksin government came into office in 2001, the centralized, control-oriented budgeting system still dominated the process" (Shah and Shen, 2007, p. 169).

14.3.2. The Role of Diagnostic Instruments

A further complicating factor is the limitations of existing diagnostic instruments for assessing the quality of budgetary institutions and systems. The best known of these instruments is the PEFA diagnostic tool that focuses on measuring the quality of financial management systems.[15] This instrument has been widely used in developing countries and emerging market economies—more than 125 countries have undertaken a PEFA assessment since 2005, and many repeat assessments have also been carried out. However, in practice, the tool was not designed to take account of the weaknesses in the institutions and governance environments critical to the improvement of budgetary systems. In principle, these institutional gaps could be covered in the narrative section of the PEFA assessment, or by an "institutional and governance review" of the kind piloted by the World Bank in the 2000s. However, such reviews tend to be resisted by national authorities, who have little incentive to open up their governance systems for public scrutiny, and relatively few have been carried out. As a result, the diagnostic information deriving from a PEFA assessment does not provide a complete basis for preparing an action plan to be used by national authorities in strengthening their budgetary institutions.

An example of incomplete information is provided by PEFA Performance Indicator 19 (PI-19), which measures the performance of a country in using open competition in awarding procurement contracts.[16] In many countries, donors have used a poor score on this indicator, alongside other diagnostic information, as evidence that more competitive procurement procedures need to be introduced and have embarked on elaborate projects to support countries in making such improvements. However, procurement is a primary source of rent seeking and remuneration for dominant elites, and the introduction of open procurement procedures is unlikely by itself to change actual practices. Thus, procurement laws in developing countries often include a provision allowing ministers to override the results of procurement competitions "in the national interest." An effective action plan for improving procurement should focus on eliminating rent-seeking behavior before it deals with inadequate competition in the procurement market. However, this path is rarely taken.

Andrews (2010) criticizes the PEFA framework, arguing that it assumes the applicability of a standard "good practice" model of public financial management, an assumption that he demonstrates to be of dubious validity. The usefulness of PEFA assessments is also diminished by the partially subjective nature of the rating system, the lack of a quality control mechanism applied on a consistent basis by all the PEFA partners, and the variability of ratings from assessment to assessment, which can be subject to political influence, especially when donors use the achievement of improved PEFA ratings as a condition for granting budget

---

[15]The assessment methodology is described in PEFA Secretariat (2005). The PEFA instrument includes 28 performance indicators covering various aspects of PFM and 3 indicators describing donor practices in providing aid.

[16]Although this indicator has been revised, it still does not really address the issues discussed here.

support to an aid-receiving country. This may encourage game playing by the government to enlarge its aid allocation.

Despite the caveats noted above, undertaking a rigorous diagnostic assessment of the existing budgetary system, including, to the extent possible, an evaluation of political economy factors, is clearly an essential precondition for building a coherent PFM reform strategy in developing countries. The PEFA framework is the best available tool, but could be improved. A comprehensive revision of the PEFA Performance Measurement Framework was launched in 2012 and should bring improvements. Some suggestions for strengthening the framework are made in Dabla-Norris and others (2010). This study proposes a new budget institutions index that recognizes the multifaceted nature of budget institutions and is broader in scope than other available indicators. The index records the quality of budget institutions along a two-dimensional framework. The first dimension covers the various stages of the budget process (planning and negotiation, approval, and execution). The second reflects five cross-cutting characteristics of the budget process, with particular emphasis on the specifics of budgeting in low-income countries. The criteria assessed include, for example, the comprehensiveness of the budget—as measured by inclusion of information on donor-financed projects and the size of off-budget expenditures; the degree of centralization of budgetary decision making; whether the budget is subject to effective rules and operational controls; the ability of the legislature to scrutinize the budget; and whether there is an effective system of internal and external control. The index allows for benchmarking against the performance of middle-income countries, across regions, and according to different institutional arrangements that deliver good fiscal performance. However, further work is needed to develop and refine the index and to evaluate its utility through field studies.

14.3.3. Prioritizing and Sequencing Reform of Budgetary Institutions

Is there a better way to plan and sequence the reform of budgetary institutions for efficient results? Schick has argued that, when improving a budget system in countries with low capacity, actions should first be aimed at "getting the basics right" (see Chapter 1). For example, the government should seek to ensure that there is effective control of inputs before seeking to control outputs, to provide good cash-based accounts before developing accrual-based accounts, and to have effective financial audit before moving to performance audit.[17] However, Schick

[17]These basic principles were included in a well-known 1998 presentation by Schick called "Look Before You Leap-Frog." Other priority actions highlighted by Schick are intended to foster an environment that supports and demands performance before introducing performance or outcome budgeting, to establish external control before introducing internal control, to establish internal control before managerial accountability, to operate a reliable accounting system before developing an automated financial management information system, to budget for work done before results, to enforce formal contracts in the market before performance contracts in the public sector, and to adopt and implement predictable budgets before insisting that managers efficiently use resources entrusted to them. See also Schick (2012).

does not present a comprehensive analytical framework for selecting his basic principles of budgeting, nor does his approach take explicit account of the political economy factors discussed above.

Related to Schick's focus on getting the basics right is the idea that some public financial management reforms are technically dependent on others for success. Pollitt and Bouckaert (2000) give some examples of "natural reform trajectories" in accounting, performance budgeting, and external audit. In accounting, for example, improvements have tended to move in stages from the development of single-entry to double-entry bookkeeping, to the establishment of a uniform accounting system across government, to the development of accounting for assets and liabilities (a rudimentary balance sheet), and eventually to the establishment of a full accrual accounting framework. Natural reform trajectories may also exist *among* the various components of the budget system. For example, the development of effective internal and external audit procedures is dependent on reliable and timely financial reports. And the existence of a sound and credible budget classification and chart of accounts is fundamental to the development of most other areas of an efficient budget and revenue administration system. However, a comprehensive framework that defines and explains these hierarchies has not yet been developed, although Tommasi (2009) makes an interesting attempt to supplement the Schick approach with practical criteria that would enable decision makers to distinguish between "basic" and more advanced reforms.

A more comprehensive strategy for sequencing PFM reform in developing countries is the so-called platform approach proposed by Brooke (2003). Rather than the traditional focus on individual components of the budget process, Brooke proposes that PFM reforms be packaged together into groups of activities or measures (platforms) that form a logical sequence (Figure 14.2). An overall reform strategy might stretch over a period of, say, 10 years, and comprise four or five of these platforms.

Each platform would last for a period of two or three years and establish a clear basis for moving to the next stage.[18] Brooke argues that the platform approach, which has some intuitive appeal, differs from existing public sector improvement strategies in several ways. First, it would provide a more structured approach to sequencing and greater clarity to governments, IFIs, and donors about their respective roles and responsibilities in the reform. Second, it would focus on the interconnection between specific measures and their ability to be mutually supportive. Third, it would encourage logical thought about the sustainable

[18] In Cambodia, for example, the government's reform plan "Strengthening Governance through Enhanced Public Financial Management" (December 2004) included four platforms, covering an 11-year period. In stage 1 (2004–06), 27 activities under 11 broad areas (budget comprehensiveness and integration, macrofiscal forecasting, streamlining spending processes, budget classification, integrated financial management information systems design, strengthening leadership within the finance ministry, redesigning the budget cycle, piloting program-based budgets, options for fiscal decentralization, information technology management strategy, and designing an asset register) and 254 separate actions were included in the program.

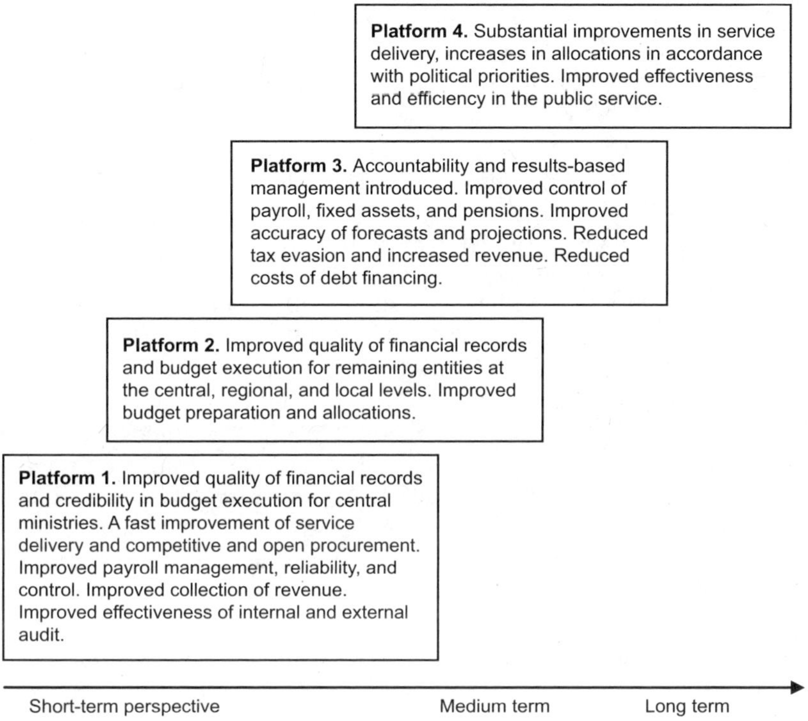

Platform 4. Substantial improvements in service delivery, increases in allocations in accordance with political priorities. Improved effectiveness and efficiency in the public service.

Platform 3. Accountability and results-based management introduced. Improved control of payroll, fixed assets, and pensions. Improved accuracy of forecasts and projections. Reduced tax evasion and increased revenue. Reduced costs of debt financing.

Platform 2. Improved quality of financial records and budget execution for remaining entities at the central, regional, and local levels. Improved budget preparation and allocations.

Platform 1. Improved quality of financial records and credibility in budget execution for central ministries. A fast improvement of service delivery and competitive and open procurement. Improved payroll management, reliability, and control. Improved collection of revenue. Improved effectiveness of internal and external audit.

Short-term perspective — Medium term — Long term

Figure 14.2 Illustration of the Platform Approach

Source: Government of Kenya, *Strategy to Revitalize Public Financial Management*, April 2006.

migration path toward technical improvements, which might ultimately be desirable, but are not realistic in the short term, and identify small steps that would create momentum for sustaining progress.

The platform approach, however, like Schick's framework, although building logically from the bottom up, offers an incomplete technocratic solution to the issue of reform design and sequencing. Following relatively successful implementation in Cambodia, as discussed by Murphy (2010), the platform approach has not been widely used and has encountered less success in other countries. As Diamond (2012a, 2012b) explains, there is a "hard" and a "soft" side to PFM reform. The hard side involves diagnosing the technical problem, prescribing the technical solution, and recommending steps to implement the technical solution. In more complex scenarios, these technical solutions will be prescribed for a range of problems and packaged together as an action plan to reform the budget process. Most of the technical assistance provided by IFIs and bilateral donors tends to focus on the hard side. However, in light of the mixed progress noted above, there has been dissatisfaction with the effectiveness of this approach, as well as demands that an improved model be developed. Complaints include the view that the reform programs are unrealistic in scope, overload countries with too many reforms, underestimate the time required for the reforms to be implemented, involve "imported" solutions not geared to country needs, and are pushed by donors with limited support from the national authorities.

According to Diamond (2012a, 2012b), a strengthened approach to designing a PFM reform program involves three elements: a recognition first, that reform needs to be geared to country circumstances and that standard technical solutions do not exist; second, that nontechnical or political economy factors[19]—the soft side—are extremely important and need to be incorporated into the design and sequencing of the reform program; and, third, that the success of reforms depends critically on how they are introduced and structured—change management has an important role to play. Andrews (2006, 2010, 2013) argues that reform is never a purely technical exercise, but is a trade-off among three dimensions: the technical PFM dimension (what needs to be done), the political demand dimension (what politicians want to be done), and the political economy or institutional dimension (how much change can realistically be achieved given the quality of a country's institutions and governance). The available "reform space," which can be quite small in practice, is determined by the intersection of these three realms.

In Diamond's view, political economy factors are important because they pose risks to reform. He further argues that it is possible to classify countries by the degree to which such risks are present. The vulnerability of a country to risk is likely to be affected by the degree of complexity of the reform considered, the time required to complete the reform, the number of organizations involved in implementing the reform, and the degree of change in behavior that is involved. Risk thus varies according to the type of reform being considered. For example, a financial management information system project involves a high degree of procedural and behavioral change, technically complex requirements, a large number of budget entities, and considerable time to implement. It is thus a high-risk reform. By contrast, the establishment of a macrofiscal unit or a debt management office requires a relatively small change in behavior and processes, is a technically simpler solution, involves only a single organization (the ministry of finance), and can be accomplished relatively fast. It is thus a low-risk reform. Low-risk projects also include the de jure reforms (changes in the legal framework) that Andrews (2010) has found predominate in low-income countries.

It may be concluded from this analysis that a strategy for reforming budgetary institutions should attempt to resolve the trade-off between the reform impact and the level of risk. Diamond recommends as a guiding principle that high-risk reforms be attempted only in a low-risk environment. He applies this principle to the various reform strategies proposed in the literature on sequencing PFM reforms. For example, he argues that the strategic or "low-lying fruit" approach, involving reforms narrow in scope, de jure, and rapidly implementable, would be a good approach in a high-risk country, but have limited impact on PFM performance. By contrast, the platform approach, which

[19] Diamond calls these factors "external," but this term seems misleading because the factors are closely related to a country's internal institutions and governance.

attempts to maximize reform impact by programming stages of PFM reform in a sequenced way, starting with more basic reforms and moving on to more complex reforms, is broad in scope, requires both de jure and de facto reforms, and involves a large number of stakeholders. This approach is thus probably viable only in a low-risk environment.

To resolve the trade-off between risk and reform impact, a composite strategy may be appropriate in low-income countries, as Diamond notes:

> For example, in high risk countries reform actions [might concentrate] on "low lying fruit" that are also locally demanded. Since it is likely that bottlenecks will exist in more than one area [of PFM], it is possible to choose to address those weakest links which match the country's risk profile: narrow reforms in higher risk countries and wider reforms in lower risk countries. Similarly, the high risk platform approach can be made less risky by allowing the re-programming of reform actions on a rolling basis depending on reform experience. Its high risk nature can also be reduced if it is front-loaded by low risk reforms, providing a basis for subsequent higher risk reform actions. This could imply, for example, adopting a "low lying fruit" approach in the first platform. (Diamond, 2012b, p. 147)

The approach proposed by Diamond seems sensible at a general level and may be useful for strategists in planning a reform program. However, it also faces a number of potential challenges if it is to be implemented. First, the concept of risk is highly subjective and difficult to measure. Risk levels cannot be determined in an absolute sense because, as noted, they depend on a range of complex relationships and interactions. Political economy factors include the informal rules and procedures that determine the actual behavior of budget entities regardless of the legal framework involved. In Andrews' striking metaphor, they represent the 90 percent of factors that are invisible below the water line in the "iceberg" of influences on PFM performance, compared with the 10 percent of formal rules that can be viewed above the surface (Andrews, 2013, p. 44). However, as noted, these informal factors are extremely important in determining behavior. External observers who have attempted to evaluate the impact of institutional factors on the behavior of budget systems have found the task challenging. Information relating to such behavior is extremely sensitive, and players in the budget process are reluctant to disclose it (Allen and Grigoli, 2012). Another problem is that risk is not stable: a change in government or other political developments can have a profound effect, for example, on the political strength of the minister of finance, that minister's relationship with other ministers and the head of state, and the influence of civil society.

Thus, while Diamond's approach offers a useful set of general principles for contemplating how a reform program should be designed—reforms should be realistic in scope, avoid the danger of overloading, be carefully timed, geared to a country's needs, and avoid the danger of donor-driven initiatives—it does not offer an operational guide for the prioritization and sequencing of reform in the real world. It seems unlikely that such a set of operational rules can ever be developed because the challenges and complexities of designing a reform program are too great, and country context is paramount.

Ultimately, the reform of budgetary institutions seems to be a slow, unending, and somewhat haphazard process, even in advanced economies. Reviewing the experience of reforms in the United Kingdom during 1960–95, commentators such as Olowo-Okere and Tomkins (1998) have concluded that the reforms were driven by a mixture of economic and financial pressures, political ideology, and pressures from the legislature and the general public (for greater accountability and transparency in the fiscal area). Political ideology became a dominant factor after 1979, when Margaret Thatcher became prime minister. Olowo-Okere and Tomkins (1998, p. 330) conclude, however, that "this continuity in the underlying pressures for change produced a broadly consistent direction of change which in hindsight seems to imply a planned sequence of events, but the exact form of development was not predictable in 1979, or even somewhat later. . . . when looking back it is nearly always possible to make sense of developments but we must not confuse that with an ability to forecast the future sequence of events in complex systems."

14.4. CONCLUSION

The core idea of this chapter is that the reform of budgetary institutions is an extremely slow and challenging process that has taken more than 200 years in advanced economies such as France, the United Kingdom, and the United States, and is still not complete. The reasons are linked to the famous doctrine, developed by North (1991) and North, Wallis, and Weingast (2006), of emerging states and the gradual transition of countries from rent-seeking states dominated by elites to open, democratic societies. Budgetary institutions are a major source of rent-seeking and rent-providing behavior in developing countries and thus exercise a strong influence on the budget process while, at the same time, containing and constraining its modernization. Reforming these institutions is difficult because the changes involve political willingness to make hard choices, and incentives for reform among politicians and public officials are weak, almost by definition. Weak ministries of finance and fragmented budgets only exacerbate these problems. For similar reasons, poor countries find it difficult to set policy priorities, which is why public sector reform programs and poverty reduction plans often mirror donor preferences.

The chapter argues that attempts to take approaches to reforming budgetary institutions that have been successful and effective in advanced economies and transplant them into the alien environment of a developing country are usually unsuccessful and can sometimes be disruptive and chaotic. Although there may be some exceptions to this view (such as emerging market economies, postconflict countries, and some developing countries with special institutional characteristics and powerful ministers of finance), they are rarely found in practice.

The chapter further argues that technocratic solutions to the design of reform strategies, such as the platform approach, have some intuitive appeal, but their sheer weight, unrealistically short timelines, and complexity may limit them as a practical tool for use in developing countries. They are also prone to capture by the agencies that provide funding and technical assistance. By contrast, the more successful improvement strategies tend to have a relatively short-term horizon; focus on a quite narrow and specific set of objectives (for example, how to correct a fiscal imbalance or a problem of arrears, or to improve budgetary reporting); and involve an incremental approach, a large element of trial and error, learning from mistakes, and "fumbling around in the dark." Andrews' (2013) problem-driven iterative adaptation model is a good example of such an approach. Successful reform requires deliberate selectivity in the choice of topics on which to focus the effort. Selection rather than sequencing is the keyword.

REFERENCES

Allen, R., 2008, "Reforming Fiscal Institutions: The Elusive Art of the Budget Advisor," *OECD Journal on Budgeting*, Vol. 8, No. 3, pp. 1–9.

———, 2009, "The Challenge of Reforming Budgetary Institutions in Developing Countries," IMF Working Paper 09/96 (Washington: International Monetary Fund).

———, and F. Grigoli, 2012, "Enhancing the Capability of Central Finance Agencies," *Economic Premise*, No. 73, pp. 1–7.

Andrews, M., 2006, "Beyond 'Best Practice' and 'Basics First' in Adopting Performance Budgeting Reform," *Public Administration and Development*, Vol. 26, No. 2, pp. 147–61.

———, 2010, "Good Government Means Different Things in Different Countries," *Governance: An International Journal of Policy, Public Administration, and Institutions*, Vol. 23, No. 1, pp. 7–35.

———, 2013, *The Limits of Institutional Reform in Development: Changing Rules for Realistic Solutions* (New York: Cambridge University Press).

Brewer, J., 1988, *The Sinews of Power: War, Money and the English State, 1688–1783* (Cambridge, Massachusetts: Harvard University Press).

Brooke, P., 2003, "Study of Measures Used to Address Weaknesses in Public Financial Management in the Context of Policy-Based Support," final report for the Public Expenditure and Financial Accountability (PEFA) Secretariat (Washington: PEFA Secretariat).

Campos, E., and S. Pradhan, 1998, *Building Blocks toward a More Effective Public Sector* (Washington: World Bank, Economic Development Institute).

Dabla-Norris, E., R. Allen, L.-F. Zanna, T. Prakash, E. Kvintradze, V. Lledo, I. Yackovlev, and S. Gollwitzer, 2010, "Budget Institutions and Fiscal Performance in Low-Income Countries," IMF Working Paper 10/80 (Washington: International Monetary Fund).

de Renzio, P., 2011, "Buying Better Governance: The Political Economy of Budget Reforms in Aid-Dependent Countries," Working Paper 2011/65 (Oxford, U.K.: University of Oxford, Global Economic Governance Program).

Diamond, J., 2012a, "Guidance Note on Sequencing PFM Reforms." Available via the Internet: https://www.pefa.org/.

———, 2012b, "Guidance Note on Sequencing PFM Reforms, Background Paper 1." Available via the Internet: https://www.pefa.org/.

Dressel, B., and J. Brumby, 2009, "Enhancing the Capabilities of Central Finance Agencies: From Diagnosis to Action" (unpublished; Washington: World Bank).

Gupta, S., G. Schwartz, S. Tareq, R. Allen, I. Adenauer, K. Fletcher, and D. Last, 2008, *Fiscal Management of Scaled-Up Aid* (Washington: International Monetary Fund).

International Bank for Reconstruction and Development (IBRD), 1960, *The Economic Development of Libya: Report of a Mission Organized by the IBRD at the Request of the Government of Libya* (Baltimore: Johns Hopkins University Press).

Kohnert, P., 2008, "The Establishment of the Fiscal Affairs Department in the IMF" (unpublished; Washington: International Monetary Fund).

Lienert, I., and F. Sarraf, 2001, "Systemic Weaknesses of Budget Management in Anglophone Africa," IMF Working Paper 01/211 (Washington: International Monetary Fund).

Murphy, P., 2010, "The Platform Approach in PFM Reform—Positive for Cambodia So Far, but Not Necessarily the Magic Bullet for All Countries," IMF Public Financial Management Blog. http://blog-pfm.imf.org/.

Murray, C., and J. Wehner, 2011, "Budgeting after 2012: What the Constitution Says" (unpublished).

Normanton, E.L., 1966, *The Accountability and Audit of Governments* (Manchester, U.K.: Manchester University Press).

North, D., 1991, "Institutions," *Journal of Economic Perspectives*, Vol. 5, No. 1, pp. 97–112.

———, J. Wallis, and B. Weingast, 2006, "A Conceptual Framework for Interpreting Recorded Human History," NBER Working Paper 12795 (Cambridge, Massachusetts: National Bureau of Economic Research).

Olowo-Okere, E., and C. Tomkins, 1998, "Understanding the Evolution of Government Financial Management Control Systems," *Accounting, Auditing & Accountability Journal*, Vol. 11, No. 3, pp. 309–31.

Peterson, S., 2011, "Plateaus Not Summits: Reforming Public Financial Management in Africa," *Public Administration and Development*, Vol. 31, No. 3, pp. 205–13.

Pollitt, C., and G. Bouckaert, 2000, *Public Management Reform: A Comparative Analysis* (Oxford, U.K.: Oxford University Press).

Public Expenditure and Financial Accountability (PEFA) Secretariat, 2005, *Public Financial Management Performance Measurement Framework* (Washington: World Bank).

Schiavo-Campo, S., 1994, "Institutional Change in the Public Sector and Transitional Economies," Discussion Paper No. 24 (Washington: World Bank).

———, 2007, "Budgeting in Post-conflict Countries," in *Budgeting and Budgetary Institutions*, ed. by A. Shah (Washington: World Bank).

———, 2009, "Potemkin Villages: The Medium-Term Expenditure Framework in Developing Countries," *Public Budgeting and Finance*, Vol. 29, No. 2, pp. 1–26.

Schick, A., 1998, *A Contemporary Approach to Public Expenditure Management* (Washington: World Bank).

———, 2012, "Basics First Is Best Practice," IMF Public Financial Management Blog. http://blog-pfm.imf.org/.

Shah, A., and C. Shen, 2007, "A Primer on Performance Budgeting," in *Budgeting and Budgetary Institutions*, ed. by A. Shah (Washington: World Bank).

Tanzi, V., 2000, "Rationalizing the Government Budget, or Why Fiscal Policy Is So Difficult," in *Economic Policy Reforms: The Second Stage*, ed. by Anne O. Krueger (Chicago: University of Chicago Press).

Tommasi, D., 2009, "Strengthening Public Expenditure Management in Developing Countries: Sequencing Issues," Available via the Internet: http://www.capacity4dev.eu.

Vani, S., 2012, "Has Global PFM Improved in the Last Decade?" IMF Public Financial Management Blog. http://blog-pfm.imf.org/.

Wehner, J., 2010, *Legislatures and the Budget Process; The Myth of Fiscal Control* (Basingstoke, U.K.: Palgrave Macmillan).

World Bank, 2011, *Enhancing the Capabilities of Central Finance Agencies,* Synthesis Report (Washington).

World Bank, Independent Evaluation Group, 2008, *Public Sector Reform: What Works and Why* (Washington: World Bank).

World Bank and Overseas Development Institute (ODI), 2011, *Public Financial Management Reform in Post-conflict States*, Synthesis Report (Washington).

Wynne, A., 2005, "Public Financial Management Reforms in Developing Countries: Lessons of Experience from Ghana, Tanzania, and Uganda," Working Paper No. 07/2005 (Harare: African Capacity Building Foundation).

Contributors

Richard Allen is an economist and public finance expert. He currently works in Washington, D.C., as a consultant with the IMF and World Bank. He previously worked for the U.K. Treasury and has held senior positions with the Organisation for Economic Co-operation and Development, Asian Development Bank, World Bank, and IMF. He is the author of many books and articles on public financial management and has advised more than 60 countries on strengthening their budgeting and public financial management systems.

Guilhem Blondy, a student of the Nelson Mandela class of the Ecole Nationale d'Administration, has a variety of experiences in public financial management as auditor at the French Court of Audit (2001–05) and advisor to France's Minister of Finance (2005–07), as well as at the IMF (2009–), but also as a practitioner in two French government agencies, IFP Energies Nouvelles (2007–09) and Voies Navigables de France, since July 2012.

Nina Budina is a Senior Economist in the IMF's European Department, having previously worked in its Fiscal Affairs Department and for its Executive Board. She was previously a senior economist at the World Bank and an advisor to the government of Romania. She holds a doctorate from University of Amsterdam. She has published on economic policy, debt, and public finances, and has contributed to the IMF's *Fiscal Monitor.*

Marco Cangiano is an Assistant Director of the IMF Fiscal Affairs Department and Visiting Scholar in the Wagner Graduate School of Public Service at New York University. Prior to joining the IMF, where he has covered a wide range of countries and the full spectrum of activities, he worked for an oil company and consulted for the Italian government. He holds degrees from the Universities of Rome and York (U.K.), and has published on fiscal policy and transparency, pension reform, tax policy, and energy economics.

Julie Cooper is an Australian Certified Practicing Accountant with more than 25 years' experience in the development and implementation of public financial management systems. She currently works for Deloitte United States and has previously worked for the IMF. She has also provided technical assistance to Ministries of Finance and line agencies and worked in Afghanistan, Australia, Egypt, South Sudan, Timor-Leste, the United Arab Emirates, the United States, and Vanuatu.

Teresa Curristine is a Senior Economist in the IMF's Fiscal Affairs Department, where she works on public financial management issues. Previously she worked for the Organisation for Economic Co-operation and Development, managing projects and teams working on several topics, including reviewing countries' budgetary systems and improving public sector efficiency. She has edited three books and published various articles on reforming budgetary institutions, performance budgeting, and public sector reform. She received her doctorate from the University of Oxford, where she also worked as lecturer.

Teresa Dabán Sánchez, a Spanish national, is a Senior Economist in the IMF's Western Hemisphere Department. At the IMF, she has worked in the design and monitoring of Fund-supported programs, surveillance consultations, and the provision of technical assistance to several countries in Latin America, Asia, and Sub-Saharan Africa. Before joining the Fund, she held several senior positions in the Central Budget Office of the Spanish Ministry of Finance in Madrid.

Richard P. (Dick) Emery Jr. is an intermittent consultant on budgeting for developing countries for the IMF, the World Bank, the Organisation for Economic Co-operation and Development, the U.S. Treasury Office of Technical Assistance, U.S. Agency for International Development contractors, and the German Development Agency. He spent 25 years at the Office of Management and Budget (the last seven as Assistant Director for Budget Review) and 11 years in the Congressional Budget Office as Chief of the Budget Process Unit.

Israel Fainboim is a Senior Economist in the IMF's Fiscal Affairs Department. He was a member of the Colombian Ministry of Finance's Council of Fiscal Advisers and Bogotá's Secretary of Finance. He was also a research associate at the leading economic policy think tank in Colombia, Fedesarrollo. A former professor of public finance, he has written articles on treasury issues, fiscal sustainability, and public investment, among other topics, and has participated in numerous technical assistance missions on public financial management.

Annalisa Fedelino is an Advisor in the IMF's Office of Budget and Planning. She has worked extensively on a number of low-income countries and emerging market economies, covering public finance issues as well as providing technical advice on intergovernmental fiscal relations.

Suzanne Flynn has been a Technical Assistance Advisor in the IMF's Fiscal Affairs Department since 2009. Having trained as an accountant in the U.K. public sector, she has advised governments on aspects of budgeting, budget execution, and financial reporting in a number of countries in Eastern Europe, the Middle East, and Africa over the past 15 years. She holds a Master's in Public Policy and Management from the University of London's School of Oriental and African Studies.

John Gardner was a successful international investment manager in bonds, currencies, and derivatives prior to joining the New Zealand Treasury in 1989. There he served as Deputy Treasurer during the foundation of the Debt Management Office, establishing a modern debt management function based on advanced portfolio management techniques comprising cost-risk analysis and asset-liability management. Since then, he has consulted on cash and debt management in over 30 countries, mainly for the IMF.

Jason Harris is a Technical Assistance Advisor in the area of public financial management in the IMF's Fiscal Affairs Department. Prior to joining the IMF, he worked in the Australian Treasury preparing the budget, as an economic and fiscal advisor to the Australian Prime Minister, and as a budget advisor in the Papua New Guinea Treasury.

Jean-Luc Hélis, after 10 years in the French Ministry of Finance, became a European Union preaccession advisor in Hungary. He joined the IMF's Fiscal Affairs Department in 2004, leading or participating in several missions to Africa, Asia, the Middle East, and Central Asia. He has been working in AFRITAC South, an IMF regional technical assistance center based in Mauritius, since June 2011.

Richard Hemming is Visiting Professor of Public Policy at the Duke Center for International Development and a consultant on fiscal policy issues. He retired from the IMF, where he was Deputy Director of the Fiscal Affairs Department, in August 2008. He has published widely on macroeconomic aspects of fiscal policy, tax policy and social security reform, and public expenditure analysis, and is joint editor of the *International Handbook of Public Financial Management.*

Richard Hughes is a Division Chief in the IMF's Fiscal Affairs Department, where his work has focused on fiscal reform in countries hit hard by the global crisis, including Iceland, Ireland, Greece, and Zimbabwe. He has also authored a number of papers on fiscal institutions and fiscal transparency. Before joining the IMF in 2008, he was a Deputy Director in the Public Spending Directorate of H.M. Treasury, where he led the 2007 Comprehensive Spending Review.

Timothy Irwin is a Senior Economist in the IMF's Fiscal Affairs Department. Before joining the IMF, he worked as an economic consultant and at the World Bank, mostly on public policy for utilities and infrastructure projects. Prior to that, he worked at the Organisation for Economic Co-operation and Development and in the New Zealand Treasury. He holds a degree in public policy from Princeton University.

Philip Joyce is Professor of Management, Finance, and Leadership in the University of Maryland's School of Public Policy. He is Editor of *Public Budgeting and Finance* and a Fellow of the National Academy of Public Administration. His research focuses on two issues—linkages between performance information and the budget, and the U.S. congressional budget process. His most recent book is *The Congressional Budget Office: Honest Numbers, Power, and Policymaking* (2011).

Kris Kauffmann, who is currently at the University of New England in Australia, was a consultant in the IMF's Fiscal Affairs Department during the drafting of this book. Before joining the IMF, he worked as a public financial management consultant, predominantly on U.S. Agency for International Development–funded projects establishing the Ministry of Finance in Kosovo. His background is in the Australian civil service, and he holds a Master's in Public Policy and Management from the University of London's School of Oriental and African Studies.

Abdul Khan is a Senior Economist in the IMF's Fiscal Affairs Department, where he is involved in providing technical assistance to member countries on public financial management. Prior to joining the IMF, he worked in Australia's Department of Finance and Administration, where he was closely involved in the implementation of an accrual-based budgeting framework and the development of the federal government's first consolidated whole-of-government financial statements.

Pokar Khemani was a Senior Economist in the IMF's Fiscal Affairs Department until July 2011 and guided budget officials on implementing public financial management reforms in Southeast Europe, Africa, and Asia. He was also the IMF's resident budget advisor in Jamaica, Malawi, Namibia, and Uganda, and also held senior positions in India's financial administration. He continues to work for the IMF as a short-term advisor in the area of public financial management for select countries.

Tidiane Kinda is an Economist in the Fiscal Policy and Surveillance Division of the IMF's Fiscal Affairs Department. He contributes to the IMF's multilateral surveillance analyses such as the *Fiscal Monitor* and the Vulnerability Exercise for Advanced Economies, as well as to other cross-country work, including on fiscal rules/institutions and debt stabilization. He worked on countries in Africa, Europe, and Latin America and was at the World Bank before joining the IMF.

Duncan Last is a U.K. national with 25 years' experience in public financial management in Africa, Europe, Asia and the Pacific, and the Caribbean, specializing in budget formulation, budget execution, and treasury management. He has advised on the design of legal frameworks for public financial management in several countries with different institutional and linguistic traditions and has also developed government financial management systems in a number of areas, including debt management, budget preparation, public investment programming, and budget execution.

Michel Lazare is an Assistant Director of the IMF's African Department. Prior to joining the IMF, he worked at the French Ministry of Finance in what was then the Forecasting Department. At the IMF, he has worked in the African and the Middle East Departments, and from 2004 to 2012, in the Fiscal Affairs Department, where he led Public Financial Management Division 2. He holds degrees from the École Supérieure des Sciences Economiques et Commerciales, the Institut d'Études Politiques de Paris, and the École Nationale d'Administration.

Gösta Ljungman is a Senior Economist in the IMF's Fiscal Affairs Department. Before joining the Fund, he worked in the Budget Department in Sweden's Ministry of Finance. He has published articles on a variety of budgeting topics.

Brian Olden is currently Deputy Chief in the IMF's Fiscal Affairs Department's Public Financial Management Division 1. From 2009 to 2012, he also served as the IMF's regional public financial management advisor in Southeast Europe. Prior to joining the IMF, he worked as a director of a consultancy firm specializing in public financial management, as Senior Treasury Manager in the Irish National Treasury Management Agency, and as Debt Manager in the Irish Department of Finance.

Murray Petrie is Director of the Economics and Strategy Group Ltd. He has also worked for the New Zealand Treasury and the IMF, and since 1998 has been a member of the IMF's panel of fiscal experts. His areas of specialization include public expenditure management, fiscal transparency, and fiscal risk management. He has also worked for the World Bank on public investment management and is actively involved in civil society initiatives to strengthen the governance of fiscal policy.

Carla Sateriale has extensively supported the IMF's public financial management research agenda, primarily through quantitative work on budget institutions and fiscal outcomes. She is currently pursuing postgraduate studies at the London School of Economics.

Andrea Schaechter is Deputy Chief of the Fiscal Policy and Surveillance Division in the IMF's Fiscal Affairs Department. She is involved in multilateral surveillance and cross-country analysis, including on fiscal rules, and contributes to the IMF's *Fiscal Monitor,* a twice-yearly IMF report that monitors and analyzes public finance developments worldwide. She has worked at the European Commission and in several other IMF departments.

Allen Schick is Distinguished University Professor of Public Policy at the University of Maryland, where he has taught since 1981. He previously served at the Brookings Institution and the Congressional Research Service. He received his bachelor's from Brooklyn College and his doctorate from Yale University. He has consulted at various international organizations, including the IMF, World Bank, Organisation for Economic Co-operation and Development, Inter-American Development Bank, and Asian Development Bank. He has worked in more than 50 countries and has published more than a dozen books and more than 200 articles and reports. He has been awarded the Guggenheim Fellowship, the Merriam Prize for lifetime contribution to political science, and the Dwight Waldo Award for contributions to public administration.

Paul Smoke is Professor of Public Finance and Planning and Director of International Programs in the Wagner Graduate School of Public Service at New York University. He previously taught at the Massachusetts Institute of Technology and worked with the Harvard Institute for International Development. His research and policy interests include fiscal reform, decentralization, and urban development. He has published extensively on these topics and has worked with a range of international organizations.

Eivind Tandberg, a Norwegian national, was a Deputy Division Chief in the IMF's Fiscal Affairs Department until 2009. He has provided technical assistance and strategic advice to a number of countries in Asia, Africa, Latin America, the Middle East, and Central and Eastern Europe. He was the IMF's regional advisor for Southeast Europe from 2005 to 2008 and its resident advisor in Bulgaria from 1998 to 2000. He also held senior posts at the Norwegian Ministry of Finance and at the World Bank, and is currently Director General of the Oslo city administration.

Holger van Eden is Deputy Division Chief in the IMF's Fiscal Affairs Department. He has worked with Ministries of Finance in Eastern Europe, Asia, Latin America, and the Caribbean on program budgeting, institutional restructuring, budget and fiscal responsibility law, and government cash management. Before joining the IMF, he worked in international consultancy and journalism and for the Dutch Ministry of Finance. He is currently editor of the IMF's public financial management blog.

Anke Weber is an Economist in the IMF's Fiscal Affairs Department. She was a principal contributor to the September 2011 and April 2012 issues of the IMF's *Fiscal Monitor*, a twice-yearly report that analyzes public finance developments worldwide. At the IMF, she has worked on several countries, including Armenia, Bulgaria, and Cyprus. She earned a doctorate from Cambridge University in 2009 and has published articles on public finances, central bank communication, and transparency.

Index

Note: Boxes, figures, notes, and tables are indicated by *b*, *f*, *n*, and *t*, respectively.